FIFTY CONTEMPORARY FILM DIRECTORS

Fifty Contemporary Film Directors examines the work of some of today's most popular and influential cinematic figures. It provides an accessible overview of each director's contribution to cinema, incorporating a discussion of their career, major works and impact. Revised throughout and with twelve new entries, this second edition is the most up-to-date introduction to the greatest film makers of the present day. The names, drawn from a range of genres and backgrounds, include:

- Martin Scorsese
- Steven Spielberg
- Sofia Coppola
- Julie Dash
- Shane Meadows
- Michael Moore
- Peter Jackson
- Guillermo del Toro
- Tim Burton
- Jackie Chan
- Ang Lee
- Pedro Almodóvar

With further reading and a filmography accompanying each entry, this comprehensive guide is indispensable to all those studying contemporary film and will appeal to anyone interested in the key individuals behind modern cinema's greatest achievements.

Yvonne Tasker is Professor of Film Studies at the University of East Anglia, UK. Her books include *Action and Adventure Cinema* (Routledge, 2004) and *Interrogating Postfeminism: Gender and the Politics of Popular Culture* (2007).

ALSO AVAILABLE FROM ROUTLEDGE

FIFTY CONTEMPORARY FILM DIRECTORS

Second Edition

Edited by
Yvonne Tasker

Routledge
Taylor & Francis Group

LONDON AND NEW YORK

First published as *Fifty Contemporary Filmmakers* 2002 by Routledge
Second edition published 2011
by Routledge
2 Park Square, Milton Park, Abingdon, Oxon OX14 4RN

Simultaneously published in the USA and Canada
by Routledge
270 Madison Avenue, New York, NY 10016

Routledge is an imprint of the Taylor & Francis Group, an informa business

Typeset in Bembo by Taylor & Francis Books
Printed and bound in Great Britain by TJ International Ltd, Padstow, Cornwall

British Library Cataloguing in Publication Data
A catalogue record for this book is available from the British Library

Library of Congress Cataloging-in-Publication Data
Fifty contemporary film directors / edited by Yvonne Tasker. – 2nd ed.
p. cm. – (Routledge key guides)
Includes filmography.
Includes bibliographical references and index.
1. Motion picture producers and directors – Biography – Dictionaries. I. Tasker, Yvonne,
1964-
PN1998.2.F53 2010
791.43023'30922 – dc22
[B]
2010008363

ISBN10: 0-415-49766-4 (hbk)
ISBN10: 0-415-55433-0 (pbk)
ISBN10: 0-203-84434-3 (ebk)

ISBN13: 978-0-415-49766-4 (hbk)
ISBN13: 978-0-415-55433-6 (pbk)
ISBN13: 978-0-203-84434-2 (ebk)

FOR MICHÈLE SCOTT – THANKS!

CONTENTS

ALPHABETICAL LIST
OF CONTENTS

CONTRIBUTORS

José Arroyo is an Associate Professor in Film Studies in the Department of Film and Television Studies at the University of Warwick where he teaches courses on Film History and Film Aesthetics. He reviews regularly for a wide variety of publications including *Sight and Sound* and *Pure Movies*.

Harry M. Benshoff is an Associate Professor of Radio, Television, and Film at the University of North Texas. His research interests include topics in film genres, film history, film theory and multi-culturalism. He has published essays on blaxploitation horror films, Hollywood LSD films, *The Talented Mr. Ripley* (1999), and *Brokeback Mountain* (2005). He is the author of *Monsters in the Closet: Homosexuality and the Horror Film* (1997). With Sean Griffin he co-authored *America on Film: Representing Race, Class, Gender and Sexuality at the Movies* (2004) and *Queer Images: A History of Gay and Lesbian Film in America* (2006).

Sue Brennan is a doctoral candidate in Women's Studies at The Ohio State University, USA. Her research focuses on representations of citizenship after 9/11 in the work of women filmmakers and writers of the South Asian and Iranian diasporas.

Anne Ciecko is an Associate Professor in the Department of Communication at the University of Massachusetts-Amherst, a core faculty member in the Interdepartmental Film Program, and director of the Graduate Film Studies Certificate Program. She has researched, taught, published, and presented widely on international cinema. She curates annual international film series and has covered international festivals in Asia, the Middle East, and Europe. Her current and ongoing research interests include international and intercultural cinema (especially emerging and resurging national cinemas); international transmedia stardom and celebrity; films, videos, and multimedia installations by women; and international film festivals.

Dr Shelley Cobb is a Teaching Fellow in Literature and Film at the University of Southampton. She received her PhD from the University of East Anglia. Her thesis is a study of women film-makers and adaptation entitled 'Revaluing Adaptation: Gender, Authority, and the Problem of Fidelity'. She teaches classes on contemporary film and gender, New Hollywood history, and film adaptation, and has published articles on *Bridget Jones's Diary* (2001), *Elizabeth* (1998), the films of Jane Campion, and on class and motherhood in celebrity culture.

Pam Cook is Professor Emerita in Film at Southampton University. She is the author of numerous publications on women and cinema, and editor of the third edition of *The Cinema Book* (2007). Her latest book is a monograph about Baz Luhrmann and world cinema (2010).

Glyn Davis is Academic Coordinator of Postgraduate Studies at Glasgow School of Art. He is the author of monographs on *Queer as Folk* (2007), *Superstar: The Karen Carpenter Story* (2008), and *Far From Heaven* (2010), as well as co-editor of the collections *Teen TV: Genre, Consumption and Identity* (2004) and *Queer TV: Theories, Histories, Politics* (2009).

Dean DeFino is Associate Professor of English and Director of Film Studies at Iona College in New Rochelle, NY. He has published on a variety of topics, from Shakespeare to *The Sopranos*, and his book on Russ Meyer's *Faster Pussycat! Kill! Kill!* for Wallflower Press will be released in 2011.

Rayna Denison is a lecturer in Film and Television Studies at the University of East Anglia, where she specialises in Asian film and television research and teaching. She has published on a range of topics including anime, children's television and comic book movies. She is currently working on two monographs: *Film Genres: Anime* and *Viewing Ang Lee: Authorship and Adaptation*.

Martin Fradley teaches at Keele University. His written work has appeared in Yvonne Tasker (ed.), *Action & Adventure Cinema* (2004), Alastair Philips and Ginette Vincendeau (eds), *Journeys of desire: European Actors in Hollywood* (2006), Stacey Abbott and Deborah Jermyn (eds), *Falling in Love Again: Romantic Comedy in Contemporary Cinema* (2009), Steffen Hantke (ed.), *American Horror film: The Genre at the Turn of the Millennium* (forthcoming 2010) and Karen Ross (ed.), *Gender, Sexuality/ies and the Media:*

Communicating Identity in a Post-Ironic Age (forthcoming). He has also published in journals such as *Film Quarterly*, *Screen* and *Film Criticism*. He is currently writing a volume on contemporary America fantasy cinema.

Aaron Gerow is Associate Professor in Japanese cinema in the Film Studies Program and the Department of East Asian Languages and Literatures at Yale University. He has published widely in a variety of languages on early, wartime and recent Japanese film, with a particular focus on issues of censorship, film reception, industrial history, representations of minorities, national cinema, film and modernity, war and cinema, documentary, and the politics of style. His monograph *Kitano Takeshi* was published in 2007 and *A Page of Madness* was published in 2008. He co-authored *Research Guide to Japanese Film Studies* (2009) with Abé Mark Nornes. His most recent book is *Visions of Japanese Modernity* (2010) is about Japanese film culture in the 1910s.

Haomin Gong is assistant professor of Chinese and Asian Studies at St. Mary's College of Maryland. His work has appeared in *Journal of Chinese Cinemas*, *China Information*, and *Asian Cinema*.

Ian Haydn Smith is Editor of the International Film Guide and Series Editor of Wallflower Press's *24 Frames to World Cinema*.

Mette Hjort is Chair Professor and Head of the Department of Visual Studies at Lingnan University in Hong Kong, and Affiliate Professor of Scandinavian Studies at the University of Washington, Seattle. She is the author of *The Strategy of Letters*, *Small Nation, Global Cinema*, *Stanley Kwan's Center Stage*, and *Lone Scherifg's Italian for Beginners* (forthcoming). She is the editor or co-editor of *Instituting Cultural Studies* (with Meaghan Morris, forthcoming), *Film and Risk* (forthcoming), *Rules and Conventions*, *Emotion and the Arts*, *Cinema and Nation*, *Purity and Provocation*, *The Postnational Self*, *The Cinema of Small Nations*, and *Dekalog 01: On The Five Obstructions*. Mette Hjort is currently working on projects in the area of environmental aesthetics, on the role of risk in various creative processes, and on the contributions made by different kinds of film schools.

Jennifer Holt is Assistant Professor of Film and Media Studies at the University of California, Santa Barbara. Her research focuses on media industries and regulatory policy. She is the co-editor of *Media Industries: History, Theory, and Method* and author of the forthcoming *Empires of Entertainment*.

Leon Hunt is a Senior Lecturer in Film and Television Studies. He is the author of *British Low Culture: From Safari Suits to Sexploitation*, *Kung Fu Cult Masters: From Bruce Lee to Crouching Tiger*, *The League of Gentlemen*, and co-editor of *East Asian Cinemas: Exploring Transnational Connections on Film*.

Mark Jancovich is Professor of Film and Television Studies at the University of East Anglia. He is the author of several books including: *Fears: American Horror in the 1950s* (MUP, 1996); *The Place of the Audience: Cultural Geographies of Film Consumption* (with Lucy Faire and Sarah Stubbings, 2003). He has edited several collections including: *Approaches to Popular Film* (with Joanne Hollows, 1995); *The Film Reader* (2001); *Quality Popular Television: Cult TV, the Industry and Fans* (with James Lyons, 2003); *Film Histories: An Introduction and Reader* (with Paul Grainge and Sharon Monteith, 2006); and *Film and Comic Books* (with Ian Gordon and Matt McAllister, 2007). He was the founder of *Scope: An Online Journal of Film Studies*; and is series editor (with Charles Acland) of the book series, Film Genres. He is currently writing a history of horror in the 1940s.

Alexandra Keller is Associate Professor of Film Studies and the Director of the Film Studies Program at Smith College, Northampton, MA. She is the author of *James Cameron*. Her next book is *The Endless Frontier: Westerns and American Identity from Reagan to W*. Her other publications address blockbuster culture, radiophony, artists and the moving image, and the avant-garde.

Chuck Kleinhans, co-founder and co-editor of Jump Cut (www. ejumpcut.org), taught in the Radio/Television/Film department at Northwestern University for over thirty years. His ongoing research reflects on the institutional and ideological nature of Hollywood and its others, especially independent, documentary, and experimental films, videos, and new media.

Peter Krämer teaches Film Studies at the University of East Anglia. He has published essays on American film and media history, and on the relationship between Hollywood and Europe, in *Screen*, *The Velvet Light Trap*, *Theatre History Studies*, the *Historical Journal of Film, Radio and Television*, *History Today*, *Film Studies*, *Scope*, *Sowi: Das Journal für Geschichte, Politik, Wirtschaft und Kultur*, the *New Review of Film and Television Studies*, *Iluminace* and numerous edited collections. He is the author of *The New Hollywood: From Bonnie and Clyde to Star Wars* (2005), and the co-editor of *Screen*

Acting (1999) and *The Silent Cinema Reader* (2004). He also co-wrote a book for children entitled *American Film: An A–Z Guide* (2003).

George S. Larke-Walsh is Senior Lecturer in Film at the University of North Texas, USA. She has published articles on Gangster films and Documentary Film. She is currently completing a book on the mythology of the Mafia in American Film and TV.

Hunju Lee is a PhD candidate in the Department of Communication at the University of Massachusetts-Amherst. Her major interests include critical cultural studies and Asian popular culture. She is completing a dissertation about Hollywood reconstruction/re-imagination of the feminine in the new Asian horror films.

Jon Lewis is a professor in the English Department at Oregon State University. He has published seven books: *The Road to Romance and Ruin: Teen Films and Youth Culture*, which won a *Choice Magazine* Academic Book of the Year Award; *Whom God Wishes to Destroy … Francis Coppola and the New Hollywood*; *The New American Cinema; Hollywood v. Hard Core: How the Struggle over Censorship Saved the Modern Film Industry*, a *New York Times* New and Noteworthy paperback; *The End of Cinema as We Know It: American Film in the Nineties, American Film: A History* and *Looking Past the Screen: Case Studies in American Film History*. Professor Lewis has appeared in two theatrically released documentaries on film censorship: *Inside Deep Throat* (2005) and *This Film is Not Yet Rated* (2006). Between 2002 and 2007, Lewis was editor of *Cinema Journal*.

James Lyons is Senior Lecturer in Film Studies at the University of Exeter. He is author of *Selling Seattle* (2004), and co-editor of *Quality Popular Television* (with Mark Jancovich, 2003) and *Multimedia Histories* (with John Plunkett, 2007). He was also a founding member of the editorial board for *Scope: An Online Journal of Film Studies*. His latest book is on the 1980s TV show *Miami Vice*.

Paul Malcolm is a film programmer for the UCLA Film & Television Archive and the Los Angeles Film Festival. He is currently completing his dissertation on the craft and culture of visual effects production.

Sebastian Manley is a PhD candidate in the School of Film and Television Studies, University of East Anglia. His research looks at the films of Hal Hartley and at independent cinema in general, with a focus on place and cultural identity.

Rosanna Maule is Associate Professor of Film Studies at Concordia University, Montreal. She is the author of *Beyond Auteurism: New Directions in Authorial Film Practices in France, Italy and Spain since the 1980s* (2008), and co-editor, with Julie Beaulieu, of *In the Dark Room: Marguerite Duras and Cinema* (2009).

Terry Moore is happily retired from the Department of Women's Studies at The Ohio State University. She continues to explore her interests in feminist and lesbian film studies and lesbians and film noir.

Diane Negra is Professor of Film Studies and Screen Culture and Head of Film Studies at University College Dublin. She is the author, editor or co-editor of *Off-White Hollywood: American Culture and Ethnic Female Stardom* (2001), *A Feminist Reader in Early Cinema* (2002), *The Irish in Us: Irishness, Performativity and Popular Culture* (2006), *Interrogating Postfeminism: Gender and the Politics of Popular Culture* (2007), *What a Girl Wants? Fantasizing the Reclamation of Self in Postfeminism* and *Old and New Media After Katrina* (2010).

Marc O'Day is course leader of the Film and Media Studies undergraduate programme at University Campus Suffolk. His research interests span fiction, film and television, with a recurring theme of the 1960s and its legacies. He has published work on the writers Angela Carter and J.G. Ballard, directors David Cronenberg and David Lynch, the TV series *The Avengers*, 'action babe' cinema, and postmodernism and television. He is currently researching issues of masculinity and honour in football.

Devin Orgeron is Associate Professor and Chair of Film Studies at North Carolina State University. He is the author of *Road Movies* and his articles have appeared in *Cinema Journal*, *The Velvet Light Trap*, *Film Quarterly* and *The Moving Image*. He is currently co-editing a collection on educational films for Oxford University Press with Dan Streible and Marsha Orgeron, and writing a book about contemporary American directors and their work in commercial advertising.

Geoff Pevere currently writes about books, media and culture for the *Toronto Star*, where he also spent ten years writing about film. His writing has also appeared in many anthologies, newspapers and magazines, and he has taught in several Canadian universities and community colleges. He has appeared on several radio and television programmes in Canada, and was the first program coordinator of the Perspective Canada program at the Toronto International Film Festival. He is the co-author of *Mondo Canuck: A Canadian Pop Culture Odyssey*, and the principle contributor to *Toronto on Film.*

Maria Pramaggiore is a Professor of Film Studies at North Carolina State University in Raleigh, NC. Her books include *Neil Jordan, Identifying Others and Performing Identities: Irish and African-American Cinema Since 1980* and *Film: A Critical Introduction* (co-authored with Tom Wallis). She has published numerous essays in journals and book collections on Irish cinema and on gender and sexuality in cinema. She is currently at work on a book on *Barry Lyndon.*

Tytti Soila is Professor of Cinema Studies and Chair of the Department of Journalism, Media and Communication at Stockholm University. She has published widely on Nordic cinema in anthologies and journals such as *Screen* and *Film International*, and is editor of *Stellar Encounters: Stardom in Popular European Cinema* (2009).

Christopher Sharrett is Professor of Communication at Seton Hall University. His recent book is a monograph on the 1950s TV western *The Rifleman*. He is editor of *Crisis Cinema: The Apocalyptic Idea in Postmodern Narrative Film*, and *Mythologies of Violence in Postmodern Media*. He is co-editor of *Planks of Reason: Essays on the Horror Film*. His work has appeared in *Cineaste, Film International, Senses of Cinema, Framework, Film Quarterly, Journal of Popular Film and Television, CineAction, Persistence of Vision*, and other publications.

Lindsay Steenberg is a lecturer in Film and Television Studies at the University of East Anglia. She has published essays on female investigators and forensic science in contemporary crime thrillers on film and television. Her wider research interests focus on the intersections of violence and gender in postfeminist and postmodern media culture.

Julian Stringer is Associate Professor of Film Studies at the University of Nottingham and coordinating editor of *Scope: An Online Journal of Film and Television Studies* (www.scope.nottingham. ac.uk). His most recent book is *Japanese Cinema: Texts and*

Contexts (co-edited with Alastair Phillips, 2007). He is currently writing a monograph on Wong Kar-wai's *In the Mood for Love.*

Yvonne Tasker is Professor of Film and Television Studies at the University of East Anglia. She is the author and editor of a number of books dealing with popular cinema and culture including most recently, with Diane Negra, the collection *Interrogating Postfeminism: Gender and the Politics of Popular Culture* (2007). Her next book, *Soldiers' Stories: Military Women in Cinema and Television since WWII,* will be published in 2011.

Sharon Lin Tay is Senior Lecturer in Film Studies at Middlesex University in London, and co-curator of the digital arts exhibition of the Finger Lakes Environmental Film Festival in upstate New York. Her book on women filmmakers and digital artists, *Women on the Edge: Twelve Political Film Practices*, was published in 2009.

Ginette Vincendeau is Professor of Film Studies at King's College London. She has written widely on French and European cinema. Among her books are *Stars and Stardom in French Cinema* (2000 and 2004), *Jean-Pierre Melville, An American in Paris* (2003) and *La Haine* (2005). She is co-editor, with Susan Hayward, of *French Film, Texts and Contexts* (1993 and 2000), with Alastair Phillips, of *Journeys of Desire, European Actors in Hollywood* (2006) and with Peter Graham, of *The New Wave: Critical Landmarks* (2009). She is currently completing a study of the South of France in film and television. Her collection of essays, *Popular French Cinema: From the Classical to the Trans-National,* will be published in 2010.

Glyn White is a Lecturer in Twentieth Century Literature and Culture at the University of Salford. He teaches an MA module called Relocating the Gangster while researching, with all due seriousness, various aspects of British and American film and television comedy towards a co-authored book called *Laughing Matters*.

Tony Williams is Professor and Area Head of Film Studies in the Department of English, Southern Illinois University at Carbondale. He has recently published *John Woo's Bullet in the Head* and is presently working on a second edition of *George A. Romero: Knight of the Living Dead*. Other projects include George A. Romero Interviews and anthologies on the work of Evans Chan and Hong Kong Neo-Noir.

Jason Wood is a film programmer and writer. Books include: *Nick Broomfield: Documenting Icons, The Faber Book of Mexican Cinema,*

100 Road Movies and *100 American Independent Films* (2nd edition). His writing also appears in *Vertigo, Little White Lies* and *Sight and Sound.*

Justin Wyatt is Senior Consultant, Primary Research at Comcast Entertainment Group. He has worked in the entertainment industry at the ABC Television Network and the consulting firm, Frank N. Magid Associates. He is the author of *High Concept: Movies and Marketing in Hollywood* (1994) and *Poison* (1998), and the co-editor of *Contemporary American Independent Film: From the Margins to the Mainstream* (2004).

Zhang Zhen teaches cinema studies at New York University. Her books include *An Amorous History of the Silver Screen, Shanghai Cinema, 1896–1937* (2005) and *The Urban Generation: Chinese Cinema and Society at the Turn of the Twenty-first Century* (2007). Zhang Zhen is also co-organiser of Chinese film series for venues such as the Film Society at the Lincoln Center for the Performing Arts and the Museum of Modern Art in New York, in addition to numerous Chinese independent documentary film programs at New York University.

ACKNOWLEDGEMENTS

The team at Routledge have been invaluable in seeing this second edition through to completion: thanks to David Avital with whom I initially worked on the project, and to Katherine Ong who took over part way. Many of the original contributors have remained involved for this edition, with new contributors coming on board as new entries have been introduced. Thanks are due to all those who not only wrote for this edition but made helpful recommendations. Devin Orgeron's entry on Wes Anderson draws on an essay originally published in *Cinema Journal* Vol 46, No. 2, 2007, and I wish to acknowledge the journal's cooperation here. Finally, I also want to thank Rachel Hall for her work on the book and for keeping me organised.

NOTES ON THE TEXT

Each essay includes a brief filmography that focuses primarily on directorial work, giving details of English titles where appropriate. Some entries also give information on other roles undertaken – such as writer, author of the screenplay, performer, composer or editor – as well as major television work. In addition to works cited in the footnotes, suggestions for further reading are given at the end of individual essays.

INTRODUCTION
Authorship in contemporary film culture and criticism

Questions of authorship (who can be said to author a film text?) have played a founding role in the development of critical writings about film, and indeed the broader academic study of the medium that is film studies. Initially these questions were bound up with an older concern – the extent to which film could or could not be viewed as something we might term 'art'. Those French, British and US critics who pioneered the study of film authorship during the 1950s, 60s and 70s sought to argue not so much that film was art – such a case had long been made for certain kinds of cinema, loosely what we now refer to under the broad heading of 'art cinema'[1] – but that popular and specifically Hollywood cinema had generated not only generic formulae, but intense and compelling cinematic works. In championing not just mavericks whose relationship to the studio system was complex and frustrating (Orson Welles, say) but those directors who thrived within its parameters (such as Hitchcock, Ford, Hawks, Sirk) authorship critics insisted on the complexity, intricacy and potential of popular filmmaking.

In the 1950s, authorship criticism sprang, as Peter Wollen put it, from a 'conviction that the American cinema was worth studying in depth' and that 'masterpieces were made ... by a whole range of authors, whose work had previously been dismissed and consigned to oblivion'.[2] It also stemmed, as James Naremore emphasises, from a passionate interest in the cinema.[3] Building on the frequently chaotic *politique des auteurs*, the auteur theory or auteurism flourished in English-language criticism of the 1960s, playing an important part in establishing the academic study of popular cinema, as well as generating passionate and close readings of films in such magazines as *Movie* in Britain and *Film Comment* in the United States. Reading the film director as an auteur meant crediting that individual with an overarching creative responsibility and vision; it also involved the understanding of the films they had directed as a coherent body of work characterised by formal and/or thematic patterns discernible by

1

the critic. Like the culture of the film festival, which rapidly gained momentum in the post-war period, authorship was always about the cultural status of film – whether reductively in the production of a canon, or polemically in an insistence on the importance of commercial or genre filmmakers such as Howard Hawks or Douglas Sirk. The most positive legacy of both the French *politique* and British and American auteurism was the establishment of a serious interest in the possibilities of popular cinema, in part through the strategic extension of a critical method associated with art cinema to other arenas.

At its simplest, authorship criticism involves the attribution of creativity to a team or, more usually, to an individual (almost always the director). The director/author is an organising presence in this view, the figure who brings together the disparate elements of a film production into a coherent form. Early authorship criticism emphasised a romantic idea of creative vision via the contention that filmmaking was potentially personal and distinctive as much as (or, at times, rather than) commercial and generic. American cinema's highly developed (and highly codified) use of the formal qualities of the shot, the mise-en-scène that was so central to authorship criticism, seemed to offer a counter to the emphasis on the screenplay as the most significant aspect of filmmaking. That is, mise-en-scène criticism suggestively proposed valuing films within a specifically *cinematic* frame of reference, rather than in terms of the cinema's relationship to other media: to literature, theatre or poetry, say. Authorship critics emphasised how revered directors were able to stamp their authority on material from any number of genres via their use of mise-en-scène and cinematography. A new orthodoxy emerged, one enshrined in Andrew Sarris's codification of great directors in American cinema.[4] Though the advent of structuralism within film studies suggested a more complex rendition of authorship, rejecting the taint of what Wollen termed the 'cult of personality', as a critical method it was increasingly contested.[5]

The limitations of ideas of cinematic authorship are by now familiar: the overly romantic figure of the individual (whether the director or some other) in a medium which is not only typically complex and collaborative, but corporate in character; the reductive reading of film as autobiography; the repression of complexity in the desire to identify an overriding stylistic or thematic unity. Thus, for example, Richard Maltby writes that the 'multiple logics and intentions that continue to impinge on the process of production ensure that authorship remains an inadequate explanation of how movies work'.[6]

For Maltby and others, the collaborative aspects of film production, particularly in highly developed commercial systems, suggested problems with attributing creativity to one individual (particularly as, for much of Hollywood history, that individual was almost always male and almost always white). As film studies became increasingly interested in understanding films within historical and industrial contexts, questions of their authored status seemed less and less relevant. These limitations are very real, as contributors to this volume are acutely aware. What does it mean, for example, to identify an individual as the one responsible for a complex entity like a film? And how might we distinguish between what is obviously a personal film in one context (for instance, Julie Dash's lengthy struggle to get *Daughters of the Dust* to cinemas[7]) from its wider significance as an innovative production in formal and thematic respects, for example, or indeed the film's status as a groundbreaking film in the terms of African-American women directors? In their attention to the institutions within which directors produce and exhibit their films, as well as discussion of the films themselves, the essays in this collection aim to contextualise individual directors and their work, acknowledging the limitations, but also the possibilities of an authorship approach.

Indeed the late 1990s and the 2000s have seen a reinvigoration of perspectives on authorship with the emergence of new scholarship and the reframing of authorship within the context of a digital age.[8] If film studies has reconsidered authorship in new ways in the last decade, this is surely in part a response to the prominence of the figure of the director. When directors with as few as two or three films to their credit are referred to, or refer to themselves, as *auteurs* then we must understand the term and what it stands for in a new way. The idea of the director as film author is a commonplace of contemporary film culture, one embraced by filmmakers themselves, by audiences and by an industry keen to target its products on the basis of previous successes. It is something of a truism that the director − promoted, interviewed, commenting on their films via DVD extras − has become something of a celebrity. Yet different work is being done by the identification of authors in the context of film festivals, in film advertising, in film criticism and in directors' own self-descriptions. So, for instance, the use of Steven Spielberg's name with respect to films he has directed or produced suggests a particular set of qualities, a brand. In contrast, Wes Anderson's self-authoring via DVD extras, discussed here by Devin Orgeron, suggests a distinct mobilisation of author discourse.[9]

The idea of the director as an impresario or self-publicist is far from new, accelerating in the American cinema of the post-war period as more directors took on the role of producer.[10] In an interview given in 1975, Victor Perkins spoke (in relation to Hawks) of 'the evasions and the image-mongering of the director, the whole projection business'.[11] What is perhaps distinctive to the contemporary scene is the scale of this phenomenon and its distribution across different sectors. As Todd Solondz notes:

> One of the things you've got going for you now is that there's more publicity for low-budget independent directors ... your name as a director is something that you can develop into a certain kind of value, so you can be less dependent on cast. When you buy a book, you look at the author.[12]

This literary analogy returns us to early writings on authorship – Alexandre Astruc's *Caméra Stylo*[13] – in a rather telling way, evoking the director's name as a factor in consumer choice. Timothy Corrigan refers to this phenomenon as the 'commerce of auteurism'.[14] The film festival, we should recall, revolves around film commerce as much as film culture: effective film criticism must consider both. Equally, whilst it is evident that young (male) directors are hyped as the new voice of independent cinema, this does not mean that the term is simply redundant; rather that we need to understand critically the process that produces some directors (and not others) as star names. Cherry Smyth cites producer Christine Vachon's comment on the marketing of *Poison* and *Swoon* in this context: 'It's just so much easier to position men as the new artistic hot potato to watch'.[15]

The specific issues faced by women directors and filmmakers highlighted by Vachon's comment point to a more general concern for a book of this kind. That is, the directors whose work is examined here operate in very different contexts – national, international and transnational – from the European art cinema to commercial film-making in the United States or Hong Kong, to television and the festival circuit. Some command vast budgets while others pursue state- or television-derived funding. Some attract critical attention only gradually, while others are scrutinised virtually from the beginning of their careers. Similarly, their work is *seen* in very different contexts, whether it is widely available through major cinema chains and rental/retail outlets (digital or otherwise), or accessible only within specialist cinemas or through film festivals. It is clear that no one model of authorship is adequate to these different contexts. Unsurprisingly, therefore, the writers in this collection approach their subjects from different perspectives: some foreground industrial factors, others thematic consistency of the director's work, for example. None the less, each essay aims to encapsulate key approaches to these directors: asking why their work matters, how they have been understood to date and how students of the cinema might meaningfully think about their work as in some way authored.

Finally, it is important to add a word on the selection process for this second edition. Commissioning new essays – on relatively young directors such as Sofia Coppola or Shane Meadows, for instance – for the book has meant excluding others, a contentious business in a field so preoccupied with lists and hierarchies. As with the 2002 edition, this collection is not offered in a spirit of exclusion or with the intention of suggesting a stable canon. I have been guided by a desire to foreground contemporary directors and filmmakers, and to acknowledge those who have attracted significant degrees of interest on the part of students, scholars, critics and filmmakers themselves, as well as audiences. I have endeavoured to foreground the work of women directors, while acknowledging that women are rarely given the opportunity to assemble the body of work (in terms of scale) associated with many male directors. The selection equally aims to acknowledge the place of commercial, as well as elite or art cinema, directors in current critical perspectives on authorship (these are not, of course, clear cut categories either). Taken together, these essays offer the reader a way into understanding the work of directors who have shaped, and are shaping, contemporary filmmaking and film culture.

Notes

1 For a useful discussion of the development of European art cinema, and its perception as an authored cinema, see Steve Neale, 'Art Cinema as Institution', *Screen* 22.1, 1981, pp. 11–39.

2 Peter Wollen, 'The Auteur Theory', in Bill Nichols (ed.) *Movies and Methods*, Berkeley, University of California Press, 1976, p. 530.

3 James Naremore, 'Authorship and the Cultural Politics of Film Criticism', *Film Quarterly*, Fall 1990, pp. 14–23.

4 See Andrew Sarris, 'Notes on the Auteur Theory in 1962', *Film Culture* Winter 1962–63. Sarris's work is reproduced widely. See for example the extract in Leo Braudy and Marshall Cohen (eds) *Film Theory and Criticism*, Oxford, Oxford University Press, 2004.

5 Peter Wollen, Conclusion to the second edition of *Signs and meaning in the Cinema*, London, Secker & Warburg, 1972, p. 167.

6 Richard Maltby, *Hollywood Cinema: An Introduction*, Oxford, Blackwell, 1995, p. 33.

7 See Terry Moore's essay on Julie Dash in this collection (p. 142).

8 For a thoughtful overview and insight into these questions see Catherine Grant, 'www.auteur.com?' *Screen*, 41:1, Spring 2000, pp. 101–8. See also Anna Notaro, 'Technology in Search of an Artist: Questions of Auteurism/Authorship and the Contemporary Cinematic Experience', *The Velvet Light Trap*, 57, Spring 2006, pp. 86–97.

9 See Devin Orgeron's essay on Wes Anderson in this collection (p. 18). And for a more detailed discussion of this aspect of Anderson's authored image, see his 'La Camera-Crayola: Authorship Comes of Age in the Cinema of Wes Anderson', *Cinema Journal*, vol. 46, no. 2, 2007, pp. 40–65.

10 Maltby writes of Hitchcock as a 'deliberate commercial creation': 'Before Hitchcock the author there was Hitchcock the marketing strategy, promoting the visibly self-conscious presence of Alfred Hitchcock in the movies he directed'. *Hollywood Cinema*, p. 438.

11 See the extracts from a 1975 *Movie* roundtable in John Caughie (ed.) *Theories of Authorship*, London, Routledge/BFI, 1981, p. 59.

12 'Van-guard Roundtable', *Premiere*, October 1998, p. 88.

13 See Ed Buscombe, 'Ideas of Authorship', in Caughie (ed.). Astruc's 'The Birth of a New Avant-garde: La Caméra-stylo' is translated in Peter Graham (ed.) *The New Wave*, London, Secker & Warburg/BFI, 1968.

14 Timothy Corrigan, *A Cinema Without Walls: Movies and Culture After Vietnam*, New Brunswick, NJ, Rutgers University Press, 1991.

15 Cherry Smyth, 'Beyond Queer Cinema: It's in her Kiss', in Liz Gibbs (ed.) *Daring to Dissent: Lesbian Culture from Margin to Mainstream*, London, Cassell, 1994. For an example of the speedy but knowing elevation of the director as star–auteur see Peter Biskind (on Quentin Tarantino), 'An Auteur is Born', *Empire*, November 1994, pp. 94–102. Christina Lane makes a similar point with respect to women directors working in the US independent scene in her 'Just another girl outside the neo-indie' in Chris Holmlund and Justin Wyatt (eds) *Contemporary American Independent Film: From the Margins to the Mainstream*, New York, Routledge, 2005, pp. 193–209.

PEDRO ALMODÓVAR

By José Arroyo

Pedro Almodóvar is a star director. As with stars, his name alone condenses a series of identities that change over time but can also be historically located. He's been first a leading light of Madrid's underground arts scene during the period of Spain's transition to democracy from 1975 to 1982, then the *enfant terrible* of Spanish Cinema in the 1980s, later the Spanish director so celebrated internationally that he becomes first synonymous with its national cinema and then eclipses it altogether: it's fair to say that more has been written about Almodóvar in English than on the rest of Spanish Cinema put together.

Now he is a grand old man of European cinema, an acknowledged master of the art. However, 'Almodóvar' signifies not only a career, or social changes, but ways of being, ways of looking and certain types of movies. His great gift has been to make those on the edges of society, the excluded, derided, the subalterns of society (in different ways and on different levels, women, gays, the deserted, the bereft, drag queens, drug addicts, social and sexual criminals) not only central to his films but to depict them in such a way that the audience empathises and sometimes even identifies with them – they not only become understandable and knowable but 'they' become 'we'. Some of the greatest female characters ever created for the cinema, often brought to life in career-defining performances by some of Spain's greatest actresses (Carmen Maura as Pepa in *Women on the Verge of a Nervous Breakdown* and Penélope Cruz as Raimunda in *Volver* to name but two) are the heart and motor of his films; and the setting for their story and the way it is told is often a marvel of mise-en-scène.

Contexts

An understanding of the political, cinematic and cultural contexts in which Almodóvar began making films is crucial to understanding his achievements and the impact of his early films. Born a decade after the Civil War, Almodóvar is part of a generation who grew up as Franco declined into old age. Important events that frame his early career are the states of emergency, which suspended civil liberties, declared by the regime in January of 1969 and December 1970 (the period when Almodóvar first moved to Madrid and which he would later use as setting for the beginning of *Live Flesh*), the assassination of Carrero Blanco, Spain's Prime Minister, which brought an end to the relative liberalisation of the *dictablanda* or soft dictatorship in 1973 and Spain's tenuous transition to Democracy from Franco's death in 1975 to the election of the Spanish Socialist Worker's Party (PSOE) in 1982. The fragility of Spain's hold on Democracy was made evident by Colonel Tejero's attempted coup in 1981. When Almodóvar says, as he has done repeatedly, that his films were made as if Franco had never existed, it doesn't mean that he was unaware of politics but that, well aware of all the risks, he still chose to make his art in freedom. It is important to remember that the titles of some of the shorts and Super-8 films he made during this period (*Dos putas ... o una historia de amor que termina en boda/ Two whores ... or a Love Story that Ends with a Wedding* or *Folle, Folle ... Fólleme Tim/ Fuck, Fuck, Fuck Me Tim* [1978]) alone would have landed him in jail a few years earlier.

Bom peeing on the policeman's wife in *Pepi, Luci, Bom* might seem merely cheeky camp, until one remembers that a few years earlier Spain had been a *military* dictatorship, or speculates on the consequences of such imagery had Colonel Tejero's coup succeeded. It is only then that that representation in *Pepi*, one of many in his early films, is revealed as the radical and subversive gesture that it is. What his early films evoke most powerfully is a sense of courage and daring made possible by youth and an emerging sense of personal and social liberation.

Almodóvar is remarkable first because he managed to make films at all – I can't think of another director of his generation who hails from the rural peasantry – and second because the films he did make were so different from anything that had been made in Spain until that time. When Almodóvar began his career, ideals of great filmmaking were seen to be exemplified by Victor Erice's *El Espíritu de la colmena/ The Spirit of the Beehive*, 1973, and Carlos Saura's *Cría cuervos/ Cría* (USA)/ *Raise Ravens* (UK), 1975. Erice and Saura's great works are densely symbolic, hermetic, allegorical art cinema made at a time when this mode of filmmaking was a way for directors and large audiences in Spain to commune in a social critique of the regime and of society. In a context in which this was seen as *the* model of, and purpose for, cinematic art, *Pepi* and *Labyrinth of Passion*, with their broad winks to Andy Warhol and John Waters; their borrowings from comic books, *Hello* Magazine, and a wide range of references from cinema and other aspects of popular culture; their scatological and corrosive humour and crude technique, not to speak of their superficiality and campness, were greeted by the critical establishment with all the shock of the new and found wanting aesthetically. As Vicente Molina-Foix has written, 'it took a long time for Almodóvar to be recognised as a great filmmaker in his own country'.[1] Luckily, Almodóvar's first features gave voice to, and found ardent support from, both an emerging youth culture and a gay subculture.

'La movida' as mode of production and consumption

Pepi and *Labyrinth* are products of a period and of a scene of which the films in turn are now the most vivid documents. The period is the transition to Democracy. 'This country is beginning to have so much Democracy, I don't know where it will end', says Luci's husband in *Pepi* ... , 'we have to give the Communists a good beating!' The scene is '*La nueva movida Madrileña*', a loose amalgamation of artists, performers and musicians who had no more in common than

8

clubbing together, a desire for the new, particularly as refracted from the fashion and music scenes in London, first glam, then punk, then the New Romantics, and a wish to shock anyone in Spain who chose to cling to outmoded ideas. Many of the artists who formed part of the scene and later became famous (Ceesepe, Fanny McNamara, Alaska y los Pegamoides, Costus etc.) contributed to and/or appeared in *Pepi* and *Labyrinth*. Though the films are still funny and they surprisingly continue to shock, they are also now imbued with a patina of nostalgia that accrues to that which is lost – the youth of the first generation of *Madrileños* since the Civil War able to explore their identities in a Democratic country where new norms of behaviour had not yet been agreed to, and with all the attendant pleasures and dangers that entails.

Pepi, shot on 16mm and blown up to 35mm for release, was made over a period of two years on a shoestring budget provided mainly by friends. It found an avid audience, particularly at the Alphaville cinema in Madrid, where it was so successful the cinema itself financed Almodóvar's second feature, *Labyrinth of Passion*. The two films became staples of the repertoire, playing at the cinema for years, often at late screenings to audiences already so fond of and familiar with the films they would voice the dialogue before the film's characters. The scene where Fanny McNamara sniffs nail polish in *Labyrinth*, for example, was received with the kind of relish and audience participation Anglo-American audiences might remember from midnight screenings of *The Rocky Horror Picture Show*.

If the screenings of *Pepi* and *Labyrinth* were the focal point of ritual happenings, Almodóvar was happening right along with them, his finger not only on the pulse of *La movida* but also constantly dipping into many other art forms. Whilst still working at his day job as a clerk for the National Telephone Company, he was also a member of the *Los Goliardos* theatre troupe, performed and recorded in a punk band (*Almodóvar y McNamara*, whose songs would become part of the soundtrack to *The Law of Desire*), wrote short stories, photonovels and created the character of Patty Diphusa for the *La Luna de Madrid* magazine.[2] All of these activities, along with what amounts to a genius for publicity in general (as is evident in the parodies of TV advertisements he inserted in almost all the early films, risking bringing the narratives to a standstill in order to get a good joke in) and self promotion in particular (still evident in the meticulous press books prepared for each new release) meant he couldn't be ignored and he wasn't. He'd become not only a director but an instantly recognisable national star.

Entering the mainstream

Dark Habits, *What Have I Done to Deserve This?* and *Matador* represent a steady progression in Almodóvar's career. *Dark Habits* was the first of his films to be produced by a 'proper' production company (Tesauro S.A., who would also go on to produce *What Have I Done to Deserve This?*); *What Have I Done...?* was his first mainstream popular and critical success; *Matador* was the first of his films to receive the funding from Spain's Ministry of Culture then essential for any mainstream filmmaking in Spain. The three films are the last he would make for outside production companies and they are instructive in what each tells us about Almodóvar's developing aesthetic.

Dark Habits is still very funny and a pleasure to watch for many reasons: the jokes, the music, the increasing evidence that Almodóvar has an eye for shot compositions that are pleasing in themselves but also progress the narrative. The actresses in the film are wonderful and now evidently a repertory company (later to be much publicised as *Las chicas Almodóvar* whose number would also include some *chicos* such as, most famously, Antonio Banderas): Cecilia Roth, Carmen Maura, Julieta Serrano had already appeared in his previous films; Antonio Banderas, Immanol Arias, Assumpta Serna, not cast here, had appeared before in earlier films and would again in later ones: Chus Lampreave makes her first appearance here and would delight audiences in Almodóvar films for years to come. The film is also interesting in that it demonstrates that Almodóvar is not infallible with actors; that the great performances in his films are collaborations for which actors need to be given their due; the proof is Cristina S. Pascual's performance as Yolanda, unarguably the worst in Almodóvar's oeuvre and deadly in a film that is essentially a vehicle for that actress.

What Have I Done to Deserve This? is the first of Almodóvar's films which may lay claim to the attention of those interested in film as an art. It's useful to see it in relation to *Trailer para amantes de lo prohibido/Trailer for Lovers of the Forbidden*, a short commissioned by Spanish television and which Almodóvar made partly to help publicise *What Have I Done...?* (the premiere of the latter appears as the conclusion of the story of the short). *Trailer* is the story of a housewife who turns to crime to support her children when her husband leaves her, before finding love with a Midnight Cowboy at the end. Most of the story is told through songs the characters mime (flamenco, disco, boleros). When characters do talk, it's in an exaggerated version of 'movie' dialogue. The film has the look and feel of a drag queen's dream after a night of debauche. It is funny and touching and, as befits a film dedicated to, amongst others, David Bowie and Olga Guillot, caused quite a stir in homes around the nation when it was shown on television. It underlines two characteristics of Almodóvar's work: camp and affect.

What Have I Done...? has all the elements audiences had by this point already come to expect of an Almodóvar film: camp humour, parodies of advertisements, a use of music that is simultaneously a send-up of and vehicle for emotion, a mix of genres and styles (in this case melodrama, suspense, neorealism), scenes that are extended quasi-vaudeville skits (the bit where the housewife helps out her prostitute neighbour with a client; the sale of her son to the dentist). Yet, in what is undoubtedly a postmodern pastiche, the film belies the claims of those such as Jameson who argue that pastiche is just empty quotation incapable of affect. The film depicts a people and a way of life (working class people in the neighbourhood of *La Concepción)*, that in spite of the spate of quotations and the absurdities of some of the situations Almodóvar places them in, remain recognisably real and very affecting. This is due primarily to two factors, Carmen Maura's magisterial performance, and Almodóvar's ability to create dialogue that is so recognisable as an embodiment of a common sense structure of feeling in everyday speech that it anchors the sometimes absurd situations to an emotional realism (something Maura's performance and the use of real locations, décor, and costumes – Almodóvar borrowed his sisters' clothing – also contribute to). It's his first great film.

Matador, his subsequent film, may be seen as a ludic exploration of key clichés of Spanishness: sex, death, religion, bullfighting. However, it's ultimately merely a fun film for casual consumption, an indicator of what Almodóvar's career might have been reduced to had his understanding of people not developed alongside his understanding of the craft of filmmaking.

The first crest

If Almodóvar had ended his career with *The Law of Desire* and *Women on the Verge of a Nervous Breakdown*, he would still have earned his place in this tome: the former was a breakthrough in representation of gays on film as well as a very funny and deeply affecting film; whilst the latter is simply one of the great comedies of the twentieth century. Filmmakers who twaddle on about being brave and taking risks should have a look at *Law* for a lesson in real courage. Who else would launch their first production company (El Deseo S.A. which

Almodóvar formed with his brother Agustín and which has since produced the rest of his films) with a gay love story in a country where homosexuality still remained taboo? Who else would have begun the film by having what seems to be the protagonist being asked to take it up the arse? However, *Law* is not only brave but a model of the type of narrative structure Almodóvar borrowed from Classical Hollywood Cinema and has kept honing in almost every film since: in *Law* each character has its opposite equivalent in the narrative (two brothers as protagonists, one gay, one transsexual; two lovers in supporting parts, a sensitive man who really prefers women, and a macho gay man; two mothers, a transsexual playing the biological mother, a straight woman playing the transsexual surrogate mother, and so on). If the desire in *Matador* was for sex, in *Law,* whilst sex plays a very important role, the desire is for love. *Law* was one of the first films to present homosexuality not as a social issue or a personal problem, nor as mere question of sex but, of love, in all its dimension, including sex. Its witty mise-en-scène, the bold bright look of the film, and its outrageous premise do not get in the way of the intensity of feeling conveyed, and are indeed part of the film's many pleasures. However, they may very well have detracted critics from appreciating the film's more serious undertones (and perhaps the director too as he would use the sub-plot with the priest as the premise for *Bad Education* later on).

Women on the Verge of a Nervous Breakdown is another film Almodóvar would later revisit (mistakenly, in *Broken Promises*). Borrowing its look from the bright Technicolor musicals and comedies of the 1950s such as *Funny Face*, its mise-en-scène from Hitchcock, and conveying an intensity of feeling through a cinephile's eye for the right film quote, most memorably Nicholas Ray's *Johnny Guitar*, *Women on the Verge* presents elegantly dressed women trying to deal practically with being left by the man they love and not quite succeeding, all to a mambo beat. It turns pain into surreal funnyness and it is, despite all its borrowings, completely original and completely brilliant. It's the film that memorably led Pauline Kael to describe Almodóvar as 'the most original pop writer-director of the eighties, he's Godard with a human face – a happy face'.[3]

Together *The Law of Desire* and *Women on the Verge of a Nervous Breakdown* are landmarks in Almodóvar's career, in the history of Spanish Cinema, and in the representation and marketing of Spain abroad. *The Law of Desire* was seen as autobiographical and became the Almodóvar film that, finally, fit the notion of 'personal filmmaking' then too narrowly defined and overvalued by Spain's critical establishment, and the film was received as an artistic breakthrough for the director. *Women on the Verge* was a culmination of the run of extraordinary popular success begun with *Matador*[4] and became the most successful Spanish film of all time to that date and the most successful foreign-language film in America in 1989, earning an Academy Award nomination for Best Foreign Film in the process (Almodóvar would only receive the award later and for another film, *All About My Mother*). Together the two films, with their bright colours, elegant design, their evocation of warmth, pleasure and passion, and the sense of freedom evident in both the characters and the filmmaking were finally enough to finish with the memory of Franco abroad. Spain was indeed different, and for foreigners, Spain was Almodóvarian.

Pop culture's not enough

After *Women on the Verge,* Almodóvar had a well-publicised argument with Carmen Maura and they ceased working together. Initially it didn't seem to have much of an effect on his films. Victoria Abril, who replaced her as lead actress and muse in Almodóvar's three subsequent films, was prettier, an undoubted star and almost as great an actress. *Tie Me Up! Tie Me Down!*, their first film together, was a financial success. It looked almost as stunning as Abril and Banderas, both superb in the film, and its story of a woman who falls for her captor caused such a sensation in America that it was given an x-rating, which in turn led Almodóvar and Miramax, the film's American distributor, to file a lawsuit that eventually resulted in a change to the film classification system and helped introduce the NC-17 rating. The film was a scandal and a popular success but it is not quite as good as we'd come to expect.

The 1990s were not kind to Almodóvar. Maura's face, with its extraordinary ability to evoke how ordinary people could be beautiful and feel deeply and complexly, had grounded Almodóvar's flights of fantasy, and without something similar, his work seemed to have lost some of its humanity. *High Heels*, with its thematic exploration of the maternal melodrama and its Sirkian mise-en-scène, is still a source of fascination for film academics, but one peels away the brightly coloured surface at the top only to find, contra Sirk, a brightly plastic heart underneath. *Kika* turned out to be a mess: audiences were more interested in Jean-Paul Gaultier's wardrobe for Victoria Abril then in the character she played. The film is redeemed only by Veronica Forqué's great comic performance and by a most daring sequence where Almodóvar stages a rape for laughs and succeeds (though this was becoming a troublesome motif in his oeuvre). Almodóvar tried a change of tack in *The Flower of My Secret*, opting for, and failing with, the romance genre, and the film remains memorable mainly for introducing Joaquín Cortez's flamenco dancing to the world.

Maturity

Live Flesh turned out to be the return to form critics wishfully attributed to *The Flower of My Secret*. It is also a considerable departure from his previous work: it's loosely based on Ruth Rendell's novel, the first time Almodóvar based an entire film on others' material; it is also the first time he cast Penélope Cruz and Angela Molina (both a revelation here in supporting parts and just as good in the later *Broken Embraces*) and his usual repertory of players is mostly absent. The film's emotional pitch is not only pulsating but trembling: it's still as generous a view of love as in earlier works, possibly even more so, but now more rueful as well. There are two scenes at least, the shootout in the apartment where David (Javier Bardem) is shot, and the love scene between Victor (Liberto Rabal) and Elena (Francesca Neri), that are superb examples of expressive mise-en-scène. In the latter, Almodóvar films the bodies of the undulating couple so that they become almost indistinguishable from each other and then moves the camera so close that they become abstract, expressing a symbolic metamorphosis of sex into love as well as representing that very moment of transformation. It's a beautiful scene in arguably Almodóvar's best film since *Women on the Verge*.

From here on Almodóvar's work just seemed to get better and better. *All About My Mother* and *Talk to Her* are widely acknowledged to be masterpieces. There's a strong claim to be made on behalf of *Bad Education* and arguably a lesser one for *Volver*, though the latter has been Almodóvar's most successful to date. All of these films, including *Broken Embraces*, are made in two modes; noir or/and the melodramatic, interesting if one thinks of the former, where a man's longing and desire for a woman brings him to the depths of despair or even death, as a male equivalent of the latter. It makes sense that these are Almodóvar's preferred modes. Melodrama, for example, cuts across genre, equally capable of conveying the tragic and the comic, eminently emotional, adept at arousing intense audience identification and capable of communicating complex processes no matter what the character's gender or sexual orientation. It's what allows us to look beyond the externals of Almodóvar's characters and begin to identify with them as people. It's also a genre of muteness where what the characters repress, the body of the film must express, as we can see in the tour-de-force that is the Shrinking Man sequence in *Talk to Her,* ideal for a master of mise-en-scène such as Almodóvar.

In this latest stage of Almodóvar's career, the key idea is probably the verb, 'to return', but almost in spiral form, a partial revisit in order to move forward. It's what Manuela does in *All About My Mother;* it's what the director (both the character Enrique Goded [Fele Martinez], and Almodóvar himself) do in *Bad Education;* it is of course the very title of *Volver,* its theme, and evident even in its execution (e.g. a return to Carmen Maura). But there's also a more literal sense of returning in these later works, often to well-known and well-loved earlier ones. Thus *All About My Mother* is a development of an idea from *The Flower of My Secret, Bad Education* taking its central story from the minor sub-plot in *Law of Desire* between the priest and the transsexual; *Broken Embraces* offers us a film within a film that is a remake of *Women on the Verge of a Nervous Breakdown* with Penélope Cruz cast in the Carmen Maura role. This return to previous preoccupations but now with greater insight and much greater skill in the craft of cinematic expression is a joy to watch and one of the great pleasures he offers audiences who have followed his career: he's not only able to make us feel, he makes us remember what we felt the first time we encountered those characters or that situation in his work previously, and we compare and mostly appreciate: he gives the audience that rare illusion that we've been accomplices in his development.

Paul Julien Smith has written that there are three issues funda-mental for any understanding of the cinema of Pedro Almodóvar: 'gender, nationality and homosexuality'.[5] He's right of course, but we must also add 'cinema' itself to that list. Not only because his work has constantly used a history of cinema as source and vehicle for expression (and because a film like *Broken Embraces* may be seen as an extended thesis on the medium itself) but because his films reward repeat, close and informed viewing. They tell us what the director himself can't or won't; that, for example, the noir hero of *Bad Education* is the paedophile priest, that the film is indeed auto-biographical. At the end of *Bad Education* the word 'passion' is the word through which the name of Enrique Goded, the fictional director in the film, merges with that of Pedro Almodóvar. And the result of Almodóvar's passion for the medium is a rare understanding of film form, almost unimaginable on the evidence of his first film, now capable of expressing an even rarer understanding and kind-hearted view of people. This combination has produced an *oeuvre*, and the career contains the unity required by the term, that for thirty years now has delighted the eye, touched the heart, tickled the funnybone and deepened our thinking and our understanding. His is an indispensable and unique body of work.

Biography

Born 24 September 1949,[6] Calzada de Calatrava, Ciudad Real, Castilla-La Mancha, Spain. His family moved to Cáceres when he was eight. He was educated first by the Silesians and then, at High School, with the Franciscans. In 1986 he founded the production company El Deseo S.A. with his brother Agustín which has produced all of his films since then as well as the work of other young directors (Isabel Coixet, Alex de la Iglesia, Lucrecia Martel and Guillermo Del Toro to mention only a few).

Notes

1 'Almodóvar tardo mucho ... en ser aceptado como oun gran cineaste en su país' (author's translation), in Vicente Molina Foix, 'Almodóvar, una fenomenología española', preface to Jean-Max Méjean, *Pedro Almodóvar*, Barcelona: Ediciones Robinbook, 2007, p. 9.

2 These stories were later collected along with other texts as *Patty Diphusa y otros textos*, Barcelona: Editorial Anagrama, 1991.

3 Pauline Kael, 'Women on the Verge of a Nervous Breakdown', *Movie Love: Complete Reviews 1988–1991*, New York, Plume, 1991, p. 23.

4 The Spanish Government's own accounting shows *Matador* to be the third most successful Spanish film of 1986. See Francisco LLinas (ed.) *4 años de cine español 1983–1986*, Madrid: Imagfic, 1987, p. 99; *The Law of Desire* came in fourth in 1987, *Women on the Verge* first in both 1988 and in 1989 and *Tie Me Up! Tie Me Down!* third in 1990. See Ferran Alberich ed., *4 años de cine español (1986–1989)*, Madrid: Imprenta de la Comunidad de Madrid, 1991, pp. 101, 129, 158 and 190 respectively.

5 Paul Julian Smith, *Vision Machines: Cinema, Literature and Sexuality in Spain and Cuba 1983–1993*, London: Verso, 1996, p. 37.

6 There is a deliberate obsfucation of Almodóvar's birth date. The press release for *Broken Embraces* would like us to think it was sometime 'in the 50's'. Antonio Holguín in *Pedro Almodóvar* (Madrid: Ediciones Cátedra, 1994) gives his birthday as the 25th of September 1951 (p. 25). Almodóvar himself told *Libération* it was the 24th of September 1952 (See Jean-Max Méjean, *Pedro Almodóvar*, trans. Caterina Berthelot, Barcelona: Ediciones Robinbooks, 2007, p. 183), The *Diccionario del cine español* (ed. José Luis Borau, Madrid: Alianza Editorial S.A. 1998), generally considered to be authoritative, gives the year as 1949 (p. 48).

Filmography (feature films for theatrical release)

Pepi, Luci, Bom y otras chicas del montón/ Pepi, Luci, Bom and Other Girls on the Heap (1980)
Laberinto de pasiones/ Labyrinth of Passion (1982)
Entre Tinieblas/ Dark Habits (1983)
¿Qué he hecho yo para merecer esto!!/ What Have I Done to Deserve This? (1984)
Matador (1986)
La ley del deseo/ The Law of Desire (1987)
Mujeres al borde de un ataque de nervios/ Women on the Verge of a Nervous Breakdown (1988)
¡Atame!/ Tie Me Up! Tie Me Down! (1989)
Tacones lejanos/ High Heels (1991)
Kika (1993)
La flor de mi secreto/ The Flower of My Secret (1995)
Carne trémula/Live Flesh (1997)
Todo sobre mi madre/ All About My Mother (1999)
Hable con ella/ Talk to Her (2002)
La mala educación/ Bad Education (2004)
Volver (2006)
Los abrazos rotos/ Broken Embraces (2009)

Shorts and Super-8

Dos putas, o historia de amor que termina en boda (1974)
Film politico (1974)
Blancor (1975)
El sueño de la estrella (1975)
Homenaje (1975)
Muerte en la carretera (1976)
Sea caritativo (1976)
Tráiler de 'Who's Afraid of Virginia Woolf?' (1976)
Sex ova, sexo viene (1977)
Folle … folle, fólleme Tim (1978)
Salomé (1978)
Tráiler para amantes de lo prohibido (1985) TV
La concejala antropófaga (2009)

Further reading

Ernesto R. Acevedo-Muñoz, *Pedro Almodóvar*, London: BFI, 2007.
Mark Allinson, *A Spanish Labyrinth: The Films of Pedro Almodóvar*, London: Tauris, 2001.
Marvin D'Lugo, *Pedro Almodóvar*, Urbana; Chicago: University of Illinois Press, 2006.
Peter William Evans, *Women on the Verge of a Nervous Breakdown*, London: BFI, 1996.

Paul Julien Smith, *Desire Unlimited: The Cinema of Pedro Almodóvar,* London: Verso, 1994.

Frédéric Strauss (ed.), *Almodóvar on Almodóvar,* Translated by Yves Baignères; additional material translated by Sam Richard, London: Faber and Faber, 1996.

Kathleen M. Vernon and Barbara Morris, *The Films of Pedro Almodóvar,* London: Greenwood Press, 1995.

Nuria Vidal, *The Films of Pedro Almodóvar,* translated by Linda Moore in collaboration with Victoria Hughes, Madrid: Instituto de la Cinematografía y las Artes Audiovisuales, Ministerio de la Cultura, 1988.

WES ANDERSON

By Devin Orgeron

In the space of six feature films since 1996, Wes Anderson has become, for better or worse, a model for contemporary cinematic authorship in the United States. His aesthetic and thematic concerns, which are decidedly consistent, are only part of the equation, though. One of a handful of American filmmakers to whom the moniker 'quirky' is regularly applied (one suspects, much to the dismay of the filmmaker himself), Anderson's films are almost absurdly recognisable. Recognisablity, in fact, is a key element in Anderson's highly orchestrated – perhaps even branded – running commentary on the theoretical and practical 'condition' of the auteur.

Populating his films with flawed but ultimately redeemable auteurs who, in the end, plot elaborate fictions in the name of a community that requires their particular intervention, Anderson's films imagine the author to be an almost inscrutable entity. The risk of narcissistic abandon always lurks in the background, yet Anderson is careful to see his singular visionaries corralled or, to use an aquatic metaphor (Anderson himself is quite fond of them), anchored to the community they serve. In this way, Anderson's fictional authors unite to protect the increasingly fragile directorial niche Anderson has carved out for himself.

Anderson's authorial logic is organised around the concept of youth and, on the surface at least, positions itself against the still quite powerful though academically unpopular myth of the solitary genius. This idea manifests itself thematically in all six of Anderson's feature films: *Bottle Rocket, Rushmore, The Royal Tenenbaums, The Life Aquatic, The Darjeeling Limited* and *Fantastic Mr. Fox.* Perhaps because his films are about childhood – literal and prolonged – they are also about family and the need, in the face of familial abandonment, to create communities in its place. Warning against the danger of smug (but usually troubled) solitude, his films repeatedly valorise the group and stand as theoretical parables for a notion of collective authorship in spite of the fact that Anderson himself has become a poster child for (and sometimes against) 'the author' in its more antiquated, singular and romantic valence.

Anderson's debut feature, *Bottle Rocket*, is a surprisingly mature examination of immaturity: its costs as well as its rewards. The film takes as its subject three apparently aimless twenty-somethings – Dignan, played by Anderson's co-writer and longtime friend Owen Wilson; Anthony, played by Luke Wilson; and Bob, played by Robert Musgrave – and their humorous wanderings down a 'criminal' career path. Dignan is the group's unlikely 'leader', orchestrating semi-climactic, cinematically derived 'scenes' and, more often than not, behaving like the group's oddly ambitious director. He is a kind of social auteur, codifying in his own way the events that mark his and his friends' lives.

Self-centered, unrealistic and irritating, there is also a sad and desperate persistence to Dignan that his friends and the viewer must respond to, a need for community and a desire for approval that find expression in his misguided and seemingly narcissistic stabs at leadership and his energised but dizzy plans. The frantic activity in *Bottle Rocket* and Anderson's later films is compensatory, covering significant gaps in the lives of his characters. Bob and Anthony, in other words, need to be directed as much as Dignan needs to direct, an idea that begins to take shape in the film's first minutes as Dignan plays out Anthony's unnecessarily elaborate 'escape' from a mental institution (we eventually learn that Anthony's residency was voluntary and he was free to exit using the building's front door at any time during his stay).

After the 'escape', Dignan shares with Anthony his meticulously organised notes outlining his seventy-five-year plan, which are written in Crayola markers and exhibit an intellect that is delightfully and seductively juvenile. Dignan's plan for the next three-quarters of a century attends to practice jobs, goals, professional ambitions, relationships and economic concerns, and is presented in a series of rapid, slightly disorienting cuts. The cuts themselves are expressive of Dignan's distracted point of view.[1] His is the work of the clinical micromanager, busily organising the little details as the larger and uncontrollable details (like family) disintegrate around him. Needless to say, Dignan's plan fails. His absurdly intricate robbery of a cold storage facility *and* his innocence are undermined by his alternate father, Mr Henry's (James Caan) only slightly more authentic criminality. Dignan's microscopic attention to detail, his trees-at-the-cost-of-the-forest logic, also governs, as we shall see, Anderson's own developing set of directorial principals.

'The world needs dreamers', Mr Henry tells Bob's brother Futureman (Andrew Wilson), publicly shaming him for his maltreatment of the boys. And, in fact, dreams form the centre of Anderson's second feature, *Rushmore*, feeding the plays that Max (Jason Schwartzman) produces at Rushmore Academy, and serving to alter his delicate self-perception. A literal author, Max, like Dignan, seeks control, appears reckless, and is often dangerously self-absorbed. And, as in the previous film, a bit of formal manipulation gives some indication as to Max's self-image.

A montage presents a series of staged tableaux of Max's various extracurricular activities, often with Max occupying center frame. The whimsical presentation of these activities indicates Max's winning and heroic view of himself. More than narcissistic, however, Max's self-perception is coloured by a desire, similar to Dignan's, to present and preserve himself in a certain light. This is Max's life as he wishes to see it: a rapidly moving series of small but monumental triumphs. In their portrait-like composition, they might also be read as imaginary surrogates for the more traditional (and for Max, painfully incomplete) family portrait; his mother, we learn later in the film, passed away when he was very young.

Max's souped-up vision of the universe guides the film, which begins with his fantasy of solving the world's hardest maths problem; is punctuated by his post-play, post-fist-in-the-nose bow before an audience he imagines howling and cheering with delight at his masterful direction; and ends somewhat more democratically with Max sharing his customised perceptual abilities with the people in his life who need it most: Mr Blume (Bill Murray) and Ms Cross (Olivia Williams). These adults, haunted by their own domestic tragedies, will learn from Max how to see differently and, in the process, Max will learn that, contrary to his dangerous self-perception, he is not alone.

Anderson's films are all about family structure, its absence, its dissolution, its rebirth, and, above all, its eccentricity. The deeply ironic Blume family portrait, which appears at key moments in *Rushmore*, is a reminder of that character's domestic disharmony, his need, quite literally, to regroup. This idea of the family portrait arises in *The Royal Tenenbaums* as well. Here, however, it becomes a principal organisational motif closely tied to the director's notions regarding authorship.

After a lengthy prologue introducing the Tenenbaum family, their complex marital history, their individual eccentricities, and Eli Cash's (here played by James Fitzgerald and later by Owen Wilson) fascination with them, a card designed to look like a page from a book appears briefly to dedicate the film to Anderson's own family. After this dedication, the film presents its conceptual problem, which is also familial. Introducing his cast of characters one at a time – twenty-two years later, as the card above informs us – Anderson allows mise-en-scène to reflect his characters' shared psychoses. Each character is introduced as an adult, preening narcissistically in front of a mirror, which is replaced to great effect by the camera itself allowing for a degree of comic eye contact with the audience. Isolation from each other and from their own feelings is what each member of the Tenenbaum family struggles against. More a series of elaborate vignettes than a cohesive narrative, *The Royal Tenenbaums* feels overpopulated and disjointed. From the enforced separation of this 'Cast of Characters' (the patriarch of the family, Royal's unmitigated selfishness was the catalyst for this systematic breakdown) until the film reaches something of a resolution, image after image and scene after scene reinforce both the idea and the problem of the fragmented family unit.

The failure of this family of creators is its inability to collaborate. It is a family composed of singular auteurs busily and joylessly plugging away at their creations until they and the family they once belonged to disintegrate. Though the struggle is certainly prolonged in *The Royal Tenenbaums*, it is yet another film in which abandoned characters attempt to compensate through creation: Eli is a hack writer of Western adventures; Margot, the Tenenbaums' adopted daughter, writes (or used to write) plays; Raleigh (Bill Murray), her husband, writes about neurological disorders; Etheline (Angelica Huston) has written about her family of geniuses; Chas's business appears nonexistent; in fact, he seems to feign *busyness*, and this could well be his 'invention'. Most interesting, however, is Richie (Luke Wilson). Richie, the once-admired-now-fallen tennis star, was once a portrait artist, though as the voice-over narration (spoken by Alec Baldwin) indicates, he 'failed to develop'. His art – distinctly Crayola and actually produced by Wes Anderson's brother Eric – fills the walls of the Tenenbaum household. Significantly, the art itself is focused on the family: a juvenile and highly fictionalised fantasy of the Tenenbaums' existence together, a pathetically cartoonish variation on another fractured family portrait.

By film's end and after a series of serio-comedic episodes (including the death of Royal who, like all of Anderson's best characters, eventually learns to temper his selfishness), the family is not only reunited, it is extended to include a cast of satellite characters who express a similar need to 'belong'. The progression is gradual, accompanied by similarly changing formal logic that moves from those previously mentioned one-shots to wider, more inclusive compositions. The group, now defined by its togetherness rather than its isolation, is glimpsed finally in an elegant and expressively wide closing group-shot, which Anderson slows down and sets to Van Morrison's appropriately inclusive 'Everyone'. The effect isn't exactly subtle, but it underscores Anderson's concerns in a manner that reflects interestingly back on his own self-image.

The Life Aquatic is similarly concerned with authorship, creation, and the importance of the group. Steve Zissou (Bill Murray) and the crew of the Belafonte are, ostensibly at least, oceanographers. More importantly, however, they are filmmakers and storytellers; their ship, which is introduced to viewers in an elaborate and breathtaking cross section, is their mobile studio. The curious and highly self-conscious fact that the film itself is shot largely at Italy's Cinecitta studios, where Fellini's *8½* was shot, and near Godard's locations for *Contempt*, plays up the film's interest in 'the process' and its occasionally numbing effects. This is a film, in other words, about the game of cinematic authorship, the sleight of hand involved, and the desperation it leaves in its wake – themes that should put one in mind of Eli Cash in *The Royal Tenenbaums*.

Team Zissou has become a product, a brand-name emblazoned not just on their decrepit ship or their heavily mediated film products, but on their gear, their correspondence stock, their action figures, and even a pinball machine. They are a parody of the stock our culture takes in the author's name and the phenomenon of celebrity. After the Italian premiere of his latest film, an elderly fan asks Zissou for his autograph. After producing a seemingly endless supply of lobby cards for the fading star to sign, however, he is told to go home and forge the rest. More than a quest for the elusive (perhaps nonexistent?) beast that killed Zissou's partner, Anderson's film is about the search for the (also perhaps nonexistent) author himself – an attempt to dig away the layers of artifice to 'reveal' some knowable entity, an attempt to find the significance behind the signature. This desire fuels Ned Plimpton's (Owen Wilson) attempt to establish a relationship with this man who might actually be his father; it motivates Jane Winslett-Richardson's (Cate Blanchett) journalistic endeavours for Oceanographic Explorer; and it is the real 'Deep Search' Zissou himself has unwittingly embarked upon.

If all of Anderson's films are about learned perceptual change, Zissou's learning curve is an unusually steep one, which results in the loss of human life. The film's penultimate scene, however, indicates Zissou's newfound realisation that the motley group he has assembled, his 'pack of strays' as he calls them, is a needful thing – an idea hinted at, as well, in Ned's new logo design, which keeps the author (represented by the large 'Z') central, though surrounded by critical alphabetic satellites. Zissou, in other words, is not alone, a fact he has forgotten over the years. The scene assembles the group together, sans the deceased Ned, within the ridiculous confines of Team Zissou's miniature submarine, Deep Search. In a posture that formed the advertising iconography for the film, the collective is foregrounded, though so is Zissou's visionary effect on the collective's imagination. A series of one-shots followed by their fantastic subjective views establishes the role Zissou's brand of fiction will play in each character's life.

The Darjeeling Limited (and its alleged short film companion/prequel, *Hotel Chevalier*) push these ideas to their breaking point. While Anderson's work has always been oddly divisive ('quirky' isn't for everyone and doesn't always age well), this feature was especially so. Consistency, as it sometimes does, has become for Anderson a liability and, it seems, the film's exotic Indian backdrop has made the case against the director all the more damning.[2] Strangely, as Anderson's productions move outward literally, the worlds he explores seem to shrink, growing more and more insular. This insularity more than anything divided the critics.

The premise is familiar enough: a family in need of spiritual reparation. Schwartzman even plays a literal author, Jack Whitman (note the obvious literary reference to the writer who opened *Leaves of Grass* with 'Song of Myself', a poem with the particularly relevant line, 'I celebrate myself and sing myself'). Where the stilted attempts at self-aggrandisement were charmingly laughable in Anderson's earlier outings, however, they run the risk of seeming troublingly trite here.

Focused on the ostensible spiritual journey of the Whitman brothers – Francis (Owen Wilson), Peter (Adrien Brody) and Jack (Jason Schwartzman) – the film's lavish, near-fetishistic mise-en-scène mirrors the brothers' privileged and myopic point of view (the 'Limited' of the film's title is subtly critical). The men aren't in India. They occupy, instead, a singularly Orientalist dreamscape of what India might do for them, and they can afford this privilege (financially if not psychically). Francis's painstakingly planned journey through the country, which is to culminate in a reunion with their mother, is a more ornate, less charming version of Dignan's seventy-five-year plan. It is a fantasy that only gradually begins to crack. The brothers see only what they want to see through much of the film, and the above-mentioned myopia is a calculated part of the film's expressive aesthetic. This is treacherous territory, though. For, as playfully critical as Anderson is of his self-absorbed characters, his own aesthetic and thematic concerns may seem similarly limited, removed from reality, and quaintly 'busy', That 'forest-for-the-trees' logic Dignan is guilty of is, at this point in Anderson's career, a defining part of his authorial signature and the 'whole' seems to be an increasingly moving target.

Dignan, Max, Royal and Zissou are potentially annoying characters, but they earn our sympathy in doses as they connect and learn to share with a world they previously had taken for granted or held in contempt. While those films critique the author function spun out of control, they also redeem the author himself and his effect on the collective imagination. In *The Darjeeling Limited*, the collective remains frustratingly restricted, and even the brothers' 'awakening' is a childish mockery of human emotion. Anderson's dedication to Satyajit Ray, which we must believe was intended sincerely, makes the synthetic emotional topography of his own imagined world stand out all the more painfully. Yet this, like his other films, is a meditation on the human need for self-reinvention. Artifice is part of the game and lends significantly to the viewer's evolving, not entirely pleasant realisation that the pointlessness of the Whitmans' struggle and its unmitigated selfishness might actually be the point.

In fact, as his career advances, Anderson's own authorial mark, his interest in creating highly stylised worlds for his highly stylised characters to inhabit, has evolved into a wry little joke on the critical importance of mise-en-scène to our understanding of the subjective auteur. Growing increasingly baroque, increasingly full of detail, the Andersonian frame threatens to consume not just its author, but the narrative, the characters involved, and perhaps even the viewer. That *Fantastic Mr. Fox* (co-written with Noah Baumbach) is fully animated would seem to indicate Anderson's desire to immerse himself, like his characters, deeper and deeper in the realm of the artificial, the 'created'. Interestingly, however, *Fantastic Mr. Fox* benefits from this more complete immersion. Where *The Darjeeling Limited* falters in its attempts to connect to the (or even *a*) real world, this world of talking creatures living in trees and below the earth is pure – and terrifically effective – metaphor. Retrospectively, we might view Anderson's other characters through this very lens.

Anderson's extracinematic endeavours have functioned, like his films, to valorise a remodeled iteration of the auteur. The cinematic creator as construct – of the studio or of the self – is certainly not a new phenomenon. Alfred Hitchcock remains a central and instructive example of the 'created creator'. The allure of the auteur as subjective and (perhaps) knowable 'reality' has become all the more alluring in the digital age where the cinematic text's 'second-life' on DVD is capable of reassigning, emphasising, or even creating authority, and giving the illusion of a privileged relationship between author and spectator. Anderson is clearly aware of this dynamic, and has continually sought to disrupt it in his extracinematic pursuits, deauthorising himself – or rather creating the illusion of deauthorisation – by situating himself within a constantly shifting pair of collectives, becoming, intermittently, both crew member and spectator. Anderson, like many contemporary directors who help to produce the extrafilmic materials on their own DVDs, projects a carefully tailored public image of himself as author, and this mediated image shares many qualities with its fictive counterparts (Dignan, Max, Royal and family, Zissou, and the Whitman Brothers), who, like him, arise as redeemed or redeemable, largely sympathetic authors, functioning, in the end, in the name of community.

Anderson's elaborate DVD packages (since *Rushmore*) as well as his public persona contribute to his image as a dependent – as opposed to an independent – filmmaker. This question of (in)dependence, so central to his fictional creations, foregrounds and valorises a romanticised notion of adolescence. Anderson, as his characters must, has learned to share – the more traditionally 'authoritative' elements of these DVD packages feature Anderson's brother's whimsical, overwhelmingly detailed drawings – and he has participated in a method of self-representation that makes his dependence on others a proud thing, the defining feature of his particular authorial strategy. In other words, the reborn auteur as exemplified by Anderson appears more prominent than ever; but his centrality – one might say his celebrity, his authority – remains in spite of attempts to document the many collaborative layers of the filmmaking enterprise. André Bazin worried about the cultish aspects of auteurism. Anderson's career so far has indicated that the cult is alive and well, though he feigns embarrassment over the whole thing.

The son of an ad-man, Anderson himself makes advertisements. His American Express promo, part of that company's 'My Life, My Card' campaign, contains an exchange that perfectly summarises the precarious, self-protected position Anderson finds himself in.

Clocking in at two minutes and featuring an unusually large cast that includes faces familiar from Anderson's feature films, the piece is simultaneously an elaborate mockery of the myth of the solitary genius and a promotion for this idea. Anderson moves through a clearly Andersonian set, talking about his life in movies and listing his accomplishments as his assistants make his film happen almost without his recognition. Holding a sandwich in one hand as he passes one of these (a banana-eating, aviator-cap-wearing young woman), Anderson says, 'can I get my snack', to which she replies (not skipping a beat and exiting the frame as quickly as she entered) 'you're eating it'. Anderson's manufactured juvenility gives the impression of a world of kids playing at movie-making, and this, along with a delightfully communal aesthetic that runs through his feature films, has sustained the Anderson cult. The cult itself may well wonder, though, whether Anderson is capable of examining the (and not just his) world.

[This entry draws from a previously published article: Devin Orgeron, 'La Camera-Crayola: Authorship Comes of Age in the Cinema of Wes Anderson', *Cinema Journal*, vol. 46, no. 2, 2007, pp. 40–65.]

Biography

Born in Houston, Texas, in 1969, Wes Anderson has established a dedicated fanbase, allowing him to continue to make his highly personal, idiosyncratic, and unusually 'busy' films. Anderson has also built a career out of publically connecting to this fanbase in the cinematic 'aftermarket' through his ironically pitched commercials, his elaborate DVD editions, his occasional critical writing, and interviews. Like Max Fischer in *Rushmore*, Anderson directed school plays, and his work so far has focused on characters who, like Max, struggle to maintain a childlike enthusiasm about a world that isn't always kind to that point of view.

Notes

1 In their three films together, Anderson and editor David Moritz have developed a cutting structure perfectly expressive of the youth perspective. Cutting on dialogue and/or action, their editorial techniques suggest hyperactivity and an underdeveloped attention span.

2 For an especially incisive if, at times, snippy article on the problem of race in this and all of Anderson's films, see Jonah Weiner (2007) 'Unbearable

Whiteness: That Queasy Feeling You Get When Watching a Wes Anderson Movie', *Slate*, Sept. 2007, accessed 27 June 2009; <http://www.slate.com/id/2174828>

Filmography

Bottle Rocket (1996)
Rushmore (1998)
The Royal Tenenbaums (2001)
The Life Aquatic with Steve Zissou (2004)
The Darjeeling Limited (2007)
Fantastic Mr. Fox (2009)

Further reading

Wes Anderson, 'My Private Screening With Pauline Kael', *The New York Times*, January 31, 1999, Arts and Leisure, pp. 20–21.
Kent Jones, 'Family Romance', *Film Comment*, vol. 37, no. 6, 2001, pp. 24–27.
Joshua Gooch, 'Making a Go of It: Paternity and Prohibition in the Films of Wes Anderson', *Cinema Journal*, vol. 47, no. 1, 2007, pp. 26–48.
Mark Olsen, 'If I can Dream: The Everlasting Boyhoods of Wes Anderson', *Film Comment*, vol. 35, no. 1, 1999, pp. 12–17.
Devin Orgeron, 'La Camera-Crayola: Authorship Comes of Age in the Cinema of Wes Anderson', *Cinema Journal*, vol. 46, no. 2, 2007, pp. 40–65.
Jonathan Romney, 'Family Albums', *Sight and Sound*, vol. 12, no. 3, 2002, pp. 12–15.

AOYAMA SHINJI

By Aaron Gerow

After decades of suffering from poor box office receipts and lack of critical acclaim, both at home and abroad, Japanese cinema enjoyed a renaissance from the 1990s on. Part of it was established directors such as Imamura Shōhei returning to the international spotlight (his *The Eel* ['Unagi', 1997] won the Cannes Film Festival), part of it was the revival of industrial fortunes with the influx of television money, but much of it was also due to the appearance of a new generation of filmmakers, ranging from Kitano Takeshi to Kawase Naomi, from Miike Takashi to Kurosawa Kiyoshi, in the 1990s. Whether this constituted a 'Nouvelle Vague' or a New Wave, words used to nominate both young directors like Truffaut, Godard, Chabrol and

Rohmer when they debuted in France around 1960, as well as such political Japanese filmmakers as Imamura, Ōshima Nagisa, Shinoda Masahiro, and Yoshida Yoshishige when they appeared around the same time, is open to debate. Was this a unified movement, sharing a worldview, politics, or perspective on cinema, or just a varied group of films that, especially in a now more a-political Japan, happened to appear at the same time? Aoyama Shinji, one of the most celebrated of these new filmmakers, is also the one who has thought about this issue the most. A director who studied under Japan's foremost film critic, Hasumi Shigehiko, at Rikkyō University, and who has published volumes of criticism and literature since graduating, even winning the prestigious Mishima Yukio Literature Prize in 2001, Aoyama has not only made challenging films, mixing art cinema with genre, fiction with documentary, long take visuals with noise music. He has become a public intellectual who thinks about what a new cinema must do, how it differs from the 'New Waves' of his elders, and the place of cinema and politics in postwar Japan. He is a filmmaker who benefits from being read as well as being seen.

His controversial debut film, *Helpless*, posed a challenge to its viewers. The shocking moment when the hero Kenji kills a diner's cook and waitress defies easy explanation. Perhaps it was a matter of mood: the teenager had witnessed a murder earlier, and had just learnt of his father's suicide. Aoyama himself has posited another reason: Kenji, as a member of a generation removed from Japan's crimes in WWII, could only recognise such guilt by reenacting them himself. Such postulations, however, are difficult to ground in a work that offers spectators little access to character psychology. Even if there are motivations for Kenji's actions, they remain beyond the spectator's reach, a point Aoyama also stresses.[1] From the start, Aoyama effectively challenged his viewers with the question of understanding such problematic individuals, such social others. We can thus think of his films as important political interventions in contemporary Japan, ones that call for a rethinking of history and a redefinition of the individual (*kojin*) on the basis of the encounter with the other (*tasha*).[2]

In a manifesto-like essay on Phillipe Garrel, Aoyama offers a political conception of the individual that is crucial to his work. To him, a truly revolutionary way of thinking – a 'nouvelle vague as a mode of thought'—is 'a discourse dueling over the sole point of how to treat the other from a political perspective, with the individual being the subject in struggle in the end'.[3] He stresses that the individual is that 'unitary existence that possesses no meaning and is a representative of nothing'—that which 'cannot be generalized or universalized'.[4] Aoyama, in a sense, is objecting to all the cultural narratives that take the individual out of specificity, and pretend to speak for it, to cram it into easy-to-understand general categories. To him, politics—the true nouvelle vague—is the 'struggle to protect the individual as an individual', to let it be itself as a singularity.[5] Since the other can also be conceived of as an individual, this is neither a self-centred politics, nor a form of radical individualism, but a politicisation of the micro-relationships between self and other: how we deal with others without imposing our ideas and meanings on them. This protection of the individual may imply a rejection of solidarity politics, but it must be considered in relation to its historical and cinematic contexts. While reflecting the deep distrust towards political narratives that has reigned among many Japanese since the left's internecine killings of the 1970s, it also participates in a resistance against the emperor system (*tennōsei*), a dominant modern discourse which effaces the other in an all-encompassing national self located around an often-unspoken term (the emperor). Applying this to cinema, Aoyama has helped criticise Koreeda Hirokazu's *Maborosi* ('Maboroshi no hikari', 1995) or Oguri Kōhei's *Sleeping Man* ('Nemuru otoko', 1996) for absorbing the self in a nature never analysed for its participation in national ideologies like the emperor system and for privileging beauty and nationalised emotions like 'mono no aware' (the sadness of things) over critique.[6]

Kenji's impenetrability should be considered as a counter to discourses that could efface his otherness, his difference, in generalised, 'known' narratives like 'alienated youth'. On a stylistic level, this opposition is effected through Aoyama's strategic use of what I call the 'detached style', a form of distantiation on the level of narration prevalent in 1990s independent Japanese cinema that utilises long-shot, long takes; generally avoids close-ups and point-of-view shots; and refrains from analysing the scene psychologically.[7] In films by Hashiguchi Ryōsuke and Suwa Nobuhiro, this style can work to detach the other from the self, but its aesthetic tendencies—composing beautiful tableaux—can in other texts like *Sleeping Man* absorb otherness in a unity of self and landscape. Aoyama's films resist such tendencies. The general avoidance of point-of-view shots, coupled with many long-shot, long takes, maintains a distance between the camera and the characters that inhibits spectator efforts to impose meanings on these individuals. At the same time, the abrupt insertion of close-ups works against the impulse to aestheticise. Even when Aoyama returns to his native Kitakyūshū in the trilogy *Helpless*, *Eureka* and *Sad Vacation*, the detached photography by his regular cameraman, Tamura Masaki, evades the nostalgic unity of character and landscape.

Constructing individuals resistant to generalised categories is thus, for Aoyama, a distinctly political issue. But it is also a cinematic one. If an individual is 'a naked state that represents nothing other than itself', then the film presenting the individual should pursue a 'materialistic cinematic practice that conflicts with what is generally called depicting humanity or "depicting emotions".'[8] In practical terms this means a cinema that rejects humanism and melodrama by avoiding explanation (*setsumei*): that leaves world and image equally bare. Aoyama in general refrains from the full explanation of not only characters, but narrative actions (such as the gangster Yasuo's 'death' in *Helpless*), and he is not alone in this tendency. While contemporary Japanese television prioritises clarity and comprehension, directors who work in the detached style prefer ambiguity. This attitude can be considered part of Hasumi's legacy. While famous for advocating cinematic specificity—to study films as films; to make films that rely only on cinematic devices—Hasumi's vision of the motion pictures, as evinced by his work on Ozu Yasujirō,[9] is not one of filmmakers using the infinite means at their disposal to overcome the limitations of cinema, but of them utilising inherently restricted means to acknowledge those limits and thus the horizon of film. This perspective constitutes part of the discursive background for both the minimalism of the detached style and the tendency to avoid explanation beyond what 'cinema' is capable of.

Significantly, Aoyama's characters toil against their own limits. Many of them—Kenji in *Helpless* and *Sad Vacation*, Mizoguchi in *WiLd LIFe*, Saga in *An Obsession*, Nagai in *Desert Moon*, Hana in *Eli, Eli, Lema Sabachthani?*—are suffering from losses, with *Eureka*, a film about survivors of a bus-jacking, being the most thorough representation of the resulting work of mourning. Hikoe Tomohiro has argued that whereas films like *Sleeping Man* exhibit symptoms of Freudian melancholy, in which the ego sets up the lost object within the ego in a form of narcissistic identification, Aoyama's characters struggle with their surroundings.[10] His heroes generally refuse to be part of an institution (Michio and Yōichi in *Two Punks* resist the yakuza life) or move out on their own (Shingo in *Shady Grove*). They do not act on the basis of metanarratives like 'humanity' or 'liberty'. The detective Saga, for instance, pursues Shimano and Kimiko not to save their lives, but simply to get his gun back. While some of those who have experienced loss, like Yasuo in *Helpless* or Asuhara in *Eli, Eli, Lema Sabachthani?*, are unable to overcome it and resort to suicide or murder, Kenji, Saga and Makoto in *Eureka* all ultimately opt to valorise the life of an other (for Kenji, Yasuo's sister; for Saga, his wife Rie; for Makoto, Kozue). Whether the object was lost in romance or violence, Aoyama's characters must overcome the lure of narcissism and recognise the existence of others. Since love has been a site for Aoyama's micro-politics of the epistemological relations between self and other, Shimano's question to Saga—'Do you know how love can be proven?'—is crucial. Shimano's answer, which is in some ways that of Rika and Yoshiki in *EM/Embalming*, is mutual annihilation. Saga does not reject this solution either: dying with another out of love is a step beyond solipsism, albeit on the paradoxical level of joining another in nothingness. Saga, however, provides an additional answer: 'live together for the rest of your lives'. It is logically a less clean solution than Shimano's, and offers no proof of the other's existence, but it represents both Aoyama's rejection of nihilism and his belief that the other is never a matter of certainty. Rika and Shingo's union in *Shady Grove*, after all, takes place in a grove that no longer exists. As their dual narration says at the conclusion, their recognition of the other, and thus confirmation of the self, is a matter of listening to a voice in the dark, of grasping uncertain handholds in the void.

This uncertainty is partially a factor of contemporary Japan. The act of recognising the other has pertinence in post-1990 Japan, where sensational juvenile crimes had sparked media discourses which maintained that young Japanese, raised in a virtual reality of video games, cellphones and manga, have ceased to acknowledge the reality of others. Aoyama, instead of endorsing such discourses' repudiation of the present, works to reconceptualise the relationship between self and other in this new age. Cellphones become not only a means of contact for Rika and Shingo, but also another variable in the complex relationship with others. Aoyama, however, does not valorise any technology. An amateur rock guitarist who has scored some of his films with Yamada Isao, Aoyama has maintained a distinction between computer synthesisers, epitomising an ordered, universal 'cognition' (*ninshiki*), and the 'self-tuned' guitars of Sonic Youth, with their individual, variable 'existence' (*sonzai*).[11] His cinema, politics and music can all in some way be said to involve this contemporary 'tuning' of 'existence' in opposition to 'cognition'.

One other aspect of this 'existence' with the other is the issue of representation. How is it possible to recognise the other given the detachment Aoyama's films evince? Some have argued that his characters resist the emotionalisation of landscape common to contemporary melancholic films by not exhibiting a substantive internality (Saga, for example, with a lost lung, is quite literally 'hollow').[12] How then are Aoyama's narratives of romance possible? The answer must consider Aoyama's effort to present the impossible. In underlining the limits of cinema, Hasumi has helped make impossibility a central issue in Japanese discourses on film, whether or not a text challenges what is impossible in cinema (*fukanōsei*) while still acknowledging those limits. Aoyama, Kurosawa Kiyoshi and others influenced by Hasumi have similarly made the representation of the unrepresentable a crucial concern of film practice. Aoyama has termed his 'marriage trilogy'—*WiLd LIFe*, *An Obsession*, and *Shady Grove*—his own experiment in 'showing the unseen'—here, love[13]— but his cinema in total can be considered an effort to weave between the representable and the unrepresentable.

One way he does that is by seeking cinematic alternatives to the forces of generalisation in representation. The Polaroid camera— photography without a negative—is thus an emblematic motif in his work, in that it is a 're-presentation' that is also a 'unique existence'. This impossible grasping of singularity in a medium that inevitably 're-presents' is what Aoyama eventually calls 'jikkan' or 'the sense of reality'. *Jikkan* is an in-between strategy of gaps and fissures, which is why he aligns it with Roland Barthes's 'third meaning', all the while distinguishing it from the processes of meaning. 'I want to call *jikkan*', he writes, 'that fragment of reality that one confronts, that "something" similar to an unknown other, an indifferent other that you can only say is there when subjectivity has been removed'.[14] Aoyama emphasises that this kind of naked reality free of subjective interpretation is a matter of representation, but '*jikkan* in representation exists as a kind of indistinct and troublesome "ghost" (*yūrei*)',[15] haunting the edges of signification because any interpreted reality is by definition no longer naked. Moving between fiction and documentary throughout his career, Aoyama ultimately seeks to represent the unrepresentable as unrepresentable, thus paradoxically summoning forth the ghost of a real but unrepresentable materiality by foregrounding the reality that makes it unrepresentable. For instance, his point-of-view structures can hint at the internality of characters, yet without denying that the representation of such internality is impossible. While he rarely uses the conventional ABA 'seer-seen-seer' structure, Aoyama can utilise ambiguous (only 'AB' without the second shot of the seer) or even impossible eyeline matches (like Kenji's last 'view' of Yasuo's car) to imply perception without completely tying the object to the subjectivity of a character.

The internality of the character is connoted without ever being denoted, raising the issue of what the other thinks while reminding viewers of the impossibility of indisputably knowing that.

Communication is also subject to this balance of possibility/ impossibility. With many of Aoyama's characters having difficulty expressing themselves, and some, like Kozue and Naoki in *Eureka*, being unable to speak after their trauma, true communication seems as impossible as knowledge of the other. In some cases, as with Akihiko (a character in *Helpless*, *Eureka* and *Sad Vacation*), an abundance of words is actually a sign of the inability to communicate; in others, it can at least represent the material fact of communication, where the fact of speech speaks of internality in terms of providing less a window onto the soul, than an opaque marker of intentionality. Aoyama has written that 'the individual is words; the individual is not the image', and by 'words' he means the materiality of language that resists the categorisable 'image' (meaning) a person can have.[16] One can think that this may figure Aoyama's own relation to words, since he not only produces literature but also makes experimental documentaries investigating the writings of novelists such as Nakagami Kenji, Natsume Sōseki, Tokuda Shūsei and Ishikawa Jun. Yet, as with *Roji: To the Alley* especially, these explore as much writing as material object as writing as signification. *Eureka* is very much a motion picture about communication, but there the model is Makoto's knocking on walls. Someone answers when he does that in the jail, but the film makes no issue of who that is and what is being communicated: the fact of communication itself is what matters. In many of his films, music offers another model of effective communication— it is even posed as the cure for the apocalyptic illness in *Eli, Eli, Lema Sabachthani?*—but importantly it is often 'noise' music free of the conventional music structures, a singularity treading the line between music and noise, signification and materiality. Interestingly, Aoyama's seven-hour documentary on the free jazz music critic Aida Akira, *AA Signature*, features dozens of interviews and live performances, but not one 'image' of Aida Akira.

Communicative acts like Makoto knocking on the wall are usually repeated in Aoyama's work. Beyond underlining that communication is as much a material as a semiotic process, they also participate in a strategy of doubling and repetition that informs Aoyama's conceptions of time and history. Significant narrative actions are often repeated (Saga visits the tunnel and Shingo 'visits' the grove twice), something that adds structure to the narrative, but also echoes the doubling of characters. Different characters are doubled through common cinematic devices or objects (Saga's gun joins him to Shimano) or through engaging in the same action (e.g., both Makoto and Naoki drive the bus). Couples are frequently mirrored, which suggests that one function of these repetitions and doublings is to establish patterns of comparison and contrast. One of the differences is generational, with Michio and Miya in *Two Punks* and Saga and Rie in *An Obsession* being in their late thirties compared to the twenties is couples of Yōichi and Yūko and Shimano and Kimiko in the same films.

Focusing on generational divisions helps Aoyama depict the emptiness and lack of place young Japanese feel, but the differences are also historicised. Generations are often mapped onto post-war Japanese history. Kenji's father was a member of the old left, and Shimano's mother a Hiroshima survivor, yet Kenji can't remember the words to 'The International'. *Helpless* is set in 1989, the year the Berlin Wall tumbled and the Shōwa Emperor Hirohito died. The end of this history means a loss of identity for Kenji's father (who commits suicide) and Yasuo (who insists his boss – his emperor – is not dead), but not for the young. They are at once removed from this history and, like the leukemia in Shimano's body, nevertheless bearing its scars. This is particularly because history, even amidst its breaks and disruptions, tends to repeat itself (the cult leader Daitokuin, in *Embalming*, engages in the human experiments he did in the notorious Unit 731). Murders and even suicides also seem to be serial events that occur again and again. *An Obsession* and *Eli, Eli, Lema Sabachthani?* suggest such repetitions are heading towards apocalypse. This circular temporality is echoed on the visual register by the circles that pervade the mise-en-scène: the wheels on the ever-present bikes, the weathercock in *Two Punks*, or the circle painting in *Embalming*.

The question to Aoyama is how individuals should relate to this circular history. Serial events like murders clearly must be stopped, but breaking the circle is not the only solution: given the choices Makoto gives to Naoki (keep riding around in a circle or stop and kill Kozue), continuing the repetition can sometimes signal an end. Nevertheless, Hiroki's life of fastidious repetition in *WiLd LIFe* must stop if he is to unite with Rie. It seems that repetition must be a form of mourning that honestly faces and overcomes the past. Akihiko is in the end unable to continue with Makoto and Kozue because, unlike them, he has never revisited the site of his own traumatic incident. Mizoguchi in *WiLd LIFe* cannot overcome past scars because the episode of his beating was hushed up. As with Makoto and his 'other bus', characters must return to the scene of the past and start over again—yet not like Daitokuin and his children, who experiment with a means to 'reset' the human psyche like a video game. That is too reminiscent of, on the one hand, Shimano's nihilistic return to nothingness, and, on the other, the cynical fiction of post-war Japan, which forgot the wartime past in order to begin anew. Aoyama's films thus confront the consequences of modern Japanese amnesia, not by narrating stories of WWII, but by firmly locating themselves in the present or its near future, histories which have suffered breaks and divisions from the past. If the scars still remain, they must be dealt with now on the level of micro-political, personal relations with the other. To Aoyama, the individual arises from these interstices of History and history,[17] from the negotiations between past and present, the personal and the social.

Alexander Jacoby has argued that a conflict exists in Aoyama's work between free will and determinism,[18] but it is important to politicise this tension. Aoyama, of course, has also repeated himself, returning to the same characters in *Helpless*, *Eureka* and *Sad Vacation*. In that, he resembles Nakagami Kenji, the subject of *Roji: To the Alley*, who penned novels featuring the same or similar characters, mostly *burakumin* stuck in a community, the Alley, where the fate of blood seems to overwhelm choice. In Nakagami, as in Aoyama, there seem to be limits to the efforts to mourn and overcome the past, but these are less philosophical issues than problems of the political nation (such as the systems which perpetuate discrimination against *burakumin*, a Japanese outcaste group). At the end of *An Obsession*, the void inside Saga remains and the death squads, ignoring Saga, continue on their lethal rampage. Saga can start anew, returning to Rie, but there is a sense that the circularity surrounding these characters has also ringed them in. One must recall the television show Akihiko tells Kenji about in *Helpless*: it is *The Prisoner*, and especially the episode where Number 6 escapes the Village only to find himself returned there. Like many other Japanese filmmakers, from Kitano Takeshi to Kurosawa Kiyoshi, who depict characters that desire to escape Japan but cannot, Aoyama conceives of Japan as the Village—the Alley—as a system that even in the global age entraps the individual through meaning and categories. That is one reason why characters like Michio in *Two Punks* run to the beach—the border—and die. It is significant, however, that Makoto and Kozue in *Eureka* turn away from the shore and head for the mountains. To Aoyama, ending the film at the coast would imply an affirmation of Japan's identity as an island system,[19] when what was needed was to 'remain here and eat it away from within'.[20]

That is what Aoyama also does in cinema: he stays within the borders of representation, of genre (yakuza film, horror, mystery, documentary, etc.), and of the Japanese system, while strategically corroding it from inside, advancing forms of singularity that mould an individual cinema which not only resists the systems that corral the individual, but which marks the personal as the starting point for political change from within.

Biography

Born on July 13, 1964, in Kitakyūshū, Fukuoka Prefecture, Kyūshū (southwestern Japan), to school-teacher parents. Attended Rikkyō University in Tokyo from 1984 to 1989, where he majored in American literature. Took courses from the critic Hasumi Shigehiko while making 8mm films in a Rikkyō film circle. Starting with *The Guard from Underground* ('Jigoku no keibiin', dir. Kurosawa Kiyoshi, 1991), worked as an assistant director on numerous films and television programs, including *The Written Face* (dir. Daniel Schmidt, 1994), *Cold Fever* (dir. Fredrik Thor Fridriksson, 1995), *BeRLin* (dir. Rijū Gō, 1995), and other Kurosawa films. Debuted as a director in 1995 with *It's Not in the Textbook!*, a made-for-video film. Has continued to write film criticism while making movies. *Eureka* won the FIPRESCI Prize and the Prize of the Ecumenical Jury at the 2000 Cannes Film Festival. With his novelisation of *Eureka* winning the coveted Mishima Yukio Literature Prize, Aoyama has also emerged as a major novelist.

Notes

1 Interview with Aoyama Shinji, 7 May 2000, Tokyo. Aoyama's previous remarks were voiced in a personal conversation in September 1997.
2 Note that to Aoyama, just as to many other contemporary Japanese intellectuals, 'tasha' refers less to the 'other' of psychoanalytic or post-colonial theory, than simply to that which is defined by alterity.
3 Aoyama Shinji, *Ware eiga o hakkenseri* (Seidosha, 2001), 22.
4 Aoyama, *Ware eiga o hakkenseri*, 27.
5 Aoyama, *Ware eiga o hakkenseri*, 28.
6 Aoyama Shinji, Yasui Yutaka and Abe Kazushige, 'Kenzaikasuru "Nihon" to iu jiko', *Cahiers du Cinema Japon* 19 (1996): 84–100.
7 See my *Kitano Takeshi* (London: BFI, 2007).
8 Aoyama, *Ware eiga o hakkenseri*, 25, 30.
9 Hasumi Shigehiko, *Kantoku Ozu Yasujirō* (Tokyo: Chikuma Shobō, 1983).

10 Hikoe Tomohiro, 'Merankorī to hiai—Aoyama Shinji no sakuhin o megutte', *Cahiers du Cinema Japon* 22 (1997): 64–76.

11 Aoyama Shinji and Inagawa Masato, 'Nihon eiga wa naze kiki o kaihisuru no ka', *Yuriika* 29.13 (October 1997): 220–21.

12 Saitō Kōji, 'Shitai no hō e: Aoyama Shinji *EM/Embalming*', *Cahiers du Cinema Japon* 28 (1999): 179.

13 Kurosawa Kiyoshi, Aoyama Shinji, Higuchi Yasuhito, Yasui Yutaka, 'Karappo no sekai—*Cure* o megutte', *Cahiers du Cinema Japon* 22 (1997): 39–40.

14 Aoyama, *Ware eiga o hakkenseri*, 326.

15 Aoyama, *Ware eiga o hakkenseri*, 325.

16 Aoyama, *Ware eiga o hakkenseri*, 26.

17 Aoyama interview.

18 Alexander Jacoby, *A Critical Handbook of Japanese Film Directors* (Berkeley: Stone Bridge Press, 2008), 7–9.

19 Aoyama interview.

20 Aoyama, *Ware eiga o hakkenseri*, 30.

Filmography

It's Not in the Textbook! / *Kyōkasho ni nai!* (1995) video

Helpless (1996) also screenplay, music

1/5 (1996) 8 min. short for the 'Celebrate Cinema 101' compilation

A Weapon in My Heart / *Waga mune ni kyōki ari* (1996) video, also screenplay, music

Chinpira / *Two Punks* (1996)

WiLd LIFe (1997) screenplay (with Satō Kumi), music

An Obsession / *Tsumetai chi* (1996) also co-producer, screenplay, music, editing (with Satō Kumi)

Shady Grove (1999) also screenplay (with Satō Kumi), music

EM / *Embalming* (1999) also screenplay (with Hashimoto Izō), music, editing (with Ueno Sōichi)

June 12 1998 (1999) video documentary

Eureka (2000) also screenplay, music, editing

Roji: To the Alley / *Roji e: Nakagami Kenji no nokoshita firumu* (2000) documentary

Desert Moon / *Tsuki no sabaku* (2001) also screenplay, editing

So as Not to Say Everything about Her Already Aged Self / *Sude ni oita kanojo no subete ni tsuite wa kataranu tame ni* (2001) video

Mike Yokohama: A Forest with No Name / *Shiritsu tantei Hama Maiku: Namae no nai mori* (2002)

The Jesus of the Ruins / *Yakeato no Iesu* (2002) television

Song of Ajima / *Ajimā no uta: Uehara Tomoko, tenjo no utagoe* (2002) documentary

The Detective Who Can Say No / *No to ieru keiji* (2003) 8 min. short for the 'Detective Festival' compilation

Like a Desperado Under the Eaves / *Nokishita no narazumono mitai ni* (2003) video, also screenplay

Days in the Shade / *Shūsei tabi nikki* (2003) video, also screenplay
Trunk (2003) web movie
So Far from the Tide / *Kairyū kara tōku hanarete* (2003) introductory video for
  Yokohama National University
Lakeside Murder Case / *Reikusaido mādā kēsu* (2004) also screenplay (with
  Fukazawa Masaki)
Eli, Eli, Lema Sabachthani? / *Eri, eri, rema sabakutani* (2005) also screenplay
AA Signature: Aquirax / *AA: Ongaku hihyōka Aida Akira* (2006) documentary
Crickets / *Koorogi* (2006)
Saddo Vakeishon / *Sad Vacation* (2007) also original story, screenplay
Little Red Riding Hood / *Le petit chaperon rouge* (2008)

Note: all above music credits with Yamada Isao

GREGG ARAKI

By Glyn Davis

Gregg Araki first attained notoriety and critical recognition in the
early 1990s with *The Living End*. Made for around $22,000 using
equipment loaned from independent filmmaking maverick Jon Jost,
its narrative centres on a pair of HIV-positive lovers (hustler Luke and
intellectual film critic Jon) on the run from Los Angeles after committing murder. In an article first published in *The Village Voice*, critic
B. Ruby Rich identified *The Living End* as one of the key texts in the
inauguration of the New Queer Cinema 'movement'. Rich saw
Araki's film as an exemplar of the 'Homo Pomo' style, an aesthetic
supposedly characterised by 'appropriation and pastiche, irony, as well
as a reworking of history with social constructionism very much in
mind'. New Queer Cinema films, claimed Rich, 'are irreverent,
energetic, alternately minimalist and excessive'. She linked Araki's
film with, among others, Todd Haynes's *Poison*, Christopher Munch's
The Hours and Times, Tom Kalin's *Swoon*, Laurie Lynd's *R.S.V.P.*,
and the Pixelvision videos of Sadie Benning.[1]
  Araki's film actually fits Rich's summary description fairly neatly. In
particular, he pays homage to his filmmaking idols throughout *The
Living End*, whether through glancing references or blatant appropriation. Jean-Luc Godard is a key figure: not only does Jon's apartment feature a poster for *Made in USA*, but the film frequently
references *Pierrot Le Fou*. (Most obviously, the names of the main
characters are Jon and Luke, though the published script identifies
them as Jon Skywalker and Luke Wayne; these surnames do not
feature in the credits or dialogue of the completed film.) Warhol is

also referenced: Jon stands in front of a poster advertising *Blow Job*, the position of his head purposefully echoing the framing of the stills behind him; Mary Woronov, who appeared in several of Warhol's films, has a cameo as an unhinged lesbian. In addition, Araki has compared *The Living End* to Howard Hawks's *Bringing Up Baby*. Indeed, the opening title card which reads 'an irresponsible movie by Gregg Araki' is a reference to film theorist Robin Wood's analysis of Hawks's film. As Araki has said, 'That movie is a screwball comedy with Cary Grant and Katharine Hepburn, but the structure of it is kind of the same as *The Living End* in that it was about this spirited, free-willed character who frees this repressed, more normal-life character. So *The Living End* sort of fit that paradigm'.[2]

Like other films of the New Queer Cinema, *The Living End* engages with both queer history and queer film history. Luke is prone to violence: he shoots at a group of thugs who threaten him, attacks a neo-Nazi using a ghettoblaster as a club, and kills a cop. Araki invites us to sympathise, even identify, with Luke. This strategy directly confronts the historical representation of queer characters by mainstream cinema as villains and murderers, a persistent and widespread practice criticised at length by Vito Russo in his seminal book *The Celluloid Closet*.[3] Where a number of films made by gay men and lesbians in the 1980s had attempted to counter such negatively-coded depictions with more 'positive images' (see, for instance, *Torchsong Trilogy* and *Desert Hearts*), some of the New Queer Cinema directors reworked and invested in these stereotypes, challenging viewers to explore their emotional and moral responses to such figures: in addition to *The Living End*, violent gay men were also placed at the centre of *Swoon* and *Poison*. At the same time, more mainstream depictions of queer killers were causing controversy: filming of *Basic Instinct* was disrupted by gay rights activists in San Francisco in 1991, and *The Silence of the Lambs* attracted criticism from a similar demographic. Queer cultural critics also weighed in: Angela Galvin, for instance, defended *Basic Instinct*, and argued in favour of the disparate ways in which individual audience members may relate to specific characters, however negatively portrayed.[4]

In addition to its challenge to the history of the representation of violent queer characters, *The Living End* also shook up the conventions of the road movie genre. It was not the only queer film of the early 1990s to do so: *My Own Private Idaho*, *Postcards from America* and *The Adventures of Priscilla, Queen of the Desert* also attempted to pervert the form. Historically, the road movie protagonist has been a white heterosexual male, escaping the pressures of urban or suburban conformity through taking to the road. The road film's narrative usually ends either with the protagonist returning home, or dying. Jon and Luke do neither: *The Living End* concludes with them sitting on a beach, staring at the sunset. And although some of the standard iconography of the road movie – a driving rock score, widescreen cinematography, shots of speeding tarmac from the position of the fender – is notably absent, Jon and Luke's passionate sex in motels and in the car itself attempts a queer usurpation of elements of the genre's topography.

Perhaps the most important aspect of *The Living End*, and the reason the film continues to be discussed almost two decades after its release, is its register of queer anger at the AIDS epidemic. Jon and Luke's nihilistic actions and attitudes are explicitly identified as a response to their diagnoses as HIV-positive: 'Don't you get it?' Luke asks Jon. 'We're totally free. We can do anything we fucking want'. *The Living End* concludes with a credits dedicating the film to 'the hundreds of thousands who've died and the hundreds of thousands more who will die because of a big white house full of Republican fuckheads'. José Arroyo has noted that HIV/AIDS is the main reason for the existence of New Queer Cinema, as well as one of the main subjects handled by the narratives of the movement's films.[5] Araki concurs:

> It was really in the cultural zeitgeist as far as it was the time of ACT UP and Queer Nation and massive protests in the street … I remember, in the late '80s, early '90s, there was just so much death in the air … AIDS is still a big problem, but the way it was just this kind of unstoppable holocaust at that time made it – the whole sense of everybody's anxiety, anger, frustration, helplessness – it all very much fed into those movies.[6]

Araki followed *The Living End* with three films sometimes referred to as his 'teenage apocalypse trilogy': *Totally Fucked Up*, *The Doom Generation*, and *Nowhere*. The first of these, like *The Living End*, had an explicit political message: it opens with a text extract from a newspaper declaring 'that 30 percent of teenagers who commit suicide are gay'. The film, broken into '15 celluloid fragments', follows six adolescent characters – three gay, two lesbian, one possibly bisexual – as they hang out, have sex, and go shopping, interspersed with video diary confessionals. Intertitles – 'and now back to our regularly scheduled program', 'can this world really be as sad as it seems?' – offer ironic commentary on the narrative, a Brechtian distancing device that interrupts the process of identification with the characters. *Totally Fucked Up* ends with one of the teens, Andy (James Duval, who stars in each of the films in the trilogy), killing himself by drinking bleach.

The Doom Generation and *Nowhere* are notably more surreal, anarchic and violent than *Totally Fucked Up*; they also look significantly different. From *The Doom Generation* onwards, Araki has developed a distinctive visual and aural aesthetic. Components of this style were in evidence earlier in his career, but the larger budgets he has worked with since the mid-1990s, and the additional assistance he has had from cinematographers, production designers and soundtrack assemblers, has enabled its fuller realisation. Visually, the aesthetic includes: a bold, even gaudy use of colour; stylised set design, including murals, road signs, rooms with décor that matches the clothing of the characters, and carefully chosen disposable pop culture artefacts (Snoopy slippers, Barbie cereal, a board game called 'Heart Throb'); exaggerated costumes, wigs, and make-up. This distinctive style extends to the casting of extras: comedian Margaret Cho, Hollywood madam Heidi Fleiss and musician Perry Farrell all appear in *The Doom Generation*, with porn star Traci Lords and *Baywatch*'s Jaason Simmons (appearing as himself) making cameos in *Nowhere*. Araki, discussing *The Doom Generation*, has noted that this aspect of his films has an intended effect:

> Well, I specifically told the casting director to fill all the smaller parts with famous faces. Because to me, the film is very surreal and hallucinogenic, and so I wanted the film to have the effect of falling asleep while the TV is on, having a nightmare where there's all these weird faces that are vaguely familiar and built on your subconscious memory of these figures.[7]

The visual styling of Araki's films is accompanied by a distinctive use of music: his soundtracks tend to feature a mixture of industrial, shoegaze and dreampop fare. Music is evidently of significant personal importance to Araki – he has said 'I'm more influenced by music than I am by movies' – and he passes this on to his characters, who talk about bands and use lyrics as lines of dialogue ('what difference does it make?' asks Luke in *The Living End*, referencing The Smiths).[8] Across his oeuvre, music by KMFDM, Ministry, Front 242, Slowdive, Red House Painters, This Mortal Coil, The Wolfgang Press, Pale Saints, Coil, Curve, Cocteau Twins, Nitzer Ebb and Nine Inch Nails recurs. The utilisation of shoegaze sounds is arguably the more interesting – reaching a peak with *Mysterious Skin*, the soundtrack for which was provided by ex-Cocteau Robin Guthrie working with Harold Budd – due to the genre's woozy register and affective power. Simon Reynolds has identified shoegaze, like earlier psychedelic musics, as androgynous, an observation which chimes with Araki's (and New Queer Cinema's) challenge to essentialist and stable identity configurations.[9]

Araki's distinctive aesthetic has caused some critics concern. Liese Spencer, for instance, wrote that:

> Art-directed to within an inch of its life, *Nowhere* could just as easily be retitled 'Nothing', its failure to engage with any real emotion not so much a comment on air-headed youth as a symptom of it ... One wouldn't want hectoring, but there's a slightly troubling lack of analysis or depth here.[10]

This critique, however, fails to recognise that Araki's teen trilogy contains clear political messages, most particularly in its depictions of the relationships between queer characters, and in its handling of identity formations. Chris Chang has noted that the six teens in *Totally Fucked Up* – for all their ironic sparring and catty commentary – are decidedly supportive of each other, forming a sort of proto-family.[11] This dynamic is made particularly explicit in one party scene, in which the two lesbians want to conceive, and ask all four boys to donate sperm. In other Araki films, the connections made between his characters may only be fleeting, but they are often intensely passionate: before Montgomery explodes at the end of *Nowhere* (in a nod to Kafka's Gregor Samsa, a giant bug bursts out of his body), he seems to have found a genuine soulmate in Dark. Araki's characters also often bond through similar experiences of disenfranchisement: in *The Doom Generation*, for instance, Jordan tells his girlfriend Amy that he is happy for drifter X to accompany them on their flight from L.A. because 'he's sort of like us. Lost. Like he doesn't fit in'.

Across the teen apocalypse trilogy, identity categories relating to sexuality become less of a concern for the characters, and more malleable. In *The Doom Generation*, Jordan and Amy go on the run with X after killing a psychotic Korean shopkeeper. As their journey progresses, Amy sleeps with X, and Jordan does not mind. X teaches Amy to experiment sexually, with tricks and methods which she then tries out on Jordan. Finally, all three have sex together in an abandoned warehouse. In other words, as the three escape from conventional society, the ideals of heteropatriarchy (monogamous couples, heterosexuality) break down, and are replaced by a different – polymorphously perverse – libidinal economy. Robin Wood has identified the depiction of this *ménage a trois*, and its interruption by violent rednecks, as 'one of the most radical statements in American cinema', calling *The Doom Generation* a 'powerfully political film'.[12]

Araki followed *Nowhere* with a creatively fallow period. *Splendor*, a sumptuously designed and shot feature focusing on another *ménage-a-trois*, bombed at the US box office, taking just over $45,000. Although the film contains some trademark Araki moments – in an early scene set at a club, Mike (Kelly Macdonald) is dressed as a giant box of tampons – the sexual politics of the film are surprisingly tame, especially in comparison with those in *The Doom Generation*. Araki next wrote and directed a pilot for an MTV series called *This Is How The World Ends*. Before production began, the budget was cut by the station from $1.5 million to $700,000, but Araki still made the drama; the pilot was not picked up for broadcast.

The release in 2004 of *Mysterious Skin* followed several years of silence from Araki. Adapted from Scott Heim's 1995 novel – the first time that Araki had worked with someone else's source material – the narrative concerns two teenagers, Neil and Brian, and the different ways in which they come to terms with being sexually abused as young boys by their Little League coach. The film features recognisable aspects of Araki's style: a shoegaze soundtrack, colourful mise-en-scène, elements of science fiction (Brian thinks he may have been abducted by aliens as a child), a focus on teenage characters. However, the distancing devices he had previously used – a mannered performance style, sardonic intertitles, patently constructed sets and costumes, cartoon violence – are absent. The acting is more conventionally naturalistic, even from the cameo oddballs (Mary Lynn Rajskub as Avalyn, for instance, the woman who claims she was experimented on by aliens). This reining in of the excesses for which he had become known meant that many critics responded favourably to *Mysterious Skin*, seeing it as a serious and mature work from a director who had previously traded in self-consiously hip, ironic, day-glo affectless confections.

As with other films about the trauma of child sexual abuse, such as *The Butterfly Effect*, *Mysterious Skin* ends with shocking revelations about exactly what was done to the boys, including the return of Brian's repressed memories of the events. Unlike *Hard Candy* or *Sleepers*, there is no retributive and cathartic act of vengeance against the paedophile, only the teenagers finding solace in each other's pain. As Neil says, in voiceover, 'I wished there was some way for us to go back and undo the past. But there wasn't. There was nothing we could do ... I wished with all my heart that we could just leave this world behind – rise like two angels in the night and magically disappear'. This ambivalent, downbeat conclusion has a similar tone to the ending of *The Living End* and the three teen apocalypse films: the final shots of each depict lead characters who have experienced severe loss and pain, and face uncertain futures.

Araki's most recent film, the stoner comedy *Smiley Face*, marked a significant shift in tone following *Mysterious Skin*:

> After *Mysterious Skin* ... I really just wanted to do something completely different. I knew my next film was not going to be this very dark, heavy drama ... I really see *Smiley Face* and *Mysterious Skin* as yin and yang to each other.[13]

Scripted by Dylan Haggerty, *Smiley Face* featured *Scary Movie* actress Anna Faris in the lead role, and received a slew of favourable reviews from *The Village Voice*, *Salon*, and other sources. Araki managed to incorporate elements of his trademark aesthetic – bold colours, hallucinatory surrealism, crazy cameos, a soundtrack in thrall to the 1990s indie scene – whilst working within the generic parameters of the stoner movie. The episodic plot follows Jane (Faris) as she accidentally ingests a vast quantity of her roommate's pot, and then attempts to replace the drugs, attend an audition, and pay a bill. She ultimately ends up having a conversation with a disembodied Roscoe Lee Browne (playing himself) on a Ferris wheel, clutching the original manuscript of *The Communist Manifesto*. Like *Dude, Where's My Car?* or *Harold and Kumar Go To White Castle*, the film wrings its comedy from the main character's mental muddiness, and the preposterous situations in which she becomes immersed. Though Araki attempted with *Smiley Face* to work outside of the queer cinema he had become associated with (the film does not contain a single queer character), the result was not a commercial success: it was poorly distributed and took less than $10,000 at the US box office.

Biography

Gregg Araki was born in Los Angeles in 1959, and grew up in Santa Barbara. He has a BA in film studies from UC Santa Barbara, and completed an MFA in film production at the University of Southern California in 1985. He worked as a music critic for *L.A. Weekly*.

Notes

1 B. Ruby Rich (1992), 'New Queer Cinema', *Sight and Sound*, Vol 2 No 9 (September), p. 32.
2 Gregg Araki, quoted in Damon Smith (2008), 'Rebel, Rebel', *Bright Lights Film Journal*, February (Issue 59), archived at http://www.brightlightsfilm.com/59/50arakiiv.html (accessed 26 June 2009).
3 Vito Russo (1987), *The Celluloid Closet: Homosexuality in the Movies* (New York: Harper, 2nd edn).
4 Angela Galvin (1994), '*Basic Instinct*: Damning Dykes', in Belinda Budge and Diane Hamer, eds, *The Good, The Bad and the Gorgeous: Popular Culture's Romance with Lesbianism* (London: Pandora), pp. 218–31.
5 José Arroyo (1994), 'Death, Desire and Identity: The Political Unconscious of "New Queer Cinema" ', in Joseph Bristow and Angie Wilson, eds, *Activating Theory: Lesbian, Gay, Bisexual Politics* (London: Lawrence and Wishart), pp. 72–98.
6 Gregg Araki, quoted in Smith, *op. cit.*
7 Gregg Araki (1995), quoted in Matthew L. Severson, 'Young, Beautiful, and F★★★ed: A Conversation with Gregg Araki and other members of *The Doom Generation*', *Bright Lights Film Journal*, Issue 15, archived online at http://www.brightlightsfilm.com/15/araki2.html (accessed 26 June 2009).
8 Ibid.
9 Simon Reynolds (1996), in Simon Reynolds and Joy Press, *The Sex Revolts: Gender, Rebellion and Rock'n'Roll* (New York: Harvard University Press), p. 172.
10 Liese Spencer (1998), 'Teenage Kicks All Through The Night', *Sight and Sound*, Vol 8 No 6, pp. 52, 37.
11 Chris Chang (1994), 'Absorbing Alternative', *Film Comment*, Vol 30 No 5, pp. 47–53.
12 Robin Wood (1998), *Sexual Politics and Narrative Film: Hollywood and Beyond* (New York: Columbia University Press), p. 339.
13 Gregg Araki, quoted in Smith, *op. cit.*

Filmography

Three Bewildered People in the Night (1987)
The Long Weekend (O' Despair) (1989)
The Living End (1992)
Totally Fucked Up (1993)
The Doom Generation (1995)
Nowhere (1997)
Splendor (1999)

This Is How The World Ends (TV) (2000)
Mysterious Skin (2004)
Smiley Face (2007)

Further reading

Gregg Araki (1994), *The Living End / Totally Fucked Up*, New York: William Morrow and Company.

Glyn Davis (2004), 'Camp and Queer and the New Queer Director: Case Study – Gregg Araki', in Michele Aaron, ed., *New Queer Cinema: A Critical Reader*, Edinburgh: Edinburgh University Press, pp. 53–67.

Roy Grundmann (1993), 'The Fantasies We Live By: Bad Boys in *Swoon* and *The Living End*', *Cineaste*, March, pp. 25–29.

Katie Mills (1997), 'Revitalising the Road Genre: *The Living End* as an AIDS Road Film', in Steven Cohan and Ina Rae Hark, eds, *The Road Movie Book*, London and New York: Routledge, pp. 307–29.

James M. Moran (1996), 'Gregg Araki: Queer Film-maker for a Queer Generation', *Film Quarterly*, Vol 50 No 1 (October), pp. 18–26.

Kimberly Yutani (1995), 'Gregg Araki and the Queer New Wave', in Russell Leong, ed., *Asian American Sexualities: Dimensions of the Gay and Lesbian Experience*, New York: Routledge, pp. 175–80.

LUC BESSON

By Rosanna Maule

As successful at the box office as he is unpopular with French and international film critics, Luc Besson is acknowledged as a significant film director almost exclusively in academic publications. Especially within the anglophone area of film-related disciplines, he is a paradigmatic case study to investigate Europe's position within the present state of global film practices and systems. Besson is correspondingly diffident of film critics, conceding interviews only to film magazines that have proven supportive of his work, such as the French *Première* and *Studio Magazine*. Otherwise, he personally sees to the promotion of his films, whether by publishing glossy books on their production history, launching vast campaigns co-sponsored by banks and media corporations, or again presenting them at selected film festivals.[1]

The discrepancies in Besson's reception history echo those relative to his position within French and international cinema. During the past decade, Besson has been regaining credibility in the international film scene. Paradoxically, the first recognition he had in his own country was the César award for best director for *Le cinquième élément*

(The Fifth Element), arguably his most characteristically mainstream and Hollywood-like film. This 'rehabilitation' process has been particularly manifest since 2000, when Besson founded Europa Corp [from now on, Europa], a French-based and internationally established production and distribution company which he owns and directs. Besson intended Europa to offer an alternative to Hollywood and France as the respective champions of commercial and cultural film offerings. The film production and distribution company targets an international film market, including Asia. The company's occasional forays into auteur and independent projects have assured Besson an important place in the international circuit of arthouse film distribution and film festivals. Significantly, in 2000 Besson was appointed Jury Director at the Cannes Festival; in 2004, he received the *Prix des Amériques* at the *Festival des Films du Monde* in Montréal as a recognition of his career achievements.

Besson is a mainstream film director whose personal style and individual approach to filmmaking collapse the boundaries between independent and corporate modes of film production. His involvement in various types of films and production systems questions the possibility of both clearly delineating the difference between 'culturally' and 'commercially' oriented film practices – in France or elsewhere – and maintaining one's autonomy as an independent player within national and international circuits of film production and distribution. Besson notoriously dismisses the French policy of 'cultural exception', which since 1993 has juxtaposed France with the United States in claiming the treatment of films as cultural products, instead of trade items. Because of his collaboration with Hollywood studios and the adoption of Hollywood-scaled production budgets and distribution strategies, he also consolidated a reputation as the most 'Americanised' European filmmaker of his generation, which he firmly rejects, claiming his professional distance from Hollywood even when he is collaborating with American companies, and stressing the difference between his individually coordinated systems of production and Hollywood's assembly line organisation. Besson moved very early in his career from small, independent productions to large scale productions and circuits of national and international film distribution and exhibition. During the 1980s and early 1990s, together with Leos Carax, Jean-Jacques Beineix and the team Jean-Pierre Jeunet/Marc Caro, he was affiliated with the *cinéma du look*, a typical product of Minister of Culture Jack Lang's efforts to boost authorial film production with the purpose of competing against Hollywood films, in both domestic and foreign markets. The *cinéma du look* marked the reaction against the art and *cinéphile* tradition of French cinema, adopting techniques and aesthetics derived from high-quality TV commercials and music videos. In so doing, this new film style brought film crews back to the studios, since the 1950s deserted by auteur-oriented filmmakers. French and international film critics associated the *cinéma du look* with a neo-baroque and post-card aesthetics, with reference to its penchant for theatricality and audio-visual effects.[2] Popular during the 1980s, the *cinéma du look* declined soon after the international success of *Nikita* (*La femme Nikita*), although it seemed to regain prestige some years later with the international success of another of Besson's films, *Léon* (*The Professional*). Even though Besson has always maintained a defiant and autonomous position within his national film context, the French film industry cherishes him as a major source of box-office receipts and of secure access to US markets. This was especially the case during the 1980s and 1990s, when Besson put into practice the efforts to reinstate France in domestic and international circuits of film distribution with high production value and spectacular films pursued by Lang (appointed Minister of Culture 1981–86 and 1988–93) and the film producer Toscan du Plantier (the head of Gaumont in the early 1980s and then of Unifrance, the state's promotional agency for French films abroad). Beginning with *Le grand bleu* (*The Big Blue*), distributed by Fox, and especially with *Nikita*, distributed by Columbia Pictures, Besson conquered the traditionally inaccessible US market. The success of the latter was such that Gaumont, France's largest production company, sold the rights to the film to Warner Bros., which released a remake only two years after the original.[3]

In the 1990s Besson's big-budget and star-studded films have defied the announced 'death' of the *cinéma du look* and the filmmaker has consolidated his reputation as a director who can appeal to the box office yet retain an independent outlook. With *Léon*, Besson moved to international co-productions: for this film, shot entirely in New York, his company Les Films du Dauphin and Gaumont joined the US major Columbia and the Japanese JVC.[4] With *Léon*, and more assertively so with *Le cinquième élément* and *Jeanne d'Arc* (*The Messenger*), Besson started to challenge Hollywood blockbusters at the level of high budgets, international and English-speaking all-star cast and crew, and global promotional campaigns. Besson's success allowed him to maintain or choose his own collaborators (including the director of photography Thierry Arbogast and the music composer Eric Serra) and to have director's cut and general supervision assured even in the most costly and complex of his American-connected film productions. In *Le cinquième element* Besson resorted to France's most notorious cartoonists, Moebius (pseudonym of Jean Giraud) and Jean Claude Mezières. The costumes provide the most manifest 'French touch' in the film's mise-en-scène, with Besson employing fashion designer Jean-Paul Gaultier. Together with Moebius's and Mezières' sets, Gaultier's costumes divert the spectator from the action-centred focus of the standard blockbuster film. In spite of this, the transition to an international dimension of film production came with some concessions to the American distribution companies. If in *Le grand bleu* and *Léon* Besson accepted the conditions of his US distributors (regarding, respectively, the musical score and the treatment of the two protagonists' relationship involving a male adult and a female adolescent), in *Le cinquième élément* he agreed to make substantial changes to his original script (changes suggested by studio-imposed US screenwriters).

In his films Besson reinstates a utopian, arguably naïve yet commercially viable conception of cinema as a medium that allows one to express personal beliefs in accessible and entertaining forms. Susan Hayward defines Besson's view of cinema's 'bardic function', aiming to please vast audiences while conveying a humanitarian, albeit pessimistic, message on the dangers that menace our society and environment in the present and in the near future.[5] At the level of production, he remains faithful to a personal working method entailing his personal input in every phase of the filmmaking process, which assures the thematic and stylistic consistency of his films. His professional proficiency, formed during his youth as a volunteer apprentice and assistant producer in the French studios and during a short residency at the Universal Studios in Los Angeles, and perfected throughout the years, allows him to plan every aspect of his complicated sets and memorise a great number of continuity shots (his preferred shooting method). Meticulous and technically competent, he supervises every detail on the set and personally monitors large crews in sets, studios and laboratories situated in different locations and continents. As Hayward stresses, Besson employs a high ratio of shots per film (an average of 1,500 against the 400 of a standard French film) and typically shoots nineteen takes a day (against an average of eight to twelve by most French directors). According to Hayward, this method reflects less the influence of Hollywood action films than an interest in the *bandes dessinées* (comic strips) which Besson adopts either as subtexts or as direct sources in many of his films, most obviously in *Le dernier combat* (*The Last Battle*), *Le cinquième élément* and in the Minimoys trilogy.

Although Besson entered the mainstream circuit at a very early age and has forged tight connections with sizeable studios – Gaumont, with which he was associated from 1984 to 1999 and from which he separated after the difficult shooting of *Jeanne d'Arc* – he remains a defender of the independent mode of production at the core of his filmmaking philosophy. He made his début feature film in 1983 with *Le dernier combat*, a low budget project financed through personal loans from friends, acquaintances and private investors. The film depicts two survivors of a nuclear conflict, fighting each other in a Paris reduced to an oasis of debris and surrounded by a desert. The theme and the hauntingly black and white cinematography – recalling Chris Marker's *La jetée* (1962) – seemed to assure Besson a place within the framework of France's new generation of film auteurs. The film, which received the Special Jury Award at the Avoriaz film festival and was praised by film critics, remains an isolated instance in Besson's production, set apart as a promising yet unrepeated proof of creative talent. In point of fact, *Le dernier combat* foreshadows motifs and elements recurring in Besson's filmic corpus. As in most of Besson's films, the protagonists are solitary outcasts dealing with a hostile social environment in which civic rules and ideals have fallen apart. Likewise, the film introduces some of the signature features in Besson's oeuvre, including the original framing, typically shot with a Cinemascope camera.

Besson distances himself from France's auteur tradition and, in response, is despised by auteur-informed film critics. By the same token, he is suspicious of French film culture and often states that his ambition is to make films for a niche audience of young spectators who are, much like him, less familiar with art or auteur films than with Hollywood blockbusters and French mainstream films.

Besson stopped directing after completing his eighth feature film *Jeanne d'Arc*, which he considers his most difficult shooting experience. During almost seven years of directorial hiatus Besson devoted himself to the film production and distribution company Europa, a studio based entirely in France, located on the director's estate properties in Paris and Normandy and financed through the reinvestment of box-office revenue from the films Besson directs and produces. Europa brought together the expertise of Pierre-Ange Le Pogam, a previous manager of Gaumont, the young producer Virginie Silla (Besson's wife since 2004), who had also previously worked at Gaumont in the international relations department, and Michel Feller, a former art house actor turned talent scout at Artmedia. Such managerial variety supports Europa's diversification of films, genres, marketing sectors and financial investments, alternating nationally and internationally distributed action films with small domestic comedies. Europa's productions range across a variety of film modes and genres: while big-budget action flicks, thrillers and comedies predominate, catering to audiences across Europe, North America, and Asia, the output also includes art cinema titles. In particular, Besson's company specialises in actors-turned-directors' projects and in sponsoring films by emerging French filmmakers, many of whom come out of his own professional team.

Besson's 2006 return to directing met with a mixed reception. *Angel-A*, starring popular French actor Jamel Debbouze, represents Besson's hugest flop to date. *Arthur et les Minimoys*, released shortly after *Angel-A*, was a huge financial success in France but received bad reviews and did very poorly in North America, even though the United States was the film's target market. The film's live action sections used a primarily American cast, including Mia Farrow and emerging child actor Freddie Highmore in the lead roles. The main animated sections of the film cost more than $80 million US and it was five years in production. For the English language version, characters were voiced by high profile performers such as Madonna, Snoop Dog, Robert De Niro and Harvey Keitel; for the French version pop stars Milène Farmer and Alain Bashung were the voices of the animated characters. An important asset for the completion of this ambitious project was the sophisticated recording studio Digital Factory, located at one of Besson's properties, a seventeenth-century castle in Normandy where the director had also filmed some sequences of *Jeanne D'Arc*. Besson fitted the property for live action shooting, and built a studio at Pantin, in the Paris suburbs, in which *Arthur et les Minimoys*'s animated sections were made. The film capitalises on one of the most popular cinematic forms now circulating in the mainstream global film market, the computer animated film. The promotional strategy employed follows that of the two most prominent animation studios: Pixar and Dreamworks. The film also borrows conventions from other films adapted from popular children novels, including *Harry Potter* (2001), *The Lord of the Rings* (Peter Jackson, 2001–3), *Eragon* (Stefen Fangmeier, 2006), and *The Chronicles of Narnia* (Andrew Adamson, 2005), a strategy which led film critics in the United States and Canada to attack both Besson's books and the script for their lack of originality, if not overt plagiarism.

Despite commercial failure in the United States, the film was none the less successful thanks to domestic support and strong box office in many European countries such as the United Kingdom,

Spain and Germany, an outcome which encouraged Besson to pursue the adaptation of the two sequels to *Arthur et les Minimoys*, the first of which was released in 2009. Besson's future directorial projects are in film animation.

Biography

Luc Besson was born 18 March 1959, in Paris, France.

Notes

1 The most remarkable examples are the books published at the release of *Le cinquième élément* and *Jeanne D'Arc*. For *Arthur et le Minimoys /Arthur and the Invisibles* in 2006) he launched a campaign financed by *Paribas* and the mobile phones company *Orange*. Some recent cases of films presented at international film festivals as culturally relevant projects are *Quand j'étais chanteur* (Xavier Giannoli, 2006) and *Michou D'Auber* (Thomas Gilou, 2007).
2 On the *cinéma du look* see, among others, Ginette Vincendeau's entry in *The Companion to French Cinema* (London: Cassell, 1996, p. 50) and the sixth chapter of Naomi Greene's book *Landscapes of Loss: The National Past in Postwar French Cinema* (Princeton, NJ: Princeton University Press, 1999, pp. 164–89). On *cinéma du look*'s neo-baroque qualities see Raphaël Bassan's 'Trois néo-baroques français', in *La Revue du cinéma* 499 (May 1989): 46–53, and Phil Powrie's *Jean-Jacques Beineix* (Manchester: Manchester University Press, 2000).
3 The film was titled *Point of No Return*, aka *The Assassin*, and starred Bridget Fonda in the main role.
4 Interestingly, *Léon* was marketed in the United States as an American film, made by the director of *Nikita*.
5 Hayward 1998.

Filmography (as director)

L'avant dernier (1981, not released)
Le dernier combat / *The Last Combat* (1983)
Subway (1985)
Le grand bleu / *The Big Blue* (1988)
Nikita / *La Femme Nikita* (1990)
Atlantis (1991)
De Serge Gainsbourg à Gainsbarre de 1958–1991 (1994) (V) (segment 'Mon légionnaire' 1988)
Léon / *The Professional* (1994)
Le cinquième element / *The Fifth Element* (1997)
Jeanne d'Arc / *The Messenger: The Story of Joan of Arc* (1999)
Angel-A (2005)

Arthur et les Minimoys / Arthur and the Invisibles (2006)
Arthur et la vengeance de Maltazard / Arthur and the Revenge of Maltazard (2009)
Arthur et la guerre des deux mondes / Arthur and the Two Worlds War (2010)
(post-production)

Further reading

Alexander, M. 1994. 'A Gaul in Hollywood'. *Variety*, 356.10: 10, October.
Aubron, H. 2006. 'Angel-A'. *Cahiers du Cinéma*, 608: 42, January.
Besson, L. 2001. 'Le plus grand défi de Luc Besson: entretien avec Jean-Pierre Lavoignant et Christophe d'Yvoire'. *Studio Magazine*, 169: 72–83.
—— 2002. 'Je n'ai plus peur: entretien avec Lionel Cartégini et Olivier de Bruyin'. *Première*, 300: 92–97.
—— 2003. 'Le système B: entretien avec Aurélien Ferenczi'. *Télérama*, 2781: 32–36, April 30.
—— 2006. Interview Luc Besson. *Première*. [online] Available: http://www. premiere.fr/premiere/magazine-et-exclus/interviews/interview-lucbesson/ (affichage)/interviewPage/(interview_id)/410269/(interviewPage_question)/9.
—— 2007. Press Conference. Montreal: Hotel Sofitel, January 5.
Bassan, R. 1989. 'Trois néo-baroques français'. *La Revue du cinéma* 499 (May): 46–53.
Bondy, J.-A. 1997. 'Le cinquième élément'. *Première*, 244: 35, juin.
Ferenczi, A. 2003. 'Sa petite entreprise ne connaît pas la crise'. *Télérama*, 2781: 36–39, April 30.
Finney, A. 1996. *The State of European Cinema: A New Dose of Reality*. London: Cassell.
Genzlinger, N. 2007. 'The Human and the Animated, Shrunk to Size'. *The New York Times* (January 12). [online] Available: http://movies2.nytimes. com/2007/01/12/movies/12art.html
Guichard, L. 2004. 'Besson un peu débouté'. *Télérama*, 2857: October, 26.
Hayward, S. 1998. *Luc Besson*. Manchester: Manchester University Press.
—— and Phil Powrie. (eds) 2007. *The Films of Luc Besson: Master of Spectacle*. Manchester: Manchester University Press.
Koehler, R. 2006. 'Arthur and the Invisibles. Arthur et les Minimoys'. *Variety*. (December 21). [online] Available: http://www.variety.com/ review/VE1117932356.html?categoryid=31&cs=1&p=
Kruger, A. 1994. 'Léon'. *Première*, 211: 40, novembre.
Lequeret, É. 2002. 'Les inconnues de l'après-Canal+ (dossier)'. *Cahiers du Cinéma*, 570: 68–71, juillet-août.
Loustalot, G. 2006. 'Angel-A'. *Première*, 348: 44, février.
Margolick, D. 2002. 'Vivendi's Mr. Universe'. *Vanity Fair*, 500: 240–77.
Maule, R. 2008. 'Made in Europa: Luc Besson and the Question of Cultural Exception in Post-auteur France'. In Maule, Rosanna, 2008. *Beyond Auteurism: New Directions in Authorial Film Practices in France, Italy and Spain since the 1980s*. Bristol: Intellect, pp. 163–87.
Mazdon, L. (ed.) 2001. *France on Film: Reflections on Popular French Cinema*. London: Wallflower Press.

Nesselson, L. 2006. 'Angel-A'. *Variety*: 23, 28, December 26.
Powrie, P. 2001. *Jean-Jacques Beineix*. Manchester: Manchester University Press.
Sarris, A. 1991. Sarris's film column. *New York Observer*, April 1.
Vincendeau, G. 1996. *The Companion to French Cinema*. London: Cassell.

KATHRYN BIGELOW

By Yvonne Tasker

The 2008 release of Iraq war movie *The Hurt Locker*, for which Kathryn Bigelow took the Director's Guild of America and Academy awards, saw this filmmaker find a contemporary setting for the violent, exhilarating cinematic spectacle with which she has long been associated. Up till this evocative war movie, Bigelow's films have been displaced from the moment by their historical setting (*The Loveless*, *Strange Days*, *The Weight of Water*, *K-19: The Widowmaker*) and/or by their use of fantasy genres and stylised imagery (as in *Near Dark*, *Blue Steel* and *Point Break*). Since her first commercial success with the film noir/vampire/Western *Near Dark*, Kathryn Bigelow has built a strong reputation and a high degree of critical interest. Typically developing her own projects, she has worked with medium to big budgets, star names and popular genres. Though rarely achieving significant box-office success, her films have continually intrigued, shocked and seduced. An art-house-oriented filmmaker who seems to revel in genres conventionally understood as both 'masculine' and artless – whether road movie, teen-pic, horror, cop thriller, action, buddy yarns, science fiction or, most recently, the war movie – Bigelow has sustained interest as a visually exciting filmmaker. As a high profile female filmmaker in an industry that remains very much male-dominated, Bigelow has provoked interest from critics who are simultaneously drawn to and repelled by the gendered dimensions of her films – the compelling strong women of *Blue Steel* and *Strange Days* on one hand, the evocation of male intimacy and violence as both intense and exclusionary on the other.

Ironically, critical interest in Bigelow's work accelerated through the 00s, a relatively difficult period for the director with the limited distribution of *The Weight of Water* and the disappointing performance of the expensive submarine movie *K-19*. With respect to Bigelow's earlier films, critics expressed ambivalence, uncertain as to whether the supposed 'breathless pace' of films like *Point Break*, indeed the high style of her work as a whole, might somehow function as a substitute for content. *Strange Days*, for instance, was read as both astonishingly creative, 'staggeringly ambitious' and basely exploitative. A visual, often visceral filmmaker, critics have also found her abilities with plotting and narrative less than convincing. One reviewer, though praising her early works *The Loveless* and *Near Dark*, called *Strange Days* 'grossly inflated visually': 'the film foams at the mouth with ideas but ultimately delivers nothing but mammoth clichés culled from a hundred other movies. The orchestration of them, however, is often quite something'.[1] That very emphasis on intense visual impact has been praised by reviewers of *The Hurt Locker*, with the exhilarating style seen as an effective evocation of the ongoing conflict in Iraq and the film as a whole felt to be a corrective against kneejerk patriotism. Like *K-19* and the earlier *Point Break*, *The Hurt Locker* foregrounds male loyalty. The film's excess – evident in the elite group's bonding through booze and violence, or in Sanborn's (Anthony Mackie) realization that he wishes to father a son – is both poignant and absurd. James's (Jeremy Renner) paternalistic involvement with the Iraqi boy nicknamed 'Beckham' culminates in a climactic scene both grotesque and emotive in which the latter's body has become a bomb and must be ripped apart.

Those critics who despair over the lack of narrative coherence and drive in Bigelow's work have a point: such films as *The Loveless* and *Blue Steel* persistently sidetrack the audience into the pleasures of looking, while none of her films could be described as particularly goal-oriented (*The Hurt Locker* ends right back at the beginning, with James returning to Iraq). Bigelow's reputation as an action auteur stems quite particularly from the fantastic set-pieces that regularly appear in her films (the bank robbery in *Point Break*; the convenience store hold-up in *Blue Steel*; the roadhouse massacre in *Near Dark*). While Bigelow might be a great director of action sequences she cannot really be described as an action filmmaker in the manner of contemporary Hollywood. In retrospect Bigelow's *The Weight of Water*, a thriller that juxtaposes a period murder case with a contemporary investigation, signaled a shift of emphasis. Indeed her subsequent films have moved away from an earlier, more experimental, hybridised use of genre, although a commitment to visual intensity (for which action serves as a shorthand) remains.

Writing of *Near Dark*, Pauline Kael comments on Bigelow's 'talent for the uncanny', pointing to her art training and film school background. Bigelow's art background has led critics to describe her work as 'painterly', feeding the notion of an ambivalent action auteur enamoured with the possibilities of the image. To some extent all Bigelow's films can be said to share an uncanny quality, something we might attribute to her peculiar situation as an experimental genre filmmaker. It is Bigelow's art-house approach to genre cinema that is most distinctive in her films up to *Strange Days*. She has spoken not only of her fascination with genre, but her interest in redefining it, creating hybrids that enable the filmmaker 'to invest ... genres with new material'. If the notion of an art-house sensibility might suggest a desire to somehow 'transcend' popular genres, Bigelow both exploits and values the genres within which she works. Moreover, from a feminist perspective, the interest of her work has as much to do with its capacity to underline the limitations of thinking about certain kinds of genres and styles as 'masculine' (what does that really mean after all?) as with their status as competent exercises in once forbidden territory.

The Loveless, Bigelow's stylish first feature, which she termed a 'psychological biker film', co-written and directed with Monty Montgomery, is perhaps her most explicitly art-house project. A pastiche of 1950s' teen movies, loaded with self-conscious allusions to the 1954 exploitation picture *The Wild One* (not least via Willem Dafoe's central performance), *The Loveless* consistently keeps the spectator at one remove from events even at their most dramatic. Long shots, an often static camera (the film is after all concerned with the perils of being stuck) and elaborate montage all contribute to this feeling of distance, as do the central characters' mannered performances of cool. The soundtrack is used at times to counterpoint the action, occasionally to almost obliterate the dialogue and to create striking effects of noise against silence (as in the final bar scene where the shots that focus on Telena are practically silent, whilst those focusing on the group in the bar are chaotic with laughter and gunfire).

For Bigelow the film functions as playful homage ('very tongue-in-cheek') in its juxtaposition of *The Wild One*, Douglas Sirk's high melodrama *Written on the Wind* (1956) and Kenneth Anger's exercise in fetishistic montage *Scorpio Rising* (1964). Borrowing its basic narrative structure and imagery from *The Wild One* – bikers stop over in a small town, bringing the community's latent tensions to the surface – the film takes its tone from the combination of elements rather than any one. More ironic than Bigelow's later work, *The Loveless* stages a commentary on the moralistic structure through which Brando's inarticulate not-all-bad biker boy learns the value of life from a good girl in a small town. Instead of salvation, Dafoe finds only corruption and an overwhelming sense of boredom. 'If you weren't born here you wouldn't have a whole lot of reason to hang around', a waitress tells him: she later performs an antiseptic striptease in the town's cocktail bar.

The Loveless combines a fetishistic attention to period detail – décor, signs, costume, design – with another sort of visual pleasure, evident in both lingering images and rapid close-ups of motorcycles, cars, leathers, tattoos, belts and bodies. The small town where Vance (Dafoe) and his friends are temporarily stalled is structured around increasingly apparent divisions of black and white, between those who stay and those who go, between adult and teenage worlds. After Vance sleeps with the boyish Telena (the androgynous female protagonist who pre-figures *Near Dark*'s Mae, *Blue Steel*'s Megan and *Point Break*'s Tyler) her sexual relationship with her corrupt father is revealed. The movie climaxes with Telena shooting her father and then herself, a suicide 'seen' through Vance's seemingly impassive face: only the soundtrack which minutes before replays her words in his head suggests to us that he may have any involvement in the events played out before him. The townsfolk project both fears and desires onto the wild ones in their midst – some parade themselves whilst others simply snatch a look (the woman whose tyre Vance changes in the opening scene, or the garage owner who tells his son: 'They're *animals*. Hell. I'd love to trade places with them for a day or two').

Road movie imagery recurs in *Near Dark* in which Caleb (Adrian Pasdar) is initiated by Mae (Jenny Wright) into the world of a vampire 'family' who transport him from the fixed life of the farm and small town into a terrifying but stimulating alternative world. The film revolves around Mae's and Caleb's mutual fascination, a relationship that brings out tensions in the vampire family since Caleb is unable or unwilling to kill, becoming increasingly dependent on Mae's ability to feed him. Alongside its 'B' movie wipes and the spectacle of gore, *Near Dark* deploys grim comedy played out through visual horror and one-liners, whilst offering a stylish and atmospheric vision of the Western landscape. For Wheeler Winston Dixon, the film is 'a trancelike fabric of sleep, slaughter, and survival, an endlessly evolving tapering of thirst and fulfillment underscored by Tangerine Dream's hypnotic, droning electronic music' (once again an evocative soundtrack is central to the film's effect).[2] If a number of Bigelow's movies suggest the formation of a romantic couple, this can raise as many questions as it answers – as with Lenny and Mace's embrace in the closing moments of *Strange Days*. *K-19* features its submariners' fond farewells to wives and girlfriends but it is the men who reunite at the end. In *The Hurt Locker*, James's very capability at his work and his addiction to danger make him unsuited to the confines of domesticity; the image of him adrift in the cereal aisle evokes his distance from the everyday, a contrast to his more certain demeanor on his return to Iraq.

As is appropriate for a filmmaker associated so much with visual spectacle and stylish showpieces, *Near Dark* revolves explicitly around the play of light as the band of vampires attempt to feed, move on and evade the sunlight. *Near Dark* uses a tenet of vampire movie mythology – daylight will destroy a vampire – to generate its central visual device. This is not to say that *Near Dark* is somehow an unusual or atypical horror film: though it is both visually stylish and original in its juxtaposition of horror and Western conventions, the film none the less exploits the existing richness of these forms. Equally, *Point Break* rehearses what are familiar cop/buddy clichés in its constitution of the outlaws as moral centre against the dryness of the FBI. The film's impact lies in the deployment of cinematic spectacle to support that opposition, right down to the final showdown on the beach. Vitality belongs to the bank-robbing/surfer outlaws led by Bodhi (Patrick Swayze) and is enacted through the exhilarating set-piece scenes of surfing (at night in one case), robbery and skydiving.

Blue Steel and *Strange Days* have both received sustained analysis, the former for its attempt to put 'a woman at the centre of a movie predominantly occupied by men',[3] the latter for its intense engagement with power and voyeurism. Co-produced by Oliver Stone, with whom Bigelow later worked on the paranoid television series *Wild Palms*, *Blue Steel* signaled a move into bigger budgets. Stylish images, atmospheric lighting and off-centre compositions contribute an uncanny, dream-like quality to the film as we watch the unfolding of serial killer Eugene's (Ron Silver) growing obsession with rookie cop Megan Turner (Jamie Lee Curtis). Atmospheric and somewhat perverse, *Blue Steel* also plays out its themes of obsession and fetishism visually – lingering over weaponry, uniforms and evocatively lit interiors. Widely – and not entirely accurately, given the evident debt to horror – reviewed as a meeting of action and woman's picture, *Blue Steel* shares the leisurely pace of *The Loveless* rather than the rapid tempo of contemporary urban action films.

The millennial noir/science fiction fantasy *Strange Days* draws on diverse generic reference points including the thriller, film noir and science fiction. The movie's tech-noir imagery and nihilistic urban vision recall scriptwriter James Cameron's breakthrough low-budget film, *The Terminator* (1984), though one of the film's most self-conscious allusions comes in the opening sequence where Hitchcock's *Vertigo* is evoked in a rooftop chase that ends in death. Preoccupied with questions of vision, voyeurism, spectacle and identity, *Strange Days* has the 'retinal fetish' nightclub as a key setting, following reluctant hero Lenny Nero's obsession with his own romantic past – he 'replays' scenes of flirtation and passion whose brightly lit qualities render them 'unreal' against the pervasive darkness of the rest of the film. The movie's themes touch on racism, addiction and social decay, before resorting to an unconvincing cheerful ending. For many critics the ending provided an indication of the shortcomings of both Bigelow and Cameron in the attempt to articulate a political sensibility within a generic context. That conundrum is also evident in *The Hurt Locker*. Like *Blue Steel* and *Strange Days*, the film plays out big themes via extraordinary images. The film exploits grotesque, visceral horror. It also leaves audiences with a lingering sense that the generic conventions of the war movie – and the military masculinity, defined by suffering and comradeship that the genre depends upon – are in some ways inadequate to the task. The pretext that 'war is a drug' is a literary and cinematic cliché, one that Bigelow's film animates via an intense immersion in the space of war. The intensity and aimlessness of that experience does not constitute a critique of these clichés. As much as any of her previous films *The Hurt Locker* demonstrates Bigelow's respect for generic conventions and her ability as a filmmaker to render them simultaneously meaningful and hollow.

Biography

Born in 1952, California, USA. Bigelow studied painting at the San Francisco Art Institute before moving to New York on a scholarship to the Whitney Museum in 1972. Her experiments with film began whilst working as an assistant to Vito Acconci, which led to a period at Columbia's Graduate Film School. Her television work includes *Wild Palms*, *Homicide: Life on the Street* and *Karen Sisco*. In 2010 she became the first woman to win the Director's Guild of America award and the Academy Award for Best Director (both for *The Hurt Locker*).

Notes

1 Derek Malcolm, *Guardian*, 29 February 1996, p. 8.
2 Wheeler Winston Dixon, *The Transparency of Spectacle: Meditations on the Moving Image*, State University of New York Press, 1998, p. 131.

3 'Walk on the Wild Side: An Interview with Kathryn Bigelow', *Monthly Film Bulletin*, November 1991, p. 313.

Filmography

The Loveless (1981) also co-writer/director (with Monty Montgomery)
Near Dark (1987) also co-writer (with Eric Red)
Blue Steel (1990) also co-writer (with Eric Red)
Point Break (1991)
Strange Days (1995)
The Weight of Water (2000)
K-19: The Widowmaker (2002) also producer
The Hurt Locker (2008) also producer

Further reading

Barry Keith Grant, 'Man's Favourite Sport: The Action Films of Kathryn Bigelow' in Yvonne Tasker (ed.) *Action and Adventure Cinema*, London, Routledge, 2004, pp. 371–84.

Christina Lane, *Feminist Hollywood: From 'Born in Flames' to 'Point Break'*, Detroit, MI, Wayne State University Press, 2000.

Needeya Islam, ' 'I Wanted to Shoot People': Genre Gender and Action in the Films of Kathryn Bigelow', in Laleen Jayamanne (ed.) *Kiss Me Deadly: Feminism and Cinema for the Moment*, Sydney, Power Publications, 1995, pp. 91–125.

Deborah Jermyn and Sean Redmond (eds) *The Cinema of Kathryn Bigelow: Hollywood Transgressor*, London, Wallflower, 2003.

Anna Powell, 'Blood on the Borders – *Near Dark* and *Blue Steel*', *Screen*, vol. 35, no. 2, 1994, pp. 136–56.

Yvonne Tasker, *Spectacular Bodies: Gender, Genre and the Action Cinema*, London, Routledge, 1993.

CHARLES BURNETT

By Chuck Kleinhans

Charles Burnett wrote and directed one widely recognised master-piece, the neorealist *Killer of Sheep*, and a major achievement in African-American film, *To Sleep with Anger*. Imbued with a deep humanist vision, a searching concern with characters facing moral and ethical decisions, and a tendency to allegorical expression, Burnett's work has gained critical regard while his career demonstrates the problems of a black American auteur working in the last quarter of the twentieth century. From an initial position as an independent feature writer/director/cameraman, Burnett has sustained his career working on a number of Hollywood and television projects which range from accomplished to banal in direction and none of which had strong commercial success.

Burnett's position can be usefully compared and contrasted with other African-American directors. Most successfully within traditional Hollywood terms, comic actor/directors such as Eddie Murphy and Keenen Ivory Wayans sustain their efforts in conventional work with cross-over in mind. Other black directors within the industry such as Albert and Allen Hughes exploited 'in the hood' and rap/hip-hop sensibilities and themes to gain box office from the racially and culturally diverse viewers who consume black youth culture with diminishing success. In contrast, Spike Lee (very much a New York, not Hollywood, director) turned himself into a celebrity auteur maintaining his distinct style and themes through obvious talent, creative versatility and a hard-sell personality.

In contrast to those working in the commercial mainstream, some independent writer/directors such as Julie Dash and Haile Gerima (*Sankofa*, 1993) mounted dramatic features deeply resonant with African-American history, won a strong critical response, and carefully promoted African-American audience interest. An even wider range of creative work has appeared from directors working in more experimental and documentary modes, often university-based such as the late Marlon Riggs, Zeinabu irene Davis and Ayoke Chenzira, or connected with the art/theatre/music world such as Camille Billops and the late Bill Gunn, or documentary and broadcasting such as Bill Greaves, and the late St. Clair Bourne.

Charles Burnett made his first feature drama, *Killer of Sheep*, as his thesis film in the UCLA MFA film program. An episodic slice of life, the film shows the daily routines of a slaughterhouse worker, Stan, interspersed with views of the Los Angeles black community's residents. Stan suffers insomnia, putting him in a liminal world of reduced affect, an emotional state echoed by exterior shots that reveal an urban landscape filled with demolished sites. Scenes with children playing form a powerful counterpoint to the actions of adults as we see the kids repeating the verbal and physical violence that the adult community exhibits as behaviour and symptom. Stan's work preparing sheep sets up an inescapable parallel – that the children are lambs being led to slaughter.

Particularly poignant moments highlight Stan's inhibited relation with his wife: she urges him to sleep and he cannot. Alone, they dance together to Dinah Washington's slow sad ballad, 'This Bitter

Earth', but the tenderness never blossoms into a physical consummation; she tries to entice him, but he is unresponsive and then his young daughter comes over and massages his shoulders – the child taking over an adult role while mother and daughter stare at each other. This dysfunctional social world finds an objective correlative in automobiles that don't work, keeping the community penned up in the ghetto. In the most memorable scene, Stan and a buddy buy a used engine on payday to rehabilitate an old car. The optimism is dashed when through their negligence the engine block hits the pavement and cracks.

The soundtrack echoes the screen action with unseen events: a menacing watchdog barking, a car starting with difficulty, police sirens, children's nursery rhymes, the jingles of an ice-cream vendor. A rich music track provides an additional counterpoint, joining commercial blues and soul with classical music and Paul Robeson's performances. Already tinged with a bitter irony for African-Americans, Robeson sings 'What is America to Me?' against images of sheep being moved to slaughter. Later slaughterhouse images play against Dinah Washington's slow love ballad, 'Unforgettable'. Yet the film does not end in naturalist despair. Rather, a bittersweet persistence of hope within this dysfunctional environment appears near the end of the film when an apparently mute young woman shyly but happily reveals to a group of women that she is pregnant. Stan continues to work, to endure, to support his family within a world of diminished opportunity.

Burnett worked on two more films that continue the closely observed study of ghetto masculinity. With *My Brother's Wedding*, another feature-length film, he served again as writer/director/cameraman, and he worked as screenwriter and cameraman on Billy Woodberry's *Bless Their Little Hearts*.[1] These films continued in the mode of production of low budget independent film. Recently re-cut by Burnett, *My Brother's Wedding* portrays a young man having to make a critical decision between the family obligation of being best man at the upscale wedding of his lawyer brother to a snooty female lawyer, and the funeral of his best friend, recently released from prison.

With more critical recognition, Burnett finally directed his screenplay *To Sleep With Anger*, leveraging a larger budget (US $1.5 million) with star Danny Glover's participation. The film changes Burnett's previous pattern of contrasting exterior cityscapes, workplace and the social space of the community to the domestic space of home and family, a contrast so pronounced in *Killer of Sheep*. This time the film is grounded in the house of a lower middle class Los Angeles family, which becomes infected with a foreign presence that slowly causes a crescendo of chaos in the family's three generations. Harry (Glover) arrives unexpectedly from 'back home' in the Deep South, is welcomed, and stays on and on. Gradually this trickster figure's presence and actions bring out the social situation's underlying contradictions and tensions until the home seems invaded by his cronies, the patriarch suddenly lies paralysed in bed, the family garden dries up, and the two adult brothers begin fighting. In the film's dramatic climax, the matriarch intervenes just in time to prevent one son from killing the other.

Harry may have more than a touch of Satan in him (flames appear on his feet at one point), but he is a minor devil at best. He works by bringing things to light that set in motion waves which loosen already unsteady structures. He's also an engaging rogue, and if our sense of justice is relieved when he dies in an accidental fall, we are also a bit regretful to see him go. Actually, he doesn't go. He dies at the start of a long weekend, and the coroner's office doesn't get around to picking up the body in the kitchen, so the family has to eat picnic style while friends and neighbors come by. Again the mood is bittersweet, with the emphasis on a comedic ending, underlined by the film's buoyant script, excellent acting, slow build up of a sense of community, and reflections on past/present, country/city and pretense/realism. Although the film visually concentrates its power by bringing all characters into the house, a key scene resonates with wider social power. Following the brothers' fight, they go to a hospital emergency room which we see filled with the physical toll of community instability.

With Burnett's next feature project, *The Glass Shield*, the writer/director adapted a former cop's account of the Los Angeles police. A black rookie is assigned to an all-white station filled with violence-prone racists; he tries to fit into an ethos of toughness and covering up police abuse but he comes to question his own position. Finally, with the unit's only woman, he works to expose the corruption, and in the process finds his life in danger from fellow officers. Finally, he loses his job. The film is marked by tense dramatic sequences and an effective use of interiors and night scenes with a haunting blue tone to the visuals. The sets lean toward the abstract (e.g., silhouetted figures against closed window blinds) and the film bends toward the allegorical. Part of this must be by design, but part results from its main actor's limited dramatic range and the script's strong black–white dichotomy in racial depiction.[2] Except for the Jewish female cop and one old jailer, all the white characters are uniformly malevolent racists and all the blacks are model upright minority citizens. The result is an awkward setup. The hero starts out as massively naive; and without any engaging rogues as counterpoint, it's very hard to figure out why he wants to be like the white guys. Part of the problem is in Burnett's adaptation of the story from an auto-biographical account of a period in which integration of the police force was still a novel matter. By the time the film appeared, big city police departments were (uneasily) integrated, and clearly, violent and corrupt cops were not just an African-American vs. Caucasian problem. Psychologically nuanced portraits of cops – black and white, male and female, rookies and veterans, moral and abusive – were widely seen on popular TV shows such as *Hill Street Blues, Homicide, Law and Order, NYPD Blue* and became part of the popular imagination. Lost in the allegoricalisation is Burnett's initial creative strength in relating community settings to social psychology and his probing issues of troubled black masculinity.

Following that last attempt at being a feature dramatic writer/director, and with his two Hollywood projects not returning their production costs, Burnett has worked only as a director. He shot three juvenile dramas for television aimed at the 'young adult' segment. *Nightjohn* is the most accomplished, set in 1830s plantation slavery South and portraying the relation between a young slave girl and an older male who teaches her the forbidden knowledge of reading. Well-crafted, the film rests on easily understood pathos to make its points. Two more Burnett projects also use dramatic senti-mentalism, but far less successfully. *Selma, Lord, Selma* presents two teens who become involved in the famous civil rights march. The film suffers badly in comparison with Spike Lee's imaginative docu-mentary examining the same period, *Four Little Girls*. In *Finding Buck McHenry* children uncover a mystery surrounding a legendary star of the Negro baseball league while clunky plot points, uneven acting and heavy handed didacticism limit the film's impact. Strong acting marks the TV mini-series drama *Oprah Winfrey Presents: The Wedding* which considers the colour and class line within the black community in the 1950s. Unevenly adapted from a late novel by Harlem Renaissance writer Dorothy West, the compelling topic seems flat-tened by the logic of television production and a mainstreamed tone. A recent romantic comedy of elders casts James Earl Jones and Vanessa Redgrave as eccentric loners who unexpectedly fall in love. Superbly shot, *The Annihilation of Fish* seems like a play adapted to film, more theatrical than cinematic. Screened at festivals, it did not find commercial release.

After the Millennium Burnett continued TV work with several projects, the most notable an episode of a Martin Scorsese-produced Public Broadcasting music documentary series, *The Blues*, where he had creative control as writer and director. He directed a well-received documentary, *Nat Turner: A Troublesome Property*, which considers the early 19th-century leader of a slave rebellion in terms of the historical record and the various and differing interpretations of Turner as a historical and literary figure. A seldom seen feature documentary *Namibia: The Struggle for Liberation*, appears from press reports to be a government-commissioned celebration of the African nation's independence movement. Burnett was announced as director of a documentary on President Obama's anthropologist mother.

Burnett's career is best understood set against the backdrop of changes in Hollywood, independent and black filmmaking. When he began studying film in 1967 contemporary black film was just getting started with Blaxploitation still to take place. When *Killer of Sheep* appeared a decade later, Hollywood began to consolidate to a dominant model of High Concept blockbuster filmmaking, but the independent feature phenomenon known as the Sundance film was still a decade away.[3] In the 1960s and 1970s black artists and intellectuals thought that, given gross misrepresentation by Hollywood, the main task was for blacks to make films about themselves. Burnett's early work fit this pattern with serious dramas set in the inner city African-American community, but the trade-off for having complete creative control was severely restricted budgets and the limited venues of art house, festival, museum and campus audiences. The temptation of 'going Hollywood' for talented artists is strong but the exchange for getting more resources tends to be working in predictable ways in predictable genres (the ghettocentric action film, the black minstrelsy comedy, etc.) and/or loss of creative control. (How Spike Lee has negotiated this tension for a productive career needs close examination.) With time, as more films starring African-Americans written and directed by African-Americans and aimed at a black audience appeared, especially in the 1990s, it became clear that the 'black audience' was not a unified entity in either sensibility, politics or market. The call to unity that was so forceful in the Civil Rights era as political rhetoric, did not have analytic power in the Millennium's reality of a consolidating global entertainment marketplace, neoliberal politics and a growing gap between inner city and middle class African-Americans. The earlier hopes by makers and critics for a distinct and forceful independent African-American film movement were earnest, but bringing it about in a capitalist film culture was elusive as the indie film sector itself imploded with changing technologies, evolving distribution/exhibition patterns, and unstable financing of a capital-intensive creative form.

Politically aware African-American filmmakers (as for feminist, Latino and gay media artists) face the dilemma of negotiating mainstream vs. independent options. Reflecting on his own experience, Burnett observed, 'The situation is such that one is always asked to compromise one's integrity, and if the socially oriented film is finally made, its showing will generally be limited and the very ones that it is made for and about will probably never see it'.[4] In *Redefining Black Film*, Mark Reid observes,

> ... production and stylistic freedoms permit black independent filmmakers to experiment with audio, visual, and performance methods that seem unrefined to audiences and film critics reared on Hollywood films. Thus, the use of non-star talent, innovative aural and visual narrative techniques, and abrupt editing (all of which are at odds with the classical Hollywood narrative style) make black independent films different in content and form from studio-distributed black films.[5]

The border between independent vision and mainstream accomplishment formed a basic controversial topic for African-American filmmakers and critics for the past 25 years. For those who have had the opportunity to work in Hollywood, the experience has its rough spots. Many of Burnett's supporters charged that *To Sleep With Anger* was sabotaged by bad distribution and publicity. Yet in discussing the film in *Framing Blackness: The African-American Image in Film*, Ed Guerrero remarks on

> ... the frustrating intersection of independent and mainstream issues debated among black filmmakers. Added to this are the overdetermining, paradoxical problems of winning broad distribution and popular box office support for a film that in its vision and style runs far beyond the colonized appetites of the sex-violence-action trained consumer audience, be it black or white.[6]

In more recent interviews Burnett has spoken of the opportunity to work on larger projects with a professionally skilled creative team and top notch acting talent, the need to make a living and support a family with one's creative work, and the desire to work regularly. His move into television, like that of Julie Dash (e.g., an episode of

Women: Stories of Passion and a romantic comedy for Black Entertainment Television) and Darnell Martin (*Homicide, ER, Oz* after her directorial debut with *I Like It Like That*) reflects what is possible in a bottom-line driven industry in which 'film artists' become 'content providers' to transnational corporations. Martin had the professional track record to direct a well financed feature again with *Cadillac Records* but the film is solidly set in a crossover strategy. In the recent phase, the most commercially successful black films by African-American directors have been projects such as *Waiting to Exhale* (d. Forest Whitaker), budgeted at US $15 million with a US theatrical return of $66.2 million and $33 million in video rentals, and *Soul Food* (d. George Tillman Jr.), a $43.5 million return on a $7.5 million budget. The most notable black writer/director indie auteur who has achieved creative control and bankability is Tyler Perry, an impresario of sentimental comedy set in the African-American community (e.g., *Madea's Family Reunion*). By and large, these filmmakers and films have not received the critical acclaim of African-American intellectuals or film scholars, critics and reviewers. Ironically, the restoration and re-release of *Killer of Sheep* and its DVD release made the film available (internationally as well) as never before, inspiring a new wave of critical appreciation for a film so different from those now being made.

Characteristically soft-spoken, Charles Burnett has moved through life, creative opportunities, and a changing situation for filmmakers with a clear conviction:

> ... it is the little personal things that begin to give a hint of the larger picture. The story has the effect of allowing us to comprehend things we cannot see, namely feelings and relationships. It may not give you answers but it will allow you to appreciate life, and maybe that is the issue, the ability to find life wonderful and mysterious. ... One has to work on how to be good, compassionate. One has to approach it like a job. Until there is a sharing of experiences, every man is an island and the inner city will always be a wasteland.[7]

Biography

Born 13 April 1944, Vicksburg, Mississippi, Burnett grew up in Los Angeles, California, USA. He attended the University of California, Los Angeles (MFA, 1977) and received the McArthur Foundation 'genius' award in 1988.

Notes

1 Chuck Kleinhans, 'Realist Melodrama and the African-American Family: Billy Woodberry's *Bless Their Little Hearts*', *Melodrama: Stage, Picture, Screen*, ed. Jacky Bratton, Jim Cook and Christine Gledhill (London: British Film Institute, 1994) pp. 157–66.
2 The classic 'rookie exposes corruption' film is Al Pacino in *Serpico* (d. Lumet, 1973). Burnett's film appeared two years after the notable *Deep Cover*, directed by African-American Bill Duke and starring Laurence Fishburne.
3 For an elaboration see Justin Wyatt, *High Concept: Movies and Marketing in Hollywood* (Austin: University of Texas Press, 1994), and my 'Independent Features: Hopes and Dreams', *New American Cinema*, ed. Jon Lewis (Durham: Duke University Press, 1998), pp. 307–27.
4 'Inner City Blues', Questions of Third Cinema, ed. Jim Pines and Paul Willemen (London: British Film Institute, 1989) p. 224.
5 Berkeley: University of California Press, 1993, p. 131.
6 Philadelphia: Temple University Press, 1993, p. 170.
7 'Inner City Blues', p. 226.

Filmography

Several Friends (1969) student film
The Horse (1973) student film
Killer of Sheep (1977) also writer, cinematographer
My Brother's Wedding (1983) also writer, cinematographer
To Sleep with Anger (1990) also writer
America Becoming (1991) also writer (with producer/writer Dai Sil Kim-Gibson)
The Glass Shield (1994) also writer
When It Rains (1995) also writer
Nightjohn (1996) Disney cable television
The Wedding/Oprah Winfrey Presents: The Wedding (1998) TV mini-series
Dr. Endesha Ida Mae Holland (1998) documentary
Selma, Lord, Selma (1999) Disney TV
The Annihilation of Fish (1999)
Olivia's Story (2000) (with producer/writer Dai Sil Kim-Gibson)
Finding Buck McHenry (2000) TV
'American Family' (2002) TV series (unknown episodes) aka 'American Family: Journey of Dreams' (USA: second season title)
Nat Turner: A Troublesome Property (2003)
'The Blues' (1 episode, 2003) 'Warming by the Devil's Fire' (2003) TV episode
For Reel? (2003) (TV)
Namibia: The Struggle for Liberation (2007)
Quiet as Kept (2007) short
Relative Stranger (2009) (TV)

Further reading

Killer of Sheep. Dir. Burnett, Charles. DVD restoration of 1977 film. 1977.

—— 'Charles Burnett: Killer of Sheep'. *Screenplays of the African American Experience.* Ed. Phillis Klotman. Bloomington, Indiana: Indiana University Press, 1991. 90–116.

James, David E. *The Most Typical Avant-Garde: History and Geography of Minor Cinemas in Los Angeles.* Berkeley: University of California Press, 2005.

Martin, Adrian. 'Counterspectacles: Teeming Life'. *Film Quarterly* 61.4 (2008): 72–3.

Martin, Michael T. 'Charles Burnett – Consummate Cinéaste', *Black Camera* 1.1 [NS] (2009), 143–70.

Massood, Paula J. 'An Aesthetic Appropriate to Conditions: Killer of Sheep, (Neo)Realism, and the Documentary Impulse'. *Wide Angle* 21.4 (1999): 20–41.

Merritt, Bishetta D. 'Charles Burnett: Creator of African American Culture on Film'. *Journal of Black Studies* 39.1 (2008): 109–28.

Skoller, Jeffrey. *Shadows, Spectres, Shards: Making History in Avant-Garde Film.* Minneapolis: University of Minnesota Press, 2005.

White, Armond. 'To Sleep with Anger'. *The Resistance: Ten Years of Pop Culture That Shook the World.* Ed. Armond White. Woodstock NY: Overlook Press, 1995.

TIM BURTON

By Yvonne Tasker

'Eccentric', 'macabre', a 'self-confessed weirdo': Tim Burton and his movies have often been characterised in similar terms. Specialising in quirky subjects, off-beat images and the darker side of popular culture, Burton has established himself as a strong visual stylist, bringing a fascination for the ghoulish (and the tacky) to the screen with flair, emotion and more than a little sentimentality. Burton sometimes gives the impression of having stumbled into the business of making movies by chance – the result of a childhood spent watching monster movies and experimenting with Super 8, followed by some lucky breaks working at Disney in the studio's period of turmoil following its founder's death. Yet though his films may be off-beat, Burton is very much part of the industry, directing distinctive yet commercially successful films. An unexpected 'player', he has worked as director, producer and consultant across fantasy genres, in animation and live-action, cinema and television. Burton has made his mark with both relatively intimate pictures (*Edward Scissorhands* and *Ed Wood*) and blockbusters (*Batman* and the sequel *Batman Returns*). His most graphically violent film is a musical – an adaptation of Sondheim's Broadway show *Sweeney Todd: The Demon Barber of Fleet Street* – while what is arguably his most sinister movie to date is an adaptation of children's classic *Charlie and the Chocolate Factory*, featuring not only Dahl's uncivil children but an elaborate Oedipal detour into dentistry and tooth decay alongside the seemingly obligatory evocation of Halloween.

As a highly *visual*, indeed at times surreal, filmmaker, it is perhaps no surprise that Burton began in animation, or that his time at Disney wasn't the most straightforward. He made two short films there: *Vincent*, which used puppets and stop-motion animation to grotesque effect, and the live-action *Frankenweenie*, in which a boy rewires his dead dog Sparky (a feature version is currently planned). Both betray a fascination with horror and fantasy imagery; *Vincent* was narrated by Vincent Prince, whilst *Frankenweenie* reworked James Whale's 1931 *Frankenstein* (both Price, as kindly creator-recluse, and the *Frankenstein* reference reappear in *Edward Scissorhands*). Though not widely seen in theatres, these shorts made an impact in terms of Burton's career, attracting small-scale critical buzz and industry interest. The extent to which Burton's visual sensibility is somehow part of, but really out of kilter with, conventional expectations – like the perverse Christmas toys gleefully manufactured by the residents of Halloween town in Burton's spectacular holiday fable *Nightmare Before Christmas* (directed by Henry Selick, but these days appearing under the title *Tim Burton's The Nightmare Before Christmas*[1]) – was already evident in these early films. *Frankenweenie* was at one stage intended to accompany the rerelease of *Pinocchio*, but these plans were scrapped after the film was rated PG in what was to become a recurrent theme in Burton's career: *Nightmare Before Christmas* was also rated PG, as was *Charlie and the Chocolate Factory*, whilst *Batman Returns* was criticised as too scary for children (the target audience for merchandising, if not for the film itself). Given this edginess, there was a certain irony in Burton's finding an unlikely home for *Ed Wood*, his biopic of the cult cross-dressing director, with Disney's Touchstone (Columbia apparently weren't happy with the use of black and white). Of course, by that point Burton had already 'returned' to Disney to produce *Nightmare Before Christmas*, an ambitious feature-length stop-motion project based on ideas and images he had initially developed whilst working at the studio (ideas which Disney therefore owned).[2]

Although gaining only limited distribution (Disney later gave it a video release), *Frankenweenie* helped get Burton his first feature: directing *Pee-Wee's Big Adventure* for Warners. A (relatively) low-budget vehicle for Paul Reuben's surreal act, the film was hugely successful commercially (though not with critics). *Pee-Wee's Big Adventure* was in some ways as much a showcase for Burton as for its star. Centred on Pee-Wee's child-man persona, the film has trademark gadgets, fantastic sets and comic special effects (with ghostly trucker 'Large Marge' the most memorable). For Ken Hanke, Herman was 'the perfect Burton hero', a figure who somehow 'could not be objected to' but was obviously 'neither quite 'normal', nor quite 'safe''.[3] The phrase evokes a quality in the director's long term collaboration with Johnny Depp, a star whose combination of quirky performance and good looks fits well with Burton's status as commercial filmmaker entranced by Gothic fantasy.

Burton followed up his success on *Pee-Wee* with *Beetlejuice*, another fantasy/comedy which employed self-consciously 'cheesy' special effects (delivered on a mini-budget in relative terms) and a wry sense of humour, and was, once again, big box office. The tale follows Adam and Barbara Maitland as they haunt their former dream home, calling on the services of the comically gruesome Betelgeuse (Michael Keaton) to evict the yuppie family with whom they ultimately learn to co-exist. The film's setpieces include a mundane after-life complete with seedy waiting room, a voracious sandworm (*Dune* on a budget) awaiting the Maitlands outside their house, and Betelgeuse himself (the film's make-up team won an Academy Award for their work). Winona Ryder's Lydia Deetz, feeling herself in tune with the macabre, mediates between the film's different worlds. Though her dark sensibility is adolescent posturing to some extent, she is the only one who can see the Maitlands. A child-woman, Lydia is one of a series of transitional figures (almost always male) in Burton's films. The easy use of effects, 'horror', comedy and sentiment – not to mention profits – finally convinced Warners to let Burton direct a major fantasy film in the shape of *Batman* (somewhat controversially with Keaton in the title role), a project he had already been working on for some time (and which had been in development for even longer; the rights had been purchased in 1979).

Even before *Batman*'s status as the event movie of 1989, Burton had acquired a cult critical following, with general and specialist fantasy-film magazines hailing his distinctive style. Of course it is in part because of his background in animation and his immersion in fantasy genres that the design and effects aspects of Tim Burton's films receive as much popular critical attention as themes or stars. This facet of his work seems particularly interesting when set against a prevailing perception of contemporary Hollywood as 'effects-driven' – the supposed triumph of spectacle over thematic complexity or character development. On the one hand, this might be said to tally with Burton's typical operation at one remove from scripting (his contribution certainly includes stories, but can more often be summed up in sketches and visual ideas). Yet it is both the total sense of visual design – the way in which, for example, effects are integrated into the film image – and the plain weirdness of the characters that command attention in the best of his films. From *Vincent* through 'Large Marge' and *Beetlejuice*'s sandworm to the complex characterisation seen in *Nightmare Before Christmas*, there is also both a raw quality and a sense of technical experimentation with the possibilities of animation and visual effects. Moreover, the effects and the imagery are firmly integrated within the fantasy world, as in the comic/grotesque physical transformations of *Beetlejuice* or, rather differently, Ichabod Crane's dreams (which feature the film's most vivid use of colour) in *Sleepy Hollow*. Some of the visual impact of Burton's movies is undoubtedly down to ongoing collaborative relationships – not only regular faces such as Johnny Depp, Jeffrey Jones and, latterly, Helena Bonham Carter, but also producer Denise Di Novi (with whom he worked up till *Ed Wood*), costume designer Colleen Atwood, visual effects/production designer Rick Heinrichs and, of course, composer Danny Elfman, who has scored almost all of Burton's features to date.

Batman's tone was markedly darker than the typical late 1980s' blockbuster, with Sam Hamm's screenplay taking its cue from the then relatively recent success of Frank Miller's graphic novel *The Dark Knight Returns*, which emphasised the tormented psychology of the caped crusader. Not that comedy is missing, more that the film carefully avoids either camp or parodic humour (of the kind later to be seen in *Mars Attacks!*). Instead, the film's humour stems primarily from the peculiarities of the scenario and its characters, from the Joker (unsurprisingly) and even from Batman himself: as Burton notes, 'it's a guy dressing up as a bat and no matter what anyone says that's weird'.[4] Keaton's Bruce Wayne is the film's straight man – haunted by the murder of his parents years before, he remains a quietly repressed rather than an extravagantly tormented figure. Disguised in both his personae, he is not an obvious hero in any way (as Kim Basinger's Vicky Vale remarks, 'You're not exactly normal, are you?'). Like the monotone nineteenth-century London of the later *Sweeney Todd*, Gotham's urban space is recognisable yet clearly fantastic in its mix of gothic and modernity – familiar enough and yet weird (that is, uncanny) enough for the version of the comic-book character played out here. Both *Batman* and *Batman Returns* situate

Keaton as a misfit rather than conventionally heroic, closer to the enemies he confronts (Joker, Catwoman, Penguin) than to the mainstream world of Gotham society. *Batman Returns* goes further, replacing the Wayne/Vale romance with the highly charged interaction between Wayne/Batman and Selina Kyle/Catwoman – a pair of cross-dressers perversely drawn together. Meanwhile, Danny DeVito's Penguin – abandoned by his parents in the opening scene – is a mutated misfit who explicitly plays to public sentiment about his status as outcast.

Though *Batman Returns* was extremely successful, it was Burton's last outing with the material as director (he was executive producer on *Batman Forever*). Press accounts differed over whether the director himself was no longer interested, or whether Warners simply felt his style was too 'dark and weird' for the franchise – a combination of the two is perhaps more likely. (All this seems particularly ironic following the success of an even bleaker version of this material in *The Dark Knight* in 2008.) *Batman* moved Burton into filmmaking on a different budgetary scale, its success allowing him to develop more off-beat projects like *Edward Scissorhands* (with Twentieth Century Fox). Burton himself moved into production at this time, working with Di Novi on his own films as well as projects such as *Nightmare Before Christmas* and *James and the Giant Peach* (1994, both directed by Henry Selick, whom Burton had first met at Disney).

Mars Attacks!, a science-fiction comedy/disaster movie pastiche based on a series of lurid trading cards from the 1960s, was Burton's return to big-budget filmmaking: an unpredictable convergence with Fox's blockbuster *Independence Day*, indicating just how far removed from the mainstream he could be. Although a hit overseas, the film did not perform particularly well at the US box office. Critics pointed to the apparent contradiction of an expensive, star-studded movie that looked so garish. More fundamentally, perhaps, the film's satire looks a little directionless, as is also the case with his *Planet of the Apes* remake (although that film certainly drew audiences). Andrew Kevin Walker's script for *Sleepy Hollow* provided an opportunity to return to gothic fantasy in a reworking of Washington Irving's 1819 tale. Here the combination of a low-budget sensibility, a strong creative team (including cinematographer Emmanuel Lubezki) and enough money to construct a small town set in Britain proved effective. A hybrid feel of atmospheric location work and evidently stagy sets, stylised action and artful cinematography, humour and gore provides the perfect backdrop for the film's thematic concerns (the gothic and the modern, illusion and reality). Another Oedipal figure, Depp's effete

Ichabod Crane, with his 'girlie' screams (he told Mark Salisbury that his performance was a combination of Roddy McDowell, Angela Lansbury and Basil Rathbone 'but a lot more girlie')[5] and peculiar investigative instruments, is also an unconventional hero, an outsider who aims to trust in reason but who is dogged by (and drawn to) the supernatural. Though in many ways a very different sort of film, *Ed Wood* offers a similar, highly polished B-movie feel, right from its elaborately crafted credit sequence, which whisks us through a gothic house, Jeffrey Jones's introduction delivered from a coffin, a grave-yard, sea monsters and flying saucers, ending on the famous Hollywood sign and panning down to Wood waiting anxiously for the press to appear for a performance of his new stage show.

Burton has spoken of Vincent Price's iconic horror films as emblematic of his antipathy towards the social:

> Growing up in suburbia, in an atmosphere that was perceived as nice and normal (but which I had other feelings about), those movies were a way to certain feelings, and I related them to the place I was growing up in.[6]

Burton's image as eccentric non-conformist couples an insistent antagonism towards the superficial appearance of normality and respectability with an interest in the freakish and weird in both everyday life and popular culture. In turn his films embrace the truism of horror and fantasy fiction, that villains are typically more interesting – certainly more complex – than clean-cut heroes, bringing out in the process the sinister aspects of what passes for normal and the potential beauty of what gets called weird. These themes are most explicitly visualised in *Edward Scissorhands* and literally embodied in the protagonist, whose half-finished physical state renders him an in-between, transitional figure (after all, like the later *Sleepy Hollow* it is a rites of passage tale of sorts). Here Vincent Price cameos as a loving (and loved) paternal figure to Edward. Themes of inclusion and exclusion are further mapped through the film's two worlds: suburbia, with its sunshine, colour and social niceties, versus the gothic of Edward's collapsing mansion on the edge of town. This is not the starkly satirical (and more explicitly sexual) vision of suburban America associated with David Lynch's films. In this fable Johnny Depp's Edward is a sensitive outsider (like Pee-Wee, a child-man) who brings funky hairstyles and elaborate topiary to suburbia, where his presence has a magical, transformative effect – at least for a time. His scissor-hands allow Edward to create fantastical shapes, but also render him dangerous; for cheerleader Kim (Winona Ryder, jokily cast here as the ultimate insider), who narrates the story to her own granddaughter, Edward offers a sensitive contrast to her lumpen boyfriend. Ultimately, although the neighbourbood masses on the gothic mansion in anger, the house isn't destroyed. In *Frankenweenie* the community realises the error of its ways – here it is simply deceived, with Edward and Kim returning to their two separate worlds.

The benign outsider is also central to *Ed Wood*, a character-driven ensemble piece (written by Scott Alexander and Larry Karaszewski) that represented a significant departure for Burton. Structured around the friendship between Ed and the washed-up, drug-addicted horror star Bela Lugosi (Martin Landau), *Ed Wood* celebrates an alternative film community in which social misfits are funny, but not played for laughs. Bill Murray's Bunny Breckinridge, Lisa Marie's Vampira, Jeffrey Jones as Criswell, and George 'The Animal' Steele as Tor Johnson are both 'special' and 'tragic' in the intensity of their self-belief (and indeed their belief in Wood). The film functions as an ode not to failure, but to a passionate love of filmmaking – a meditation on the more bizarre aspects of the film industry. Although framed by Wood's cult status as a 'bad' filmmaker, Depp plays Wood as an upbeat, optimistic figure, almost a visionary – his ecstatic face, lit up by the cinema screen or by the act of directing, serving as one of the film's recurrent images. Moreover, Ed's anxieties rarely surface explicitly, just as we see only brief glimpses of the negative or amused responses of others (the executives watching *Glen or Glenda*, say, or Delores/Sarah Jessica Parker's angry outburst at the wrap party for *Bride of the Atom*).

Wood's cross-dressing is never presented as freakish, despite the fact that his declaration to Kathy (Patricia Arquette) takes place in the darkness of a 'spook house' fairground ride. Instead, the film deals with a marginal showbiz world in which Wood and his associates form their own society and pursue their own dreams, staging a fantasy meeting between a frustrated Wood and his inspiration, Orson Welles (played here by Vincent D'Onofrio). The line between fantasy – tall tales – and emotional realities is central to *Big Fish*, a film once more preoccupied with fathers and sons; the film's voiceover tells us early on that 'It doesn't make sense and most of it never happened'. As Sweeney Todd, Depp enacts a different, if in many ways no less romantic vision of outsider status as a figure driven by the desire for revenge. Suggesting a bleaker outcome, *Sweeney Todd* offers no community of outsiders of the kind celebrated in *Ed Wood*. In contrast to the tentative couple who step into the modern world of *Sleepy Hollow*, or the sentimental whimsy of *Corpse Bride* (in which the Gothic potential of the meeting between the living and the dead is swept aside in a series of teaching/comic reunions), *Sweeney Todd* ends on a gruesome image of destruction and loss (the putative couple formed by Johanna and Anthony remain offscreen).

Perhaps what stands out most about Burton's films is the combination of technical experimentation and visual innovation with strongly emotive storylines. Sentiment shifts the films away from being exercises in style, whilst attention to design and visual flair prevents them from seeming too self-indulgent in their narratives of troubled male protagonists. Like other filmmakers of his generation, Burton shows himself aware of cinema's past – hence the allusions in films and interviews to Whales's *Frankenstein*, the Poe horror cycle with Vincent Price, to Hammer, monster movies, Fellini, Harryhausen and Expressionist imagery. Yet the films usually manage to avoid getting bogged down in either heavy-handed references or smug irony. Hammer, as Salisbury notes, provides a reference point for *Sleepy Hollow*, a feeling to aim towards rather than a blueprint.[7] While American cinema too often seems characterised by a purposeless – or at best nihilistic – irony, Burton's movies are both dark and weird and yet invested with emotion: postmodern Gothic, exercises in heart-warming horror.

Biography

Born in Burbank, California, in 1958, he attended the California Institute of the Arts before working with Disney and moving on to direct features. His television work includes serving as executive producer on Spielberg's animated *Family Dog* series. In 1997 Burton published an illustrated collection of short stories and poems, *The Melancholy Death of Oyster Boy & Other Stories*.

Notes

1 This attribution of Burton as author/brand led to more confusion in the promotion of Henry Selick's 2009 *Coraline* as 'From the Director of *Tim Burton's Nightmare Before Christmas*'.

2 'I love stop motion', says Burton. 'There's a certain beauty to it, yet it's unreal at the same time. It has reality. Especially on a project like *Nightmare*, where the characters are so unreal, it makes them more believable, more solid'. Frank Thompson, *Tim Burton's The Nightmare Before Christmas: The Film, the Art, the Vision*, New York, Hyperion, 1993, p. 11.

3 Ken Hanke, 'Tim Burton', *Films in Review* vol. 43, no. 11/12, 1992, p. 380.

4 Mark Salisbury (ed.) *Burton on Burton*, London, Faber and Faber (2nd edition), 2000, p. 75.

5 Mark Salisbury, 'The American Nightmare', *Guardian*, 1999, 17 December, pp. 2–3.

6 Mark Salisbury, 2000, *op. cit.* p. 4.

7 Mark Salisbury, 1999, *op. cit.*

Filmography

Vincent (1982) short
Frankenweenie (1984) short
Pee-Wee's Big Adventure (1985)
Beetlejuice (1988)
Batman (1989)
Edward Scissorhands (1990) also story, producer
Batman Returns (1992) also producer
Tim Burton's The Nightmare Before Christmas (1993, Henry Selick) as producer
Ed Wood (1994)
Mars Attacks! (1996)
Sleepy Hollow (1999)
Planet of the Apes (2001)
Big Fish (2003)
Charlie and the Chocolate Factory (2005)
Corpse Bride (2005)
Sweeney Todd: The Demon Barber of Fleet Street (2007)

Further reading

Lawrence French, 'Tim Burton's *Ed Wood*', *Cinefantastique*, vols 25 and 26, no. 6/1, 1994/5, pp. 10–18 and 112–20.

Alison McMahon, *The Films of Tim Burton*, London: Continuum, 2005.

Stephen Pizzello, 'Head Trip', *American Cinematographer*, December 1999, pp. 54–59.

Taylor L. White, 'Making of Tim Burton's *Beetlejuice* and his other bizarre gems', *Cinefantastique*, vol. 20, no. 1/2, November 1989, pp. 64–85.

JAMES CAMERON

By Alexandra Keller

> Every time I make a movie, everybody says it's the most expensive film in the film industry.
>
> James Cameron[1]

In 1997, *Titanic*, at the time the most expensive film ever made, also became the highest grossing film in history. It still ranks among the most lauded, by both critics and audiences. In 2009, James Cameron made *Avatar*, which, within little more than two months of its release, became the highest grossing film in history, just edging out Cameron's last outing as a fiction feature film director twelve years before. The film has been estimated to have cost between US $240 million and $300 million, likely making it the most expensive film ever made. These statistics, not very meaningful in themselves, point to the interesting figure that Cameron is. He is recognised both as an important director in the context of blockbuster cinema and also as the maker of the two most popular dramas ever made, making him a rare blockbuster auteur. One may use the designation 'auteur' only in the loosest way with Cameron. In the traditional sense, as initiated in the 1950s by André Bazin and his colleagues at *Cahiers du cinéma*, as subsequently debated in the 1960s in the United States by Andrew Sarris and Pauline Kael, and revised in the 1970s (this time off the Continent) by Peter Wollen, Cameron is only provisionally an artist, and certainly one whose entrance into either the famed Pantheon (Hawks, Ford) or even Sarris's Far Side of Paradise (Sirk) is questionable. Nevertheless, Cameron has a true genius for special effects, technological ingenuity, and an extraordinary knack for giving the spectator a remarkably physical, visceral viewing experience. On the one hand, Cameron is responsible for some of the most innovative techniques and indelible images in contemporary cinema. When *Titanic* called for underwater camera movement impossible with existing equipment, he simply invented what he needed, and there is no doubt that the sight of the Terminator (Arnold Schwarzenegger) removing his own eye has become iconic. *Avatar*, whose technology Cameron was integrally involved in developing, has revived the possibility that 3-D might be a viable technology for *all* film exhibition, not just select stories.

However, on the other hand, Cameron is often legitimately seen as a megalomaniac lurching around a large pit of money, and his films can be not just expensive but offensive. *True Lies*, in which Schwarzenegger plays an American secret agent single-handedly battling hordes of generic, hysterical Arab terrorists offends like few films since *Birth of a Nation* (1915), but with none of the sustaining film historical interest that D.W. Griffith's film offers. (In some respects it is worse – we are supposed to have a significantly shorter fuse concerning racism now than in 1915. Certainly the film reads rather differently since 9/11 and its aftermath.) *Avatar* has come under fire from both the Right and the Left for its potential colonial, and even, racist undertones. (Cameron even got a slap on the wrist from the Vatican for inciting Deism with the film.) His technological achievements and visual and thematic consistency notwithstanding, Cameron merits consideration for two interrelated reasons. First, he is responsible for many of the most expensive films ever made, as well as the two highest grossing films in history. (*Titanic* also tied the record for most Academy Awards won; though nominated for nine Academy Awards, *Avatar* ultimately took home only three.[2]) Second, though Canadian by birth, he may be the most symptomatic director of American mainstream cinema of his generation, and the one whose films best reflect the vertical reintegration of Hollywood in the context of globalisation.

Prior to *Titanic*, it was possible to say that Cameron's genre was science fiction or action (or some combination of the two), but *Titanic*, at US $1.85 billion in gross receipts, appeared to be a radical departure.[3] This generic difference makes auteur criticism a useful framework for discussing Cameron as a director. As a set of organising principles, it helps address how *Titanic*, a film that seems anomalous in the largely sci-fi and action-oriented works of the Cameron *œuvre*, is actually very much in the Cameron groove. Increasingly, Cameron's groove has been money itself. Just as John Ford made his mark in the Western and Alfred Hitchcock spoke through the thriller, so Cameron, once called the Cecil B. DeMille of his generation,[4] seems to have gravitated toward the blockbuster, and in so doing has helped redefine radically what that genre is. Not least, he has continually pushed the limits on budgets: *Titanic*, dubbed Cameron's $200-million art film by Fox CEO Bill Mechanic,[5] required the funding of two studios, 20th Century Fox and Paramount, and clinched the proposition that the more money spent on a film, the more it was likely to make – a precedent set by Cameron three times before with *The Abyss*, *Terminator 2: Judgment Day* and *True Lies*.[6] Atypical of most blockbuster films in that it was neither science fiction nor action, *Titanic*, at the time the most expensive and most profitable film of all time, has nevertheless become something of a Golden Mean for blockbuster cinema. In this sense, one may legitimately argue that whatever other themes Cameron concerns himself with from film to film, one of his favourite subjects is the transparent cinematic representation of capital, and his access to and control over it.[7]

In this, among other things, Cameron is a decidedly post-studio director. In other ways he more typifies the patterns of the Classical

Hollywood studio system. His favourite film is *The Wizard of Oz* (1939), but the film that sparked his desire to make movies was Stanley Kubrick's *2001: A Space Odyssey* (1969), which he saw ten times on its release. Cameron was born in Canada and raised near Niagara Falls. Frequent trips to the Royal Ontario Museum in Toronto, where he sketched antiquities, helped him become a skilled illustrator.[8] At the age of 17, his family relocated to Los Angeles, where Cameron, after false starts in college majoring in both physics and English literature, became a truck driver. In 1979 he went to work for B-movie king Roger Corman, who also helped jump-start the careers of Martin Scorsese, Francis Ford Coppola, Ron Howard and Jonathan Demme, among others. Here Cameron first began to hone his special effects techniques. Officially, his first directorial effort was *Piranha II: The Spawning*, but Cameron was fired from the project after twelve days, though his name was kept on the film. Cameron himself considers *The Terminator* his directorial debut.

It has been called 'the most important and influential film of the 80s',[9] and *The Terminator* set crucial precedents in Cameron's career. It was the beginning of the collaboration between Cameron and body-builder turned actor Arnold Schwarzenegger, which has so far yielded four films (*The Terminator*, *Terminator 2*, *True Lies* and *Terminator 2 3-D: Battle Across Time*), and, though it seems less likely since Schwarzenegger's election as governor of California in 2003, may produce more.[10] It was also the first time Cameron had complete control over a film from story idea to script to production deal to locations to storyboarding to special effects to editing, a control he has seldom if ever relinquished. *The Terminator* also marks the start of Cameron's fascination with violence, technology, strong women, money, and the nexus of representation and history. It established what is probably the strongest thematic thread in Cameron's work— his signature, if he has one: a preoccupation with vision. There is no film, *Titanic* included, in which the spectator's intense cinematic pleasure is not echoed by an equally intense consideration of visuality within the diegesis: in *The Terminator* it is the cyborg's field of vision, in *Aliens* it is also the vision of the aliens themselves. In *The Abyss* the non-terrestrial intelligent life forms show the humans a 'movie' in order to show them reality. *True Lies* constantly deploys surveillance equipment (from hi-tech infrared cameras to a low-tech dentist's mirror), and *Titanic* shows us the eponymous ship early on via cameras in remote operated underwater vehicles. In *Avatar* human vision is completely relocated into another species as the human characters, in a deep sleep, experience the world through their Na'vi avatars.

Each of these visual manoeuvers reflects Cameron's preoccupation with constructing his films in meta-visual ways – ways that are entirely available for the viewer's enjoyment. This meta-visuality is typically produced through tropes of mediated vision (about which more later).

Any one of Cameron's films lends itself easily (some more than others) to readings both progressive and conservative. For example, Cameron seems at once suspicious of both Big Government and Big Business. In film after film he takes a dim view of the power of government and the inevitability of big business to screw things up. In *The Terminator* and *Terminator 2*, government and corporations get into bed together, and the result is nuclear war and a race of genocidal cyborgs. In *The Abyss*, the Navy and a multinational oil company are revealed as morally bankrupt by the extraterrestrials living under the ocean floor. In *True Lies*, Schwarzenegger's government operative actually has to disobey orders to get the job done. In *Titanic*, it is clear that the corporate-driven desire to bring the ship across the Atlantic in record time leads directly to the disaster. In *Avatar*, 'The Corporation', with the enthusiastic cooperation of the military, nearly destroys an entire planet just to extract Unobtanium (read: oil) from below its surface.

Yet seen as a group these simultaneous readings are not possible. The more of Cameron's films one sees, the more his conservative ideology comes to the fore, ironically in his apparent attachment to strong women characters set in male-addressed cinema. *Titanic* may be exceptional in Cameron's work for a fan base mainly consisting in teenage, Leonardo DiCaprio-addled girls, but this does not mean that his earlier and subsequent science fiction and action films, masculinist though they are at a generic level, have not actively invited female spectators.

If Cameron has other consistencies in his films, one of the most important remains his heroic, and very often physically powerful, female protagonists. If *The Terminator*'s Sarah Connor (Linda Hamilton) is the first of these heroines, she is latent until *Terminator 2*, at which point her extremely muscular body competes with Schwarzenegger's for the spectator's attention and admiration. In between, Cameron made *Aliens*, which turned Sigourney Weaver's Ellen Ripley from Ridley Scott's more measured, stately and almost intellectual force in *Alien* (1979) into a contemplatively pumped up rebel who, it happens, has spent some time training at the Yale Drama School. In *The Abyss*, Lindsey (Mary Elizabeth Mastrantonio) seems to take an almost existential pleasure in relentlessly being called a bitch – what in Cameron's world you would apparently have to be to design, build, manage and save a colossal oil-rig-cum-deep-sea-exploration-unit. In *True Lies*, even Jamie Lee Curtis's Little Susie Homemaker character, Helen Tasker, is man enough to throw punches not only at the enemy (male and female) but also at her husband, for lying to her so patronizingly all these years. *Avatar* has three strong women. Sigourney Weaver is now the eminent researcher, Dr Grace Augustine (a resonant name indeed), chain-smoking and Cassandra-like, the first and last word on the Na'vi, the ten-foot-tall blue inhabitants of the planet Pandora. Trudy Chacon (Michelle Rodriguez), a powerful reiteration of Private Vasquez (Jenette Goldstein) in *Aliens* (though far less butch), flies a mean helicopter and flies in the face of the tyrannical Colonel Quaritch (Stephen Lang), switching her allegiances to the Na'vi cause. Where in previous Cameron films the female alien presence has always been predatory, here the Na'vi warrior princess Neytiri (Zoë Saldana) teaches the hero Jake Sully (Sam Worthington, coincidentally one of the stars of *Terminator: Salvation*) everything he needs to know about the Na'vi, including how to fly their pterodactyl-like creatures.

But Lindsey is still a bitch, softening only when her estranged husband Bud (Ed Harris) finally hails her as 'wife' from 20,000 leagues under the sea. Helen may become a gun-toting, helicopter-hopping fury of a woman, but her climactic battle is a catfight *par excellence* with a seductive villainess (Tia Carerre). Ripley's major motivation to heroic action is almost exclusively maternal, and she can only dispense with the alien queen when the showdown is framed in mother versus mother terms. *Terminator 2* sees Sarah Connor, for all her action hero antics, as nowhere near as good a mother to her son as Schwarzenegger's Terminator. Grace Augustine and Trudy Chacon are collateral damage, single women sacrificing their lives for the couple that Jake and Neytiri have become. Thus, Cameron's fierce women are always pressed back into the service of patriarchy, pleasantly reaffirming the way things are in a manner equally palatable to both women and men. Time after time, Cameron has his heroines use their spunk and force to maintain the status quo.

In *Titanic*, Kate Winslet's high-spirited heiress, Rose, initially seems to lack the physical force of Cameron's previous heroines (though she has an exemplary turn-of-the-century feminist social stance),[11] but as the ship goes down, she seems as unstoppable as the Terminator in her efforts to free her lover from his watery prison below decks. She is as independent, wilful, smart, sexy and idiosyncratically beautiful[12] as Cameron's previous leading women. And yet again, Rose, a powerful but pleasing figure of the feminine, ultimately serves both patriarchy and the owning classes she appears to spurn in favour of Jack and all he represents. All Cameron films have a kind of bait-and-switch when it comes to their heroines, and ultimately many of Cameron's narratives provide the viewer with the Classical Hollywood closure of the heterosexual couple's union, as well as the (re)constitution of the nuclear family, though often with a dystopic twist.

In *The Terminator*, love-struck Kyle Reese (Michael Biehn) succeeds in his mission of impregnating Sarah Connor before he is killed. In *The Abyss*, Lindsey and Bud are reunited in a finale that seems specifically to be an aquatic response to both *Close Encounters of the Third Kind* (1977) and *E.T. The Extra-Terrestrial* (1982), one that seeks to erase the heartbreak of separation of the latter film. In *Titanic*, Rose and Jack find true love, consummate it, and Jack (like Kyle) sacrifices his life for hers.[13] In *Terminator 2*, Sarah and John Connor and the T-101 (Schwarzenegger) briefly comprise the happy family unit, and again, the sacrificial figure is the father rather than the mother. In *Aliens*, the makeshift family of Ripley, Hicks (Michael Biehn again) and Newt (Carrie Henn) survives, though Hicks has sustained critical injuries. And in the ultimate happy ending, Schwarzenegger having rescued his daughter from a skyscraper in a military jet, *True Lies'* Helen and Harry Tasker have their happily-ever-after kiss in front of an atomic mushroom cloud.

In a film in which, Cameron claims, almost everything was supposed to be received tongue-in-cheek ('And you know what?' he once quipped, 'I'm not a P.C., candy-assed director'),[14] this mushroom cloud kiss instantiates his fascination with the failure or betrayal of state of the art technology, and yet, using state of the art technology – often of his own invention – he neither questions nor problematises it, or his use of it, to bring this fascination forward. There is good technology and bad technology in Cameron films, and this is distinct from the good and bad people who wield it. (The Terminator and the Na'vi avatars are interesting examples of both technology and its user wrapped into one.) Moreover, while much is made of his frequent use of firearms and high body counts, the technology that fascinates Cameron most is not the technology of death, but the technology of representation.

The extent to which Cameron frequently sees representation as more real than the real is the extent to which he often refers (somewhat obliquely) to history and politics as if they are mere accessories.

Image in Cameron's films is more real – or more revealing – than reality. This, of course, is a sleight of hand symptomatic of a television-era director, three of whose films have been serials (*The Terminator*, *Terminator 2, Aliens*. Cameron has a sequel to *Avatar* in the works as well).[15] If image says more about reality than reality, then Cameron has it both ways – his metaimages supersede the reality of the films, and yet it is clear that the film as a whole is itself an image which supersedes the reality of the film audience. This particularly post-modern relationship of representation and real is seen in each of his films in a remarkably consistent way.

Among the many other important tropes of a Cameron film, perhaps the most crucial is the notion of prosthetic vision, and its implications. Cameron has never made a film without prosthetic vision. *Titanic* is no exception, and here, where it is least obvious, it might be most important. For in *Titanic*, Cameron's use of prosthetic vision manifests what Robert Burgoyne and Alison Landsburg call 'prosthetic memory' which 'describe[s] the way mass cultural technologies of memory enable individuals to experience, as if they were memories, events through which they themselves did not live.'[16] The implications of *Titanic*'s prosthetic memory may be less dire than Burgoyne's exemplar, *Forrest Gump* (1994), simply because the event itself does not have the import of 'The Sixties'. But the note it strikes is no less false, and may be even more so since it is part of a larger aesthetic tradition presented under the sign of Cameron.[17]

In *The Terminator* we are presented early on with the now famous red field of Schwarzenegger's cyborg vision. All visual information is mediated, and text breaks the world down into data – animal, vegetable, mineral, terminal. It is a method of negotiating the world visually that is distinctly non-human, distinctly technological. In *Aliens*, Ripley sees a great deal of the initial Marine incursion on a number of video screens, which transmit what each soldier sees (as well as the vital signs of each – *Terminator* redux), as she sits safely inside a protective vehicle. Cameron specifically aligns her view with that of Corporal Hicks's camera, a character with whom she will later form a couple. In *The Abyss*, in a direct precursor to *Titanic*, there are little video camera rovers that swim through the depths of the ocean, moving ahead of divers, a pair of scouting eyes through which Bud and Lindsey see both the oceanscape and, at times, each other. In *Terminator 2*, the cybervision is back, but in addition there is also a lengthy scene in which we observe Sarah Connor undergo some slightly sadistic psychiatric testing. Our vision is often mediated by a video screen, which highlights the clinical power and detachment of her doctor, but it also shows us a pathos the doctor cannot see. In addition to all the high-tech, highfalutin night sights befitting a secret agent's mission in *True Lies*, the *Terminator 2* video probe repeats itself as Schwarzenegger anonymously verbally tortures his own wife, who sits behind a two-way mirror. The audience often sees her through a video feed and the glass simultaneously, as well as on a television screen that abstracts her image to highlight heat-emitting areas – predictably, tears. In *Avatar* the prosthetic vision is now tied to the complete prosthetic body. Every part of the human save the mind has been replaced by his or her avatar. We can go further and include *Strange Days* (1995), the script he wrote and produced for his then-wife Kathryn Bigelow.[18] The film's foundational premise revolves around the ability to 'jack in', or plug other people's visual and sensory experiences, which have been stored on disc, directly into one's own brain, a kind of hyped-up virtual reality complete with snuff films. In all of these films, this prosthetic vision simultaneously, and often para-doxically, both further distances the spectator by adding another layer of vision to the experience of watching a film, and brings her closer, by reminding us through this now-conventional coding that we are, in fact, engaged in the act of watching a movie.

This thematic of mediated vision reappears in *Titanic* as Bill Paxton, captain of the present-day dive crew, cynically delivers a dramatic, made-for-the-Discovery-channel narrative to accompany the roving camera's investigations into the ship. But prosthetic vision in *Titanic* is not just the technological, it is the historiographic as well. The visual aid technologies embodied by the underwater Mir exploration crafts which lead the crew (remaining safe and dry inside their submersible) to the safe in which lies the drawing of young Rose, not only moves the crew (and the spectator) between viewing paradigms, but also between two eras. And this, too, is typical of Cameron.

Why? For one thing, with the exception of *Aliens* and *Avatar*, these films all take place in the present, and *Titanic* is no exception. Cameron, whatever else he is, is not a modernist, nor even simply a post-modernist. He is a *presentist*, and this is especially evident in *Titanic*, his single period piece, his one and only foray into history and the past. As *New Yorker* critic Anthony Lane pointed out in his review of *Titanic*, the film about a sinking ship was actually more like the two *Terminator* films than it was a 'fresh departure' from them, because in all three, Cameron is 'obsessed by the bending and shaping of time'.[19] And this obsession with time becomes, in the case of *Titanic*, an obsession with history.

This obsession with history brings us back to Cameron's symptomatic nature: the assertions, both visual and thematic, that Cameron makes in his films carry with them their own repudiation or counter-criticism. His heroines are stronger than his heroes, but their strength is used to uphold patriarchy. His assertion that facts are facts is undermined by his repeated use of images that supersede what they represent. And in what may be his most interesting contradiction as a director, his films constantly criticise government and especially big business, and yet this latter is precisely what James Cameron is and does.

These investigations sustain in Cameron's newest project, *Avatar*, his first fiction feature film since *Titanic*. Cameron wrote the script in 1995 – before *Titanic* – and worked to develop the technology until it could be filmed as written. Indeed, in the wake of *Titanic*, James Cameron's next projects were documentaries that continued *Titanic's* engagement with the deep sea – but they were not blockbusters, nor were they designed, really, to sustain Cameron's high profile. The public rather saw him performing himself in a proliferation of film and television roles, from the series finale of *Mad about You* (1998), to *The Muse* (in which he came to Sharon Stone's Muse for creative inspiration), to his appearance on several episodes of the HBO series *Entourage* (2005–6, in which he directed the central character, an actor, in a fictional blockbuster version of *Aquaman* – though some media outlets mistakenly reported its release as true). Like *Aliens*, *Avatar* is set in the future. It is certainly as technologically innovative as his previous films. He has developed a new 3-D high definition technology for the film, and new motion capture technology. (Cameron is also working on a 3-D version of *Titanic*.) If not the most expensive film on record, and it well may be, it is still Cameron's own most expensive film. Before *Avatar's* release Cameron said, 'I don't think I'll beat *Titanic's* [box office] record, and I don't think anyone else will for a while. I'll be happy if this film makes money relative to its budget'.[20] Whether that was protective modesty or a misreading of reality, he was very wrong. The story, about Jake Sully, a paraplegic veteran who inhabits an alien body on a 22nd-century mining planet, Pandora (recalling *Aliens* and *The Abyss*), rings a wide range of familiar narrative bells from *Dune* to *Pocahontas* to *Dances with Wolves*. It brings the prosthetic qualities of Cameron's films, visual and otherwise, to a new extreme. The combination of the story – a familiar critique of the Military Industrial Complex, corporate greed and ecological recklessness – and the exorbitantly expensive technology required to produce that story bring Cameron's ideological wet knots into further relief than ever. *Time* magazine technology writer Joshua Quittner, one of the few to have seen sequences of the film before its release, described the experience: 'I couldn't tell what was real and what was animated – even knowing that the 9-ft.-tall blue, dappled dude couldn't possibly be real. The scenes were so startling and absorbing that the following morning, I had the peculiar sensation of wanting to return there, as if Pandora were real.'[21] Though the script was first drafted in 1995, the disabled war veteran protagonist is certainly an apropos figure for current times (as is the struggle over environmental resources), and given the symptomatic nature of Cameron's career, *Avatar* is likely to resonate, though whether it does so as escapist fantasy or as more of a critical relationship to the current Iraq and Afghanistan conflicts and the global climate crisis is yet to be seen.

Biography

Born Kapuskasing, Ontario, Canada, 16 August 1954, Cameron moved to Los Angeles, USA, in 1971. He was apprenticed with Roger Corman as a set designer, art director, miniature set-builder and process projection supervisor. Cameron made both the first $100-million film (*True Lies*) and the first $200-million film (*Titanic*). He has been married and divorced four times: Sarah Williams (1974–85), Gale Anne Hurd (1985–89, producer of the Cameron projects *The Terminator*, *Aliens*, *The Abyss* and *Terminator 2*), Kathryn Bigelow (1989–91) and Linda Hamilton (1997–99). He married Suzy Amis, who starred in *Titanic*, in 2000. He has four children. He has retained his Canadian citizenship.

Notes

1 Quoted in John H. Richardson, 'Magnificent Obsession', *Premiere*, 1997 (December), pp. 125ff., p. 128.
2 Nominated for fourteen awards, *Titanic* won eleven, including Best Picture.
3 *Titanic* has grossed over $1.8 billion in theatres worldwide, and an additional $1.2 billion in worldwide video and DVD sales and rentals.
4 Brian D. Johnson, 'Titanic Ambition: A Canadian Sails Hollywood's High Seas', *Maclean's*, 8 December 1997, vol. 110, no. 49, p. 86.
5 Cameron himself has often referred to it as his $200-million 'chick flick'.
6 *Titanic* is often compared to *Gone with the Wind* in its sweeping epic proportions, and to *Cleopatra* in its runaway expense; Cameron himself has repeatedly drawn parallels between himself and *Dr Zhivago* director

David Lean. But in 1939 MGM carried the financial burden of *Gone with the Wind* on its own, and cooperated with another studio only to borrow Clark Gable from Columbia. *Avatar*'s budget is still a matter of speculation, though James Gianopulos, co-chairman and CEO of Fox Filmed Entertainment, has allowed that the film is the most expensive the studio has ever made.

7 Indeed, Cameron's extraordinary success with *Titanic*, in spite of its cost overruns and bloated budget, began the template for subsequent action films whose budgets exceeded *Titanic*'s, such as Peter Jackson's remake of *King Kong* (2005) at $207 million and the first to set a new budget record, and both *Terminator 3: Rise of the Machines* (Jonathan Mostow, 2003, $200m) and *Terminator Salvation* (McG, 2009, $200m) – neither of which was directed by Cameron. Currently the most expensive film ever made is *Pirates of the Caribbean: At World's End* (Gore Verbinski, 2007), costing a reported $300m.

8 He storyboards most of his films, also sketching the portraits of Rose attributed to artist Jack Dawson in *Titanic*.

9 Sean French, *The Terminator*, BFI Modern Classics Series (London: BFI Publishing, 1996), p. 9. *Esquire* magazine also selected it as its film of the 1980s.

10 Schwarzenegger is the best known, but not the only actor with whom Cameron has worked repeatedly. Others include Michael Biehn, Bill Paxton and, of course, ex-wife Linda Hamilton.

11 This feminist voice is not so difficult for Cameron to accord Rose, since the turn of the century of the film's plot is 100 years before that of the film's release.

12 Cameron has never cast a typically beautiful female star in any of his films. Linda Hamilton, Sigourney Weaver, Mary Elizabeth Mastrantonio, Jamie Lee Curtis and Kate Winslet are, in a variety of ways, gratifyingly wide of the mark of what audiences seem to want in their Hollywood femininity—young, or re-cut and liposuctioned to look it, buxom, and yet stick-thin everywhere else, delicately bobbed nose, and blonde, blonde, blonde.

13 Jack's death is not the tragic ending for Rose that it first appears to be. It is a commonplace of feminist criticism of the film that Rose always knew that Jack would disappoint her in the end. As Katha Pollitt asked in *The Nation*, 'How many happy artists' wives do you know?' Katha Pollitt, 'Women and Children First', *The Nation*, 30 March 1998, p. 9.

14 Brian D. Johnson, op. cit., p. 87.

15 A sequel to *True Lies* is reportedly in the works.

16 Robert Burgoyne, *Film Nation: Hollywood Looks to U.S. History*, Minneapolis, University of Minnesota Press, 1997, p. 105. See also Alison Landsburg, 'Prosthetic Memory: *Total Recall* and *Blade Runner*', *Body and Society*, nos 3–4, 1995.

17 Indeed, in *Titanic*, Cameron seems to equate memory, even a fictitious one, with experience. As Cameron stand-in Bill Paxton's contemporary ocean explorer asks the older Rose (Gloria Stewart) in an early scene, 'Are you ready to go back to *Titanic*?'

18 Musing on his four wives, producer Gale Anne Hurd, director Kathryn Bigelow, actress Linda Hamilton, and unknown (to the industry) wife number one—on whom the character of Sarah Connor was based—we must retool that old adage to say that, in Cameron's case, behind every great man there are several great women.

19 Anthony Lane, 'The Shipping News: *Titanic* raises the Stakes of the Spectacular', *The New Yorker*, 15 December 1997, pp. 156–7.

20 'Q&A with James Cameron', Rebecca Winters Keegan, *Time*, Thursday, Jan. 11, 2007. http://www.time.com/time/arts/article/0,8599, 1576622,00. html

21 Josh Quittner, 'Are 3-D Movies Ready for Their Closeup?' *Time*, Thursday, March 19, 2009. http://www.time.com/time/magazine/article/0,9171,1886541–43,00.html

Filmography

Piranha II: The Spawning (1981)
The Terminator (1984) also writer
Aliens (1986) also story and writer
The Abyss (1989) also writer
Terminator 2: Judgment Day (1991) also writer
True Lies (1994) also writer
Terminator 2 3–D: Battle Across Time (1996) also writer
Titanic (1997) also writer
Ghosts of the Abyss (documentary, 2003)
Aliens of the Deep (documentary, 2005)
Avatar (2009) also writer

Further reading

Joe Abbott, 'They Came from Beyond the Center: Ideology and Political Textuality in the Radical Science Fiction Films of James Cameron', *Literature Film Quarterly*, vol. 22, no. 1, 1994, pp. 21–8.

Tim Blackmore, ' "Is this going to be another bug hunt?" S-F Tradition Versus Biology-as-destiny in James Cameron's "Aliens"', *Journal of Popular Culture*, vol. 29, no. 4, 1996, pp. 211–27.

Todd F. Davis and Kenneth Womack, 'Narrating the Ship of Dreams: The Ethics of Sentimentality in James Cameron's *Titanic*', *Journal of Popular Film and Television*, Vol. 29, no. 1, Spring 2001, pp. 42–8.

Thomas Doherty, 'Genre, Gender and the *Aliens* Trilogy', in *The Dread of Difference* (Austin: University of Texas Press, 1996), Barry Keith Grant (ed.), 181–99.

Sean French, *The Terminator*, BFI Modern Classics Series (London: BFI Publishing, 1996).

Krin Gabbard, '*Aliens* and the New Family Romance', *Post Script: Essays in Film and the Humanities* vol. 8, no. 1, 1988, 29–42.

Nancy Griffin, 'James Cameron is the Scariest Man in Hollywood', *Esquire*, vol. 128, no. 6, 1997, pp. 98ff.

Christopher Heard, *Dreaming Aloud: The Life and Films of James Cameron*, New York, Doubleday, 1998.

Alexandra Keller, *James Cameron*, London: Routledge, 2006.

Constance Penley et al. (eds) *Close Encounters: Film, Feminism and Science Fiction*, Minneapolis, University of Minnesota Press, 1991.

Gaylyn Studlar and Kevin S. Sandler (eds), *Titanic: Anatomy of a Blockbuster*, New Brunswick, NJ: Rutgers University Press, 1999.

Amy Taubin, 'The "Alien" Trilogy from Feminism to Aids', in *Women and Film: A Sight and Sound Reader*, Pam Cook and Philip Dodd (eds), Philadelphia: Temple University Press, 1993, pp. 93–6. Originally published in *Sight and Sound*, July 1992, vol. 2, number 3.

Anne Thompson, 'Cameron's Way', *Premiere*, August 1997, pp. 63ff.

JANE CAMPION

By Shelley Cobb

As the first (and to date only) female filmmaker to have won the Palme d'Or at the Cannes Film Festival, and one of only three to be nominated for the Best Director Academy Award, for *The Piano*, Jane Campion is regularly held up in reviews and criticism as an exceptional example of individual female success in contemporary cinema. Her films, particularly her shorts and features, have been nominated for and won several other awards; the most recent film, and her fifth feature, *Bright Star*, about the doomed love affair of the Romantic poet John Keats and his neighbour Fanny Brawne, brought Campion her third nomination for the Palme d'Or in a year that included films by Quentin Tarantino, Ang Lee, Lars Von Trier, Mike Leigh, Michael Haneke and Pedro Almodóvar. *Variety* called the lineup a 'who's-who of revered Riviera regulars' and 'Cannes' biggest heavyweight auteur smackdown in recent years'.[1] This return to one of the highest profile film festivals and into the contest for one of the most prestigious awards for cinema raises her exceptionality again; as the only woman director amongst the 'auteurs' nominated, Campion, it seems to many, 'still stands at the head of a field of one'.[2]

Until *Bright Star*'s Cannes nomination, Campion's status as the standard bearer for women directors and her entry into 'the pantheon of great filmmakers' depended largely on the stand-out success of *The Piano* with its multiple awards, critical acclaim, and commercial success. Screened beyond the typical art house cinema circuit for a foreign costume drama, the film made forty million dollars in US theatres from a seven million dollar budget. The collective signs of crossover success for an international independent art film (Golden Palm win, critical praise, box-office profit and Academy Award nominations) made it, as Dana Polan argues, 'a key work in our historical moment', a stand out in its acquisition of both cultural capital and actual capital.[3] The film's traversing of the differing expectations of art and mainstream cinema reception is reflected in its hybridity as it mixes the conventions of the mainstream woman's film with the aesthetics of European art cinema within the mise-en-scène of a Victorian costume drama. The fusion of these disparate elements seems to have set the template for the feature films that have followed, each of which 'share[s] the generic concerns of family melodramas or women's films ... [and] maps onto the affective diffusions of melodrama the perceptual confusions of the surreal'.[4]

The Piano, of course, was neither Campion's first film nor her first to receive an award. Three of her short films made while at film school in Australia were accepted at Cannes in 1986 – *Peel*, *Passionless Moments*, and *A Girl's Own Story* – *Peel* won the Palme d'Or for Best Short Film, an earlier 'first woman' win. Looking back, we can see the beginnings of Campion's inclination to mix women's stories, family melodrama and art cinema aesthetics in these shorts. *Peel* centres on the red-headed Pye family – Tim, his sister Katie and Tim's son Ben – as they drive through the Australian country on a hot summer's day. Tim stops the car and demands that Ben walk back down the busy and litter-strewn road from where they have come, to pick up the orange peel that he has been indolently throwing out the window. Katie is frustrated by their altercation as it will make her miss her favorite TV show. Ben marches down the road and then disappears from sight. Tim goes after him, and upon their return to the car, they find Katie peeling an orange and leaving the peel on the road. They insist that she pick it up before they leave; she refuses. The film ends just as Ben has jumped onto the roof of the car. The film's subtitle is 'An Exercise in Discipline'. The title and cast list appear in between shots of the road and cars speeding by, and then the caption 'A TRUE STORY/A TRUE FAMILY' appears.

The demand for a son's discipline, a child's need for adults to be disciplined, and the familial power play and stand off that results from these conflicts are reflected in the film's opening tight shots within the car that shift perspective from Ben to Katie and to Tim. The father/son power dynamic is fought out between brother/sister arguments over a piece of land they might buy and getting home on time. This visual use of constricted space is turned inside out at the end of the film, when, through the point of view of passing cars, we see Katie sitting in the front seat, Tim leaning against the back bumper and Ben jumping on the roof of the car. The vying for relational power within the family and the contrast between cramped spaces and the outdoors and the tension between movement and stasis are ongoing thematic concerns and stylistic practices within Campion's oeuvre. And yet, the film keeps any potential moralising at bay with its droll sensibility. The same can be said for the more disturbing *A Girl's Own Story*, which concerns several teenage girls growing up in 1960s Australia. One girl's parents are constantly fighting, and the father is severely and oppressively depressed. Another gets dumped by her best friend for a more popular girl. The last falls pregnant by her own brother and is sent away to an unwed mothers' home. The film's subject might easily lend itself to melo-dramatic moralising but this is held in check by the film's forays into dark comedy and its often awkward framing and moments of surreal visual expression, such as the closing image of a girl ice skating, superimposed over the faces of each of the girls to whom this short film has given a story. Campion continued her focus on girls with the 1986 tele-feature *Two Friends*, which narrates, in reverse chronological order, the breakdown of the close friendship of two teenage girls.

Campion's first feature film, which screened in competition at Cannes, *Sweetie* (1986), also focuses on the difficult relationship between two women, but in this film they are sisters. Kay and Sweetie/Dawn have strongly contrasting personalities. Kay is con-sidered socially awkward by her peers, but she seems more self-contained than awkward, if maybe a bit reserved. She steals Louis from his fiancée because he has a lock of hair that falls over a mole above his eye, forming a question mark, fulfilling the prediction made by the fortune teller at the beginning of the film that her destiny lies with a man with a question mark on his face. Kay is also afraid of trees (she rips from their yard a sapling Louis had planted in honour of their love). Sweetie appears on Kay and Louis's doorstep one day with her druggie boyfriend/producer, who's supposedly going to launch Sweetie's singing career. Sweetie is emotionally erratic, often infantile in her expression of desires and needs, and regularly manic. The film hints at an inappropriate sexual relationship between Sweetie and her father. Their mother has left their father to cook on a ranch for jackaroos, so Sweetie has nowhere to stay but with Kay. Kay cannot stand Sweetie's lack of emotional control or the amount of space she takes up in the house, which further impedes the already dwindling sexual relationship between Louis and Kay. At one point, in a fit of frustration, Sweetie chews several glass horse figurines from a beloved collection kept by Kay.

The turmoil between the sisters and the disorder within their family reaches a climax when Sweetie assaults their tenuous grasp on middle-class respectability by barricading herself in the tree house in her parents' yard, naked. The old tree house collapses, killing Sweetie, evoking Kay's fear of trees and indirectly referencing her removal of the tree Louis planted for her. After the funeral there is a tentative reunion between Kay and Louis. The film ends with Kay and Sweetie's father standing in his yard, looking at the tree. We then see what seems to be his memory of a young, red-haired Sweetie, wearing a pink dress and singing (off key) 'Every beat of my heart'. Although Sweetie's performance is marked by tacky, childlike naivety, with her frilly dress and robot hand movements that mimic the words of the song, the performance appears purposeful in its attempt to catch her audience's attention. Sweetie's lack of emotional maturity as an adult seems entrenched in a need to perform for her father that he has always encouraged, but the end seems only to state this fact rather than place blame on either of them. Despite the parallels with *Peel* – sibling rivalries and family power plays – *Sweetie* was received badly. Reportedly, at a press screening, it was booed. The film is uncompromising in the ways that it withholds sympathy for and judgment of any of the characters. Even as Kay and Louis (as well as Kay's parents) are reunited, Sweetie's death resolves nothing. The source of her psychological suffering is never explained fully nor is the trauma she inflicts on her family justified by the conclusion.

Sweetie has been critically reclaimed since Campion's following successes, but at the time, Campion's response to the difficult reception of the film was to return to television to make the adaptation of Janet Frame's autobiography, *An Angel at My Table*, which was subsequently given a general release in theatres outside Australia. The story of the New Zealand writer's life through its beginnings in poverty to her time in a mental hospital and a near lobotomy to her triumphant success as an award winning author is significantly more cheering than *Sweetie* and went some way to restoring Campion's reputation amongst critics.

Three years later the film that made Campion's name screened at Cannes; *The Piano* received immediate, widespread and lavish critical praise. Its fusion of art cinema aesthetics, conventions of the costume drama, and the narrative affect of melodrama continually serves as the catalyst for a variety of, often conflicting, readings of the film, and

The Piano has acquired, since its release, a central place in the ongoing debates concerning art cinema, the woman's film, female audiences, female authorship, romance, feminism and postfeminism. As a film made by a woman about a woman and her desires that has a strongly emotive female fanbase, *The Piano*, Dana Polan argues, 'has come to be seen as one of the supreme signposts of the art of feminine sensibility'.[5] The combination of the film's high profile 'femaleness' with its critical and commercial achievements has never been duplicated by Campion or any other woman director, doubling the meaning of 'one' in the claim that she stands at the 'head of a field of one' – she is not only the one woman director to achieve such a combination of success, only one of her films has achieved such heights. After the success of *The Piano*, interviewers and reviewers remarked upon the 'immense anticipation for [Campion's] next film'.[6] In hindsight it might seem that, after the sensation of *The Piano*, whatever choice Campion made would pale in comparison. Her adaptation of Henry James's *The Portrait of a Lady* was criticised for being cold and distant and cramped. Campion was accused of 'playing it safe' with another costume drama, as well as of compromising her auteur identity by adapting a classic novel. However, a few critics at the time saw something more radical in the film's style, with its canted angles, tight compositions, cluttered mise-en-scène, and fantasy sequences. Structured by an emphasis on the female body and erotic touch, it maps the aesthetics of the surreal onto the conventions of the heritage film. Robert Sklar argues that Campion's *Portrait* 'presents a new way of thinking about movie adaptations of literature' because 'it does not avow fidelity to the novel and its historical era' – a judgement that has since been corroborated by many critical analyses of the film.[7]

Campion moved away from the costume drama and returned to the setting of the Australian suburbs and a focus on the discontents of the middle-class family with *Holy Smoke*, starring Kate Winslet and Harvey Keitel. Ruth (Winslet), a young woman traveling through India, joins a cult and enters into a spiritual union, as do dozens of other followers, with its leader, Baba. The Bollywood-style cartoonishness of her conversion/union contrasts with the cartoonish banalities of her middle class family, heightened by the kitschiness of their suburban home. Lying about her father's health, Ruth's mother connives to get her daughter home, where the extended family ambushes her on the family ranch and demands that she submit to PJ's (Keitel's) cult de-programming. For many critics, despite this plot, *Holy Smoke* was ultimately a film about the 'battle of the sexes'.[8] Both Dana Polan and Kathleen McHugh argue that the film reconstructs the genre conventions of the screwball comedy in its power play between a man and a woman, both of whom use sex and words to try and get 'one-up' over the other.[9] Again, Campion maps the aesthetics of the surreal onto the expectations of a mainstream genre form – particularly notable is PJ's desert fuelled hallucination of Ruth as a six-armed Hindu goddess. This splicing of surrealist moments with mainstream generic conventions avoids any melodramatic moralising of Ruth as a victim in her relationship with PJ.

In many of Campion's films this refusal to moralise and to victimise often comes within a plot initially structured on the premise of woman as victim, inviting, at first, moral judgement of her independence. This is especially true of *In the Cut*. Adapted from the crime thriller by Susannah Moore, the film is a neo-noir detective fiction centred on Frannie (Meg Ryan), a literature teacher and collector of words that she finds on her daily commute through New York City. Frannie has an affair with a police detective investigating a serial killer who leaves engagement rings on his victims' fingers whose bodies have been 'disarticulated' – a word the detective uses which fascinates Frannie. The film may have the plot machinations of a thriller, but Campion keeps the pace slow and includes what could be seen as 'artsy' moments: the romance of Frannie's parents is shown as a black and white silent film of Victorian ice skaters, a romance that ends starkly but with a flourish as her mother's legs are cut in two by her father's ice skates. Sex, romance and danger are intertwined throughout the film. Frannie, while looking for the restroom in a bar, watches a woman on her knees fellate a man in a dark corner; the man turns out to be the serial killer. Pointing out that female voyeurism is common in the erotic thriller, Linda Ruth Williams argues that *In the Cut* can be read as existing within that genre's paradigms in addition to its categorisation as an art film and a woman's film. However, the clear shot of an exposed, erect penis is extremely uncommon in non-pornographic film, and it shocked some viewers.[10] More frustrating for some critics is that Frannie wanders in a dreamlike state throughout the film despite the many sexual threats she faces, including an ex-boyfriend who stalks her, an angry male student who is writing a paper trying to prove John Wayne Gacy innocent, and her romantic involvement with Detective Malloy despite the fact that she suspects him of being the killer. The film's threats reach their peak when Frannie's sister, who lives above a strip joint, is found disarticulated and with a ring on her finger. At the film's climax Frannie seduces Malloy and handcuffs him to some pipes in her apartment, but their sex game ends abruptly when she finds a charm from her bracelet that was lost when the killer attacked her earlier. Frannie leaves him, but ends up in the company of the killer. In a departure from the novel Frannie effects her own rescue, shooting the killer as he attempts to slip the infamous ring on her finger.

Ryan portrays Frannie with a look and a manner that evokes Jane Fonda in *Klute* (1971), while the narrative is reminiscent of *Looking for Mr. Goodbar* (1977), in which Diane Keaton plays a teacher who spends her nights cruising bars looking for sex. The likenesses to 1970s neo-noirs may not be coincidence; Sue Thornham argues that the film's 'yoking together [of] multiple and often shockingly disparate references and registers' evokes a feminist tradition of 're-vision' and 'thinking back'.[11] However, the current postfeminist era is particularly fraught for the female filmmaker whose exceptional status marks her out as exemplary of feminist success for individual women and the exception that proves the rule of women's 'normal' choices made in general (e.g., choosing children means not choosing a high-powered career). Campion, like many high-profile women, must navigate the contradictions of the current postfeminist climate in which some feminist tenets, such as equal pay for equal work, have become, apparently, 'common sense' while the idea of feminism and feminist politics is vilified, marking any women who claim feminism as out-of-date angry whiners, and any individual woman's success is haunted by the spectre of affirmative action. After the initial critical euphoria over *The Piano*, a backlash ensued and *New York Magazine* declared that 'it arrives with this feminist baggage, or presumed feminist message, that probably shuts people up'.[12] Despite this censure, Campion's films consistently refuse to be didactic, so it may be no surprise that when asked, in an interview, if 'one could call [her] a feminist director', Campion responded, 'I have to admit that I no longer know what this means or expresses.'[13]

And yet, in her analysis of *In the Cut*, Thornham argues that 're-authoring is not such a simple matter. Women may be producers and consumers of romance, but then they always have been, and men retain control of the twin poles of high culture and the language of the street.'[14] The gendered nature of power and control is inherent to all of Campion's films, including her short film 'The Lady Bug' which was one of 35 shorts made by film directors in honor of Cannes's 60th anniversary. In it, a woman dressed up as an insect gets stamped on in a movie-theatre. In an AP release, Campion said it was 'a metaphor for women in the film world'.[15] She added, 'I just think this is the way the world is, that men control the money, and they decide who they're going to give it to.'[16] And yet, as

Thornham argues, 'in insisting on the difficulties of female authorship, Campion's film[s] also declare ... its possibility' – a possibility that the director might hope would soon end her reign at the head of the field of one.

Biography

Jane Campion was born 30 April 1954 in Wellington, New Zealand. She graduated with a BA in Anthropology from Victoria University, Wellington, and a BA from Sydney College of the Arts, where she majored in painting. She created her first short films at the Australian School of Film and Television in the early 1980s. She won the Academy Award for Best Original Screenplay in 1993 for *The Piano*. She lives in Sydney, Australia, with her daughter Alice.

Notes

1 Derek Elley and John Hopewell, 'Cannes unveils lineup: heavyweight auteurs vie for Palme d'Or', *Variety*, 23 April 2009, http://www.variety. com/article/VR1118002762.html?categoryid = 19& cs = 1 (accessed 23 May 2009).
2 Charlotte Higgins, 'Cannes contender Jane Campion gives clarion call to women directors', *The Guardian Online*, 15 May 2009, http:// www.guardian.co.uk/film/2009/may/15/jane-campion-cannes-film-festival (accessed 23 May 2009).
3 Dana Polan, *Jane Campion*, London: BFI, 2001, 4.
4 Kathleen McHugh, *Jane Campion*, Urbana: University of Illinois Press, 2007, 50.
5 Polan, op. cit., 7.
6 Susan Saccoccia, 'Portrait of a Lady and Her Films', in Virginia Wright Wexman, ed., *Jane Campion: Interviews*, Jackson: University of Mississippi Press, 1999, 201.
7 Robert Sklar, 'A Novel Approach to Movie-Making', B7.
8 Bob Graham, ' "Holy" Possessed by Earthly Spirit: Winslet, Keitel Star in Campion's Unusual Tale', *San Francisco Chronicle*, Friday 11 February 1999, C-3.
9 See McHugh, 109, and Polan, 142–56.
10 Linda Ruth Williams, *The Erotic Thriller in Contemporary Cinema*, Edinburgh: Edinburgh University Press, 2005, 420.
11 Sue Thornham, ' "Starting to Feel Like a Chick": Re-visioning Romance in *In the Cut*', *Feminist Media Studies*, 7, no.1 (March 2007): 44.
12 William Grimes, 'After a First Wave of Raves, *The Piano* Slips Into a Trough', *The New York Times*, 10 May 1994, Section: Movies.
13 Heike-Melba Fendel, 'How Women Live Their Lives', in Wexman, op. cit., 87.

14 Thornham, op. cit., 44.
15 Thornham, op. cit., 44.
16 Associated Press, 'Campion's take on the dearth of women filmmakers', *The Baltimore Sun*, 21 May 2007, http://www.baltimoresun.com/enter tainment/movies/bal-to.jane21may21,0,7548445.story (accessed 27 May 2007).

Filmography

A Girl's Own Story (1984)
Two Friends (1986)
Sweetie (1989)
An Angel at My Table (1990)
The Piano (1993)
The Portrait of a Lady (1996)
Holy Smoke! (1999)
In the Cut (2003)
Chacun son cinéma (Segment: *Lady Bug*) (2007)
8 (Segment: *The Water Diary*) (2008)
Bright Star (2009)

Further reading

McHugh, Kathleen. *Jane Campion (Contemporary Film Directors)*. University of Illinois Press, 2007.
Polan, Dana. *Jane Campion*. BFI, 2008.
Wexman, Virginia Wright, ed. *Jane Campion: Interviews*. University of Mississippi Press, (1999).

GURINDER CHADHA

By Rayna Denison

Gurinder Chadha has been described as the 'queen of the multi': a filmmaker who embodies contemporary British multiculturalism and has thus reaped rewards at the multiplex.[1] However, despite this notion of Chadha as 'multi', she is a filmmaker whose cultural identity is, while hybridised, more fixed than fluid in nature. Strenuous attempts at early self-definition placed Chadha as a film-maker who recognised the political (and the economic) value in rendering herself as a marginal figure within British culture.[2] As articles and interviews have regularly noted, Chadha was born in Africa, and has lived in Britain since the 1960s, but her self-defined identity comes from her ethnicity. Her identity is usually described as diasporic; her Sikh Punjabi family found themselves geographically displaced after India gained independence from the British, and they resettled in Southall, London, after a period in Kenya. Chadha has carefully sculpted and maintained a conceptualisation of herself as a filmmaker whose South Asian Britishness provides her with a distinct vision of the world. While she is without question Britain's most successful female ethnic director to date (and possibly the most successful female British director regardless of ethnicity), the question here is just how deeply notions of nationality and ethnicity have impacted on her filmmaking, and how she balances between the political and her self conceptualisation as a 'populist' filmmaker.[3]

Chadha emerged from a period in the 1980s and 1990s in which previously marginalised minorities were actively encouraged to make films about their experiences of diasporic British life. Government initiatives and workshops were created in this period, and television's Channel 4 was also instrumental in exploring the potential audiences for diasporic British filmmaking.[4] These initiatives foregrounded the importance of ethnicity and hybridised British identities in a period in which British political leaders were looking to emphasise the always already hybridised nature of British culture itself. Indeed, British Prime Minister Tony Blair wrote to Chadha after seeing *Bend It Like Beckham*, declaring, 'We loved it, loved it, because this is my Britain'.[5]

While *Bend It Like Beckham* may have been in line with Blair's version of a multicultural Britain, the film's positive tone and happy ending were a refinement of Chadha's more radical set of previous political visions of Britain. Starting in radio journalism before moving into filmmaking, Chadha's filmmaking has, seemingly, become *less* of a personalised view of her own British Asian identity as time has passed. Certainly her early documentary and narrative shorts, *I'm British But ...* and *A Nice Arrangement*, overtly deal with the nature of British Asian identity and the difficulty of what Danette Dimarco and J. Sunita Peacock have discussed as the intercultural performance of British Asian subjectivity.[6] The former documentary examined the importance of British Bhangra music to young Asians across the different British nations, asking how they define themselves in relation to the notion of British and 'home' cultures. *A Nice Arrangement*, which Chadha co-wrote with Meera Syal (who also collaborated with her on her breakthrough feature *Bhaji on the Beach*) is a brief examination of the choices open to British Asian women in relation to marriage which, without judging its characters, demonstrates the inherent tensions between Indian tradition and the lived experience of modern British Asian women. From these tightly focused shorts that deal exclusively with British Asian identity and life, Chadha's works have slowly expanded outwards taking in transnational cultural exchange, non-Asian identity crises and globalised notions of space and home.

Chadha's shift from localised, multicultural concerns to more global or universal representation schema chimes with a shift noted by June Givanni in relation to what she terms Black or Urban Film in Britain:

> The multifaceted identity of being black and British and a woman or gay was expressed in an issue-based agenda in many films in the 1980s. As their repertoire and aspirations grew, cultural specificity, cultural hybridity, and agendas beyond the cultural meant that some filmmakers were redefining themselves, what they do, and where their work fit.[7]

This shift is certainly visible in Chadha's films, which have become progressively wider in scope and less specifically British Asian in focus. From her early work on *Bhaji on the Beach* to her most recent *Angus, Thongs and Perfect Snogging* it is possible to trace the expanding interests of a filmmaker exploring different aspects of identity. Chadha's films have grown from an early interest in understanding 'home' and the tensions between the divergent positions taken up by British Asian community members, to her current modification of her concerns into more specific interest in gender issues and clashes between generations of women who understand nationality and femininity in divergent ways.

This is a second and rather more constant aspect of Chadha's work: a consistent focus on women, particularly on British Asian women. Roy writes that 'Chadha plays on different forms of marginalization – based on ethnicity, gender, sexuality or class – that might throw up new meanings of community'.[8] However, while these forms of marginalisation are present throughout Chadha's cinema, her larger concern is with women and their cultural marginalisation. For example, *What's Cooking?*, perhaps the most overlooked of Chadha's films to date, is, while a film about multi-generational gatherings of families on Thanksgiving, centrally preoccupied with its female characters: its most famous American stars are women, including Kyra Sedgwick and Julianna Margulies, who play a lesbian couple struggling to be accepted at a Thanksgiving dinner that includes extended family. Perhaps the most striking character is Elizabeth Avila, played by Mercedes Ruehl, an American Hispanic whose traditional male family members (her son and ex-husband) attempt to manipulate the celebrations in order to prevent her from maintaining her post-divorce freedom and happiness. Convincing performances and complex characterisation highlight, in a relatively short space of time, conflict between traditional masculinity and women's romantic/economic freedom. In the four vignettes that make up *What's Cooking?*, Chadha and her co-writer husband Paul Mayeda Berges frequently use multi-generational family structures to consistently question the position of women in American society, across America's racial, ethnic and sexual categorisations of women.

Justine Ashby has noted that it is within these storytelling confines that women frequently become both protagonist and antagonist in Chadha's films. Citing the mothers of *Bend It Like Beckham*, she writes:

> not only are the mothers figured as more sexist than their husbands, but when each father finally puts his foot down and insists that their wives support their daughters' ambitions, the fathers strike a blow for 'girl power', on the one hand, while reasserting their more traditional power as head of the family, on the other.[9]

The problem of women seems to be, however, more one of generational clashes between value systems than one of women per se. In *Bhaji on the Beach*, for example, the 'aunties' play a similar role, with the oldest amongst them reacting strongest to the news that the young Hashida has fallen pregnant to her black boyfriend, calling her a 'whore'. The distance between generations is likewise a central problematic carried over from Austen's *Pride and Prejudice* into Chadha's *Bride and Prejudice*. In that film, Darcy's mother displays her cultural intolerance of the Indian Elizabeth, Lalita, while Lalita's mother insists that her well-educated and capable daughter must find a husband. Perhaps, though, female generational conflict is most strikingly visible in Chadha's *Angus, Thongs and Perfect Snogging*, wherein the central character Georgia's lack of communication with her mother and squabbling with an older girl at school cause her to believe her parents are divorcing and (temporarily) cost Georgia her closest group of friends.

The consistency with which Chadha produces inter-generational and female-centred conflicts, however, need not be read as entirely negative. Instead it is possible to view these inter-generational conflicts through their positive resolutions, as Chadha consistently punishes inflexible women and rewards those willing to accept change and difference. Moreover, male agency in Chadha's films is severely reduced, with many of the major character types being fulfilled by women. This being the case, it is perhaps unsurprising that Chadha's cinema offers a wide range of female character types, both positive and negative, that go beyond those populating much of the rest of contemporary cinema. Significantly, in Chadha's films women are key characters because, as Chadha and Syal state through character dialogue in *Bhaji on the Beach*, women struggle 'between the double yoke of racism and sexism'. This doubled marginalisation, through race and gender, has created a liminal space in which Chadha explores the possibilities of female representation. The doubled marginalisation of, particularly ethnic, women also links back to issues of nationality and cultural collectivism in diaspora. In presenting a range of British Asian female characters Chadha gives space and a voice to otherwise marginalised debates about British Asian cultures and their relationship to broader women's cultures. These characters and debates are a key component in Chadha's global crossover appeal.

British Asian women's roles are only one aspect of the way in which Chadha has created a cinema of multicultural representation, however. The blending of cultures in Chadha's films takes on many guises, and ones which chime with Hamid Naficy's claims about accented cinema:

> At the same time that accented films emphasize visual fetishes of homeland and the past (landscape, monuments, photographs, souvenirs, letters), as well as visual markers of difference and belonging (posture, look, style of dress and behavior), they equally stress the oral, the vocal, and the musical – that is accents, intonations, voices, music, and songs, which also demarcate individual and collective identities.[10]

Examining the first of Naficy's categories, 'fetishes of homeland' and tradition are carefully highlighted across Chadha's cinema. For example, representations of the Golden Temple at Amritsar in India appear in *Bhaji on the Beach* and *Bend It Like Beckham* and the temple itself is displayed as an establishing shot early in *Bride and Prejudice*. Chadha draws attention to all of these moments of display through her DVD commentary tracks for the films, discussing how a picture of the Golden Temple is now in her mother's home; or, how she used her mother's statue of the temple in *Bend It Like Beckham*. Tradition, family and images of Indian culture become bound up in complex ways in these films, with the geographical markers of one nation made part of the cultural experience of another, if largely through facsimile.

However, Chadha's cinema also invests in notions of the 'homeland' through her uses of language, of music and of Bollywood cinema. In terms of the former, Roy has discussed Chadha's use of often unsubtitled Punjabi language in *Bend It Like Beckham* as a 'refusal to translate the local vernacular as an acknowledgement of the 'untranslatability' of cultural difference'.[11] Language becomes a site of cultural difference, but also of tradition and passion according to Roy, while classed notions of British language also heavily inflect Chadha's presentation of a 'multicultural' British identity. In fact the British Asianness often displayed in Chadha's films borrows from a single London community, her own, in Southall. Frequently, party scenes, dances and weddings in Chadha's films are peopled by her family and members of the community in which she grew up, creating a distinctive, small-scale notion of British Asianness.

British Asianness also has a distinctive impact on the aural nature of Chadha's cinema, with Bhangra playing a significant role in her films from *I'm British But ...* onwards. However, as her concerns have begun to take in white British culture and more globalised film forms like Bollywood and the musical, Chadha's provision of music has also altered significantly. For example, Christine Geraghty has discussed the use of musical 'numbers' at the end of Chadha's films to offer a 'deconstruction which invites the audience to recognise the work that has gone into the film' but significantly one which 'is presented as a communal experience, a utopian moment which embraces the audience at the very point at which they have to abandon the film and the cinema'.[12] The utopian experience of music in Chadha's films goes further than this implies, however, and examples of multicultural transnationalism can be found throughout Chadha's soundtracks. Examples like the Indian language versions of 'Hot, Hot, Hot' and 'Summer Holiday' used in *Bend It Like Beckham* and *Bhaji on the Beach* respectively work to combine the linguistic registers of Punjabi, Hindi and English while naturalising the existence of multinational musical types and styles across the films in question. More obvious still is the use of Hindi film music producers and English language lyrics for the majority of the songs in *Bride and Prejudice*. While the staging of the songs often owes as much, if not more, to the Hollywood musical as it does to popular Indian cinema, the use of English lyrics over Indian musical tracks performs a similar role to the inclusion of translated songs in other films. Essentially, the fusion created between language and musical style works to create a series of utopian border-crossing moments that transcend issues of national film style in Chadha's filmmaking.

In fact, Chadha has regularly referenced and used popular Hindi cinema (or Bollywood) in her films. Bollywood becomes a literal fantasy in *Bhaji on the Beach*, wherein one of the central characters, Asha, has headaches that lead her to hallucinate Bollywood intrusions into her reality. A single film, *Purab Aur Paschim* (*East and West*, 1970) has been quoted several times in Chadha's films. Cheryl A. Wilson writes that 'Bollywood also becomes a "setting": the fight between Darcy and Wickham [in *Bride and Prejudice*] takes place in a theatre during a Bollywood film festival and mirrors the fight onscreen'.[13] In this instance *Purab Aur Paschim* is used to visually link Chadha's film back to earlier popular Bollywood cinema in a humorous but also culturally authenticating fashion. However, despite its potentially globalised or transnational nature, the Bollywood inflections of *Bride and Prejudice* were carefully managed and Chadha actually produced two versions of the film, one for the English-speaking market and one for India. The main difference between the two, according to Chadha's DVD commentary, was that many of the songs were cut down for the English-language version. While this is suggestive of Chadha's cultural sensitivity, it also implies limits to the transnationality of her filmmaking style, with competing aesthetics rather than a single global one.

However, as a 'populist' filmmaker, Chadha's is a cinema intended in conception to cross borders. Consequently, Chadha's filmmaking has struck a balance between a set of performed diasporic identities and normative modes of (Hollywood) filmmaking. Chadha's cinema functions as a 'multicultural reading of mass-mediated culture', and attempts to 'explore the repressed ethnic and racial contradictions, transgressing the segregationist discourse on ethnic representation as limited to either third-world films or to narratives depicting peoples of color'.[14] However, this balance comes at the cost of her earlier, more politicised stance on British Asian identity. In the commentary for *Bend It Like Beckham*, Chadha cites the humour in her films as a problem for those seeking a political cinema in her works:

> People sometimes think when you make a film about people you don't often see on the screen like Indian people, like girls or whatever, you know, people think that it's going to be very issue based and very earnest. ... In fact that's what we're trying to [do, to] subvert you all the time, subvert what you expect.

Humour is largely the means through which Chadha maintains her populism as a filmmaker, and the subversiveness of her films, whether positive, in terms of British Asian representation, or negative, as with the mothers in *Bend It Like Beckham*, seems intended as a challenge to the seriousness of other urban and black filmmakers' products.

However, this could disguise the ways in which Chadha is performing her diasporic identity in almost every film she makes. The casual way in which she attempts to make British Asian representation more normative and indicative of contemporary Britain is particularly interesting in these regards. For *Angus, Thongs and Perfect Snogging*, for instance, she changed one of the central characters, Ellen, into a British Asian girl played by Manjeeven Grewel.

> We made her Indian and that's worked out really well in the film and it's sort of modernised it and updated it and made it a much truer picture of Britain. She adds a kind of innocence because Manjeeven is a very young girly 14-year-old.

British Asianness in Chadha's vision has thus progressed from a position of marginality to one of 'modernity' and 'truth'. In her fascinating matter-of-fact commentary, Chadha's inclusion of the British Asian actress in this role is naturalised and seemingly unquestioned as a 'normal' part of representing contemporary Britain. However, Ellen is the only British Asian in the film, and there are no other major characters of colour at all. To conclude, then, the naturalisation of British Asian representation through Chadha's work has also seen a reduction in the number of British Asians in her films, as they share screen time with white Britain. This is not intended, however, as a criticism, but rather as a reflection on the ways in which Chadha has maintained other aspects of her filmmaking style (an interest in multi-generational representations of women and a fascination with music's role in filmmaking) above and beyond her desire to represent her own personal racial and ethnic politics. It is this that makes her a potent directorial force – different elements of her filmmaking 'vision' may be foregrounded at different times without a loss of cultural relevance.

Biography

Gurinder Chadha was born in Africa in 1960 before her family settled in England. Chadha has been writing and directing films and television since 1990, gradually helming more mainstream projects.

Though this article has focused on her directorial career, Chadha has also written or co-written her scripts, and additionally wrote the screenplay for *The Mistress of Spices* (2005) starring Aishwarya Rai. Her next film is a co-production between her own Bend It Films and The Indian Film Company, called *It's a Wonderful Afterlife*, and marks a return to Chadha's focus on the British Asian community in London.

Notes

1 Jigna Desai, *Beyond Bollywood: The Cultural Politics of South Asian Diaspora*, New York: Routledge, 2004: p. 68.
2 Susan Koshy and Gurinder Chadha, 'Turning Color: A Conversation with Gurinder Chadha', *Transition* 72 (1996): pp. 148–61.
3 Koshy, 1996; Christine Geraghty, 'Jane Austen meets Gurinder Chadha: Hybridity and Intertextuality in *Bride and Prejudice*', *South Asian Popular Culture* 4.2 (Oct 2006): pp. 163–68, p. 167. See also Geraghty, *Now a Major Motion Picture: Film Adaptations of Literature and Drama*, Lanham, Maryland: Rowman and Littlefield, 2008.
4 Desai, *op. cit.*, p. 46.
5 Quoted in Justine Ashby, 'Postfeminism in the British Frame', *Cinema Journal* 44.2 (Winter 2005): pp. 127–33, p. 130.
6 Danette Dimarco and J. Sunita Peacock, 'The *Bhadramahila* and Adaptation in Meera Syal's and Gurinder Chadha's *Bhaji on the Beach*', *Mosaic* 41.4 (Dec 2008): pp. 161–78, p. 169.
7 June Givanni, 'A Curator's Conundrum: Programming "Black Film" in 1980s–1990s Britain', *The Moving Image* 4.1 (Spring 2004): pp. 60–75, p. 70.
8 Anjali Gera Roy, 'Translating Difference in *Bend it Like Beckham*', *New Cinemas: Journal of Contemporary Film* 4.1 (2006): pp. 55–66, p. 58.
9 Ashby, *op. cit.*
10 Hamid Naficy, *An Accented Cinema: Exilic and Diasporic Filmmaking*, Princeton, NJ: Princeton University Press, 2001, pp. 24–5.
11 Roy, *op. cit.*, pp. 55–6.
12 Geraghty, *op. cit.*, 2006, p. 167.
13 Cheryl A. Wilson, '*Bride and Prejudice*: A Bollywood Comedy of Manners', *Literature/Film Quarterly* 34.4 (2006): pp. 323–31, p. 330.
14 Ella Shohat, 'Ethnicities-in-Relation: Toward a Multicultural Reading of American Cinema', in Lester D Friedman, ed., *Unspeakable Images: Ethnicity and the American Cinema*, Urbana, Il: University of Illinois Press, 1991, p. 221.

Filmography

I'm British But … (1990)
Bhaji on the Beach (1993)
A Nice Arrangement (1994)

JACKIE CHAN

By Leon Hunt

More so than even Bruce Lee or John Woo, Jackie Chan came to represent the global image of 'Hong Kong Cinema'; a hyperkinetic, breathless national cinema fashioned by impossibly limber and fearless performers, and by prodigiously inventive choreographers (Chan, significantly, was both). 'No Fear. No Stuntman. No Equal', proclaimed the English-language posters for *Rumble in the Bronx*, underlining both the supposedly 'universal' aspects of his films and those qualities Hollywood could not deliver. Built into this, however, was the implication that Hollywood once *did* deliver such 'uncomplicated' pleasures, as is evidenced in numerous references to silent cinema (Keaton, Chaplin, Lloyd) or classic Hollywood musicals (those of Gene Kelly, in particular). This cast Chan as Hollywood's 'lost innocence', an alternative to 'high concepts' and (most importantly) special effects – his admirers often portrayed him as a filmmaking throwback – 'cliff-hanger, kung fu and Keystone cops all in one'.[1] Certainly, the silent cinema/Hollywood musical comparisons, while limited, stand as a reminder that there is more to cinematic pleasure than the classical 'well-made film'. In Chan's best-loved films, the text is often the set-piece – no Chan book, his autobiography included, is complete without a list of his ten best fights or ten best stunts. This suggests a kind of 'cinema of attractions', or what David Bordwell calls an 'ecstatic cinema', which transports spectators 'into a realm of rapt, electric apprehension of sheerly pictorial and auditory momentum'.[2] The danger is, however, that such accounts can easily conspire with a patronising 'trash aesthetic', celebrating Hong Kong as a mindless guilty pleasure; never mind the quality, feel the stunts.

Chan's warmth, vulnerability, and mixture of comedy and action have sometimes been celebrated as an antidote to the machismo and heartless irony of Western action cinema, but his persona is also rooted in culturally specific conceptions of masculinity and heroism. Steve Fore sees Chan's films as a negotiation of 'certain contradictions characteristic of Hong Kong culture', mediating between a need for individual action and 'respect for the value of nurturing a group orientation based on altruism and humility'.[3] This is a considerable part of Chan-fandom, too – magazines like *Screen Power: The Jackie Chan Magazine* emphasise his work for charity, and his love for and friendliness towards his fans – qualities which support rather than contradict his bravery and martial arts skills.

References to Keaton, Chaplin and Kelly point to another key aspect of Chan's public persona, namely the star-auteur as performative genius. Chan's filmography encompasses a multiplicity of filmmaking roles – director, producer, choreographer, stuntman, vocal talent in animated features – and his role is rarely confined to performer alone. This array of talents is partly attributable to the multi-skilling of Chinese Opera, in which Chan was trained as a child. Behind-the-scenes projects like *Jackie Chan: My Stunts* explore his 'creative process' (improvisation and brainstorming with his stunt team, a choreographic emphasis on 'rhythm' and tempo) and promote the stuntman as star, choreographer as auteur, self-endangerment as popular art. Chan's reputation hinged on 'control', even over those films which he did not nominally direct; several of his directors have walked off his films, willingly or otherwise. He has found it harder to exercise such control over his Hollywood films. The failure of his early US vehicles, *The Big Brawl* and *The Protector*, is popularly attributed to the blind hubris of B-movie hacks who thought they knew better, but more mainstream directors like Brett Ratner have also kept Chan's obsessive perfectionism in check. Relatively speaking, Chan is one of Hong Kong's most expensive filmmakers; costly period re-creations, international settings, but more importantly for the legend, fights which in his prime took months to film, multiple takes and, of course, lengthy stays in hospital. *Miracles* (a re-creation of 1930s' Hong Kong, inspired by Capra's *A Pocketful of Miracles*, 1961) and *Operation Condor* (a rambling desert adventure filmed in Morocco and the Sahara), in particular, have taken on the reputation of expensive *follies de grandeur* – the former higher in grandeur, the latter more of a folly.

Chan's popularity is one of the paradoxes of global popular culture; for many years prior to his belated Hollywood breakthrough, he managed to be a cult figure and an international superstar at the same time. Prior to *Rumble in the Bronx* (released in the US in 1996), he was little more than a cult figure in the West, a cult fostered mainly through video. Elsewhere, he could justly claim to be the biggest star in the world, with a vast following around the globe. 'In

Asia ... I am *Jurassic Park*. I am *E.T.*', Chan once claimed.[4] But in another sense that is precisely what he *is not* – 'We are very poor ... The only choice I have is dangerous stunts'.[5] Chan had eventually to change his tune as digital effects proliferated in Chinese action films and years of hard-hitting stunts took their toll, but there is something irresistible about the 'real' body pitted against the tyranny of the digital, the Drunken Master versus the *Titanic*. But Chan is no cinematic primitive – his control over camera placement and (largely invisible) editing is as meticulous as his control over bodies in motion, and his multiple takes often function as 'action replays' of jaw-droppingly 'real' (read: dangerous) on-set events. Rather, Chan astutely gauged those elements of Hong Kong cinema that Hollywood could not absorb or copy. For Chan, cinema is primarily in the service of the body. In Renee Witterstaetter's entertaining hagiography, his filmography constitutes an autobiography of his body, both its performative achievements and 'a chronological account of every broken bone and crushed head, broken finger and twisted knee'.[6]

Few Hong Kong filmmakers have enjoyed Chan's longevity. His career spans the most significant period in Hong Kong cinema – from the Mandarin-language kung fu films of the 1970s (Hong Kong cinema's first global export) to the 'new' Cantonese cinema of the 1980s and 1990s, which looked to Hong Kong itself for its thematic and narrative content; from the 'Crown Colony's' economic 'miracle' to its postcolonial status as China's Special Administrative Region. There is a set-piece in most Chan films where he is attacked from all sides, parrying furiously, receiving as many blows as he successfully blocks or returns – the culture-shock of an ever-mutating environment translated into a flurry of high-impact action. Neither Hong Kong's return to Chinese sovereignty nor his belated success in Hollywood stopped him making films in the declining Hong Kong cinema; he continues to work in both industries, even though neither career has been entirely satisfactory in recent years. One senses that he would like to abandon his Hollywood career and make globally successful films from his Hong Kong base. But compared to such shrewd Chinese blockbusters as *Crouching Tiger, Hidden Dragon* (2000) and *Kung Fu Hustle* (2004), Chan's recent attempts at transnational blockbusters look clumsy and misjudged.

Chan's career grew out of an already dying genre, the kung fu film. His earliest star vehicles were lacklustre period films for former Bruce Lee director Lo Wei, and his breakthrough came in two kung fu comedies directed by Yuen Wo-ping, *Snake in the Eagle's Shadow* and

Drunken Master. In the latter, he reinvented Cantonese folk hero Wong Fei-hung as a pre-legend juvenile delinquent – in one scene, he sees off an opponent by farting in his face. Both films were variations on the 'master–pupil' theme, which had been popular since the mid-1970s and which was being given an increasingly comic twist. His early films as director were essentially reworkings of his breakthrough hits, made with the larger budgets Golden Harvest studios could provide, but the failure of *Dragon Lord* suggested that even comic martial arts films had run their course for now. Subsequently, he was instrumental in creating a hybridised comedy-action film with hair-raising stunts and meticulous choreography, but Chan never lost sight of the martial arts film's 'difference' from Western spectacle, its performative virtuosity and the centrality of the body-in-motion. By the time of *Project A*, the emphasis was equally on the body-in-danger – falls from clocktowers, hanging from a moving bus by an umbrella handle (*Police Story*) or dangling from a helicopter (*Police Story 3*) – all injuries replayed in end credits out-takes. If one looks for evidence of 'maturity', then *Project A* is probably Chan's breakthrough film. Not only is it more enjoyable than any film has a right to be, but it displays a penchant for period recreation and a new interest in Hong Kong rather than the kung fu film's mythical China. The film is set in turn-of-the-century Hong Kong and pits Chan's coastal guard Dragon Ma (aided by Yuen Biao and Sammo Hung) against a conspiracy of pirates and corrupt British officials. This is where the 'silent cinema' comparisons begin – the film includes a virtuoso comic bicycle chase and a Lloyd-inspired clocktower sequence. There is a new variety to the fight choreography, too, ranging from riotous bar-room brawls to an extended fight with the pirate leader full of hyperbolic sound effects, slow-motion leaps and Beijing Opera acrobatics.

Chan developed another series with *Police Story*, usually seen as his riposte to the 'rogue cop' posturing of *The Protector*. The stunts are as breathtaking as ever – Part 1 is the final word on the pleasures of breaking glass and demolishing shopping malls. In *The Protector,* he had played a Chinese American cop visiting Hong Kong on a mission, whereas *Police Story* re-casts him as a much more local 'protector'. Nevertheless, there clings to his mostly genial cop a lingering sense of 'Dirty Jackie' from the earlier film, particularly in a gruelling opening shootout. The generosity and 'social responsibility' of Chan's period films is sometimes undercut by a certain callousness in some of his modern-day ones – what are we to make of his character's destruction of a refugee shantytown during a car chase as Part

1's opening 'spectacle', or the grotesquely stereotyped deaf-mute heavy in Part 2? *The Armour of God*, an Indiana Jones-type adventure filmed in Europe, represents another important development in that Chan's films began to transmute into travelogues with intermittent action scenes. The film almost killed Chan when one stunt went wrong – to add insult to nearly fatal injury, it is a hard movie to like (not least for its racism). *Operation Condor* was an expensive sequel and one excess too many for Golden Harvest, but Chan was displaying a growing weakness for colourless internationalism with yawning longeurs in between his films' set-pieces.

Although hardly one of his most distinguished films, *Rumble in the Bronx* holds an important place in the Chan biography. Fore provides an illuminating account of how it was modified for and promoted to US multiplexes – the new version played down Chan's physical comedy (always a sticking point in his 'crossover') and those self-effacing aspects of his star persona that conflicted with him being a straight action performer.[7] *Rush Hour*, his Hollywood reboot, seems more comfortable with both the 'nice guy' persona and the comedy, even if the latter is toned down (especially in comparison with Chris Tucker's mugging). Interestingly, the action is the casualty; Chan had to work with American stunt co-ordinator Terry Leonard for reasons of both safety and expense. While the comedy westerns *Shanghai Noon/Knights* seem as ill-at-ease with Chan's 'Chineseness' as the *Rush Hour* series, they at least give him a less aggressively competitive co-star (Owen Wilson) and allow him to display his choreographic and performative skills to greater effect, not least when facing off against Donnie Yen in the second film. *The Forbidden Kingdom*, Chan's long-awaited pairing with Jet Li, is the most interesting of his Hollywood films, attempting to re-fashion the *wuxia* (Martial Arts Chivalry) fantasy film for an anglophone audience. While undoubtedly orientalist in its exotic fairy-tale China, it offers effective dual roles for both stars. If the role of Chan's American co-stars has usually been to help him 'become American', he finds a genuine chemistry with Li and reprises his 'Drunken' kung fu during their duel.

Chan's career overlaps significantly with that of Sammo Hung Kam-bo. Hung was the oldest member of the 'Seven Little Fortunes', the Beijing Opera troupe in which Chan trained as a child. Hung, like Chan, became a prolific star, director, producer and choreographer, and a key influence on the Hong Kong action film. Chan and Hung appeared together in numerous films including the *Lucky Stars* series, *Dragons Forever* and Chan's own *Project A*, usually accompanied by a third 'Little Fortune', the agile Yuen Biao, and sometimes by a fourth, wiry Yuen Wah, as the villain. They are part of the last generation of Opera performers to make their mark on popular cinema. Hung is as talented as Chan and their styles have some similarities, but he is even less of a conventional leading man (one film title tells all – *Enter the Fat Dragon*) and never enjoyed the same level of adulation. Hung, Chan and another important choreographer-director from an Opera background, Yuen Wo-ping, represent an intermediate stage in martial arts cinema. Bruce Lee had consolidated a demand for 'real' martial artists, both in front of and behind the camera, and this 'authenticity' was guaranteed by extended takes and wide framing of the action. Hung, Chan and Yuen shifted this 'authenticity' away from the kung fu itself to a new kind of hard physical action, away from traditional styles and towards a mixture of operatic tumbling, high impact stuntwork and self-effacing comedy. Yuen has proven the most adaptable of Hong Kong choreographers, with recent credits that include *The Matrix*, *Crouching Tiger* and *Kill Bill*.

Since the early 1990s, Chan's most frequent Hong Kong collaborators have been Stanley Tong and Benny Chan, both 'safe pairs of hands' in curbing some of his excesses without diluting his trademark style. Chan's last truly great film was a more fractious collaboration with Shaw Brothers veteran Lau Kar-leung (Mandarin name: Liu Jialiang). Lau is the epitome of 1970s'-style authenticity, and the glorious *Drunken Master II* saw Chan performing a range of genuine southern kung fu moves, including the eponymous 'Drunken Boxing'. Thematically, the film bore some similarities to the *Once Upon a Time in China* films (which also dealt with Wong Fei-hung) – colonialist villains, Wong Fei-hung's coming of age – but the style was very different. Chan has likened Lau's style to classical music – 'very traditional' – and his own to jazz,[8] and Lau reportedly walked off the set before the film's completion. But the film is more seamless than either might like to think and offered two incongruously old-fashioned figures giving the 'new wave' a run for its money.

Physical performers are fated to decline – if they aren't prematurely snuffed out like Bruce Lee – and Chan has borne this more gracefully than many. To the chagrin of some long term fans, he has had to make his peace with digital effects, most jarringly in the film *Tuxedo*, and stunt doubles have become more common. While the younger Chan got by on boyish charm and athleticism, there have been intermittent signs of an ambition to be taken more seriously as a character actor and vacate the martial arts throne for younger performers like the Thai star Tony Jaa, often seen as the 'new Jackie Chan'. In *New Police Story*, Chan plays a disgraced alcoholic cop trying to regain his dignity while pursuing a gang of youthful villains, while his most recent film *Shinjuku Incident* has been touted as the star's most serious bid to date for acting credibility. As an action filmmaker, Chan's glories are mostly in the past, but it would be unwise to write off one of Hong Kong cinema's most formidable and durable talents.

Biography

Chan Kong-sang ('Born in Hong Kong') was born in 1954, in Hong Kong. In 1962 he joined the Beijing Opera School and studied under teacher Yu Cha Yuen, and subsequently performed (as 'Yuen Lo') in the Seven Little Fortunes opera troupe. He played a handful of child roles in Hong Kong films, but his film career began in earnest as a stuntman in the early 1970s. Chan was groomed as a replacement for Bruce Lee by producer-director Lo Wei and renamed Sing Lung ('Becoming a Dragon'). However, his real breakthrough came while on loan to Seasonal films – *Snake in the Eagle's Shadow* and *Drunken Master* (both 1978) made him a star. His signing to Golden Harvest in 1980 made him the biggest star in Asia and he blossomed as a director/choreographer. Chan achieved international success with the dubbed, re-edited version of *Rumble in the Bronx*, a success consolidated by his first Hollywood-produced hit, *Rush Hour*.

Notes

1 Renee Witterstaetter, *Dying For Action: The Life and Films of Jackie Chan*, London, Ebury Press, 1998, p. 5.
2 David Bordwell, 'Aesthetics in Action: Kung Fu, Gunplay, and Cinematic Expressivity', in 21st Hong Kong International Film Festival, *Hong Kong Cinema Retrospective: 50 Years of Electric Shadows*, Hong Kong, Urban Council of Hong Kong, 1997, p. 88.
3 Steve Fore, 'Jackie Chan and the Cultural Dynamics of Global Entertainment', in Sheldon Hsiao-peng Lu (ed.) *Transnational Chinese Cinemas: Identity, Nationhood, Gender*, Honolulu, University of Hawaii Press, 1997, pp. 239–62 and p. 254.
4 Fredric Dannen and Barry Long, *Hong Kong Babylon: An Insider's Guide to the Hollywood of the East*, London, Faber, 1997, p. 3.
5 Renee Witterstaetter, *op. cit.*, p. 53.
6 Ibid., p. vii.

7 Steve Fore, *op. cit.*

8 Jackie Chan and Jeff Yang, *I Am Jackie Chan: My Life in Action*, New York, Ballantine, 1998, p. 361.

Filmography

(All Hong Kong productions unless otherwise indicated)

As leading performer/director/choreographer (directed by Chan unless indicated otherwise)

The Little Tiger of Canton / Master with Cracked Fingers (Chin Tsin, 1971)
New Fist of Fury (Lo Wei, 1976)
Shaolin Wooden Men (Lo Wei, 1976)
Killer Meteor (Wang Yu, 1977)
To Kill with Intrigue (Lo Wei, 1977)
Snake and Crane Arts of Shaolin (Lo Wei, 1978)
Half a Loaf of Kung Fu (Chen Chi-hwa, 1978)
Magnificent Bodyguards (Lo Wei, 1978)
Dragon Fist (Lo Wei, 1978)
Snake in the Eagle's Shadow (Yuen Wo-ping, 1978)
Drunken Master (Yuen Wo-ping, 1978)
Spiritual Kung Fu (1978)
Fearless Hyena (1979)
The Young Master (1980)
Fearless Hyena II (Lo Wei, 1980)
The Big Brawl / Battlecreek Brawl (Robert Clouse, HK/US 1980)
Cannonball Run (Hal Needham, US 1981; supporting role, intended to break into the US market)
Fantasy Mission Force (Chu Yen Ping, 1982)
Ninja Wars (Mitsumisa Saito, Japan 1982)
Dragon Lord (1982)
Project A (1983)
Winners and Sinners (Sammo Hung, 1983)
Cannonball Run II (Hal Needham, US 1983)
Wheels on Meals (Sammo Hung, 1984)
My Lucky Stars (Sammo Hung, 1985)
Twinkle, Twinkle, Lucky Stars (Sammo Hung, 1985)
The Protector (James Glickenhaus, HK/US 1985)
Police Story (1985)
Heart of the Dragon / First Mission (Sammo Hung, 1985)
Armour of God (1986)
Dragons Forever (Sammo Hung, 1987)
Project A II (1987)
Police Story II (1987)
Mr. Canton and Lady Rose / Miracles / Miracle (1989)

Armour of God II: Operation Condor / Operation Condor (1990)
Island of Fire (Chu Yen-ping, 1991)
Twin Dragons (Tsui Hark, Ringo Lam, 1991)
Police Story III: Supercop (Stanley Tong, 1992)
City Hunter (Wong Jing, 1993)
Crime Story (Kirk Wong, 1993)
Drunken Master II (Lau Kar-leung, aka Liu jialiang, 1994)
Rumble in the Bronx (Stanley Tong, 1994)
Thunderbolt (Gordon Chan, 1995)
Police Story IV: First Strike / First Strike (Stanley Tong, 1996)
Mr. Nice Guy (Sammo Hung, 1997)
Burn Hollywood Burn ('an Alan Smithee film' [Arthur Hiller], US 1997)
Rush Hour (Brett Ratner, US 1998)
Who Am I? (Benny Chan, Jackie Chan, 1998)
Gorgeous (Vincent Kok, 1998)
Shanghai Noon (Tom Dey, US 2000)
Rush Hour 2 (Brett Ratner, US 2001)
The Accidental Spy (Teddy Chan, 2001)
The Tuxedo (Kevin Donovan, US 2002)
The Medallion (Gordon Chan, 2003)
Shanghai Knights (David Dobkin, US 2003)
Traces of a Dragon: Jackie Chan and his Lost Family (Mabel Cheung, 2003)
New Police Story (Benny Chan, 2004)
Around the World in 80 Days (Frank Coraci, US 2004)
The Myth (Stanley Tong, 2005)
Rob-B-Hood (Benny Chan, 2006)
Rush Hour 3 (Brett Ratner, US 2007)
The Forbidden Kingdom (Rob Minkoff, US 2008)
Kung Fu Panda (Mark Osborne and John Stevenson, US 2008) Vocal
    performance as Monkey
Shinjuku Incident (Derek Yee, 2008)

Television/video

Jackie Chan: My Story (1998)
Jackie Chan: My Stunts (1999)

Further reading

Steve Fore, 'Life Imitates Art: Home and Dislocation in the Films of Jackie Chan' in Esther Yau (ed.) *At Full Speed: Hong Kong Cinema in a Borderless World*, Minneapolis and London, University of Minnesota Press, 2001, pp. 115–41.

Leon Hunt, *Kung Fu Cult Masters: From Bruce Lee to Crouching Tiger*, London, Wallflower 2003.

Craig Reid, 'An Evening with Jackie Chan' (interview), *Bright Lights Film Journal*, 13, 1994, pp. 18–25.

Ramie Tateishi, 'Jackie Chan and the Re-invention of Tradition', *Asian Cinema*, 10/1, pp. 78–84.

THE COEN BROTHERS

By Jon Lewis

Part I: Independence and auteurism

The Coen brothers have made thirteen films: *Blood Simple, Raising Arizona, Miller's Crossing, Barton Fink, The Hudsucker Proxy, Fargo, The Big Lebowski, O Brother, Where Art Thou? The Man Who Wasn't There, Intolerable Cruelty, The Ladykillers, No Country for Old Men* and *Burn After Reading*. Based on the widely held industry formula that a movie needs to gross three times its production budget to make anyone any money, only two qualify as hits. After winning a couple of Oscars, *Fargo* grossed $25 million off a $7 million budget.[1] And the Coens' 2008 Best Picture winner *No Country for Old Men* grossed $75 million off a $25 million production budget.

Several of their films have been box office bombs. Their biggest budget film, *Intolerable Cruelty*, was made for $60 million (thanks to over-the-line costs for star actors like George Clooney and Catherine Zeta-Jones) and grossed roughly half that amount. Though it starred one of Hollywood's most bankable stars, Tom Hanks, *The Ladykillers* also lost money. And the arch retooling of *Double Indemnity*, *The Man Who Wasn't There*, grossed a mere $7 million despite an ensemble cast including *The Sopranos'* James Gandolfini, Scarlet Johansson and Billy Bob Thornton. The key question with regard to the Coens is not so much how they've managed to stay *independent* for so long – whatever independence really means these days – but how for over two decades have they continued to find money to make movies at all?

Independent film, alternative film, has to be understood, as Chuck Kleinhans reminds us, as a relational term.[2] Certain films are made independent of, or provide an alternative to, what might be called the dominant Hollywood cinema. Independence is also a relative term; it is never *complete* so long as a feature is screened in commercial theatres or on pay or network TV, so long as the film is made available on video and laserdisk and DVD, so long as it has an MPAA rating classification.

Indie films, historically, have been defined by the two principal and intersecting characteristics of the movies as a medium. Such a definition regards specific matters of content (plot, style, a 'productive' relationship with the PCA, MPPDA, MPAA, CARA)[3] and cash, as it is made evident on screen, and as it regards the way a film is plat-formed or presented to the public. Two Hollywood adages are worth considering here. The first is a bastardisation of an H.L. Menken quip: 'When they say it's not about the money, it's about the money'. (Menken's line was about politics: 'When they say it's not about sex, it's about sex'. Menken was nothing if not prophetic.) The second Hollywoodism seems even more to the point here: 'You take the money, you lose control'. We have come to suspect that inde-pendence has something to do with a refusal to make concessions. But such a refusal is bottomed on the relative commercial incon-sequence of independent projects. Historians and filmgoers have come to look to independent film as the last refuge of auteurism ... films made with a signature style that would have been difficult to make in a studio industry committed to a collaborative, assembly-line mode of production.

Since the mid-1980s auteurism and independence in the new Hollywood have intersected in interesting ways. The Coens seem to provide a useful case study in this critical intersection. The two brothers produce, direct and write all their films. The amount of real control they exert over *their* films seems fairly extensive. Their ability to finance movies when most of the stuff they make flops at the box office suggests an auteurist project, a body of work assembled some-how independent of the profit motive. Is it, then, in the consistent commercial failure of their films that the term 'independent' is implied?

Thirteen films over twenty-five years, only two of which have made money, only one of which has made *real money* ... what is it about the Coen brothers that keeps them in the grid? gets them access to financing? keeps them interesting? Two possible answers, both tied more or less to the old-fashioned notion of the auteur. First, the stu-dios know what to expect from the Coens. The two brothers have, in the old-fashioned auteurist sense of the term, a signature style. Second, they have, to borrow a term coined by the film scholar Tim Corrigan, successfully exploited the 'commerce of auteurism'.[4] They have been able, despite the box office numbers, to maintain a sort of auteur-celebrity. And that auteur-celebrity ensures a connection of sorts to a young(er) generation of filmgoers who can be targeted in the short term and are coveted for the long term health of the industry.

The Coen brothers 'burst upon the scene' in 1984 with their first film, *Blood Simple*. It premiered at the New York Film Festival where audiences 'cheered themselves hoarse' – or so *Film Comment* columnist Elliot Stein reported at the time. The film's popularity was in Stein's view the result of a kind of knee-jerk anti-elitism. *Blood Simple* was 'considerably less rarefied' than the other titles on the festival programme and the cheering crowd mistook genius for simple difference. The Coen brothers' film, Stein concluded, was unlike the rest of the festival fare because it wasn't (good enough to be) a festival film.

Stein focused on the young auteurs' signature, over-the-top visual style: 'Boy do the Coen brothers have style. Amplified chunks of face are shoved up close to our dumbstruck gaze, prosaic household objects are given the fisheye and magically attain ominous connotations that don't mean anything in particular … Most of this *vacant virtuosity* is what the American screen can't get enough of and emphatically doesn't need'.[5] What Stein failed to acknowledge was that the Coen brothers' 'virtuosity' was in and of itself a significant accomplishment given the film's tiny budget and the brothers' relative inexperience. A second, related problem for Stein was the art house audiences' willingness, even anxiousness, to be *entertained*. What makes the Coen brothers so important in contemporary American cinema is their insistence that an independent film need not be high-brow, need not take itself so seriously, need not require any real sophistication to appreciate and understand. Indie films can be fun.

Stein's fears concerning the impact of *Blood Simple* were soon realised as more widely read critics celebrated the film and its auteurs. Richard Corliss, writing for *Time*, wrote: '*Blood Simple* (the title comes from Dashiell Hammett) works tense, elegant variations on a theme as old as the fall; it subverts the film noir genre in order to revitalize it; it offers the satisfactions and surprises of a conniving visual style. Most important, it displays the whirligig wit of two young men … in a debut film as scarifyingly assured as any since Orson Welles was just this wide'.[6] David Ansen, writing for *Newsweek*, was no less enthusiastic. He described the film as 'at once a bated breath thriller and a comedy as black as they come – the most inventive and original thriller in many a moon'.[7]

Writing after the *Time* and *Newsweek* reviews hit the newsstands, the *New Yorker*'s Pauline Kael, who by this point in time was using her 'Current Cinema' column to lament the state of post-auteur renaissance Hollywood, joined Stein in savaging *Blood Simple*, blasting the critics who mistook the film for real art. *Blood Simple* 'is so derivative, it isn't a thriller', she wrote, 'it's a crude ghoulish comedy on thriller scenes'. Kael described *Blood Simple* as 'a splatter art movie', a quip that accurately calls attention to the Coens' roots in 1960s exploitation films. In conclusion, Kael, like Stein, damned the Coens for their stylistic audacity, which, she argued, served a small and stupid narrative: 'What is at work here is [nothing more than] a visually sophisticated form of gross out humor'.

Kael's objections to the film spoke to larger concerns about 'third generation auteurs'. Coppola, Altman and Scorsese spearheaded the first wave and their films, according to Kael's scheme, were mostly terrific and original and modernist. The second generation was led by Spielberg and Lucas who crassly traded on their talent in service of simple and simplistic Hollywood entertainment and pretty much subverted the success of the first wave. The third generation (of which the Coens are a part) had less talent than the first two. These young auteurs possessed an encyclopedic knowledge of cinema and TV but little practical or experiential knowledge of anything else. These *post-modern* filmmakers, Kael opined, pointlessly shattered genre categories. They made films composed of allusions not images or themes or plots. Their films were ahistorical and ironic; in-jokes for a new in-crowd. 'What's the glory of making films outside the industry', Kael mused, 'if they're Hollywood films at heart?'[8]

Part II: Fishmongers and big men in tights: A quick look at the Coen Brothers' films

There are two keys to all the films: pace and critical distance. *Blood Simple* is dead slow – a complete reversal on the hectic, urban noir universe. Much the same can be said about *Barton Fink*, *Miller's Crossing*, *Fargo*, *The Man Who Wasn't There* and *No Country for Old Men*. *Hudsucker Proxy* and *Intolerable Cruelty* are fast like the screwball films they ape. *The Ladykillers*, a remake of the 1955 Alexander Mackendrick comedy, released with the tagline 'The Most Befuddled Set of Assorted Thugs That Ever Fouled Up a Million Dollar Bank Robbery', and *O Brother Where Art Thou*, which riffs on Preston Sturges's 1941 Hollywood farce *Sullivan's Travels* and Homer's *Odyssey* are manic to such an extent that their recycled plots seem wholly secondary to the slapstick. The two more or less original comedies *Raising Arizona* and *The Big Lebowski* are similarly manic and irreverent.

Though the auteurs themselves are university educated sons of college professors, their films are all about stupid people. One needn't worry about the Coens 'killing all their darlings'. They're all too willing to see any and all of their characters suffer through most anything for a laugh, for a cool image, for a gross-out effect. In her review of *Blood Simple*, Pauline Kael found a formal explanation for this critical distance. '[*Blood Simple*] has the pattern of farce', Kael wrote, 'a bedroom farce except that the people sneaking into each other's homes have vicious rather than amorous intentions'.[9] Such a subtle tweaking of genre has become the Coen brothers' distinct auteur signature and the basis for their claims to authorial independence. Their tendency to find farcical the very sort of everyday idiocy and violence of American culture that other more mainstream directors glorify or at the very least sensationalise forms the foundation of an original social commentary – a commentary that emerges despite the pervasive irony and the filmmakers' cheeky games with style.

The mostly hapless characters in the Coen brothers' films find themselves in familiar genre predicaments but react in crazy, stupid ways. Ray finds Marty's 'corpse' in the café office in *Blood Simple* and tries to clean up the crime scene. He succeeds only in making a bigger mess, spreading Marty's blood onto every surface in the room. Then, like so many other characters in Coen brothers' films, Ray comically botches an attempt to dispose of the body. The Snoats brothers in *Raising Arizona* stumble through a bank-robbery, then leave behind the baby they've kidnapped for ransom. Norville Barnes, the proxy in *Hudsucker Proxy*, is a dupe and a moron from Muncie! The film borrows liberally from *Meet John Doe*: the promise of a holiday suicide, the exploitation of an innocent by a 'dame from the newspaper'. Tim Robbins (who plays Norville) is tall enough for the Gary Cooper role in the Capra film, but seems instead modelled on another 1940s' dupe, the dimwitted Dick Powell character in Preston Sturges's *Christmas in July*. And then there's Jerry in *Fargo*, whose plot to change the life he has and deserves (as a wimp and a moron) ends much as all such plots launched by characters in the Coen brothers' films end: in butchered bodies and wrecked cars. He resorts to crime (the kidnapping for ransom of his own wife) because his plan to get out of an embezzlement mess – to build a parking lot – goes awry. There are at least four scenes set in parking lots in the film. All four are important set pieces that feature hundreds of empty parking spaces.

In *The Big Lebowski*, there are the so-called nihilist kidnappers (who are neither nihilist nor are they kidnappers) and the ill-fated Donnie who is told to 'shut the fuck up' all film long and for good reason. When Walter and the Dude locate the Dude's car (and the million dollars supposedly tucked in a briefcase on the back seat), Donnie points out that the car-thief's house is near a hamburger joint he really likes. They both tell Donnie to 'shut the fuck up' because he is missing the gravity of the situation: the $1 million in lost cash has suddenly been found. But the joke doesn't end there. All three men sit through a ridiculous one-man dance recital given by the Dude's landlord before they exit to retrieve the money. By that point, they're hungry and, as Donnie suggested, decide to stop for burgers on the way. Near the end of the film, Donnie dies in a parking lot confrontation that has nothing to do with him or the one thing he seems to care about, bowling. Bowling may be on the rise again here in the U.S., but what, the Coen brothers ask, do we really think about men who bowl and take it seriously? The focus on stupid people doing stupid things enables the Coen brothers to tweak genre formula. In *Burn after Reading*, for example, they undermine the traditionally earnest political intrigue by involving members of the national security apparatus (NSA, CIA, FBI, and U.S. Marshals office) in a plot hatched by the hapless employees at a second rate gym. The film hinges less on national security than on private fantasy: the government workers are busy sleeping with each others' spouses (without much in the way of practical gain or pleasure). And the gym employee behind the whole operation, one Linda Litzke (played by Coen veteran Frances McDormand), is willing to engage in blackmail, breaking and entering, theft, even murder in order to get the elective cosmetic surgery her insurance company has refused to cover. In the Coens' peculiar universe, Linda is the inevitable domestic terrorist.

The Coen brothers are especially unkind to people like themselves: upper-mid-westerners and Jews. Like David Lynch, who grew up for a time in Montana and then bitterly satirised small town mean-spiritedness and dimwittedness in *Twin Peaks* and *Blue Velvet*, the Coens use 'place' evocatively and satirically. The Coens were brought up in Minnesota, a place they describe as a 'bleak windswept tundra, resembling Siberia except for its Ford dealerships and Hardees restaurants'.[10] The simple folk who stumble their way through the complex plot of *Fargo* speak in a dialect and at a pace that seems not only foreign but other-wordly. The film is populated by stupid people who are stupid simply because they live in the upper-mid-west. The Coens make similar use of rural Texas; empty landscapes for people with empty heads. The screenplay for *Blood Simple* opens with a single sentence to set the scene: 'An opening voice-over plays against dissolving Texas landscapes – broad, bare, and lifeless'. *No Country for Old Men*, released over two decades later, blithely repeats the insult.

As to the Jewish question, a more worrisome self-loathing emerges. First and foremost there's *Barton Fink*, a film that offers caustic stereotypes of a Jewish commie-artiste (Barton), a lunatic Jewish studio boss named Lipnick, who introduces himself as 'bigger and meaner than any other kike in this town', and a motor mouthed Jewish studio producer. Recall that *Barton Fink* won the Grand Prix at Cannes. An American film with anti-Semitic caricatures in France! ... Need I say more?

Two other prominent Jewish characters appear in Coen brothers films. Bernie Birnbaum, 'the Shmata kid' in *Miller's Crossing*, is, we're told, 'ethically kinda shaky'. Bernie's a *player* with loyalty to no one except himself. And then there's Walter in *The Big Lebowski*, a recent convert who has taken to Judaism with a seriousness that makes no sense to the Dude or, apparently, to the Coens. When the Dude asks Walter to drive on the Sabbath, Walter contemplates the notion of transgressing '3,000 years of beautiful tradition from Moses to Sandy Koufax'. What, we might ask here, isn't a joke to the Coens?

The flesh is weak in these films, but sex is seldom at issue. Even the films that are loosely about sex or sexual relations – *Intolerable Cruelty* and *Burn after Reading* – connect sex not to pleasure but to humiliation. The bodily functions that seem to interest the Coens most are those that involve convulsive vomiting or spurting blood. Marty throws up blood and food several times in *Blood Simple*. The writer Bill Mayhew (based on William Faulkner) is introduced in *Barton Fink* puking in the commissary bathroom. Charlie (whose ears ooze pus) throws up when he sees Audrey dead in Barton's hotel room (though we later discover that Charlie has killed her).

Bloody violence in the Coen brothers' films is pervasive and explicit. As Kael suggests, theirs is a 'splatter art cinema', an alternative film project rooted in exploitation genre pictures. We see a knife stabbed through the detective's hand (à la *Godfather*) in *Blood Simple*. *Raising Arizona* climaxes with a fifteen-minute fight between Hi and the Snoats – a fight that is capped when the bounty hunter Smalls is blown to bits. Casper murders the Dane with a fireplace shovel in *Miller's Crossing*. Walter bites off the ear of one of the nihilists in *The Big Lebowski*. And the stoic hired killer Anton Chigurh in *No Country for Old Men* fashions for himself an air-powered gun modelled on a device used to stun cattle before their throats are slit in the slaughter house. The Coens have little use for the clean kill.

Graphic violence is also a key element in the comedies. In *The Big Lebowski*, a film played entirely for laughs, the on-screen violence is so outrageous it's often funny. Two thugs burst into the Dude's apartment and find him in the bathtub. When the Dude can't answer their questions, they drop a marmot in the water. We watch and laugh and squirm. As Freud suggests – as is self-evident, really – things are funny when they happen to someone else.

Fargo goes the furthest into the splatter tradition and it is one of the two most profitable Coen brothers' films. One of the kidnappers, Gaer, shoots a cop in the face in the opening scene of the movie. Carl, Gaer's partner, is then shot in the face by Jerry's father-in-law. Near the end of the film, Gaer kills Carl and feeds his dead body into a wood chipper. There's a morbid (and often morbidly funny) preoccupation with the disposal of bodies: in *Fargo, Blood Simple, Barton Fink, Miller's Crossing, The Man Who Wasn't There* and *Burn After Reading* the plots turn on the success or failure to dispose of a body properly, completely, finally.

The Coen brothers use voice-over extensively in several of their films, including *Blood Simple, Raising Arizona, Hudsucker Proxy*, and *The Big Lebowski* – but mostly just to set things up. In all but one of the films mentioned above it's the voice of a minor, even tangential character, like the all-knowing Moses, who works in the bowels of the Hudsucker building in *Hudsucker Proxy*, or the cowpoke in *The Big Lebowski*. Unlike traditional first-person narration which invites the audience to feel close to a character (who speaks directly to us), these narrators stand in for the Coens, wryly observing the ridiculous behaviour of everyone else in the film.

Dream sequences abound, often to unsettling effect. Abby dreams that Marty is still alive in *Blood Simple*. Tom's dream of 'a foolish man chasing his hat' opens *Miller's Crossing* and foreshadows the film's final scene. Barton Fink hallucinates with disturbing regularity. At one point, while reading the *Book of Daniel*, he finds instead the key to his script about 'fishmongers and big men in tights'. Norville in *The Hudsucker Proxy* dreams up a romantic dance number. The set-piece is staged to accompany an aria from Bizet's *Carmen*. In *The Big Lebowski,* the Dude dreams he's flying above the city. Then, like Norville, he finds himself a performer in a Busby Berkeley-like production number. The Dude's dream – like so many of the dreams realised on screen by the brothers Coen – is framed by the movies.

The Coen brothers seem prepared to keep us at a distance from the action in their films, so much so that it is difficult to know what if anything should be taken seriously. The films are populated less by characters than by comic grotesques. The level of humour is often adolescent, but that is not to say that it isn't also funny. The best or worst of such grotesqueries can be found in *The Big Lebowski*, a film that has spawned a loyal cult following. There's the paedophile, bowling-ace Jesus, the scriptwriter in the iron lung, the German techo-nihilists, the crippled millionaire, the loopy cowpoke narrator. At a moment of understandable frustration in the film, the Dude tries to talk some sense to the performance artist Maud (who wants the Dude to father a child with her) and says: 'I'm sorry your stepmother is a nympho, but what's that got to do with me'. The remark is at once comical and revealing. It is comical because the Dude is accurately summarising (and satirising) Maud's motivation as a character. And it is revealing because it makes obvious the adolescent preoccupation of two brothers whose development, like that of so many filmmakers these days, has been arrested someplace in and at the movies.

Full disclosure: Like the Coen brothers, I too am a suburban Jewish white boy. Ethan is my age; Joel three years younger. So I am anxious to believe that the critical, ironic distance that pervades their films and speaks so keenly to my own sense of humour adds up to something more than just a refusal to leave adolescence, and the movies of our adolescence, behind. To that end, I defer to Devin McKinney and his revealing—albeit mostly negative—review of *Fargo*: 'The spin which the Coens give our expectation of and need for empathy amounts to an existential reversal, given that empathy as a literary idea is commonly understood as a unifying agent … At their most original, the Coens have exercised the darker, more difficult impulse to unite characters and audience not in the warmth of common affirmation [which I'd argue is the stuff of most mainstream films], but in the chill of common alienation'.[11] It is in this shared desire for irony over false sincerity, for messy innovation over some neater, slicker product, for alienation over some insultingly stupid happy ending that the Coen brothers' work has spoken so keenly to a lot of men and women of my generation. Their independence, then, seems less a matter of fact than a matter of critical position. They're not commercial or mainstream because they don't want to be. And for lots of folks of my generation, that's pretty cool.

Biography

Joel Coen was born in 1954 and Ethan Coen in 1957, both in Minnesota, USA.

Notes

1 *Fargo* won for the Coen brothers a Best Original Screenplay Oscar. Frances McDormand, who played Marge, the very pregnant police-woman who solves the case, won Best Actress.
2 Chuck Kleinhans, 'Independent Features: Hopes and Dreams', in *The New American Cinema*, edited by Jon Lewis (Durham, NC: Duke University Press, 1998), pp. 308–9.
3 A quick key to the acronyms: PCA stands for the Production Code Administration (which supervised, as in censored, production from 1930–68), MPPDA stands for the Motion Picture Producers and Distributors Association (the organisation which regulated the business of making films in the United States between the two world wars), MPAA stands for the Motion Pictures Association of America, which replaced the MPPDA after the Second World War (just in time to institute the blacklist) and CARA stands for the Code and Rating Association or Classification and Rating Association, which was formed by the MPAA in 1968 to implement a new film classification system (G, M, R and X – now G, PG, PG-13, R and NC-17).
4 See: Timothy Corrigan, *A Cinema Without Walls* (New Brunswick, NJ: Rutgers University Press, 1991), pp. 101–36.
5 Elliot Stein, 'New York Film Festival' (review), *Film Comment* 20 (November/December, 1984), p. 67.
6 Richard Corliss, 'Same Old Song', *Time*, January 28, 1985, p. 90.
7 David Ansen, 'The Coens: Partners in Crime', *Newsweek*, January 21, 1985, p. 74.
8 Pauline Kael, 'The Current Cinema', *The New Yorker*, February 25, 1985, pp. 81–3.
9 Pauline Kael, 'The Current Cinema', p. 81.
10 Ethan Coen and Joel Cohen, *Fargo*, (London: Faber and Faber, 1996), p. x.
11 Devin McKinney, *'Fargo'* (film review), *Film Quarterly,* Fall 1996, p. 34.

Filmography

Blood Simple (1985)
Raising Arizona (1987)
Miller's Crossing (1990)
Barton Fink (1991)
The Hudsucker Proxy (1994)
Fargo (1996)
The Big Lebowski (1998)
O Brother, Where Art Thou? (2000)
The Man Who Wasn't There (2001)
Intolerable Cruelty (2003)
The Ladykillers (2004)
No Country for Old Men (2007)
Burn After Reading (2008)

Further reading

William Rodney Allen, *The Coen Brothers: Interviews* (Jackson, MS, University Press of Mississippi, 2006).

Joel Coen and Ethan Coen, *Blood Simple*, London, St Martins Press, 1989.

——*Raising Arizona*, London, St Martins Press, 1989.

——*The Hudsucker Proxy*, London, Faber and Faber, 1994.

——*Barton Fink and Miller's Crossing*, London, Faber and Faber, 1995.

——*The Big Lebowski*, London, Faber and Faber, 1998.

Cathleen Falsani, *The Dude Abides: The Gospel According to the Coen Brothers* (Grand Rapids, MI, Zondervan, 2009).

Emmanuel Levy, *Cinema of Outsiders*, New York, New York University Press, 1999.

William Luhr, ed., *The Coen Brothers' Fargo* (Cambridge, Cambridge University Press, 2003).

R. Barton Palmer, 'Blood Simple: Defining the Commercial/Independent Text', *Persistence of Vision*, no. 6, 1988.

J.M. Tyree and Ben Walters, *The Big Lebowski* (London, BFI, 2008).

Paul Woods (ed.) *Blood Siblings*, New Jersey, Plexus Books, 2000.

SOFIA COPPOLA

By Pam Cook

Sofia Coppola is an actress, director, producer and screenwriter. She is the daughter of designer/documentarist Eleanor Coppola and film-making legend Francis Ford Coppola, one of the 'movie brats' who helped to change American cinema in the 1970s. The Coppola family dynasty is extensive,[1] forming a close-knit network whose members frequently collaborate with one another. These personal connections have played an important part in Sofia Coppola's creative develop-ment, and they continue to define her output. In particular, her father features strongly as mentor, and as producer and executive producer on her films through his company American Zoetrope, which nurtures new talent. These illustrious credentials have been both help and hindrance. On one hand, Sofia Coppola has benefited from exceptional levels of support and encouragement that many young filmmakers only dream of. On the other, her father's monu-mental reputation for landmark titles such as *The Godfather* trilogy (1972, 1974, 1990) and *Apocalypse Now* (1979) casts a long shadow, acting as a benchmark against which her own work is judged. In addition, the fact that she appears to enjoy preferential treatment has provoked disproportionate amounts of malice and envy from critics.

The 'family circle' as a model of production is interesting in the context of contemporary American cinema, where structural changes generated by the formation of global media conglomerates and the rise of the mini-majors in the 1990s resulted in the proliferation of different kinds and degrees of independence, opening up a space at the edges of the mainstream known as 'Indiewood'.[2] Since *Lost in Translation*, Sofia Coppola's feature films have received financial backing from independent production companies such as American Zoetrope, mini-majors such as Focus Features and major studios such as Columbia Pictures, with involvement from Japanese company Tohokushinsha Film. The Coppola family nexus is one of a series of interlocking production operations at varying distances from the mainstream. Arguably, this enables Sofia Coppola to enjoy a high level of artistic autonomy while taking advantage of studio marketing and distribution. Equally, her position in what might be seen as a de-centred production context has an impact on her style and choice of projects.

Sofia Coppola began her film career as an actress, with an uncredited appearance as the baby boy in the baptism sequence of *The Godfather*. Throughout the 1970s and 1980s she took small parts in a number of her father's films and acted occasionally in television. In 1989 she co-scripted and worked on costumes for Francis Ford Coppola's segment of New York Stories, 'Life Without Zoe'. Then in 1990 she replaced Winona Ryder as Mary Corleone in *The Godfather Part III*. The unnecessarily hostile response to her performance led her to try out different directions; she attended the Cal Arts Fine Art program, studied photography for a while, co-hosted a short-lived television magazine show (Hi Octane, 1994) with friend Zoe Cassavetes, appeared in cameo roles in music videos and set up a successful clothing company called Milk Fed in Japan with another close friend, Stephanie Hayman. In 1996 she co-directed the 28-minute comedy short *Bed, Bath and Beyond*, which was shot on video. Coppola and Hayman co-wrote *Lick the Star*, a 14-minute 16mm black-and-white film set in the clique-ridden high-school world. Coppola's solo directorial debut, which she also co-produced, aired on Bravo and the Independent Film Channel in the United States. It brought together her interests in fashion, popular music and generational conflict and contained many of the ideas explored in the later features. The alienation of the young heroine was visualised in a travelling shot of her looking out of the window of her parents' car, an image that recurs in *The Virgin Suicides*, *Lost in Translation* and *Marie Antoinette*. A high shot of the teenage girls lying on the ground in a star, or wheel, formation was repeated in *The Virgin Suicides*. *Lick the Star* was influenced by the controversial novel *Flowers in the Attic*, which was at the centre of the story and inspired the poisoning plot. Like the novel, Coppola's film used first-person narration to provide a child's perspective on events. *Flowers in the Attic* was a Gothic tale of children abandoned, abused and poisoned; *Lick the Star*, which revolved around the amoral cruelty of an elite group of girls, was similarly disturbing in its depiction of the murderous fantasies lurking beneath the surface of American high-school life. The ostracisation of the group's leader by fellow students led to her suicide attempt, and her journal was pointedly named 'An American Biography'.

Lick the Star was a stylish, confident achievement that paved the way for Coppola's first feature, *The Virgin Suicides*. Both films were dominated by dark themes of youthful alienation, obsession, senseless cruelty and death, preoccupations that have been traced to the traumatic effect on Coppola of the 1986 speedboat accident in which her beloved elder brother Gian-Carlo was killed. She has acknowledged that life events have a significant impact on her work, and this has become an important factor in building her profile as an intensely personal auteur. *The Virgin Suicides* was adapted by Coppola from the novel by Jeffrey Eugenides, which was set in the 1970s and used first-person plural narration to tell the story from the perspective of a group of adolescent boys, now adults, who became obsessed with the inexplicable suicides of five teenage sisters from a strict Catholic family. Coppola employed first-person voice-over by one of the boys to relate the story and the unsuccessful attempts by the suburban community to piece together the reasons for the girls' actions. The visual style had a hazy, dream-like quality that subtly transmitted the surface beauty of the sisters and their apparently idyllic lives, conjuring up a lost past that remained impenetrable, as the male characters sifted through the girls' intimate possessions for clues. These relics, far from providing the truth, were fetish-objects that resisted interpretation. A gulf of incomprehension opened up between peer groups and generations that revealed the emptiness and despair at the heart of American family and community life. The soundtrack, a mix of 1970s and 1990s popular music, underscored the aura of emotional angst. The bleakness and nihilism of the film's vision of conventional society, and the tentative attempts of the protagonists to make connections, were also features of Coppola's next two projects. In light of the importance in her own life of strong family bonds, the pessimism underlying the depiction of family and community in *The Virgin Suicides* was intriguing. The deceptive nature of surface reality and social ritual became a key theme for Coppola, perhaps indicating an awareness of the ephemeral quality of existence.

Coppola's first feature was well received by the press, and was nominated for a host of awards, among them the Young Hollywood best director, MTV best new filmmaker, the Las Vegas Film Critics Society best director, best female newcomer and best adapted screenplay, and Empire (UK) best debut.[3] She followed it up with a comedy that she wrote, produced and directed, set in Tokyo and starring Bill Murray as an aging movie star commissioned to film a whiskey commercial, with Scarlett Johansson as the young wife Charlotte accompanying her photographer husband on a celebrity photo-shoot. From the start, Coppola was intent on persuading Murray to play Bob Harris, declaring that without him the film would not get made. The notoriously difficult actor was evasive, and it was only due to extreme persistence on the part of the director that he eventually agreed. This episode is often used to indicate the tenacity that lies behind Coppola's ultra-feminine exterior. The title *Lost in Translation* evoked the emotional and psychological anomie of the American protagonists, adrift in an alien culture that they failed to understand. Their situation was the basis for some hilarious comic set-pieces in which insurmountable obstacles of language and social differences led to farcical outcomes. The absurdity of these sequences was set against the genuine loneliness of the lead characters, trapped in unhappy marriages and drawn together by their sense of being at the mercy of events. Despite the proliferation of Japanese stereotypes, it was the Americans who were the main targets of the comedy, and it was their inability to connect with the world outside themselves that was thrown into relief by the cross-cultural drama. Although Bob and Charlotte were the focus of audience empathy, they both had unsympathetic qualities of narcissism, elitism and isolationism that were at the root of their alienation. Their sense of detachment, which preceded their encounter with Tokyo, was part of their national identity and could be seen as a comment by Coppola on American culture. Their budding romance may have enabled them to find temporary solace; certainly Coppola's treatment of their separation and farewell seemed to see their brief liaison as having a positive effect on their lives. But it also suggested loss and resignation; indeed, the open-ended narrative offered little in the way of resolution or indication of what might happen next.

The episodic, inconclusive storyline and passive protagonists of *Lost in Translation* were closer to European art cinema than to mainstream Hollywood. From the 1960s Hollywood was increasingly influenced by art-cinema aesthetics, particularly in the independent sector, where formal devices and themes emerged that transformed classical norms. The enigmatic narratives and aimless characters of European art cinema were incorporated into Hollywood movies, producing films whose meandering plots and unfulfilled quests expressed a sense of national disillusionment. European art cinema also depended on the presence of auteurs whose personal vision shaped their body of work, which was seen as a coherent whole. In the context of contemporary global media production, the European-style auteur has become progressively important as a way of branding a filmmaker's oeuvre as art, giving it a recognisable niche identity that can be used in promotional campaigns. Coppola is clearly aware of the significance of this strategy; she has frequently acknowledged the influence of art-cinema aesthetics on her work, and has compared it to the Nouvelle Vague.[4] She insists on creative autonomy and emphasises the personal nature of her films as part of her auteurist credentials. She also has strong European connections; she lives in Paris with her partner Thomas Mars, a member of the French rock band Phoenix, and their daughter Romy. Coppola's affinities with European art cinema are demonstrated by her reliance on the ambiguity of the image, which is deployed for its formal and affective qualities rather than as the repository of truth and meaning; by her focus on ambivalent characters who are often morally flawed; and by her use of an equivocal style that refuses to allow the viewer a settled position from which to understand the film. Her work has an elusive quality that is also a feature of her directorial persona, which is perceived as low-key and relaxed in comparison with that of her ebullient father.[5]

Coppola's laid-back image adds to the aura of 'cool' that surrounds her, which is consolidated by her celebrity status as fashion icon.[6] Her life and films are regularly covered in style magazines such as *Vogue*, *Vanity Fair* and *Dazed and Confused*. She is associated with a new creative elite that spans areas of popular culture such as fashion, music, art and film, enabling commercial tie-ins in a range of media sites. In contemporary cinema, 'Hollywood' as a centre has given way to a conglomerate culture comprising diverse interrelated operations that feed one another, so that it has become difficult to consider any single element in isolation. Coppola's work and persona have emerged from this de-centred context, and almost seem to embody it. Her filmmaking technique oscillates between the observational distance and 'let's see what happens now' ethos of cinéma vérité, the intimacy of home movies, and highly stylised collages of images and music. The fragmented feel of *The Virgin Suicides*, *Lost in Translation* and *Marie*

Antoinette suggests an incomplete serial oeuvre motivated more by the director's personal creative journey than by narrative or genre constraints. This impression is reinforced by Coppola's habit of leaving sentences unfinished in interviews, which has become something of a trademark.[7] The close connections between her life, persona and films are essential to the fabrication of the Sofia Coppola brand that operates across different media to promote her work and, crucially, to give it a distinctive identity. This identity is directly, and deliberately, opposed to that of patriarch Francis Ford Coppola. The construction of Sofia Coppola's 'feminine' image is based on seemingly irreconcilable contradictions between passive and active; dilettantism and determination; trivial pursuits and serious intent; fragility and toughness; effortlessness and drive; and naturalness and artifice. This multifaceted persona matches the diversity of her activities as filmmaker, music video and commercials director,[8] photographer, actress, fashion model and costume designer.

The critical acclaim for *Lost in Translation* established Coppola's artistic credentials and consolidated her international celebrity status. The film picked up a plethora of prestigious award nominations, including Golden Globes for best picture, best screenplay and best director, and Independent Spirit awards for best director, best feature and best screenplay.[9] In 2004 Coppola became the first American woman to be nominated for an Academy Award as best director.[10] She was also nominated as co-producer for best picture, and she won the award for best original screenplay. As a result of these accolades she was invited to join the Academy of Motion Picture Arts and Sciences and was hailed as one of Hollywood's most powerful women. Her next project was an ambitious costume drama about the early life of Marie Antoinette, inspired by Antonia Fraser's sympathetic biography of the teenage Austrian princess who married into the French royal family in the run-up to the Revolution and became the subject of malicious hate campaigns. Coppola crafted a highly personal film in her idiosyncratic, impressionistic style, presenting historical events from the subjective perspective of the naive young heroine, played by Kirsten Dunst, who was completely out of her depth among the hierarchical rituals and vicious gossip machinery of the Versailles court. The production's elegant, lush visual design was deliberately anachronistic, to the extent of including a modern-day trainer among the array of exquisite Manolo Blahnik-devised period shoes worn by Marie Antoinette and her friends. The soundtrack was compiled from strident post-punk and New Romantic songs with a sprinkling of classical music, and there were disruptive moments of travesty, as when a crude portrait of the queen daubed with the slogan 'Queen of Deficit' appeared onscreen. Coppola depicted Marie Antoinette as a misunderstood figure who sought escape from her isolation and unhappiness in fashion, music and theatre, creating herself as celebrity icon. The young queen's grisly demise on the guillotine was held at bay, with the film ending on an elegiac note as Marie Antoinette and her family fled Versailles to escape the advancing revolutionaries. *Marie Antoinette* featured many of the motifs of the earlier films, and was a characteristically adventurous, off-kilter work. However, not everyone appreciated Coppola's playful approach to her subject, and critics were sharply divided.

Despite the controversy surrounding *Marie Antoinette*, it was entirely consistent with Coppola's auteurist concerns. Echoing the experiences of the film's heroine, Coppola has forged a distinctive identity and personal style that refuses to conform to expectations of how powerful Hollywood filmmakers, male or female, should behave. The challenge she presents to the male-dominated industry is not aggressively confrontational; rather, through its very femininity it undermines the authoritarian ethos and hierarchical working practices of Hollywood, conjuring up a very different model of creativity from that of the overbearing male genius.[11] With *Marie Antoinette*, the trilogy of works that centred on drifting protagonists in search of fulfillment came to an end. Rumors that Coppola's next project would be an adaptation of Sarah Waters's lesbian novel *Tipping the Velvet* were unfounded; she is currently writing, producing and directing a comedy titled *Somewhere*, set in Hollywood, about a hell-raising actor who is forced to re-examine his life after a surprise visit from his 11-year-old daughter. It will be produced by American Zoetrope, with involvement from Focus Features, French company Pathé and Tohokushinsha Film.[12]

Biography

Born 14 May 1971, Sofia Coppola is an actress, director, producer and screenwriter.

Notes

1 See 'Coppola family tree' in Wikipedia, The Free Encyclopedia: <http://en.wikipedia.org/w/index.php?title=Coppola_family_tree&oldid=292245871>. Accessed 26 May 2009.
2 See Geoff King, *Indiewood USA: Where Hollywood Meets Independent Cinema*, London, I. B. Tauris, 2009.

3 Full awards history available on the ImDb The Virgin Suicides entry at: <http://www.imdb.com/>. Accessed 27 May 2009.

4 See for example Sean O'Hagan, 'Sofia Coppola', *Observer* 8 October 2006, Features section, p. 5. Available online at: <http://www.guardian.co.uk/film/2006/oct/08/features.review1>. Accessed 28 May 2009.

5 See Evgenia Peretz, 'Something about Sofia', *Vanity Fair* September 2006, p. 237.

6 Coppola is credited with being the inspiration for fashion designer Marc Jacobs, who used her as the face of one of his fragrances and named a handbag after her. He is also a close friend.

7 See Peretz, 'Something about Sofia', p. 184.

8 In 2008 Coppola directed a commercial for Dior's Miss Dior Chérie fragrance. For a list of music videos directed by Coppola, see 'Sofia Coppola' page in Wikipedia, The Free Encyclopedia: <http://en.wikipedia.org/w/index.php?title=Sofia_Coppola&oldid=292851490>. Accessed 28 May 2009.

9 Full awards history available on the ImDb Lost in Translation entry at: <http://www.imdb.com/>. Accessed 28 May 2009.

10 Only two women besides Coppola have been nominated for the best director Academy Award: Jane Campion and Lina Wertmuller.

11 See Lynn Hirschberg, 'The Coppola smart mob', *New York Times Magazine* 31 August 2003, available online at: <http://www.nytimes.com/2003/08/31/magazine/31COPPOLA.html?pagewanted=1>. Accessed 28 May 2009.

12 See company details for Somewhere on IMDB: <http://www.imdb.com/>. Accessed 31 May 2009.

Filmography

Bed, Bath and Beyond (1996) short, co-director
Lick the Star (1998) short film
The Virgin Suicides (1999)
Lost in Translation (2003)
Marie Antoinette (2006)

Further reading

Pam Cook, 'Portrait of a Lady: Sofia Coppola', *Sight and Sound* 16 (11), November 2006, pp. 36–40.

Wendy Haslem, 'Neon Gothic: *Lost in Translation*', *Senses of Cinema* no. 31, April–June 2004. Available online at: <http://archive.sensesofcinema.com/contents/04/31/lost_in_translation.html>. Accessed 31 May 2009.

Anna Rogers, 'Sofia Coppola', *Senses of Cinema* no. 45, October–December 2007. Available online at: <http://archive.sensesofcinema.com/contents/archive/index.html>. Accessed 31 May 2009.

Sharon Lin Tay, *Women on the Edge: Twelve Political Film Practices*, London: Palgrave, 2009.

DAVID CRONENBERG

By Marc O'Day

Canadian director David Cronenberg is the most controversial auteur to emerge from the post-1968 horror/science fiction boom. Belonging to a generation of maverick outsiders who made their names in low-budget horror (George Romero, Wes Craven, John Carpenter), he has sustained and developed his career to the point where he is now securely regarded as a major contemporary auteur. A mild, conformist family man in person, he has never entirely thrown off the lurid reputation of Dave 'Deprave' Cronenberg, the 'King of Venereal Horror' and the 'Baron of Blood', which was quickly established with his early shockers *Shivers*, *Rabid*, *The Brood*, *Scanners* and *Videodrome*. Subsequently he branched out in other directions, including more commercial productions such as *The Dead Zone*, *The Fly*, *A History of Violence* and, to an extent, *Eastern Promises*, and the more openly arty and character-centred adaptations *Dead Ringers*, *Naked Lunch*, *M. Butterfly*, *Crash* and *Spider*. While some of these films downplay body horror in favour of aesthetic and psychological contemplation, they are still examples of nightmare cinema, the out of genre horror movie which first came to prominence in the 1980s.[1] In fact, for all their visceral gore, the early films are also intellectual and experimental and the later ones still often include a bodily gross-out factor; and without doubt Cronenberg's *œuvre* reveals remarkable continuities.

One reason for this is that Cronenberg is an author as well as an auteur: initially he penned original screenplays and from the mid-1980s he adapted from pre-existing sources (sometimes in partnership). Since *eXistenZ*, however, his most recent screenplay to date, he has relied on others to adapt or produce scripts for his films. He is steeped in literature and philosophy, from Nabokov and Burroughs to Nietzsche and Wittgenstein. He wrote his first, three-page 'novel' at the age of 10, won a short story prize as a college freshman, and intended to become a novelist until he discovered the magic of film through the work of his University of Toronto student peer David Sector. For much of his work he has been able to exercise total control over his projects, while it has sometimes been the case that films which he had little or no hand in writing – for example, *Fast Company*, *The Dead Zone* and *M. Butterfly* – have (rightly or wrongly) been labelled 'unCronenbergian'.

A second reason is the clinical gaze which informs the look and style of Cronenberg's films. This may partly stem from his lifelong passion for science in general and biochemistry in particular. No doubt mischievously, Cronenberg has identified himself with the bespectacled Mantle twins in the early scenes of *Dead Ringers*, whose childlike yet ultimately lethal fascination with the mysteries of sex, reproduction and the human (especially female) body is dramatised by their early experiment in 'inter-ovular surgery'. He began studying biochemistry at university before switching to English because he found his tutors' academic approach too dull. He is a scientist-artist, whose work has repeatedly been viewed as cool and detached, favouring deadpan acting, distancing the spectator and refusing the consolations of identification. Such apparent coldness and aloofness have sometimes been equated with a reifying and pornographic consciousness, seen as analogous to scientific method. Yet equally discernible in the films is a range of emotions, from icy fury (*The Brood*) and black comedy (*Shivers*) to restrained celebration (*A History of Violence*) and accessible sentimentality (*The Fly*). Promoting *Crash*, Cronenberg expressed his surprise that for him it had become a very emotional movie.

Writing and the clinical/emotional gaze fuse in Cronenberg's conception of cinema as a hotline to the contemporary patriarchal unconscious. As Michael O'Pray[2] and others have argued, his films give symbolic and narrative shape to primitive unconscious fantasies and fears, centring on the human subject as a traumatised body and/or mind, playing out horror's pervasive themes of separation, ageing, disease, violence, invasion, decay and death in a series of metaphors which detail grotesque and abject bodily and psychic mutation. Whilst feminist critics have produced some of the very best Cronenberg criticism (see below), they have also attacked his work for its hostility towards women, and it is certainly the case that patriarchal fantasies and anxieties surrounding gender difference provide its symbolic foundation (as they do for much of the horror genre and mainstream cinema more generally). Nevertheless, it can be argued that they are as critical of as they are collusive with the issues of male desire and control they exhibit, and that although men and masculine-coded institutions are the source of the mutations in the movies, the effects on individuals' bodies and psyches increasingly centre on male transformation, often through a problematic feminisation of male characters and increasingly with attention to homosexual as much as heterosexual desire (albeit marked by repression and homophobia which might be claimed to complement the work's alleged misogyny). Perhaps Cronenberg's films should come with the health warning: 'caution: men and the patriarchal unconscious at work'.

Critics from Robin Wood to Jonathan Crane[3] have noticed that a generative formula underlies Cronenberg's screenplays, based on the trope of the mad scientist drawn from *Frankenstein*: a male scientist (usually with a bizarre name), often located in a formal institution (also with a bizarre name), invents something which is of potential benefit to humanity but turns out to have disastrous consequences. This formula fits a remarkable number of the films, from the early shorts *Stereo* and *Crimes of the Future* right up to *eXistenZ*. Thus in Cronenberg's debut feature *Shivers* aphrodisiac parasites, invented by Dr Emil Hobbes (Fred Doederlin) and shaped like penile turds, pass between the denizens of a luxury high-rise block, turning them into rapacious Romero-like zombies who gleefully embody the polymorphous perverse. The fictional Starliner Towers apartment complex (in reality just outside Montreal) is an alienated bourgeois space awaiting (deserving?) sexual apocalypse. The relentless narrative begins with Hobbes assaulting, cutting open and pouring acid into the belly of the young woman in whom he has implanted the parasite, before slitting his own throat. If the film's most memorable instants (for a heterosexual male spectator?) centre on women's bodies – the parasite swimming between Betts' (Barbara Steele) legs, or passing up her oesophagus and down Janine Tudor's (Susan Petrie) in a hedonistic moment of seduction – it is nevertheless male birth images played through the body of Janine's husband, Nick (Allan Migicovsky), which are most consistently developed. Bugs move about under his stomach and ooze disgustingly from his mouth, mutant offspring which (or is it whom?) he addresses affectionately: 'Come on boy! Come on fella! You and me are going to be good friends'. This is Cronenberg's philosophy entirely.

Men's anxiety and envy concerning women's reproductive powers motivate Cronenberg's best movies to date, *The Brood*, *The Fly* and *Dead Ringers*, which may be termed the 'Womb Trilogy'. As Barbara Creed and Helen W. Robbins have demonstrated, these films offer elaborate womb fantasies, manifesting both horror at women's power to create life and male attempts to destroy, emulate or control it: indeed, this is arguably the power, possessed in religious discourse by God and in aesthetics by the Artist, which all Cronenberg's mad scientists seek to acquire.[4] *The Brood* is family horror set in and around a bleak, wintry Toronto: its images seem cold enough to freeze and cut. The mad scientist is Dr Hal Raglan (Oliver Reed), head of the Somafree Institute of Psychoplasmics, where residents learn to externalise their psychic traumas on their own bodies. His star patient, Nola Carveth (Samantha Eggar), was abused as a child and is estranged from her husband Frank (Art Hindle), who determines to gain custody of their young daughter Candy (Cindy Hinds) when she returns from a visit to her mother covered in bruises. Howard Shore's dissonant music underscores the brutal murders of those against whom Nola has grievances – including, eventually, Raglan himself – by the Brood, snow-suit-clad 'children' with an uncanny resemblance to Candy (and to the killer dwarf in Roeg's *Don't Look Now*, 1973). The climax reveals, in an abject spectacle witnessed by Frank, that the Brood are mutants born from a literally hysterical womb on the outside of Nola's body. The sight of Nola, kneeling in hieratic white robes, biting open the sac and licking her latest 'child' clean, is another landmark in visceral cinema (one trimmed by the censor), not least because of its close proximity to the mess of natural birth. Written during his own marital break-up and child custody battle, Cronenberg has called *The Brood* his *Kramer versus Kramer* and acknowledged the rage ('the brood') at its heart as his own.

In *The Fly* and *Dead Ringers* too the scientists die – but the women survive. *The Fly*, made on a (by Cronenberg's standards huge) budget of US$10 million, remains his most popular film to date (although *A History of Violence* also has a considerable following). Casting relatively big name stars, Jeff Goldblum and Geena Davis (then romantically involved), in the roles of techno-magician Seth Brundle and science journalist Veronica 'Ronny' Quaife, it combines gross-out horror with a moving love triangle melodrama (the third is Ronny's ex-lover magazine boss Stathis Borans [John Getz]). Inventor of a womb-like 'designer phone booth' which can transfer matter, at the outset Seth can only teleport inanimate objects (Ronnie's erotically charged stocking) but when he learns about 'the flesh', he is able to teleport first a baboon and then, in a fit of drunken pique when he thinks that Ronnie has abandoned him for Borans, himself, along with a common housefly with which he becomes genetically spliced. Cue an affecting mutation from charming, naïve geek to repulsive hybrid species, which may be interpreted as a metaphor for AIDS, BSE or other diseases, but which literally (from Ronnie's perspective) shows your loved one ageing rapidly and horribly as you look on helplessly. Seth's hubris infects Ronnie too; in his sexual athlete phase he impregnates her, and the nightmare sequence in which she is delivered of a hideous maggot by none other than the director himself – in due acknowledgement of his own art as a case of rampant womb envy? – is a shocking monstrous birth fantasy. *The Fly* is moving because horror iconography serves and develops the tragic love story, as when Brundlefly resembles the Hunchback of Notre Dame claiming his Esmerelda, or (having fused with his own creation, the telepod), in his final, terrible mutant form he pleads for release with still-soulful eyes.

Dead Ringers, for many Cronenberg's masterpiece to date (it won a Genie Award for Best Film and Screenplay and the Los Angeles Film Critic's Award for Best Director), is womb envy cinema *par excellence*. Its sombre tragic narrative charts, through obsessively controlled *mise-en-scène* and pacing, the decline of identical gynaecologist twins Elliot and Beverly Mantle (both played by Jeremy Irons). Specialising in female fertility, the Mantles are fascinated by 'trifurcate' actress Claire Niveau (Genevieve Bujold), a 'mutant' woman who destabilises their lives when she threatens to separate them, since she is the first thing which they have not been able to share fully. They are, it seems, two bodies with one soul: the film's most explicit horror sequence depicts them organically joined at the abdomen like Siamese twins, with Claire biting through the tissue. The film's melancholy chronicle of control and loss is traced by the transition from their 1967 prize-winning Mantle Retractor (though even back then, their tutor remarks 'it might be fine for a cadaver but it won't work with a living person') to Bev's invention, twenty years later, of 'gynaecological instruments for operating on mutant women', his use of which finally gets the twins banned from practice. As Elliot (now feminised as 'Ellie') takes drugs to 'synchronise' himself with Bev, Bev uses the instruments to try and separate them in reality, opening up his own twin where his womb should be and killing him. Their unresolved masochistic desires have re-figured them as the real mutant women, the true objects of their lifelong gynaecological quest.

The closing shot of *Dead Ringers*, the half-naked Bev draped over Ellie, plays as an almost Derek Jarman-like queer tableau and raises the question of gay desire in Cronenberg's cinema. Though still little dwelt upon – Barbara Creed's work again being a notable exception[5] – there is a persistent strain of homoerotic imagery, running from the sensibility of Cronenberg's gay friend Ron Mlodzik which suffuses *Stereo* and *Crimes of the Future* through *Dead Ringers* (surely Bev and Ellie are 'really' gay?) and *eXistenZ* (Willem Dafoe 'plugging' Jude Law) on into the man-on-man gun and knives violence of *A History of Violence* and *Eastern Promises*. Just where we might expect 'out' queer Cronenberg, however, as in his adaptations of Burroughs's *Naked Lunch* and J.G. Ballard's *Crash*, it is the powerful hetero-sexuality of his concerns which is overbearingly stressed, suggesting a strong contradiction between homosexual desire and homophobic repression. For all the gay erotics of male collaboration that might be read into Cronenberg's *Fly*-like 'fusion' with Burroughs, for instance, the film downplays the homosexuality of its source, foregrounding Joan Lee's/Frost's (Judy Davis) role as literary muse and offering in its one gay coupling, the ruthless decadent Cloquet (Julian Sands) taking the beautiful boy Kiki (Joseph Scorsiani), certainly the film's most grotesque horror image. Similarly, while Ballard's circular novel can be read as the love letter of the narrator Ballard to his perverse mentor, the scientist Vaughan, and its sexual encounters peak with their intercourse (admittedly only after they have dropped some acid), Cronenberg somewhat marginalises all this, restructuring the plot to focus on the Ballards' marriage and the quest to initiate the pristine Catherine (Deborah Kara Unger) into the erotic cult of car crash wounds (see Sinclair and Creed for counter-arguments to this[6]). *M. Butterfly* also, among the least discussed and assimilated of the films, unfolds what is literally a homosexual affair, between a French diplomat (Jeremy Irons, again) and a Beijing Opera male to female impersonator (John Lone), under the guise of heterosexuality (once again see Creed for a persuasive reading).

Mutation and perverse desire continue in *Spider, A History of Violence* and *Eastern Promises*, which J. Hoberman[7] has grouped together as 'murderous family dramas' and which are explicitly concerned with male power and violence. *A History of Violence* and *Eastern Promises* use the thriller format to counterpoint the destinies of the conventional heterosexual family and the homoerotic male gangster family; both are gangster films (the latter explicitly) and each narrative is jolted forward by scenes of extraordinary male violence. The energy and ingenuity which formerly went into Cronenberg's fantasy special effects is here deployed in the service of a bleak naturalism representing the brutalised male body. *Violence*, financed mainly by New Line Cinema, unfolds the return of the repressed into the life of upright small town family man Tom Stall (Viggo Mortensen) after he becomes a reluctant all-American Hero by killing two criminals who hold up his cosy diner in Millbrook, Indiana. The media spotlight brings unwanted attention from gangsters who repeatedly claim that Tom is Joey Cusack, brother of criminal magnate Richie Cusack (William Hurt), whom Joey had crossed in his Philadelphia past and run out on to avoid the consequences. To survive, Tom must release the monster within him and face his destiny; it's a version of Jekyll and Hyde done with the ethos of *Dirty Harry* (1971). The sexual politics of the nuclear family and the gangster family are both contrasted and related in the sequences of sex between Tom/Joey and his wife Edie (Maria Bello), in which the contradictory but inter-dependent dynamics of love and hate are all too apparent, and the homoerotic bonding between the two brothers before their final face off. The homoerotic dynamic is further foregrounded in *Promises*, which features Mortensen again in a remarkable performance as double agent Nikolai Luzhin, who rises to power in the London-based Russian mafia clan the Vory V Zakone by serving the honour-bound gangster codes of the charming and evil patriarch Semyon (Armin Mueller-Stahl) and by protecting his dissolute gay son Kirill (Vincent Cassell). He also protects midwife Anna Khitrova (Naomi Watts), who accidentally stumbles into this male world when she finds Semyon's restaurant card in the diary of a young Russian woman who died in childbirth. Power is written on the body of the male gangster; his tattoos inscribe the history of his criminal life. One of the film's key scenes displays the semi-naked Nikolai for the eyes of the clan elders as they choose to accept him into the fold; in another, set in a Finsbury Park bathhouse, he is naked as he fights for his life against vengeful Chechens armed with linoleum cutting knives. It's an extraordinary *tour de force* of action cinema which sur-faces physically the rage for control and supremacy which has run through much of Cronenberg's cinema.

The minimalist and hermetic *Spider* inhabits the mind of its epony-mous schizophrenic hero (Ralph Fiennes), released from a long-term mental institution to a halfway house in London's East End where he grew up as a child. Adapted by Patrick McGrath from his novel, its investigation of male psychopathology is pure Cronenberg territory and it sits alongside *Dead Ringers* in uncovering the problem of 'woman' and sexual difference – here, the classically Freudian splitting of the mother into nurturer and castrator, the Madonna and whore complex – at the root of male sickness. Such a blunt statement of the illness, though, scarcely does justice to the haunting, symbolic, tor-tuous and melancholy unfolding of Spider's repressed memories: from the opening title sequence, featuring peeling walls with shapes that could be spiders, shrouds or Rorschach blots, through the virtuoso acting of Fiennes, Miranda Richardson (in no fewer than three roles), Gabriel Byrne and Lynn Redgrave, to the sombre design and atmo-sphere created by Cronenberg's regular team (is there a composer since Bernard Herrmann who has contributed more to the distinctive texture of a director's body of work than Howard Shore?), *Spider* is a dramatic masterpiece – almost no one saw it, none of the leading makers or actors were even paid for it – which charts the distance

Cronenberg has travelled from mad scientist to mad Everyman; in a sense, no distance at all.

Biography

Cronenberg was born in Toronto, Canada, in 1943. He was educated at the University of Toronto, and gained a BA in Literature in 1967.

Notes

1 See Kim Newman, *Nightmare Movies*, London, Bloomsbury, 1988.
2 Michael O'Pray, 'Primitive Fantasies in Cronenberg's Films', in Wayne Drew (ed.), *BFI Dossier 21: David Cronenberg*, London, BFI Publishing, 1984, pp. 48–53.
3 Robin Wood, 'Cronenberg: A Dissenting View', in Piers Handling (ed.), *The Shape of Rage: The Films of David Cronenberg*, Toronto, Academy of Canadian Cinema, General Publishing Company, 1983, pp. 115–35; Jonathan Crane, 'A Body Apart: Cronenberg and Genre', in Michael Grant (ed.), *The Modern Fantastic: The Films of David Cronenberg*, Trowbridge, Flicks Books, 2000, pp. 50–68.
4 Barbara Creed, *The Monstrous Feminine: Film, Feminism, Psychoanalysis*, London, Routledge, 1993, pp. 43–58; Creed, 'Phallic Panic: Male Hysteria and *Dead Ringers*', *Screen*, 31, 2, Summer 1990, pp. 125–46; Helen W. Robbins, ' 'More Human Than I Am Alone': Womb Envy in David Cronenberg's *The Fly* and *Dead Ringers*', in Steven Cohan and Ina Rae Hark (eds), *Screening the Male: Exploring Masculinities in Hollywood Cinema*, London, Routledge, 1993, pp. 134–47.
5 Barbara Creed, 'The Naked Crunch: Cronenberg's Homoerotic Bodies', in Grant, *op. cit.*, pp. 84–101.
6 Iain Sinclair, *Crash: David Cronenberg's Post-mortem on J. G. Ballard's 'Trajectory of Fate'*, London, BFI Publishing, 1999; Creed, ibid.
7 J. Hoberman, 'Still Cronenberg', *The Village Voice*, 4 September 2007.

Filmography

Transfer (1966) short
From the Drain (1967) short
Stereo (1969)
Crimes of the Future (1970)
Shivers (1975)
Rabid (1976)
Fast Company (1979)
The Brood (1979)
Scanners (1980)
Videodrome (1982)
The Dead Zone (1983)

The Fly (1986)
Dead Ringers (1988)
Naked Lunch (1991)
M. Butterfly (1993)
Crash (1996)
eXistenZ (1999)
Spider (2002)
A History of Violence (2005)
Eastern Promises (2007)

Further reading

Martin Barker et al., *The 'Crash' Controversy*, London, Wallflower Press, 2001.

Mark Browning, *David Cronenberg: Author or Film-Maker?*, Bristol, Intellect Books, 2007.

Michael Grant, *'Dead Ringers'*, Trowbridge, Flick Books, 1997.

Ernest Mathijs, *The Cinema of David Cronenberg: From Baron of Blood to Cultural Hero*, London, Wallflower Press, 2008.

Peter Morris, *David Cronenberg: A Delicate Balance*, Toronto, ECW Press, 1994.

Chris Rodley (ed.), *Cronenberg on Cronenberg*, London, Faber and Faber, 1996 (rev. edn).

JULIE DASH

By Terry Moore

Writer, producer and director of the critically acclaimed *Daughters of the Dust*, Julie Dash was the first African-American female to have a feature-length film in theatrical distribution. Named Film of the Century by the Newark Black Film Festival, *Daughters of the Dust* embodies the radical potential of narrative cinema in its reclamation of African-American history and culture, its negotiation of the intersection of gender and race, and its construction of African-American female subjectivity. It exemplifies what Toni Cade Bambara has called 'oppositional cinema', a re-vision of narrative film from a female-centred, Africentric perspective.[1]

In all of her work, Dash's desire is to 'redefine images of black women'.[2] Her breakthrough black-and-white short, *Illusions*, not only explicitly challenges the sexism and racism of mainstream cinema, but also theorises and exemplifies an 'oppositional' narrative film. Set in Hollywood in 1942, the year the NAACP met with studios to convince them that more African-Americans should be positioned on- and off-screen, *Illusions* focuses on Mignon Dupree (Lonette McKee). An African-American studio executive passing as white, Mignon 'want[s] to use the power of the motion picture'.[3] Dash expresses a similar ambition:

> [*Illusions*] intentionally mimics the form and conventions of Hollywood films of the thirties and forties. But by embedding certain foreign objects in the form – the protagonist Mignon, for example – I've attempted to throw the form into relief, hopefully making all of the sexist and racist assumptions of that form stick out.[4]

Illusions opens with a quote from Ralph Ellison's 'The Shadow and the Act' in a voice-over juxtaposed with a swirling Oscar, followed by a cut to documentary footage of white soldiers, and shortly thereafter, to an African-American janitor cleaning the glass on the outer door of the white studio executive's office. These four components clearly delineate the extant racial perimeters of mainstream cinema (and US society), as well as the transformative possibility of this cinema that *Illusions* takes as its theme. The voice-over ('to direct an attack upon Hollywood would indeed be to confuse portrayal with action, image with reality. In the beginning was not the shadow, but the act, and the province of Hollywood is not action, but illusion') acknowledges the racism of Hollywood film, but also emphasises that such depictions mirror the racism of the society which produces such films. The 'reality' of society's racism is depicted by the African-American janitor in a subservient position outside the studio door, excluded from the inner sanctum of Hollywood power just as an African-American presence is excluded from Hollywood's screen. While the twirling Oscar acknowledges the recognition and fame garnered by Hollywood films, implying the power of images, the presence of the documentary footage, snippets from the province of the cinema of the 'real', demonstrates how easily subjective imagery elides into 'objective' reality: no African-American soldiers appear in this footage.

Thus the film's opening moments acknowledge both the power of cinematic illusion and its exclusionary foundations. *Illusions* is not simply an attack upon racism in Hollywood and US society; it also theorises the possibility of a transformative narrative cinema which would give voice to the voiceless and make the absent present (making visible the heretofore 'invisible man', the African-American janitor). If, as the passing Mignon observes, her studio cohorts 'see me, but they cannot recognise me', *Illusions* assures that its audience will 'recognise' her. And, in recognising her, the audience also recognises the possibility of African-American female subjectivity.

This recognition comes through Mignon's relationship with an African-American singer, Ester Jeeter (Rosanne Katon). Although Ester dreams of being on screen, she makes her living dubbing the singing voices of white stars. When the sound on a new musical is out of synch, Ester is hired to dub the blonde star's musical number with Mignon in charge of the process. We see Mignon standing behind the glass of the recording booth, looking out into the studio, but positioned between the reflections of two white male sound engineers. Ambiguity predominates: Mignon towers over them, but is contained by their reflections. Moments afterward, Mignon's gaze frames Ester and the microphone on the left and the dubbing room film screen on the right, blank (and white) at first and later filled with the blonde actress lip-synching. As Judith Mayne has elucidated, while the Hollywood screen functions as a barrier, what Mignon imagines and what the viewer literally sees is a new film with Ester as subject.[5] The subsequent cuts from a close-up of the white star to close-ups of Ester make explicit that what we are watching is a new cinema, born from the relationship between Ester and Mignon, negotiated through African-American female spectatorship, and predicated on making 'real' African-American female subjectivity.

After the dubbing session, Mignon and Ester (who immediately recognises Mignon as an African-American woman) stand together at the doorway of a huge sound stage sharing their dreams and aspirations about the movies. Shot from the interior of the building, the foreground of the frame is black, with their figures silhouetted in an extreme long shot against the intense whiteness of the sunlight outside the doorway. Mignon tells Ester, 'There's no joy in the seduction of false images'. However, the composition of the shot implies that they are poised on the threshold of possibility. With their backs to the blinding white state of current cinema, they stare into the blackness of the sound stage and the potentiality of a new Black cinema is foregrounded, just as the promise of a cinema which centres its gaze on Ester and Mignon is affirmed. The Black Filmmaker Foundation's Film of the Decade, *Illusions* is a particularly important film in Dash's career, foregrounding characteristics central to her work: her espousal of narrative, revelry in the pleasure of the visual, embrace of 'Afro-American expressive traditions', and her delight in the representation of the diverse beauty of African-American women.[6]

Dash's first experience with film came as a high school student in the late 1960s when she attended an after-school programme at the Studio Museum in Harlem. Fascinated by the 'mechanics' of film-making and inspired by the works of African-American women writers like Toni Cade Bambara and Toni Morrison, she became a film production major at City College.[7] In particular, she was influenced by Bambara's circular narrative structures and deviation from the 'male Western narrative', and by Morrison's 'depth of character'.[8] After producing her first film, *Working Models for Success*, a promotional documentary for the New York Urban Coalition, she discovered that 'people in the community want[ed] to see a *story*', and she resolved to work with narrative film.[9]

Upon graduation, Dash journeyed to Los Angeles and the American Film Institute. At the AFI, one of her teachers, Slavko Vorkapich, the well-known montagist, greatly influenced her sense of film aesthetics. Also influential, however, were her fellow students, half of whom came from outside the States. She found their 'non-western', non-formulaic work 'bold' and filled with more 'dynamic' shots than typical Hollywood films.[10] The seven-minute experimental dance film, *Four Women*, reflects these concerns in its interpretation of the Nina Simone ballad. In 1978, *Four Women* received the gold medal for Women in Film at the Miami International Film Festival, the first of Dash's many awards.

Dash then attended UCLA's graduate film school. In the midst of the social and political upheaval of the period, the university was challenged by its students. Out of this struggle, the Black Independent filmmaking movement at UCLA was born. Named the 'L.A. Rebellion' by film scholar Clyde Taylor, it had as its goal the establishment of an 'independent Black film enterprise that was true to their cultural roots and contested the falsification of African American history by Hollywood'.[11] Dash, Alile Sharon Larkin, Bill Woodberry and Bernard Nichols were part of the 'second wave' who 'screened and discussed socially conscious cinema from directors like Satyajit Ray, Yasujiro Ozu, Ousmane Sembene, Humberto Solas, and Sara Gomez'.[12] Their influence is evident in Dash's *Diary of an African Nun*, an adaptation of a story by Alice Walker. This lyrical film, in which 'the protagonist struggles with the conflict that develops when her adopted Christian beliefs are intruded upon by the traditional African beliefs of her community', gained Dash a Director's Guild Award for student film.[13]

Four Women, Diary of an African Nun and *Illusions* exemplify the evolution of Dash's vision. All acknowledge a black female spectator, de-centre the white male gaze, and revel in a story-telling tradition that dates from the first African griot. They are critically important not only in terms of the history of black independent film, but in terms of the history of *all* independent film. *Diary of an African Nun* and *Illusions*, in particular, demonstrated not only the transformative power and radical potential of narrative film, but also posed a challenge to the unacknowledged racism of the feminist film movement. By engaging with the intersection of race and gender (and later, sexual identity) in her films, Dash spurred the creation of an inclusive feminist film movement.

It was, however, Dash's first full-length feature film, *Daughters of the Dust*, which transformed forever the face (literally and figuratively) of independent filmmaking. Here, her gifts of story-telling and visual aesthetics come to full fruition in a film which Greg Tate has called 'an unparalleled and unprecedented achievement in terms of both world cinema and African aesthetics'.[14] Set in 1902 at Ibo Landing in the Sea Islands, off the coast of Georgia and South Carolina, *Daughters of the Dust* is the story of the Peazant family and the northern migration of some of its members. As a stopping place before slaves were taken to the slave market in Charleston, the Sea Islands, because of their isolation from the mainland, have the 'strongest retention of African culture', as reflected in the Gullah culture's dialect, food and rituals.[15]

Steeped in a history, myth and tradition never before seen in full-length narrative film, *Daughters of the Dust* focuses on the women in the family (their characters based on African deities). The camera celebrates the beauty of their diversity by lingering on a broad range of skin tones, hairstyles and body types. The head of the family and its spiritual centre is the elderly Nana Peazant (Cora Lee Day), an ex-slave who worries that, in moving away from this land, her family will also move away from the ancestors, and thus, the traditions, histories and other 'scraps of memories' which have given the family the strength to triumph over slavery, Reconstruction, and beyond. Recognising that her family 'ain't going to no land of milk and honey', Nana calls on the ancestors to help ensure that the family's connection with them is honoured and maintained. The ancestors send the Unborn Child (Kai-Lynn Warren) of Eli and Eula Peazant (Alva Rogers and Adisa Anderson) both to help Nana and to reconcile Eli and Eula, who are in turmoil because the pregnant Eula was raped by a white man. Although the Unborn Child represents the future, it is a future predicated on the necessity of remembering the past.

Neither the Unborn Child, nor Nana Peazant, are able to touch and transform Haagar (Kaycee Moore), who married into the Peazant family and who becomes Nana's nemesis. Haagar, anxious to move away from Nana Peazant and her 'hoodoo mess', is eager to embrace the urban North. Other Peazant women are poised between the beliefs of the two. Viola (Cheryl Lynn Bruce), who has returned from the North with a photographer, Mr Snead (Tommy Hicks), in order to document the Peazant family's leave-taking, is fearful of Nana's beliefs because of the Baptist Christianity she has adopted. She urges a renunciation of the old ways, but, unlike Haagar, her respect for Nana makes it difficult for her to sever her connection. Yellow Mary (Barbara-O), the most urbane of the Peazant women, also has returned from her journeys for this special occasion. Accompanied by her lover, Trula (Trula Hoosier), she is scorned by most of the older women (except Nana) because of her light complexion, because of this 'thing' (Trula) she brought with her, and because she got 'ruint' and is a prostitute. At the end of the film, with the intercession of Nana, the Unborn Child and the ancestors, all of the Peazant family, except Trula and Haagar, maintain their connection to the old ways and 'old souls' and in so doing are given the strength to carry on.

Encompassing diverse aspects of African-American culture and history, *Daughters of the Dust* refers to the ongoing history of the rape of black women by white men; the anti-lynching movement; the entwined history of Native Americans and African-Americans; the varieties of African-American religions; the importance of myth and oral tradition to African-American culture; the enrichment of US culture through African and African-American traditions, language and philosophy; the attempted infestation of African-American culture with white patriarchal ideology; the depiction of an agrarian African-American history; and so on. In its depiction of this suppressed history, and bolstered by years of intensive research, the film overflows with ethnographic detail, but its ideology, script, structure and cinematography are far removed from both the purview of ethnographic cinema and the conventions of mainstream narrative cinema.[16] The structure is not plot-driven; the story 'unravels [in] much the same way that an African griot would recount a family's history'.[17] In addition to this 'Africentric grounding', Dash uses multiple voice-overs, and, in collaboration with cinematographer Arthur Jafa, and production designer, Kerry Marshall, utilises 'multiple point-of-view camera work'; 'wide-angled and deep-focus shots in which no one becomes a backdrop to anyone else's drama'; camera placement inside groups, rather than outside looking in; and off-centre framing of characters, as well as deep-focus long shots and extreme long shots, so that the environment seems to become a character, too.[18] The production was shot exclusively in natural light. Jafa, 'question [ing] … whether the standard of twenty-four frames per second rate is kinesthetically the best for rendering the black experience', frequently slows down certain scenes, emphasising spirituality and the connection between the present and the future to the past and the ancestors.[19]

Dash's vision was not welcomed with open arms or wallets; as Erhart notes, *Daughters of the Dust* 'is less a product of its time than a product in spite of its time'.[20] Inspired by her own Gullah family and by photos of African-American women taken in the early twentieth century by James Van Der Zee, Dash first conceptualised the film in 1975. In 1986, after eleven years of research, Dash was ready to shoot the film, but could get only enough funding to shoot a sample. Hopeful that actually seeing what the film would look like would generate funds, Dash, even with the sample, a completed script and an award-winning filmography, was unable to secure money from either Hollywood or European sources. Eventually she received $800,000 from the Public Broadcasting System's *American Playhouse* and began shooting late in 1989 – with only twenty-eight days in which to complete the film and no money for post-production. In the following year Dash worked on editing, completing the final cut at the end of 1990 with grants from the Rockefeller Foundation and the National Black Programming Consortium.

Dash encountered the same problems with distributors that she had with investors. She later speculated that since 'role-playing' can be a part of the viewing experience, white men, including distributors, '[did] not want to be a black woman for two hours. That's two hours too long'.[21] Distributors told her that there was no market for such a film, so she took it to film festivals – including Sundance (where it received the award for best cinematography), Munich, London and Toronto. Finally, it was picked up by a small New York distributing company, Kino International, and opened in January 1992.

As with the potential investors and distributors before them, some white reviewers had a problem with the film. B. Ruby Rich, likening it to Isaac Julien's *Looking for Langston* and Lourdes Portillo's and Susana Muñoz's *La Ofrenda: The Days of the Dead*, notes that white critics attacked these films for their beauty. 'People of color are expected to produce films of victimization', she writes, positing that because these films 'look at the richness of their cultures instead of their poverty', the films evoke 'aesthetic envy' from white critics.[22] None the less, upon its release, *Daughters of the Dust* sold out in theatres across the US. Even with non-comprehending white critics and without an expensive advertising campaign or bookings into multiplex theatres, during its first year of release, *Daughters of the Dust* grossed over $1 million.

In spite of the success of *Daughters of the Dust* and its being named to the Library of Congress National Film Registry in 2004, Dash has yet to be given the opportunity to direct another theatrical feature film. In the 1990s, she directed a number of music videos for African-American artists; made two shorts, both for the Public Broadcasting System: *Relatives*, a dance film featuring Ishmael Huston Jones, and *Praise House*, performed by Urban Bush Women; directed two feature-length films for the cable network, Black Entertainment Television: *Incognito* and *Funny Valentines*; and wrote and directed a segment of HBO's *Subway Stories* and Showtime's *Women: Stories of Passion*. She also published a novel, *Daughters of the Dust*, that revisited the Peazant family. Her direction of television movies continued in 2000 with an MTV original movie, *Love Song*, and 2002 with CBS's *The Rosa Parks Story*. The latter film, a moving biography of the civil rights hero, garnered many awards and nominations, including the NAACP Image Award, an Emmy nomination for its star, Angela Bassett, and The Directors Guild of America nomination for Outstanding Directorial Achievement for Dash, making her the first African-American woman nominated in the category of Primetime Movies Made for Television. In 2004 she directed another historically-based short film, *Brothers of the Borderland*, for the National Underground Railroad Freedom Center about two members of the Underground Railroad, John Parker and Rev. John Rankin, and their efforts to help runaway slaves. In 2007, Dash received the Lifetime Achievement Award from the UK's Images of Black Women Film Festival.

While the importance of Dash's cinematic achievements cannot be overestimated, it is telling, and unfortunate, that she has not secured more financial support to write and direct her own films. She 'sees herself as in and out of Hollywood' because she uses its crews and would use its money, but does not want to 'duplicate the Hollywood popcorn fodder'.[23] She explains: 'I want to do the films that *I* want to do' and is 'not locked into features; for me it's about making films and showing Black women in ways that have not been seen before. It's about moving people, about disseminating information'.[24] To that end, she founded Geechee Girls Multimedia in order to develop interactive media applications, but she also continues her work in film. She is at work on a documentary, *Glory Days*, that documents the history of African-American women from their perspective, and two feature narrative films written by Jeanne Marie Scarpazza: *The Scarapist*, a suspense film about therapist abuse, and *Making Angels*, a story of five women artists living in the Algonquin Hotel.[25] Inspired by black women filmmakers of the past and present, and with or without support from Hollywood, Dash will continue to create a profound and influential cinematic legacy.[26] Mignon and Ester were left poised on the threshold of cinematic possibility, but Julie Dash has taken her camera through that doorway and has shown us the promise of African-American women's cinema.

Biography

Julie Dash was born in New York City, USA, in 1952. In 1969 she attended the Studio Museum of Harlem before undertaking a BA in Film Production at the City College of New York. She then attended the Center for Advanced Film Studies at the American Film Institute and received an MFA from UCLA.

Acknowledgement

Thanks to Mijoung Chang at Women Make Movies, distributor of *Illusions*, *Praise House* and *The Cinematic Jazz of Julie Dash*, for providing me with video copies. Contact information: http://www.wmm.com/

Notes

1 Toni Cade Bambara, 'Preface', in Julie Dash, *Daughters of the Dust: The Making of an African-American Woman's Film*, New York, New Press, 1992, p. xiii.

2 J.M. Redding and V. Brownworth, *Film Fatales: Independent Women Directors*, Seattle, Seal Press, 1997, p. 192.

3 Julie Dash, *Illusions*, in P. Klotman (ed.) *Screenplays of the African American Experience*, Bloomington, Indiana University Press, 1991, p. 212.

4 K. Harris, 'New Images: An Interview with Julie Dash and Alile Sharon Larkin', *Independent* 9, 10, 1986, p. 18.

5 Judith Mayne, *The Woman at the Keyhole*, Bloomington, Indiana University Press, 1990, p. 64.

6 K. Harris, *op. cit.*

7 H. Baker Jr and Julie Dash (1992) 'Not Without My Daughters: A Conversation with Julie Dash and Houston Baker, Jr'., *Transition 57*, 1992, p. 153.

8 Ibid., pp. 150–1.
9 Ibid., pp. 154.
10 Ibid., p. 158.
11 C. Taylor, 'The L.A. Rebellion: New Spirit in American Film', *Black Film Review*, no. 2, 1986, pp. 11 and 29; N. Masilela, 'The Los Angeles School of Black Filmmakers', in M. Diawara (ed.) *Black American Cinema*, New York, Routledge, 1993, pp. 107–8.
12 Julie Dash, 1995, *op. cit.*
13 Dash, in K. Harris, *op. cit.*, p. 18.
14 Greg Tate, 'Of Homegirl Goddesses and Geechee Women: The Africentric Cinema of Julie Dash', *The Village Voice*, 4 June 1991, pp. 72.
15 Julie Dash, *Daughters of the Dust: The Making of an African American Woman's Film*, New York, New Press, 1992, p. 6.
16 bell hooks calls it 'mythopoetic'; bell hooks, *Black Looks: Race and Representation*, Boston, South End Press, 1992, p. 29.
17 Julie Dash and bell hooks, 'Dialogue between bell hooks and Julie Dash', in Julie Dash, *Daughters of the Dust: The Making of an African American Woman's Film*, New York, New Press, 1992, p. 32.
18 Toni Cade Bambara, *op. cit.*
19 Ibid., p. xv.
20 J. Erhart, 'Picturing *What If*: Julie Dash's Speculative Fiction', *Camera Obscura*, no. 38, 1996, p. 117.
21 See Y. Welbon's film, *The Cinematic Jazz of Julie Dash* (1992) and 'Calling the Shots: Black Women Directors Take the Helm', *Independent*, 15, 2, pp. 18–21.
22 B. Ruby Rich, 'In the Eyes of the Beholder', *The Village Voice*, 28 January 1992, pp. 60 and 65.
23 Y. Welbon, *op. cit.*; J.M. Redding and V. Brownworth, *op. cit.*, p. 201.
24 Y. Welbon, *op. cit.*; Z.I. Davis, 'An Interview with Julie Dash', *Wide Angle*, 13, 3–4, p. 115.
25 Janus Adams. 'Glory Days'. 12 November 2008. *New York Women in Film and Television*. 15 May 2009 <http://www.nywift.org/article.aspx?ID=831>; Bobby Tanzillo, 'Ambitious Spicuzza Draws Inspiration from Artistic Family'. *OnMilwaukee.com* 29 April 2003. 21 June 2009 <http://staff. onmilwaukee.com/buzz/articles/jspicuzza.html>; <http://www.seasonsandmuse.com>; 'The Scarapist'. 26 July 2008. 21 June 2009 <http://www.indiegogo.com/The-Scarapist?account_id=1803&iggref=ttag>.
26 Julie Dash, 1995, *op. cit.*

Filmography

Working Models of Success (1973)
Four Women (1975)
Diary of an African Nun (1977)
Illusions (1982)
Breaking the Silence (1988)

Phyllis Wheatley (1989)
Preventing Cancer (1989)
Relatives (1990)
Praise House (1991)
Daughters of the Dust (1992)
Breaths (1994)
Subway Stories: Tales from the Underground: Sax Cantor Riff (1997)
Women: Stories of Passion: Grip Till It Hurts (1997)
Funny Valentines (1999)
Incognito (1999)
Love Song (2000)
The Rosa Parks Story (2002)
Brothers of the Borderland (2004)

Further reading

F.L. Aldama, *Postethnic Narrative Criticism: Magicorealism in Oscar 'Zeta' Acosta, Ana Castillo, Julie Dash, Hanif Kureishi, and Salman Rushdie*. Austin, TX, U of Texas Press, 2003.

T.C. Bambara, 'Reading the Signs, Empowering the Eye: *Daughters of the Dust* and the Black Independent Cinema Movement', in M. Diawara (ed.) *Black American Cinema*, New York, Routledge, 1993.

J. Bobo, *Black Women as Cultural Readers*, New York, Columbia University Press, 1995.

J. Dash, *Daughters of the Dust: The Making of an African American Woman's Film*, New York, New Press, 1992.

——*Daughters of the Dust*, New York, Dutton, 1997.

——'Making Movies That Matter: A Conversation with Julie Dash', *Black Camera*, vol. 22, no. 1, 2007, pp. 4–12.

——*Geechee Girls Multimedia*. 2008. 10 June 2009 <http://www.geechee.tv/>.

M. Diawara, *Black American Cinema*, New York, Routledge, 1993.

G.A. Foster, *Women Filmmakers of the African and Asian Diaspora*, Carbondale, Southern Illinois University Press, 1997.

G. Gibson-Hudson, 'Aspects of Black Feminist Cultural Ideology in Films by Black Independent Artists', in D. Carson, L. Dittmar and J.R. Welsch (eds) *Multiple Voices in Feminist Film Criticism*, Minneapolis, University of Minnesota Press, 1994.

A. Gourdine, 'Fashioning the Body [as] Politic in Julie Dash's *Daughters of the Dust*, *African American Review*, vol. 38, no. 3, 2004, pp. 499–511.

S.V. Hartman and F.J. Griffin, 'Are You as Colored as That Negro? The Politics of Being Seen in Julie Dash's *Illusions*', *Black American Literature Forum*, vol. 25, no. 2, 1991, pp. 361–73.

J. Hobson, 'Viewing in the Dark', *Women's Studies Quarterly*, vol.30, no. 1/2, 2002, pp. 45–59.

S.C. Kaplan, 'Souls at the Crossroads, Africans on the Water: The Politics of Diasporic Melancholia', *Callaloo: A Journal of African Diaspora Arts and Letters*, vol. 30, no. 2, 2007, pp. 511–26.

A.S. Larkin, 'Black Women Film-makers Defining Ourselves: Feminism in Our Own Voice', in E.D. Pribram (ed.) *Female Spectators: Looking at Film and Television*, New York, Verso, 1988.

J.S. Ryan, 'Outing the Black Feminist Filmmaker in Julie Dash's *Illusions*', *Signs: Journal of Women in Culture & Society*, vol. 30, no.1, 2004, pp. 1319–44.

V. Smith, *Representing Blackness: Issues in Film and Video*, New Brunswick, NJ, Rutgers University Press, 1997.

C.A. Streeter, 'Was Your Mama a Mulatto? Notes toward a Theory of Racialized Sexuality in Gayl Jones's *Corregidora* and Julie Dash's *Daughters of the Dust' Callaloo: A Journal of African Diaspora Arts and Letters*, vol. 27, no. 3, 2004, pp. 768–87.

N.E. Wright, 'Property Rights and Possession in *Daughters of the Dust*', *MELUS*, vol. 33, no. 3, 2008, pp. 11–25.

G. Tate and A. Jafa, 'La Venus Negre', *Artforum*, vol. 30, no. 1, pp. 90–3.

GUILLERMO DEL TORO

By Lindsay Steenberg

Mexican born filmmaker, screenwriter and make-up artist, Guillermo del Toro has a self-confessed passion for Goya, ghost stories, and B-films. It is unsurprising, then, that his body of work uses a visual lexicon of the grotesque and the uncanny to tell its horrifying fairy/folk tales about political violence, spiritual truth and the troubled transformations of adolescence.

Many of his films are explicitly philosophical. Two begin with expansive moral musings: *Hellboy*'s opening voiceover asks what distinguishes men from monsters, while that in *The Devil's Backbone* asks what makes a ghost. *Pan's Labyrinth* reads as a parable about personal and political sacrifice. *Mimic* and *Blade II* are cautionary tales about humans (or vampires) meddling with nature through genetics. *Hellboy II: The Golden Army* includes an environmental moral to its fable about the conflict between humans and elves. All of these stories, and del Toro's body of work more broadly, explore humanity's place within a crumbling universe and the responsibilities we have in preserving its balance and preventing its disintegration. Yet he shies away from a Manichean imagining of a world divided into good and evil; or a straightforward struggle between man and monster. His villains are rarely without (quasi-) justifiable motives and are typically treated with sympathy for their doomed situation. Heroes (and heroines) are generally children or adolescents confused and, at times, misled by the supernatural or humans making understandable but horrifying misjudgements.

Del Toro describes his films, particularly the Spanish language films, as 'academic'[1] and political. With respect to *The Devil's Backbone*, written as his thesis for a screenwriting class, he says:

> I think that all politics is fantasy. I've always been fascinated with it. In film you can choose a fable of some kind to shine light on an important element of politics instead of just making a movie … the way I see things all fantasies have a political standard. And what better way to get to know a particular reality than to make a really good fantasy out of it![2]

Despite this commitment to political critique through cinema, del Toro's films often privilege the universality of the fairytale and the redemptive possibilities of fatherhood.[3] Frequently, the paternalist lessons of the fairytale push the political charge of the narratives to the background.

While fatherhood, fairytales and political fables are structuring elements across his work, many critics separate del Toro's films into two categories – the critically acclaimed Spanish language political allegories (*Cronos*, *The Devil's Backbone*, *Pan's Labyrinth*) on the one side and Hollywood genre pictures (*Mimic*, *Blade II*, *Hellboy* and *The Golden Army*) on the other. In a 2006 interview, del Toro reinforced this dichotomy, but added that the comic book adaptation *Hellboy* allowed him to explore a more personal vision within the Hollywood system. Despite the obvious distinctions between his Spanish and English language films, dividing del Toro's work into two opposing camps is an oversimplification. This is primarily because del Toro's 'art' films are also genre pictures. Additionally, because del Toro is involved in many aspects of all of his films (as director, screenwriter, special effects designer and, occasionally, as producer) the visual grammar of his films is remarkably consistent with a persistent use of catholic iconography, clockwork machines and insect motifs.

Rather than hinting at the monstrous through chiaroscuro effects, del Toro captures it in full frame. Indeed he has complained about the much-repeated assumption that the best horror films are those that only hint at the monster, hiding it from the spectator's scrutiny. Rather, he says: 'I'm from the school that likes to show the creatures. I love these movies! Representing fear physically in the movie is a celebration of my kind of film … You don't buy the ticket to see the movie star; you buy it to see the monster. He's the star'.[4] Nor does he save these monsters for the denouement of his films – the insect-people of *Mimic*, the mythical creatures of *Pan's Labyrinth* and the ghost in *The Devil's Backbone* are all revealed to the spectator relatively early. Del Toro describes the monsters of the American studio system as 'castrated',[5] assigning his supernatural creatures more violent potency and claiming that they are revealed (visually and psychologically) in more depth. Their bodies, and their motivations, are displayed for the other characters and for the spectator.

One of his most memorable monsters appears in the first of his Spanish language films to receive international attention, 1993's *Cronos*. This film sees antique dealer and grandfather Jesus Gris develop a kind of addiction to the clockwork machine (the cronos device)[6] which turns him into a vampire. In scenes of almost erotic intensity, Jesus repeatedly places the cronos device on his skin and allows it to drain his blood. While at first he appears to find a new vitality through the device, Jesus's body and appetites soon become more and more monstrous (he licks blood off a bathroom sink at a party and his skin gradually turns to grey and begins to fall off). The revulsion inspired by Jesus's transforming body parallels an entrenched and resonant fear of ageing by framing it as a traumatic and literal death in life. Yet Jesus is not the true monster of the film. Neither is the curious insect-fuelled prosthetic device which transforms him. Rather, the villain is a terminally ill millionaire who longs for immortality, and his plastic surgery-obsessed (and ironically named) nephew, Angel. What humanises Jesus, and differentiates him from the vampires featured in other horror films, is his relationship to his granddaughter, Aurora, who loves and cares for him despite his transformation. In a tense but touching sequence, Aurora puts her ailing and vampiric grandfather to bed in her toy chest. Ultimately, Jesus fights his urges, retains his human soul and dies because he will not harm his granddaughter.

As in Victor Erice's *Spirit of the Beehive* (1973), which is often invoked when discussing del Toro's Spanish language films, monsters speak particularly to children. Because they inhabit a liminal space between childhood and adulthood, the adolescent in del Toro's world is in a privileged position to mediate (and transgress) the borders between reality and fantasy; between the living and the dead and between a personal rite of passage and the public world of political upheaval. Ofelia, heroine of del Toro's most lauded work, *Pan's Labyrinth*, is representative of these mediating adolescents. Set against the backdrop of the Spanish civil war, *Pan's Labyrinth* follows fairytale-fixated Ofelia in her struggle against her fascist stepfather and her quest (guided by the ambiguous faun, Pan) to return to her true place in the underworld. Ofelia is the centre around which the fantastic and political worlds circulate. Her experience of violence is the force that holds them together. In the allegorical economy of *Pan's Labyrinth*, Ofelia's body, on the edge of the transformations of adolescence, registers the violence of the political situation: first as witness, then as victim. Del Toro frames the poetic tragedy of Ofelia's death as a kind of homecoming, and uses this as a coda to the film's political message. Del Toro's films often use suffering adolescents as stand-ins for the masses caught in political machinations beyond their control – from the murdered orphan, Santi, in *The Devil's Backbone*, to the man-child-demon, Hellboy, in the eponymous franchise.

Del Toro's films do not shy away from showing violence perpetrated against, or witnessed by, youths or children. Rather, violence is an essential part of the adolescence imagined in del Toro's worlds and an integral part of the Grimmian sensibility[7] of his cinematic fairytales. Del Toro describes his use of the horror genre as 'an extension of the fairytale'.[8] The journeys of characters like Ofelia in *Pan's Labyrinth* and Carlos in *The Devil's Backbone*, require violence for their moral lessons, as well as for their fairytale qualities. Adolescence does not protect del Toro's protagonists from an experience of fantastical or political violence, rather they seem to be particularly attuned to it – suggesting a kind of rite of passage articulated in brutal ways. This bloody coming-of-age resonates with del Toro's own history as a witness to violence in Guadalajara.

In interviews, del Toro often comments on the importance of violence to his work. He believes that it is important not to shield children from representations of violence. He insists that revealing danger and horror in film is a way to 'give us our dosage of fear in a safe way. It's a vaccine against all the real horrors out there'.[9] This view of violence stems in part from del Toro's own experiences of violence as a child:

> I think I have seen more cadavers in Mexico than people see working in the New York City morgue. I've just been exposed to these kinds of things and they have left their mark on my life as a director of horror movies.[10]

Del Toro's personal experiences of violence, and his method of using them in his filmmaking, are tied to his experience as a father. He acknowledges that his experience of fatherhood has taught him not to over-protect children from images of violence.[11] He is passionate in his belief that a good father does not shield his children from the varied experiences of the world, including its horrifying aspects.

Themes of fatherhood are an integral, but often ignored, element in del Toro's work. Much of Ofelia's journey is informed by a longing for her 'true' father and the violence perpetrated by her 'false' stepfather. The redemptive capacity of fatherhood, particularly those who act as father-figures, goes some way to answering the questions posed by the opening voiceover in *The Devil's Backbone* and *Hellboy*: it is the ghost of Dr. Casares who watches over and protects the orphans from the fascists and it is Hellboy's adopted father who provides him with the choice of becoming a demon or a man. This choice is later reinforced when Hellboy discovers he is to become a father himself in *The Golden Army*. The grandfather of *Cronos* is transformed into a vampire by an insect-powered clockwork device. Yet his granddaughter loves him despite his increasingly monstrous body and drives. It is the potential parenthood of the lead scientists in *Mimic* that balances their deadly mistake in engineering and releasing a hoard of carnivorous insects. Likewise, in *Blade II*, the father–son relationship between vampire hybrid Blade and his mentor, Whistler, humanises him and distinguishes him from the perverse familial system of the vampires. In del Toro's world, benevolent paternalism plays a critical role in managing the violence of both mythic and political realities.

What most obviously distinguishes a Guillermo del Toro film is its attention to the details of the monstrous and the fantastic. Creatures like the duplicitous Pan, the kitten-loving Hellboy, the humanoid 'Judas' bugs from *Mimic* and the drowned ghost in *The Devil's Backbone* have an unearthly, and perhaps even un-Hollywood, quality to them. Clockwork devices like the golden army and the insect-powered cronos device propel worlds where the laws of physics are sublimated into the circular laws of the mythical and the allegorical. Here the adolescent witnesses a violent world that is only redeemed by flawed but earnest attempts at fathering. The transnational success of these films is due in some part to del Toro's combination of mythic themes and imagery with narratives about political strife and an honesty in the representation of the brutal violence so much a part of both worlds.

Biography

Born on October 9, 1964 in Guadalajara, Mexico, Guillermo del Toro ran film workshops from the age of fifteen and later co-founded the Film Studies Centre and the Muestra del Cine Mexicano in Guadalajara. Del Toro began his screen career on Mexican television (writing, directing and supervising special effects) and studied make-up and special effects under Academy Award winning make-up artist, Dick Smith. He received international recognition and the Cannes critics' prize for his first feature, *Cronos*. In addition to creating his own special effects company, Necropia, del Toro is also a founding member of two notable Latin-American production companies, Tequila Gang and, more recently, Cha Cha Cha Films (distributed through Universal Pictures) with Alfonso Cuarón and Alejandro González Iñárritu. Del Toro is the author of a Spanish language book on Alfred Hitchcock and the co-author of the vampire novel, *The Strain*. He is a director, screenwriter, make-up artist and special effects supervisor, and has also produced several films, most notably *El orfanato – The Orphanage* (Bayona 2007).

Notes

1 Kimberly Chun, 'What is a Ghost? An Interview with Guillermo del Toro', *Cineaste,* Spring 2002, p. 28.
2 Jaime Perales Contreras, 'The New Master of Horror Movies', *Américas*, vol. 16, no. 2, March/April 2008, p. 60.
3 Michael Atkinson describes this as 'folkloric materialism' in which 'people's rebellions and socialists movements are subordinated to the patterns and ordeals of a hero's quest and the archetypal agonies of traumatized childhood'. 'Moral Horrors in Guillermo Del Toro's *Pan's Labyrinth*. The Supernatural Realm Mirrors Man's Inhumanity to Man', *Film Comment*, vol. 43, no. 1, January/February 2007, p. 53.
4 Contreras, *op. cit.*, p. 61.
5 Ibid.
6 According to Jason Wood, Del Toro sold his van to raise the money to pay for the cronos device.
7 Atkinson, *op. cit.*, p. 50.
8 Jason Wood, 'Guillermo Del Toro', *Telling Stories: Contemporary World Filmmakers in Interview*, Wallflower Press, 2006, p. 36.
9 Kimberly Chun, 'What is a Ghost? An Interview with Guillermo del Toro', *Cineaste,* Spring 2002, p. 31.
10 Contreras, *op. cit.*
11 Chun, *op. cit.*

Filmography

Doña Lupe (1985) also writer – short film
Geometria (1987) also writer – short film
Cronos (1993) also writer
Mimic (1997) also writer

El espinazo del diablo – The Devil's Backbone (2001) also writer/producer
Blade II (2002)
Hellboy (2004) also writer
El laberinto del fauno – Pan's Labyrinth (2006) also writer/producer
Hellboy II: The Golden Army (2008) also writer

Further reading

Michael Atkinson, 'Moral Horrors in Guillermo Del Toro's *Pan's Labyrinth*. The Supernatural Realm Mirrors Man's Inhumanity to Man', *Film Comment*, vol. 43, no. 1, January/February 2007, pp. 50–3.

Kimberly Chun, 'What is a Ghost? An Interview with Guillermo del Toro', *Cineaste,* Spring 2002, pp. 28–31.

Ann Davies, 'The Beautiful and the Monstrous Masculine: The Male Body and Horror in *El espinazo del diablo* (Guillermo del Toro 2001)', *Studies in Hispanic Cinemas*, vol. 3, no. 3, pp. 135–47.

Antonio Lazaro-Reboll, 'The Transnational Reception of *El espinazo del diablo* (Guillermo del Toro 2001)', *Hispanic Research Journal*, vol. 8, no. 1, February 2007, pp. 39–51.

Brad O'Brien, 'Fulcanelli as a Vampiric Frankenstein and Jesus as his Vampire Monster: The Frankenstein and Dracula Myths in Guillermo Del Toro's *Cronos*', in Richard J. Hand and Jay McRoy (eds) *Monstrous Adaptations: Generic and Thematic Mutations in Horror Films*, Manchester University Press, 2007, pp. 172–80.

Jaime Perales Contreras, 'The New Master of Horror Movies', *Américas*, vol. 16, no. 2, March/April 2008, pp. 60–1.

Paul Julian Smith, 'Pan's Labyrinth (El laberinto del fauno)', *Film Quarterly*, vol. 60, no. 4, pp. 4–9.

Jason Wood, 'Guillermo Del Toro', *Telling Stories: Contemporary World Filmmakers in Interview,* Wallflower Press, 2006, pp. 29–47.

ATOM EGOYAN

By Geoff Pevere

> Have you ever noticed that the things you want are the things that slip away?
>
> *Exotica*

In a disconcerting departure from the novel it is based on, the film of *Felicia's Journey*, written and directed by Canadian Atom Egoyan, leaves off somewhere near home. Not literally, but in the sense of an arrival at a place where everything will finally be all right. Home as safe harbour, the welcoming embrace of closure. Having barely escaped an ' unspeakable fate at the hands of the fussy serial killer Hilditch (who, in yet another arresting flight from William Trevor's novel, has freed his quarry in a fit of near-evangelical remorse), the Irish runaway Felicia is seen in the film's final moments tending shrubbery and attending to young mothers in a public park. She is a glowing, happy nurturer, earthbound and family-oriented, the embodiment of all that is good in the idea of home. Compare this to the book's final destination, which drops us on the step of madness, that most unhome-like of dwellings, yet the place where Trevor insists both Felicia and Hilditch must be left. The finicky killer is driven to suicide as a result of the girl's escape (and not, as the movie suggests, because of a cold splash of spiritual reckoning), while she is left to an even more chilling fate. When we last encounter Felicia in Trevor's book, she is mad, feral and – much to the point of the novel if not the film – homeless. 'She seeks no meaning in the thoughts that occur to her', Trevor writes of Felicia, 'any more than she searches for one in her purposeless journey, or finds a pattern in the muddle of time and people, but still the thoughts are there'. Felicia's journey has been 'purposeless', bereft of destination and direction. The opposite, one might say, of the journey she takes in Egoyan's film, which leaves her not only safe but wiser. Clearly her experience with the murderer Hilditch has lifted her to a more caring and sensitive station in life: a place where children and shrubbery grow, but only if properly tended. Like Hilditch, who kills himself after recognising his own evil, Felicia has been transformed by the revelation of horror. She has found serenity and peace, which means her journey has been anything but purposeless.

These matters are worth stressing for the purposes of fixing Atom Egoyan's position as a 'Canadian' artist. Where the Irish novelist Trevor's conception of Felicia's journey leaves the young woman like a vessel adrift on remorseless seas, the Canadian filmmaker sees her safely home to port. Even at the risk of what might be judged, if not the film's failure, at least its dramatic good sense. For while the novel's bleak ending at least follows a certain cold logic – wherein Felicia's fate is the inevitable outcome of a predatory world, as embodied by the epicurean obsessions of the more benignly Hannibal Lecterish killer Hilditch – Egoyan's ultimately upbeat adaptation smacks of an over-determined optimism, an unconvincing attempt to spread a little sunshine in a tomb. But the attempt is revealing, for if it fails to illuminate the darkness surrounding it – and Hilditch's last-minute, pre-suicidal conversion verges on gallows hysteria – it at least sheds some light on the role certain national predilections may play in the worldview of one of the most internationally conspicuous of Canadian artists. (Atom Egoyan is currently the most internationally celebrated English Canadian director since Cronenberg. He is as close as a filmmaker can get to being a household name in Canada; that is, slightly better known than dead prime ministers but not nearly as well known as living hockey players.) If we are to understand Atom Egoyan as a Canadian artist – with all the self-conscious uncertainties such an enterprise implies – we could do much worse than start with the idea of home. And the determination, in the case of *Felicia's Journey*, even at the expense of dramatic consistency and emotional logic, to get there.

Like many Canadian artists, Egoyan's work has frequently articulated the difficulty of basic human affinities, the almost pathological absence of rootedness which has also been widely described as alienation. And in this, if in little else on the level of apparent articulation (he is, if nothing else, a highly non-traditional stylist), his work explores and extends one of the most deeply abiding themes in Canadian movies. From the homeland-seeking ethnographic odysseys of Quebecois documentarist Pierre Perrault (*Pour la suite du monde, L'Acadie, L'Acadie!?!*, for example), to the wrenching coming of age experienced by the adolescent protagonist of Claude Jutra's *Mon oncle Antoine*; and from the lost highway of Donald Shebib's *Goin' Down the Road* to the existential black holes probed in the work of directors as disparate as Cronenberg and Michael Snow, Canadian films have demonstrated a distinctive fascination with the vacuous elusiveness of self and place. (One of the most astute questions ever posed of Canadian experience was asked by Canadian literary scholar Northrop Frye: 'Where', he famously wondered, 'is here?') And, when self is defined by external parameters – as, in Canadian movies, it so often is – this elusiveness extends to a sense of place. In many movies made by Canadian filmmakers, and in just about every movie made by the Cairo-born, British Columbia-raised Egoyan, there is literally no place like home. There are many means of accounting for this persistent condition of spiritual drift in Canadian movies, but it may perhaps suffice in this context to suggest that, in their concern with inescapable solitude, Canadian movies (ironically enough) are not alone. Indeed, as the possible consequence of clinging to an expanse of landscape that is as vast as it is unyielding (and where the most significant geological entity is called the 'Canadian Shield'), Canadians have developed a telling tendency to the anxiety of imminent disappearance, as though one must constantly cling for fear of losing purchase and falling off.

But losing purchase of what? Falling off what? And clinging to what? It is an existential paradox of the first order: the only greater fear than losing one's grip is not knowing if there is anything to grip in the first place. In *Calendar*, which Egoyan shot in Armenia with Russian money, the director plays a photographer whose lens frames the dissolution of his own marriage. His wife is falling in love with an Armenian tour guide, and her husband feels a frosty nothingness in the face of it. The setting may be a long way from the Canadian Shield, but the sentiment expressed is right at home: 'What I really feel like doing is standing here and watching', the photographer's narration coldly states. 'Watching while the two of you leave me and disappear into the landscape I'm about to photograph'.

To the extent that something like a mythological undercurrent exists in Canadian culture (and perhaps it is because it does not that these anxieties thrive), it is pretty much stuck on this possibility of drift. To grow up and be educated here in the 1960s and 1970s, as I did, was to be constantly reminded of the tenuousness of one's hold. The country was forever (and remains) on the verge of doing a deconfederating Humpty Dumpty: losing its delicate balance and shattering to miserable little pieces. Seminal Canadian volumes, of the kind anyone passing through the public school system must confront, had titles which prodded constant attentiveness to the danger of what lay just beyond the timberline: Susannah Moodie's pioneer classic *Roughing It in the Bush*, Farley Mowat's school curriculum staple *Lost in the Barrens*, W.O. Mitchell's *Who Has Seen the Wind?*, Pierre Berton's *The National Dream*, Margaret Atwood's *Survival*. Indeed, the latter, a key work of identity-carving literary criticism, merely gave scholarly credence to what many Canadians probably felt in the chill of their bones anyway, that is, that the single most prominent and abiding theme in Canadian literature was the monumental challenge of just getting by – of trying not to let this unforgiving and infinite landscape swallow you up or blow you away.

If the landscape provides a particularly vivid metaphor for the rocky, settler-deflecting uninhabitability of the country (tellingly, there are few more forbidding schools of landscape painting than Canada's renowned 'Group of Seven'), it also expresses the echoey vastness of the role played by alienation in Canadian cultural life. Egoyan is Canadian, of course, which argues for his consideration in the context of certain general tendencies apparent in the country's national culture. But, as an Egyptian-born Armenian, Egoyan also compels us to consider his alienation from an already alienated culture. His films have developed a singular tone of *communicatus interruptus*, in which the primary form of experience defining the relations between characters is what they cannot communicate to each other. (His adaptation of Samuel Beckett's *Krapp's Last Tape* seems ideally suited for Egoyan's fascination with the space between words.)

As a Canadian filmmaker, Egoyan practises a domestic art-form which has never enjoyed much popularity or currency with Canadians, who have historically preferred Hollywood movies to their own, and who thus find Canadian films alienating. (More than one observer has likened the status of Canadian movies to that of a foreign cinema in its own country.) Moreover, he is a Canadian filmmaker whose archly non-naturalistic aesthetic has broken considerably with the so-called 'traditions' of Canadian filmmaking, which have tended toward docu-dramatic realism – a legacy which is partly accounted for by the non-commercial haven provided by the National Film Board, a largely non-fiction-producing institution whose once pervasive influence was in steep decline by the early 1980s when Egoyan began making films. To sum up, he is a non-native Canadian filmmaker working in a marginal medium in a non-traditional way who makes movies which people from other countries tend to get more excited about than Canadians do (as Egoyan's serial invitations to festivals like Cannes, Berlin and Venice attest), all of which leaves his work at the point where alienation disappears over the horizon and becomes something else. Something vaster and more infinite: alienation ad infinitum. And you don't get much more Canadian than that.

Nor does it get you any closer to home, which is not an idea likely to thrive under such circumstances of marauding detachment. Canada is a place to get lost in, the United States a place to call home. Thus, while the root of American mythology (the border-spanning mirror inverse of Canada) ploughs beneath the concept of homesteading, making a garden of civilisation from an untamed wilderness, the rootlessness of Canadian mythology springs from the impossibility of laying down stakes. Home on such a landscape is never secure: it can never win against nature, and nature is never less than stubbornly opposed to it. While it is true to say that nations in all parts of the world have felt the cultural influence of America, and perhaps truer to suggest that cinema is one of those areas where this influence has been felt most acutely, no national entity has had – or could have – the experience of English Canada, the only country to live right snug upside the United States and speak the same language. Needless to say, this has had its effects – effects which ripple right through the entirety of Canadian culture and history, from the revealing 'settlement' of the Canadian west to the particular tone and form taken by Egoyan's movies.

Which may not be as random a conceptual span as it appears: there is a connection, particularly if you place any significance in the relations between history, culture, nationalism and popular myth. If one accepts western settlement as the key event of American popular mythology – the seed planted in the wilderness from which everything that is essential to America's self-image grew – one must also consider the peculiarly refracted shadow this has cast upon Canada, a country that shares the northern extension of America's continental west but not its western mythology. Or, more to the point perhaps, it shares exactly the same mythology which, unlike the region's weather, tends to blow north. Which is to say that Canada may have a west, but it has no Western. Or not one it can call its own. Fearing an outbreak on the Queen's soil of the kind of unpleasant business that characterised the Indian Wars in America, Canada's first Prime Minister, Sir John A. Macdonald, created a special police force to precede Canadian settlers and pre-empt their mixing it up with the newly established Dominion's aboriginal populations. In so doing, Macdonald not only created Canada's most enduring symbol of tenacious, top-down Canadian dullness – the Mountie: anti-outlaw, anti-cowboy, anti-sex, anti-fun – he pre-empted a northern-style Wild West. Moreover, in the process he also undercut any possibility that Canada might develop a national mythology based on Manifest Destiny, individualism, or ritualistic codes of honour and retributive justice. Instead of cowboys, that is, Canada got cops. Thus a country was born which, to this day, is renowned for its virtues of compromise, diplomacy and politeness. The Nice Guy Next Door of the first world. Not that this is necessarily a bad thing (one John Wayne-producing nation should do for us all), but it has played havoc in the country's development of a sense of national destiny.

In Canada, where no deep mythological roots have been permitted to grow, everything is open for discussion and debate. (And few topics are debated more vigorously or tirelessly than the issue of national identity.) Out of the West, with its blood, lawlessness, genocide and bone-simple code of survival, America drew its most potent and elementary mythological archetypes, and one of these was the raw sentimental poetry of home – what the West was fought and won for. As an idea, America was as inevitable and natural as home, and home was America. Home was where your journey took you, what you risked danger for, the end of all suffering. In narrative terms, Manifest Destiny was the ultimate Happy Ending. Endings were made happy not just by the literal appearance of Home, Sweet Home, they could be made so by the implication of home: marriage would do, a brilliant sunrise, a clinched embrace on a railway platform. To be delivered to a happy ending was to be dropped safely on the doorstep of home, and the very threshold of a national idea. And, in Canada, we didn't have it. In Winnipeg director Guy Maddin's 1992 movie *Careful* – a truly great Canadian title – an entire social system grows out of the fact that, if anyone belonging to the movie's mythical alpine community makes too much noise, an avalanche could sweep everybody off the mountain and into oblivion: if you speak up too loudly, or surrender to too much raw feeling, you could kill everyone around you. It seems a singularly Canadian theme, as is the subject of one of the totemically Canadian pop band The Tragically Hip's most anthemic songs. Called 'Fifty Mission Cap', it is inspired by the true story of a hockey player who, within days of leading his team to the national championships of the national sport, simply disappeared, fell off the edge of national experience never to be heard from again. It would seem that, for Canadians, no degree of skill or notoriety is insurance against the fear of simply being inhaled one day by the landscape.

With the exception of *The Sweet Hereafter*, in which a school bus full of children is swept off a mountain road and swallowed up by a partially frozen lake, the slipperiness of place in Egoyan's films has been articulated in terms more spiritual and psychological than physical. In fact, it has most often expressed itself as a kind of chronic *ennui*, a vague but crippling condition of terminal disconnectedness. In his first feature, *Next of Kin* (made in 1984, and the first of several to deal with the pregnantly troubled relations between adolescents and adults), the protagonist – the only child of a well-to-do Toronto WASP couple – is so disengaged from his actual family that he seeks (and creates) a surrogate one, in the form of an Armenian family (a reflection on Egoyan's Armenian heritage) to whom he presents himself as a long-lost son. In *Family Viewing* another teenager seeks to avenge a sense of domestic betrayal by taking revenge against the divorced father who has been erasing the archive of family videotapes. (Videotape, and its status as instantly disposable artificial memory, figures prominently in Egoyan's early work.) In *Speaking Parts*, the medium of disengagement is again video, as a number of characters peripherally involved in a film production struggle to establish virtual connections where actual ties are absent. In *The Adjuster*, the protagonist is an insurance adjuster whose own familial displacement is (futilely, as it turns out) compensated by his determination to play surrogate patriarchal saviour to families with whom his business puts him in an unequally dependent relationship. He needs broken homes to feel that he is putting something together.

Exotica traces a similar cycle of doomed domestic simulation, as a father whose daughter has been kidnapped and murdered establishes a creepy paternal relationship (foreshadowing, in less overtly predatory terms, the Hilditch–Felicia relationship) with a teenage stripper with whom he becomes obsessed. Even *The Sweet Hereafter*, with its more literal evocation of a killing landscape, is ultimately about doomed and tortured patriarchal imperative: unblessed home-building. Based on Russell Banks's melancholy novel, it follows a troubled lawyer's attempts to relieve his own sense of paternal failure (his daughter is a suicidal drug addict) by playing conniving saviour to the families bereaved by the accident. Indeed, if there is a single dramatic pre-occupation to Egoyan's work, it is the desperate attempt to build something like home, usually through the medium of something like family. It is an attempt bound to fail due to the most elementary of engineering oversights: homes without foundations collapse. Sooner or later the weight of their own artifice brings them down. Interestingly, however, Egoyan's films have consistently been marked by a kind of melodramatic pose of closure, moments of final punc-tuation so archly articulated that they seem to mock the very idea of happy endings, and thus the possibility of home itself: the kiss that summons the end credits in *Speaking Parts*, the haunted suburban pastoral that concludes *Exotica*, the hand stretched before the flame (of a burning home) in *The Adjuster*. Even *The Sweet Hereafter*, which carefully wraps up its narrative strands by weaving together moments that suggest a form of peace beyond catastrophe, contains a distant rumble of doubt: the final image, of the young woman we know will be crippled and sexually abused after the flashback we are seeing, undercuts the very notion of an unbitter sweetness hereafter: she has yet to face the horror of that mountain ride. An ending yes, but happy? Not quite.

The ending of *Felicia's Journey*, on the other hand, strikes no mere momentary attitude of contentment. On the contrary, like Hilditch pleading desperately for Felicia to 'let the healing start' before releas-ing her to the rich soil of a nurturing future, the film seems almost hysterically determined to convince us that everything that we have seen – the systematic cruelty, loneliness, disappointment, heartbreak and alienation – can be swept away in an instant of soul-cleansing clarity. Strangely then, while it would appear to be intended as the least ironic of Egoyan's happy endings, it is the one that most desperately seems so: it registers as if it were a dream of a happy ending, a vision of peace and home that might visit someone for whom such ideas are, and can never be, more than fantasies, momentary and necessary escapes from the oppressive reality bearing down. It seems, that is, the type of fantasy that the mad Felicia at the conclusion of Trevor's book might have before falling asleep in another alley on another hopeless night, or that which a Canadian filmmaker like Egoyan, otherwise so deeply disinclined to believe in such ideas, might have of the impossible dream of a place like home.

Addendum: Ten years on

As far as the basic concepts expressed in the foregoing essay are concerned, not a whole lot has changed for either Atom Egoyan or the country he calls – albeit self-consciously – home. While there may be certain superficial adjustments to both – Egoyan's critical cache has waned somewhat as he approaches 50, and he is now nearly as likely to be directing operas as he is movies; and Canada is, if anything, a more multicultural hotbed of conflicting ideas of 'Canadianness' – the basic presumptions governing both are in place. Which is to say, Atom Egoyan still tends to make movies about the struggle for something like home, while Canada remains a place where such struggles inevitably lead artists down the sucking existential vortex of alienation. If anything, the defining conundrum of Egoyan's work, which is how one marks a meaningful sense of place in a world where the tools for doing so permit such wanton fabrication and self-erasure, is only more vexing now than it was a decade ago. Interestingly, as Canada in the early twenty-first century has seemed to relinquish some of its zeal for cohesive national identity in tandem with its increasing status as a place anyone (theoretically anyway) can call home – one of the more successful home-made TV series of the twenty-first century's new decade was called *Little Mosque on the Prairie* – Egoyan's own pursuit of existential cohesion has only drawn him that much further from anything resembling a beaten path – including his own.

But it has also resulted in a certain crisis of uncertainty in his work – there was uncertainty before, but it was at least a strangely confident uncertainty – and this is nowhere more evident than in the recurring instances in his recent work of the question – not always literal, but always looming – 'What the hell are we doing here?' By mid-career, the questions that animated the young filmmaker, and which were ultimately optimistic in their concern for the status of the individual soul in the global machine, now seem more paralysing than provocative. By 2009, it looked as though the filmmaker might have self-questioned himself right into a corner. The decade began with *Ararat*, Egoyan's long dreamed-about film addressing the Armenian genocide. But it is Egoyan's Armenian genocide that is the subject here, which means that the movie is not about history but is a movie about a movie that is stricken by questions of history: who writes it? Who owns it? And what becomes of what is left out? *Ararat* is an historical movie about the impossibility of being precisely that, a self-inscribing void that projects Egoyan's previously rather intimate explorations of ontological meaninglessness on a world-historical scale.

Echoing *Calendar* is *Citadel*, a documentary made by Egoyan on the occasion of his wife Arsinee Khanjian's first visit to Beirut, Lebanon, since civil war forced her departure, as a teenager, 28 years previously. Narrated by Egoyan and addressed to his and Khanjian's son Arshile, *Citadel* is fascinating, penetrating and intelligent, but it ultimately stumbles backward onto the spear of its own self-consciousness. As Egoyan follows his wife on pilgrimages to childhood places which largely are no longer there, and as he opens his frame to include the history of the 1982 civil war that brought his future bride to Canada, Egoyan gradually begins to question the entire enterprise of not only what he's doing but what we're making of it. By the end, *Citadel* crosses the line between documentary and drama with the introduction of a sensational development that is later revealed to be bogus. Its stated point? To prove how easily fooled we are, and thus how pointless any attempt is at capturing anything other than, as the movie itself suggests, 'pure light' with a camera.

Where the Truth Lies is Egoyan's most nakedly commercial project, and it too becomes impaled on the question of fundamental meaninglessness. Based on a pulp novel written by the pop singer turned author Rupert Holmes, the story concerns a journalistic investigation into the apparent murder of a young woman in a hotel suite occupied by one-half of a Martin and Lewis-esque musical comedy team played by Kevin Bacon and Colin Firth. Also at first blink a stretch for the filmmaker, Egoyan's interest in the material is hardly difficult to divine. *Where the Truth Lies* is ultimately about the utter relativity of truth, which means it is also a mystery that disdains mystery and a thriller at paralysing odds with its own thrills.

In apparent retreat from the drubbing widely taken by *Where the Truth Lies*, Egoyan returned at least to early-period form with *Adoration*, a movie that reconfigures many of the mediated-family melodramatic tropes of *Next of Kin*, *Family Viewing* and *Speaking Parts* – with traces of *The Sweet Hereafter* also present and accounted for. The story of a teenage boy who fabricates a false identity for himself on the internet as a means of re-writing a family history steeped in misunderstanding, resentment and disgrace, the movie at least feels like the purest Egoyan piece since *The Adjuster*. But it also seems less like a reclamation than a retreat, and although the circumstances (post 9/11) and the technology (the web) belong to the new century, the artist's response seems stuck on the pre-millenial side of the historical divide.

Perhaps it was inevitable that an artist who dedicated himself to the question of action forestalled by technologically-induced existential crisis would himself one day become stuck. But stuck and stopped are two different things, and Egoyan is far too talented and intelligent a filmmaker to presume stalled for good. If anything, it's a question of finding new questions to ask. For the time being, Egoyan has apparently ventured as far as he can by wondering if there's any point to expecting anything other than relative realities from recorded interventions. If there's anything beyond the lens, it lies somewhere outside of truth. Now knowing what we can't see, Atom Egoyan's challenge would seem to be imagining what we can.

Biography

Born in Egypt, in 1960, Egoyan was raised and works in Canada.

Filmography

(All Canadian production unless otherwise indicated)

Next of Kin (1984)
Family Viewing (1987)
Speaking Parts (1989)
The Adjuster (1991)
Calendar (1993)
Exotica (1994)
The Sweet Hereafter (1997)
Felicia's Journey (Canada/UK, 1999)
Krapp's Last Tape (Canada/UK, 2000)
Ararat (2002)
Citadel (2004)
Where the Truth Lies (2005)
Adoration (2008)

Further reading

Carole Desbarats, Daniele Riviere and Jacinto Lageira, *Atom Egoyan*, Paris, Dis Voir, 1993.

Atom Egoyan, *Exotica: The Screenplay*, Toronto, Coach House Press, 1995.

Geoff Pevere and Greig Dymond, *Mondo Canuck: A Canadian Pop Culture Odyssey*, Toronto, Prentice-Hall Canada, 1996.

DAVID FINCHER

By Devin Orgeron

David Fincher is something of an anomaly: a big-budget, commercial, Hollywood filmmaker whose films are large, high-concept, and star-laden. Like Stanley Kubrick before him, however, Fincher manages, from within the system, to make films that are critical not only of 'The System' but of *systems* more generally. His films are especially apprehensive about his generation's apparent desire for a highly suspect, largely compensatory brand of stability and structure, and in this way the link to Kubrick is not mere fancy. Fincher's themes of alienation and discontent, as well as the visual design of his films, descend in marked ways from his predecessor. And, like Kubrick's, Fincher's films, most especially *Fight Club*, have been the subject of much heated debate, particularly over the filmmaker's possible contributions to that which he purports to critique. To what degree, critics ask, are his films a celebration of their sometimes violent, anarchistic subjects?

Fincher rose to popular and critical prominence with *Seven*, a film that chronicles an aging and thoroughly disenchanted Detective Sommerset's (Morgan Freeman) attempts to retire peacefully from the profession that brought him to the end of his psychological rope. A series of highly structured murders enacted according to the seven deadly sins, and the as-yet uncorrupted moral outlook of his younger partner, Detective Mills (Brad Pitt), however, slowly reactivate Sommerset, causing both men to reflect upon their ability to effect change. The film moves well beyond the potential pitfalls of the bi-racial buddy/cop film Hollywood continues to produce. Like all of Fincher's films to date, *Seven* is at its best in its critique of late twentieth century complacency, or as the Deadly Sins would have it, *apathy*. John Doe (Kevin Spacey), the film's serial murderer, enacts his rage toward a society grown comfortable in its moral bankruptcy upon the bodies of his victims. Sommerset, also repulsed by the city, perhaps even the world, seeks not revenge or punishment, but escape.

His own disgust nearly forces him to the ultimate act of complacency: dropping out altogether, leaving the force, the city, and his past behind. The film's visual design, its acute attention to the mise-en-scène of the contemporary urban space and its instability and violence, lends significantly to these, Fincher's larger, less generically bound themes.

The Kubrickian notion of man alone in the universe he's created for himself is a theme Fincher's films return to repeatedly, and in *Seven* this feeling of isolation finds its visual expression in Fincher and director of photography Darius Khondji's wide angle, shallow-focus cinematography. Space is engulfing, threatening to absorb the individual and trap him in his anonymity. Fincher reduces the details of the mise-en-scène, transforming them into an all-encompassing, amorphous blanket behind his centrally composed, smaller-than-life protagonists. This idea is foregrounded in Fincher's decision to locate *Seven* in an anonymous city, a sort of stripped down 'any-city' with no defining physical or historical characteristics (save for its constant, sheeting rainfall). The individual, Fincher's films repeatedly suggest, is at risk of disappearing in an indifferent, contemporary world.

A less commercially successful but equally engaged film, *The Game*, continues *Seven*'s central critique of complacency; it is also the prototype for his subsequent foray into the realm of chaos and hyperreality, *Fight Club*. *The Game* assigns a class to complacency: the rich. Fincher has arranged the narrative details so that there is satisfaction in watching our hapless protagonist Nicholas Van Orton (Michael Douglas) shaken, in classic Hitchcockian fashion, to his very foundation; it is no coincidence that Fincher's film, like *Vertigo* (1958), is set in San Francisco. *The Game*, however, shares more in common with Hitchcock's more popular thriller *North by Northwest* (1959). Like our introduction to Roger Thornhill (Cary Grant), our introduction to Nicholas is not an especially favorable one. He is arrogant, aloof, conspicuously wealthy; however he is also, like Hitchcock's character, redeemable. Nicholas's brother Conrad (Sean Penn), the younger and more reckless of the two, serves in the film as his saviour, enlisting Nicholas in a complex game as part of a bizarre and extravagant birthday gift. The game, which to Nicholas is indistinguishable from reality and causes him to question his relationship *to* reality, quite literally forces Nicholas to *hit bottom*, an idea at the heart of *Fight Club*. Nicholas emerges, by game's and film's end, reborn and separate from his comfortable, predictable, safe, and seemingly emotionless existence. The game has humanised him.

As with *Seven*, *The Game* is muted in both light and colour. It is also a film that perpetuates what are clearly the thematic obsessions of its director. Fincher, as critics have been fast to point out, is simultaneously fascinated and repulsed by the American city and it, more than John Doe's false moral superiority in *Seven* or Nicholas's comfortable, classed existence in *The Game*, is the enemy, the destroyer of men. The city plays a central role in *Fight Club* and *Panic Room* also; and *Zodiac* in Fincher's hands becomes more a tragic city-symphony than a violent serial killer biopic.

At a glance, the bulk of Fincher's work appears to be primarily interested in the psychological and emotional state of the contemporary American male, seemingly at the expense of fully developed female characters. Writing about Gwyneth Paltrow's portrayal of Mills's wife Tracy in *Seven*, Amy Taubin compares the character's 'saintly domesticity' to the women in John Ford's films.[1] As with Ford's women, who gaze upon their men as they engage in activities of mobility, there is a distinct sense that behind this static gaze lies a more complete, more complex knowledge of the American family, its dissolution, its decay. Fincher's men act, often recklessly, but his women *know*.

In *Seven*, Mills's wife Tracy is murdered before she has the opportunity to inform her husband of her pregnancy and after tearfully divulging her secret to Sommerset. Tracy discloses a fear that Sommerset himself admits to giving in to many years previously: the fear of bringing another being into the city. The city, *Seven* suggests, has made Ford's romanticised agrarian domesticity an impossibility. John Doe also speaks to this failure in *Seven*, informing Mills that before he murdered Tracy he attempted to 'play husband' with her, though unsuccessfully.

The family's vulnerability is explored most acutely in *Panic Room* where the connection to John Ford's *The Searchers* is literalised and urbanised, though here the viewer's point of view is aligned throughout with the threatened and abandoned women themselves. Recent divorcee Meg Altman (Jodie Foster) and her daughter Sarah's (Kristen Stewart) search for a new home in New York City, and their ultimate decision (not without some heated debate) to move into an enormous brownstone with a panic room (a sort of internal fortress installed by the home's previous owner, a rich, eccentric invalid) are the net result of an act of male abandonment. Unlike *Seven*, which ends in irreparable fragmentation, Fincher goes to great lengths in this film to restore familial unity.

The room itself functions as a metaphor for a machine-like male 'logic' Meg has grown to distrust and Sarah still views as a form of protection. But the room, like Fincher's men, fails, becoming a trap to the claustrophobic woman and her diabetic daughter when a gang of semi-competent burglars attempts to liberate the room (their hiding place) of its previous owner's wealth. Fincher's familial thesis is underscored by the gang's 'leader', Junior (Jared Leto), who is the previous owner's grandson. Redemption comes in the form of Meg's former husband, Stephen, who responds to her panicked call and, perhaps for his prior transgressions, is beaten within an inch of his life. The film ends (thankfully) before the family is reunited, but the implied outcome is clear enough.

In *The Game*, Fincher's interest in the family is focused even more squarely on the theme of abandonment. Nicholas is divorced. His bachelor's existence is captured in much the same way Sommerset's is in *Seven* (though differently marked by class). His home is a fortress to himself and his obsessive selfhood, characterisations implied by widely composed shots that highlight the vastness of his immediate space (though it pre-dates *Panic Room*, one wouldn't be at all surprised to find a similar room in Nicholas's conspicuously safe mansion). Gated and enormous, it, like the city, threatens to swallow its occupant. His housekeeper, Ilsa (Carol Baker), functions more like a mother than a maid. The evening of his birthday she prepares for him a child's plate (though under a stunning silver lid) of a hamburger and French fries; a cupcake with a candle serves as dessert. Nicholas, in spite of his existence in a seemingly adult world, is trapped in the realm of his own problematic childhood (an idea literalised in 2008's Academy Award contender, *The Curious Case of Benjamin Button*). The suicide of Nicholas's father is presented in the film as a supreme act of familial abandonment, one that forced Nicholas to prematurely assume an adult role and the presumed rituals that come with that role. Fatherlessness, then, is partly to blame for Nicholas's condition, though it is combined with a highly routinised misunderstanding of masculinity.

Nicholas is sick but salvageable. The Zodiac Killer is just sick, but the disease is the same one that afflicts all of Fincher's men: obsession, routine, mechanisation, and a need (seldom spoken and always per-verted) to step out from behind the anonymity of contemporary existence. No newcomer to working with digital technology, Fincher uses it in *Zodiac* to great effect. Those blankets of blankness and artifice that characterise his earlier work seem even more alien (and alienating) here; indeed, Fincher's crime-scene aesthetic may well put one in mind of Errol Morris's much-discussed 'recreations' of the crime in *The Thin Blue Line* (1988).

Fincher's film, as I've suggested, is a fractured city symphony – maybe even a dirge. Like the city symphonies that predate it, *Zodiac*'s 'musicality' is premised on parallel forms. The film is about the Zodiac Killer, it's true, but the obsessions that grow in the wake of those infamous 1970s murders are also Fincher's subject. Robert Graysmith (Jake Gyllenhaal), the cartoonist-turned-sleuth at the film's centre, is sympathetic, smart, and likeable in an aw-shucks kind of way, but his involvement in the case pulls him deeper and deeper into precisely the kind of sociopathic existence Fincher's work examines so intently. His obsession becomes an act of abandonment, and his wife Melanie (Chloe Sevigny) and children are the casualities. Male obsession and the women and children in its wake are also critical ideas in *Seven* and *Fight Club*.

Zodiac doesn't linger on the theme of fractured human relationships, but the effect is palpable. After 157 minutes even the viewer is left feeling isolated, removed from the very characters and events the film purports to be about. Robert Downey Jr's Paul Avery eventually expatriates himself to a docked boat, paralleling the viewer's own enforced distance, the killer's alienation, and Graysmith's antisocial obsession. *The Curious Case of Benjamin Button*, on the other hand, is a veritable treatise on abandonment and isolation.

An initial act of paternal abandonment spins Benjamin's (Brad Pitt) entire universe into reverse. Parentless, he populates his life with an array of surrogate mothers – Queenie (Taraji P. Henson) and Daisy (Cate Blanchett) both 'raise' him at different points in his odd 'progression', and point up the absurdity of his struggle to be independent. One is reminded of *Fight Club*'s reduction of the male predicament to 'a generation of men raised by women' and of Nicholas's perpetual childhood in *The Game*. The film contains some of Fincher's best female characters yet (Benjamin's story, one must recall, is told from Daisy's point of view), and seems to underscore Fincher's interest in men whose personal trajectory is interrupted by the cowardice of other men. Benjamin can find community nowhere, and the film's 166 minutes are, more than anything, a tragically protracted realisation of this fact. Based on an F. Scott Fitzgerald story of the same name, the reverse-ageing idea feels like a literary conceit problematically literalised through the quasi-indexical magic of digital cinema. But the viewer's visual engagement with Benjamin's hyperbolised solitary existence is key, for in the end Benjamin retreats from us – and our varying degrees of revulsion – as well.

Though *Benjamin Button* is unquestionably the director's most ambitious film to date, Fincher's ideas about the state of the individual in contemporary society are even more articulately realised in *Fight Club*. Very much in keeping with Fincher's interest in the contemporary state of masculinity, *Fight Club* is reminiscent of Stanley Kubrick's most controversial film, *A Clockwork Orange* (1971), both in theme and in popular and critical reception. It is a film steeped in 'ultraviolence'. It is a film about men who, on the surface, seem indifferent to women and fully invested in male relationships defined by acts of violence. It is also a film critical of its own audience. Where *Benjamin Button* punishes the viewer for conditionally accepting and identifying with the film's protagonist at his most Brad Pitt-like moments, *Fight Club* is critical of an audience that accepts the idea of 'Tyler Durden' too readily. Our un-named narrator (Edward Norton), who occasionally refers to himself in his voiceover monologues as some organ or another belonging to 'Jack' (an idea gleaned from a stack of similarly narrated magazines he finds), is what Susan Faludi identifies as the personification of 'the modern male predicament: he's fatherless, trapped in a cubicle in an anonymous job, trying to glean an identity from Ikea brochures, entertainment magazines and self-help gatherings. Jack traverses a barren landscape familiar to many men who must contend with a world stripped of socially useful male roles and saturated with commercial images of masculinity'.[2] Faludi's argument that the film is ultimately 'a quasi-feminist tale' relies upon her reading of the film's seemingly very old-Hollywood ending where our hitherto uninterested narrator joins hands (and forces) with the film's only female character, Marla (Helena Bonham Carter), whose neurotic existence outside of 'the system' has remained invisible to the narrator until film's end.

The narrator's literalised doppelganger (the ambitious literalisation of a difficult literary conceit here is more successful than it is in *Benjamin Button*), Tyler Durden (Brad Pitt), *is* the commercial image of masculinity, one that the narrator buys into in precisely the way he buys into Ikea's vision of personal space. The narrator's myopic and narcissistic obsession with his own alter ego consumes his life and blinds him to Marla who, the film suggests, is the more appropriate 'object choice'. Tyler (Fincher's decision to cast Pitt in this role is a stroke of genius) is another commodity in a culture that fetishises commodities; he is the narrator's media-derived fantasy of independent masculinity. He is Hollywood's version of the individualist; he is pretty, strong, and maintains an animalistically active and emotionless sex-life with Marla. Tyler's connection to the world of film is hinted at in his late-night job as a porn-splicing projectionist. His role as *image*, however, functions more provocatively. His image is introduced in the film one frame at a time, a feature virtually (but not entirely) unnoticeable without viewing the film on DVD and pausing on these single inserted frames. He operates, like the penises he splices into children's films, at the subliminal level. At one point in the film, Tyler's image addresses the audience directly, shaking the cinematic frame containing him as he does so and exposing the sprocket holes at either edge. Tyler is film; film is seductive. And, through much of *Fight Club*, Tyler's warped ideas about hitting bottom are likewise seductive both to our narrator (whose imagination has created Tyler) and to the viewer. There is something appealingly base in Tyler's philosophical stance, at the centre of which are the clubs themselves. Late-night, bare-knuckled, male exclusive basement brawls, Fight Club contests are simple, brutal and, to the contestants, affirming in their ability to reclaim some mythic sense of the masculine individual. Project Mayhem, an anarchistic branch of the clubs, proposes to extend exponentially Tyler's brand of primitivism by leveling the corporate world and balancing the economic playing field. The seductiveness of these ideas, however, spins out of control.

Men, the film suggests, are in a precarious state in contemporary American culture, where even the notion of individuality is a product of consumer culture. Fight Club and Project Mayhem are flawed because their organisational logic descends from the very structures their members seek to escape (perverted reiterations of mainstream organisation are central to *Seven* and *Zodiac* as well). Fight Club becomes a franchise and Project Mayhem an exceedingly fascistic and militaristic operation reminiscent of Kubrick's vision of boot camp in *Full Metal Jacket* (1987). While the narrator's fight is ultimately an internal one (in a twist on the logic of Vietnam, he must shoot himself in order to save himself), the film is careful not to blame the *individual* for his own unravelling.

As the beginning of this essay suggests, it is ultimately the system – in this case, an inescapable, corrupting, capitalist system – that has undone the individual. Even Fincher's debut feature film, *Alien 3*, a film the director all but disowns as he did not oversee the final cut, contains remnants of what have come to be Fincher's central themes. *Alien*ation and family (particularly of the maternal sort) are larger-than-life issues in the entire *Alien* series. The series is also critical of the capitalist system and, Fincher's film perhaps more than any other in the series, focuses on this problem by positing, in microcosmic form, a generation (or penal colony) of men abandoned by and alienated from the system they helped to build. The outpost in *Alien 3* is an extension of Fincher's decaying urban landscape.

Herein, however, lies a fundamental problem. Fincher, in spite of his acute critiques of consumer culture, has also participated in it to varying degrees. He made his foray into visual culture in the early 1980s, working for George Lucas (an acknowledged hero of the young filmmaker-to-be) and Industrial Light and Magic. This largely technical work served as Fincher's film school. From ILM, Fincher began a career directing advertisements for major organisations (the 'smoking fetus' campaign for the American Cancer Society in the 1980s was an early sign of his genius) and music videos for A-list pop-stars. Fincher was one of the founding members of the super-slick production company Propaganda Films, nomenclature that hints at a sense of irony that runs through his work and the work of his peers. An iteration of this influential firm, now called Anonymous Content, also has a feature film division and Fincher is one of the company's touted directors. Far from anonymous, Anonymous has pioneered a new era of boutique-style, *authored* advertisements and videos. Fincher's relationship to the image is thus a complicated one. He is not a 'sellout' as that term has traditionally been used. He is, rather, the perfect model of postmodern *image infatuation*. Fincher's almost childlike love for things that look cool, most obviously and endearingly revealed in the director's voiceover comments on the DVD versions of his own work, keeps him working in a more broadly conceived visual realm than many of his predecessors. Errol Morris, who also makes television advertisements, has referred to them as the haiku of the West. Fincher's relationship to the form might be less poetic. His commercial work, however, like Morris's, exhibits a love for the image, disconnected from its possible relationship to products or profits.

Biography

David Fincher was born in Denver, Colorado, in 1962. He has directed seven feature films to date and has been an active part of a new wave of image-makers who work consistently in advertising and music videos. Working for Industrial Light and Magic in the early 1980s, Fincher contributed optical effects for *Twice Upon a Time* (1983), *The Return of the Jedi* (1983), *Indiana Jones and the Temple of Doom* (1984), and *The NeverEnding Story* (1984) and began to hone a distinct visual style and a penchant for experimentation that follows the filmmaker to this day. Fincher is both an aesthetic perfectionist and an adroit Hollywood deal-broker whose skills in both categories keep his roster of current projects or projects under consideration unusually full.

Notes

1 Amy Taubin, 'The Allure of Decay', *Sight and Sound*, vol. 6, no. 1, 1996, p. 23.
2 Susan Faludi, 'It's *Thelma and Louise* for Guys', *Newsweek*, 25 October, 1999, p. 89.

Filmography

Alien 3 (1992)
Seven (1995)
The Game (1997)
Fight Club (1999)
Panic Room (2002)
Zodiac (2007)
The Curious Case of Benjamin Button (2008)

Further reading

Ilsa J. Bick, ' 'Well, I guess I Must Make You Nervous': Woman and the Space of *Alien 3*', *Post Script: Essays in Film and the Humanities*, vol. 14, nos 1 and 2 (Fall 1994, Winter/Spring 1995), pp. 45–58.
Chris Drake, 'Inside the Light', *Sight and Sound*, vol. 6, no. 4, 1996, pp. 18–20.
Richard Dyer, 'Kill and Kill Again', *Sight and Sound*, vol. 7, no. 9, 1997, pp. 14–17.
——, *Seven*, London, BFI Publishing, 1999.
Graham Fuller, 'Up the Hill Backwards', *Sight and Sound*, vol. 19, no. 3, 2009, pp. 26–7, 29.
Steve Macek, 'Places of Horror: Fincher's *Seven* and Fear of the City in Recent Hollywood Film', *College Literature*, Special Issue 26, no. 1, 1999, pp. 81–97.
Amy Taubin, 'So Good it Hurts', *Sight and Sound*, vol. 9, no. 11, 1999, pp. 16–18.
Linda Ruth Williams, 'Mother Courage', *Sight and Sound*, vol. 12, no. 5, 2002, pp. 12–14.
John Wrathall, '*Seven*: a Film Review', *Sight and Sound*, vol. 6, no. 1, 1996, pp. 49–50.

HAL HARTLEY

By Sebastian Manley

Since the modest success of his 1989 debut feature, *The Unbelievable Truth*, Hal Hartley has worked almost exclusively at the low end of the 'independent' film sector, making distinctive low-budget films with limited distribution prospects. His films are often discussed in terms of their characters: an array of eccentrics, hipsters, philosophers and lost souls – each with a gift for poetic contemplation and deadpan witticisms. He has also provided the independent film world with some of its most unusual and memorable images of New York, from the flattened, faintly fantastical landscapes of the early Long Island features, to the 'Europeanised' city streets of *Amateur*, to the futuristic Manhattan of *The Girl From Monday*. Hartley is the sole writer and director of all of his ten feature films, and has often served as his own composer, producer and editor. Yet if his working practices and artistic fixations are suggestive of an American auteur, there is also a sense in which Hartley refuses to play the game of industrial authorial cinema, making surprising artistic detours and repeatedly declining the chance to 'graduate' to a more prestigious division of indie film-making. Comprising ten features, twelve short films, several music videos, an art exhibition piece (*The Other Also*, 1997), a play (*Soon*, 1998) and, most recently, an opera (*La Commedia*, 2008), Hartley's artistic output is marked by a restless dissatisfaction with the mechanics of storytelling and style in contemporary film culture.

Hartley's idiosyncrasies as a director have not made for an easy course through the production–distribution process, and many of his films have received only narrow and short theatrical releases. Only in the early stages of his career did Hartley seem to embody the combination of hip weirdness and accessibility required for sustained visibility in the independent world: his first three features, *The Unbelievable Truth*, *Trust* and *Simple Men*, rode a wave of critical goodwill and festival buzz, and established their director as an influential presence in the indie scene developing on the edges of Hollywood. Picked up by Miramax in 1989, *The Unbelievable Truth* was an attractive product for an industry just beginning to realise the potential of alternative, low-budget films to secure mainstream audiences. As with Steven Soderbergh's more famous 1989 debut, *sex, lies, & videotape*, much of the appeal lay in the details of production. Even in independent film terms, the budget was ludicrously low: Hartley remembers deliberately *overstating* the figure at $200,000, in fear that distributors would not take seriously a film costing just $75,000. Moreover, the money was put up by Hartley's boss at the TV company for which he was working – an amateur funding story of the sort beloved by press notes compilers which was widely reproduced in journalistic coverage.

The film itself, an off-beat satire on suburbia and the commercial power system, draws on the aesthetics of European art cinema while narrating a familiar (if quirkily individualised) story of familial malcontent and youthful rebellion. It follows teenage heroine Audry, played with typical subtlety by the late indie actress and director Adrienne Shelly, as she struggles with her feelings of alienation and powerlessness – expressed in particular through her fear of an impending nuclear apocalypse. Audry is differentiated from both the blue-collar and white-collar (commuter) classes of Long Island by her all-black dress-code, 'essentially the default bohemian uniform of the 1980s', according to Jeffrey Sconce, and signifying a conscious aversion to the triviality and commerciality of mainstream fashion.[1] Audry's bohemian credentials, though, are put in doubt as she embarks on a career in fashion modelling, moving away to the city and leaving behind her soul mate Josh (Robert John Burke), an austerely dressed auto-mechanic with a criminal past. The film invites us to admire Audry's adventurous rejection of suburban routine (more commonly the privilege of male characters in independent film), while at the same time presenting her new life as an unfortunate capitulation to capitalism and its unfulfilling value system. *The Unbelievable Truth*'s romantic close has Audry and Josh reunited as she signs away her money and annuls all the personal and financial deals she has made with her father. Thus the film anticipates a number of early 1990s' films, including *Slacker* (1991) and *Reality Bites* (1994), concerned with the 'dropping out' of young Americans from the 'American Dream' of economic opportunity and upward mobility so aggressively promoted by the Reagan administration of the 1980s.

Similar concerns with work and suburban ennui figure in *Trust* and *Simple Men*: together with *The Unbelievable Truth* these films form what is often referred to as Hartley's 'Long Island trilogy'. Still among his most accomplished and poignant films, each stands as an early entry in the now populous genre of the satirical suburb film (spanning low-budget indies like *Spanking the Monkey* and *SubUrbia* and box-office successes like *The Truman Show* and *American Beauty*), centring the tropes of isolation and strangeness. Yet there is a particularising impulse at the heart of Hartley's films which betrays his intense identification with Long Island. The setting of *The Unbelievable Truth* and *Trust* and of part of *Simple Men* is Hartley's hometown, Lindenhurst – a small, middle-class and mostly white town on the southern shore of Suffolk County. A place of strange landscapes, bizarre tabloid crime and oddly melancholy anger, the Long Island of these films is both recognisable and highly personalised, drawing together popular notions of the region and Hartley's own memories of the small town in which he grew up (typically, Hartley accounts are unflattering, to say the least: in a 1992 profile he characterised Long Island as a 'corridor without a door at the other end'[2]). *Trust*, a melancholy portrait of a town hit by the 1990–91 recession, supplements its gritty, everyday realism – the plot touches on the compromises and disappointments involved in both nine-to-five labour and family life – with a strange subplot about the case of a kidnapped baby, solved, after some detective work, by the female protagonist Maria. *Simple Men* charts the journey of two brothers looking for their father, an alleged terrorist and former baseball personality on the run in rural Long Island. More readily associated with the American city, lurid crimes of this nature are an everyday part of small-town life in Hartley's films. Coming at exactly the time when Long Island was capturing headlines in the national press for a series of unusual murders and other violent crimes – a supposed trend exemplified by the so-called 'Long Island Lolita' case involving Amy Fisher, convicted for shooting the wife of her lover Joey Buttafuoco – the films offer a particular tabloid frisson that remains a marketable quality.

Amateur was Hartley's first full-length film to be set entirely in New York City, although SoHo and Brooklyn had provided the settings for the early shorts *Ambition*, a Godardian pastiche with a striking colour scheme, and *Theory of Achievement*, an affectionate essay of wannabe artist-intellectuals struggling despite their privilege to realise their ambitions. No less than the earlier suburban dramas, *Amateur* is an examination of personal identity and the vexations of intimate relationships, mapped here onto the broader canvas of the city. The film's male protagonist, Thomas (Martin Donovan), is an amnesiac; with the help of Isabelle (Isabelle Huppert), a former nun with aspirations of being a writer of pornography, he slowly unearths his own unsavoury personal history as a violent misogynist working under the aegis of a transnational pornographic film business. Hartley exploits the New York City setting to formulate an explicit critique of America's consolidated corporate order. Thomas is pursued by two suited heavies emblematic of corporate power and wholesale commodification – bureaucratic and executive, they are also practised in torture and talk casually of the female body as a 'useful' article of trade – who have been sent to retrieve sensitive materials used in a blackmailing attempt.

One of the most talked about features of *Amateur* was Isabelle Huppert, the first 'star' to be associated with Hartley's film world and its mainly repertory casts. Huppert's prominent career as an actress in European arthouse films haunts both her character (lines such as 'I'm coldly intellectual. Too pale. Altogether too ethereal' play overtly on her star image – with just a little too much ostentation for some critics[3]) and the film itself, which plays out its expressionist noir drama on the narrow cobblestone streets of a strangely European New York. Indeed, Hartley's work is very often characterised by a 'European' style of design and performance: Huppert is just one of the more obvious examples of this influence. If Hartley's films share one stylistic feature it is their preference for flattened, deadpanned performances. Offering a kind a performance more associated with European theatre (and particularly the 'Theatre of the Absurd' grouping of playwrights) than cinema, actors deliver their dialogue – aphorisms, repetitions and odd juxtapositions informing the most memorable exchanges – in an unmodulated tone of voice, while maintaining an unusually impassive expression. Beyond this 'blank' acting style, the films exploit a large range of striking devices which function in various ways to subvert the 'classical' style of Hollywood cinema: the static long shots and leisurely editing of the Long Island features; the unexpected dance sequences in *Simple Men* and the short *Surviving Desire*; the dramatic night-time exterior shots in *Amateur*, filmed by cinematographer Michael Spiller with the use of a blue gel; the woozy DV camerawork in *The Book of Life* and *The Girl From Monday*, replete with light distortion, blurred visuals, tints and freeze frames.

As a satirical and inquiring filmmaker, Hartley has always been concerned to explore the personal dilemmas of his protagonists within specific social contexts – an impulse that informs both small-scale dramas like *Trust* (whose image of a line of people waiting with their TVs outside a repair shop is as striking a symbol of the national recession as any in early 1990s' cinema) and bigger, more obviously political films like *Amateur* and *The Girl From Monday*. If Hartley is a committed stylist – and an often brilliant one at that – then he also knows that stylisation and social commentary need not be confined to separate types of filmmaking. In an interview about *No Such Thing*, Hartley suggested that his filming of a 'monster movie' was linked to the idea that the fantasy genres, with their emphasis on artifice and spectacle, can provide a framework for social critique: 'it's funny but you have to be more fantastic to talk about reality, like *Godzilla*'.[4] Thus the film contemplates the social via metaphor and unusual juxtapositions – an approach shared by the millennial religious fantasy *The Book of Life* and *The Girl From Monday*, the final entry in Hartley's loose trilogy of fantastical films.

Declining the opportunity to bring a harsh, vérité-style realism to horror/sci-fi material, or to extend a psychological explanation for traditionally supernatural phenomena (both common strategies among independents working in fantastical genres), Hartley's films present instead an entertaining gloss on contemporary society and politics, making strange the world as it 'naturally' is. Of these three films, *No Such Thing* stands out as in many ways the most unusual and surprising. Originally conceived as a low-budget production making use of overseas financing, the film was eventually made with Francis Ford Coppola's production company American Zoetrope, in conjunction with MGM/UA, for a $5 million price tag – Hartley's largest budget by some way. Press accounts and Hartley's own comments suggest that MGM had reservations about the film's playability to mainstream audiences, and put pressure on Hartley to make modifications and even a re-cut; ultimately, the film gained a theatrical release of just three weeks (the contractual minimum) and met with a lukewarm critical reception. Indeed, *No Such Thing*, notwithstanding its star cast (Helen Mirren, Julie Christie) and impressive make-up effects for the 'monster', frustrates many of the expectations associated with larger-budget 'Indiewood' productions, preserving Hartley's longstanding preference for highly stylised performances and offering a sometimes awkward mix of melodrama and satire. But there is much to admire in this caustic fable about the political power of the media industry, from the rarely filmed Icelandic 'black desert' landscapes, to the entertaining jeremiads of the Monster, played by Robert John Burke as a typically Hartleyan melancholic.

With *The Girl From Monday*, a low-tech science-fiction art film in the tradition of Godard's *Alphaville*, Truffaut's *Fahrenheit 451* and John Sayles's *The Brother From Another Planet* (1984), Hartley returned to a more low-stakes and less accountable form of filmmaking. The extent to which Hartley's artistic independence is dependent on a high level of economic savvy is evident in *The Girl From Monday*'s production–distribution history: Hartley financed and (for the first time) self-distributed the film through his own Possible Films company, removing most institutional pressures from the production process and increasing the scope for low-budget experimentation. Famously parsimonious and open to the increasing opportunities for overseas investment, Hartley is unusual among low-profile independents in finding enough money to fund regular personal projects – and this without taking on the 'gun-for-hire' writing or script-doctoring work that often provides funding for marginal filmmakers. One way in which Hartley has kept up his commitment to innovative filmmaking is through producing short films. Like David Lynch and a few other experimental but principally industrial independents, Hartley has made shorts throughout his career, taking advantage of the low costs of production (aside from the obvious savings, actors can agree to be paid a low wage under the Screen Actors Guild's 'limited exhibition' contract) to put together short-form sketches or 'essays' that supplement, prefigure or expand upon his narrative features. Characteristically, the short films dwell on questions of place and identity: in Hartley's 16mm graduation film, *Kid*, a boy yearns to leave Lindenhurst for the city; in *Flirt*, later combined with two more short films to create a three-part omnibus, Bill Sage's character mulls over the nature of love and commitment; and in *NYC 3/94*, New York City is imagined as a war zone, shaking to the sound of machine-gun fire.

While Hartley remains a productive and provocative director, his recent films have represented a tough sell to an increasingly crowded independent film sector. Distribution and box-office returns for films such as *The Girl From Monday* and *Fay Grim* have been limited, while newspapers and journals tend to allocate the films minor review slots, if they review them at all. It is hard to account for Hartley's diminished presence in the independent scene without considering the dimensions of place and cultural identity so central to his work. If the successful Long Island films turn on ideas of community and regional roots, the later films favour urban, corporate settings and move characters across national boundaries: think of the Iceland-set sequences in *No Such Thing* and the plot of *Fay Grim*, which follows Parker Posey's Fay from Queens in New York to Paris and beyond. A complex and sometimes prolix tale of international espionage, *Fay Grim* is the seven-years-on sequel to the well-received suburban epic *Henry Fool* – although the two films differ quite drastically in scope and tone. While *Henry Fool* reprises the theme of familial dysfunction in suburbia explored in the Long Island trilogy (with a more 'cult' feeling, owing to an emphasis on taboo sex and gross-out humour), *Fay Grim* relates a bewilderingly intricate story of CIA initiatives, double-crosses and geopolitical conflicts, held together by Posey's performance as a resourceful single mother from Queens dragooned into an espionage mission she has little hope of understanding.

Definitive in its decentring of place, *Fay Grim* lacks the familiar regional detail that characterises Hartley's most popular films. The abiding impression is of obfuscation, anxiety and ambiguity: when a CIA agent suggests to Fay's son that his mother may have defected to the 'other side', his exasperated response is to ask 'The other side of what?' The restlessness and oddball humour of *Fay Grim* did little to impress reviewers, but Hartley's most recent film preserves many of the most distinct and satisfying features of his cinema: the centring of philosophical and often unruly protagonists, the questioning of traditional cultural roles and conventions (there are surely few character 'types' less well represented in the espionage thriller than the working class single mother), the blend of stylisation and social observation. At a time when American independent cinema can seem as invested in star casting and aimless hyperbole as much mainstream fare – albeit with a marked tone of cynicism – Hartley works in a distinctly minor-key mode. His films about idiosyncratic Americans in recognisable but somehow unfamiliar places are as marginal as they are inventive: self-conscious efforts to move beyond the more familiar varieties of independent filmmaking.

Biography

Born in Islip, New York, in 1959, Hal Hartley grew up in Lindenhurst, a working-class town on Long Island. After attending the Massachusetts College of Art in Boston for a year in the late 1970s, he applied to the State University of New York at Purchase film school, where he produced his thesis film, *Kid*, in 1984. Working at a TV company which made public service announcements, Hartley was provided with the budget for a full-length film by his boss, Jerome Brownstein. Since making his debut, *The Unbelievable Truth*, Hartley has worked mainly in America and Europe as a filmmaker and film teacher.

Notes

1 See Jeffrey Sconce, 'Irony, nihilism, and the new American 'smart' film', *Screen*, vol. 43, no. 4, 2002, pp. 355–6.
2 Jed Springan, 'Hartley's Edge', *Elle*, September 1992.
3 Jonathan Romney writes that 'Huppert's oddly stunned delivery only underlines the archness of lines that wink at her image'. 'Isabelle Huppert: Mysterious? Moi?', *Independent on Sunday*, 27 February 2005, pp. 10–11.
4 Peter Sobczynski, 'An Interview With Hal Hartley', *24FPS*, date not given. See www.24fpsmagazine.com/Archive/Hartley.html

Filmography

As director/screenwriter (All US productions unless otherwise stated)

Kid (1984) short
The Cartographer's Girlfriend (1987) short
Dogs (1988) short

The Unbelievable Truth (1989, 90 min)
Trust (UK/US, 1990, 107 min)
Surviving Desire (1991) short
Ambition (1991) short
Theory of Achievement (1991) short
Simple Men (Italy/UK/US, 1992, 105 min)
Flirt (1993) short
Opera No.1 (1994) short
NYC 3/94 (1994) short
Amateur (US/UK/France, 1994, 105 min)
Flirt (US/Germany/Japan, 1995, 85 min)
Henry Fool (1997, 137 min)
The Other Also (1997) short
The Book of Life (France/US, 1998, 63 min)
The New Math(s) (UK, 2000) short
Kimono (Germany, 2000) short
No Such Thing (Iceland, US, 2001, 102 min)
The Sisters of Mercy (2004) short
The Girl From Monday (2005, 84 min)
Fay Grim (US/Germany, 2006, 118 min)

Further reading

Geoff Andrew, *Stranger Than Paradise: Maverick Film-makers in Recent American Cinema*, London, Prion, 1998.

Ryan Gilbey, 'Pulling the Pin on Hal Hartley', in Jim Hillier (ed.), *American Independent Cinema*, London, British Film Institute Publishing, 2001, pp. 142–5.

Kent Jones, 'Hal Hartley: The Book I Read Was in Your Eyes', *Film Comment*, vol. 32, no. 4, 1996, pp. 68–72.

Kenneth Kaleta and Hal Hartley, *True Fiction Pictures & Possible Films*, New York, Soft Skull Press, 2008.

Donald Lyons, 'Around Long Island', in *Independent Visions: A Critical Introduction to Recent Independent American Film*, New York, Ballantine Books, 1994, pp. 36–56.

Jason Wood, *Hal Hartley*, Harpenden, Herts, Pocket Essentials, 2003.

Justin Wyatt, 'The Particularity and Peculiarity of Hal Hartley', *Film Quarterly*, vol. 52, no. 1, 1998, pp. 2–6.

TODD HAYNES

By Justin Wyatt

A man must dream a long time in order to act with grandeur, and dreaming is nursed in darkness.

The above quote from Jean Genet, infamous French novelist, play-wright, filmmaker and outlaw, closes Haynes's feature debut *Poison*. The words offer a call to action for those alienated and isolated from mainstream society, the major theme of the film, but even more so they perfectly capture the audacity of this filmmaker. For Haynes, 'acting with grandeur' is a given through works that challenge, confuse and surprise audiences, even those accustomed to the world of art-house cinema.

Within the popular and academic worlds of film criticism, Haynes enjoys an enthusiastic following, with critics lauding his films as groundbreaking, visionary and bold. For the general public, however, he remains a cult figure. Only one of his films, *Far from Heaven*, has achieved breakthrough recognition among the public, garnering solid art-house box office gross ($29 million world-wide) and four Academy Award nominations. Haynes's marginal status as a filmmaker in com-mercial terms is perhaps not surprising. The uncompromising approach to narration and the dense cinematic style make the Haynes films daunting for some, but rich for those willing to take the journey.

As the writer and director of all his projects, Haynes has been able to guide each film carefully through all stages of development. His career is distinguished, however, by important collaborations with producer Christine Vachon, actress Julianne Moore, editor and actor James Lyons and cinematographer Maryse Alberti. Vachon, in particular, plays a pivotal and continuing role in Haynes's career, producing all of his projects from *Poison* onward.

After graduating from Brown University's programme in art/semiotics in 1985, Haynes co-founded Apparatus Productions with Vachon and Barry Ellsworth. Essentially a re-granting organisation, Apparatus helped to fund those makers of short films who would not be competitive through the usual granting routes. As part of his post-graduate film production training at Bard College, Haynes made *Superstar: The Karen Carpenter Story*, a 43-minute mock documentary, acted entirely by Barbie and Ken dolls, telling the rise and fall, the fall was due to anorexia, of saccharine pop singer Karen Carpenter. The notoriety of the project – Haynes withdrew the film from distribution due to legal injunctions from the Carpenter family – was matched by Haynes's first feature, *Poison*, inspired by both Jean Genet and the AIDS epidemic. *Poison* moves between three interconnecting stories: 'Hero', a television-style documentary about patricide; 'Horror', a hyperbolic 1950s-style horror/science fiction parody about a scientist who becomes a leper sex killer after ingesting the 'sex drive' in liquid form; and 'Homo', the most direct connection to Genet, a florid examination of power and romantic obsession between two prisoners in 1930s France. After winning the Grand Jury prize at the Sundance Film Festival, *Poison* was targeted by the religious right, particularly Donald Wildmon's American Family Association, who objected to the film's small completion grant from the National Endowment for the Arts.

While raising money for his next feature, Haynes wrote and directed the short television film *Dottie Gets Spanked* for the ITVS series, 'Television Families'. Like *Poison*, *Dottie* paints a picture of an outsider, 6-year-old Steven, obsessed almost equally with television sitcom star Dottie Frank and spanking as a form of discipline. Steven's escape through his endless drawings of Dottie and his visit to her television show set represent important moments of happiness for the child, already alienated from his father for his 'inappropriate' interests and fascinations. Haynes's heroine, Carol White, in his next feature, *Safe*, is also defined, first and foremost, by alienation. Set in the near past of 1987, the austere and completely restrained *Safe* vividly depicts Carol's disintegration: an upper-middle-class suburban housewife in the San Fernando Valley, Carol begins to suffer from amorphous environmental illness, reacting toxically to everyday chemicals and stimulants in her environment. Medical doctors and psychiatrists fail to reverse Carol's deterioration, and she flees to Wrenwood, an alternative healing centre led by a New Age guru supposedly suffering from both chemical sensitivity and HIV-related infections.

Stylistically, *Safe* is distinguished by deliberate pacing, controlled setting and minimalism, parameters that are polar opposites to the cinematic traits of *Velvet Goldmine*. That film's fictional glam-rock world is, by design, excessive, energetic and highly stylised. Haynes's juxtaposition of opulent visuals (including Sandy Powell's Oscar-nominated costume designs), a hip star cast and original soundtrack aided the presentation of the world considerably. *Velvet Goldmine* is structured around reporter Arthur's investigation into a missing figure, fictional British glam-rock star Brian Slade (Jonathan Rhys-Meyers). As Arthur (Christian Bale) interviews Slade's previous manager, his ex-wife and others associated with the androgynous star, the film's structural parallels to Welles's *Citizen Kane* (1941) become obvious. As the reporter recreates Slade's meteoric rise and fall, capped by the fake on-stage murder of the star at a London concert, Arthur is forced to confront his own adolescent fascination with glam, his confused sexuality, and his brief liaison with Slade's muse, American rock star Curt Wild (Ewan McGregor). *Velvet Goldmine* follows *Poison* in its interest in gay history, with Haynes locating Oscar Wilde, rather than Genet, as the film's spiritual father. Writing gay history as part of a fictional glam-rock exploration left mainstream audiences and some critics merely perplexed.

Haynes's next effort continued his experimentation with narration and character identification. *Far from Heaven* evoked the expansive melodramas of Douglas Sirk such as *Written on the Wind* (1956), *Magnificent Obsession* (1954) and *All that Heaven Allows* (1955). Taking place in the affluent Connecticut suburbs of the late 1950s, *Far from Heaven* centres on housewife Cathy Whitaker (Julianne Moore), the caring and sheltered wife of sales executive Frank (Dennis Quaid). In the course of a few weeks, Cathy undergoes a personal transformation caused by dual forces: the realisation of her husband's homosexuality and her friendship, mild flirtation and eventual unrequited love for her black gardener Raymond Deagan (Dennis Haysbert). Beautifully designed and shot with a pristine elegance, the film shows the difficulty of even considering intimacy across racial lines and homosexual ones. The denouement sticks to the classic melodramas of the 1950s by reinforcing the status quo and showing that 'illicit' love must exist either in the shadows or not at all. Critically and commercially, *Far from Heaven* broke new ground for Haynes, garnering good domestic commercial reception and four Oscar nominations. While *Far from Heaven* is controlled and precise in its design, development and mise-en-scène, Haynes's next feature, *I'm Not There*, recalls the wild abandonment of *Velvet Goldmine*. Originally titled *I'm Not There: Suppositions on a Film Concerning Dylan*, the film tackles the remarkable project of folk singer Bob Dylan's life. Using a conceit which recently appeared in Solondz's *Palindromes*, Haynes casts multiple actors to portray different aspects and incarnations of Dylan's public and private persona: the poet Arthur (Ben Whislaw), the young African-American hobo Woody (Marcus Carl Franklin), the folk singer Jack (Christian Bale), the transforming international star Jude (Cate Blanchett), the philandering actor Robbie (Heath Ledger), and the reclusive Western outlaw Billy (Richard Gere). Like *Poison*, Haynes tells these stories in a non-linear fashion, cutting between glimpses and segments of Dylan's different 'lives' at will.

Echoing one of his heroes, Rainer Werner Fassbinder, Haynes's work is perhaps most significant for the relationship between formal experimentation and audience reception. Very few American directors of his generation evidence this kind of interest in narration, problematising audience expectations and orientations. The form of experimentation varies considerably, but audiences are always asked to question their notion about cinematic storytelling and character as part of the exercise. The origins for this may be located in having

Superstar cast entirely with Barbie and Ken dolls. In some ways, the choice is obvious: tell the story of the most saccharine pop group of the 1970s using plastic figures, a camp gag at first glance. Yet *Superstar* cannot be reduced merely to camp or kitsch. Haynes dramatises the film using the dictates of the star story and the 'disease-of-the-week' television movie, allowing for some intertitles, voice-over narration and inserted documentary footage. The dramatic force of the genres, our desire to connect with Karen Carpenter and our empathetic response to her battle with anorexia eventually make the film emotionally affecting and moving rather than a camp tale using dolls as its cast. Of course, the immediate response of viewing the family/star drama played with dolls is laughter, particularly given that the tale is depicted in a straightforward manner. Haynes's clear feeling for Karen and her pressures soon becomes evident. Moving from an immediate response of laughter and superiority to the sincere emotional one at Karen's demise is one of the film's most extraordinary accomplishments, forged through realising that audiences want to identify so much with character and narrative that even plastic dolls will not derail this engagement.

Poison offers a different formal experiment through its interlacing of three stories of social outsiders. Nevertheless, just as *Superstar* shifts between disengaging (through the dolls) and bonding (through the narrative trajectory and genres) with the audience, *Poison* confronts the viewers through its joining of the three stories. The editing moves between three starkly different stories told in contrasting styles (black-and-white exploitation in 'Horror'; lush colour and intimate surroundings in 'Homo'; and blank television documentary for 'Hero'). Audiences are forced to make the connections between the stories, some of which are obvious, others much more subtle. Haynes cuts, for example, from Dr. Graves mistakenly ingesting the sex drive ('Horror') to a shot of the suburban homes in Richie's neighbourhood ('Hero') with the voice-over narration, 'the quiet community of Glenville was stunned'. While the narration refers to Richie's patricide and disappearance, the statement could just as readily refer to the 'stunned' community reaction to Graves's physical deterioration and disease. Other omnibus films – *Aria, Flirt, Three Cases of Murder* – tell sequential stories in full, yet Haynes's structure challenges viewers to build connections and to seek meaning. As with all Haynes's work, *Poison* is so dense in its style, structure and themes that multiple viewing is required.

Haynes's remaining work – *Safe, Velvet Goldmine, Far from Heaven* and *I'm Not There* – continues the stylistic experiments, but these films also push Haynes's innovations in terms of character and audience identification much further. With *Safe*, we learn very little of Carol White's history and motivations, curious since the film is centred so squarely on the one character. Except for a single voice-over of Carol narrating one of her letters, Haynes offers almost nothing to anchor her character. She is defined by her milieu (upper middle class, San Fernando Valley), primary role ('home-maker'), and her bland, pretty good looks. Carol's identity equals these simple components, nothing more. We are left with a character study without the character. As an alternative, Haynes examines the ways through which cultural and social factors construct Carol as a character. Stylistically, Haynes matches the empty lead with medium and long shots. On occasion, Haynes hints at a close shot, such as the scene where Carol faints for the first time outside the kitchen. The camera moves closer, as if a close-up were the ultimate goal, but stops at a medium shot before abruptly cutting to the next scene. The close-up, critical for connecting the audience to the emotions of the character, is withheld.

Velvet Goldmine also revolves around a structuring absence, the missing Brian Slade. Just as *Safe* confounds viewers with a heroine blank, empty and reflective, *Velvet Goldmine*'s glam world is recreated, ten years on, by the boring and staid reporter Arthur. Rather than presenting Slade's stardom directly, Haynes refracts the action through Arthur so that we learn only snippets of Slade's life, with many elements and pieces clearly missing. Slade remains an enigma, even once his 'new identity' has been revealed at the end of the film. While many filmmakers would have foregrounded the glamorous and exotic Slade and Curt Wild, their exploits and liaisons, Haynes is perhaps more interested in Arthur, the reporter and fan whose life has been altered forever by glam-rock.

Borrowing a page from the career of Fassbinder, Haynes's reworking of melodrama evoking the Sirk films creates provocative and contradictory ways for the viewer to connect with characters. Fassbinder generally placed the Sirkian melodrama and conflict in a contemporary German setting, immediately complicating the familial and romantic pressures within the stories. Haynes, on the other hand, chooses to recreate the 1950s suburban setting directly, using a 'perfect housewife' and her stereotypically masculine husband as the leads in his romantic drama. The tension is created through the mix of styles, veering between conventions of the 1950s melodrama (e.g., the lush Elmer Bernstein musical score, the central romantic conflict) and contemporary filmmaking (e.g., the explicit theme of homosexuality, the stylised mise-en-scène). Cathy Whitaker, the heroine, is central to this destabilisation of style and expectations. Julianne Moore's formidable performance is based around committing to arch readings of 'clichéd' 1950s dialogue. At first, the performance seems like it might be a parody of the Sirk heroines, with the actress condescending to the role. However, it becomes clear that Moore is simultaneously seeking to portray the real emotion and heartache at the core of Cathy's situation. Again, just like the style of the film overall, the performance confounds expectations, making the viewer connect deeply with a stereotype and showing the emotional truths underlying typical melodrama.

Most audaciously, Haynes divides the central 'character' of Bob Dylan in *I'm Not There* into six different characters. Rather than casting different actors to represent Dylan at different points in his life, Haynes complicates the structure even further by having actors play entirely different characters who may comment on unique Dylan personas but who clearly cannot facilitate a smooth transition from one stage of his life to the next. So, for instance, Christian Bale plays Dylan as Jack, a burgeoning coffee house folk singer, while at the height of his international fame, the character – now Jude – is portrayed by Cate Blanchett. While there is some similarity in appearance, the characters are actually fairly different in demeanor, attitude and action. This is augmented by the acting style, with Bale portraying his character in a naturalistic way, while Blanchett favors a broader, more exaggerated style of presentation. Haynes offers very little to draw connections between the characters, leaving the viewer to seek the intersection between these side-by-side characters. The approach to character reflects the difficulty, or even the impossibility, of assigning meaning to Bob Dylan. Of course, a director refusing to pinpoint a central character for the audience complicates traditional character identification for viewers. This is precisely the point, however. Haynes wants us to investigate our own process of identifying with characters and narrative by making the process so torturous through his 'multiple' main characters.

Haynes's experiments in narrative, narration and character are not empty exercises. Indeed, the formal experimentation follows from Haynes's sustained critique of the dominant ideology. This critique centres on the social structures designed to omit and ostracise certain people and groups from the mainstream of society. *Superstar*, for instance, clearly depicts how Karen Carpenter's family and the ingrained desire to be part of a 'perfect family' contribute greatly to her bulimia and anorexia. Haynes dramatises this brilliantly with the shot of Karen waking up in the hospital after fainting on stage due to her bulimia: from Karen's point of view, the family members hover over the bed creating a spectacle of oppression for the fatigued young woman. Similarly, the shifts in style in *Poison* and *I'm Not There* and the narrative structure of *Velvet Goldmine* are motivated by a desire to avoid traditional storytelling structures of classical and post-classical cinema and to investigate how these traits are complicit with dominant society. For Haynes to offer alternatives for those alienated and marginalised, he must forge a new filmmaking language, upsetting the norms of cinematic storytelling.

For many critics, the desire to locate a space for those on the margins would be reduced to Haynes's status as one of the leading 'New Queer Cinema' directors. Tellingly, none of Haynes's films however address the contemporary lifestyle of gays and lesbians. Haynes completely avoids the form of labelling that limits his work and the characters contained within it. To label is to limit the possibilities and opportunities for interpretation. Labelling also permits those in power to feel secure with clear boundaries separating those within and those outside the realms of power. Consider Steven from *Dottie Gets Spanked* and the leading characters (Slade, Wild, Arthur, Mandy) in *Velvet Goldmine*; none can be adequately typed or contained through sexual labels. The categories fail as a means to define the characters and their actions. The one openly gay contemporary character (self-help guru Peter in *Safe*) also fails to adhere to a comfortable position for a gay character created by a gay director. Narratively, Peter could be presented as Carol's saviour, the person who can make Carol love herself enough to cure her chemical sensitivity. Haynes deliberately undercuts Peter by suggesting that he is self-involved, manipulative and perhaps a fraud. Consequently, even the 'out' gay character in a Haynes film is typed more by social and economic power than by sexuality as defining characteristic. Haynes denies the simple affirmative role models dictated by some in gay culture, a refusal that further complicates audience identification.

This emphasis on Haynes's play with audience expectations and cinematic conventions may suggest that the films are cool, ironic and detached. Haynes is nevertheless, at the core, a deeply compassionate filmmaker. This can be gauged from the critical moments when outsiders do gain control: Steven burying the naughty drawing of Dottie getting spanked; Richie Beacon killing his father and flying from the bedroom window in *Poison*; and Arthur imagining a bold declaration of his sexuality to his parents in *Velvet Goldmine*. These attempts to empower the disenfranchised often take place in a fantasy world created by the characters apart from their tormentors. Haynes's ability to depict this world so expertly signals his total conviction in reclaiming the boundaries for those pushed to the side by dominant forces. Through presenting this reclamation project in such a formally experimental style, Haynes evoked the Russian Formalists' claim for the function of art in our lives, defamiliarisation. In film after film, the director makes the familiar 'unfamiliar' and, in the process, helps to restore our own sense of the unusual, unexpected, and beautiful within the everyday.

Biography

Todd Haynes was born 2 January 1961, in Los Angeles, USA.

Filmography

Superstar: The Karen Carpenter Story (co-written with Cynthia Schneider, 1987)
Poison (1991)
Dottie Gets Spanked (1993)
Safe (1995)
Velvet Goldmine (1998)
Far from Heaven (2002)
I'm Not There (2007)

Further reading

M. Dargis, 'Endangered Zone', *The Village Voice*, 4 July 1995, pp. 38–40.
M.A. Doane, 'Pathos and Pathology: The Cinema of Todd Haynes', *Camera Obscura*, 19, 3, 2004, pp. 1–21.
R. Grundmann, 'How Clean Was My Valley: Todd Haynes' Safe', *Cineaste* 21, 1995, pp. 22–5.
T. Haynes, *Velvet Goldmine*, New York, Hyperion Books, 1998.
T. Haynes, *Far from Heaven, Safe, Superstar: The Karen Carpenter Story*, New York: Grove Press, 2003.
N. James, 'American Voyeur', *Sight and Sound*, Sept. 1998, pp. 8–10.
B. Kruger, 'Into Thin Air: Karen Carpenter Superstar', *Artforum*, vol. 26, no. 4, 1987, pp. 107–8.
M. Laskawy, 'Poison at the Box Office: An Interview with Todd Haynes', *Cineaste*, 18, 1991, pp. 38–9.
J. Morrison, *The Cinema of Todd Haynes: All That Heaven Allows*, London, Wallflower Press, 2007.
E. O'Neill, 'Poison-ous Queers: Violence and Social Order', *Spectator*, 1994, pp. 9–29.
J. Savage, 'Tasteful Tales', *Sight and Sound*, October 1991, pp. 15–17.

J. Wyatt, 'Cinematic/Sexual Transgression: An Interview with Todd Haynes', *Film Quarterly*, vol. 46, no. 3, 1993, pp. 2–8.

J. Wyatt, *Poison*, Trowbridge, Flicks Books, 1998.

PETER JACKSON

By Paul Malcolm

In its 1989 review of Peter Jackson's debut feature, the cheekily-titled, cannibal splatter-fest, *Bad Taste*, *Gorezone* magazine ventured to predict that 'Peter Jackson may become known as New Zealand's answer to Lucio Fulci'.[1] How Jackson has since become known as New Zealand's answer to Steven Spielberg is one of the more fascinating stories of recent commercial cinema. Jackson's rise, during the 1990s, from Pukerua Bay fanboy to Academy Award-winning producer and director, speaks not only to his abilities as a filmmaker and business person but a number of other compelling features of the contemporary global film industry, including the enduring power of genre in the international marketplace, the impact of digital technologies on the global flow of film production and the role of the internet and fan culture in movie production and marketing. While Jackson has not yet achieved the kind of commercial clout that would allow him to bankroll a studio start-up the size of DreamWorks, beginning with the *Lord of the Rings* trilogy, his productions alone count for a sizeable portion of New Zealand's offshore production revenues, close to NZ$370 million in 2007, while the visual and special effects company he co-founded, Weta, is an internationally recognised post-production facility. The extent to which Jackson has been able to get Hollywood to come to him is matched, however, in the degree to which Jackson has conformed his own sensibilities to Hollywood. While his career might be cast as that of an outsider triumphing over the studios – particularly by any governmental agency hoping to develop its own national creative industries – it is also emblematic of Hollywood's continued stylistic dominance in the digital age.

Jackson's first three features, *Bad Taste*, *Meet the Feebles* and *Braindead*, are each a gleeful pastiche of the horror, comedy and fantasy films Jackson devoured as a teenager, each made with the stated purpose of pushing the limits of the acceptable on screen. Along with director Sam Rami's *Evil Dead* trilogy, Frank Henenlotter's *Basket Case* (1982) and Stuart Gordon's *Re-Animator* (1985), these films came to be identified with what some critics described as a horror sub-genre, the gore-comedy.[2] Even among such auspicious company as Rami and Henenlotter, however, Jackson stood out for the viscera-greased, slip-and-slide velocity of his generic excesses. *Bad Taste*, in which the agents of an alien fast food corporation hope humans will be the next galactic taste sensation, set the model as a science fiction/zombie/cannibal/action/horror comedy in which parodic film references range from *The Day the Earth Stood Still* (1951) to *The Texas Chainsaw Massacre* (1974) and *The Evil Dead* (1981). While *Meet the Feebles* might be simply described as a satire of the backstage musical with puppets, the sheer number of ribald offences against felt and foam that Jackson commits to film in just ninety-four minutes represents something of a Bahktinian-level world record for carnivalesque carnality. In *Braindead*, in which the bite of a Sumatran Rat-Monkey, imported to Wellington from Skull Island, triggers a zombie pandemic, a seemingly humble parish priest spins into action against an undead mob, shouting, 'I kick ass for the Lord', a nod to Jackson's then recent enthusiasm for Jackie Chan. In each film, the sheer volume of guts and gags is, itself, the final punch line. In this context, the climax of *Braindead*, in which a long-suffering son is swallowed whole into the gaping belly of his gargantuan zombiefied mother, is more richly read less as a sign of Jackson's own subconscious mother issues bubbling over, than as a conscious apeing and rim shot recognition of the increasingly monstrous figures of the feminine that became a central trope of the horror genre since Alfred Hitchcock's *Psycho* (1960).

To laugh instead of wince at such grizzly imagery requires a fan's appreciation, one that Jackson has appealed to both on screen and off throughout his career. Beginning with his very first interviews Jackson constructed an image of himself as a film fan turned director who 'makes movies that I would want to see'. It is an integral part of Jackson's personal mythology that cinephilia took serious hold of him in 1971 when he first saw Merian C. Cooper and Ernest B. Schoedsack's *King Kong* (1933) on the family television at the age of nine. A steady diet of *The Thunderbirds*, *Monty Python's Flying Circus*, Buster Keaton films and the stop-motion animation of Ray Harryhausen followed throughout his adolescence which, as the story goes, inspired him to take up his parents' Super 8 camera and begin shooting effects-driven mini-epics in his backyard. Along the way, Jackson became a devotee of Forrest J. Ackerman's *Famous Monsters of Filmland* magazine which encouraged a participatory fan culture amongst its readership with 'How To' articles and interviews with classic Hollywood's effects practitioners that placed an emphasis on craft and technique. Jackson's early films encourage and reward such fan knowledge through on-screen intertexuality and the acquisition of production details found in the pages of the kind of fan magazines that Jackson grew up on. References to George A. Romero's *Night of the Living Dead* (1968) are obvious enough in *Bad Taste* and *Braindead* to any aficionado of the genre. Other in-jokes require something more. Early on in *Bad Taste*, for example, Jackson, in one of two on-screen roles he plays, witnesses the first dollops of what will soon become a wave of spilt brains and remarks, 'I hope I'm not the poor bastard who's got to clean that up'. While Jackson may or may not have been the poor bastard who cleaned up the mess, as the sole make-up artist on the shoot he definitely concocted the gruesome special effects that went into it. It's an in-joke that emerges, not simply through repeated viewings, but through the acquisition of extra textual knowledge about the film's production. Such self-referential jokes appear throughout Jackson's films and pay dividends for a particular mode of viewing: that of the fan.

Underpinning all of the generic chaos and intertexuality of his first three features is Jackson's visual style, a pell-mell suturing of swooping zooms, extreme close-ups, oblique angles and hand-held tracking shots that create a vertiginous playground for all the unmoored generic elements. It is a low-budget style under the influence of Sam Rami and Terry Gilliam that strives to conceal meagre sets and smooth over rough performances as much as create a sense of atmosphere and tone. A key element in the development of this style was the 16mm Bolex camera that Jackson purchased in 1983 with the aim of stepping into professional production. In *Bad Taste*, Jackson exploited the camera's compact size and minimal weight by constructing his own crane and a Steadicam-style rig, reproducing the equipment, if not yet the production values, of Hollywood.

By the time that Jackson had purchased his Bolex, filmmakers such as Roger Donaldson (*Sleeping Dogs*, *Smash Palace*) and Geoff Murphy (*Utu*) had already gained attention for themselves and New Zealand's fledgling film industry on the international stage. The following year, Vincent Ward's *Vigil* (1984) would be the first New Zealand film selected for the Cannes Film Festival. Jackson's career, however, would not be determined by the selection committees of the auteur driven festival circuit, at least not until *Heavenly Creatures*. Instead, he made his reputation in the carnivalesque capitalism of the Marché du Film at Cannes where *Bad Taste* made its world premiere. When he first applied to the New Zealand Film Commission, founded in 1978, for completion funds on *Bad Taste*, Jackson anticipated the argument that his splatter-fest was not a 'proper' kind of film. As he wrote in his application:

> One subject I would like to touch upon is the question of 'Is it culture?' Yes. It is. Cinema is an art form, and art is culture … I am a New Zealander and proud of it. I have as much right to make whatever film I please and it is just as much a New Zealand Film as anyone else's.

This early exchange with the Film Commission, which eventually provided $15,000 for *Bad Taste*'s completion, is perfectly in tune with the raw, unchanneled adolescent energies coursing through the film itself, which become a flood in *Meet the Feebles*. While it would be difficult to argue that Jackson was a politically or ideologically motivated filmmaker, he nevertheless aims, however scattershot, to tweak the presumptions of authority wherever it lies on the political spectrum. *Bad Taste* and *Meet the Feebles* are littered with AIDS jokes and politically incorrect racial and gender caricatures, while the extreme gore of both films represents a full-scale assault on the forces of cultural conservatism. There is, in other words, something to offend everyone just beyond the films' intended audiences. In *Bad Taste* and *Meet the Feebles*, though, the objects of these assaults are never represented on screen. This changes with *Braindead* when Jackson positions a culturally conservative vision of New Zealand society as the central target of his satire. Of Jackson's first five features, only *Meet the Feebles* is set in an unspecified locale, with recognisable references to New Zealand itself becoming increasingly prominent from *Braindead* through *Heavenly Creatures* and *Forgotten Silver*. As New Zealand becomes more specific as a place in his films, Jackson comes into sharper focus as a cultural critic, bringing his primordial fan boy frustrations with middle-brow disdain to bear on increasingly specific social forces.

Braindead was Jackson's first period piece, and the decision to set the film in 1957 was, as Jackson has explained, a pragmatic one to provide a believable context for the story of a grown man, Lionel, who must struggle to escape the influence of his domineering mother, Vera, if he wants to be with the girl of his dreams. That Lionel's liberation also involved doing battle against a horde of undead zombies – including a monstrous baby born from the union of two undead corpses – was not enough, apparently, to strain credulity on its own. Be that as it may, the shift to 1957 allows Jackson to expand on the always assumed, but always off-screen, targets of his previous films. Where *Bad Taste* found Jackson mocking off-screen religious conservatives – as when his character, Derek, chainsaws his way, head to bum, through the centre of the chief alien, to emerge at the other side with a gore soaked grin: 'I've been born again' – Lionel's mother, Vera, in *Braindead* embodies the type on screen. As the recently elected treasurer of the Wellington Ladies Welfare League (WLWL), Vera craves an ideal of respectability that refuses a place even for dust in her Victorian home. Early in the film, Vera shouts at Lionel as he toils away in the garden, 'Does this look like a well maintained frontage?' The line takes on an ironic twist when Vera's own well-maintained façade begins to slip away, literally, as the rat-monkey's bite gradually transforms her into the undead. During a luncheon with the president of the WLWL and her boorish husband, the conversation turns to the 'younger generation' and the need for 'another war' just before a contaminated Vera's ear slips off her head and into her custard, pearl earring and all.

Viewing *Braindead* as a horror satire of bourgeois convention and hypocrisy, the gap grows a little narrower between this zombie period piece and Jackson's next feature, the decidedly art house *Heavenly Creatures*. Based on one of New Zealand's most infamous crimes, the Parker-Hulme Murder in 1954, it was Jackson's conscious attempt to escape the 'splatter director' label he once sought so hard to gain. At the same time, it finds him re-working and re-contextualising a number of recurring themes and techniques and the film remains his most complex. In adapting the story of Pauline Parker (Melanie Lynskey) and Juliet Hulme (Kate Winslet), a pair of teenage girls who murdered Parker's mother, Honora, in a park in Christchurch, New Zealand, with a brick wrapped in an old stocking, Jackson assays the class and social divisions of New Zealand society – Pauline's family was local and working-class, Juliet raised by upper-class, British intellectuals – sexual paranoia and the seductive nature of private fantasy.

Almost immediately in *Heavenly Creatures*, Jackson reveals a more sophisticated cinematic approach to representing the duality and duplicity of small town New Zealand life. The film opens with a period documentary cheerfully extolling the joys of Christchurch, dissolving into the screams of young women and the blood spattered figures of Pauline and Juliet fleeing in seeming terror up a garden path. The cut produces a striking and careful contrast that deepens as the film unfolds. Jackson confronts the town's sunny image with a darker reality at work beneath but, as we learn more about the events leading up to the unsettling moment on the pathway, the town's manufactured image of itself seems a lot like the make-believe world that Pauline and Juliet escape into themselves. Having met in boarding school, Pauline and Juliet bonded quickly over their shared experiences with childhood ailments and had soon constructed an elaborate fantasy world for themselves which they called Borovnia. As their parents begin to eye their intense and intimate relationship with growing discomfort and suspicion, Pauline and Juliet recede deeper and deeper into the imaginative realm they keep stoked with a steady diet of movies and romantic literature. Even as Jackson refuses to posit an explanation for the girls' actions – contemporaneous explanations for the murder ranged from insanity to lesbianism (with the implicit assumption, at the time, that they were essentially two sides of the same coin) – he explicitly links the girls' passionate brand of fandom to their status as social outsiders. The liberated realm of Borovnia acts as a counterweight to the repressive and neglectful worlds of the parents. Jackson underscores this relationship visually by following standardised shot patterns throughout the film while the dutch angles and swooping movements that dominate his previous works are here reserved for those specific sequences illuminating the girls' flights of imaginative reverie. But even as Jackson uses these moments of punctuation to heighten a sense of the ecstatic nature of the girls' fandom, he signals his willingness to subsume his own more wild stylistic gestures to a conventional style. When Jackson initially wrote to the New Zealand Film Commission to seek funding for *Heavenly Creatures*, he was sure to insist that his art house film would be something different: 'All of my instincts are commercial … When I say I want to make strides as a director, it's in the direction of James Cameron and Steven Spielberg, not Peter Greenaway'. While Pauline and Juliet's plan to escape to Hollywood never came to pass, Jackson's soon would. Before beginning his first Hollywood studio producer project, *The Frighteners*, however, Jackson took one jab at the cultural gatekeepers of New Zealand with a project for television, the faux-documentary, *Forgotten Silver*.

For anyone who still doubted after *Heavenly Creatures* that Jackson's filmic vocabulary was limited to the horror genre, *Forgotten Silver* underscored that the source of the slapstick in Jackson's gore-comedy films were the knockabout antics of Buster Keaton while it revealed an intimate familiarity with the documentary form. Slicing and dicing the documentary's claims to authority, Jackson re-writes the histories of both New Zealand and cinema through the fictional figure of Colin McKenzie (Thomas Robins) who, but for the vagaries of fate, should have been hailed as a key figure, if not *the* key figure in the development of silent cinema. That some, including historians and scholars, actually fell for Jackson's hoax says as much, perhaps, about national longing as about Jackson's skills as a prankster, but the film nevertheless stands as a brilliant work of cinematic manipulation. Some episodes from McKenzie's life are impossibly absurd – as when the still teenage McKenzie invents his own homemade process for making film stock and is subsequently arrested for trying to procure enough chicken eggs to shoot the world's first feature film – but Jackson's faux history does not depend on veracity. Rather, Jackson relies on sincerity over authenticity, affection over accuracy to put over his joke. If any cultural guardian who would deny the pleasures of genre was susceptible enough to champion the career of Colin McKenzie, Jackson could claim proof, once and for all, that story was indeed king.

Forgotten Silver would be Jackson's last film set specifically in New Zealand for some time to come. While his next project, *The Frighteners*, was shot in New Zealand, the story was set in small town America. In many ways, Jackson's first Hollywood studio production revealed the limits of his ability to translate his native sensibilities into a foreign milieu. Produced by Robert Zemeckis (*Who Framed Roger Rabbit?*, *Death Becomes Her*) whose own sensibilities lean toward the kind of genre blending that so animated Jackson early in his career, *The Frighteners* was intended as a horror-comedy on a Hollywood scale. Michael J. Fox stars as Frank Bannister, a conman posing as a ghost-busting psychic who employs real ghosts to spook his marks. Though Jackson had convinced his Hollywood partners that New Zealand would be a suitable stand-in for a coastal American burg, *The Frighteners* never feels entirely grounded. Jokes about the Public Works Department in *Bad Taste* may have fallen on deaf international ears but the film always feels deeply rooted in the local. In *The Frighteners*, Jackson and longtime partner and co-screenwriter Fran Walsh never find the proper footing for either the film's horror or its humour. An acerbic jab about gun crime in Los Angeles, for instance, feels desperately regurgitated, while a rape joke – 'I like it when they lie still like that' – would have backfired even in *Meet the Feebles*. Unable to get the humour right, Jackson loses control of the darkness at the heart of Fox's character, an emotionally scarred and haunted man, and the whole film comes crashing down. Awkward narrative devices that might have been overlooked in the general rough hewn nature of Jackson's low budget work become glaring pot holes amid more polished production values. Nevertheless, Universal felt it had a *Back to the Future*-sized hit on its hands and moved *The Frighteners* off its original Halloween release date to open as a summer tent-pole film, thus sealing its fate as Jackson's least successful film.

If *The Frighteners* was a commercial and critical failure, it nevertheless established Weta, Jackson's then fledgling effects house, as an international post-production facility. In order to create the ghostly digital visual effects that would be used in the film, Weta embarked on a major expansion that brought technology and talent from abroad. As Jackson's agent at the time, Ken Kamins, explains, Jackson and Weta found that they 'could create an ad hoc effects company by leasing equipment from Silicon Graphics and then going to unemployed animators throughout the world and enticing them to come to New Zealand'.[3] Arguably, it was New Line Cinema's confidence in Weta and its proprietary innovations – including the crowd rendering software, Massive – which allowed Jackson to shake off the disappointment of *The Frighteners* and keep his next project, *The Lord of the Rings* trilogy, a home grown production.

No matter what Jackson may accomplish over the rest of his career, *The Lord of the Rings* trilogy will define him as a filmmaker for the foreseeable future. Indeed, on the news in 2009 that Jackson would be writing and executive producing two films based on Tolkien's *The Hobbit*, to be directed by Guillermo del Toro, Jackson's fate seemed as bound to The One Ring as was Frodo's. Taken as a whole, *The Fellowship of the Ring*, *The Two Towers* and *The Return of the King* are a monumental achievement of adaptation, management and technical artistry. Jackson, however, never feels entirely comfortable working on an epic scale. The fantasy genre is particularly ill-suited for the brand of intertextual play that marks all of Jackson's previous works, especially a fantasy film set in the richly detailed but hermetically sealed world of J.R.R. Tolkien. While Jackson effectively captures the grand sweep of Tolkien's sprawling narrative, his attempts to blend action, drama and comedy in individual sequences result in more than a few awkward bumps along the way. Throughout, there is a marked tension between the classic Hollywood style that Jackson has assumed and his seemingly more natural inclination toward postmodern pastiche and parody. Ever the craftsman, Jackson proves far more successful at achieving a seamless on-screen integration of digital and traditional visual effects techniques in a hybrid production that often made as much use of models and miniatures and forced perspective as it did algorithms and performance capture. Through a canny Internet campaign, Jackson proved equally adept at yoking the participatory fan culture he grew out of to New Line Cinema's marketing of the films. By feeding information to unofficial fan sites, such as TheOneRing.net and Harry Knowles's 'Ain't It Cool News', Jackson cultivated a community around the production and promotion of the films, a community that became invested in the films' ultimate success. The fan culture that was formed around the trilogy before the release of *Fellowship* became a particularly fascinating centre of debate after the film opened internationally in December 2001 in the wake of the September 11th attacks on the World Trade Center, and various groups struggled to fix the meaning of the film and the trilogy as a whole, within the context of the Bush administration's War on Terror. Jackson, for the most part, tried to ride above this textual fray – 'The idea of interpreting films to mean whatever you wish them to mean is a pastime in which I've never taken much interest',[4] he has said – while preparing his next film, *King Kong*.

If the *LOTR* trilogy currently defines Jackson's career, *King Kong* brought it full-circle, returning to the material that first inspired him to take up a camera in the first place. Jackson's adaptation with regular *LOTR* co-screenwriters Fran Walsh and Phillipa Boyens remains relatively faithful to the original as Jackson retains the character of filmmaker Carl Denham (Jack Black), jettisoned and replaced by an oil company executive in Dino De Laurentiis's 1976 remake. Jackson, in fact, expands on the original narrative's show business context with additional characters, such as screenwriter Jack Driscoll (Adrien Brody), now the human love interest for Naomi Watts's Ann Darrow, and Bruce Baxter, the narcissistic leading man of Denham's film within the film. Back on the familiar generic terrain of the action horror film, Jackson takes intertextual liberties anew, peppering the script with film references, including a sight gag involving *Braindead*'s Sumatran Rat-Monkey. The joyful, if irreverent, cinephilia that fuels so much of his early output, however, is here tempered by an acerbic insider's critique of *King Kong*'s other outsized monster, Hollywood.

While Jackson positions Driscoll and Denham as the age-old combatants Art and Commerce, the film as a whole falls, not unexpectedly, squarely on the side of Denham-style spectacle. In addition to expanding the cast of characters, Jackson extends whole action sequences from the original, multiplying exponentially the island's dinosaur population while reinstating the original film's fabled 'Spider Pit Sequence' which, legend has it, was deemed too horrifying for 1933 audiences. Where Jackson's efforts to out-gore his horror heroes in *Bad Taste* and *Braindead* played as giddy celebrations of low-budget ingenuity, it is hard not to read his mobilisation of a blockbuster budget in *King Kong* to out-do Cooper and Schoedsack as excessive triumphalist chest-beating in opposition to the narrative's more humanist intentions. Such, however, is the nature of the beast.

Throughout his career, Jackson has kept both his fans and his critics off guard and his decision to follow up *Kong* with an adaptation of Alice Sebold's best selling novel *The Lovely Bones,* about a girl who witnesses as a ghost the aftermath of her own murder on her family, continues to keep them guessing. It is becoming clearer, however, that post-*LOTR*, Jackson aims to chart a career path similar to Spielberg's, moving between tentpole commercial projects capable of keeping his Wellington infrastructure up and running while taking on more personal outings that nevertheless fall within the limits of Hollywood marketability. With a slew of high-profile producing credits already in the works, including *The Hobbit* and the Spielberg-directed *The Adventures of Tintin: Secret of the Unicorn*, Jackson remains a most unlikely force to be reckoned with.

Biography

Peter Jackson was born in 1961 in Pukerua Bay, New Zealand. Interested in pursuing a career in film from childhood, Jackson left school after the sixth form but could only find work as a photo-engraver at the Wellington Evening Post. He continued shooting films on the weekends with friends, eventually completing his first feature, *Bad Taste*, in 1987. A string of commercial and critical successes followed culminating in Jackson winning the Oscar for Best Director in 2004 for *The Lord of the Rings: The Return of the King*.

Notes

1 Paul A Woods (ed.), *Peter Jackson: From Gore to Mordor*. London, Plexus Publishing Ltd., 2005, p. 27.
2 Donato Totaro, 'Your Mother Ate my Dog! Peter Jackson and Gore-Gag Comedy'. *Séquences*, Jan./Feb. vol. 176, 1995, pp. 22–7.
3 Brian Sibley, *Peter Jackson: A Film-maker's Journey*. London, HarperCollins, 2006, p. 308.
4 Ibid., p. 539.

Filmography

The Valley (1976) (Short)
Bad Taste (1987)
Meet the Feebles (1989)

Braindead (1992) a.k.a. *Dead Alive*
Heavenly Creatures (1994)
Forgotten Silver (1995)
The Frighteners (1996)
The Lord of the Rings: The Fellowship of the Ring (2001)
The Lord of the Rings: The Two Towers (2002)
The Lord of the Rings: The Return of the King (2003)
King Kong (2005)
Crossing the Line (2008) (Short)
The Lovely Bones (2009)

Further reading

Harriet Margolis, *Studying the Event Film: The Lord of the Rings*, Manchester, Manchester University Press, 2008.
Kristin Thompson, *The Frodo Franchise: The Lord of the Rings and Modern Hollywood*, Los Angeles, University of California Press, 2007.

JIM JARMUSCH

By Jason Wood

The independent spirit

American independent cinema is a complex, contradictory and frequently elusive term. Jim Hillier captures its essence, describing it as being something that is different from the mainstream in either economic, aesthetic or stylistic terms. This definition acts as a perfect introduction to the films of Jim Jarmusch, a contemporary American filmmaker still very much out in the field whose continuing engagement with figures on the margins of society and the gaps and pauses that form the backbone of ordinary life could be said to encapsulate the spirit of independent filmmaking.

A contemporary of John Sayles, who has also cast his shadow on films made outside of the studio system, Jarmusch is routinely described as the most influential independent filmmaker since John Cassavetes (a director for whom Jarmusch has expressed admiration). Both are actor-led filmmakers[1] whose work is infused with a cinematic sensibility that stretches beyond U.S. borders. Jarmusch, like Cassavetes, has always insisted on economic autonomy, taking an active role in how his films are distributed and marketed and placing himself in the rare position of retaining the rights to the negatives of his work[2] and its future exploitation.

A 17-year-old Jarmusch left Ohio for New York City fuelled by aspirations to become a writer. A literature student at Columbia University, he spent a semester in Paris and awakened a passion for foreign language cinema after becoming a regular habitué at the cinematheque. The discovery of film as a medium that offered an engagement with cultural diversity would become a cornerstone of Jarmusch's work. With his prematurely white hair, Jarmusch became a distinctive fixture on the New York underground circuit, pouring his energies into making music, joining a band called the Del-Byzanteens. Sound and vision were to become inseparable in his work, and like other independent figures such as Hal Hartley, David Lynch and Kelly Reichardt – perhaps the most recent filmmaker in whom his influence can be detected – Jarmusch would be considerably involved in the score, working with artists as diverse as Neil Young (also the subject of Jarmusch's somewhat atypical 1997 concert movie, *The Year of the Horse*), RZA (responsible for the outstanding *Ghost Dog: The Way of the Samurai* soundtrack) and Mulatu Astatke (the Ethiopian jazz of *Broken Flowers*).

Unsure of his direction (a trait that can be ascribed to many of his characters) Jarmusch applied to graduate film school at New York University. Critical of his time at NYU (he claims to have had to 'unlearn a lot of the things they tried to teach us'[3]), Jarmusch did however form alliances, with Nicholas Ray and Tom DiCillo. DiCillo would act as the cinematographer on Jarmusch's first two features before finding his own success as director with *Johnny Suede* (1991).

Permanent Vacation, Jarmusch's feature debut, began life as a final thesis. The institution's criticism of the project led to Jarmusch's decision to drop out, taking his film with him. Made for just $15,000, the film, subsequently expanded to 80 minutes, centres on an apathetic drifter (Christopher Parker) who, inspired by the improvisational jazz of his all-time hero Charlie Parker, meanders around New York City, ostensibly to visit his estranged mother. Perhaps most notable for DiCillo's artful cinematography, which lends the bustling Metropolis a surreal sheen, and its saxophone score courtesy of Lounge Lizard John Lurie, *Permanent Vacation* suggested an artist still grappling for an individual sense of expression.

The year it all changed

John Pierson situates *Stranger Than Paradise* as modern American independent cinema's point of origin. He details the film's bargain basement budget and its organic and original aesthetic – a synthesis of

Ozu, Rivette and punk rock sensibilities – that made it 'identifiably European and quintessentially American at the same time'.[4] Originating as a 30-minute short shot over a weekend on leftover stock gifted by Wim Wenders[5] following the completion of *The State of Things* (1982), *Stranger Than Paradise* screened on portable projectors at clubs throughout New York in order to attract further finance. Later shown at the Hof Festival in Germany, the short captured the attention of Paul Bartel and chocolate impresario Otto Grokenberger, who provided the completion funding that extricated Jarmusch from his soured relationship with Gray City Films, Wenders's distribution company.

Exploring the effects of an unwanted visit from a Hungarian cousin (Eszter Balint) on detached, taciturn New Yorker Willie (John Lurie) and his gambling buddy Eddy (Richard Edson), the film offers a perceptive look at exile, existential solitude and the possibilities of communication beyond cultural differences. Jarmusch also studies the effects of geography on human emotions, tracking the trio as they travel from New York, to snowy Cleveland and then on to an out-of-season Florida.

Shot for $110,000, $10,000 of which went towards securing the use of Screamin' Jay Hawkins's 'I put a Spell on You', *Stranger Than Paradise* was immediately set apart by DiCillo's elegant black and white photography and its part poignant, part comic minimalism which serves to magnify the import of every gesture and wry comment. Originating the technique of dividing his films into chapters ('The New World', 'One year later' and 'Paradise'), Jarmusch employs a discrete approach to style and grammar, with no dissolves, cuts or wipes in the long, uninterrupted stationary scenes in which the film proceeds. A masterclass in understatement, the film made a telling contribution to the casting process with Jarmusch avoiding Screen Actors Guild members in favour of character types and figures with whom he was familiar from the downtown punk scene.

The recipient of sustained critical approval, Jarmusch became the first American to win the Cannes Camera d'Or for best first feature. Zeroing in on the zeitgeist, *Stranger Than Paradise* was picked up for distribution by the Samuel Goldwyn Company and played for over a year in cinemas. It was subsequently a cultural event throughout Europe and Japan (a sustained source of future funding), where Jarmusch was immediately canonised as a guru of cool. A seismic influence on the way American independent films were made, distributed and marketed (the poster audaciously proclaimed 'a new American film by Jim Jarmusch'), the determinedly spare style perfectly captured the relationship between aesthetics and economy.

Down By Law, Jarmusch's third feature, fine-tuned the director's distinctive approach to genre and convention, beginning as a tale defined by an authentic urban naturalism before taking a scenic detour through the prison movie, noir thriller and fairytale romance. Jarmusch also brings his own esoteric sensibility to bear on the buddy movie, crafting a comic and characteristically offbeat variant in which miscommunication, a common theme for Jarmusch, is key.

The film charts the exploits of two New Orleans deadbeats: pimp Jack (John Lurie, who again provides the film's score) and radio DJ Zack (Tom Waits), both of whom are framed by the corrupt local police for crimes they unwittingly commit. Thrown together in jail, their hothead similarities breed a simmering antagonism until the pair finds a fresh butt for their sniping in new cellmate Roberto (Roberto Benigni), a diminutive Italian tourist and alleged murderer with a passion for Robert Frost and Walt Whitman. Ridiculed for his rudimentary grasp of English, Roberto ultimately acts as a solidifying force, leading his fellow inmates to freedom across a Southern bayou.

Robby Müller's high contrast black and white photography captures both the seediness of late night New Orleans, and the eerie beauty of the swamps in which the men seek freedom. The contrasting performance styles of the leading players is effective, with Benigni's over-the-top gesticulating and energetic fizz lending the film a broader accessibility that led some to define the humour as lowbrow. Indeed, many of Roberto's idiosyncratic interpretations of the English language such as 'I ham a good egg' raise an easy-won smile but there's also depth and poignancy too, as in his mantra 'it's a sad and beautiful world'.

Down by Law shares with subsequent Jarmusch pictures an arresting tripartite structure (before prison, in prison, after prison) and a wry exploration of American culture colliding with foreign elements. Again, Jarmusch favours tone and atmosphere over narrative and action, omitting vital details concerning the jailbreak. The defining style is almost absurdly minimalist, a term the director rejects, preferring 'reduced'; in literary terms, one may think of Jarmusch as cinema's Raymond Carver. The film remains the director's favourite of his own movies, largely for the celebratory atmosphere in which it was shot.

Minimalism on a global scale

Mystery Train offered a continuing observation of America and American popular culture through the eyes of outsiders in a narrative comprised of three separate but interconnecting stories which take place over the course of the same evening. The film was described by Jarmusch on its release as 'a minimalist's version of *The Canterbury Tales*'.[6]

A temporal comedy set in Memphis, Tennessee, the stories ('Far From Yokohama', 'A Ghost', and 'Lost in Space') begin with a laconic Japanese couple whose love of rock 'n' roll has inspired a pilgrimage to Elvis's home. After touring Sun Studios, the couple (Masatoshi Nagase and Youki Kudoh) check into the Arcade Hotel. The liveliest thing about the establishment is the night clerk (Screamin' Jay Hawkins) and his wide-eyed bellboy (Cinqué Lee). Also checking in for the night is an Italian woman, Luisa (Nicoletta Braschi) on the eve of flying to Rome with the ashes of her husband. Luisa finds that things really do go bump in the night when she receives a visit from Elvis's ghost. Meanwhile, in a parallel universe somewhere across town, drunken fugitives (led by Joe Strummer and Steve Buscemi) head for the Arcade after holding up a liquor store.

Although the episodic structure is something of a ruse as the characters never really meet with the three stories 'just separate cars pulled by the same train',[7] it does exemplify the director's 'restlessly experimental interest in the method and structure of cinematic storytelling'.[8] Jarmusch is however no chilly formalist.

Again working with Robby Müller and rarely straying from the crisply composed and resolutely still tableaux, Jarmusch does however draw upon a more colourful palette, using lurid reds (a neon sign and Mitsuko's crimson lipstick, later smeared across the lips of her impassive lover) evocative of the paintings of Edward Hopper. The spirit of Hopper lives on in the film's nocturnal setting and its fascination with characters that, even when in the company of others, seem utterly alone.

Jarmusch assembled an impressive international array of actors (including Gena Rowlands, Giancarlo Esposito, Winona Ryder, Armin Mueller-Stahl, Beatrice Dalle, and Roberto Benigni) for *Night on Earth*, a quintet of one-act plays featuring five cities, five taxicabs and a multitude of strangers in the night.

In Los Angeles, a casting agent tries to convince a streetwise female cabbie that she is tailor made for the movies. In New York, an initially irascible black passenger becomes convinced that his inexperienced and hopelessly lost German driver will never make it to Brooklyn without his assistance. In Paris, a taxi driver from the Ivory Coast ejects his rowdy cargo in favour of a no-nonsense blind woman. In Rome, the talkative driver recounts his sexual proclivities in explicit detail, much to the consternation of the priest occupying the back seat. Meanwhile, in a freezing Helsinki dawn, the occupants of a taxi become engaged in an unofficial competition to see just who has the most tragic tale to tell. Despite insisting that he had no real desire to revisit vignettes, his international standing and ability to secure funding from various international territories partly precipitated the project. Another contributing factor was the director's interest in language coupled with the opportunity, following the experience of 'Far From Yokohama', to shoot in foreign tongues.

Continuing the director's interest in shared differences and similarities, the film allows blindness to function as a motif regarding receptivity to the perspectives and experiences of others. This is pronounced in the Paris sequence where the driver (Isaach de Bankolé) views his fare's lack of vision as a form of weakness. 'Can you drive?' he asks. 'Can you?' she fires back. Not without humour, but still underpinned by a palpable sense of urban displacement and global ennui, accentuated by the melancholic Tom Waits score, *Night on Earth* also demonstrated the director's ability to work with stars without compromising his standing.

Journeys into genre

Reverting to a single narrative, but retaining a focus upon exiles and outsiders, *Dead Man* (a western, albeit one filtered through Jarmusch's existential sensibility) signalled a shift in Jarmusch's work with a more determined foray into genre. The story of a physical and spiritual journey into unfamiliar terrain, Johnny Depp stars as William Blake, a newly orphaned accountant who leaves his Cleveland home to take up a position at a metal works in a violent and desolate frontier town. Informed by owner Mr. Dickerson (a bizarre cameo from Robert Mitchum in his final screen performance) that his position has been filled, Blake seeks solace in the arms of a prostitute. Forced to defend himself against her jealous lover (Gabriel Byrne), who also happens to be Dickerson's son, Blake is badly wounded and flees into the wilderness where a Native American named Nobody (Gary Farmer) tends his wounds. Mistaking his charge for the English poet, Nobody helps him evade the bounty hunters on his trail and assumes the role of guide during Blake's passage to the spirit world.

Reunited with Robby Müller, the atmospheric black and white photography and attentiveness to period detail bestows the authenticity of a genuine historical artefact. The soundtrack is also notable, with Neil Young recording direct to picture and without interruption.

Filled with a density of ideas, which no doubt contributed to the muted critical reaction, *Dead Man* contrasts new and old world values to offer a biting commentary on modern American morality. Jarmusch's most explicitly political work, the film considers the contemporary obsession with fame, money and violence. When asked why she keeps a pistol by her bed, the prostitute with whom Blake lays comments, 'Cause this is America'. Juxtaposing surrealist and macabre black comedy (Iggy Pop appears in drag) with images of extreme violence, the film's obsession with death may have also tempered its box office potential. The release proved tortuous, with Harvey Weinstein's Miramax adopting a contemptuous strategy after Jarmusch refused to re-cut the film in order to secure a wider audience.[9] The director would not make another film for four years.

Boasting a Philosophical Consultant amongst its credits, *Ghost Dog: The Way of the Samurai* retains the spiritual bent central to *Dead Man*, incorporating quotations from the 18th-century samurai manual *Hagakure* while re-invigorating the hit man genre. A shrewd look at the dichotomy between ancient and modern values, it depicts an increasingly industrialised world in which, as its central protagonist puts it: 'Everything seems to be changing around us'.

The protagonist, the eponymous Ghost Dog (Forest Whitaker), is a professional assassin and self-taught samurai who follows a strict physical and moral regime. Famed for his ability to come and go without attracting attention, Ghost Dog has dedicated his services to Louie (John Tormey), a low-level crime boss who once saved his life. Living alone, Ghost Dog receives instruction via carrier pigeon and has so far carried out twelve flawless hits. The thirteenth, the execution of one of Louie's mobster associates, develops complications when the victim's girlfriend (Tricia Vessey), who is also the daughter of mafia don Ray Vargo (Henry Silva), catches a glimpse of the killer's face. When Ghost Dog's own death is ordered as atonement, the silent warrior harnesses his powers of survival to methodically wipe out his former employers.

Widely interpreted as a riff on the emancipation of black con-sciousness, the central character was written with Whitaker in mind and in part inspired by the actor's own interest in martial arts and Eastern philosophy. A further source of inspiration was Jean Pierre Melville's *Le Samourai* (1967), with Melville, alongside Akira Kurosawa and Seijun Suzuki, appearing in the credits. Referencing Melville's emotionally disengaged protagonist, who also devours samurai texts, Jarmusch makes clear the cinematic lineage of his mobster characters by casting character actors associated with the gangster genre. *Ghost Dog* however deviates from type, portraying the ageing cronies as henpecked husbands and fathers who seek quiet solace in TV re-runs of classic kids' cartoons.

Although Robby Müller's camerawork incorporates more tracking shots for the action sequences, *Ghost Dog* offers little advance on Jarmusch's trademark minimalism. Abiding themes are revisited too: the synthesis of various aspects of cultural entities (black, mafia and samurai culture) and how language need not be a barrier to understanding and communication. This becomes paramount as the film progresses, with Ghost Dog forming an alliance with a Haitian ice-cream vendor (Isaach de Bankolé, one of numerous actors with whom the director works repeatedly), who speaks only French. More positively received than *Dead Man*,[10] it is somewhat ironic, and typically 'Jarmuschian', that without abandoning his practices or his principles the director incrementally inched towards a wider audience.

All there is is this

Coffee and Cigarettes began in 1986 when Jarmusch was asked to create a short film for *Saturday Night Live*. The result, *Strange to Meet You*, starred Roberto Benigini and Steven Wright. Shot by Tom DiCillo, the film was selected for numerous international festivals. The short set the stage for what would become a long-term and ongoing project, a series of conversations which, as *Coffee and Cigarettes*, would be linked by theme and style into one feature-length film. Filmed in black and white, all the pieces employed consistent visual motifs as part of a unifying structure, whilst Jarmusch's screenplay worked a host of variations on the basic idea of centring on the title's twin pleasures/addictions. Many of those asked to appear were friends, but some, such as Steve Coogan or Cate Blanchett, were simply people Jarmusch aspired to work with. Though at times the actors appear to be playing themselves, the scripts were either completely fictional or at most exaggerated versions of personalities and personas.

The second instalment of *Coffee and Cigarettes* was shot in 1989 whilst Jarmusch was in Memphis filming *Mystery Train*. It featured two actors from the film, Cinqué Lee and Steve Buscemi, and Lee's sister Joie. The film, titled *Twins* when incorporated into the final feature, played at festivals as *Coffee and Cigarettes: Memphis Version*. In 1992 Jarmusch filmed a third segment in Northern California, *Coffee and Cigarettes: Somewhere in California*, starring Tom Waits and Iggy Pop as two musicians who bristle over a diner jukebox. Frederick Elmes undertook photography duties and the film won the Golden

Palm at the 1993 Cannes Film Festival as Best Short Film. Returning to New York, Jarmusch shot two more scenes in a single day (*Renée* and *No Problem*). The remaining six parts were completed over two weeks in early 1993: *Those Things'll Kill Ya*, *Cousins*, *Jack Shows Meg His Tesla Coil* (featuring Jack and Meg White of The White Stripes), *Cousins?* (the compendium's stand-out sequence), *Delirium* (with GZA, RZA and a hyped Bill Murray drinking coffee straight from the pot) and *Champagne*.

Broken Flowers, Jarmusch's return to a single, extended narrative feature, maintained both the director's relationship with the hangdog Bill Murray – in many ways the director's ideal leading man – and the lighter tone of *Coffee and Cigarettes*. Dumped by his latest lover (Julie Delpy), Don Johnston (Murray) is resigned to a life left to his own devices. However, the ageing bachelor is instead compelled to reflect on his past when he receives a mysterious pink letter from a former lover informing him that he has a 19-year-old son who may now be searching for his father. Don is urged to investigate this 'mystery' by his closest friend, neighbour and local amateur sleuth, Winston (Jeffrey Wright). Hesitant to travel, the independently wealthy Don is persuaded to embark on a cross-country trek in search of clues from four former flames (Frances Conroy, Jessica Lange, Sharon Stone, and a very much against type Tilda Swinton). Unannounced visits to each hold new surprises as Don haphazardly confronts his past, his present, and the possibilities for the future.

Combining mirth (the lead character is an obvious riff on Don Juan and an amusing reference to *Miami Vice* star Don Johnson) and melancholy to engaging effect, *Broken Flowers* grapples in characteristic Jarmusch fashion with the failures and disappointments of life, with all the characters in the film to some degree linked by the opportunities that have slipped through their fingers. But a combination of deftly chosen star performers, a more linear road movie structure (all Jarmusch's films betray similarities with the structure of classic road movies)[11] and a dampening of the line of philosophical enquiry at the heart of both *Dead Man* and *Ghost Dog* made *Broken Flowers* a more palatable commercial prospect. As such, the film remains the director's only genuine box-office success, achieving a U.S. gross of \$13.7 million (in the UK it took a shade under £2 million).

There is of course a knowing artificiality and implausibility at play, a constant facet of the director's work that arises from his preference for character over plot. But there is also a pronounced emotional generosity at the heart of *Broken Flowers*. Perhaps the result of a mellowing on the part of its maker, who when he made the film was not so far in age from his central character, it certainly makes for an utterly charming, generous work. Dedicated to Jean Eustache, the film of course has its serious and sombre side, offering a chastening portrait of the ageing process and the speed at which life moves. Asked to proffer his wisdom on the meaning of life by the teenager who may or may not be his son, Don responds sagely, 'The past is gone. I know that. The future isn't here yet, whatever it may bring. All there is is this.' It's a statement that offers a fitting summation of life as seen by Jim Jarmusch.

The story doesn't quite finish here. Jarmusch continues to remain active even during an economic climate hostile to independent film production. The director's latest feature, *The Limits of Control*, unseen by the writer at the time this article was completed, is the story of a mysterious loner (Isaach de Bankolé) whose activities remain meticulously outside the law. Sent on an unspecified assignment, the man undertakes a dreamlike journey in which he will traverse both Europe (the film is set in France and Spain) and his own consciousness. Shot by Christopher Doyle, the film is described by Jarmusch in the accompanying press notes as his attempt to remake John Boorman's *Point Blank* (1967) via Jacques Rivette and Antonioni. Writing in *Screen International*, Mike Goodridge critiques the film as a retreat from the commercial breakthrough of *Broken Flowers*, tagging it as an 'extreme art film as obscure and elliptical as anything he's [Jarmusch] ever made' (*The Limits of Control*, *Screen International* review, 24th April 2009). The film is at the time of writing without a UK distributor.

Biography

Born in Akron, Ohio, in 1953.

Notes

1 Cassavetes was also an actor, appearing in studio pictures such as Aldrich's *The Dirty Dozen* (1967) and Polanski's *Rosemary's Baby* (1968) and then ploughing his fee back into his own productions. Jarmusch has also appeared in a number of cameo roles, most frequently for friends and fellow independent directors.

2 The only film to which Jarmusch has not retained the negative is *The Year of the Horse*, a surprisingly conventional mix of concert performances and backstage interviews with Neil Young and his band, Crazy Horse.

3 David E Williams, 'Interview with Jim Jarmusch', *Film Threat*, Issue 5, August 1992, p. 17.

4 John Pierson, *Spike, Mike, Slackers and Dykes*, 1996, p. 25.

5 Jarmusch worked as the assistant to Wenders on *Lightning Over Water* (1980). Jarmusch would also display a good eye for assistants, later hiring, amongst others, Claire Denis. Denis worked with Jarmusch on *Down by Law* and also served Wenders on *Paris, Texas* (1984) and *Wings of Desire* (1987).

6 Reproduced from www.Jim-Jarmusch.net (an unofficial website but still a valuable resource tool for all things Jarmusch).

7 (*Dead Man*, London, BFI Publishing, 2000) Ibid.

8 Geoff Andrew, *Directors A–Z*, p.104.

9 A transcendental film that continues to grow in stature, *Dead Man* is the subject of a monograph by Jonathan Rosenbaum.

10 J Hoberman, in a largely positive review, described the film as 'impeccably shot and sensationally scored' and as containing enough moments of 'throwaway brilliance to suggest the filmmaker's capacity to rise from the Dead' (J. Hoberman, 'Promised Lands', *Village Voice*, 14 May, 1996).

11 Though *Dead Man* is considered a western, it also incorporates road movie elements. The films of Jim Jarmusch exist in a world pretty much all of their very own but they all to some degree share some similarities with the classic road movie structure. Suffice to say, they can be considered road movies with one flat tyre.

Filmography

Permanent Vacation (1980) also writer
Stranger Than Paradise (1984) also writer
Coffee and Cigarettes (1986) also writer
Down by Law (1986) also writer
Mystery Train (1989) also writer
Red Hot and Blue (1990) (TV) (segment 'It's All Right With Me')
Night on Earth (1991) also writer
Dead Man (1995) also writer
Year of the Horse (1997) also writer
Ghost Dog: The Way of the Samurai (1999) also writer
Ten Minutes Older: The Trumpet (2002) (segment 'Int. Trailer Night') also writer
Coffee and Cigarettes (2003) also writer
Broken Flowers (2005) also writer
The Limits of Control (2009) also writer

Further reading

Allon, Yoram, Del Cullen and Hannah Patterson (eds), *The Wallflower Critical Guide to Contemporary North American Directors* (London: Wallflower), 2000.

Andrew, Geoff, *Stranger Than Paradise: Maverick Filmmakers in Recent American Cinema* (London: Prion Books Ltd), 1998.

Andrew, Geoff, *Directors A–Z* (London: Prion Books Ltd), 1999.

Bradshaw, Peter, review of *Broken Flowers*, *The Guardian*, Friday October 21st, 2005.

DiCillo, Tom, *Living In Oblivion and Eating Crow: A Filmmaker's Diary* (London: Faber and Faber), 1995.

Goodridge, Mike, review of *The Limits of Control*, *Screen International*, 24th April 2009.

Hillier, Jim (ed.), *American Independent Cinema, A Sight and Sound Reader* (London: BFI Publishing), 2001.

Hoberman, J., 'Into the Void', essay review of *Ghost Dog: The Way of the Samurai*, *The Village Voice*, February 29th, 2000.

Hoskyns, Barney, *Lowside of the Road, A Life of Tom Waits* (London: Faber), 2009.

Keogh, Peter, *Home and Away*, reproduced in Hillier 2001.

Pierson, John, *Spike Mike Slackers & Dykes: A Guided Tour across a Decade of Independent American Cinema* (London: Faber and Faber), 1996.

Rosen, Dan with Peter Hamilton, *Off Hollywood: The Making and Marketing of Independent Films* (New York: Grove Press), 1990.

Winter, Jessica, *The Rough Guide to American Independent Film* (London: Rough Guides Ltd), 2006.

NEIL JORDAN

By Maria Pramaggiore

Neil Jordan wrote his way into international cinema. Having come of age during the 1950s and 1960s in Ireland – which was, during those decades, an insular, impoverished country whose chequered film history had been dominated by foreigners – perhaps there was no other way. Jordan wrote short stories while working as a jazz musician, a London day labourer, and an actor, carousing with the likes of Stephen Rea, Colm Meany, Gabriel Byrne, Liam Neeson, Jim Sheridan and Ciaran Hinds at Dublin's Project Theatre in the 1970s. He won the Guardian Fiction Prize for his collection, *A Night in Tunisia*, in 1976, and landed his first job in the film industry writing dialogue as a script consultant for John Boorman's *Excalibur* (1981). Jordan also directed a making-of documentary for the film, perhaps his first and last foray into conventional realism.

Jordan admits that he was simultaneously inspired and inhibited by the weighty tradition of Irish writing.[1] That centuries-long and diverse literary heritage – whose rich satirical and gothic elements pervade Jordan's work – encompasses the radical experiments of Beckett, O'Brien and Joyce, the poetics of Yeats, the gothic tales of Stoker and Le Fanu, the farcical theatricality of Boucicault, the satire of Swift, and the visionary *aisling*, or dream poem, of the seventeenth-century bards. In particular, Swift's rapacious wit and O'Brien's self-conscious genre blending are evident in the archly ironic tone that often infiltrates Jordan's films; equally consistent, however, is the director's profound engagement with the gothically-inflected mysteries of love and loss, memory and time.

Whereas literary giants cast a long shadow over contemporary Irish writers, Ireland's cinematic lineage was not nearly as well developed. Jordan, along with countless other cineastes in Ireland and abroad, grew up believing that John Ford's returned immigrant saga, *The Quiet Man* (1952), was an Irish film.[2] A member of the first genera-tion of indigenous Irish filmmakers, Jordan produces films that often challenge stereotypes about Irish culture and redress Ireland's status as a colony within international cinema. Jordan's cohort includes Bob Quinn (who made the first Irish language feature film, *Poitín*, in 1978), Cathal Black, Thaddeus O'Sullivan, Jim Sheridan and Pat Murphy. All of these directors repudiate the pastoral innocence and implied (or explicit) primitivism that characterises numerous American and British films made in and about Ireland.

With formative influences that range across British, American and French cinema, Jordan's work chafes at the limitations of genre and national cinema paradigms. His films exhibit impatience with boundaries of all kinds, as critics have noted.[3] Although frequently identified as an Irish director, most of Jordan's films do not focus on Irish themes; even the films that address Ireland's history, and speci-fically, the role of the Irish Republican Army, examine the personal and emotional devastation wrought by political violence rather than the broader social ramifications (*Angel*, *The Crying Game*, *Michael Collins*, *Breakfast on Pluto*).

Jordan may be unique among major international film directors in that he has continued to write. He has published four novels that are, characteristically, set in dreamy worlds where time feels suspended and the dead never come to their final rest: *The Past* (1979), *The Dream of a Beast* (1983), *Sunrise with Sea Monster* (1994) and *Shade* (2004). In addition, he has written or co-written screenplays for more than half of the films he has directed to date.

Whereas Jordan expresses himself in fiction through the whispered tones of the confessional, his prose conjuring up solitary figures and barely perceptible ghosts, his cinematic voice is sumptuous and con-veys the extravagance of the opera and carnival. Jordan's expressionist tendencies are apparent in terms of sound design alone. He often blends popular songs and original scores (frequently working with Eliot Goldenthal), orchestrating the mixture precisely for maximum emotional impact. He relies on particular musical favorites to induce nostalgia and a false sense of security – it's no coincidence that so many of his films share their titles with familiar songs, including *Mona Lisa*, *The Crying Game*, *In Dreams*, *The Butcher Boy*, *Breakfast on Pluto* – only to engineer a startling reversal of fortune that leaves his protagonists, and the audience, devastated. In *Mona Lisa*, for example, Nat King Cole's worshipful ballad about the singer's slightly unapproachable object of affection acquires a sinister tone when Jordan situates it within a film about the traffic in women. Michael Kamen's original score for that film samples notes from 'Mona Lisa' and from another Cole hit, 'When I Fall in Love … It Will Be Forever', a technique that drives home the obsessive love of the film's protagonist.

Jordan's visual style is similarly multi-layered, dynamic and opulent: whether he is darkly retelling children's fairy tales about gothic monsters in *The Company of Wolves*, *Interview with the Vampire* or *In Dreams*, or tracing the harrowing effects of political violence in *Angel*, *Michael Collins* or *Breakfast on Pluto*, Jordan imbues even realistic settings with saturated colors, visually arresting symbols and slow moving pans, evoking a sense of uncanny enchantment reminiscent of the work of Jean Cocteau, Michael Powell and Emeric Pressberger. When Neil Gaiman announced in early 2009 that Jordan would direct an adaptation of Gaiman's Newbury award-winning *The Graveyard Book*, about a young boy adopted by graveyard-dwelling spirits, he cited the visual design of *The Company of Wolves*, a film whose uncanny nightmare landscape is populated by brutal and seductive werewolves and grotesquely exaggerated children's toys.[4]

Jordan is adept at turning an actual location into a 'nowheresville':[5] a place of indeterminate time and geography where nothing turns out to be what it initially appears to be. *The Good Thief*, Jordan's remake of Jean Pierre Melville's *Bob Le Flambeur*, draws a stark visual contrast between Nice's seedy neon-lit criminal underworld and the sun-bleached opulence of Monte Carlo's casinos, yet both are spaces of illusion. The film's central metaphor revolves around gambling, and, in particular, the ability to engineer an elaborate bluff. Bob (Nick Nolte), like many Jordan characters, is a performer and a fabulist; even characters who are not musicians or actors find themselves enjoined at some point, usually by a cataclysmic event, to reconstruct their identities. Whether Bob is trying his luck at *chemin de fer* or passing off a fake Picasso as the real thing, he improvises stories as he goes along.

In this film, like most of Jordan's work, reflective images of all kinds, and particularly glass and mirrors, along with photographs and paintings, occupy a place of prominence in the mise-en-scène. His jewel-like, polished interiors reflect light and complicate the basic act of seeing; in exterior sequences, the atmosphere itself acquires a velvety thickness and a texture, absorbing light and obscuring vision in a different way. The smoky London streets of *The End of the Affair*, the rain-soaked forests of the northeastern United States in *In Dreams*, and the hazy, sun-drenched beach in *The Miracle* all thwart Jordan's protagonists' ability to comprehend the world around them.

His films frequently take shape around solitary characters who are possessed by the past, or by their own guilty obsessions, a trope that appropriately calls up associations with Hitchcock, and, most notably, *Vertigo*. In keeping with Jordan's interest in dark subjects of violence, death, revenge, addiction and madness, his films explore, but rarely indict, characters whose fates are determined by their intensely fertile, if not delirious, imaginations. One case in point is an iconic dream sequence from *The Butcher Boy* that superimposes a mushroom cloud over a postcard-perfect image of a lake reminiscent of the Lakes of Killarney, blending the prospect of nuclear Armageddon with Irish tourism and comic book kitsch. Yet this expressionist amalgam makes perfect sense within the mad mental logic of young Francie Brady, a boy whose abusive, alcoholic father consigns him to a Catholic home for boys after his mother commits suicide. Francie's magical, comical and horrifying visions suggest his tenuous connection to reality (a reality that itself seems a bit skewed, as in one scene the people in his town gather to await a visitation from the Virgin Mary) but also provide the only world in which Francie can affect the course of his destiny. Jordan's most critically acclaimed work, *The Butcher Boy*, is part historical account of the schizophrenic cultural politics of postwar Ireland and part gaily surreal psychodrama. Jordan's slate of Irish themed films, comprising *The Butcher Boy*, *Angel*, *High Spirits*, *The Miracle*, *Michael Collins*, *Breakfast on Pluto* and *Ondine*, seems to offer the perfect outlet for the director's penchant for expressionism and operatic excess.

Jordan's investigation of dangerous emotions generates more than simple melodrama. His first film, *Angel*, offers an example of the director's powerful allusiveness, his constant gesturing toward a subtext, be it sublime, profane, or both. The film juxtaposes the grittiest of contemporary realities with the redemptive potential of art, even art that is crass and commercial. The screenplay, which Jordan wrote, concerns a musician whose band is caught up in the Troubles in Northern Ireland. After a gig at the Dreamland Ballroom, a tacky dance hall and otherworldy locale whose name recalls William Trevor's story 'The Ballroom of Romance', the saxophonist Danny (Stephen Rea – a frequent Jordan collaborator) trades his instrument for an automatic weapon, at one point prowling the lush green countryside in his ridiculous pink silk stage outfit as he exacts his revenge. The film's soundtrack is punctuated by the sentimental ballad 'Danny Boy' and by Verdi's *Requiem*, aural notes whose repetition signifies the downward spiral of the narrative and suggests the way that Danny's life is defined by practices of violence that he neither seeks out nor understands. In fact, every action he takes only makes matters worse. Here Jordan draws upon a European cinema tradition of absurdist doom, evident in Roman Polanski's *Chinatown*, a downbeat neo-noir thriller that presages the spatial dislocation and circular narrative structure of many Jordan films. Although they emphasise their own recursiveness, Jordan's narratives inevitably fail to return to a prelapsarian normalcy: after the disruptions of the 'dark carnival' that Jordan summons, resolutions rarely assume a benign form.[6]

Jordan followed *Angel* with two films that marked the beginning of his long collaboration with British producer Stephen Woolley: *The Company of Wolves* and the thriller, *Mona Lisa*. Although *Mona Lisa*'s generic indebtedness to the British gangster film was made plain in the casting of Michael Caine as the aptly named Mortwell, the head of a London drugs and prostitution syndicate, Jordan nevertheless manages to evoke a compelling dream world within the context of this urban crime drama. Notably, he continues to develop the character of the male fantasist who clings to his illusions until they are inevitably and violently torn away. His hapless protagonist George (Bob Hoskins), a petty criminal ex-con and driver for the mob, dwells in a whimsical parallel universe, assisted by his partner in crime, Thomas (Robbie Coltrane), who deals in contraband religious kitsch. George imagines himself as St. George on a white horse, gallantly serving his beautiful lady love Simone (Cathy Tyson), a high priced prostitute who is using him to search for her lover, another sex worker in Mortwell's organisation. George gallantly conveys Simone to her appointments in a chariot, his prized Jaguar, all the while failing to notice what the views of nighttime London through his windshield, or the glimpses of Simone in his rear view mirror, make plain. His feverish delusions about Romantic love and valor are quixotic and self-destructive.

The painful shattering of illusions is an omnipresent theme in Jordan's work. *The Crying Game*, the film that earned Jordan not only an international reputation but also an Academy Award for Best Original Screenplay, traces the exploits of Fergus (Stephen Rea), a reluctant IRA volunteer who attempts to assuage his guilt at the death of a black British soldier taken hostage, but instead finds his pre-conceived notions of national and sexual politics challenged when he subsequently becomes involved with his hostage's lover Dil, whom he learns is a transvestite after he has fallen in love with her. The film pays homage to Robert Bresson in the casting of a non-actor to play Dil, and in its concluding scene, where the romance between Fergus and Dil remains both intact and suspended, due to the former's incarceration. Like *Mona Lisa*, *The Crying Game* dismantles hetero-sexual masculinity, exposing its ideology, and equally important, its effects, examining the way masculinity structures practices of racial and national identity. The traditional assumptions regarding race, gender and nationality that Jordan's violent men cling to are not merely quaintly retrograde belief systems, but dangerous ideologies that enable exploitative social practices.

The Crying Game – with its spectacular scenes of military assault and political assassinations and equally dramatic scenes of unconventional sexual attraction – serves as a powerful rejoinder to conventional stereo-types of Irish innocence and pastoralism. In terms of film history, it also reflects the industry trends in production and distribution in the 1980s and 1990s that put writer-directors like Neil Jordan on the map. Jordan's career – like those of contemporaries Ang Lee and Steven Soderbergh – has oscillated between small independent films and major Hollywood productions and has moved between and among thriller, comedy and horror genres. Jordan's invitation to the A-list was the result of the unlikely marriage between Palace Productions, Woolley's company, which had declared bankruptcy when *The Crying Game* was released, and Miramax, Bob and Harvey Weinstein's company, whose acquisition of *The Crying Game* was an early coup that proved essential to its rise as an independent film juggernaut in the 1990s.

For Jordan, however, forays into Hollywood (where creative con-trol can be compromised) have yielded equivocal results: in the late 1980s after *Mona Lisa*, he made two comedies that were poorly received by critics and at the box office: *High Spirits*, a whimsical Irish riff on *Ghostbusters*, and *We're No Angels*, an unlikely Bogart remake starring Robert DeNiro and Sean Penn as escaped convicts masquer-ading as priests. After his underdog success with *The Crying Game*,

Jordan was invited to direct Anne Rice's *Interview with the Vampire*, which earned $220 million internationally and remains his only bona fide blockbuster to date, largely due to the pre-sold audience for Rice's novels. In 1999, Jordan returned to Hollywood to direct *In Dreams*, a hallucinatory horror film about a serial killer (played by Robert Downey Jr., struggling with his own demons at the time) who infiltrates the mind of a children's book illustrator (Annette Bening). The film offers some of the most spectacularly baroque images of psychic possession and child abuse ever committed to film and it was a dismal failure at the box office. In 2005, Jordan directed *The Brave One*, a revenge thriller starring Jodie Foster as a woman who hunts down her fiancé's killers; despite strong performances by Foster and by Terrence Howard as a sympathetic detective, the film earned lukewarm reviews and a modest box office.

If Jordan's best-known film is *Interview with the Vampire*, a lavish production that emphasises the trope of vampire as celebrity – these supernatural creatures are eternally gorgeous, yet they are also hideously dependent upon the lifeblood of the common people – his most controversial film remains the Irish epic *Michael Collins*. The production raised hackles in Ireland and the UK because the circumstances surrounding the Irish War for Independence are still hotly debated and deeply felt. The resurgence of IRA violence during the production added to the controversy. In many ways, *Michael Collins* illustrates the difficulty of categorising Jordan's approach to filmmaking or his *oeuvre*. The film deals with a specific era in Irish history, but Jordan is more interested in examining the personal lives of Collins and his associates than in glorifying a national hero. The film was shot on location in Dublin and draws upon a reservoir of Irish acting talent in the persons of Liam Neeson, Stephen Rea and Sean McGinley, yet Hollywood megastar Julia Roberts plays Collins's lover, Kitty Kiernan, and Jordan's screenplay and visual design borrow heavily from the Hollywood gangster film, most notably Coppola's *The Godfather*. Rather than approaching this real-life saga with a documentary sensibility, Jordan treats Collins as something of an enigma, a resurrected ghost. He opens the film with the leader's death and proceeds retrospectively, with a frame that is reminiscent of Welles's *Citizen Kane*. Finally, he introduces gothic elements into a story of asymmetrical warfare, treating Collins's guerilla army as spectres haunting an ashy Dublin cityscape. As Neil Jordan continues to make films – high productivity being a constant in Jordan's career – his choice to work in diverse contexts and with varied subject matter seems unlikely to eclipse his ability to envision quotidian reality as potentially magical.

Biography

Neil Jordan was born in 1950 near Sligo, Ireland. He attended university at UCD and established the Irish Writers' Cooperative in 1974. He has five children and lives near Dublin with his second wife Brenda Rawn and their two sons.

Notes

1 Maria Pramaggiore, *Neil Jordan*. Urbana and Chicago: University of Illinois Press, 2008, p. 153.
2 Ibid., p. 152.
3 See Kevin Rockett and Emer Rockett, *Neil Jordan: Exploring Boundaries*. Dublin: Liffey Press, 2002; Jenny O'Connor, 'Repositioning Irish-America: Neil Jordan's American-Irish and the Value of the Interstice' in Ruth Barton (ed.) *Screening Irish-America: Representing Irish-America in Film and Television*. Dublin: Irish Academic Press, 2009.
4 'Neil Gaiman Pleased With *The Graveyard Book*'s Director'. ReelzChannel. com. February 4, 2009. www.reelzchannel.com/movie-news/2708/neil-gaiman-pleased-with-the-graveyard-books-director
5 Director's Commentary, *The Good Thief*.
6 Carole Zucker, (ed). *The Cinema of Neil Jordan: Dark Carnival*. London: Wallflower Press, 2008.

Filmography

Angel (1982)
The Company of Wolves (1984)
Mona Lisa (1986)
High Spirits (1988)
We're No Angels (1989)
The Miracle (1991)
The Crying Game (1992)
Interview with the Vampire (1994)
Michael Collins (1996)
The Butcher Boy (1997)
The End of the Affair (1999)
In Dreams (1999)
Not I (2000)
The Good Thief (2002)
Breakfast on Pluto (2005)
The Brave One (2007)

Ondine (2009)
The Graveyard Book (pre-production)

Further reading

Cullingford, Elizabeth Butler. 'Virgins and Mothers: Sinead O'Connor, Neil Jordan, and *The Butcher Boy*'. *The Yale Journal of Criticism*, 15.1 (Spring 2002), 185–210.

McCabe, Colin. *The Butcher Boy*. Cork: Cork University Press, 2007.

McIlroy, Brian. *Horror International*, ed. Steven Jay Schneider and Tony Williams. Detroit: Wayne State University Press, 2005.

Rockett, Kevin and Emer Rockett. *Neil Jordan: Exploring Boundaries*. Dublin: The Liffey Press, 2002.

AKI KAURISMÄKI

By Tytti Soila

The motor of this essay exploring the films of Aki Kaurismäki is 'genealogical curiosity', perhaps against better judgement since I cannot but agree with Mikhail Iampolski's insistence that it is impossible to establish an authentic source behind the choices that result in a work of art.[1] However, confronted with a phenomenon, our curiosity demands exegesis. As Andrew Sarris put the inevitable question: 'That was a good movie, who directed it?' Less sophisticated, perhaps, but to the point.[2] This essay is posited between a pragmatic quest for an explanation and an acknowledgement of the folly of such endeavour, i.e. between the questions of *how* and *why bother*, to travesty Sarris. Though Aki Kaurismäki has, from the beginning of his career, consistently sabotaged any proposal of meaning or intent behind his work, none the less, his films are full of cues referring to prior knowledge of Finnish history, popular culture, celebrities, and suchlike – all in a sense begging explanation. It is difficult to say how audiences lacking such prior knowledge read his films, a question that brings about a third, relational aspect, namely a question: *(to) whom*? Umberto Eco discusses levels of reader positions declaring that a text does not always invite everybody to the same party. Although certain types of text select some readers over others (preferring intertextually conscious readers), for Eco this does not mean the exclusion of those less well read.[3] Understanding is analogous: a fact worth remembering since many maintain that it is difficult to understand Kaurismäki's films without familiarity with the 'Finnish mindset'.[4]

Such an approach may be explained by the nation's cultural geography: existing on the borderline between the cultural and political power blocks of East and West, Finns have always defined themselves by exclusion: 'We are not Swedish, we will not become Russian – so let us be Finnish!' Today Finnishness attempts to define itself as a part of the European community with the demolished worldview of the former Soviet Union and an onrushing Americanism in the background. Kaurismäki's films reflect this reorientation in condensed image-frames, exposing visual reminiscences from an earlier period of national identity crisis when the setup seemed to be much more clear-cut. But in many other ways, the stories created by him and his crew speak to all people in a tangible way. As I wish to argue below, his films express sentiments and reflections on modernity that may be applicable everywhere.

Person/a

Initially Aki Kaurismäki was perceived as the younger part of the unity of 'The Kaurismäki Brothers', a unity that impacted the entire cinema culture of Finland during the 1980s. There was significant interest in the brothers' work from the beginning. The short, *Valehtelija* (*Liar*) – older brother Mika's exam film, released in 1981 – won a prize at the Tampere film festival. *Saimaa-ilmiö* (*The Saimaa Gesture*), *Jackpot* and *Arvottomat* (*The Worthless*) were all immediately hailed as inventive, creative and ingenious, confirming Aki's and Mika's position in the country's cultural life.

The idea of the 'Kaurismäki Brothers' prevailed long after the two developed independent careers. Aki inclined towards the absurd using an interview strategy of making a statement on a topic, immediately contradicting it and finally finishing the sentence with ' … I don't know, who cares?' Mika Kaurismäki showed himself more willing to discuss his work in accessible terms and headlines have offered a more conventional image (such as 'I am a Restless Soul' or 'Rootless Adventurer', preferably next to a photo of him on a motor bike[5] depicting him as a fervent intellectual deeply involved in his work.[6]) Aki, in his turn – and at least in a Finnish context – has conveyed his sense of social responsibility in general, and more particularly concerns regarding working conditions in the film industry. On the other hand, his public behaviour is increasingly identified with the Finnish brand of romantic artist: that is, a heavy drinking scoundrel. Few pictures or stories of his family relations circulate in public. Instead, he has painstakingly worked on his public image in line with his cinematic universe.[7]

The fashioning of the public persona of Aki Kaurismäki began – intentionally or not – with the exceptional productivity the brothers showed. Their industriousness vindicated their bashing of the Finnish politicians responsible for the administration of state support, and the county's cultural politics altogether ('Finnish culture is dead – we are old men').[8] As the brothers gave interviews together, they used a kind of nonsensical jargon mixed with critical remarks about Finnish life, film politics and the film production business. 'American cinema is dead, the European one is dying – and I am not feeling particularly well either!', said Aki in 1986.[9]

Story

Aki Kaurismäki has stressed that the story is the main component of his filmmaking: 'You do not make films about ideas, you make films about stories'.[10] Crucially, Kaurismäki's films derive from and comment on classic melodrama. What may be called the commonsensical mechanisms of melodrama – ritualisation, repetition, proverbial sayings, clichés, its employment of history and memory – involve a stylised and naturalised commitment to past actions and behaviour, allowing explorations of relationships between the past and the present.[11] Classic film melodrama is, then, a part of the public sphere where all kinds of hegemonic struggles take place. In a sense, as Fassbinder's work has shown, modernist films perform similar functions. As Marcia Landy writes: 'The insertion of a modernist perspective, the notion of increasing self-consciousness, serves to impose a new narrative of progress, replacing action with self-awareness on the part of the auteur and his handling of the genre'.[12]

In Kaurismäki's films the story however often holds a secondary position to cinematic space. In fact it is constructed as a *critical space* allowing the integration of political, social and economic power structures. The orchestration of the narrative, the emphasis on muteness and the excessive use of music (not to mention all the cues and references) refer to the commonsensical functions of the melodramatic thought in a heightened, self-conscious way. Thus, for instance, the excess in *Tulitikkutehtaan tyttö* (*The Match Factory Girl*) is *inverted excess*. Instead of exposure of abundance (of colours, forms, décor), a Kaurismäki film presents a *mise-en-scène* that is highly stylised, archaic and minimalist. *The Match Factory Girl* is the story of the monotonous life of Iiris, who divides her time between her parents, her work and modest moments of entertainment. The story ends when she poisons her parents.

Milieu

While Mika Kaurismäki has moved from Finland through Hollywood to Brazil, Aki has remained faithful to Finnish localities, at least as a backdrop for his stories. Thus, for instance, many of his films begin with a montage from a workplace such as a factory, a mine or a depot. Or to be more precise: his films are preoccupied with past milieus at the fringes of Finnish cities. Obsolete settings harmonise with another recurrent milieu, namely places of transit, 'spaces-in-between', such as staircases, locker-rooms, supermarkets, jails, cars – even boats: all places where one naturally encounters strangers.

In shots of the city, central perspective street sights dominate. Occasionally, a building is posited in relation to the camera so it reminds of a backdrop in an outdated theatre scene, in front of which the characters perform. In exteriors shot in the countryside, the scenery is characterised by horizontal lines just like the side-strips on big, American cars from the 1950s (another Aki Kaurismäki sign). The flat landscape of Finnish Ostrobothnia with a black ribbon of forest separating the grey fields and equally grey skies from each other – or a sand shore with the layer of rocks behind as in *Ariel* – look equally artificial. The boundary of Kaurismäki's cinematic realm is Helsinki harbour. Even if, for example, the Leningrad Cowboys go to America, the milieus they visit bear a striking resemblance to the scenery in his Finnish-based films.

The archetypal Aki Kaurismäki setting is, however, a cafeteria. Understood as a sign, a reminder for post-war Finnish audiences of the shared past, its 1950s design signals a period of transition from agrarian to city life. Such cafeterias were characteristic of small Finnish communities and working class quarters of the cities where the Kaurismäki children grew up. Ubiquitous and pleasantly anonymous, they became meeting places for post-war teenagers and, later in the 1970s, for beer-drinking outcasts. A cafeteria may be a place of degradation as in *Kauas pilvet karkaavat* (*Drifting Clouds*) where Ilona, a former maître-d' of the finest restaurant in the city, finally finds herself working on odd terms: 'The place hasn't even got a name!' she cries out in humiliation. Or it may be a haven as in *Mies vailla menneisyyttä* (*The Man without a Past*), where the main character M is served a free meal. In this story, a working man from the countryside comes to the city looking for work but gets robbed and beaten upon his arrival. He survives the assault but loses his memory; the story is about how, little by little, he creates an identity for himself.

Actors

Aki Kaurismäki started his career as an actor in films directed by his brother. Early on, both contested that 'acting' should be avoided in films,[13] and that actors should avoid identifying themselves too deeply with the role.[14] Whilst he was a student in Tampere, known for its 'red' university in the early 1970s as well as for its prominent theatres, interest in Bertolt Brecht reigned in Finland. Even small township theatres staged *The Threepenny Opera* and *Caucasian Chalk Circle* and *verfremdung* was discussed in student cafés. It is most likely that Brecht's idea of an epic or dialectic theatre as opposed to a dramatic/illusionist one influenced both him and Mika (who studied in Berlin at the time).

Aki Kaurismäki obviously likes to work with the same actors, or rather, with the same people, as he knowingly mixes professional actors with amateurs in his films. Why, he asks, replace a good actor just because you are making a new film. What characterises a good actor seems to be more difficult to establish: Kaurismäki said that he liked to work with Matti Pellonpää because he was the only Finnish male actor who looked like a sad rat. When Pellonpää died, Aki was working on the script of *Drifting Clouds*. Unable to think of a male replacement, he rewrote the script and cast a woman, Kati Outinen.

For Brecht, it was important to emphasise human relations, provoking audiences to draw intellectual conclusions instead of becoming emotionally attached to what they saw on the stage.[15] The main responsibility lay, in Brecht's opinion, with the actor who should regard him/herself as a narrator; a person who would only *quote* the character he/she was playing. In consequence, the few lines uttered by the actors in Kaurismäki's films sound literary, indeed like quotes, and the acting recalls poses in a *tableau vivant*.

Humanity

According to the public fantasy both at home and abroad, Finns are taciturn and lonely people, frozen into numb silence in the arctic chill. 'The myth about Finnish people depicts them as strong witches, intrepid soldiers and beautiful women. Even the export of cultural products supports these prejudices. Aki himself supports the image of such Finns in an excellent manner', writes a journalist not entirely pleased with this state of affairs.[16]

Yet, difficulties with expressing feelings do not indicate their absence: the obvious lack of eloquent verbal expression in

Kaurismäki's films only proclaims that they are to be found elsewhere. Desire is omnipresent. It is sealed in the evasive gazes and in the music: most particularly in Finnish popular music such as the tango. *The Match Factory Girl*, for instance, a film that contains only twenty-four lines of dialogue, presents a well known Finnish tango from the first bar to the last: Iiris visits a dance hall, the camera is placed in the doorway and registers the band in three steady takes.

Tangos are a crucial part of Finnish popular culture and folklore. The melody sung in this film tells of the singer's yearning for the land beyond the vast sea: a far away land of ever-blooming flowers where warm wind sweeps over sunny beaches. The singer is lamenting because he is 'a prisoner of the earth, without wings', unable to fly over to where love calls him. The words create a stunning discrepancy with the rigidity of the dance hall. Furthermore, the conflict invades the musical performance: the drummer maintains the flat rhythm with a steady, stiff beat and the incompetence of the musical performance stands in conspicuous contrast to the words. The drums are an ancient symbol of male sexuality. It has sometimes been said that the yearning words of a tango are the only means for the Finnish man to express his tender thoughts, his only way to declare what he really feels for his woman as he moves around the dance hall floor.[17] In this scene the musical performance becomes an expression for both his feelings and his inability to assert them.

Finnish film critics have called the 1980s to the mid-1990s the age of 'Male Odyssey', with a succession of films made by young men, describing a young man's search for adulthood (or death). Though Kaurismäki's films are part of this Odyssey, when we examine how men and all-male groups relate to their environment and to women, it is clear that they portray a bankrupt masculinity. Such films as *Juha* showcase a corrupt and destructive male image. Juha is a canonic Finnish story from 1911 of an elderly man who leads a happy life in the woods with his young wife Marja. A wandering young Russian persuades Marja to run away with him. Juha grabs his axe and sets forth to look for the pair. Marja returns to Juha but confesses her love for Shemeikka. Juha cannot live with the deceit and, after killing Shemeikka, drowns himself in the rapids.

In *Juha*, our sympathies are with the older man; and even *Calamari Union*, as well as *Leningrad Cowboys* and its sequels, adopts a parodic distance to young men. Assembled in tight groups, they wander the streets of Helsinki or Midwestern US towns, fast and heedless. Dressed in white shirts and thin black neckties, dark coats and Rayban sunglasses, they resemble penguins on the seashore (perhaps it is a coincidence that both have their habitat in Polar regions?). Both films can be read as an ironic portrait of a cultural Male Odyssey in the West. The hollowness of any such fellowship and its feebly defined goals is demonstrated in a scene where the manager of Leningrad Cowboys, sitting in the front seat of the car, finishes his beer and throws the can over his shoulder; it hits the statue-like face of a band member, producing no reaction. The Cowboys are equated with the empty beer-cans in the back seat. In fact, their eccentricity – expressed in their clothes and excessive black pompadours – seems to offer the only discernible value.

Male Odyssey films typically feature few women (or any other antithetic pole to relate to), but in a film like *Juha*, the limitations of the male image are exposed precisely in its relation to femininity. In this film a man's relation to a woman is reduced to its two basic patriarchal figures: either an infantile dependency (Juha) – the flip side of which is uncontrolled aggression – or sexual exploitation (Shemeikka). Both reduce woman to an object, but are also destroyed. Shemeikka dies by Juha's axe – a weapon as primitive as the man himself – whereas, in this version of the story, Juha is shot by his rival and perishes on the city dump. Marja, in turn, survives and, embracing her child, boards a train.

Music

Music is undoubtedly of crucial importance for Aki Kaurismäki's films, and he picks freely from fine opera to the idiosyncrasies of the popular range of the Finnish 1950s. Significant for Kaurismäki is that he oftentimes lets the musical piece be performed from beginning to end, underlining the interplay between melody, lyrics and the performance itself. This is the case in regard to the abovementioned tango in *The Match Factory Girl*, but especially in *The Man without a Past*, the different musical performances carry a significance beyond a mere recital: they become entertainment numbers as in musicals, another classic film genre with its roots in melodrama.

At the end of *The Man without a Past* a song called Monrepos is performed by the elderly Salvation Army Officer, accompanied by the Army Band. In the film, she reveals that in her youth, she, too, 'used to sing a bit'. In reality, the actor, Annikki Tähti, was one of the most popular singers in the country in the mid-1900s. The song, a slow waltz by Toivo Kärki, was a tremendous hit. The lyrics concern the memory of a park in the city of Viborg that was yielded to Russia in the 1944 peace treaty. The greenery of the park is associated with melancholic contemplation while roaming over its bridges and its 'natural' fields. The song identifies the park as the singer's own fantasyland, and the singer remembers the reveries but no particular person.

The actual image, here, is 'objective', perceivable in the present. The face of the singer is marked by a lived life, covered with deep wrinkles and lines – but her smile is still lovely and fully recognisable from the fan-magazines of yesteryear. Her voice cracks toward the ends of the verses but she still keeps the tune, letting the melody linger steadfast over the vowels. Her phrasing is perfect, reaching the peak of the tones, thus bonding the past and its representations, as well as the actuality of the performance together. The recollections themselves are real and present, and that makes it possible to make the beauty of the by-gone times tangible. In the absence, then, there is presence.[18]

Yet, M does not seem that interested in finding his past but instead, he tries to create himself a future. The past remains for the spectator to construct, as it is produced from the bits and pieces of the popular culture of the 1950s and 1960s that Kaurismäki has arranged – a bricolage recognisable at least if the spectator happens to be a Finnish–born person brought up during the period in question, or earlier. So in that sense, the past is less M's and more the spectators' and Kaurismäki's own. However, to return to Umberto Eco and his notion of differently educated spectators, it is possible to generalise from the idea of Kaurismäki's films if they are seen as musicals or melodramas of a kind.

Richard Dyer suggests that the categories of utopian sensibility expressed in the musical are related to specific inadequacies of the society.[19] He holds that the 'sensibility' part of the musical consists of the aesthetic forms intrinsic in the medium itself: the spectacle, the entertainment. Further, he considers utopianism as a central thrust of entertainment. It provides the image of 'something better' to escape into that our daily lives do not provide: 'alternatives, hopes and wishes – that are the stuff of utopia'.[20] I would suggest that the 'spectacle' of a Kaurismäki film and its inverted excess works in a similar manner, speaking to the spectator about a utopian realm of the dream-come-true. In such a sense, in spite of the fact that he has spoken of his latest three features as a 'loser trilogy', it feels so comforting when Koistinen, at the end of *Laitakaupungin valot* (*Lights in the Dusk*), beaten into pieces, sits in the gravel in the harbour and mumbles: 'I'm not going to die of this', while his hand reaches that of his friend Aila. It is not just an expression of the special brand of Finnish 'go' (sisu) but, actually, universal hope.

Biography

Aki Kaurismäki was born in Finland, 1957.

Notes

1 Mikhail Iampolski, *The Memory of Tiresias, Intertextuality and Film*, Berkeley, CA, University of California Press, 1998, p. 15.
2 Andrew Sarris, 'Towards a Theory of Film History' in Bill Nichols (ed.) *Movies and Methods*, Berkeley and Los Angeles, CA, University of California Press, 1976, p. 250.
3 Umberto Eco, *Tankar om litteratur*, Stockholm, Norstedts, 2002, p. 192.
4 *Turun Sanomat* 2 April 1993.
5 Satakunnan Kansa, 10 June 1990.
6 Me Naiset, 1996.
7 Marcia Landy, *Cinematic Uses of the Past*, Minneapolis and London, Minnesota University Press, 1996, p. 22.
8 Oulu-lehti 14 October 1982.
9 Jyväskylän Ylioppilaslehti, 13/1986.
10 Iltalehti 2 March 1996.
11 Marcia Landy, op.cit., pp. 19–23.
12 Ibid. p. 85.
13 Etelä-Suomen Sanomat 960302.14 Lapin Kansa 13 August 85.
14 Martin Esslin, *Brecht, the Man and his Work*, New York, Norton and Co., 1971, pp. 140–1.
15 Turun Sanomat 2 April 1993.
16 M.A. Numminen, *Tango är min passion*, Helsinki, Schildts, 1999.
17 Tytti Soila, 'Fragment av det fortidige i Aki Kaurismäkis Mannen uten minne' in Susanne Brinch and Anne Gjelsvik (eds), *Veier tillbake: Filmhistoriske perspektiv*, Kristiansand, Høyskolefølaget, 2009, p. 142.
18 Richard Dyer, *Only entertainment*, London, Routledge, 1992, p. 26.
19 Ibid. p. 18.
20 Ibid.

Filmography

Saimaa-ilmiö (1981)
Rikos ja rangaistus/Crime and Punishment (1983)
Calamari Union (1985)
Varjoja paratiisissa/Shadows in Paradise (1986)
Hamlet liikemaailmassa/Hamlet Goes Business (1987)
Thru the Wire (1987)
Rich Little Bitch (1987)
Ariel (1988)
Leningrad Cowboys Go America (1989)
Tulitikkutehtaan tyttö/The Match Factory Girl (1990)

I Hired a Contract Killer (1990)
Those were the days (1991)
Boheemielämää/Bohemian Life (1992)
These Boots (1992)
Pidä huivista kiinni, Tatjana/Take Care of Your Scarf Tatiana (1994)
Leningrad Cowboys Meet Moses (1994)
Total Balalaika Show (1994)
Kauas pilvet karkaavat/Drifting Clouds (1996)
Juha (1999)
Mies vailla menneisyyttä/The Man Without a Past (2002)
Laitakaupungin valot/Lights in the Dusk (2006)

ABBAS KIAROSTAMI

By Sharon Lin Tay

In the 1990s, the international film festival circuit provided the context for Kiarostami's emergence as a world renowned Iranian filmmaker. Hailed as the successor to Jean-Luc Godard[1] and the 'standard bearer of the new Iranian cinema',[2] Kiarostami continues to make works that please, fascinate and frustrate in equal measure. It is difficult to imagine the context of reception for Iranian films at a time when opportunities for a glimpse into Iranian culture and society were rare. Western audiences' whetted appetites for narratives, images and subjects from an alien and exotic culture, especially when they turned out to be so warm and brilliant, have now been assuaged given the proliferation of contemporary Iranian filmmaking. The ready availability of contemporary Iranian films, through cinematic releases and DVD distribution, has to an extent made contemporary Iranian cinema familiar, even banal, to the outside world. Yet, this may not be a bad thing. Considering the political focus on the Middle East since the derided 'War on Terror' launched by the Bush Administration from 2001, the social realism that many Iranian films advocate serves to neutralise the adverse and dehumanising publicity that Iran specifically, and the Middle East in general, receive in the mainstream Western media given the conduct of international politics and diplomacy. In other words, there is a discernible transition in the reception of the New Iranian cinema: from cultural fetish within the film festival circuit to paid up member of world film culture. This essay looks at the ways in which Kiarostami's filmmaking practice might give credence to this perspective on the New Iranian cinema.

Social realism

Kiarostami's early films, made under the aegis of the Institute for the Development of Children and Young Adults during the Shah's regime in Iran, focus on children. His first short, *Bread and Alley*, is about a boy walking along an alley kicking a ball who is stopped by a ferocious dog in his path. Seeing a herd of cows and a cyclist go past, he thinks of a way to carry on his journey. He then decides to follow at the back of an old man who next goes past, which works for a while until the man's path diverges from his. Again confronted by the dog, he throws it some bread, they become friends, and the dog follows him for the rest of the way with its tail wagging. The boy gets home and the dog awaits its next victim: this time, another boy carrying a dish that he is trying not to drop. *Bread and Alley* was followed by a series of other shorts, such as *Recess* and *Two Solutions for One Problem*. *Recess* follows a boy who is punished at school for breaking a glass window with his ball and who wanders off at recess. *Two Solutions for One Problem* plays out two scenarios of what happens after one boy finds out that his friend has torn his copy book. In one scenario, they proceed to break each other's things and get into a brawl. In the other, they repair the book with a stick of glue and remain friends. These simple stories belie the allegorical potential of Kiarostami's narratives, so much so that they have been criticised for catering to 'superficial morality, characterized by easy hopes, cheap emotions and inexpensive good deeds' instead of 'concentrating on deeper Iranian and Islamic mystic values'.[3] Yet, these shorts culminate in the feature-length *Where is My Friend's Home*, about the adventures of a boy who tries to deliver his classmate's copy book to his home so as to save his friend from the teacher's wrath the next day.

The influence of Italian neo-realism in these films is unmistakable. Kiarostami's investments in the seemingly insignificant stories and the minutiae of everyday life imbue these early films with a humanism that matures into the social realism evident in the later work. *Close-up* tells the story of a trickster who masquerades as Mohsen Makhmalbaf, another acclaimed Iranian filmmaker, and gains the trust of a family, the Ahankhah, who are eager to be involved in a film project. Using a mixture of real and staged footage, *Close-up* shows the fraud being exposed and records the court proceedings (with permission from the rather sympathetic judge) where the trickster, Sabzian, tells his side of the story. Unemployment has forced Sabzian into duplicity for several good meals and some dignity, given how Makhmalbaf's *The Cyclist* (1987) speaks to him about the bleakness of his own life. The family withdraws all charges because they empathise with Sabzian's plight. The film ends with the real Makhmalbaf making an appearance to fetch Sabzian on his motorbike to apologise at the Ahankhah residence. In *Taste of Cherry,* the protagonist drives his Range Rover over a desolate landscape looking for someone desperate enough to help him commit suicide in exchange for money. The characters he propositions have their own problems: a poor young farmer-turned-soldier, a seminary student who moonlights as a labourer, and an old taxidermist who needs money for his child's medical fees. The characters that the protagonist meets in *Taste of Cherry* are the casualties and by-products of conflicts in the region, and the film is delicate in its registration of these geopolitical tensions and difficulties: the security guard who offers tea, and his seminarian friend, are Afghani refugees; the young soldier is Kurdish, an identity to which a particular set of political anxieties is attributed; the rag and bone man collecting plastic is a migrant who sends home his meagre earnings; the taxidermist, Mr Bagheri, tells a Turkish joke after making sure that the protagonist is not Turkish. Departing from an Iranian context, *Tickets*, a collaboration between Kiarostami, Ken Loach and Ermanno Olmi, consists of three interlocking narratives set on a train. Such a collaboration between these filmmakers – Iranian, British and Italian respectively – seems inevitable, given that each is partial to neo-realist influences and social realist themes. Once again, the narratives are simple: an old professor rouses himself from his daydreams to bring a glass of warm milk to a crying baby in the adjacent carriage after witnessing a family's maltreatment by some soldiers on duty; at the end of his tether, a community service volunteer abandons an abusive old lady with whom he is travelling; and a trio of Scottish football hooligans who find themselves robbed of a ticket do a good deed after learning about the plight of the immigrant family that the professor first helped.

Kiarostami's characters often form the underbelly of society or are shown to be subject to adverse circumstances. *Under the Olive Trees,* for instance, is built around characters in the aftermath of an earthquake, many of whom have lost everything. In one of the film's most poignant moments, a woman given a ride in the lorry could not produce an address at which Mrs Shiva, the set director, could locate her daughter for a part in the film. She simply says, 'I have no address. Nothing'. The woman driver in *Ten* and the various characters she picks up are also seen to be driven to the verge of despair by their circumstances: the cynical prostitute who overturns the driver's questions and assumptions about her professional choice; the two women at the end of love affairs; and the old lady who displaces her sufferings by religious piety. *Ten* is reminiscent of *Taste of Cherry* in its use of the car as a semi-enclosed mobile space that facilitates the interaction between private circumstances and public discourses. The woman driver's son, with his torrent of abuse for his mother, contradicts the view that children are used in Kiarostami's films to tell stories of easy hopes and cheap moralities, and is instead shown to be imprinted with, and a perpetrator of, cultural misogyny. Yet, upon these sympathetic characters and narratives that Kiarostami creates are placed a burden of representation that is beyond reasonable, particularly given international festival audiences' expectations that these films provide the opportunity of a glimpse into Iranian society and culture. Kiarostami's response to this heavy burden of representation appears to be the almost obsessive self-referentiality with which he permeates his films, often addressing cinematic practices and aesthetics as well as questioning the notion of realism. In general, though, reflexivity is a stylistic feature inherent in many contemporary Iranian films. Ahmad Sadri attributes the reflexivity of Iranian cinema to the historical role of intellectuals in revolutionary Iran who live to see their utopian visions result in an ultra-conservative regime run by clerics and that infringes basic rights and freedom.[4] So as to not have these sorts of consequences ever again, Sadri argues that Iranian filmmakers take upon themselves, as part of the intelligentsia, to meditate 'on the dialogue of the author – not as the writer of an impersonal text, but as an agent in full human flesh – and the society'. While this sort of authorial commentary and distanciation is far from new, Sadri notes that Iranian reflexivity and distanciation are none the less unique in their limpidness due to historical imperatives.

Circumventing the burdens of representation

Kiarostami's reflexivity begins with the ways in which he foregrounds himself as the director in films such as *Close-up, And Life Goes On, Under the Olive Trees* and *Taste of Cherry*. While *Under the Olive Trees* and *And Life Goes On* use proxies for Kiarostami in the films, *Taste of Cherry* concludes with footages of the production process in which Kiarostami appears. In *Close Up*, the audience learns that Makhmalbaf's appearance outside the court house to pick up Sabzian is choreographed and results in anxious conversations between crew members on walkie-talkies when things do not go as planned. Kiarostami's authorship is not so much seen in terms of a creative individual responsible for a work of art. Instead, his authorship is more in a postmodern vein, where the auteur is 'present in the text as a cinematic effect'.[5] The filmmaking process is made conspicuous by the collapse of the real into the fictional, as a result bringing to the fore issues of documentary aesthetics, realism and representation. Many characters in Kiarostami's films assume the names of the actors who play them. Are Mrs Shiva, Hossein and Tahereh in *Under the Olive Trees* playing themselves? They are, and they aren't. Are Kiarostami's films somehow meant to be documents of Iranian life and reflect the lives of the actors playing in them? To an extent, perhaps. *And Life Goes On,* the second instalment of the Koker trilogy, refers back to its predecessor and goes on a fictitious search for the two child actors in *Where is My Friend's Home. Close-up* relies heavily on constructing the filmmaking process as part of the film. This self-referentiality renders irrelevant the question of what is real and what is fictitious, and challenges the notion that cinema represents reality. To a large extent, this relieves the burden of representation on Kiarostami's films without requiring that they relinquish their fair share of the responsibility of representation.

While the prevalence of self-referential strategies in Kiarostami's films may have been necessitated by the social and political contexts of their production, his exploration of the potential of cinema for communication, as well as the dynamics of the relationship between film and spectator, gesture to a broader project beyond the perimeters of Iranian cinema. In Spring 2005, the Iran Heritage Foundation organised a series of events in London featuring a retrospective of both Kiarostami's cinematic and his non-cinematic outputs. A comparative study of his non-cinematic works in relation to his more abstract later films such as *Five* and *Shirin* would validate Kiarostami as a theorist of, and experimenter with, the cinematic form.

The installation *Kiarostami's Ta'ziyeh* references traditional Iranian theatre and considers the interaction between film and spectator. In the London version of this installation (it was also staged in Rome and Brussels), the *ta'ziyeh* was shown on a large screen, behind which are two other screens that depict close-ups of Iranian peasants whose facial expressions react to the action of the play. In other words, one would watch both the drama that is screened and the reactions of the theatre audience in this installation, thereby layering on another level of reflexivity. This *ta'ziyeh* installation bears an uncanny resemblance to *Shirin*, the latest of Kiarostami's increasingly esoteric and pared down films. Just over ninety minutes long, *Shirin* is a series of portraits of women who are watching a film in what looks like a cinema auditorium. The camera would cut from one woman to another, registering their expressions and actions, as they concentrate on watching what we presume to be a film that we do not see but only hear. Doubts would be raised as to whether the set-up in *Shirin* is ironic or tongue-in-cheek, given that a strong female voice-over provides the narrative more in the fashion of a radio drama, along with accompanying sound effects, than it would if it were a film. The audience comprise both young and old women who all wear headscarves, as one would imagine to be the case in an Iranian cinema auditorium, even though these women all seem to be unusually beautiful. (They turn out to be professional actors, and if one looks closely enough, one would recognise the French actress Juilette Binoche in the audience.) Like the *ta'ziyeh* installation that seeks recourse to an ancient Iranian theatrical tradition, *Shirin* is based on Persian folklore about star crossed lovers and the woman's ultimate sacrifice. Both the *ta'ziyeh* installation and *Shirin* emphasise the audiences' emotional investment with the respective narratives, signalling the centrality of the contract between the director and his audience in Kiarostami's works as that which provides the basis for his films to observe, critique and engage.

As part of the 2005 retrospective, an installation entitled *Forest Without Leaves* was staged in the foyer of London's Victoria & Albert museum. Tall tubular structures masquerade as tree trunks: these structures are carefully papered over with the texture of bark and are raised from the brown carpet that covered the floor. In all, the installation recalls the yellowish-green and parched Iranian landscapes in Kiarostami's films, for example, the last shot in *Through the Olive Trees* where an aerial view shows Hussein, the protagonist, chasing after the girl of his dreams through a forest of olive trees and across a vast green landscape. This installation evokes an enchanted forest, a feeling in part achieved by the delayed edge effected by the reflective walls and the diffused lighting that emanates from the ceiling. As nature and trees are important recurring motifs in Kiarostami's works, the artifice of *Forest Without Leaves* was that which paradoxically brought the natural landscape to the fore. Kiarostami notes in the programme accompanying the retrospective that only when nature is framed and placed as artifice in a museum, or similar environments, do we recover the ability to observe. In much the same way, *Shirin* is a film that is deprived of images so that we may contemplate the cinema and different ways of seeing in their absence. *Five*, another recent film that would perplex audiences about its purpose, records five seemingly random scenes along the coast of the Caspian Sea. They include a piece of driftwood tossed about by the waves; people walking on the promenade bordering the coastline; wild dogs in the distance; ducks strolling up and down the beach in single file; and the moon accompanied by the sound of frogs croaking. Shot on digital, *Five* defies genre, narrative and form; and once again suggests Kiarostami's thoughts on spectatorship as he manipulates, cheats and deceives his audiences of the film's intent. Sometimes, he does this to hilarious effect, as with the ducks that are forced to wade across in front of the camera in a strangely meditative film; in the process Kiarostami reaffirms his contract with his audiences while reserving the right to play with them.

Biography

Born 22 June 1940, Teheran, Iran. Kiarostami studied to be a painter at Teheran University and subsequently worked as an illustrator and designer for advertisements and children's books. In 1969, he set up the cinema department in the Institute for Intellectual Development of Children and Young Adults under the patronage of the Empress Faraah. The following year, he made his first short film *Bread and Alley*.

Notes

1 Philip Lopate, 'New York', *Film Comment* November – December 1997, p. 60.
2 Farah Nayeri, 'Iranian Cinema: What Happened in Between', *Sight and Sound* 3/12, 26–28, p. 26.
3 Hamid Naficy, 'Islamizing Film Culture in Iran', in Samih K. Farsoun and Mehrdad Mashayekhi (eds) *Iran: Political Culture in the Islamic Republic*. London and New York: Routledge, 178–213, p. 199.
4 Ahmad Sadri, *Searchers: The New Iranian Cinema*. http://www.iranian. com/Sep96/Arts/NewCinema/NewCinema.html (Accessed 1 June 2009).
5 Dudley Andrew, 'The Unauthorized Auteur Today', in Robert Stam and Toby Miller (eds) *Film Theory: An Anthology*. Massachusetts. Blackwell, 2000, p. 26.

Filmography

Bread and Alley (1970, 12 mins)
Breaktime (1972, 17 mins)
The Experience (1973, 60 mins)
The Traveller (1974, 74 mins)
Two Solutions for One Problem (1975, 5 mins)
So Can I (1975, 4 mins)
The Colours (1976, 15 mins)
The Wedding Suit (1976, 54 mins)

The Report (1977, 112 mins)
Tribute to Teachers (1977, 30 mins)
Solution (1978, 11 mins)
Jahan Nama Palace (1978, 30 mins)
Case No. 1, Case No. 2 (1979, 53 mins)
Toothache (1980, 23 mins)
Regularly or Irregularly (1981, 15 mins)
The Chorus (1982, 17 mins)
Fellow Citizen (1983, 52 mins)
First Graders (1984, 84 mins)
Where is — Friend's Home? (1987, 87 mins)
Homework (1989, 85 mins)
Close-up (1990, 100 mins)
And Life Goes On (1992, 91 mins)
Under the Olive Trees (1994, 103 mins)
Taste of Cherry (1997, 95 mins)
The Wind Will Carry Us (1999, 118 mins)
Ten (2002, 91 mins)
Five, Dedicated to Ozu (2003, 74 mins)
Tickets (with Ken Loach and Ermanno Olmi, 2005, 109 mins)
Shirin (2008, 92 mins)

ANG LEE

By Ian Haydn Smith

At the beginning of Ang Lee's *The Ice Storm*, one of the central characters, Paul Hood, reflects on the nature of the family and its place in the world: 'Your family is the void you emerge from and the place you return to when you die. And that's the paradox. The closer you're drawn back in, the deeper into the void you go'. The paradoxical permanency of the family is a central tenet of Lee's work. He has referred to himself as 'a filmmaker who does family dramas'.[1] With the aid of long-term producer/screenwriter partner James Schamus, Lee has shown himself to be one of the most accomplished contemporary practitioners of the melodrama.

In recent year's Lee's work has become increasingly diverse, moving away from the simple categories of the earlier Taiwanese co-productions,[2] known as his 'Father Knows Best' trilogy, and the films that occupied a territory that Schamus termed the 'cinema of quality', part of 'that body of 'classy' Hollywood movies that borrows its middlebrow legitimacy from its literary pedigree'.[3] Seemingly unconnected thematically, although displaying a marked progression in both the complexity of Schamus's writing and Lee's fluid direction, Lee's work continues to express an interest in the potentially transgressive situations that impact family life, be it the simple act of leaving home, the emotional ravages of civil war, the damage caused by domestic abuse or larger societal changes. Even at his most commercial, tackling an ungainly summer blockbuster such as *Hulk*, Lee still manages to imbue his films with concern for the survival of the family unit. At its heart, Lee's work attempts to analyse the social order of each given society, whether based on ethnicity, sexuality, age or class, mainly within the context of the family drama.

In interviews, Lee emphasises the cultural diversity of his background, which has had a profound impact upon his work: 'I talk English and turn around and speak Chinese to someone else. It's hard for us to look at a specific event from an American or a Chinese or even an Asian-American point of view. It's always a mixture'.[4] *Pushing Hands*, *The Wedding Banquet* and *Eat Drink Man Woman* use the collision of differing cultural attitudes to sexuality and age to expose the cracks in the veneer of the ostensibly stable family structure. The most complex example of this approach can be found in *Eat Drink Man Woman*. Lee's only film to be set in Taiwan, it centres on the seemingly traditional relationship between a widowed master chef and his three grown-up daughters. Tracing the breakdown of the Chu family as each daughter leaves home to build a life and family of her own, the drama gradually edges towards the climactic final family dinner, where Mr Chu reveals a secret that irreversibly changes the future of the family, and each member's relationship with one another. Oscillating between domestic farce and a more serious rumination on the loss of traditional values held dear by Mr Chu, the film ends with – or resigns itself to – an acknowledgment that each individual and his/her values are as important as those of the family unit.

Eat Drink Man Woman expands on Lee's first two films in using the traditional Chinese archetype of the father-figure as the focal point of the drama; and as Peter Matthews points out, all three films are 'scrupulously poised between celebrating and chastising our modernity for its loosening of the ties that bind'.[5] In *Pushing Hands*, the father travels from Taiwan to live in his son's house, but is eventually forced to find his own accommodation because the family ties that existed in his homeland are considered less important in America. Similarly, in *The Wedding Banquet*, Gao's parents return from New York to their home in Taiwan having reluctantly accepted their son's homosexuality. At the end of both films, there is a note of regret that acknowledges what has been lost in order for modernity, and the new set of values accompanying it, to survive. In *Eat Drink Man Woman*, Lee uses the strained relations between Mr Chu and his middle daughter, Jia-Chen, to explore generational conflict. Unable to accept each other's lifestyles, they avoid all forms of communication with each other. It is only when the two generations recognise, if not accept, each other's way of life that any future happiness, no matter how small, can be guaranteed.

The use of food as a metaphor for domestic strife is a recurrent feature of Lee's work. Its preparation and presentation links values and traditions, both old and new, and is the catalyst that ignites familial differences and generational conflict. In *Pushing Hands*, the contrasting meals of the elderly tai-chi teacher and his American daughter-in-law symbolise the cultural and generational differences between them. For Gao and Simon in *The Wedding Banquet*, any intruder into the domestic intimacy of their immaculately clean kitchen poses a threat to their future happiness together. And for the three daughters in *Eat Drink Man Woman*, the traditional family dinner represents the imposition of their father's patriarchal values. Moreover, Mr Chu's inability to taste the food he eats symbolises his unwillingness to accept the world around him as it is, and not what he wants it to be. When he tells a friend that 'people today don't appreciate the exquisite art of cooking', he is referring to the disappearance of the values he has always used to make sense of the world. The new values are embodied in his daughters, who work in fast-food restaurants, marry without their father's consent and would rather live alone than with their family. It is only when he accepts the inevitability of change that Mr Chu regains his ability to taste and, as a result, is able to display his affection for Jia-Chien.

The notion of shifting values is pushed even further in Lee's sexually explicit Second World War drama, *Lust, Caution*. His second win at the Venice Film Festival, Lee's espionage drama transforms a young woman – a remarkable performance by newcomer Tang Wei – from a student to a spy for the resistance who, in order to cement her new identity, embarks on a sexual relationship with the Secret Service head of the Chinese collaborationist government. Eschewing histrionics in favour of a cool, detached account of the relationship, the film's originality lies in its attempt to present the drama and, more specifically, the heated sex scenes, from the female character's point of view. The family this time are the group of students who join forces to fight their oppressors, but it is in the sex scenes that attracted so much controversy that the film's ambitions were pronounced. As Lee commented,

The story is written by a woman from a woman's point of view, and Wong Chia Chi [Tang Wei] is a strong character. I think this provides a fresh angle on female sexuality, especially when contrasted with the political aspect, which is usually very patriarchal.

War has imposed new values on the hitherto traditional society and with it a new role for the female central character. At the same time, Lee offered a more historical – and personal – perspective on his reasons for adapting Ellen Chang's short story:

In my culture, there's a tradition that when you're in an over-whelming situation and you don't know what to do, you put yourself in a woman's shoes. I guess this makes it easier for me in a dramatic situation to identify more with women than men. I'm not macho, I'm not a Mel Gibson sort of person.[6]

Lee's previous film is a testament to this last comment. Arguably his most acclaimed film, *Brokeback Mountain* successfully presented what was sacrilegious to some: a gay western. Adapted from Annie Proulx's short story, Larry McMurtry and Diana Ossana's screenplay had been working its way through various studios for a number of years. Widely admired, its subject matter nevertheless caused some concern amongst those who felt an audience would balk at a love story between two cowboys. Perhaps because of Lee's image as an 'outsider' who worked with ease both in Hollywood and outside it, Lee and James Schamus were able to get the project off the ground. With a cast that featured some of Hollywood's finest young talent and unwilling to compromise Proulx's vision, Lee not only redefined an almost moribund genre, it offered his most stark account of the frailty of human relationships. Ennis and Jack's relationship over decades transgresses the norms of a strictly regimented society and the rules of mainstream Hollywood entertainment. A significant commercial success for Lee and a winner at the 2006 Academy Awards, albeit not without controversy (after winning Best Screenplay and Director, the film lost out to Paul Haggis's *Crash* for Best Film, which prompted a vitriolic article by Proulx, claiming 'We should have known the conservative heffalump academy voters would have rather different ideas of what was stirring contemporary culture'.[7]), the film draws more from the westerns of the 1970s, such as Peter Fonda's *The Hired Hand* and Robert Benton's *Bad Company*, than from the classic period of Ford and Hawks. More surprisingly, despite its reputation as 'the gay western' and the controversy it attracted, the film's power lies in its understatement and subtlety. A quietly devastating portrayal of forbidden love, Lee's sensitive handling of the script draws one further into Ennis and Jack's world until, like those characters, we realise there is no hope left, only broken dreams and a few cherished memories.

Thoughts of an earlier, happier life haunt Ben Hood, one of the central characters in Lee and Schamus's moving adaptation of Rick Moody's *The Ice Storm*. The Hoods, a seemingly perfect image of the American family, gather together for the Thanksgiving dinner, and Ben announces that 'it's great that we can all be together', asking daughter Wendy to say grace. Instead, she offers a petulant criticism of her parent's values. One of the many scenes of domestic strife in the film, Wendy's comments chip away at her family's Rockwellian façade to reveal that the Hoods have not been 'together' for a very long time. Over the course of the weekend, this façade will crumble entirely. Ben's secret affair with his neighbour, Janey Carver, will become public knowledge, his wife will despise him for his dishonesty, his desire for a perfect family life will be shattered forever, and a young boy will die.

The Ice Storm is a caustic account of 1970s Connecticut society gone awry, focussing on two families, the Hoods and the Carvers. In exploring the generational differences between the characters, it looks back to themes raised in Lee's earlier films. However, the tone is more sombre, particularly in the way the film questions the adults' responsibility both for their own behaviour and for that of their children. Their apparent unwillingness to assume any responsibility has resulted in the increasing gulf between and within generations. Jim Carver announces his return from a business trip only to be greeted with indifference by his sons, who had failed to notice his absence. Even Jim's wife greets him coldly. Having been emotionally frozen for so long in a relationship where she appears to be little more than a social accessory to her husband, she is concerned that he has disturbed her reading rather than happy at his return. Relations are hardly better in the Hood residence where son Paul would rather be in boarding school and his sister's extra-curricular activities elicit little interest from her parents.

Through its focus on the characters' lack of involvement in each other's lives, the film paints a portrait of the loneliness and suffering they all experience. Ultimately, it takes the death of a family member to rouse these characters from their emotional somnambulism, only to realise that any hope of reconciliation has long passed.

The 'stifling' closure of this social world is manifested throughout *The Ice Storm* by the pathetic fallacy of the frozen landscape, against which the drama is played out. When the actions of the adults are at their most negative, destroying the social fabric of the New Canaan community, the natural forces reach their most positive with devastating consequences; the aftermath of the ice storm results in the electrocution of Mikey Carver.

A number of critics have highlighted the increasing maturity of Lee's visual style.[8] While the frenetic restaurant scenes in *Eat Drink Man Woman* and the period settings of *Sense and Sensibility* showed Lee to be adept at creating striking images, it is with *The Ice Storm* that he most effectively uses mise-en-scène to project the inner turmoil of the characters onto the environment around them. The interiors exhibit a cool, ascetic sheen, influenced as much by the depthless unreality of the photo-realist movement, as by the sterile bricolage of 1970s' artefacts that populate the sparse, soulless spaces.[9] Lee defends his stylised approach as a way of creating an atmosphere that his previous mode of directing would not have allowed:

> I think this sort of intense material needs a style, otherwise it wouldn't hold up. Because nature, in its naked structure, is so patchy, you have to make visual parallels and pull the film together carefully … In this film you're watching a progression of moments, so it's more artificial – or artsy, if you will – than the others I've made.[10]

Highly praised for its style and the quality of the performances, *The Ice Storm* has, more than any of Lee's previous films, been criticised for an apparent conservatism. Peter Matthews was one of a number of critics who saw Lee's melodramatic tableaux as deeply conservative, accusing Lee and Schamus of blunting the satirical sword by which novelist Rick Moody attacks his characters, and opting instead for an oblique assault upon the liberal values of the previous decade.[11] Openly admitting that he was interested in making a film that was 'both provocative and conservative at the same time',[12] Lee is more disposed to absolve the characters of their actions, preferring to place the blame on society. To borrow from Elsaesser, fault lies at the 'social and existential level, away from the arbitrary and finally obtuse logic of private motives and individualized psychology'.[13]

Julian North has also identified a strong conservative vein running through Lee's *Sense and Sensibility*, claiming that the adaptation capitalises 'on the subversiveness of [Austen's] work, but more so on the fact that her subversiveness may be so safely contained'.[14] For instance, the glamorisation of Colonel Brandon as a romantic hero, comparable with Willoughby himself, renders Marianne's fate more attractive than it appears in the novel. Although she is obliged to marry him for future financial security, the film implies that she commits herself to him out of a deep affection. Much of North's criticism is levelled at Emma Thompson's script, particularly given that Lee was brought in as a 'gun for hire'. Yet the film's pre-occupation with patriarchal power and the role of the family certainly echoes the themes of his previous films, in which he had more involvement. The film is also significant for its phenomenal critical and commercial success, earning Thompson an Academy Award for Best Adapted Screenplay in 1996 and paving the way for the funding of Lee's subsequent films, *The Ice Storm* and *Ride with the Devil*.

Based on Daniel Woodrell's *Woe to Live On*, *Ride with the Devil* is an elegiac account of the life of a German immigrant, Jake Roedel, as he travels with Confederate Bushwackers during the American Civil War. He is accompanied by Daniel Holt, a freed black slave. By following the Confederates, Lee documents the loss of tradition, no matter how unpalatable that tradition is, in the face of modernisation, this time enforced by the Unionist government. Although thematically linked to Lee's earlier work, the film differs in its emphasis on the physical, as well as emotional, drama. Moments of intimacy are inter-cut with epic battle scenes between the Bushwackers and Jayhawkers (the bands of Unionist irregulars enlisted to hunt down their Confederate rivals). The world of Roedel and his friends is representative of the larger battle being waged across the fragmented nation. The fight for freedom is reduced to the ambitions and hopes of individual men and women: Jake's dream of a peaceful life; his love's desire for a family; and Daniel's search for his place in the world amidst the ravages of a bloody war.

The search for identity lies at the heart of Lee's most problematic film. *Hulk* was one of the major blockbuster attractions of the 2003 summer season. Lee hinted that he was making the film at the end of his 2001 commercial short, *Chosen*, which was filmed as part of the BMW sponsored series, *The Hire*.[15] The anticipation for the film was high due to the success of *Crouching Tiger, Hidden Dragon*. The winner of the 2000 Best Foreign Language Film Academy Award, *Crouching Tiger* once again dealt with the conflict between tradition and modernity. It also cemented Lee's reputation as a director who could balance high emotions with action, whilst successfully avoiding mawkish sentimentality or over-the-top pyrotechnics. The performances by the four leads (Chow Yun-Fat, Michelle Yeoh, Zhang Ziyi and Chang Chen) also reaffirmed Lee's status as one of the best directors of actors. With a relatively small budget, *Crouching Tiger* created a magical yet troubled world where the warriors' attempts to achieve happiness in their emotional lives is stymied by their allegiance to the honour of their craft and the complexities of the moral codes binding them to their social status. It is Lee's understanding of these conflicts, and his seamless integration of them within an action-packed narrative, that elevates the film above the many inferior swordplay films that followed in its wake. *Crouching Tiger*'s runaway success – it remains Lee's biggest commercial hit – gave him carte blanche for his next project.

As an attempt to create a blockbuster arthouse film with a budget in excess of $100 million, *Hulk* is, at the very least, a fascinating failure. Once again, family lies at the heart of the narrative. Bruce Banner's overdosing on Gamma rays, resulting in his transformation into a mass of CGI trickery whenever he becomes angry, may on the surface be the central mystery of the Marvel adaptation. However, the real mystery is to be found in Bruce's past and the disappearance of his father. Brilliantly employing the same narrative techniques of a comic book, with arguably the best use of split screen in a mainstream Hollywood film since Brian DePalma's *Carrie*, Lee's film nevertheless fails in its attempt to ground a real story in a genre that is anything but. The result is a mélange of badly realised set pieces and unconvincing scenes featuring actors who, for the first time in any of the director's films, do not appear comfortable in their roles. Whereas *Crouching Tiger* and *Ride with the Devil* balanced action and drama with a deft touch, *Hulk* appears to lack any control, particularly in the film's chaotic climax.

An analysis of the family is at the heart of Ang Lee's most recent film, *Taking Woodstock*. An interesting, albeit less vital, companion to *The Ice Storm*, it looks back to the concert that defined the decade that Ben Hood and his friends sorely missed out on. Inspired by the real story of how the legendary concert came to be, James Schamus's script acknowledges the Woodstock as the last moment of idealistic abandon before the events of Altamont and the arrival of a darker, bleaker decade took their toll. Rather than focus on the festival itself, *Taking Woodstock* tells the story of the family whose small motel became the base for the organisers. The film then builds towards the inevitable climax of the festival itself. In light of his recent work, it could be seen as something of a confection for Lee. It is certainly less focused and more episodic than his previous work. However, it offers a fine reminder of Lee's gift for blending comedy and drama, particularly in drawing out the eccentric characters of the Woodstock audience, many of whom were scarred by their involvement in Vietnam. And when viewed as part of his larger body of work, from *The Wedding Banquet* to *Brokeback Mountain*, it is another fascinating addition to an intriguing mosaic of American family life. After eleven films, and with the possible adaptation of Alain Renais's musical *Au Connait La Chanson* and Yann Martel's *Life of Pi* to look forward to, there is little doubt that Ang Lee remains 'the most mysterious talent at large in American cinema'.[16]

Biography

Ang Lee was born in Taiwan in 1954. He received a BFA from the University of Illinois and an MFA in Film Production from New York University, graduating in 1984. Lee won the Best Director and Best Film award at the 1984 NYU student film festival for his graduation short *Fine Line*.

Notes

1 O. Moverman, 'The Angle on Ang Lee', *Interview*, September 1997, p. 65.
2 The films were produced by The Central Motion Picture Corporation and Good Machine, the company owned at the time by Ted Hope and James Schamus.
3 James Schamus, *The Ice Storm*, London, Nick Hern Books, 1997, p. xi.
4 *Filmmaker*, vol. 11, no. 4, 1993, p. 22.
5 P. Matthews, 'Ride with the Devil', *Sight and Sound*, December 1999, p. 35. Lee claims to have used his father as a model for the three patriarchs in *Pushing Hands*, *the Wedding Banquet* and *Eat Drink Man Woman*. More than just a parent, Lee has stated that the father figure in Chinese society is the 'symbol of how tradition works' (O. Moverman, *op cit.*, p. 68).
6 Rebecca Davies, 'Interview: Ang Lee', *New Statesman*, 3 January 2008, www.newstatesman.com/film/2008/01/lust-caution-ang-lee-sex-china.
7 Annie Proulx, 'Blood on the Red Carpet', *The Guardian*, 11 March 2006, p. 3.
8 P. Matthews, 'The Big Freeze', *Sight and Sound*, February 1988, p. 14.
9 Lee acknowledges the influence of the Photo-realist movement on the visual style of *The Ice Storm* (interview with I. Blair, 'The Ice Storm', *Film and Video*, October 1997, p. 68).
10 O. Moverman, *op. cit.*, p. 68.
11 P. Matthews, 1998, p. 14.
12 I. Blair, *op. cit.*
13 Thomas Elsaesser, 'Tales of Sound and Fury: Observations on the Family Melodrama' in B.K. Grant (ed) *Film Genre Reader II*, Texas, University of Texas Press, 1995, p. 374.
14 J. North, *Conservative Austen, Radical Austen: 'Sense and Sensibility' from Text to Screen*, London, Routledge, 1999, p. 49.

15 Produced by BMW and overseen by David Fincher, the series also featured short films by John Frankenheimer, Wong Kar-wai, Guy Ritchie and Alejandro González Iñárritu.
16 P. Matthews, 1999, p. 35.

Filmography

Pushing Hands / *Tui shou* (Taiwan/US, 1992)
The Wedding Banquet / *Xiyan* (Taiwan/US, 1993)
Eat Drink Man Woman / *Yin shih nan nyu* (Taiwan/US, 1994)
Sense and Sensibility (US/UK, 1995)
The Ice Storm (US, 1997)
Ride with the Devil (US, 1999)
Crouching Tiger, Hidden Dragon / *Wo hu cang long* (China/Hong Kong/ Taiwan/US, 2000)
Chosen (short, US, 2001)
Hulk (US, 2003)
Brokeback Mountain (US, 2005)
Lust, Caution / *Se jie* (US/China/Taiwan/Hong Kong, 2007)
Taking Woodstock (US, 2009)

SPIKE LEE

By Yvonne Tasker

In a filmmaking career spanning a quarter of a century, Spike Lee has produced and performed in challenging drama, worked with – and rendered somehow distinct – an array of familiar genres and forms (musical, comedy, crime, thriller, biopic), and developed as an accomplished documentarist. Working across multiple forms – and across film and television – Lee's work is both extraordinarily diverse and connected by key themes and visual tropes: urban experience and the evocation of New York City in particular; racism in America and its connections to institutions, money and power; the possibilities of music as a prominent component of the texture of film; men and masculinity, defined by themes of responsibility, failure and reconciliation.

Even while working across such a range of genres, his films typically combine and exceed any one of the labels which we might attach to them: think of the high-colour musical number in his black-and-white début feature *She's Gotta Have It*, or the charged combination of domestic melodrama and urban life in *Jungle Fever*, or the juxtaposition of documentary-style and rites-of-passage road movie that is *Get on the Bus*. More recent films such as *She Hate Me* and *Miracle at*

St. Anna attempt to combine numerous contrasting plotlines in an attempt perhaps to suggest the connectedness of that which movies (and culture) more often keep apart. Combining political energy, a bold formalist style, perceptive use of music and sound commercial skills, Spike Lee has established himself as one of the most prominent figures working in US film culture.

An African-American filmmaker whose work contends and engages with race in contemporary America, with history and with histories of representation, Lee's work innovates within a film industry that has erased, caricatured or exploited (packaged as a commodity) Black experience and culture. Back in 1989 fellow filmmaker Reginald Hudlin commented, 'Spike's films are evidence that you can make quality black films or even art films, and still make money'.[1] Since his breakthrough success with the low-budget, new-wave inspired *She's Gotta Have It*, Lee has not only kept working (hard enough for a filmmaker so explicitly antagonistic to mainstream images and studio culture) but kept up a commentary on Hollywood's representation of African-Americans through interventions, commentary and, of course, his movies. Criticising the erasure of African-American servicemen from Hollywood's rendition of WWII – his comments on Eastwood's well-received Iwo Jima movies – Lee's commercial success with *Inside Man* allowed him to suggest an alternative war story (one characteristically extending beyond the war itself) in *Miracle at St. Anna*.

Bamboozled remains his most explicit commentary on the industry in which he works – a satire on the US television (and film) industry in which writer Pierre Delacroix (Damon Wayons) launches a modern minstrel show which proves a perverse hit. While *Bamboozled* tackled the industry in direct terms,[2] he had essayed the territory in *Girl 6* (written by Suzan Lori-Parks), a film book-ended by two exploitative audition scenes featuring Theresa Randle, the first in New York with director Q.T. (Quentin Tarantino), the second with Ron Silver in Los Angeles. The majority of the film is taken up with Randle's telephone sex-work as Girl 6 – a different (but the film suggests, related) kind of performance – and the crisis of identity that it provokes. *Girl 6* is also punctuated by celebrity cameos and by sequences – just a little bit too sharp to be simply deemed affectionate – in which Lee evokes the stars and genres of the past (Randle as Dorothy Dandrige in *Carmen Jones*, as a Grier-esque action heroine 'Lovely Brown' and as the daughter in sitcom family *The Jeffersons* – Lee plays the father). Lee's documentary portrait of Jim Brown, *Jim Brown: All American* (made for HBO), further explores the way in which ideas about race shaped the early film roles of the former athlete. Such a concern with representation foregrounds a long-standing feature of Lee's work – an awareness of the work performed by stereotypes together with a willingness to mobilise such types to his own ends.

Lee's visibility, indeed his star persona as a filmmaker, is bound up with a commitment to popular filmmaking, or at the very least to getting his films seen. From the start, Lee realised the importance of promotion in terms of gaining an audience for his films and getting them talked about. A New York Film School graduate, Lee appeared on the scene just as the commercial possibilities of the developing independent sector – hip, low-budget films could make significant profits relative to their costs – were beginning to become evident. His thesis film, *Joe's Bed-Stuy Barbershop: We Cut Heads*, won acclaim; however, funding collapsed on his follow-up project. This struggle to secure a budget which would enable him to make the high-profile films he wished to would be a consistent feature of Lee's career (he established his production company, 40 Acres and a Mule Filmworks, early on).

It is difficult to discuss Spike Lee's significance without thinking about the context of Black filmmaking in the United States.[3] Through the latter part of the 1980s – as Lee was beginning his career – it became clear that certain kinds of black subject matter could find commercial backing. As *Get on the Bus*'s student filmmaker Xavier (Hill Harper) wryly says: 'They sum us up with the four R's: rap, rape, rob and riot'. Lee acknowledges his talent for publicity, presenting it as a necessary counter to the film industry's typical fail-ure to successfully promote the work of African-American filmmakers ('marketing is an integral part of my filmmaking').[4] Distribution and marketing – both theatrical and through video and DVD release – have become areas of contention in a context where executives seem to have fixed ideas about where and, crucially, how well, black-themed films will play. Lee steered clear of drugs until *Jungle Fever* in which Samuel L. Jackson's Gator tears at the illusions of the central family (the end credits of *She's Gotta Have It* proclaim: 'This film contains no Jerri curls!!! and no drugs!!!'). Interviewed about *Clockers*, Lee showed an acute awareness of the limitations of 'the whole gangsta-hip-hop, urban-drug genre film', but also of the daily presence of imagery on the news associating young black men with drugs and criminality: 'I just hope that people will see some of the insights they might not see on the news at 6 and 11'.[5] Thus the film is concerned to explore the psychological complexity of protagonist Strike's (Mekhi Phifer) choices as much as the acute social issues surrounding drug use, to open up familiar media images.

Like fellow New Yorker Martin Scorsese (who served as executive producer on *Clockers*), Lee is independent in spirit, an innovative mainstream filmmaker (questioning and controversial, Lee can also be rather conventional – not least in the portrayal of relationships between men and women). When a three-picture deal with Island collapsed, he quickly signed with Columbia for his second feature, *School Daze*, a celebration and interrogation of black college life. Lee wrote at the time that '*School Daze* is my arrival in the big leagues', and that the relationship represented 'an ideal situation for an independent filmmaker working with a studio'.[6] (Later he would criticise Columbia's marketing campaign.) He has worked with Universal, Warner Bros, 20th Century Fox, Disney's Touchstone and HBO. Lee's very public challenges to the industry form an important part of his persona – for instance, securing backing from African-American celebrities when *Malcolm X* (a film he took over from Norman Jewison after extensive lobbying) went over budget and Warners would not back the lengthy epic (it was finally released with a running time of over three hours). And as a credit at the end of Columbia's *Get on the Bus* informs us, the film 'was completely funded by 15 African-American Men'.

It was Lee's third feature, still his most accomplished, which established him as a major presence. *Do the Right Thing* follows twenty-four hours in the life of a Brooklyn neighbourhood on the hottest day of the year. Shot in bold colour, the film shifts between key locations on the block – Sal's pizzeria, a Korean-owned grocery store, a radio station, the street itself – foregrounding the uneasy relationships, whether romantic, professional or antagonistic, between the block's different ages and ethnic groupings. The film's compelling treatment of racism – institutional on the part of the police, casual or personal in the life of the block – was crafted into an elegant screenplay making effective use of an ensemble cast; the film gained event status in the US. *Do the Right Thing* aims to dramatise the complexity of racism through multiple characters with whom we are invited to sympathise or to judge. Lee's intense involvement in media discussions of the film was crucial in questioning the very terms in which the film was discussed: why was there so much focus on the destruction of property (Sal's pizzeria) rather than people (Radio Raheem's death at the hands of the police); why was the *absence* of drugs an issue – 'do those interviewers ask the people who made *Rain Man* or *Wall Street* why they did not include drugs in their pictures?' asked Lee.[7]

Whilst there is a realist impulse at the heart of Lee's stylised cinema, evident in his evocative portraits of urban life, he is primarily a story-teller and sometimes a rather fantastic one at that. In a 1986 interview, Lee said with typical assurance: 'I wanted to see black stories on the screen and I figured the only way that was going to happen was if I put them there'. By 1991, a similar rhetoric was combined with allusions to art cinema:

> I try to show African-American culture on screen. Every group, every culture and ethnic group needs to see itself on screen. What black filmmakers can do is show our culture on screen the same way Fellini's done for Italians and Kurosawa's done for the Japanese.[8]

As his nod to international art cinema suggests, though popular in style, Lee's films are typically more complex than they have been given credit for. So much attention has been paid to fixing the political meaning of Lee's persona and films that his status as a filmmaker can get sidelined. If one word could describe Lee's style it would be restless: from the mobile camera and dollies to jump cuts and montage sequences. The films are replete with striking visual devices – direct address to camera, canted frames in *Do the Right Thing*, multiple film stocks in *Get on the Bus*, the fragmented flashbacks of *He Got Game*, overhead shots which flatten out space, or those conversations staged with both performers facing the camera – again disrupting conventional expectations of how film space works.

Thoroughly identified with New York, Lee's work is never less than public and social in its dimensions, even when focused on familial drama. In *Jungle Fever*, for example, Flipper's (Wesley Snipes) and Angie's (Annabella Sciorra) mutual fascination is mapped explicitly through the urban geography of New York. Moreover, their lives are lived in public – watchful, unseen neighbours turn a playful row into a police incident. The later *Crooklyn* – widely reviewed as an autobiographical portrait of 1970s Brooklyn (the script, co-written by Lee, his sister Joie and brother Cinque, featured a jazz musician father and schoolteacher mother) – maps a process whereby Carolyn's (Alfre Woodard) responsibilities are shouldered by 10-year-old Troy (Zelda Harris). Women with responsibilities are in the background of both *Do the Right Thing* (Mookie's girlfriend Tina and son Hector) and *Jungle Fever*, but at the centre of *Crooklyn*. Yet the film is an uneasy mix of tragedy (Carolyn's death) and comedy (the scenes set in the South where Troy is dispatched during her mother's illness), of cliché and genuine innovation. *Summer of Sam* is a period portrait of a frenzied city under siege during the summer of 1977. Typically, Lee avoids the clichés of contemporary serial-killer cinema, sketching the life, rituals and suspicions of an Italian-American neighbourhood; the film culminates in Berkowitz's arrest cross-cut with the community's attack on an outsider within, punk rocker and part-time stripper Ritchie (Adrien Brody). The later *25th Hour* offers an almost elegiac take on the city as the film's central character Monty (Edward Norton), who will start a prison term for drug dealing the following day, ponders how he got to this point in his life. Although an adaptation, the film's meandering pace and violent imagery echoes those scripted by Lee.

Lee's concerns with Black history have led in a variety of directions. After the success of his first five features, Lee embarked on an epic film based on the life of Muslim leader Malcolm X – his biggest studio project to date, featuring Denzel Washington in the title role. Perhaps inevitably, given the political and historical significance of Malcolm X, debate over the way in which Lee presented his story was fierce. The question of how to interpret Malcolm X's life for a mass audience centred on a perception that Lee's popular style could not convey the complexity of the subject. Lee talked of the need for a David Lean-style epic, remaining true to his vision of a popular narrative cinema. Many critics were surprised that he opted for such a conventional format, setting aside many of the formal flourishes associated with his earlier films. Perhaps this was a sign that Lee took his task seriously.[9] Both an historical film and an intervention, Lee's film insists on the contemporary significance of Malcolm X; the opening sequence shows Malcolm speaking over images of a burning American flag intercut with footage of the Rodney King beating, while the closing montage, featuring Nelson Mandela, takes us from Malcolm X's funeral to schoolrooms in the contemporary US and South Africa.

Both the possibilities and the limitations of mainstream production are foregrounded in the contrast between the epic *Malcolm X* and Lee's powerful Oscar-nominated documentary, *Four Little Girls*. Achieving only a limited release, the film uses the 1963 bombing of a Birmingham Baptist church to stage a complex portrait of the Civil Rights movement of the early 1960s. Promoting the film, Lee said:

> I never thought about making a movie as opposed to a documentary because I've seen how similar race [issues] films get distorted. I could have reached a larger audience with a proper

movie but I felt that this story was so important and needed to be told.[10]

This distinction between documentary and 'proper' filmmaking is suggestive; some stories, Lee seems to argue, are effectively too compelling to be worked through in his characteristic multiple plot form. Lee has continued to develop his work in documentary, notably with the two part film for HBO *When the Levees Broke: A Requiem in Four Acts*, a devastating excavation of the impact of Hurricane Katrina and the government's response to that crisis. Though Lee is a vocal presence in film culture – and in his films – as a documentarist he typically remains in the background, rarely intervening explicitly in interviews for instance. Such a distance allows Lee's subjects to speak and is somewhat at odds with the more frenetic documentary style associated with, say, Michael Moore.

Writing of what she regards as the missed opportunity of *Malcolm X*, bell hooks comments that Lee too often remains with the familiar:

> No matter how daring his films, how transgressive their subject matter, to have a predictable success he provided viewers with stock images. Uncompromising in his commitment to create images of black males that challenge shallow perceptions and bring the issue of racism to the screen, he conforms to the status quo when it comes to images of females.[11]

The limitations of Lee's broad-brush style have most often been discussed in relation to his female characters, from the controversial rape scene in *She's Gotta Have It* on. As Douglas Kellner notes,[12] Lee's films tend to restrict women to a private rather than a public sphere – from Indigo (Joie Lee) and Clarke (Cynda Williams) competing over star performer Bleek in *Mo' Better Blues* to the mother/daughter narrative of *Crooklyn*. *Girl 6* ultimately turns in on itself, ending with Theresa Randle walking out of her Los Angeles audition (and over Dorothy Dandridge's star on the pavement) before disappearing into the crowds outside a theatre where *Girl 6* is announced on the marquee. Randle's audition monologue – finally recited in full in these closing scenes – is none other than Nola Darling's opening address to camera from *She's Gotta Have It*: a self-referential moment whose circularity points up the limited spaces open to black women in film. The maternally driven lesbians impregnated by Jack (Anthony Mackie) in *She Hate Me* provide a context against which the film's drama of corporate corruption is played out. For hooks, Lee 'is at his creative best in scenes highlighting black males. Portraying black masculinity through a spectrum of complex and diverse portraits, he does not allow audiences to hold a stereotypical image'.[13] It would certainly be fair to say that Lee's preoccupations are with black masculinity and with communities of men – perhaps the reason why *Get on the Bus* (written by Reggie Rock Bythewood), which follows a diverse group of men as their coach takes them across country to the Million Man march in Washington, is so effective. *Miracle at St. Anna* explores the tensions between its central characters, soldiers in a US military, which seems to disregard their very existence.

While Lee's characters are boldly sketched, the men can move beyond stereotype (not always though), looking past the easy assumptions of mainstream movies. At a more general level, Lee's films make use of multiple characters. The main protagonists do not bear the sole weight of the narrative since they are firmly grounded in a community – sometimes supportive, sometimes antagonistic, but none the less a space for discourse and exchange. Consider the way that issues are talked out/about across characters in such films as *Do the Right Thing, Get On the Bus, Jungle Fever or Summer of Sam*. In these definitively urban films – even the relationship-oriented, distinctly middle-class world of *Jungle Fever* – exchanges take place in public places from the street itself to social spaces such as bars and restaurants. Lee's own pivotal role as Mookie in *Do the Right Thing* is indicative here; his job takes him through all the film's key spaces. Initially a spectator and occasional commentator, he finally becomes involved.

Like music, dialogue is central to Lee's work. Of *Jungle Fever* Lee remarked: 'The people in this film are constantly talking about identity, where they belong'.[14] That observation also has pertinence for his documentaries in which ordinary citizens and extraordinary people/celebrities are given leave to speak, reflecting on their sense of personal history and the histories they have lived through. In Lee's films more generally people are constantly talking, shouting, listening, understanding and misunderstanding – communication (and its failure) is at the centre of his work.

Biography

Born Shelton Jackson Lee, in Atlanta, USA, in 1957, to jazz musician Bill and schoolteacher Jacquelyn. The family moved to Brooklyn, New York, within a few years. Lee studied mass communications at Morehouse College and film at New York University.

Notes

1 Thulani Davis, 'Local Hero: Workin' 40 Acres and a Mule in Brooklyn', *American Film*, vol. 14, no. 9, 1989, p. 27.

2 His student film, *The Answer*, was about a black filmmaker who remakes *The Birth of a Nation* (D.W. Griffith's 1915 canonical civil war epic in which the Ku Klux Klan are the heroes). Troy Patterson links this early endeavour to *Bamboozled* ('About Face', *Entertainment Weekly*, 20 October 2000, p. 43).

3 See Ed Guerrero, *Framing Blackness*, Philadelphia, PA, Temple University Press, 1993.

4 Spike Lee, *By Any Means Necessary: The Trials and Tribulations of the Making of 'Malcolm X'* ... , London, Vintage, 1993, p. 21.

5 'Spike', *Premiere*, vol. 9, no. 2, 1995, p. 108.

6 Spike Lee, 'Class Act', *American Film*, vol. 13, no. 4, 1988, p. 59.

7 Mark A. Reid (ed.) *Spike Lee's 'Do the Right Thing'*, Cambridge, Cambridge University Press, 1997, p. 148.

8 Janice Mosier Richolson, 'He's Gotta Have It: An Interview with Spike Lee', *Cineaste*, vol. 18, no. 4, 1991, p. 12.

9 Not that this impressed many of his critics – see the various views collected in the 'Malcolm X Symposium', *Cineaste*, vol. 19, no. 4, 1993, pp. 4–24.

10 Ronke Adeyemi, 'Spike Lee Interview', *Black Film Bulletin*, Spring 1999, p. 5.

11 bell hooks, 'Malcolm X Symposium', *op. cit.*, p. 14.

12 Mark A. Reid, *op. cit.*, p. 94.

13 bell hooks, *op. cit.*, p. 13.

14 In Richolson, *op. cit.*, p. 13.

Filmography

She's Gotta Have It (1986)
School Daze (1988)
Do the Right Thing (1989)
Mo' Better Blues (1990)
Jungle Fever (1991)
Malcolm X (1992)
Crooklyn (1994)
Clockers (1995)
Get on the Bus (1996)
Girl 6 (1996)
Four Little Girls (1997)
He Got Game (1998)
Summer of Sam (1999)
The Original Kings of Comedy (2000)
Bamboozled (2000)
A Huey P. Newton Story (2001) television
Jim Brown: All American (2002) television

25th Hour (2002)
She Hate Me (2004)
Sucker Free City (2004) television
Inside Man (2006)
When the Levees Broke: A Requiem in Four Acts (2006) television
M.O.N.Y. (2008) television
Miracle at St. Anna (2008)
Passing Strange (2009) television
Kobe Doin' Work (2009) television

Further reading

Manthia Diawara (ed.), *Black American Cinema*, London, Routledge/AFI, 1993.

Cynthia Fuchs (ed.), *Spike Lee: Interviews*, University Press of Mississippi, 2002.

Ed Guerrero, *Do the Right Thing*, London, BFI, 2008.

Paula Massood (ed.), *The Spike Lee Reader*, Temple University Press, 2008.

Mark A. Reid, *Spike Lee's 'Do the Right Thing'*, Cambridge University Press, 1998.

DAVID LYNCH

By Marc O'Day

David Lynch has arguably been the foremost romantic filmmaker to come out of America in the last forty years. Love him or loathe him, he is an edge director who has elaborated a distinctive vision of the mythical, wholesome American innocent's encounter with darkness, decay and evil across a range of film and art/media contexts, from cinema, television, video, animation and the web to painting, drawing, photography, performance art, comic strips and popular music. The most famous examples of his cinematic style are, of course, *Blue Velvet*, where naïve Jeffrey Beaumont (Kyle MacLachlan) descends into the violent world of sexual perversion and criminality lurking just beneath the surface of Lumberton's bland suburban normality, and its television sibling, *Twin Peaks*, with MacLachlan as FBI Special Agent Dale Cooper investigating the brutal sex murder of Prom Queen Laura Palmer (Sheryl Lee). But the dark romantic encounter between seemingly idyllic innocence and corrupting evil can be found throughout his œuvre, from the low-budget *Eraserhead* and his first commercial success *The Elephant Man*, through the gargantuan flop *Dune*, to the 1990s' movies *Wild at Heart*, *Twin Peaks: Fire Walk with Me* and *Lost Highway* and the overtly woman-centred *Mulholland Drive* and *Inland Empire*.

The myth of the lost romantic also underpins Lynch's public persona, in concert with an emphasis on a self-taught, well-nigh Emersonian pragmatic self-reliance. In interviews he comes across as the charming all-American boy who had an idyllic, if peripatetic, 1950s childhood, much of it spent accompanying his woodsman scientist father in his work around the forests bounding small towns of the Pacific Northwest (towns which he describes in very similar terms to the surface conformity of Lumberton and Twin Peaks), and who was frightened by the city when he visited his maternal grandparents in Brooklyn. From an early age, he claims that:

> I learned that just beneath the surface there's another world, and still different worlds as you dig deeper. I knew it as a kid, but I couldn't find the proof. It was just a kind of feeling. There is goodness in blue skies and flowers, but another force – a wild pain and decay – also accompanies everything.[1]

This captures Lynch's poetics of Weirdness, laying equal stress on upholding the idyll's value – apparently he really believes the small-town 1950s were great, just as he really believes in American innocence and the transcendence of romantic love – and on the threatening inevitability of the darker worlds which lie beneath it and may inhabit or overtake it.

Lynch's dark romanticism informs his aesthetic sensibility, his cinematic style, his handling of genres redolent with the romantic mode – European surrealism and art cinema, gothic/horror, noir and melodrama in particular – and the pervasive theme of the Freudian family romance which binds much of his work. He distrusts words and formal learning, refuses to analyse his work because this may spoil its mystery, and gets his ideas from a process which amounts to a form of guided daydreaming, apprehending sensory visual or aural images from the unconscious or, as he sometimes, suggests, 'the ether' (also, as a long-time practitioner of transcendental meditation he writes about the effect it has had on his creativity in his 2006 book *Catching the Big Fish*). Lynch's imagination is at once concretely sensuous and self-consciously intuitive and atavistic; almost the romantic artist as creative seer, he is interested in orchestrating visual and aural effects to evoke a certain mood, aura, atmosphere or association, often one of dis-ease, the uncanny or the sublime, rather than in producing coherent cause-and-effect narratives. The archetypal Lynch scene possesses the quality of a dream/nightmare (sometimes it *is* a dream/nightmare), making strange the familiar, shifting us to an unfamiliar world, or articulating a vision of the strange world, often with a terrible and terrifying beauty. Consider the birth and death sequences in *The Elephant Man*; Cooper's dream of the dwarf dancing under strobe lights in *Twin Peaks*' Red Room; Laura's journey into the painting on her bedroom wall in *Twin Peaks: Fire Walk with Me*; Fred's (Bill Pullman) foreboding meeting with the Mystery Man (Robert Blake) at the party in *Lost Highway*; much of *Inland Empire*; and just about all of *Eraserhead*.

Lynch's romantic vision, giving rein to a dissident conservatism, often alights upon the family idyll and its desecration. Drawing on childhood fears and fantasies, his films return repeatedly to parent – child and sibling relations, exploring the ambivalent bonds of love and hate, power and desire which fuel the dynamic of the family and its roles. *Blue Velvet*'s Oedipal fantasy scenario is explicit and *Twin Peaks* multiplies plots and supernaturalism around the incest at the heart of the all-American Palmer family, with the movie, Laura's last days, displaying the trauma which the series sought to investigate and reveal. But try these, too. His early short *The Grandmother* is a child's view of birth and his compensatory fantasy – the creation of a special grandmother – against the cruelty of his parents. *Eraserhead* features Henry Spencer's (John Nance) attempts to cope with the monstrous baby which he has allegedly fathered. *The Elephant Man* is suffused with John Merrick's (John Hurt) fantasies of his beautiful mother and his incestuous desire for return to her. *Dune* works to position Paul Atreides (Kyle MacLachlan) as the privileged male in an extended family of women. *Wild at Heart*'s Sailor (Nicholas Cage) and Lula (Laura Dern) are more grown up than Lula's wicked mother Marietta (Diane Ladd), who invokes bad fathers to prevent their union. *Lost Highway* is structured around the bad father-figure, Mr Eddy/Dick Laurant (Robert Loggia), thwarting the heroes' access to the femme fatale Patricia Arquette figure, split as the brunette Renee and blonde Alice. Cackling parents and duplicitous parental substitutes oversee the decline of Betty/Diane (Naomi Watts) in *Mulholland Drive*, and one reading of Nicki Grace's (Laura Dern) slide from Southern belle to prostitute within the film within-the-film in *Inland Empire* might place her mourning over her dead son at the root of her dislocation.

Unusually among his contemporaries, Lynch was an art school student; he has continued to paint, take photographs and make installations throughout his more illustrious cinematic career, and a major retrospective of his work, *The Air is on Fire*, was held at the

Fondation Cartier, Paris, in 2007. His love of Edward Hopper and Francis Bacon is discernible in the *mise-en-scène* and ambience of his films. His move into filmmaking came from a desire to bring his paintings to life, to build a world and furnish it with motion and sound, and he learned the mechanics of the trade very much by trial and error. The early films comprise a mini monstrous-births-and-deaths cycle within the broader trend which ran from *Rosemary's Baby* to *Alien* and also chart his emergence from art-house obscurity to surprising mainstream success.

Following on from his initial shorts, *The Alphabet* and *The Grandmother*, *Eraserhead* became the cult underground masterpiece of 1970s hideous infant cinema. Begun in 1971 with an American Film Institute grant and filmed mainly at night using friends as cast and crew, Lynch worked intermittently for five years to complete this black-and-white expressionist nightmare, the grotesque tale of vacationing printer Henry, whose neurotic girlfriend Mary X (Charlotte Stewart) is delivered of a mutant creature which the couple have to care for in Henry's rundown bedsit. It opens with an elaborate conception fantasy: as Henry floats horizontally in space, a worm-like form − possibly an umbilical cord (they are everywhere in the movie) − issues from his mouth, before plunging into a pool on a planet when the scarred Man in the Planet (Jack Fisk) pulls a lever. What follows is just as surreal. Henry, the innocent with a phallic coiffure, waddles around the desolate landscape (actually Los Angeles factory-lands) like a perplexed silent film comedian. His apartment contains trademark mounds of earth and a hairy-cheeked woman (Laurel Near) who inhabits a vaudeville stage behind the radiator. When he enters this world, the monstrous baby knocks off his head, which is turned into pencil erasers. And, in the dénouement, when he cuts open the bandages protecting the limbless infant, it expands into a threatening serpent, the world of the opening explodes and, in a flash of blinding white light, Henry is united with the Lady in the Radiator. The movie's claustrophobic atmosphere is augmented by long-time collaborator Alan Splet's ambient soundtrack, which presses the spectator back into intense solipsistic isolation.

Also in black and white, *The Elephant Man* was adapted from accounts of the real John Merrick and shot in London with British theatrical actors. The contrast in directorial control between hippie cottage industry filmmaking and Hollywood-financed commercial production could scarcely be greater but the film still exhibits distinctly Lynchian trademarks. Its narrative, of course, is more readable than its predecessors': eminent surgeon Frederick Treves (Anthony

Hopkins) rescues sideshow exhibit Merrick, afflicted from birth with neurofibromatosis which has caused grotesque physical deformity, makes him a home and a family at the London Hospital and introduces him to London society. Merrick turns out to be educated and chivalric in his desire to be a gentleman and a courtly ladies' man. Yet atmosphere is as important as story, and reality at any moment can slip away into gothic or the uncanny. An initial nightmare sequence matches images of a woman's face, elephants marauding, a hideous rape, smoke and a baby's cry to a garish Splet soundtrack; only later do we realise that this is Merrick's vision of his own monstrous conception. It is answered by the transcendent closure, his pantheistic reunion with his idealised mother on his deathbed, her voice reassuringly intoning that 'nothing will die'. The film is wonderful melodrama (it was nominated for no less than eight Oscars, although it landed none).

It's a tribute to Lynch's toughness that, following the commercial failure of the big budget space opera *Dune* – a sci-fi blockbuster beset with adaptation and technical problems, which Lynch later disowned – he rebuilt his career with the works for which he is still best known: the small-town murder mysteries *Blue Velvet* and *Twin Peaks*. *Blue Velvet*, widely regarded as his masterpiece to date (it won the National Society of Film Critics Awards for Best Film, Best Director, Best Supporting Actor [Dennis Hopper] and Best Cinematography), is a cruel romantic fairytale with a postmodern air of pastiche. Jeffrey Beaumont is the archetypal Lynch innocent (MacLachlan is Lynch's most abiding alter-ego, though Laura Dern may be catching him following *Inland Empire*), launched on a quest into sexual awakening by the discovery of a severed human ear (itself the entrance to another world) and the clue provided by Detective Williams's pure all-American daughter Sandy (Dern) that it may be linked to exotic nightclub singer Dorothy Vallens (Isabella Rossellini). The celebrated opening establishes the bizarre small-town locale of Lumberton with a deft yet surreal economy, shifting us from the shimmering blue curtain (evoking other realms of desire) into an arena counterpointing images of dream-like 1950s suburban bliss (white picket fences, friendly firemen waving in slow motion, the safe middlebrow house with its neat lawn) with others which are disturbing and threatening (a hand holding a gun on the television screen, Mr Beaumont's mysterious seizure as he waters the garden, the descent into the bug-infested horror beneath that neat lawn). Equally famous is the 'primal scene' sequence where Jeffrey, secreted in Dorothy's closet, voyeur-istically spies on the sadomasochistic sexual ritual enacted by psychotic hoodlum Frank Booth (Hopper) and Dorothy, in which the roles of parent and child are fluid and only the sexual fetish of blue velvet (another umbilical cord?) enables Frank's sexual pleasure. The film also marked the emergence of allegedly postmodern trends in recycling, using the classic pop standards 'Blue Velvet' and 'In Dreams' in a manner which had thematic resonance but which could also lead to the synergy of soundtrack CDs and promotional tie-ins and restaging 1950s iconography with a tone at once naïvely innocent and mockingly self-knowing. The latter led to a view of Lynch as a sophisticated postmodern cynic. But if this is the case, it is surely only the disappointed flip-side of his thorough-going romanticism.

Twin Peaks crosses the small town murder mystery formula with a compendium of film and television genres, from film noir and supernatural horror to situation comedy and soap opera. The series format allows for the rich development of the Twin Peaks community and, while the central plot, with its increasingly supernatural twists, grounds the drama in sombre darkness (its lineage leads to *The X Files*), there is also an off-beat humour and magic which is ordinary and accessible (and continues in a series like *Northern Exposure*). Marketed as quality television from a cinematic auteur, *Twin Peaks* arguably works because of – and not in spite of – its soap ingredients, due to the brilliant collaboration between Lynch (who directed six of the thirty episodes, with a writing credit on four), Mark Frost (later creator of *Desperate Housewives*) and composer Angelo Badalamenti. As Biancamaria Fontana argues, its form most closely resembles the nineteenth-century feuilleton, the lengthy saga published in weekly instalments in the popular press, which drew on stereotypes (the shining knight, the sinning woman) and the exotic intrigues of the romance mode to build multi-genre entertainments with cryptic clues and strong cliffhangers.[2] As such, its delights derive from traditional popular fare as much as from intertextual postmodern cleverness. The movie prequel to the series, *Twin Peaks: Fire Walk with Me*, however, was released after public interest had dwindled and it sank at the box office.

With his star in the ascendant, Lynch speedily filmed *Wild at Heart*, a brash, episodic, rock'n'roll-fuelled tribute to the power of love. Mixing noir, comedy and fantasy within the couple-on-the-run road movie frame tale of Sailor and Lula's flight to the South, pursued by a private detective and gangsters set in motion by Lula's jealous mother, it plays as a pop-video-style tribute to Americana: leopard-skin jacketed Sailor is an Elvis look-and-sound-alike; sex-pot Lula is a joyous inversion of *Blue Velvet*'s doe-eyed Sandy; Bobby Peru

(Willem Dafoe) is a close cousin to Frank Booth; and Sheryl Lee briefly appears as the Good Fairy from *The Wizard of Oz*. The night-time sequence where the lovers, cruising to the sound of Chris Isaak's 'Wicked Game', come upon a beautiful, dying car-wreck victim (Sherilyn Fenn) by the side of the road, is one of the most haunting in Lynch's cinema. Winner of the Golden Palm at Cannes, *Wild at Heart* was nevertheless attacked as mere style over substance, as mindlessly glorified sexualised violence and as inadvertent self-parody.

Lost Highway mixes horror and noir, exploring the theme of the double as troubled saxophonist Fred Madison mysteriously transforms into younger garage worker Pete Dayton (Balthazar Getty) after he has been convicted of savagely murdering his wife Renee (he later transforms back again). Their worlds are held together by metaphorical links and encounters with the same or similar people and situations: Renee and Alice are both played by Patricia Arquette, who may or may not be the same woman; Robert Loggia's demonic gangster goes by two names, Dick Laurant and Mr Eddy, but is the same person; and crucial experiences for both Fred and Pete occur in the luxury house of porn filmmaker Andy (Michael Massee). The initial 'Fred' segment, set largely in his and Renee's Bauhaus-style home (apparently part of Lynch's condominium in LA), is a brooding distillation of psychic disintegration and the uncanny. The shift to the familiar suburban landscape when Fred segues into the innocent Pete – an avatar of Jeffrey Beaumont and the high school kids in *Twin Peaks* – is at once a relief and a dissipation.

The Straight Story is a breath of fresh air in the Lynch canon. A delightful film of profound simplicity, it tells of self-reliant 70-something Alvin Straight's (Richard Farnsworth) journey from Iowa to Wisconsin to visit his long-lost brother Lyle (Harry Dean Stanton), who has suffered a stroke. The first Lynch film which he had no hand in writing – it was scripted by John Roach and Lynch's then-partner and editor Mary Sweeney – in it he indulges eccentric American wholesomeness unencumbered by darkness. Alvin's pre-ferred mode of transport is a motor-driven lawnmower (with trailer) and the slow-paced travelogue affords opportunities aplenty to meet up with off-beat people, including a hysterical woman who loves deer but keeps on running them over. At once a celebration of the middle-American landscape and traditional rural American values – Alvin is, at heart, a cowboy – *The Straight Story* recalls *The Elephant Man* when Alvin contemplates the ineffable mystery of the stars in the night sky with his daughter Rose (Sissy Spacek) and, at the close, in deep silence with Lyle.

The 2000s have witnessed the 'dark' Lynch on top form again in the woman-centred tours de force *Mulholland Drive* and *Inland Empire*, focusing on Hollywood actresses split across fractured identities and recalling Lynch's suffering women in *Blue Velvet* and *Lost Highway*. *Mulholland Drive*, which won Lynch Best Director prizes from Cannes and the New York Film Critics' Association, started life as a rejected ABC television pilot in the *Twin Peaks* vein. Lynch rescued it with the aid of Studio Canal Plus money and new footage shot more than a year after the original. Like *Blue Velvet*, it is a dream/nightmare of the fall from innocence, in which plucky blonde ingénue Betty Elms, a contemporary would-be Grace Kelly or Doris Day, falls under the spell of amnesiac brunette femme fatale Rita (Laura Elena Harring) – but when the two seek to discover who Rita 'really' is, reality apparently turns out to be sordid and sad. Betty, perhaps, is the benign projection of Diane Selwyn, a drug-addicted prostitute and hanger-on lover of film star Camilla Rhodes (Harring) – whose dream is a Freudian family romance which the film's last third brutally deconstructs. Classic Lynchian motifs abound: a supernatural Mafia-like conspiracy to control the casting in Adam Kesher's (Justin Theroux) latest film, overseen by the malignant Cowboy (Lafayette Montgomery) and Mr Roque (Michael J. Anderson); electricity buzzing and terrifying forays around corners and into shadows and black; and the ongoing opposition between light and darkness, grace and the fall. Generically the film again straddles horror and noir, satire and musical, absurd comedy and plangent tragedy. Lynch's own observation that for him it is a love story suggests a possible emotional grounding: after Betty and Rita (in a blonde wig which makes her look like Betty) make love, Betty's twice-whispered 'I love you' elicits no reply.[3]

Co-produced by Laura Dern herself and shot on grainy digital video, the epic *Inland Empire* takes *Mulholland Drive*'s dream/nightmare logic further in Lynch's most experimental feature since *Eraserhead*. She plays Nikki Grace, an actress cast as Southern belle Susan Blue in the movie *On High in Blue Tomorrows*: it turns out to be an adaptation of a Polish film left incomplete because the original folktale on which it itself was based was subject to a gypsy curse and the leads in the film were reputedly murdered. Dern-as-Grace-as-Blue splits further, into a Sunset Strip prostitute who meets a violent end and also the wife of a Polish worker, one among a cachet of threatening and jealous men who resemble the vampiric phantom (Krzysztof Majchrzak), another avatar of Lynch's sinister other-worldly orchestrators. With Dern's unique ontological presence as the common denominator throughout, *Empire* unfolds as a set of fragmentary scenarios where reality, film, fiction and fantasy mix (Lynch even incorporates bits of his *Rabbits* online sitcom); as spectators we have to go with the surreal and uncanny flow, allowing ourselves to be subject to scenarios and correspondences which are by turns constricting, oppressive, threatening, suspenseful and frightening, but also mysterious, comic, absurd and beautiful. At the close Grace is back in the mansion parlour where we first encounter her, yet she is joined by many of the figures she has encountered throughout her journey. She looks radiantly content but her expression is perhaps comparable to Laura's at the end of *Fire Walk with Me*: beatific happiness but after death – Nikki, it seems, has achieved her State of Grace but we don't know where – or who – she 'is'.

Now in his sixties, Lynch has been in it for the long haul: those ideas from the ether keep grabbing him and he keeps forming them into unique and disturbing cinematic visions. While his work can be dismissed as modish, sexist or too often merely clever – that perpetual adolescent romantic in him? – such criticism chooses not to engage with the haunting power of the images, sounds, moods and textures in his work. Indeed, as the recent monographs by Todd McGowan, Jeff Johnson and Slavoj Žižek among others attest, he is at present securely canonised as one of the leading American directors of his generation, worthy of mention in the same breath as several of his own favourite directors: Tati, Fellini, Bergman, Kubrick.[4] As Michael Atkinson put it, on the release of *Inland Empire*, Lynch may be 'our greatest and most uncompromising *sui generiste*'.[5]

Biography

David Lynch was born in Missoula, Montana, USA, in 1946. He was educated at Corcoran School of Art (*circa* 1964), Boston Museum School (1965), Pennsylvania Academy of Fine Art (1965–69) and the American Film Institute Centre for Advanced Studies (1970), studying under Frank Daniel.

Notes

1 Chris Rodley (ed.) *Lynch on Lynch*, rev. edn, London, Faber and Faber, 2005, p. 8.

2 Biancamaria Fontana, 'Kin Peaks', *Guardian*, 14 March 1991, p. 27.

3 Rodley, *op cit.*, p. 289.

4 See Todd McGowan, *The Impossible David Lynch*, New York, Columbia University Press, 2007; Jeff Johnson, *Pervert in the Pulpit: Morality in the*

Works of David Lynch, Jefferson, N.C. and London, McFarland, 2004; Slavoj Žižek, *The Art of the Ridiculous Sublime: On David Lynch's 'Lost Highway'*, Seattle, Walter Chapin Center for the Humanities, University of Washington, 2002.

5 Michael Atkinson, '*Inland Empire*', *Sight and Sound*, Volume 17, Issue 4, April 2007, p. 68.

Filmography

The Alphabet (1968) short
The Grandmother (1970) short
Eraserhead (1976)
The Elephant Man (1980)
Dune (1984)
Blue Velvet (1986)
Twin Peaks (1989–91) television serial, thirty episodes
Wild at Heart (1990)
Twin Peaks: Fire Walk with Me (1992)
Lost Highway (1997)
The Straight Story (1999)
Mulholland Drive (2001)
Inland Empire (2006)

Further reading

John Alexander, *The Films of David Lynch*, London, Letts, 1993.
Michael Atkinson, *Blue Velvet*, London, BFI Publishing, 1997.
Michael Chion, *David Lynch*, London, BFI Publishing, 2006.
Charles Drazin, *Charles Drazin on 'Blue Velvet'*, London, Bloomsbury, 2000.
Kenneth C. Kaleta, *David Lynch*, New York, Twayne, 1993.
David Lavery, *Critical Approaches to Twin Peaks*, Detroit, MI, Wayne State University Press, 1994.
Martha P. Nochimson, *The Passion of David Lynch: Wild at Heart in Hollywood*, Austin, University of Texas Press, 1997.
Erica Sheen and Annette Davison, eds, *The Cinema of David Lynch: American Dreams, Nightmare Visions*, London: Wallflower Press, 2004.

MICHAEL MANN

By Christopher Sharrett

It can be argued that Michael Mann is the quintessential postmodern director, but in ways that may be seen as unflattering both to him and the whole notion of the postmodern. He is perhaps the artist most closely associated with the introduction of 'rock video stylistics' to cinema, especially after his hit 1980s TV crime show *Miami Vice* (he was executive producer) began to show its impact. The show's high gloss, slick fashions, pounding rock score and hyperkinetic editing evidenced the increased influence of advertising culture on the commercial entertainment industry during the age of Reagan, and the predominance of business in American life. But this facile view places an unfair burden on Mann. The attributes associated with Mann were plentiful on the mediascape before he arrived, with little of the particular focus that makes Mann indeed a chronicler and annotator of the postmodern sensibility, and a figure with whom to reckon. And Mann's sensibility has little in common with morning-in-America Reaganism; episodes of *Miami Vice* and *Crime Story* are often about the failure and contradictions of the justice system, and the tensions within the male group, at times portrayed as intrinsically evil.

I won't bother the reader with new definitions of postmodernism, the debate about which has persisted ad nauseum in publications in and out of academe to such an extent that I must assume a degree of familiarity with the ways that the new landscape, with its cybernetic culture and highly mediated and commodified environment, constitutes a transition from the relatively industrialised mid-twentieth century to the present moment.[1] Michael Mann is a representative artist of postmodern cinema in ways that make him very distinct from some of his contemporaries also associated with postmodernity. While filmmakers such as David Lynch and Quentin Tarantino focus on a meretricious destruction of linear narrative coupled to incessant allusions, all driven by aloof, snide nihilism, Mann's work looks rather straightforward and generic (to the point that many accuse him of merely puffing up old formulas), with rather few references to other works nor to the cinematic apparatus itself (one may argue that allusionism is important to *Public Enemies*). Instead, Mann's work depends on some of the realist conventions of both the plastic arts and the European cinema to create a sense of elegy for civilisation as it enters the realm of postmodernity. The pervasive sense of anguish in his films, embodied in many operatic largos, suggests his basic humanism and his roots in the modernist tradition. Perhaps as important, Mann's commitment to genre points to his relationship to classical Hollywood, and his interest in engaging in dialogue with and inflecting – rather than merely alluding to – genre conventions and film history.

Mann's elegies are often highly problematical. He is much concerned with the fading of the male subject in the climate of postindustrial society, as this subject is swallowed up by a sense of hyperalienation that Mann captures with an eye trained in the graphic arts, and a visual style that owes as much to painting and architecture as to cinema. His concern for the eclipse of the male, overwhelmed by a culture showing the effects of a corporatised 'world system',[2] has little in common with Angry White Male films of the last two decades (*Fatal Attraction* [1987], *Falling Down* [1992]), especially given the very European *angoisse* of his films. His sensibility seems to have more affinities with the abrogation of the hero's centrality in the nine-teenth-century novel[3] than with the rightist cinematic ideologues of the Reagan-Bush-Clinton-Bush era, and yet one comes away won-dering if Mann's work is yet another critique of capital from the right,[4] with its sense of a lost era subsumed by a cruel technological present. Mann's nostalgic sense of the eclipse of the male subject is mitigated by his questioning of the demarcation of self and other (in, for example, the near-disintegration of Will Graham in *Manhunter*, in the notion that inside and outside are interchangeable as the bar-barism of the penal system has equivalence with the normal bourgeois world in *Thief*; in the feeling of dissolution at the end of *Heat* and *Collateral*; and the dismissal of the all-encompassing corporate world and their compromised democratic institutions at the end of *The Insider*).

Mann's films are also notable for their sense of the abject, and the transgressive penetrating bourgeois life (the photos of a bloody crime scene slipping from Will Graham's file, terrifying a child in *Manhunter*; the photo of a young girl's body stuffed in a trash can in *Heat*). In Mann, a brutal world is suddenly interrupted by something so horrific as to seem out of place even in the context of the world's assump-tions. Many of the bloody or otherwise horrific still lifes and set pieces in Mann's films have the matter-of-fact preciousness of much postmodern art, suggesting the loss of affect much discussed by chroniclers of the new sensibility.

Mann's films for the most part end badly, and feature wretched, largely ineffectual protagonists overwhelmed by circumstance. His bleak vision makes his work share something in common with, say, the horror films of the 1970s, which saw civilisation at a dead end but could not posit any alternative vision.[5] Mann's representation of the crisis is not nearly as visceral as that of the horror genre; his sense of the postmodern *cul de sac* comes across in the delineation of his cine-matic landscape. While traduced for being too entranced with style, Mann is an artist whose sense of the world is manifest precisely in the realisation of style. Like Antonioni – especially *The Eclipse* (1962),

Red Desert (1964) and *Zabriskie Point* (1969) – Mann sets his narratives against carefully constructed *mise-en-scène* emphasising his characters' alienation. Many of Mann's images recall the paintings of David Hockney, Eric Fischl, Robert Longo, or that perennial influence, Edward Hopper, with lonely subjects framed by cityscapes, industrial wastelands, bodies of water, or large bay windows, the images often photographed with heavy blue or amber casts to convey an icy or autumnal effect.[6] These carefully-composed images are plentiful: Frank seated in front of a deep blue stockade fence, reading a letter from Okla in *Thief*; Will Graham staring at himself in a restaurant window in *Manhunter*; Neil and Chris talking, framed by a glass wall that overlooks the Pacific in *Heat*; Vincent Hanna and his cops standing in an overlit industrial complex in *Heat*; Jeffrey Wigand seated alone in a nicely-appointed but very eerie hotel room in *The Insider*; Muhammed Ali standing on a rooftop in *Ali*; Vincent alone and dying in the subway car in the operatic finale to *Collateral*. The hyperalienation that forms the emotional context of Mann's eulogies is bolstered by his eclectic use of industrial/techno/ambient/neo-goth music on his soundtracks. Tangerine Dream, Einsturzende Neubauten, Lisa Gerard, The Kronos Quartet, Moby, The Reds, and other post-modern artists provide an aural correlate to a kind of unrelenting claustrophobia that is Mann's view of postmodernity. The music underscores the aridity of the current world (again, *Red Desert* comes to mind), while also providing numerous largos and *longeurs* that demonstrate the director's essential romanticism (the prolonged male *pieta* at the end of *Heat* is a notable example). The aura of suffocation that suffuses Mann's work provides a utopian/dystopian dialectic that brackets the struggles of his characters.

Such a focus is evidenced in his first film, *Thief*, with its protagonist, the ex-con and high-line safecracker Frank (James Caan) seeking a normal life by creating, rather irrationally, an impromptu family as if to affirm to the remains of his inner life a sense of utopia. The movie establishes Mann as a poet of the city and the suburbs, which is why I exclude from these remarks *The Keep* and *The Last of the Mohicans*, works which have their successes and identifiable Mann character-istics, yet seem outside the world that Mann has delineated as his own (although I would note that *Mohicans* seems in part about envisioning a lost world implicit in *Thief* and the rest of Mann's output). *Thief* emphasises men in factories, prisons, bars, suburban living rooms, used car lots, in the bowels and webworks of warehouses and hi-tech office buildings. The film has a strong 'men at work' theme, from the pulsating opening scene of Frank's safecracking (replete with protective goggles and various tools), to the spectacular final heist, with Frank and his partners clad in asbestos, burning through a vault with an eight-thousand-degree thermal lance, filling the image with sparks – the moment evokes socialist realism. When Leo holds back Frank's cut from the theft, Frank complains that Leo (Robert Prodsky) profits from 'the yield of [my] labor'. When the cops who want a percentage of Frank's action rough him up, he says 'Have you guys ever heard of working for a living?' Frank's notion of hard work, like the instant family he creates with Jesse (Tuesday Weld), suggests the bankruptcy of the American Dream. The notion of the ex-con trying to enter bourgeois life is deeply entrenched in the crime genre, dating at least to *High Sierra* (1941). But in *High Sierra* the criminal is locked out largely by the consequences of his own decisions; in *Thief* the very desire to mimic normality brings consequences, since the normal world is itself criminal (as Frank tells the still-imprisoned Okla [Willie Nelson], 'It's real fuckin' weird out there'). The cruelty of the everyday bourgeois world is represented everywhere, such as in the failed attempt by Frank and Jesse to adopt a child (which pushes Frank further into the arms of the Mafia); the police beating; the judge at the parole of Okla; Okla's sudden death; the conflation of organised crime with nine-to-five business life. Frank's Last Stand at the end of the film is as much about erasing himself and his bogus vision of a peaceful world as it is about taking revenge on Leo and the mobsters. Frank tells Jesse to leave in an especially unnerving moment, given his insistent and rather boyishly naïve courtship of her. He blows up his home and businesses before proceeding with the murder of Leo. The final scene has nothing of the 'apotheosis effect' that allows the gangster a final moment of glory. Frank's burning of his car dealership ('Rocket Used Cars') is a rather surreal moment; the camera tracks past random burning vehicles in a sequence reminiscent of J.G. Ballard, and Frank's explosion of his home and tavern recall *Zabriskie Point*, as the utopia of consumerism becomes the apocalypse of self-abrogation. Frank pauses to throw away the photomontage he carries in his pocket, which he has glanced at earlier and displayed proudly to Jesse. The montage, featuring images of his mentor Okla, a mother and child, dead bodies, and other scraps from his miserable 'state raised' life, is Frank's modernist utopian gesture, his pulling together of the disparate elements of his fractured world. In the film's landscape, Frank's montage looks outdated and naïve, like the jacket art of *Sgt. Pepper's Lonely Hearts Club Band* (perhaps the key appropriation of the utopianism of montage by pop culture). While Frank survives the shoot-out with

Leo's thugs, he enjoys no release or vindication, but merely disappears into the night in Mann's most brutal conclusion.

The conclusion to *Manhunter* isn't nearly as bleak, but the film conveys even more so than *Thief* a sense of the protagonist's entrapment, and of the questionable status of the normal, bourgeois world. FBI agent Will Graham (William Petersen) is besieged from all sides: his key enemies are less his manipulative boss Jack Crawford (Dennis Farina, a Mann regular in film and TV), or his serial killer nemeses Hannibal Lecter (Brian Cox) and Francis Dollarhyde (Tom Noonan), than his own tormented consciousness. Graham's special gift, for which he is dragooned back into active duty by his superiors after suffering a physical and emotional breakdown, is his ability to understand the sensibility (and therefore methods) of the serial killer. Unlike 'the man who knows Indians' who populates numerous westerns (*The Searchers*),[7] Graham's gift is a curse, especially as it blurs his sense of self and other, of difference. *Manhunter* is among the postmodern crime films to have special connections with the horror film, at least in its challenge to the notion of the monstrous.[8] The challenge poses a sense of entrapment to Graham that is figured, as in all of Mann's films, by the association of the protagonist with landscape and architecture. After an upsetting conversation with the wily Hannibal Lecter, Graham literally runs from a bone-white, Panopticon-like prison. One sequence has him descending in an elevator in Atlanta's Peachtree Plaza, a John Portman building very much like the Bonaventure Hotel in Los Angeles, the model *par excellence* of postmodern alienation.[9] As in most of Mann's work, the natural world is figured as ambiguous, photographed in a way that gives to it a hyperreal, synthetic quality, suggesting its fusion with industrial civilisation. Examples in *Manhunter* include the early meeting of Graham and Crawford by the edge of the sea, each man seated on opposite ends of a piece of driftwood. Similar images appear in *Heat* and *The Insider* — it is interesting that such scenes in these films show the steady sealing-off of nature, as if to suggest the increased suffocation of humanity (the empty beachfront house of Neil in *Heat*; the grey, windswept beach and rooftops of *The Insider*, from which Lowell Bergman makes his impassioned phone calls; the confining taxi of Max in *Collateral*). In *Manhunter*, nature is hardly more than a wishdream fabrication, like Frank's photomontage in *Thief*. Will Graham is regularly engaged in important conversations within the crassest settings, such as his explanation to his son of his psychological problems as the two stand in the cereal aisle of a supermarket.

Graham's pursuit of Francis Dollarhyde is marked by the notion that serial murder, as horrendous as it is, is bracketed by a world out of joint, and responsible for the production of monsters. Graham recognises this when he speaks to Crawford of Dollarhyde: 'This started from an abused child, a battered infant'. Mann shows Dollarhyde as ominous, but with an authentic (if fractured) poetic sensibility, with his artifice and Blakean citations. The most evocative moment is Dollarhyde taking the blind Reba (Joan Allen) to a zoo veterinarian, in whose office she pets a sleeping, sickly tiger. Dollarhyde is enraptured by this moment of sensitivity as much as Reba, as the film draws the spectator toward a sense of the murderer's rage at a cruel civilisation. The eventual vanquishing of Dollarhyde returns Graham and his family to normality at the coda, but the film's essential premises defining the normal have been so unsettling that the hero's victory seems tenuous.

Heat, based on a teleplay entitled *L.A. Takedown*, was until *The Insider* Mann's most ambitious film, even (perhaps especially) considering the aspirations of *The Last of the Mohicans*. The film was subtitled in its ad copy 'A Los Angeles Crime Saga', bringing charges of pretension, especially considering the film's roots in a TV script. But the film's operatic aspect, with its emphasis on some of the features mentioned earlier (the *longeurs* enhanced by a highly eclectic and atmospheric musical score; the shots of lonely individuals carefully framed within postmodern geometry), suggest Mann's concern for conveying a mood and tone as much as storytelling, features that, as suggested, make his work cinematic in a very European sense. The 'reunion' of Robert De Niro and Al Pacino, not seen in the same film since *Godfather II*, was one of the film's selling points effectively exploited by Mann, especially in support of the film's strong homosocial/homoerotic (if conflicted and necessarily misogynist) theme. These rather similar, Method-informed 'sons of Brando' portray characters who continue Mann's notion of the thin line between self and other. Vincent Hanna (Pacino) is a cop in relentless pursuit of gang leader Neil McCauley (DeNiro). Both men lead troubled lives in a postmodern landscape saturated with Prozac, cable television news, cybernetic technologies, broken families, child neglect, child murder. Both men are self-absorbed pragmatists who neglect or abuse their mates (and are rather dismissive of women overall), and it is here that Mann complicates our regard for his elegy, centred on the demise of the male group.

Heat is Mann's most sustained preoccupation with the fading centrality of the male, conveyed with Mann's usual melancholy but with more than usual influence from the men-with-their-backs-to-the-wall cinema of an earlier epoch (Ford, Hawks, Aldrich, Peckinpah). When Neil's gang recognises that the police are onto their plans, they decide to proceed anyway, an affirmation of the male self basic to a director like Peckinpah. Michael (Tom Sizemore) tells Neil: 'I go with you Neil, fuck it, whatever!', a proclamation recalling several scenes from *The Wild Bunch*. The gang's Last Stand after the botched bank robbery also harks to the western, but perhaps with close attention to the homoerotic subtext of Last Stand narratives,[10] especially as we see the close bond between Neil and his young acolyte Chris (played by a blonde, pouty-mouthed Val Kilmer), a relationship basic to the story. Just as basic to this dynamic is Vincent's obsession with Neil. The idea of the dedicated cop pursuing his *doppelganger* has deep roots in crime fiction, but here the theme looks especially hyperbolic when we observe Vincent's home life. Again, the basic situation looks highly generic – the overly-dedicated cop and his neglected wife – until Mann uses it for something of a tirade about the effects of a (feminised) postmodern condition on the male. One of Justine's (Diane Venora) complaints seems Baudrillardian: ('You sift the detritus, you look for signs of passing, the scent of your prey'). She later tells Vincent that, although she is 'stoned on grass and Prozac', she has more humanity than her husband, with whom she needs to 'get closure' by her affair. Vincent explodes, complaining to Justine's boyfriend Ralph about the 'dead-tech bullshit post-modern' house (Justine's from her last divorce) he has been forced to live in. He destroys his TV – his last emblem of domesticity – as he goes back to the pursuit of Neil. After his brief reunion with Justine following her daughter's near suicide, Justine sets him free, and Vincent literally floats blithely (the soundtrack suddenly silent to emphasise the privileged moment) back to battle – that is, back to the world of men. The prolonged trackdown and final shootout between Vincent and Neil, culminating in the homoerotic tableau, with Vincent holding the hand of the dead Neil, underscores this rather obsessive elegy for the male and the forms of art that have portrayed his tragedy (e.g., *The Death of Thomas Chatterton*). An apocalyptic, operatic techno composition by Moby ('God Moving Over the Face of the Waters') accompanies Neil's death and the end credits.

Male bonding, with its pronounced homoerotic overtones, becomes a constant in Mann. In *Collateral*, a hitman named Vincent (Tom Cruise) forces a cabbie named Max (Jaime Foxx) to drive him around L.A., assisting him in a series of assassinations. The demands of

Vincent on Max seem less about making Max understand the power of his inner self (associated more with masculine power than realising one's 'true dreams') than in providing a pretext for the relationship of the two men. The world through which they travel is again Los Angeles, a grim cityscape suggesting the frontier at trail's end (we see coyotes in the street) photographed with digital process, illuminated by sodium vapour streetlamps, giving a surreal aspect. The Vincent – Max bonding is threatened less by the urban denizens who are Vincent's targets than by the feminine (Jada Pinkett Smith) and Max's increasing doubts about the nature of the normal world. The heterosexual couple is restored at film's end, but the *angoisse*, complete with surging score, is centred on the demise of Vincent and the male relationship. The relationship of Crockett (Colin Farrell) and Tubbs (Jamie Foxx) in Mann's film version of *Miami Vice* is equally troubled; this Miami is another nightworld, not the pastel playland of the TV series. The bleak vision might be said to flow naturally from the stylistic demands of neo-noir, the genre that frames the film. *Miami Vice* offers a world overtaken by crime syndicates, where trust in institutions has eroded. But most crucial is the threatened status of the male buddy construct basic to American fiction. At the end, the bourgeois couple is only partially restored – Tubbs's love interest survives a gunfight, Crockett's disappears into the night.

The Insider is perhaps Mann's most accomplished work, embodying fully the elegaic, melancholy sensibility informing all of his work, and offering a compelling example of political postmodernism. The film's political aspect derives to some extent from the Capraesque one-man-against-the-system paranoid populism revived in the 1990s primarily by Oliver Stone. While Stone's work is a fairly radical dissent aimed at the Cold War military-industrial state, it is burdened by overwrought nostalgia for a golden moment (Kennedy's Camelot) of an earlier America. Mann's tendencies toward nostalgia have been jettisoned in *The Insider*, his anxieties centred on the very specific power of contemporary global corporatism. The disorienting authority of this new power is perhaps best represented in the film's Internet web page,[11] which downloads with a rapid series of 'flash' pictures showing oblique images of the film's many locales ('int. a house in Lebanon. day'; 'int. a Brown and Williamson laboratory. day'; 'int. CBS News studio. night'). The images suggest well the film's sense of a disparate simultaneity in the new global system that the individual subject can just barely grasp.

The film is based on the very contemporary real-life story of Jeffrey Wigand, a senior biochemist for Brown and Williamson, one of the biggest of the Big Tobacco corporate conglomerates. In 1995, a disgruntled Wigand, recently fired by Brown and Williamson, gave information to the CBS newsmagazine *60 Minutes* about the company's attempts to make addicts of consumers, in the process poisoning them. CBS convinced *60 Minutes* to shelve the story due basically to the company's dense entanglements with Big Tobacco. The programme's producer, Lowell Bergman, goes into bat for Wigand, pitting sectors of the media and corporate capital against each other until the show is finally aired. More than in Mann's previous work, the male protagonist is made nearly irrelevant by the dizzying effect of the postmodern transnational corporate state. Bergman (Al Pacino) wanders nearly blind through the events of the story, a notion suggested in the Middle East establishing sequence where Bergman is brought blindfolded to Hezbollah headquarters in Lebanon to arrange an interview. At first the immediate establishing of the East as Other (so typical of post-Cold War cinema) seems highly problematical, until the scene suddenly changes and the Other is transmuted into Brown and Williamson CEO Thomas Sandefur (Michael Gambon). As Bergman enters into Wigand's (Russell Crowe) life, he seems a mere ancillary appendage to an array of video monitors, cellphones, fax machines, computers, and other gadgets that function as metaphors for the corporate arena. East and West become fused in the transnational mediascape, although Mann doesn't allow the situation to dissolve into some free-floating paranoia in the face of the new mediascape and capitalist structure. This extremely topical story is so familiar as to be almost banal, yet Mann turns it into his grandest opera yet, with a dramatic, near-liturgical score by Lisa Gerard and Pieter Bourke. The impulse in this project flows from the banality of evil in the postmodern, corporatised world, with its features at once benign, impervious and incomprehensible. The Lebanon opening is accompanied by a percussion-driven composition entitled 'Tempest', which quickly conveys the idea that this establishing sequence is less about the Middle East crisis – one of those constant media field days – than the maelstrom that is the current technological/ media/corporate environment. During Wigand's testimony, and later during the appearance of the Big Tobacco giants in Congress (as Wigand loses all), the Gerard/Bourke piece 'Sacrifice' fills the soundtrack with a dolorous requiem for the postmodern world. Although the world eventually hears Wigand's *60 Minutes* story, which saves him from total marginalisation, the film is by no mean a vindication of the media and the other institutions with which they are interlocked. When the show finally airs, we note that spectators in airports and bars are barely conscious of its import; after a bitter interchange at CBS, Bergman leaves the building, the movement of the scene shifting to slow motion – as it did when Wigand was fired by Sandefur. Mann suggests that the public is inured to the mediascape, and the most good-hearted players within the corporate/media state (the film notes that Bergman was a former radical journalist for *Ramparts*) are fairly insignificant against current capitalist assumptions.

Mann's latest film at the time of writing is *Public Enemies*, which might be read as a kind of prequel to his sagas about the male group, - especially *Heat*, since it deals with John Dillinger (Johnny Depp) and the legendary criminals of the Great Depression, whose myths seem foundational to notions of masculinity in the crime film. Dillinger's relationship to his nemesis, FBI agent Melvin Purvis (Christian Bale), corresponds very roughly to the McCauley/Hanna relationship in *Heat*. The men are fascinated with each other, respecting the other's competence. Purvis, like Hanna, is compelled by the chase. The Hanna/Neil meeting at the diner in *Heat* has its equivalent in the Purvis/Dillinger meeting at the Tuscon jail. But the moment is far more perverse than the equivalent moment in *Heat*. Dillinger shouts to Purvis that he needs a new line of work; the remark causes Purvis to stop in his tracks, alone in shadow. The dialogue foreshadows Purvis's eventual suicide, a victim of the system he slavishly serves. The moment also acknowledges his essential barbarism, which exceeds Dillinger's (obvious in Purvis's murder of Pretty Boy Floyd, and his recruitment of professional killers from the Deep South to help wage the 'war on crime'). The emblem of the establishment is the FBI, embodied in its effete, tyrannical founder, J. Edgar Hoover, who is concerned with little more than self-promotion. There is a strong hint of what Hoover and the FBI will become, although the political dimension here is set aside.

The film seems a bit opportunistic in the casting of boyish Johnny Depp as John Dillinger. Depp's box office popularity overrode other considerations, such as the fact that the real Dillinger looked like a mature man, not the surly young 'teen rebel' figure incarnated by Depp (although Depp is actually older than Dillinger at the time of the gangster's death). Unlike most of Mann's crime films, *Public Enemies* is mostly a daylight film; it is less concerned than *Heat*, *Collateral* or *Miami Vice* with the nighttime underworld as metaphor of the unconscious. Like *Heat*, *The Insider*, *Collateral* and *Miami Vice*, *Public Enemies* has a strong operatic quality, its long 'arias' centred on homage for the male group and male beauty. Dante Spinotti's photography (in high definition) gives the detailed period sets a hyperreal quality suggesting that we are watching a compilation of images from the Hollywood past, not a 'docudrama' attempting to replicate history (for all of Mann's emphasis on detail), giving the film some of postmodernism's more superficial and indulgent aspects. The very title, taken from the source book by Bryan Burrough, evokes William Wellman's key crime film of 1931.

Mann's continued eulogising of the male subject raises more than a few questions about his political focus, especially as he cannot seem to posit a world outside of patriarchy, even in its decayed, postmodern moment. Yet this decay seems fairly absolute, making Mann's vision hark to an earlier (post-Watergate) cinema that encouraged the critical faculties of the audience, and looked beneath the façade of the existing order of things.[12] His work evokes nothing less than a revisiting of some of Howard Hawks's essential fixations on the male group, amplified by an aesthetic that puts me in mind of Visconti, who was certainly unabashed in his study of the contradictions of the male group, its erotic dimension combined with its horrid viciousness.

Biography

Born Chicago, 5 Feb. 1943. Attended University of Wisconsin, London International Film School.

Notes

1 Useful descriptions of postmodernism are Fredric Jameson, *Postmodernism, or, The Cultural Logic of Late Capitalism* (Durham: Duke University Press, 1991); Steven Connor, *Postmodernist Culture: An Introduction to Theories of the Contemporary* (Oxford and New York: Basil Blackwell, 1989); David Harvey, *The Condition of Postmodernity* (Oxford and Cambridge: Basil Blackwell, 1989).

2 This topic is the subject of Fredric Jameson, *The Geopolitical Aesthetic: Cinema and Space in the World System* (Bloomington: Indiana University Press, 1992).

3 Of some relevance is Mario Praz's elegy for the romantic hero in *The Hero in Eclipse in Victorian Fiction* (London: Oxford University Press, 1956).

4 An important discussion of the phenomenon is George Steiner's introduction to Dostoevsky's *The Gambler* and *Notes from Underground* (New York: The Heritage Press, 1967).

5 See Robin Wood, *Hollywood from Vietnam to Reagan* (New York: Columbia University Press, 1986), pp. 70–135.

6 The reader is invited to compare Mann's compositions to the art featured in, for example, Charles Jencks, *Post-Modernism: The New Classicism in Art and Architecture* (New York: Rizzoli, 1987).

7 This notion is developed at length in the work of Richard Slotkin, especially *Gunfighter Nation: The Myth of the Frontier in Twentieth-Century America* (New York: HarperCollins, 1993).

8 The best discussion I have seen on the politics of *Manhunter* and its relation to the horror film is Tony Williams, *Hearths of Darkness: The Family in the American Horror Film* (New Jersey: Fairleigh Dickinson University Press, 1996), pp. 255–9. I fully agree with Williams that Mann's portrayal of the monstrous is far more sophisticated than that other, very ballyhooed Hannibal Lecter narrative, *The Silence of the Lambs*.

9 Jameson has a rather famous discourse on the Bonaventure and Portman in *Postmodernism, or, The Cultural Logic of Late Capitalism*.

10 Last Stand narratives and the ideology underneath them are developed in Slotkin's *Gunfighter Nation*, and in his earlier *The Fatal Environment: The Myth of the Frontier in the Age of Industrialization, 1800–1890* (Middletown, CT: Wesleyan University Press, 1985).

11 www.theinsider-themovie.com

12 Mann's cinema seems to have much in common with the 'incoherent texts' of the 1970s, with their conflicted ideological positions. See Robin Wood, *op. cit.*, pp. 46–70.

Filmography

Thief (1981) also writer
The Keep (1983) also writer
Manhunter (1986) also writer
The Last of the Mohicans (1992)
Heat (1995) also writer
The Insider (1999) also producer
Ali (2002)
Collateral (2004) also producer
Miami Vice (2006) also writer and producer
Public Enemies (2009) also writer

Television

Starsky and Hutch (TV series, 1975, writer)
Vega$ (series, 1978)
The Jericho Mile (1979) also writer, producer
Miami Vice (series, 1984) also executive producer
Crime Story (series, 1986) also executive producer
Band of the Hand (1986) also producer
L.A. Takedown (1989) also writer, producer-director
Drug Wars: The Camarena Story (mini-series, 1990) also executive producer
Drug Wars: The Cocaine Cartel (1992) also executive producer.

SHANE MEADOWS

By Martin Fradley

> *I live up north. If I lived down in London I'd just be part of what was going on. What I retain is a belief in my own work. I can't be bought out ... and if people don't like it I couldn't care.*
>
> Shane Meadows[1]

> Ta, duck
>
> Richard (Paddy Considine), *Dead Man's Shoes*

Since the earliest written features on Shane Meadows, it has become standard practice to describe the director as 'Nottingham-based' while only making fleeting reference to his unremarkable birthplace in Staffordshire. It is perhaps fitting that metropolitan presumptuousness has disassociated this ardently regionalist filmmaker from the quasi-rural milieu which so deeply informs his work. Indeed, the visual, thematic and autobiographical specificity of Meadows's output stems not from the relative sophistication of Nottingham, but instead from the considerably less urbane environs of Uttoxeter. A small market town situated in the agrarian hinterland between Derby and Stoke-on-Trent, Uttoxeter's *uber*-provinciality was the butt of a notoriously long-running joke in BBC sketch show *A Bit of Fry and Laurie* (1986–95). Irrefutably, however, it is the formative experience of growing up on the social and geographical margins which has directly shaped Meadows's creative sensibility and distinctive worldview.

Deeply and perennially unfashionable, the region of the United Kingdom known as the Midlands has what is best described as a limited cinematic heritage. Beyond the kitchen-sink drama of *Saturday Night and Sunday Morning* (1960), this amorphous geographical area has traditionally been given a wide berth by British filmmakers. In Meadows's hands, however, the forgotten communities and anonymous spaces of central England have been given a singular cinematic voice. Sharply attuned to the daily rhythms, colourful vernacular and often unconventional lifestyles of these regional non-places, Meadows's affectionate semi-autobiographical stories have an intuitive understanding of both character and locale. While all of his films prior to the breakthrough success of *This is England* have a contemporary setting, the director has repeatedly ascribed the experience of coming of age in the heyday of Thatcherism with particular significance. 'I think my 1980s is a richer time to draw on for me than any other',[2] he has remarked. Although

This is England remains the closest Meadows has come to overt political statement, his *oeuvre* has from the outset insistently registered the long-term social costs of Thatcherite policies upon peripheral working-class communities.

Alan Clarke, Ken Loach and Mike Leigh are all regularly cited as major influences on Meadows, a director whose debt to the social realist tradition is self-evident. Yet Meadows is fundamentally a product of the 1980s' conflicting ideologies. Bolshie and independent in spirit, the director is both creative romantic and self-made businessman. A working-class idealist who began his career making zero-budget short films on borrowed video equipment, Meadows is also pragmatic enough to have directed adverts for McDonalds. With no formal training, Meadows is a cinematic entrepreneur who has continued to employ family and friends as a way of maintaining his autonomy from the restrictions of mainstream filmmaking. Eschewing the individualistic trappings of auteurism, Meadows espouses a collaborative working method that is founded upon a communal ethos. 'What I had with my short films was very much a family environment – I did a lot of the cooking and that sort of thing … I try to create an environment where anyone can deliver a really good performance'.[3] Like the emphasis on community and mutuality in his films, at the heart of Meadows's creative practice is a fundamentally humanist belief in the benefits of reciprocity. A staunch autodidact, Meadows advocates an unpretentious DIY approach which continues to manifest itself in films such as *The Stairwell*, a 15-second short filmed on a mobile phone. 'There are people out there who won't make a film unless they can shoot on 16mm', Meadows scoffs. 'Well, I think "fuck off, then".'[4]

Meadows's early experiments with video culminated in 1996 with two attention-grabbing films, consolidating his reputation as an intriguing young talent. Funny and irreverent, both *Where's the Money, Ronnie?* and *Smalltime* are appropriately frugal glimpses into lives eked out under the social radar. Capturing a lifestyle the youthful Meadows knew well, they depict a world of opportunist rogues and shell-suited chancers – socioeconomic *survivalists* in an age of neo-liberal consensus. The dissolute wit of Meadows's initial output is encapsulated by *Smalltime*'s unofficial tagline: 'We rob from the rich … and sell to the poor at half-price'. Much of the energy and ramshackle charm of these early shorts stems from the naturalistic, semi-improvised performances of Meadows and his non-professional cast of friends and acquaintances. The director has regularly cited *Mean Streets* (1973) as a key influence, and while the epithet

'Staffordshire's Scorsese' is best delivered with tongue pressed firmly in cheek, Meadows's is similarly alert to the coarse verbal interchanges and licentious habits of Britain's underclass. 'Authenticity' is a contentious and provisional term, of course, but there are few contemporary British filmmakers with Meadows's genuine understanding of the communities he represents. This narrow social focus leaves the director open to accusations of parochialism, but it is precisely his continued attentiveness to the colloquial minutiae of ordinary provincial lives that has steadily earned Meadows's so much affection.

Featuring many of the young performers from his early films and co-written with childhood friend Paul Fraser, *TwentyFourSeven* was Meadows's first full-length feature. Marked out by cinematographer Ashley Rowe's strikingly beautiful black and white photography, *TwentyFourSeven* is the story of Alan Darcy (Bob Hoskins), a middle-aged idealist who attempts to foster solidarity and self-esteem amongst the disaffected young men of a nameless Midlands town. A bittersweet tale of directionless youth and the disastrous legacy of Thatcherism on small working-class communities, it is easy to see Darcy as Meadows's alter-ego. Founding an amateur boxing club, Darcy acts as a nurturing paternal figure in a world otherwise filled with selfish, cruel and ineffectual fathers. Tutoring the local dispossessed how to productively channel their aggression and frustration, Darcy's altruism eventually proves out of tune with the dominant ethos of contemporary Britain. In common with many of Meadows's films, *TwentyFourSeven* culminates in an ugly and horrifically realistic bout of self-destructive violence. Based on his own experiences as a member of a boxing club in Uttoxeter, it is clear that Meadows's identifies as much with the plight of the town's demoralised young men as he does with Darcy's social conscience. By turns sad, tender and funny, *TwentyFourSeven* is a simple but surprisingly mature piece of work. Heartfelt and affecting, it remains a powerful and visually accomplished debut.

Fraser and Meadows's shared history, growing up as neighbours, provides the autobiographical basis for the friendship between Romeo (Andrew Shimm) and Gavin (Ben Marshall) in *A Room for Romeo Brass*. The film also granted a conspicuous screen debut to Paddy Considine, as the eccentric Morell, another of Meadows's teenage friends from Staffordshire. Forming a bond with the two boys, Morell is an entertaining and initially amiable character who provides quasi-paternal solace for Romeo in the absence of his own father. Ostensibly a raucous suburban comedy, the film's humour is offset by Morell's increasingly unhinged behaviour as he becomes infatuated with Romeo's older sister. Meadows's rural milieu is again characterised by stasis and stifled ambition, but this world of social limitations is ultimately redeemed by the enduring warmth of friendship and familial bonds. Much like *TwentyFourSeven*, the success of *A Room for Romeo Brass* rests upon the unrefined verisimilitude of the performances. Combining brash charm with vulnerability, the effortlessly charismatic Shimm proves himself more than equipped to register the film's abrupt shifts in tone. Elsewhere, Morell is one of Meadows's many disturbed and potentially violent male characters. Visual allusions to *Taxi Driver* (1976) reiterate Morell's obsessively sociopathic behaviour, with Considine re-imagining Travis Bickle if he had been raised on the mean streets of Burton-on-Trent. The characterisation is far from one-dimensional, however. Seemingly autistic and living alone in his dead father's house, Morell is ultimately as tragic as he is menacing. Despite winning over critics, *A Room for Romeo Brass* suffered from wayward distribution and struggled at the box office; it is nevertheless an exemplary slice of Shane's world.

The intrusion of outsiders upon otherwise self-contained social worlds is a recurrent theme in Meadows's work. Dubbed 'a *tinned* spaghetti western', the interloper in *Once Upon a Time in the Midlands* is feckless Scottish hoodlum Jimmy (Robert Carlyle). Descending unannounced, Jimmy's unexpected arrival in a quiet Midlands suburb creates a disruptive love triangle between himself, former girlfriend Shirley (Shirley Henderson) and current beau Dek (Rhys Ifans). Despite its title and sub-Morricone score, *Once Upon a Time …* fails to live up to the comic potential of its *faux* mythic pretensions. It is widely considered to be the director's weakest film; Meadows's seems hampered by a substantial production budget and the unfamiliar baggage of a starry cast. Denied final cut and unable to work with his preferred improvisational freedom, the production of *Once Upon a Time …* restricted Meadows's organic creative style. Although the film foregrounds his trademark semi-detached *mise-en-scène*, it lacks the self-assurance and emotional resonance of Meadows's best work. Not that the director's signature is entirely absent: a surreal heist in which a gang of stocking-clad Glaswegians wrestle with a pair of clowns in a quiet cul-de-sac is gloriously absurd. Such moments are rare, however, and the sense of outside interference with Meadows's circumscribed universe is palpable. *Once Upon a Time …* 's random amalgamation of accents is indicative of the compromised nature of the project. A sequence in which adopted siblings Jimmy and Carol (Kathy Burke) greet each other fondly with Staffordshire's favoured term of affection – '*duck*' – is a case in point. Displacing the specificities of local dialect and incongruously delivered in Glaswegian burr and estuary squawk, the scene *sounds* in retrospect like a self-lacerating in-joke.

Meadows's has made no secret of the fact that the low-budget production of *Dead Man's Shoes* was a deliberate reaction to the unhappy experience of making *Once Upon a Time in the Midlands*. Filmed in just three weeks, *Dead Man's Shoes* marked a return to the semi-improvised territory favoured by the director. Both disturbing and darkly comic, *Dead Man's Shoes* straddles numerous genres (revenge melodrama; Brit-western; rural horror film; surreal black comedy) whilst carefully honing Meadows's colloquial idiosyncrasies. Echoed by the eclectic soundtrack, the film's unnerving shifts in mood reflect broader themes of guilt, chemically-induced disorientation and patho-logical violence. Exuding sociopathic menace, co-writer Considine plays Richard, a former soldier who returns to his small hometown to exact murderous revenge on the locals who tormented his simple-minded younger brother (Toby Kebbell).

As ever, the richness of the director's craft is located beyond the sparse plot. Meadows's depiction of smalltown drug-dealers renders the temporal vacuum and torpid hedonism of dole culture with the experiential detail of the long-term participant. An assortment of profligate 30-somethings perpetually caught in the no-income trap of *Smalltime*, the clique hunted down by Richard embodies the film's schizophrenic tone. While flashbacks expose them as cruel and sadistic, the laddish rabble of amiable degenerates are the film's main source of humour. Inelegantly wasted, characters like Herbie, Soz and Tuff snort unidentified powders, take the piss, leer over low-rent porn, and pass out in front of the TV as a matter of course. Meadows's ear for earthy dialect also remains as precise as ever. 'Proper Uttoxeter con-versation that', he muses appreciatively on the director's commentary. 'You can hardly even tell what they're saying'.

The demotic insularity that Meadows's detects in the improvised dialogue is apt. Despite its sweeping backdrop, *Dead Man's Shoes'* abiding atmosphere is one of psycho-geographical claustrophobia. Shot on location amidst the stark, rain-sodden beauty of Meadows's rural badlands, *Dead Man's Shoes'* bleak imagery exemplifies the director's tactile visual sensibility. A far cry from the verdant idyll happily traversed by boyhood friends in *A Room for Romeo Brass*, Meadows's imbues the prosaic, unloved spaces of the Midlands with a haunting sense of the uncanny. Full of subdued expressionist mourning, this is a world of neglected places and neglected lives. The film's mundane visual detritus – the dank grey of council houses;

abandoned farm buildings; desolate country lanes – is imbued with an unarticulated sorrow. Like *High Plains Drifter* (1973) transposed to the Midlands, Meadows's re-imagines his native landscape as an amoral gothic wilderness. The sense of fatalism is appropriate: *all* the characters walk in dead men's shoes. Meadows's ends with a gloomily ostentatious aerial shot of the film's sprawling locale – an uncharacteristic metaphysical flourish which underscores the doubling of psychological interiority and rural expanse.

Featuring a virtually all-male cast, *Dead Man's Shoes* is illustrative of Meadows's career-long preoccupation with the failings of working-class manhood. Ranging from stilted immaturity through to violent psychosis, masculinity is a consistently troubled terrain in Meadows's films. A critical and commercial triumph, 1980s period piece *This is England* continued the director's interrogation of the emotional and psychological dysfunction of adult males. His father having perished in the Falklands, Shaun (Thomas Turgoose) is – like so many of Meadows's characters – a disoriented young man in need of paternal guidance. Embraced by the local skinhead gang, Shaun must choose between symbolic *paterfamilias* gentle, jocular Woody (Joe Gilgun) and the more authoritative magnetism of Combo (Stephen Graham). Exuding a confused jumble of hateful right-wing invective and personal vulnerability, Combo's surface charisma and National Front rhetoric seduce Turgoose's unhappy *naïf*. Shaun's painful rite of passage is soon completed as Combo's self-loathing and impotent rage manifests itself in a furious racist assault on Milky (Shimm). Like the incoherent neo-fascist politics he espouses, Combo's physical brutality – like that of Darcy, Morell and Richard before him – is futile, providing only an illusory and nihilistic sense of empowerment. With a resurgence of far-right politics on the home front and British servicemen still occupying Afghanistan and Iraq, *This is England*'s release in 2007 seemed timely and appropriate. Scored by the multicultural sounds of ska and framed with bleak archival footage from the Falklands, the film quietly stresses the depressingly atavistic continuum between traditional forms of masculinity, violence and the ideological intolerance of nationalism.

It is tempting to critique the apparent conservatism underpinning Meadows's preoccupation with the breakdown of the nuclear family and the recurrent *motif* of the absent and/or ineffectual father. Yet while the director is certainly no apologist for the failings of his male characters, he clearly understands low self-esteem and dysfunctional behaviour to be symptoms of social fragmentation. As previously witnessed in *TwentyFourSeven*, … *Romeo Brass* and *Dead Man's Shoes*, the intimated link between social deprivation, mental illness and self-destructive violence is rarely far from the surface. Although *This is England*'s contemporary resonance attracted much commentary, the film is best understood as a reiteration of Meadows's core themes. The director's valorisation of social bonds is emblematised by the film's evocative celebration of youthful tribalism, sartorial nouse and class-based communality. Almost as a corrective to Meadows's trademark gendered predilections, young women are significantly prevalent in the skinhead's social order. Transcending the potential limitations of her role as Woody's girlfriend, Lol (Vicky McClure) is a striking and assertive presence. In shaving Shaun's hair, Lol figuratively enacts a subcultural baptism – a gesture conferring membership of a pro-social collective built upon an ethos of tolerance and inclusivity.

Meadows's next film, *Somers Town,* saw him return to the monochrome aesthetic and understated visual poetry of *TwentyFourSeven.* Initially conceived as a promotional short for Eurostar, *Somers Town* is archetypal Meadows's: an impressionistic sketch of burgeoning friendship between young men on the cusp of adulthood. The film focuses upon a seemingly mismatched duo – rough-diamond Tommo (Turgoose) and sensitive Polish immigrant Marek (Piotr Jagiello) – who both fall for beautiful French waitress Maria (Elisa Lasowski). Again teasing precociously naturalistic performances from his young actors, *Somers Town*'s wistful ambience is compounded by the gently melancholic soundtrack of Staffordshire *compadre* and regular collaborator Gavin Clarke. The narrative is slight, but *Somers Town*'s lyrical evocation of mood – loneliness, dislocation, the sickening potency of first love – is unequivocal.

Set in a little-known district of London, admirers balked at the director abandoning his beloved Midlands. But *Somers Town* is unmistakably Meadows's world: impoverishment is tolerated with expediency and humour; banknotes are retrieved from the crotch of grubby y-fronts; entire sequences are based around the comic deferral of bowel movements. A scene in which Tommo is caught furtively masturbating over Marek's cherished photographs of Maria perfectly synopsises Meadows's competing impulses: heartfelt artistry versus toilet humour. London is traditionally a magnet for ambitious dreamers from the provinces, but Meadows's capital is no wonderland. Tommo's exiled Midlander only manages footsteps from Euston before he is mugged by Burberry-clad urchins. The looming bulk of St Pancras offers a way *out*, the promise of blissful escape from what Meadows's disparagingly refers to as '*that fucking place*'.[5] The film shifts abruptly to colour for the wordlessly happy final reel in Paris; in a shrewd double move, Meadows's appeases his sponsors whilst covertly offering London a terse single-fingered salute.

Somers Town drew mixed reviews, some critics arguing that Meadows's was treading water. His next film, *Le Donk & Scor-zay-zee*, suggested that the director was unrepentant. Reprising a character developed in earlier shorts, *Le Donk* ... was an irreverent mockumentary starring Considine as 'Donk', a former roadie-turned-managerial-*impressario*. Largely improvised and completed in a brisk five-day shoot, *Le Donk* ... bristles with vivacious wit and a refreshing lack of self-importance. As an extended in-joke between old mates, however, it raises the question of whether Meadows's is interested in pushing himself beyond his comfort zone. Current evidence would suggest not. Again starring Considine, *King of the Gypsies* – a long-cherished biopic of Uttoxeter's bare-knuckle boxing champion Bartley Gorman – is planned as his biggest production to date. Still in his thirties, Meadows's appears content – for now – to continue excavating the unexpected riches of his provincial origins.

Biography

Shane Meadows's was born in Uttoxeter, Staffordshire, on 26th December 1972. He has produced work for British television and numerous short films in addition to his feature-length output. *This is England* won the award for Best British Film at the 2008 BAFTAs.

Notes

1 Geoffrey Macnab, 'The natural', *Sight & Sound* 8:3 (March 1998): p. 16.
2 Nick James, 'At the edge of England', *Sight & Sound* 17:5 (May 2007): p. 41.
3 Macnab, op. cit.: p. 14.
4 Ibid.: p. 16.
5 http://www.bbc.co.uk/stoke/content/articles/2004/10/12/
  shane_meadows_feature.shtml

Filmography

Where's the Money, Ronnie? (short, 1996)
Smalltime (short, 1996)
TwentyFourSeven (1997)
A Room for Romeo Brass (1999)
Once Upon a Time in the Midlands (2002)
Dead Man's Shoes (2004)
Northern Soul (short, 2004)

The Stairwell (short, 2005)
This is England (2006)
Somers Town (2008)
Le Donk & Scor-zay-zee (2009)

Further reading

William Brown, 'Not Flagwaving but Flagdrowning, or Postcards from Post-Britain' in Robert Murphy (ed.), *The British Cinema Book* (3rd Edition) (London: BFI, 2009): pp. 408–16.

Jon Savage, 'New boots and rants', *Sight & Sound* 17:5 (May 2007): pp. 38–42.

HAYAO MIYAZAKI

By Rayna Denison

Hayao Miyazaki provides a version of the film author that complicates conceptualisations of filmmakers-as-directors. As a filmmaker he rose through the ranks of Japanese animation, from lowly beginnings as an in-betweener (filling in the less important movements between key shots) at Toei Animation to become Japan's pre-eminent prestige animation film director. But this belies the sheer variety of roles that Miyazaki has performed, and continues to span, from the creative to the industrial. For, as well as being a film director, Miyazaki is also a high profile producer for Studio Ghibli, which he co-founded with Isao Takahata. Miyazaki therefore poses certain challenges to contemporary studies of authorship that still tend to place the title of 'author' in the hands of the film director. In some respects, Miyazaki's ability to control the images onscreen (famously and laboriously so for *Princess Mononoke* where he reportedly re-drew 80,000 frames of animation himself)[1] far outstrips that of most of his live-action contemporaries. However, animation does not function industrially in the same ways as live-action filmmaking, forcing attention onto directors as rare 'real' figures that can be used to promote films. Hayao Miyazaki's filmmaking therefore lies at a crossroads between the creative myths of the 'total filmmaker', as Krutnik terms it,[2] and the industrial necessities of filmmaking in a highly competitive animation environment.

Discussions of Miyazaki's filmmaking have tended to focus on certain traits of his filmmaking style, particularly on his young female (shōjo) heroines, his use of fantasy, his didacticism around the environment and activism in Japanese youth cultures and on his love of flight and flying machines.[3] These well-discussed traits of Miyazaki's animation have been used to explain his importance, but they fall short of explaining Miyazaki's impact on animation, which is much more difficult to define. Certainly, however, Miyazaki's close working relationship with his supporting animation staff at Studio Ghibli, who are hired as permanent staff members and not just on a film-by-film basis, means that there is a consistency to his animation style unusual in Japanese animation, and this has played a major role in his global recognition as a producer of 'quality' animated films.

In these regards, three issues beyond those cited above seem distinctive in Miyazaki's Ghibli films. First, Miyazaki emphasises movement. Whether it is characters in flight, as with Kiki in *Kiki's Delivery Service* struggling to fly over a European townscape, or characters moving along the ground, as with Ashitaka riding Yakkle, bounding across the lush landscapes of *Princess Mononoke*, Miyazaki's characters are often dramatically mobile ones. Second, and linked to this first, is an unusual exaggeration of a typical Japanese anime conceit of producing highly detailed background drawings. Consequently, Miyazaki's films are famous for their backgrounds, for their rich colour schemes, often making use of pastel shades in his films for younger audiences, and for their detailed representations of landscapes, large-scale buildings (such as the castle in *Howl's Moving Castle* or the Yuya bath house in *Spirited Away*) and flying machines. *Porco Rosso*'s immaculate reproductions of early planes provide just one example of the latter. Finally, Miyazaki's films often take place in distinctive pastiches of 'other' places, be they re-imagined fantasies of Japanese history (as in *Princess Mononoke*), or amalgams of different European locations from the Welsh mining village in *Castle in the Sky* to Kiki and Howl's less defined European homes. The distinctive aesthetic look of Miyazaki's Ghibli films is a significant part of his filmmaking, but it would be wrong to assume that aesthetics are the only reason for his global success.

The negotiation of the meanings of Hayao Miyazaki's films have been a prominent part of global animation culture since (at least) the release of *Princess Mononoke* in 1997. Famously, in anime circles, when Disney produced the first version of their English-language trailer promoting the film and showed it to fans belonging to the online Nausicaa.net group (a version of which is still available at http://www.nausicaa.net/miyazaki/mh/relmedia.html), there was uproar, not least over the fact that Disney's voice over artist had mispronounced Miyazaki's surname. From these humble beginnings to multiple award wins for his subsequent feature, *Spirited Away*, including an

Academy Award, Miyazaki soon became a globally recognised 'Master' animator. What has remained obscure about Miyazaki, however, is how he is viewed in Japan.

Success in the Japanese market is crucial for maintaining Miyazaki's global directorial and artistic filmmaking reputation. Japan is always the testing ground for his films' potential success, being released there sometimes years in advance of their distribution to other parts of the world. For example, the Academy Award won by Miyazaki for Best Animated Feature for *Spirited Away* was at the Oscars in 2003, whereas the film was released in Japan in July 2001. Part of this delay is down to the re-production time taken to provide new American-English voice tracks for Miyazaki's films, but it remains the case that the primary market for Miyazaki's animation, in both profit and early promotional terms, is Japan. Despite this, Miyazaki's reputation there, how he actively promotes his films, and how his name is mobilised in relation to their marketing, has long been an overlooked aspect of his filmmaking persona. The remainder of this essay will therefore represent an initial bid to map some of the changes in Miyazaki's reputation and promotion as a filmmaker in Japan, with a view to examining the ways in which he is deployed both as a brand name and as a creative locus for his, and others', films.

It was early in Miyazaki's directorial career that those marketing his films began to place value on his potential as a brand name. Masanari Tokuyama, a prominent figure in Ghibli's early advertising team, has claimed that it was after the success of *Nausicaa of the Valley of the Winds*, a fantasy based on Miyazaki's original manga comic book, that Miyazaki's name brand value was recognised. In interview he states,

> Miya-san's (director Hayao Miyazaki) name seemed to be becoming widely known and an assessment of him as a great director began to be born. ... the basic policy, it was based on the previous product base, and it was the case that we emphasised the point of 'It is the newest film from that Miyazaki'.[4]

Most advertisements for Miyazaki's subsequent films consequently refer back to *Nausicaa of the Valley of the Wind* as an origin point for his filmmaking style. By mobilising Miyazaki's back catalogue in this fashion, the advertisers are able to create an associative brand for Miyazaki's cinema that plays on audience nostalgia for his previous hit films. In effect, associative branding like this works to create Miyazaki's films as a subgenre.

Miyazaki's importance to his studio can be read from its advertising following the release of the double-bill of features which he shared with Takahata in 1988: *Grave of the Fireflies* and *My Neighbour Totoro*. The double-bill paired Miyazaki's nostalgic fantasy of pastoral Japanese life in the 1950s with Takahata's harrowing melodramatic tale of two war orphans slowly starving to death in the chaos of World War II Japan. Subsequent to this double-bill's success, Miyazaki's centrality to Studio Ghibli was literally written on its products, with his Totoro character used as the company's logo from the release of *Porco Rosso* in 1992. Moreover, following the double bill, Miyazaki's extra-directorial roles behind the scenes at Studio Ghibli also became highly visible in its advertising. For example, multiple advertisements and posters were produced for Takahata's *Only Yesterday* (*Omohide Poro Poro*, 1991) which featured Miyazaki's name as the film's producer before listing Takahata as director.

Miyazaki's name was also listed more prominently than director Yoshifumi Kondo's for the 1995 Studio Ghibli release *Whispers of the Heart*. For that film, Miyazaki's multiple roles as producer, scriptwriter and storyboard artist were listed first. In one sense these examples concur with the approach of contemporary academics writing about the commercialisation of the auteur; for example, with Timothy Corrigan's claim that 'what defines this group is a recognition, either foisted upon them or chosen by them, that the celebrity of their agency produces and promotes a text that invariably exceeds the movie itself'.[5] Exceeding even his agency as a director, in these cases, Miyazaki's celebrity agency becomes a hallmark of quality and success, appended to the work of less well-known (or in the case of Takahata, perhaps less populist) directors, even in cases where his levels of involvement with the production are questionable, and even where other directors might have a greater claim to authorship.

Another way in which Miyazaki's brand name has been promoted can be seen in *Princess Mononoke*, for which his studio labelled him a 'genius'. An historical epic, based in fourteenth-century Japan, the film was also an environmental fable focusing on the unbalancing of the relationship between man and the environment, as embodied by animal gods. It is also probably Miyazaki's most adult oriented film to date, with significant moments of bloodshed and violence; a departure from his often whimsical or nostalgic modes of filmmaking. In *Princess Mononoke*'s advertising, a copy slogan was added that read: '13 years since *Nausicaa of the Valley of the Winds*, genius Hayao Miyazaki's ferociously passionate film sweeps across the world!' This slogan was used repeatedly in *Princess Mononoke*'s advertising and also seems to have been proliferated in other print materials relating to it, with portions of the slogan repeated in magazine articles at the time. Significantly, duration of success and global success are hyperbolically linked to Miyazaki's status not as a filmmaker, but as a 'genius'. While such hyperbole is a standard element of film advertising, the use of this term, in conjunction with Miyazaki's claims that *Princess Mononoke* would be his last film, helped to foster a sense of scarcity and uniqueness around it, perhaps suggesting some of the reasons why *Princess Mononoke* was to go on to break all Japanese box office records.[6]

This appending to *Princess Mononoke*'s advertising of Miyazaki's name brand was complemented by his high profile in the broader reception culture of Japan at the time. *Princess Mononoke* marked a turning point in Miyazaki's filmmaking not merely because it broke Japanese box office records, but also because it, arguably, marked his emergence (through a distribution deal with Disney) into the global animation markets. However, within Japan, Miyazaki was still being positioned dependently and contextually; he was still being made sense of in relation to Japanese film culture. In order to assess Miyazaki's position within the Japanese film industry, this section will examine how the Japanese press contextualised Miyazaki on the release of *Princess Mononoke*.

Any conception of Miyazaki as some kind of pre-eminent Japanese auteur must be tempered by the knowledge of his problematic positioning within Japanese cinema's pantheon of directors.[7] Time and again in the promotion of *Princess Mononoke* the spectres of previous 'great' Japanese directors are used to qualify Miyazaki's place in the limelight. Though these were at times calculated insertions by Studio Ghibli, used to add gravitas to their new film, there were positive and negative outcomes from such associations. Chief amongst these comparisons were ones of Miyazaki with Akira Kurosawa and with Osamu Tezuka. Kurosawa has been widely credited with bringing Japanese cinema to the attention of Western critical audiences, following the success of *Rashomon* at the 1951 Venice Film Festival, and with strongly influencing the Western genre with films like *Seven Samurai* (1954) and *Yojimbo* (1960). Osamu Tezuka, similarly, is perhaps Japan's most famous manga (comic book) author, credited with pioneering a new style of manga and developing techniques for animation production in Japan that have greatly influenced Japan's contemporary markets for both media.[8] *Kinema Jumpo*, Japan's foremost film journal, examined at length the shared ground between *Princess Mononoke* and Kurosawa's *Seven Samurai*.[9] For example, it quotes Miyazaki as saying of himself and his contemporaries that 'if we want to make a period drama, we have to go beyond this [*Seven Samurai*], to surpass it', claiming that others, but not himself, had been spellbound by the film.[10]

Miyazaki courted this comparison with Kurosawa in general and *Seven Samurai* in particular throughout the promotional phase of *Princess Mononoke*'s release. It is evident for example in a further promotional piece by Studio Ghibli. Therein Miyazaki comments:

> I like Akira Kurosawa's *Seven Samurai* very much. Because *Seven Samurai* reflects the Zeitgeist of its period, I think it's a very good film and it reflects reality well. However, if I make a film now then it [unfortunately] falls under the spell of *Seven Samurai*.[11]

Miyazaki's recognition of the sway Kurosawa holds over the period drama (*jidaigeki*) genre in Japanese filmmaking is vital here for two reasons. First, it recalls Kurosawa's own brand of filmmaking and creates through that brand, and *Seven Samurai* explicitly, points of similarity and disparity with *Princess Mononoke*. Kurosawa's brand is mobilised here to raise and discuss issues like quality and realism, which are then subsequently applied to Miyazaki's rendering of history in *Princess Mononoke*. The association allowed *Princess Mononoke* to lay claim to some of the gravitas and reflected glory of its predecessors in Kurosawa's oeuvre. Likewise, in summoning the ghost of Kurosawa, Miyazaki too was able to bask in reflected glory. The periodisation is important here. Kurosawa's career entered a permanent downturn in the 1980s, which is the same decade in which Miyazaki began producing his increasingly successful features for Ghibli.

Kurosawa was not, however, the only spirit haunting *Princess Mononoke*. *Kinema Jumpo*'s special issue on *Princess Mononoke* also contained an article discussing Osamu Tezuka's influence on Miyazaki.[12] In fact, the latter portion of this article takes care to trace not just the relationship between Tezuka and Miyazaki but also the role that Disney played in the films of each. At several points its author, Jun Ishiko, differentiates Miyazaki from these other prominent animators, claiming, for instance, that 'Miyazaki denies such facile humanism by Disney and in his works he maintains a more complex humanism that you need to battle and claim'.[13] However, this distinction is maintained alongside appeals to Japanese, and indeed American, animation cultural authorities. To this end the article finishes: 'I wish Osamu Tezuka could have watched it [*Princess Mononoke*]'.[14] Therefore, Miyazaki is mobilised not only as the maker of a particular brand of animated films, but also in comparison to other brand name animators like Tezuka and Disney. Through such branding and brand association, Miyazaki's films are differentiated and elevated. Miyazaki's *Princess Mononoke* is thereby granted a privileged and well-delineated place in the Japanese filmmaking pantheon.

Through a negotiation of Japan's history of film and animation, and through careful deployment of globalised branding techniques, Hayao Miyazaki would appear to be understood not simply as a 'master' of animation techniques as he is in the West, but also as a composite figure; as a director, a producer, a scriptwriter, and as part of an industry that is still looking to categorise and place him. By examining *Princess Mononoke* as a turning point in his career, we can see how Miyazaki has become associated with those at the very pinnacles of Japanese film and manga history, and additionally, with those at the highest peaks of global animation culture. Consequently, this brief introduction to Miyazaki's meanings in Japan has demonstrated that what is understood of Miyazaki outside Japan is akin to ripples spreading out from a pebble dropped in a lake. Miyazaki's primary impact is in his home market and it is there that he performs complex negotiations within and beyond his studio to help maintain and increase his global status.

Biography

Born January 5, 1941, in Tokyo, Japan.

Notes

1 For more on Ghibli's Japanese Marketing see: Rayna Denison, *Cultural Traffic in Japanese Anime: The Meanings of Promotion, Reception and Exhibition Circuits in* Princess Mononoke, Thesis: University of Nottingham, 2005.

2 Frank Krutnik, 'Jerry Lewis: the Deformation of the Comic', *Film Quarterly*, vol. 48 no. 1 (Fall 1994): pp. 12–26.

3 Helen McCarthy, *Hayao Miyazaki: Master of Animation: Films, Themes, Artistry*. Berkeley, CA: Stone Bridge Press, 1999; Susan J. Napier, 'The Enchantment of Estrangement: The *Shōjo* in the World of Hayao Miyazaki', *Anime from Akira to Howl's Moving Castle: Experiencing Contemporary Japanese Animation*, New York: Palgrave Macmillan, 2005, pp. 151–68.

4 Emphasis mine. Yoshiharu Tokugi and Shinkai Nakashima, eds, 'The Concept of 'That Miyazaki's New Film', *Have you seen the newpaper advertisements for Nausicaa? The 18 year history of Ghibli's Newspaper Advertising*. Tokyo: Tokuma Shoten, 2002, p. 146.

5 Timothy Corrigan, 'Auteurs and the New Hollywood', Jon Lewis, ed., *The New American Cinema*, Durham, NC: Duke University Press, 1998, p. 51.

6 Tomomo Katsuda, '*E.T.* Outdone by *Princess Mononoke*', *Mainichi Shimbun*, 31 October 1997, sec. 14: 30. *Shimbun* is the Japanese for 'newspaper' and is left untranslated here for clarity.

7 This said, however, there is a certain reverence shown to Miyazaki by the Japanese press. See: Hayao Miyazaki, 'The Fight between the Furious Gods and Humans', *Kinema Jumpo* 1233 (2 September 1997): p. 2. The same introduction also appears in other places in the promotion. See: *Roman Album: Princess Mononoke*, Animage Publishing, 1 November 1997: p. 8; or, Studio Ghibli Publishing, *Princess Mononoke*, 12 July 1997: p. 1.

8 Frederick L. Schodt, *The Astro Boy Essays: Osamu Tezuka, Mighty Atom, Manga/Anime Revolution*, Berkeley, CA: Stone Bridge Press, 2007.

9 Taketarou Nishimura, 'Hayao Miyazaki and Akira Kurosawa: Has *Princess Mononoke* surpassed *Seven Samurai*?', *Kinema Jumpo* 1233 (2 September 1997): pp. 71–3.

10 Nishimura, 'Hayao Miyazaki and Akira Kurosawa', p. 72. A similar quote appears in an issue of *Kinema Jumpo* in a discussion between Miyazaki and film critic Sato Tadao, 'Discussion: Hayao Miyazaki and Tadao Sato', *Kinema Jumpo* 1233 (2 September 1997): p. 33.

11 'A New Light at the Turning Point of a Period – Hayao Miyazaki Talks about *Princess Mononoke*', *Yomiuri Shimbun*, 25 June 1997, sec. 2: p. 17.

12 Jun Ishiko, 'Hayao Miyazaki and Osamu Tezuka: Simple and Complex Approaches to Humanism – The Metamorphoses of Two Men', *Kinema Jumpo* 1233 (2 September 1997): pp. 66–70.

13 Ibid.: p. 70.

14 Ibid.

Filmography

Lupin III: Castle of Cagliostro/Rupan sansei: Kariosutoro no shiro (1979)
Nausicaa of the Valley of the Wind/Kaze no Tani no Naushika (1984)
Castle in the Sky/Tenkuu no Shiro Rapyuta (1986)
My Neighbour Totoro/Tonari no Totoro (1988)
Kiki's Delivery Service/Majou no Takyubin (1989)
Porco Rosso/Kurenai no Buta (1992)
Princess Mononoke/Mononokehime (1997)
Spirited Away/Sen to Chihiro no Kamikakushi (2001)
Howl's Moving Castle/Haoru no Ugokushiro (2004)
Ponyo at the Cliffs by the Sea/Gake no Ue no Ponyo (2008)

Further reading

John Grant, 'Hayao Miyazaki', *Masters of Animation*. London: BT Batsford, 2001, pp. 161–71.

Helen McCarthy, *Hayao Miyazaki: Master of Animation: Films, Themes, Artistry.* Berkeley, CA: Stone Bridge Press, 1999.

Susan J. Napier, *Anime from Akira to Howl's Moving Castle: Experiencing Contemporary Japanese Animation,* New York: Palgrave Macmillan, 2005.

MICHAEL MOORE

By Diane Negra

One of the most commercially successful documentary filmmakers of all time, Michael Moore is strongly associated with a cinema of umbrage, a protest cinema directed toward monopolistic state and industry practices and the conditions of neoliberal citizenship. His films, television series, books and public appearances consistently seek to funnel attention to the social casualties of free market turbo-capitalism, upholding and extending traditionally liberal notions of speaking truth to power. Moore's aptitude for highlighting the absurdities produced by neoliberal economies has helped to secure the high profile of the contemporary advocacy documentary.

The singularity of Moore's position has been underscored by numerous critics. As Christopher Sharrett and William Luhr have observed, 'He stands virtually alone, not as a filmmaker who inter-rogates social and corporate power, but as one able to place such films into the multiplexes of America'.[1] Moore's efforts to chronicle the dying American Dream and the deepening inequalities of life in the United States have made him a lightning rod for the political right, for documentary purists and for those (including some segments of the left) who view his filmmaking tactics as manipulative and/or counter-productive. Under the presidency of George W. Bush, when right-wing cable news culture assumed an unprecedented centrality and prominence in American political discourse, Moore became a widely excoriated figure even as his films drew large audiences. Film efforts to critically interrogate and/or discredit Moore's methods include *Michael Moore Hates America* (2004) and (in a play on Chomsky) *Manufacturing Dissent* (2007).

As a first-time filmmaker, Moore experienced 'out of nowhere' success with *Roger & Me* in 1989, a film whose ostensible raison d'etre is to chronicle the director's efforts to obtain an interview with then General Motors chairman Roger Smith to discuss the social carnage resulting from GM's reduction of operations in Moore's hometown of Flint, Michigan. The film installs a core set of concerns: the indifference of the powerful to the plight of workers, the fallacy of market fundamentalism and the audacious imposition of faux rhetorics of recovery and boosterism onto wrecked economies. Also noteworthy in the film perhaps are the limits of Moore's critique; as Paul Arthur has observed, 'a willingness to actually take apart and examine the conventions by which authority is inscribed – as opposed to making sport of them – is largely absent'.[2]

Roger & Me was released in a year that was noteworthy for the (re-)energising of American independent cinema. With ample publicity given to the fact that the film had been funded through a home mortgage and the proceeds of a court settlement for wrongful dismissal, Moore was positioned as part of a generation of filmmakers including Hal Hartley and Richard Linklater for whom narratives of financial improvisation were a significant part of the authenticating discourses that came to accompany a new wave of American independent feature production. Moore held in common with many such filmmakers a concern with his home region, and in some respects *Roger & Me* pointed the way toward an emphatically regionalist American independent cinema to come (associated with such filmmakers as Hartley, Kevin Smith and Robert Rodriguez).

In the intervening thirteen years between the sensational success of *Roger & Me* and Moore's next hit film, the filmmaker released the fictional (though highly politically minded) *Canadian Bacon* in 1995 and *The Big One*, a documentary account of Moore's book tour in support of *Downsize This!: Random Threats from an Unarmed American*, and wrote, directed and hosted the television series *The Awful Truth*, a socially critical news magazine spoof. Upon the release of *Bowling for Columbine* in 2002 Moore regained the national spotlight with a film that challenged simplistic and evasive cultural explanations for the killings at Columbine High School in 1999, re-framing the massacre as an episode demanding contextualisation within a long national history of compensatory violence and challenging the hegemony of second amendment-based weapons advocacy in the United States.

Bowling for Columbine was followed up by Moore's most contentious film, *Fahrenheit 9/11*, which tracks the ideological contours of the 'War on Terror', making the case that the Bush Administration preyed upon public fears after 9/11 to further its political and financial interests, presented distorted and deceptive rationales for war in Iraq and sheltered political allies including members of the bin Laden family. Released in a year that would see a second successive disputed presidential election and the subject of a wrangle over distribution between Miramax and its parent company Disney that raised questions of censorship, the film moved Moore into an even more prominent role in public discourse, establishing him for some as a political truth-teller and canny diagnostician of the nation's failings while for others he became a symbol of disloyalty and liberal instigation in a time of national crisis. *Fahrenheit 9/11* holds in common with virtually all of Moore's films a desire to challenge conventional accounts of political and financial power in America, but (despite returning to Flint to explore the impact of military recruitment in blighted neighborhoods there) it represents a significant step away from the localism that had been a key feature of Moore's earlier films where notions of the national were consistently interwoven with a local focus. Emphatically working from a definition of national community that he had not previously formulated in such an aggressive and stark fashion, Moore produced a film that is striking not only for its outrage but for its sense of despair about the condition of American democracy, and it seems clear that *Fahrenheit 9/11* spoke to a growing sense of political disenchantment and concern in American life that would be given further impetus a year later as a result of the events of Hurricane Katrina.

Following on in 2007, *Sicko* finds Moore exploring the healthcare crisis in America, inviting critical reflection on the bureaucratic, inefficient and profit-driven US system which is unfavourably compared with those of nations such as France, Britain and Cuba. Near the close of the film, in a characteristically ironic gesture, a po-faced Moore gathers together a group of uninsured Americans (some of whom have health conditions brought on by the conditions at Ground Zero) and travels by boat to the US military base in Guantanamo Bay, Cuba, in hopes of getting access to the government-sponsored healthcare given to detainees. When a siren from the base deters the group, they are subsequently provided with medical treatment for free in Havana.

As Robert Hunt has characterised it, Moore's cinematic practice involves 'guerilla interview techniques, ironic use of stock footage and music, and, most significantly, the creation of an on-screen persona'.[3] His debut film, *Roger & Me*, appeared at a time of greater formal experimentation in documentary in which the category saw 'an unprecedented degree of hybridization. Materials, techniques and modes of address are borrowed not only from earlier documentary styles but from the American avant-garde and from Hollywood as well'.[4] For Steven Mintz, Moore has centred the rise of 'docutainment, the treatment of non-fiction topics using all the tools of high production feature films, including animation, fast-motion photography, graphics, montage and rock music'.[5] This form would seem to straddle previously discrete cinematic categories and emerged in an era (as Mintz observes) in which documentaries seemed increasingly to fill a void in the US marketplace left behind by diminishing interest in foreign releases and a widely-held belief that Hollywood was making far fewer films tailored to adult interests and sensibilities. As Michael Chanan argues,

> while the dominant culture of the multiplex has become mired in special-effects cornucopia of puerile wish-fulfillment, full of bully-boy violence and conspicuous destruction, fairytale romance and the obligatory happy ending, an answer to this loss of reality is found at the margins in a restoration of documentary, which deals in the actuality of the social and historical world of everyday life.[6]

The new advocacy documentaries like *Roger & Me* and Errol Morris's *The Thin Blue Line* (1990) thus appeared to gratify a public appetite for 'serious' films that accommodated a contemporary audience's aesthetic and narrative expectations.

Moore has sometimes been criticised as being politically fatuous and ideologically reductive; arguably, a pronounced failing of Moore's films is the desire to idealise and simplify other national cultures (frequently Canadian culture, but also Cuban and British cultures in films like *Sicko*) in order to point up US social and economic failings. The writer/director/producer has come in for criticism for strategic omissions, factual slipperiness and for a cherry-picking informational approach on virtually all of his films and has also been widely critiqued for his abandonment of traditional documentary codes of neutrality. Emblematic of the kinds of criticisms of what the filmmaker would regard as legitimate license, and others as a violation of core documentary traditions, was a controversy over a bank promotion featured in the gun-control documentary *Bowling for Columbine* where, in exchange for opening a checquing account, Moore is see-mingly presented on the spot with a rifle by a bank teller. Critics have alleged that Moore staged the gift presentation in a deceptive manner, eliding a number of security procedures put in place by the bank so as to make it appear that customers simply walked into a bank branch and walked out brandishing a new gun. Similarly, debate occurred around a set of temporal manipulations in *Roger & Me* whereby events that took place prior to the GM layoffs are presented as if they occurred afterward and as a function of the cuts. Another concern that has sometimes been raised turns on whether Moore's films (perhaps unwittingly) objectify their working-class subjects. (Rhonda Britton, the 'pets or meat' woman struggling to make a living in *Roger & Me*, might offer evidence of this phenomenon). A distaste for Moore's ambush interviewing was perhaps most apparent in widespread criticism of his appearance (waving the photo of a young girl killed by gunfire) at the home of elderly national icon (and right-wing gun enthusiast) Charlton Heston in *Bowling for Columbine*.

Critics have observed that Moore demonstrates stylistic and thematic affinities with filmmakers like Tony Buba, Nick Broomfield and Ross McElwee, whose films according to Michael Chanan 'represent a mode of political reportage in which the film-maker's personality invades the film, which consequently becomes highly performative; the style, which has strong resonance in the US, is highly gendered but also adopts a satirical and ironic stance'.[7] Bearing these points in mind, Moore's own relationship to celebrity nevertheless appears to be a problematic concern. His disputed political position and the growing gap between his own socioeconomic position and the people Moore presents himself to be speaking for is a frequent element of criticism. Yet Moore's films have long been inseparable from his public persona as a white everyman, and working class schlub (which he sustains even while collecting high speaking fees for his public appearances). Moore's overweight body and decidedly unglamorous appearance have factored in all of his films beginning with *Roger & Me*, in which the director dons a large orange smock to have his 'colors' analysed by a wardrobe consultant. The exuberant style and outraged demeanor Moore displays in his efforts to demand accountability from public figures positions him as strikingly apart from the 'coolness' cultivated by so many contemporary independent film directors. Of course, Moore's performance of the faux naïf is more complex and strategic than some critics allow for. Arthur shrewdly observes that 'Moore's social solidarity is grounded in a trope of technical awkwardness'.[8] Such a characterisation may be less true now but it is worth remembering that the trailer for *Roger & Me* began with Moore feigning technical incompetence by asking if his microphone is on. Those who fault Moore for flouting the documentary code may also adhere to an overly narrow definition of documentary, one that neglects the full spectrum of films made under this rubric. Indeed, some critics have located in Moore a radical critique of traditional documentary's claims to objectivity and neutrality. For Stella Bruzzi, Moore is one of a cadre of documentary practitioners who hold to 'an established tradition of the performer-director'[9] and who seek to 'accentuate, not mask, the means of production because they realize that such a masquerade is impossibly utopian'.[10]

In addition to their box office success, Moore's films have been significantly critically lauded: *Bowling for Columbine* won the Academy Award for Best Documentary in 2002 and *Fahrenheit 9/11* was awarded the Palme D'Or at Cannes in 2004. (Though some of the limits on tolerance for full-fledged political conversations were signalled in the booing with which Moore's political diatribe from the podium was met when he claimed the Oscar.) Overall, the filmmaker who David Denby has referred to as an 'an absurdist of outrage'[11] seems to be thriving in the early twenty-first century. One of a number of past and present social critics of the left such as Studs Terkel, Noam Chomsky, Barbara Ehrenreich and Naomi Klein whose profiles have been significantly raised in recent years, Moore perhaps stands out even amongst this group as a practitioner of a cultural criticism that is so evidently financially gainful.

Moore's now eminent status as a provocateur whose films regularly shape cultural conversations about hot topic issues is confirmed not only by his own continuing output (at this writing *Capitalism: A Love Story* is arriving in theatres in what would appear to be another well-judged act of release timing given the global recession) but also by an influence that is increasingly apparent in a succeeding generation of filmmakers. In the films of Morgan Spurlock (*Super Size Me* [2004] and *Where in the World is Osama Bin Laden?* [2008]) the centrality of the director's persona and concern with political and social matters echo Moore's signature style and approach. Similarly, it would be hard to deny the influence of Moore in the robust success in recent years of television comedy news franchises like *The Daily Show* and *The Colbert Report*. When *The Daily Show* host Jon Stewart aggressively challenged financial huckster Jim Cramer in a sensational broadcast in March, 2009, it was hard not to see some traces of Moore's brand of pointed corporate confrontation. Later that year the election of comedian Al Franken to the US Senate pointed to a similarly broad blurring of absurdist comedy and political intervention of the kind associated with Moore.

Michael Moore seems potentially poised to flourish in the climate of the global recession which has thus far given credence to many of the director's concerns. Despite the charges of ideological reductionism levelled against him, it is hard to fault his efforts to direct attention to those who are dispossessed from the American Dream and to argue for greater accountability from public and corporate officials. Ultimately the forcefulness with which Moore has frequently been denunciated speaks to the filmmaker's role as a cultural instigator, one who has consistently denominated those features of contemporary US culture that challenge the national self-image of a flourishing and fair democracy. There is an undeniable power in the images and accounts generated by a filmmaker who seeks to engage (however problematically) the issues of class disparity and economic inequity that remain so obdurately unacknowledged in American national culture.

Biography

Michael Francis Moore was born on April 23, 1954, in Flint, Michigan, into an Irish-American Catholic family with multi-generational ties both to General Motors and the labour union United Automobile Workers (UAW). After working as founder of a magazine in Michigan, Moore was hired as editor at *Mother Jones*, later winning a judgement against the magazine for wrongful dismissal. Moore put the proceeds from the suit toward his first film *Roger & Me*, the success of which launched his filmmaking career which has run alongside other creative ventures, including occasionally directing music videos and the television series *TV Nation* and *The Awful Truth* which aired in the United States and Britain in 1994–95 and 1999–2000 respectively. Moore is the author of a number of best-selling books including *Downsize This!* (1996), *Stupid White Men* (2001) and *Dude, Where's My Country?* (2003), and appears regularly as a paid speaker and media commentator.

Notes

1 Christopher Sharrett and William Luhr. '*Bowling for Columbine*: A Review'. In *New Challenges for Documentary*. Eds Alan Rosenthal and John Corner. Manchester: Manchester University Press, 2005, pp. 253–9, p. 253.

2 Arthur, Paul. 'Jargons of Authenticity (Three American Moments)'. In *Theorizing Documentary*. Ed. Michael Renov. New York and London: Routledge, 1993, pp. 108–34, p. 128.

3 Robert Hunt, 'Michael Moore'. *Encyclopedia of the Documentary Film*. Ed. Ian Aitken, New York: Routledge, 2006, pp. 925–7, p. 925.

4 Paul *op. cit.,* p. 127.

5 Steven Mintz, 'Michael Moore and the Re-Birth of the Documentary', *Film & History* 35(2) (2005), pp. 10–11, p. 11.

6 Michael Chanan, *The Politics of Documentary*. London: BFI, 2007, p. 7.

7 Ibid., p. 12.

8 Arthur, pp. 130–1.

9 Stella Bruzzi, *New Documentary: A Critical Introduction*. London: Routledge, 2007, p. 163.

10 Ibid., p. 155.

11 David Denby, 'Do No Harm'. *The New Yorker* July 2, 2007, pp. 84–5, p. 84.

Filmography

Roger and Me (1989)
Pets or Meat: The Return to Flint (1992)
Canadian Bacon (1995)
The Big One (1997)
Bowling for Columbine (2002)
Fahrenheit 9/11 (2004)
Sicko (2007)
Capitalism: A Love Story (2009)

MIRA NAIR

By Sue Brennan

Mira Nair is one of the most prominent and successful South Asian women directors working in film today. Born in India, educated at Harvard, and now living between New York and Uganda, Nair is what Hamid Naficy calls an 'interstitial' filmmaker, creating films 'astride and in the interstices of social formations and cinematic practices'.[1] Her films use a variety of transnational localities, modes of production and representational techniques, which serve as the foundation of Nair's distinctly hybridised and deterritorialised form of filmmaking. Nair, more than just an independent filmmaker or a cosmopolitan director, takes up themes of geographic and cultural interstitiality in her films, exploring the topics of exile, diasporic communities, intercultural romance, homelessness and transnational migration. The subjects of her films often exist on the margins of their social worlds; focused on the subjectivities of immigrants, women, sex workers, and street children in both India and the United States, Nair's films draw inspiration, she says, from 'those that are considered to be on the outside'.[2]

Nair's interstitial status also complicates the roles of identity and location in interpreting her voice as a filmmaker. Neither simply an 'Indian' nor an 'American' director, she has created a directorial gaze and style that repeatedly blur the boundaries between insider and outsider. Her frequent use of cinema vérité techniques and her penchant for lush, vivid costuming and visual effects are sites of both praise and critique, garnering disapproval from critics who see her filmmaking as exploitative or misinformed. South Asian critics, for example, consider Nair a type of native informant, offering Western audiences exoticised or abject images of the Third World. In the West, on the other hand, her films have come under fire for promoting a type of apolitical and romanticised multiculturalism.[3] These criticisms also testify to Nair's strength as a filmmaker, namely her ability to provoke viewers and challenge their understandings of place, culture and identity in creating – and watching – film.

Nair began her career as a documentary filmmaker, producing four short films before turning to narrative feature film. Trained in the techniques of cinema vérité at Harvard, her documentaries focus on 'observing truth' in various interstitial spaces.[4] The first of these films, *Jama Masjid Street Journal*, is an 18-minute short that chronicles the male-dominated street life around the Jama Masjid (or Great Mosque) in the old city of Delhi. In her next two documentaries, *So Far From India* and *Children of a Desired Sex*, Nair examines two distinct experiences of in-between-ness: the struggle of an immigrant living between his new home in the United States and his family in India, and the role of amniocentesis in the selective abortion of female fetuses in India. Both films foreground Nair's adeptness in humanising the flow of capital, culture and technology across a modern and globalised world, a theme also reflected in Nair's most commercially and critically successfully documentary, *India Cabaret*. *India Cabaret* documents the ordinary lives of female cabaret dancers working and living in a suburb of Mumbai. Nair lived with the dancers for two months, following them into their homes and communities in an effort to expose what she perceived as the artificial boundary 'that divides good women from so-called not good women' in contemporary urban India.[5]

Feeling constrained by the lack of audience and creative control in documentary film, Nair ventured into feature film with *Salaam Bombay!*[6] The film follows Krishna, a young boy living on the streets of Mumbai (formerly Bombay) whose job as a 'tea boy' draws him into the dysfunction of a nearby brothel. In *Salaam Bombay!*, Nair combines the extemporaneous style of cinema vérité with the dramatic effects of a narrative-driven film. It was filmed entirely on location in Mumbai, the story of Krishna shaped from anecdotes told to Nair and screenwriter Sooni Taraporevala during their research for the film.[7] During filming Nair took advantage of the city's social geographies, shooting in working brothels, middle class homes, and street festivals. *Salaam Bombay!*, however, generally offers a view of Mumbai from the perspective of its subaltern subjects. Nair draws from the interstices of Mumbai's urban landscape, repeating images of winding alleyways, dark brothel stairwells, and shadowy corners in order to highlight the immobility of its young characters.

Nair's filmmaking met criticism from critics 'who felt she pandered to the West with images of a destitute and victimized India in her role as native informant or cultural insider'.[8] Despite her focus on subaltern subjects, Nair does not hold them up to the West in pity or shame. Her use of untrained actors (many of the performers were themselves street children), combined with a guerilla-style shoot, allowed Nair to extract brazen, honest and nuanced performances from the young actors that propel the film beyond an exploitative or Orientalist gaze. The subjects of *Salaam Bombay!* emerge as agents in the shifting networks of global and local, improvising an existence through work, theft and everything in between.

Salaam Bombay! garnered critical acclaim in the West, including an Oscar nomination and a Golden Camera Award at the Cannes Film Festival. While Nair became sought after as a studio director, she parlayed the success of her first feature into funding and a distributor for another independent project, *Mississippi Masala*. The film marks a significant shift in locality for the filmmaker, who turned her gaze away from India and toward its diasporas in Uganda and the American south. The film's dual focus highlights her continued interest in marginalised groups: *Mississippi Masala* confronts the exile of South Asian Ugandans under Idi Amin, as well as the economic and cultural marginalisation of South Asians living in the small town of Greenwood, Mississippi.

In *Mississippi Masala*, hybridity (as both theme and form) is at the foundation of Nair's interstitial perspective. Working with screen-writer Sooni Taraporevala again, Nair clearly draws inspiration from Hindi cinema's Masala (or 'mix') films, weaving family melodrama, comedy and historical drama into the film's star-crossed romance between Mina (Sarita Choudhury), the daughter of Indian-Ugandan nationals sent into exile, and Demetrius (Denzel Washington), an African-American man who owns a local carpet cleaning business. Meanwhile, Mina's father Jay (Roshan Seth) is obsessed with reclaiming his property in Kampala lost during Amin's reign. While Jay eventually gets his home back, Mina and Demetrius's relationship is condemned by their respective families and extended communities, instigating a series of events that inspire Demetrius and Mina to leave Greenwood.

Much of the film's emphasis on hybridity revolves around Mina, who self-identifies as a 'masala'. Mina, equally at home in a salwar kameez or a Bob Marley t-shirt and jeans, is also a 'mix' of national and ethnic identities that intentionally complicate the roles of race and place in forging ethnic identity in the United States. Mina, for example, argues that her home is not India but Africa; when Demetrius's brother balks at her claim, she notes that the experience of being an Indian who has never been to India is similar to the displacement he and Demetrius feel as African-Americans who have not been to Africa. Critics praised Nair's multiculturalist take on Mina and the anti-racist message embedded in her romance with Demetrius. Yet the film also met criticism from feminists in the South Asian diaspora, who admonished Nair for her apolitical and exotified representations of South Asian American femininity[9]. While they condemned *Mississippi Masala* as Orientalist exoticism masquerading as feel-good multiculturalism, the scholarly and critical attention it received made Nair the most prominent cinematic voice to represent the South Asian diaspora in the United States.

After the success of *Salaam Bombay!* and *Mississippi Masala*, Nair's status as a feature film director also grew. She directed her first studio film, *The Perez Family*, for the Samuel Goldwyn Company in 1995, starring Marisa Tomei, Alfred Molina and Anjelica Huston as an impromptu family of Cuban refugees. She then returned to India to direct *Kama Sutra: A Tale of Love*, a film she co-wrote and co-produced in conjunction with Channel Four Films. Part costume drama, part erotic romance, *Kama Sutra* features Sarita Choudhury and Indira Varma as sexual rivals in 16th-century Mughal India. The film's sexually explicit content prompted its banning in India, which Nair challenged in a protracted court battle with the Indian government.[10]

True to her interstitial roots, Nair's filmmaking is bound to neither form nor medium. She has directed two made-for-television movies, *My Own Country* and *Hysterical Blindness*, along with several short films and documentaries: *The Laughing Club of India*, short features for the films *9'11'01* and *New York, I Love You*, and *Migration*, a 17-minute short about AIDS awareness in India made in conjunction with the AIDS Jaago ('AIDS awake') project.[11] These pieces, although varied in content, address many of the same themes of interstitiality as Nair's feature films, including the experiences of exile and marginalisation. The low-risk, low-budget format of short film offers Nair more latitude as a filmmaker, and she often takes up topics too politicised for feature filmmaking in her shorter works. For *9'11'01* French producer Alain Brigand assembled eleven filmmakers from around the world, including Nair, to each create a short film lasting 11 minutes and 9 seconds. Nair's short told the true story of Mohammad Salman Hamdani, a Pakistani-American mistakenly identified as a fugitive terrorist after 9/11 and later lauded as a hero after his remains were found at Ground Zero. Her choice of Hamdani's story for the film underscores her willingness to unabashedly address a topic considered marginal – and even taboo – in the post-9/11 nation. While criticised as cloying and superficial, it clearly exposes the dangers of nationalist rhetoric in an otherwise patriotic moment.[12]

Determined to shed the creative and editorial restrictions attached to big-budget filmmaking, Nair vowed her next feature film would make 'something out of nothing' through 'self-imposed leanness' and creative loyalty only to herself.[13] The result, *Monsoon Wedding*, is perhaps Nair's most complete and innovative vision of interstitial filmmaking. The film begins in Delhi three days before the arranged nuptials of young Delhian Aditi (Vasundhara Das), and her NRI (non-resident Indian) groom-to-be, Hemant (Parvin Dabas). It revisits many of the same topics of Nair's previous work – women's sexual subjectivity, family conflict, and the role of diaspora in shaping modern Indian identity – but presents them in a breezy hybrid of a comedic ensemble film and a Bollywood wedding film. Critics have compared the style of Nair's filmmaking in *Monsoon Wedding* to Altman, and certainly the film's lack of exposition, large cast of characters, and the chaotic merging of two families are all nods to his *A Wedding* (1978). Nair's characters, however, are also products of a modernised and globalised Delhi, moving easily between Punjabi, Hindi and English throughout the film.

In making *Monsoon Wedding*, Nair aimed to direct a film that appealed to both Indian and Western audiences, and it is the spectacle of the Punjabi wedding that serves as a site of localised and transnational identification.[14] The wedding is a familiar trope in Bollywood film, offering a point of identification for viewers in India and a potential site of nostalgia for diasporian audiences. Utilising the format of a narrative-driven Hollywood feature film, however, Nair transforms the unfolding of Aditi and Hemant's union into a universalised, multicultural site of consumption for mainstream Western audiences.[15] Nair also presents Aditi's bourgeois Delhi family as a product of a modern and cosmopolitan India. Their conflicts challenge the romanticised patriarchal family celebrated in Bollywood films, as well as the Orientalist vision of India as backward and anti-modern. Aditi, for example, is not a 'traditional' Indian bride; she agrees to the arranged marriage in order to escape from a doomed love affair with a married man. For Nair, however, the wedding is a site through which modern subjectivity merges with cultural tradition, including the heteronormative, male-headed family unit. Aditi's marriage to Hemant draws her back into the structure of the patriarchal family without compromising her cosmopolitan self. He is clearly the better choice for Aditi, linked to a progressive masculinity in touch with the needs of a modern Indian woman.

Monsoon Wedding was an international hit, earning the Golden Lion at the Venice Film Festival and a Golden Globe nomination. Its success propelled Nair's career forward and into a series of high-profile directing jobs, starting with the adaptation of James Thackeray's *Vanity Fair*. Nair captures the elaborate opulence of Thackeray's world in the film's elaborate costuming and its stunning images of Regency England. Film critics, however, panned Nair's uncharacteristically modern interpretation of the novel's central character, Becky Sharp (portrayed by star Reese Witherspoon).[16] Her attempt to reference England's (as well as Thackeray's) colonial ties to South Asia in a series of Bollywood-style dance numbers also fell flat with both audiences and critics. *Vanity Fair* confirms Nair's attraction to the stories of plucky, ambitious women: she notes an identification with Becky's desire to survive, despite the hostile conditions in which she must live.[17]

Nair's studios projects like *The Perez Family* and *Vanity Fair* often lack the grit and liveliness of her independent films. She seems, however, to have struck a balance between the demands of bigger-budget filmmaking and her own vision with her adaptation of Jhumpa Lahiri's *The Namesake*. Spanning some 30 years, the film describes the journey of a young Bengali graduate student Ashoke Ganguli (Irrfan Khan) and his wife Ashima (Tabu) to the United States, and the growth and maturation of their son Gogol (informally named after the Russian author). Departing from the novel's emphasis on assimilation, Nair recreates a history of South Asian American citizenship that is distinctly transnational in scope, unfolding against the sociopolitical backdrops of New York and Calcutta. In *The Namesake*, the trials of marriage, childbirth, education and death all play out in and between the two cities. The film's reoccurring signifiers of transit and travel become powerful symbols of the economic, social and emotional ties immigrant families rely upon in order to sustain connections with various versions of home.

Nair's casting choices reflect her focus on global connection: she paired Bollywood stars Tabu and Irrfan Khan as Ashima and Ashoke with American actor Kal Penn as Gogol. It is a casting choice that effectively captures Gogol's ambivalence toward the inaccessible and foreign world of his parents. He struggles against the Bengali traditions and customs they follow, only to feel clumsy and alienated in the Anglo-centric world of his friends, and later his girlfriends. Not simply a matter of an intercultural generation gap, the sparse narration and melancholy tone convey a type of aimlessness that follows Gogol throughout his life, preventing him from feeling comfortable anywhere. His awkwardness presents an interesting bookend to the heavily criticised hybridity of *Mississippi Masala*'s Mina. With Gogol, Nair seems to respond to critics of Mina, suggesting that the mythology of the 'model minority' is as fabricated as the spectacle of multiculturalism.

Nair's latest studio project is the Fox Searchlight biopic *Amelia* starring Hillary Swank, Richard Gere and Ewan McGregor. After 30 years of filmmaking, Nair is not simply an interstitial filmmaker. Her commercial and critical success have secured her status as a skilled and sought after director in Hollywood and abroad. In the shift between studio 'director-for-hire' and independent filmmaker, however, Nair's films still retain characteristics of interstitial filmmaking, including a devotion to geographies – and narratives – of the in-between.

Nair's legacy also highlights the financial, ethical and creative challenges of making films between continents and modes of production. Conversely, Nair's best work accentuates the rewards of these relationships: the creation of dialogues and connections across cultures, and the articulation of voices otherwise marginalised in mainstream filmmaking. Throughout her career Nair has shaped images of India and the Indian diaspora for audiences around the world. More importantly, the prominence of South Asian women screenwriters, directors and producers currently engaged in interstitial modes of filmmaking is directly indebted to Nair's vision and success as a filmmaker.

Biography

Mira Nair was born in 1957 in Bhubaneswar, India. Educated at Delhi University and Harvard University, she has directed over twenty documentary, short and feature films. She founded her own production company, Mirabai Films, in 1989, and in 2005 started Maishi, a filmmaking workshop devoted to fostering filmmakers from East Africa and South Asia. An Adjunct Assistant Professor of Film at Columbia University, Nair lives in both New York City and Kampala, Uganda.

Notes

1 Hamid Naficy, *An Accented Cinema*, Princeton, Princeton University Press, 2001, p. 4.
2 'Mira Nair', *guardian.co.uk*, June 12, 2002, online, available <http://www.guardian.co.uk/film/2002/jun/12/guardianinterviewsatbfisouthbank1> (accessed 1 June 2009).

3 See Arora Poonam, 'The Production of Third World Subjects for First World Consumption: *Salaam Bombay* and *Parama*', in *Multiple Voices in Feminist Film Criticism*, Diane Carson, Linda Dittmar, and Janice Welsh (eds), Minneapolis, University of Minnesota Press, 1994, pp. 293–304, and Jigna Desai, *Beyond Bollywood: The Cultural Politics of South Asian Diasporic Film*, New York, Routledge, 2004.

4 Mira Nair, commentary, *Salaam Bombay!*, Dir. Mira Nair, 1988, DVD, MGM Home Entertainment, 2003.

5 Ibid.

6 Ibid.

7 John Kenneth Muir, *Mercy in her Eyes: The Films of Mira Nair*, New York, Applause Theatre and Cinema Books, 2006, p. 38.

8 Jigna Desai, *op. cit,* p. 47.

9 See Kum K. Bhavnani, 'Organic Hybridity or Commodification of Hybridity? Comments on *Mississippi Masala*', *Meridians,* vol. 1, no. 1, 2000, pp. 187–203; bell hooks and Anuradha Dingwaney, '*Mississippi Masala*', Z Magazine, July–August 1992, pp. 41–3; and Binta Mehta, 'Emigrants Twice Displaced: Race, Color, and Identity in Mira Nair's *Mississippi Masala*', in *Multiculturalism, Postcoloniality, and Transnational Media*, Ella Shohat and Robert Stam (eds), New Brunswick, Rutgers University Press, 2003, pp. 153–69.

10 John Kenneth Muir, *op. cit.*, p. 127.

11 Uma Thurman received a Golden Globe for her role in *Hysterical Blindness*.

12 Peter Matthews, 'One Day in September', *Sight and Sound*, vol. 13, no. 1, 2003, pp. 32–3.

13 Mira Nair, commentary, *Monsoon Wedding*, dir. Mira Nair, 2001, DVD, Universal Studios, 2002.

14 Ibid.

15 Jigna Desai, *op. cit.*, p. 221.

16 Stephen Holden, 'Becky Sharp Again Weaves her Wily Web', *The New York Times*, September 1, 2004, Section E, p. 1.

17 Nair, *op. cit.*

Filmography

Jama Masjid Street Journal (1979) documentary
So Far from India (1983) documentary
Children of a Desired Sex (1985) documentary
India Cabaret (1986) documentary
Salaam Bombay! (1988)
Mississippi Masala (1991)
The Day Mercedes Became a Hat (1993)
The Perez Family (1995)
Kama Sutra: A Tale of Love (1996)
My Own Country (1998) television movie
The Laughing Club of India (1999) television documentary

Monsoon Wedding (2001)
Hysterical Blindness (2002) television movie
11'09'01 (2002) Segment 'India'
Still, The Children Are Here (2003) documentary
Vanity Fair (2004)
The Namesake (2006)
Migration (2007)
8 (2008) Segment 'How Can It Be?'
New York, I Love You (2009) Segment 'Kosher Vegetarian'
Amelia (2009)

Further reading

Gwendolyn Foster, *Women Filmmakers of the African and Asian Diaspora: Decolonizing the Gaze, Locating Subjectivity*, Carbondale, Southern Illinois University Press, 1997.

Gayatri Gopinath, *Impossible Desires: Queer Diasporas and South Asian Public Cultures*, Durham, Duke University Press, 2005.

Jhumpa Lahiri and Mira Nair, *The Namesake: A Portrait of the Film by Mira Nair Based on the Novel by Jhumpa Lahiri*, New York, Newmarket Press, 2006.

Gita Rajan, 'Constructing-Contesting Masculinities: Trends in South Asian Cinema', *Signs: Journal of Woman in Culture and Society*, vol. 3, no. 4, 2006, pp. 1099–124.

Urmila Seshagiri, 'At the Crossroads of Two Empires: Mira Nair's Mississippi Masala and the Limits of Hybridity', *Journal of Asian American Studies*, June 2003, pp. 177–98.

Andrea Stuart, 'Mira Nair: A New Hybrid Cinema', in Pam Cook and Philip Dodd (eds) *Women and Film: A Sight and Sound Reader*, Philadelphia, PA, Temple University Press, 1993, pp. 210–16.

FRANÇOIS OZON

By Ginette Vincendeau

In the landscape of contemporary French cinema François Ozon occupies a unique place, marked by hybridity, transformation and provocation. Here is a filmmaker who likes to cross borders: in the course of two prolific decades (nineteen shorts and ten features since 1989) he has ranged from gay and 'extreme' short and medium-length films to a star-laden comic musical such as *8 femmes/8 Women*, as well as austere auteur work, for instance *Le Temps qui reste/Time to Leave*. He has played with shock tactics, outrageous stories, Hollywood pastiche and gender fluidity, and ventured into English-language production with *Angel*, claiming, 'I don't want to get bored … I need to have the impression of taking risks, to go into the unknown'.[1] Indeed, as one reviewer put it in relation to his controversial 2009 'social fantasy' *Ricky*, 'the maker of *8 femmes* loves to take spectators into territories they never dreamt of visiting'.[2] Critical opinion has seen this variously as creative risk-taking or gratuitous desire to shock, but there is no denying Ozon's stature in today's French cinema and on the international scene.

Ozon crosses borders in other ways too. As France's first openly gay mainstream director, his popular success at home has to some extent relied on the erasure of his queer identity, while the latter is central to the scholarly interest he has elicited, especially outside France. At the same time the taboo-breaking nature of much of his work is accompanied by both ambiguity and a disregard for political correctness. Thus the daring and eclecticism that give Ozon's work its high profile also mean that he fits uneasily within established critical paradigms, whether classic European auteur cinema, international queer cinema, 'Young French Cinema' or 'New French Extremism'. Although it would be reductive to argue for a single theme or visual style running through his work, echoes and resonances do link his shorts and features across his career, in particular the exploration of mourning and eroticism, a desire to shock coupled with a willingness to explore difficult or rebarbative characters (as he admitted, 'People have found my characters unsympathetic'.[3]) Stylistically, Ozon's disparate films are also, up to a point, united by cinephilia, pastiche and theatricality and above all uncertainty of tone, oscillating between seriousness and frivolity, irony and emotion, reality and fantasy.

Early shock tactics

Ozon's apprenticeship was both classic and unusual. In time-honoured French fashion he followed studies at the Parisian film school FEMIS with a number of short films before graduating to features. But he also took a postgraduate degree in film studies, the legacy of which can be seen in his ostentatious cinephilia. This includes straightforward tributes, such as *Gouttes d'eau sur pierres brûlantes/Water Drops on Burning Rocks*, the adaptation of a Fassbinder play, and homage to Hollywood melodrama. *8 femmes* explicitly recalls *The Women* in plot and hothouse atmosphere, and several films (especially *8 femmes* and *Angel*) reference the heightened passions and visual excess of the melodramas of Douglas Sirk and Vincente Minnelli, more postmodern pastiche than New Wave reverence. He conceded, 'I feel I belong to a generation which absorbed all influences and put them all on the same plane'.[4] Both *Sous le sable* and *Swimming Pool* have been compared to Hitchcock in the way they build suspense – although Mark Hain argues for more subtle links between the two directors, in terms of how they both 'investigate the dread of sexual difference, the imbalance of power within the patriarchal system symptomatic of this dread and repression of sexuality (particularly 'transgressive' sexualities) ultimately resulting in antisocial actions'.[5]

Concern with sexuality and 'antisocial actions', combined with reflections on the medium, have been at the heart of Ozon's work from the beginning. The first ten years of his career (until *Sitcom*) while still in his twenties were an intense period of experimentation, in which he confronted homosexuality head on – still a relative rarity in French cinema at the time – and made films in a variety of formats, from super-8 and video to 35mm (a comprehensive examination of these is now possible thanks to their availability on DVD).

Ozon's first short, *Photo de famille*, reflects on photography as social practice, using members of his own family to stage murder scenes, thus anticipating *Sitcom*. Later, *La Petite mort* moves the ratchet up with images of men's faces in the throes of sexual orgasm, as well as of the hero taking pictures of the naked body of his dying father. But perhaps the most 'shocking' aspect of the film is, as Max Cavitch puts it, that in the film 'mourning *is* an erotic narrative',[6] a theme that Ozon will return to in *Sous le sable*. The medium-length *Regarde la mer/Look at the Sea* represents Ozon at his most provocative, with its delight in the abject (shots of feces in a toilet bowl, of a woman using a toothbrush dipped in it, images of a murdered woman's mutilated body). But if this film, and later *Sitcom*, placed him squarely with the 'New French Extremism', with directors like Gaspar Noë and Catherine Breillat, Ozon's cinema can by no means be fitted neatly under this label.

In his early career Ozon also approached same-sex desire in characteristically eclectic ways. In *Une robe d'été*, he offers a joyful, affirmative take on the topic, deliberately moving away from the socially anchored films of Cyril Collard or Patrick Mimouni towards something more playful: 'After the guilt-inducing period when we thought AIDs had rendered sexuality impossible, this joyful vision was timely … In my short films homosexuality is given as itself, it is not problematised'.[7] He makes the same point about his later feature *8 femmes*, which features a lesbian sub-plot: 'The point was to show [homosexual pleasure] in a natural manner, without guilt-making, without trying to shock'.[8] Yet in *Les Amants criminels/Criminal Lovers*, homosexuality is anything but 'natural' and guilt-free; instead it is intimately connected to violence and murder. The homosexual relation, in which a rough older man called 'the forest ogre' initiates the young Luc is presented as escape from a 'castrating' young woman, Alice. Even taking into account the distanciation afforded by the framing of the story as fairy tale, it is difficult to ignore the cynicism and misogyny of the film, as well as its potential to feed homophobia. As Mark Hain says, 'Whether not offering a condemnation of whatever socially-motivated oppression/repression led to the murder in *Criminal Lovers* can be considered irresponsible or gay-negative will be a matter of conjecture for future critics'.[9]

While *Les Amants criminels* did badly at the box-office, the previous year's *Sitcom* was the breakthrough film which revealed Ozon to a wider audience. Described as 'a black farce that delights in breaking every taboo in the book',[10] *Sitcom* shifted the provocation of the early shorts to a 'Buñuelian' comic demolition of bourgeois family values, couching a series of outrageous scenes in black farce, in a colourful and deliberately artificial décor. A laboratory rat brought home by the father of a 'normal' bourgeois suburban family causes chaos. Among the taboos the film gleefully takes on are incest, paedophilia, group sex and bestiality. Besides the son's 'coming out' as gay, there is attempted suicide, maiming, the cooking and eating of the rat, and the death of the father after he has returned as a 'giant rat'. Andrew Asibong sees *Sitcom* as 'a simultaneously playful and caustic critique of the hypocrisy of contemporary French social relations',[11] but, more often, critics, like Frédéric Bonnaud, judged it gratuitous provocation and adolescent childplay 'devoid of any substance',[12] while Alain Brassart has condemned its 'contemptuous'[13] attitude towards its characters. Either way, *Sitcom* put Ozon on the map and marked his move to more mainstream and more mature projects.

Ozon's femmes

One key motif links the feature films Ozon made from *Sous le sable* onwards, namely the portrayal of female characters who are 'strong' in terms of their domination of the narrative and of the actresses who embody them. Even *5x2*, a film about the disintegration of a heterosexual couple can be described, as Robert Sklar argues, as 'another 'feminine film project' in that audience sympathy seems directed almost entirely toward the wife'.[14] Ozon's films undoubtedly show a fascination with women, in particular ageing women (*Sous le sable, Swimming Pool, 8 femmes*). He is revered by actresses for this reason and Charlotte Rampling's career certainly enjoyed a second flowering thanks to *Sous le sable* and *Swimming Pool*.

With these two films, Ozon's auteur credentials also rose exponentially, as critics saluted his move to a tasteful cinema of psychological exploration among sophisticated middle-class characters. In *Sous le sable* Rampling plays a university professor whose husband inexplicably vanishes while on holiday, the film then charting her increasingly disturbing denial of his disappearance. In *Swimming Pool* the same actress embodies a thriller writer jilted by her publisher-lover who is struggling to overcome her writer's block. The arrival at the Provençal villa where she is staying of the publisher's young and sexy daughter (Ludivine Sagnier) reawakens her own sexuality and creativity, but also has other dramatic consequences including murder. While Ozon is unusual in allotting extensive screen space to glamorous older women, there is a ferocious undercurrent of misogyny in these two films, as there is in the more playful *8 femmes*, and it is perhaps no accident that these three movies have been his most popular to date.

In his book on homosexuality in French cinema, Alain Brassart forcefully states his position when he analyses Ozon's work under the chapter heading, 'A gay misogyny: Ozon, Chéreau and a few others'. Where many saw sensitive portrayals of desiring and desirable older women, or a psychoanalytically-based exploration of loss and mourning in mid-life crisis,[15] Brassart sees the failure of portraying autonomous female subjectivity. It is true that in *Sous le sable* and *Swimming Pool* Rampling's characters forever mourn the loss of their youth and sexual power, while in both cases their professional activity is trivialised. In *Sous le sable* her lecturing consists of reading out bits from Virginia Woolf's *The Waves*. She is depicted at length as an empty creature, a wife who gave up research to devote herself to a husband, yet turns out to have known very little about him (including the fact that he was clinically depressed). Despite Ozon's claim to have aimed at letting the spectator 'inside this woman's head',[16] we never have access to her thoughts, so while she elicits sympathy, identification with her is not possible, except in her status as a 'failure'. In *Swimming Pool*, Rampling's professional activity is taken more seriously, no doubt in part because Ozon uses her identity as a writer as a *mise-en-abyme* of his own creative process ('*Swimming Pool* reflects my personal obsessions about creating, and, since it's a film about inspiration, contains many references to my other work'.[17]). Yet here again the trigger for the story is the fact that her lover has rejected her, and the beginning of the film shows her as a drab, sad single woman looking after her father, rather than the successful novelist she is meant to be. And her renaissance at the end is *shown* to be more sexual than creative. This being said, *Swimming Pool* and *Sous le sable*, in the best tradition of European auteur cinema, are accomplished stylistically, projecting a vivid sense of space, developing nuanced psychological dynamics between the characters (helped by first-rate performances), and building up gripping narratives of suspense and mystery. Ozon also uses imaginative cinematic techniques to bring to life the films' subtle toeing of the line between reality and fantasy, such as making the dead husband magically appear in *Sous le sable*, or the deployment of location, as in the use of the eponymous swimming pool.

Part of the difficulty in deciphering Ozon's sexual politics is his deliberate ambiguity. Offering either blank pastiche or enigmatic narratives, and distancing action through theatricality or overlaps between reality and fantasy, he adopts a typical postmodern posture which discourages interpretation. This is particularly true of *8 femmes*, Ozon's most successful film at the box-office, with a dream cast of French stars (Catherine Deneuve, Isabelle Huppert, Emmanuelle Béart and Fanny Ardant among them). Adapted from an obscure French play from the 1960s, and emulating Cukor's *The Women* in the total absence of men from the screen, Ozon's film offers a parody of the country house plot: eight women holed up in a mansion around the body of the one man, who has been murdered. His wife, daughters, mother, etc. bicker over 'who done it', cut off by snow and severed telephone wires, in a series of ludicrous twists, stopping only to each sing a song – until we find that the murder itself was part of an intricate plot. The women are all potentially guilty and all embody sexist stereotypes (the 'French maid', the grasping wife, the maiden aunt, etc.). Brassart and others have linked Ozon to Chabrol in his quasi-scientific examination of women as fascinating 'monsters', in turn vapid and evil – as in Chabrol's own *Les Bonnes femmes* (1960). Similarly, the inclusion of the lesbian sub-plot and famous kiss between Catherine Deneuve and Fanny Ardant have been criticised as token.[18] Yet at the same time the high theatricality and the singing warn us not to take any of it seriously – unlike *Sous le sable* and *Swimming Pool*, which use predominantly naturalistic mise-en-scène. Like its popular songs, *8 femmes* invites us to read true emotions under a frivolous theatrical exterior. It is a highly pleasurable visual feast, with lush colours, extraordinary attention to (reconstituted) period costume and star turns. Deneuve probably delivered the most lucid comment on the film and on Ozon's sexual politics, when she said, 'I am not sure Ozon likes women, but he likes actresses'.[19]

Critical roller-coaster

After his run of three hits (*Sous le sable*, *8 femmes*, *Swimming Pool*), Ozon's more recent record has been hit and miss. *5x2* and *Le Temps qui reste/Time to Leave* returned to the more austere auteur style of *Sous le sable*, with less popular success though more critical approval, especially with *Le Temps qui reste*, an extended reflection on love and death, pleasure and mourning. The film's young gay hero learns early on that he is about to die of cancer and, in classic fashion, uses the time left to reassess his relationships to both male lovers and members of his family; particularly memorable is his visit to his grandmother (Jeanne Moreau). Whereas his portrayals of women in *Sous le sable* and *Swimming Pool* were marked by fascination but also estrangement, and in *5x2* the back-to-front narrative distanced the action more than it afforded deeper spectator knowledge, Ozon's depiction of the male hero of *Le Temps qui reste* succeeds in evoking immediacy and tenderness, and the young man (played by Melvil Poupaud) is possibly his most classically rounded character.

Ozon nevertheless returned to women with *Angel*, an ambitious, though critically unsuccessful, international production (14m euros) based on an Elizabeth Taylor novel and shot in English. True to form, the film is equally interested in the fate of its unconventional Victorian heroine as it is in Hollywood melodrama and nineteenth-century romantic fiction. *Angel* tells the story of an impoverished girl, Angelica ('Angel'), from a dreary English provincial town, who becomes rich and successful through writing lurid sentimental novels. She falls in love with an unsuccessful painter, Esmé, who ends up deserting her and committing suicide, while Esmé's sister Nora becomes her faithful secretary in whose arms she dies at the end of the film. Angel is a particularly 'unsympathetic' character, a difficult woman who listens to no advice and uses her fame and wealth to dominate all around her. As in *Swimming Pool*, it is tempting to see her, a writer, as a stand-in for the director, someone who succeeds at her art by being oblivious to notions of 'good taste' and conventions (both social and literary). Yet here too romance overwhelms the heroine and in the second half of the film the fun of her 'bad girl' persona is overtaken by her identity as unhappy lover.

After the lukewarm reception of *Angel*, in 2009 *Ricky* baffled critics and bombed at the French box-office, despite starring local celebrity

Alexandra Lamy, well-known for her television and theatre work. *Ricky*, based on a short story by Rose Tremain, tells the story of a young working-class couple (Lamy and Sergi Lopez) whose child is a baby boy ... with wings. The fact that reviewers had to reach for references ranging from the Dardenne Brothers to Walt Disney to make sense of *Ricky* is telling about the film's hybridity, in which fantasy grows, like Ricky's wings, out of a social realist story set in a bleak *banlieue*. Clearly Ozon's penchant for blurring the boundaries between 'reality' and 'fantasy' this time had gone too far. In 2001 Frédéric Bonnaud saw Ozon as having attained the status of that most valued commodity in French cinema, a 'bankable auteur'.[20] Yet his roller-coaster relationship with critics and audiences shows that his love of experiment, or of gratuitous provocation depending on your point of view, still places him in a precarious position. But the fact remains that he has in just 20 years produced an unparalleled, original body of work, in turn fun, outrageous, moving and thought-provoking, but certainly never dull.

Biography

François Ozon was born in November 1967 in Paris. He studied there, attending Paris I university and the FEMIS film school.

Notes

1 François Ozon, interview with Eithne O'Neill, *Positif* 553, March 2007, p. 25.
2 Pascal Mérigeau, 'Et vole le bébé!', *Le Nouvel observateur*, No. 2309, 5 February 2009 [no page number].
3 François Ozon, interview with Eithne O'Neill, *Positif* 553, March 2007, p. 23.
4 François Ozon, in *Positif* 492, February 2002, cited in Alain Brassart, *L'Homosexualité dans le cinéma français* (Paris: Le Nouveau monde, 2007), p. 197.
5 Mark Hain, 'Explicit Ambiguity: Sexual Identity, Hitchcockian Criticism, and the Films of François Ozon', *Quarterly Review of Film and Video*, No. 24, 2007, pp. 279–80.
6 Max Cavitch, 'Sex after death: François Ozon's libidinal invasions', *Screen*, No. 48:3, Autumn 2007, p. 324.
7 Philippe Rouyer and Claire Vassé, 'François Ozon, La vérité des corps', *Positif*, No. 521/522, July/August 2004, p. 41.
8 Philippe Rouyer and Claire Vassé, 'François Ozon, La vérité des corps', *Positif*, No. 521/522, July/August 2004, p. 45.

9 Mark Hain, 'Explicit Ambiguity: Sexual Identity, Hitchcockian Criticism, and the Films of François Ozon', *Quarterly Review of Film and Video*, No. 24, 2007, p. 287.

10 Cited in Richard Falcon, 'Reality is too shocking', *Sight and Sound*, No. 18:9, January 1999, p. 11.

11 Andrew Asibong, 'Meat, Murder, Metamorphosis: The Transformational Ethics of François Ozon', *French Studies*, Vol. LIX, No. 2, p. 207.

12 Frédéric Bonnaud, 'François Ozon: Wannabe Auteur Makes Good', *Film Comment*, vol. 37, no. 4, July–August 2001, p. 53.

13 Alain Brassart, *L'Homosexualité dans le cinéma français* (Paris: Le Nouveau monde, 2007), p. 196.

14 Robert Sklar, 'Sex, Violence, and Power in the Family: An Interview with François Ozon', *Cineaste*, Fall 2005, p. 48.

15 Diana Diamond, 'Loss, Mourning and Desire in Midlife, François Ozon's *Under the Sand* and *Swimming Pool*', in Andrea Sabbadini (ed.), *The Couch and the Silver Screen, Psychoanalytical Reflections on European Cinema* (Taylor & Francis, 2007), pp. 145–59.

16 François Ozon, in Sheila Johnston, 'Death every day', *Sight and Sound*, No. 11:4, April 2001, p. 13.

17 François Ozon, quoted in Thibault Schilt, 'François Ozon', *Sensesofcinema*, http://archive.sensesofcinema.com/contents/directors/04/ozon.html#16

18 Lucille Cairns, *Sapphism on Screen in French and Francophone Cinema* (Edinburgh: Edinburgh University Press, 2006).

19 Catherine Deneuve, in 'L'Arbre de Noël d'Ozon', *Libération*, February 2002.

20 Frédéric Bonnaud, 'François Ozon: Wannabe Auteur Makes Good', *Film Comment*, vol. 37, no. 4, July–August 2001, p. 53.

Filmography

Short films

Photo de famille (1988)
Les Doigts dans le ventre (1988)
Mes parents un jour d'été (1990)
Une goutte de sang (1991)
Peau contre peau (1991)
Le Trou madame (1991)
Deux plus un (1991)
Thomas reconstitué (1992)
Victor (1993)
Une rose entre nous (1994)
Action vérité/Truth or Dare (1994)
La Petite mort (1995)
Jospin s'éclaire (1995)
Une robe d'été/A Summer Dress (1996)
L'Homme idéal (1996)
Regarde la mer (1997)
Scènes de lit (1998)

X2000 (1998)
Un lever de rideau/A Curtain Raiser (2006)

Feature films

Sitcom (1998)
Les Amants criminels/Criminal Lovers (1999)
Gouttes d'eau sur pierres brûlantes/Water Drops on Burning Rocks (2000)
Sous le sable/Under the Sand (2000)
8 femmes/8 Women (2002)
Swimming Pool (2003)
5x2/Five Times Two (2004)
Le Temps qui reste/Time to Leave (2005)
Angel (2007)
Ricky (2009)

PARK CHAN-WOOK

By Anne Ciecko and Hunju Lee

With Park Chan-wook's long-planned vampire feature *Thirst* (2009), one of South Korean cinema's foremost stylists recovered a top spot at the domestic box-office while polarising critics, marking another round of daring cinematic viscerality. At this stage in his career, a Park Chan-wook film fuses name-recognition appeal with bizarrely inventive aesthetic exploration. *Thirst* focuses on a priest played by Song Kang-ho who is transformed into a vampire after being infected by a deadly virus as a result of a medical experiment, subsequently becoming sexually entangled with his best friend's wife. In addition to displaying Park's versatility and ongoing risk-taking, the movie (shot in Korea and Australia) represented a new international co-production relationship as the first Korean film to be co-financed from the pre-production stage by a Hollywood major studio, Universal Pictures, in partnership with the distributor Focus Features and Korea's leading studio CJ Entertainment. *Thirst* also continues a pattern of boundary-pushing – through its use of sexual imagery, Catholic religious icon-ography, nudity (especially male full frontal), and a provocative (and censored) ad campaign including the teaser trailer and movie poster. *Thirst* shared the 2009 Cannes Film Festival Jury Prize, a controversial choice, and Park's second Cannes win. Previously, *Old Boy* took the Grand Prix in 2003, with the jury panel famously headed that year by Quentin Tarantino. Since that time, Park has been continually courted by Hollywood, yet continues to chase his dream projects on his own terms. His work is highly personal, featuring complex narratives, an overt play with genre elements coupled with resistance to generic classification, excessively over-the-top brio – all leading to the ubiquitous possibility of alienation of audiences and/or critics.

Park is one of the most prominent Korean filmmakers of his generation, helping to dynamize the film industry and the reputation of Korean cinema at home and abroad, at a time when Korean films have fared well domestically (with record market shares) and internationally, garnering critical praise and festival successes. He has been a vocal proponent for the maintenance of a screen quota ensuring homegrown films are played in Korean theatres. For the past decade, he has been a central figure in the New Korean Cinema and the global *hanryu*, or Korean Wave, starting with his stunning third feature *Joint Security Area* (2000) which became Korea's (then) most expensive production and all-time box-office record-holder, helping to put contemporary Korean cinema in the international spotlight. A suspenseful and deftly crafted military thriller with shades of poignant dark humour set at the 38th Parallel in the village of Panmunjom at the 'Bridge of No Return', *Joint Security Area* is an adaptation of Park Sang-yun's novel *DMZ* about a tragic shooting involving four North and South Korean soldiers who, it is revealed, had become unlikely friends. The film expanded the cinematic image repertoire of the divided peninsula through humanising images of North Koreans (with a central role played by popular actor Song Kang-ho), *Rashomon*-like storytelling with multiple flashbacks from contradictory points-of-view (these framed by a military investigation), and extraordinary cinematography with the first Korean use of Super-35 film format, a Hollywood standard.[1] Park's filmmaking – especially his 'Vengeance Trilogy' – has earned a prominent place in the pantheon of the so-called Asian 'Extreme Cinema', a transdiscursive branding term used by critics, distributors and exhibitors, and cult fans for films by directors such as Japan's Takashi Miike, Hideo Nakata, 'Beat' Takeshi Kitano, and the late Kinji Fukasaku, the Hong Kong-born Pang brothers, and fellow Korean directors Kim Ki-duk and Kim Ji-woon.[2]

Park has an innate affinity for visual expression, narrative structure, and filmic exploration of human psychology – although it took years for his unique talents to be recognized. Park has described Hitchcock's *Vertigo* as the movie that catalysed his desire to become a filmmaker, noting as other influences the writers Sophocles, Shakespeare, Kafka, Dostoevsky, Balzac, Zola, Stendhal, Austin, Philip K. Dick,

Roger Zelazny and Kurt Vonnegut.[3] Fittingly, his films are filled with existentially stimulating elements: doubled identities and trans-formations, abjection and bodily violence, tragedy and heroism, intense emotionalism and romanticism, crime and punishment (and atonement), incarceration and isolation, sympathy and guilt, black humour and red colour motifs, absurd comedy and witty dialogue, ecstatic horror and obsessive fantasy. In interviews Park additionally cites the following favourite directors: Don Siegel (especially *The Killers* with Lee Marvin[4]), Robert Aldrich, Sam Fuller, Monte Hellman and other American 'B' film directors, Ingmar Bergman and Roman Polanski, and, emphatically, Kim Ki-young, the Korean director who made the 1960 classic shocker *The Housemaid* and its remake *The Woman of Fire '82*.[5] (A proponent for wider acknowledgement of the contributions of Korean filmmakers, Park has also asserted that if the underrecognised Kim was making films today, he would be considered one of the greatest directors in the world.[6]) Park's own films (particularly their postmodern nonlinear narratives, elements of violence, and genre pastiche) have been compared with the work of fellow contemporary directors Quentin Tarantino, the filmmaker whose endorsement helped solidify his international profile as an auteur, David Fincher and Christopher Nolan. However, there was a long gestation period before Park's directorial skills had the opportunity to be fully born.

Park did not have formal training as a filmmaker; he learned his craft on film sets. After graduation from college, Park worked as an assistant director on films by Yu Yeong-Jin (*Kkamdong*, 1988) and Kwak Jae-yong (*Watercolor Painting on a Rainy Day*, 1989) before writing and directing his own first feature in 1992, a critically dis-paraged gangster melodrama with abysmal box office receipts. *The Moon is … the Sun's Dream* is a noir-ish film about two brothers who live totally different lives: Ha-young, a photographer trained in France, and his younger brother, Moo-hoon, a junior gangster. Moo-hoon and his boss's moll Eeun-ju run away together after stealing money from the boss, but are caught and Eeun-ju is sent to a whorehouse. Rescued by Moo-hoon and hidden in Ha-Young's studio, a love triangle ensues. Finally, Moo-Hoon is killed by his boss's men after murdering his boss, and Eeun-Ju becomes a successful model with Ha-Young's support.

The Moon is … the Sun's Dream features the type of meticulous mise-en-scène displayed in Park's later films. The film also experi-ments with destabilising use of music and cinematography, unsettling spectators' identification with characters. However it is marred by an incoherent narrative, the male protagonist's awkward performance (Lee Seung-chul, a Korean pop music idol at the time), and exaggerated theatrical narration. In a Korean newspaper, Park essentially disowned his earliest work, asserting that if a DVD collection for all films he had made to date was produced, he would want to dispose of the first and second ones, *The Moon is … the Sun's Dream* and *Saminjo* (aka *Trio*).[7] *The Moon is … the Sun's Dream* was reportedly not the film Park wanted to make for his debut; he couldn't get his desired project to the production stage because the political story about the mysterious murder of a union buster confronted early 1990s Korean censorship on ideological grounds. Discouraged by his experiences, Park almost gave up working as a director, and didn't make another film for five years.

The crime caper comedy *Saminjo* (1997; aka *Trio*) was also largely ignored by audiences. Yet the ways in which *Saminjo* weaves social criticism and black comedy (as well as mixing road movie and action conventions) demonstrates genealogical stylistic links with his later films, especially anticipating his Vengeance Trilogy, for which it can be seen as precursor. *Saminjo* tells the story of three accidentally-linked people, two men and a woman, who solve their problems in socially unacceptable ways, collectively hatching a plot to rob a bank: Han, a poor saxophone player in a cabaret who has had to sell his instrument; Moon, the ex-gunman who stole his boss's weapon; and Maria, who dreamed of becoming a nun but now works as a waitress. She had a daughter (now missing), after being raped by her father. *Saminjo* includes the use of outrageously mismatched humour at grim moments which is now considered one of Park's trademarks, and demonstrates the director's avowed affinity with the work of B-movie directors. (For example, in a scene in *Sympathy for Mr. Vengeance*, a drowned daughter appears to her grieving father and makes a joke about her tragic death, saying, 'Daddy, you should have given me swimming lessons sooner'.) *Saminjo* is a kind of satire about the economic structure and family violence in 1990s Korea. In spite of the poor box-office record and critical reviews, the producer Sim Jae-Myung discovered Park's talents through this film and asked him to direct the big-budget *JSA*.[8]

An exemplar of the new Korean blockbuster, *Joint Security Area* (2000) explores the mystery of the death of two North Koreans at the De-Militarized Zone, with an investigation of the incident by a Swiss military officer (daughter of a Swiss mother and a Korean expatriate father who turns out to have been North Korean) in which contradictory depositions of the surviving North and South Korean soldiers do not equate with the number of bullets fired. A story of the development of an unlikely friendship emerges which resonated with South Korean public sentiment about brotherhood and desire for reunification, while also fearing the threat of possible violence – themes also explored in other contemporary Korean blockbusters that explosively invigorated the local industry and national cinematic pride at a time of economic downturn, including the espionage actioner *Shiri* (Kang Je-kyu, 1999).

During the years before he attained a high profile reputation as a filmmaker in Korea and internationally, Park wrote criticism (attaining a formidable reputation as a critic in print and on television), worked as a video store clerk, and continued his film industry apprenticeship. While trying to pique producers' interest in his projects, he made a short film called *Simpan* (*Judgment*, 1999) with plot twists and themes anticipating his trilogy. A family attempts to identify a young woman's body after an earthquake (and a government compensation agreement) and the mortician recognises her as his own daughter; both daughters had run away from their respective parents years before. Park formed a screenwriting collaboration with director/ actor/musician/writer Lee Moo-yeong who shares writing credits on *JSA* and 2002's *Sympathy for Mr. Vengeance*. Park also scripted – although he declined to direct the long-in-development *The Anarchist* (2000 Yu Yong-sik), an ambitious action film set in Japan-occupied Shanghai in the 1920s that was the first Chinese/Korean co-production and shot entirely in China; and he co-wrote Lee's directorial debut *The Humanist* (2001).

Park's critical and cult reputation solidified with his graphically violent sequence of films *Sympathy for Mr. Vengeance* (2002), *Old Boy* (2003) and *Lady Vengeance* (2005). His articulate discussion of the evolution of the trilogy in interviews, the distribution of the three films packaged as a boxed set in UK company Tartan's Asia Extreme catalogue (which also includes other titles representing extreme action, passion and horror), and serious examinations of his work by Korean and international film critics and theorists are among the many factors that have contributed to his auteur profile. As Korean critic Kim Young-jin has asserted, Park Chan-wook 'accepts genre convention without losing his authorial tension', and his work is dynamically fueled by 'the irony of negativity gathered from a secessionist approach toward goal-oriented narrative'.[9] Like *Thirst* and *JSA*, *Sympathy for Mr. Vengeance* features a central performance by Song Kang-ho. Ryu, a deaf-mute, seeks to acquire a kidney for his ailing sister and is scammed by a gang of organ traffickers. A spiralling cycle of violence ensues after Ryu and his girlfriend kidnap the daughter of a wealthy industrialist (played by Song) and the girl is accidentally killed.

As Park has evolved as a filmmaker, he has developed his own actors' repertory with roles (often very challenging) for Song, Shin Ha-kyun, Choi Min-sik, Lee Young-ae, and Kang Hye-jeong. Park also co-founded Korea's first in-house production company, Egg Films, with fellow directors Bae Chang-ho, Kwak Jae-yong, Lee Young-jae and Lee Mu-young.[10] As part of this group, he wrote *A Bizarre Love Triangle* (2002), directed by Lee. Park also participated in the National Human Rights Commission of Korea-produced omnibus *If You Were Me* (2003) with the film 'N.E.P.A.L'. (acronym for 'Never Ending Peace And Love') based on the true story of Chandra Gurung, a migrant labourer who ends up in a mental hospital for six years when she is mistakenly diagnosed as schizophrenic; she looks Korean and no one understands her tribal language.

The trope of incarceration recurs in Park's brilliant breakthrough *Old Boy* which met with both critical acclaim and commercial success. Based on a Japanese manga by Nobuaki Minegishi and Garon Tsuchiya, *Old Boy* stars Choi Min-sik as Oh Dae-su, imprisoned for fifteen years without understanding the motivation of his captor, who seeks an explanation and revenge upon his release. 'I want to tell you my story', Oh Dae-su insists as he grabs tight hold of the necktie of a suicidal man leaning back precariously from the top of a building in the very first scene of the film. Likewise the film metaphorically grabs its viewer by the throat from its opening images. Cinematography and editing contribute to the sense of a distinctive consolidated Park Chan-wook style, and collaborations with cinematographer Chung Chung-hoon and film editor Kim Sang-beom on *Old Boy* and multiple other Park-helmed films help to achieve this.

While Park is a decidedly Korean director at a time of national pride in the Korean film industry, *Old Boy*'s manga roots underscore a transnational and pan-Asian dimension to his filmmaking, further explored via Park's contribution to the *Three … Extremes* omnibus (together with Fruit Chan from Hong Kong and Takashi Miike from Japan, a co-productive initiative produced by the Hong Kong company Applause Pictures). Park's 'Cut' is an ironically self-reflexive film about a director making a vampire movie who is captured and tortured by a homicidal 'fan'. The film set is designed to look like his own lavish home, and he carries the music soundtrack through different locations – from the set to his car and his home. The intruder, a poor extra who was in five of the director's films, grotesquely parallels the filmmaker's work, with the cut referring to the director's god-like authority and extreme acts of reel/real violence and confession. The diegetic film director's morality is tested when he is forced to make the choice between saving his pianist wife's fingers or killing a child (a boy dressed as a girl who is revealed to be the intruder's son), which turns out to be another meta-layered scenario of atonement.

The complex drama of family is again at the crux of *Lady Vengeance*, where for the first time he centres the narrative around a strong female character. Lee Geum-ja (played by *hanryu* superstar Lee Young-Ae) is a seemingly reformed and beatific female prisoner who was falsely convicted and imprisoned for a crime she did not commit, the murder of a schoolboy, so that she could save the life of her infant daughter. Lee Geum-ja, upon her release, reunites with her daughter (who had been adopted by an Australian couple) and enlists a network of allies and parents of child-victims to enact a vigilante plan of revenge against the mass murderer who framed her (sadistic schoolteacher Mr. Baek, played by Choi Min-sik). The sumptuous mise-en-scène is again symbolically sensitive to colour. Post-prison, the once-demure Geum-ja reinvents herself as an icy-seeming, red eyeshadow and lipstick-wearing, high heel-donning, cigarette smoking femme fatale. She is employed as a baker (an expertise honed in prison) who crafts exquisite desserts such as the red and white cake she serves to the parents post-execution of Mr. Baek, and a white confection she offers to her daughter at the end of the film (paralleling the Christmas tofu she is gifted by Christian well-wishers upon release from prison) with the advice to remain innocent; she buries her own face in the cake as her daughter embraces her amidst the falling snow.

Park's next feature, *I'm a Cyborg, But That's OK*, departs from the mordant imagry of the trilogy with an arguably hopeful, surreal comedy romance that nevertheless weaves through some familiar stylistic threads, tropes of human 'monsters' and transgression of societal norms with images of hyper-stylised techno-violence. A waif-like young woman in a mental institution, Cha Young-goon, communicates with vending machines and fluorescent lights and believes she is a robot. Flashback sequences elliptically reveal her past (a trauma regarding her beloved grandmother with a fetish for radishes and listening to the radio and familial intolerance for her behaviours, and an empathic breakdown in a transistor assembly plant where she slices her wrist and attempts to insert wires) and the backgrounds of her fellow patients, including a handsome (but mask-wearing) klepto-maniac and electronics expert Park Il-soon (played by popstar Rain). Young-goon licks batteries to 'recharge', planning Terminator-like vengeance on the medical staff in the institution 'white 'uns' (played out in elaborate fantasy sequences where bullets shoot from her fingers) – who symbolically represent the people who took away her Grandma, and steadfastly refuses to eat. Park Il-soon, who falls in love with her, feeds her fantasies while also developing a plan to bring her back from the verge of starvation. While largely dismissed by critics and audiences as a curious trifle, *I'm a Cyborg, But That's OK* can be viewed as a redemptive interventionist love story in a fatalistic cinematic universe, and a colourful gem in Park's impressively sparkling, but sometimes blindingly and numbingly intense, oeuvre. In addition to his own films *I'm a Cyborg, But That's OK* and *Thirst*, Park has also nurtured a new generation of Korean filmmakers, serving as producer and co-screenwriter with female director Lee Kyoung-mi's debut *Crush and Blush* (2008), a darkly comic feature about an outcast female high school teacher. Adding to the intertextual fun, he also had a cameo walk-on role, together with fellow Korean blockbuster director Bong Joon-ho. Park is also producing Bong's latest film, and seems certain to continue making distinctive films that engage, and sometimes even enrage, viewers' minds, emotions and senses.

Biography

Born in 1963 in the city of Jecheon in North Chungcheong province, South Korea, Park Chan-wook earned a Philosophy degree from Sogang University, a Catholic institution in Seoul where he initially intended to become an art critic, and where he began to write film reviews and founded a film club. He has directed eight features to date, and has also worked as a screenwriter, producer and film critic.

Notes

1 James Mudge, 'Park Chan Wook's Aesthetics of Violence', *YumCha! Asian Emtertainment Reviews and Features*, http://www.yesasia.com/us/yumcha/park-chan-wooks-aesthetics-of-violence/0-0-0-arid.56-en/featured-article.html

2 Chi Yun-Shin, 'Art of Branding: Tartan "Asia Extreme Films"', *Jump Cut* 50 (Spring 2008).

3 Mark Russell, 'Park Chan-Wook, Filmmaker', *The Hollywood Reporter* May 24, 2004, http://www.hollywoodreporter.com/hr/search/article_display.jsp?vnu_content_id=1000552276

4 Park Chan Wook Q&A, *Time Out London* February 9, 2006, http://www.timeout.com/film/news/916/

5 Q&A: Park Chan Wook, *The Hollywood Reporter* May 13, 2009, http://www.hollywoodreporter.com/hr/content_display/features/interviews_profiles/e3i641dc7e691e8df844b116cd4ec7235fd

6 Carl Davis, 'Old Boy Director Disses Vengeance, Looks Toward Upcoming Cyborg-Teen Comedy', mtv.com August 22, 2005, http://www.mtv.com/movies/news/articles/1508066/08222005/story.jhtml
7 Yoo Jae-Suck, 'Do you Know the forgotten debut films of the famous filmmakers?', *Chosun.com*, April 18, 2009, http://news.chosun.com/site/data/html_dir/2009/04/17/2009041701249.html (Korean Source).
8 'An Interview with Park Chan-Wook, "Hitchcock changed my life"', *HanKyerye*, May 27, 2004, http://news.naver.com/main/read.nhn?mode=LSD&mid=sec&sid1=106&oid=028&aid=0000061311 (Korean Source).
9 Kim Young-jin, *Park Chan-wook* [Korean Film Directors series], trans. Colin A. Mouat (Korean Film Council [KOFIC], 2007), p. 69.
10 Darcey Paquet, 'Five Korean directors team to form Egg Films', *Screendaily.com* 28 October 2001, http://www.screendaily.com/five-korean-directors-team-to-form-egg-films/407325.article

Filmography

The Moon is ... the Sun's Dream (1992)
Saminjo (1997)
Simpan (*Judgement*, 1999)
JSA: Joint Security Area (2000)
Sympathy for Mr. Vengeance (2002)
If You Were Me (2003) segment: 'N.E.P.A.L'. ('Never Ending Peace and Love')
Old Boy (2003)
'Cut' (2004) segment: *Three ... Extremes*
Lady Vengeance (2005)
I'm a Cyborg, But That's OK (2006)
Thirst (2009)

Further reading

Anne Ciecko, 'Ways to Sink the *Titanic*: Contemporary Box-Office Successes in the Philippines, Thailand, and South Korea', *Tamkang Review* Vol. XXXIII No.2 (Winter 2002): pp. 1–29.
Kim Kyung Hun, ' "Tell the Kitchen That There's Too Much *Buchu* in the Dumpling": Reading Park Chan-wook's "Unknowable" Old Boy', *Korean Journal* (Spring 2006): pp. 84–108.
Hyangjin Lee, 'South Korea: Film on the Global Stage', *Contemporary Asian Cinema: Popular Culture in a Global Frame*, ed. Anne Ciecko (Berg, 2006), pp. 182–92.
Nikki J.Y. Lee, 'Salute to Mr. Vengeance!: The Making of a Transnational Auteur Park Chan Wook', *East Asian Cinemas: Exploring Transnational Connections on Film*, eds Leon Hunt and Leung Wing-Fai (L.B. Taurus, 2008), p. 203–19.
Jonathan Romney, 'Sympathy for the Devil', *Artforum International* 44.9 (May 2006): pp. 270 (8).
Julian Stringer, ed., *Movie Blockbusters* (Routledge, 2003).

B.M. Yecies and D. Chambers, 'Double Take on Vengeance: Journey Through the Syncopatic Editing Style of *Sympathy for Mr. Vengeance*', *New Korean Cinema Series* Vol.10 (Seoul: Yonsei Institute of Media Arts, 2006), pp. 135–58.

SALLY POTTER

By Anne Ciecko

As one of the foremost woman directors and formally experimental cinematic innovators to have emerged in the UK in the last thirty-plus years, Sally Potter can be viewed as a British, European and global filmmaker; her work marks a fascinating career trajectory inside and out of Britain, in and around the medium of film.

The films she has made in the new millennium have challenged audiences and critics alike; and her originality of voice is undeniable regardless of the scale of her projects, from excessively dressed-up to radically stripped-down. At one end of the spectrum, a British–French co-production with reportedly the biggest budget for a European woman filmmaker, *The Man Who Cried* (2000), continued to imagine the feature film as a composite artwork with a strong emphasis on music, meticulous production design and lavish cinematography (the late Sasha Vierny's final work), original screen-writing by Potter, and an international cast and characters (including Hollywood actors Christina Ricci and Johnny Depp). Set in Europe during the 1930s, the melodrama centres around the story of a displaced young Jewish woman and her relationships with a Romany Gypsy man, a Russian dancer and an Italian opera singer. While some questioned aspects of its execution, *The Man Who Cried* manages to speak powerfully to questions of racial/ethnic oppression, exile and diaspora.

In contrast, *Yes* (2004) had a decidedly lower budget and exhibits more direct intimacy – and was famously scripted by Potter in iambic pentameter verse. Illustrative of Potter's need to make 'personal, poetic and political' films,[1] *Yes* is a powerful post-911 intellectual and erotic meditation on the state of the world through a cross-cultural, cross-ethnic, cross-class love story starring Joan Allen as 'She', a middle-aged Northern Ireland-born American-raised biologist living in London in a sterile marriage with an adulterous husband, and Simon Abkarian as 'He', a Lebanese refugee trained as a doctor who works in a restaurant kitchen. *Yes* mixes eclectic cinematography (shot on Super-16 film by Alexei Rodionov with unusual camera movements and angles, a variety of lenses, slowed and elliptically speeded motion) and diverse music (including original compositions Potter co-created with longtime collaborator Fred Frith). The narrative unfolds with the affair and the rhythms of dialogue (sometimes via characters' confessional interior monologues, and interspersed with extended direct address monologues by a housekeeper played by Shirley Henderson) that reveals their backgrounds and perspectives about the world, their embrace of life, and the limits and possibilities of human understanding. Adding another layer of extra-textual commentary, Potter began a film diary weblog as she travelled the world with *Yes*, and she continues to use its latest incarnation as a forum for discussing ideas about the art of filmmaking.

Most recently, Potter's *Rage* is a satirical critique of the fashion industry and a murder mystery, framed as a cellphone documentary made by a kid as a school project. The film has been critically discussed as an example of the new 'naked', 'poor', 'barefoot', or 'kitchen table' cinema (the first a term coined by a Reuters journalist covering the film at its Berlin premiere, the rest of them terms used by Potter herself) – a 'no-waste' film that doesn't flaunt its (modest) budget and that has been picked up for multi-territory multi-platform release including broadband and mobile phone, in addition to traditional theatrical exhibition.[2] A UK–US co-production shot in New York and London with British and American actors (including Jude Law as a transsexual supermodel), *Rage* consists only of a sequence of short interviews/monologues. Ironically it shares the title and fits the description of the film Sally Potter's director character (played by Potter herself) attempted and failed to make in her previous film, *The Tango Lesson*.

The Tango Lesson (1997) self-reflexively addresses issues of internationalisation and interdisciplinarity. What does it mean to be a multi-tasking woman filmmaker in contemporary Britain? A film about making a film, created in the wake of her breakthrough art-house hit *Orlando*, *The Tango Lesson* is written, produced and performed (acted/danced/sung) by Potter. It chronicles the story of a woman director who, while writing a screenplay for a would-be Hollywood movie, ends up taking tango lessons and making a very different film about the process. As the director enacts the professional and personal dance of an independent contemporary woman filmmaker, learning to tango becomes an apt metaphor. Shot in Buenos Aires, Paris and London – with funding from Argentina, France, Japan, Germany, the Netherlands and the United Kingdom (including the Arts Council of England and the European Co-Production Fund) – *The Tango Lesson* is both a British film and a truly international co-production. Yet at the same time it is also an exemplar of independent filmmaking by a woman; the development of Sally Potter's multifaceted career connects with the experiences of other woman filmmakers in the UK, and the narrative of the emergence of contemporary 'British' cinema.

The history of British cinema as it is currently written gives limited attention to woman feature filmmakers (with Muriel Box and Wendy Toye as rare exceptions, both of whom successfully directed studio feature films in the 1950s and 1960s).[3] An increasing number of English, Irish, Welsh and Scottish woman directors have emerged in the past four decades.[4] British women have had the opportunity to helm films largely as a result of workshops, training programmes and collaborative efforts with other makers; television opportunities for feature film production; advocacy organisations such as Women in Film and Television UK; and funding and production schemes within the British Film Institute (in the 1990s) and elsewhere. Contemporary television and filmmaking in Britain remain profoundly interlinked. Women in Britain have traditionally found work within the television industry, although the glass ceiling has restricted directorial positions within certain genres and upper-level administration; documentary as a filmic/televisual genre has historically proven to be one space where women have been able to make relative inroads within the industry and stay active as filmmakers.[5]

Sally Potter's career in film, television and dance/music performance has been about claiming the tools of representation and blurring genre boundaries. Potter began her career as a filmmaker after leaving school at the age of 16. Her training-ground was the London Film-makers' Co-op, which provided support for the making of experimental film, distribution and exhibition opportunities for women's films. At the Co-op Potter made what she has called mostly short 'abstract visual poems'.[6]

With initiatives led by women's movements in the 1970s and the Workshop Declaration (made between the trade union ACTT, the British Film Institute and Channel 4 television) in the 1980s, woman filmmakers also participated in the creation of production units such as Four Corners Film Workshop, London Women's Centre/WAVES (Women's Audio Visual Education Scheme), WITCH (Women's Independent Cinema House) in Liverpool, the Leeds Animation Workshop, Sheffield Independent Film and Television (formerly the Sheffield Film Co-op), Derry Film and Video, and Women's Media Resource Project (London). Woman feature filmmakers also emerged out of the so-called black British collectives such as Ceddo, Sankofa, and Black Audio Film Collective. The workshop movement had its roots in collective practice and, often feminist politics.[7] These alternative modes of production also allowed for the possibility of expression of diverse, culturally marginalised British voices, and the films which were produced often actively engaged with discourses of hybrid identities, employing new aesthetic models, different from Hollywood and the European art cinema. Throughout the 1970s, more British college and polytechnic film courses were developed, and women have continued to graduate from the National Film School. British women also established women's film distribution organisations such as London Women's Film Group, Circles, Cinema of Women, and more recently, Cinenova (Europe's only women's film distributor which, like its sister organisation Women make Movies in the United States, currently distributes some of Sally Potter's work). Film festival activities also promoted the work of woman filmmakers in Britain, and have assisted in the rewriting of the history of British cinema.[8] In 1972, Laura Mulvey, Claire Johnston and Lynda Miles co-organised the landmark Women's Event at the Edinburgh Film Festival, the first time a collection of films by women had been showcased at a major exhibition venue in the UK. The same year, the influential London Women's Film Group, a production and advocacy organisation, was formed.

Throughout the 1980s and 1990s, woman programmers did important work in exposing audiences to films by British woman directors. For example, Sally Potter was represented in Sheila Whitaker's series 'A Century of Women's Film-Making' at the National Film Theatre in London in 1996–97. *Orlando* was also on the roster in a 1995 season of films by women and a documentary film called 'Reel Women' televised on Channel 4. (However, *Orlando* was the only British feature included, and Potter and Gurinder Chadha were the only British directors interviewed in the 'Reel Women' documentary.) Women in Film and Television UK was established in the early 1980s as a non-profit support organisation for women in the film and television industry, and Cinewomen was established in 1990s to raise the profile of women working in film, video and television, and hosted Britain's longest running annual women's film festival. Sally Potter has been widely celebrated as a model for independent filmmaking at women's film festivals in the UK and internationally.

Following her early work with the London Film Co-op, Potter trained as an interdisciplinary performance artist, dancer and musician. During the 1970s, she toured with the Limited Dance Company and the Feminist Improvisation Group. (There are some interesting parallels between Potter and American avant-garde director Yvonne Rainer *vis-à-vis* the connection between dance performance and film.) With her experimental film *Thriller*, funded by the Arts Council of Great Britain, Potter attempts to subvert the opera *La Bohème*, telling the story from Mimi's point of view – foregrounding issues of gender and race (with Mimi played by black actress Collette Laffont, who stars with dancer Rose English), deconstructing the popular Hollywood genre of film noir (with references to Hitchcock) and positioning the heroine as a detective. *Thriller* became a catalytic text for nascent feminist film theory which began to evolve in the 1970s, and which celebrated counter-cinematic/avant-garde/experimental alternatives to the dominant filmmaking paradigm. British theorist and film and video artist Laura Mulvey's influential essay, 'Visual Pleasure and the Narrative Cinema', offered a re-evaluation of the classical Hollywood paradigms of representation of the female body.[9] Potter's film work (and Mulvey's own) extends this deconstruction to the practice of filmmaking. Feminist film theorists – including Doane, Fischer, Kuhn, Kaplan, Cook, Mellencamp and others – have argued that Potter's *Thriller*, together with films like Laura Mulvey and Peter Wollen's *Riddles of the Sphinx*, provides a new model for feminist filmmaking which radically reinscribes the female body.[10] The subsequent feature films written and directed by Potter, while still displaying a feminist politics and commenting on gender roles, are more cohesive, viewer-friendly and 'mainstream' in narrative terms.

All of Potter's films can arguably be seen as meta-commentaries on the role of the (female) film story-teller, consistently challenging formal narrative strategies and genres, while also aiming for increasingly accessible visual and auditory pleasure in the synthesis – or rather, choreography – of image and sound. Such an evolution is demonstrated in Potter's short fanciful film *The London Story*, a spy story as a dance musical.

Woman producers have been instrumental in developing film and television projects and partnerships for women in Britain, as in the film collaborations of Philippa Giles (producer), Beeban Kidron (director) and Jeannette Winterson (writer), with such projects as the acclaimed *Oranges Are Not the Only Fruit*, a three-part BBC television film, and the less fortunate *Great Moments in Aviation*. Potter has worked as producer/director/writer; she founded and developed a production company with Christopher Sheppard called Adventure Pictures, which produced her features *Orlando*, *The Tango Lesson*, *The Man Who Cried*, *Yes*, and *Rage*. Like many other woman filmmakers, Potter has used television as a forum for non-feature work, especially documentary – including the four-part Channel 4 series on emotions and cinematic representations, *Tears, Laughter, Fear, and Rage*, produced by Sara Radcliffe (Working Title Productions). Potter's series uses interviews with a wide range of personalities and film-clips from mostly British films to explore the nature of human affect, and to find a space for emotions in the personal and collective British consciousness. Potter's work has consistently created its own spaces in terms of funding and film form (genre, visual style, modes of performance, etc.). The Channel 4 documentary, *I Am Ox, I Am Horse, I Am Man, I Am Woman*, produced by Adventure Pictures and directed by Potter, examines some of the absent histories of the post-Soviet film industry uncovered by Potter during her attempts to find locations and funds for her epic feature *Orlando* – the director's own struggle to gain industrial support for feature filmmaking and to find her own place within a national cinema. This documentary chronicles the labours of women within the Soviet film industry; images of women on film also become a way to examine the history of women in the Soviet Union.

While her peers Beeban Kidron and Antonia Bird managed with varying degrees of success to move between commercial Hollywood (*To Wong Foo, Mad Love*) and BBC-funded British films (*Great Moments in Aviation, Priest*), through the 1990s, Potter consistently avoided the lure of Hollywood and the mainstream, and her British/international features found theatrical life in the arthouse rather than the multiplex. Potter's first feature, a genre-bending revisionist twist on the musical *The Gold Diggers*, was financed by the British Film Institute, shot in Iceland and London (another multinational production in terms of location), and had an all-woman cast and crew, including star Julie Christie and independent filmmaker Babette Mangote as cinematographer. It was more visually and narratively experimental than her later feature films and was not generally well received. *The Gold Diggers*, an interesting remake and revision of Busby Berkeley's Warner Brothers musical *Gold Diggers of 1933*, reached limited audiences but deserves critical attention for its attempts to bridge the gap between theoretical investigations and artistic practices. During the Thatcher era in Britain (1979–90), woman filmmakers such as Lezli-An Barrett (*Business as Usual*, 1987) and Jan Worth (*Doll's Eye*, 1982) made first features informed by overtly feminist sensibilities, highly critical of socio-economic issues which impact upon women's lives and labour. Neither Barrett nor Worth has to date made a follow-up feature, while after *The Gold Diggers* Potter was considered too risky by potential financiers.

Eight years in the making, Potter's second feature, *Orlando*, an adaptation of Virginia Woolf's novel, triumphed on the international art-house circuit. Pam Cook called the film 'a positive way forward for British cinema'[11] and Potter herself has acknowledged that this film enabled her to 'find her feet' as a director.[12] British films of the post-Thatcher 1990s consistently expressed confusion about Britain's status as a nation, and about British identities. Thatcherism resisted European consolidation based on the assertion of cultural and linguistic differences between nations, and an anxiety around the question of sovereignty. However, postmodern geopolitical shifts made the re-imagination of the national cinemas of Europe (and the idea of European Community) a necessity. Potter's adaptation of *Orlando* conducts sophisticated boundary-crossings of nation, gender and genre. In the film, Tilda Swinton plays the title character who changes sex throughout centuries of British history in a wry, winking performance (including moments of direct address to the camera); Quentin Crisp is ironically cast as Queen Elizabeth. The film adaptation of Woolf's fictional biography (itself a *roman-à-clef* of the author's female lover) updates the end of the novel to contemporary England, giving Orlando a daughter who in the film's final scene uses a video camera, a metaphor for a new way of seeing the world in the postmodern electronic age. The lush visual fabric of *Orlando* connects Potter's work with the modernist art films of British contemporaries such as Peter Greenaway and the late Derek Jarman. In production terms, Potter also employs Greenaway's production designers, Jarman's long-time collaborator, actress Tilda Swinton, and costume designer Sandy Powell (who worked with both Jarman and Greenaway). *Orlando* is in dialogue with (bending the rules of) the genre of the British costume/heritage films, which have successfully sold England to the international market.[13] In the introduction to her film script, Potter asks,

> But what of Orlando's change of sex, which provides the most extraordinary narrative twist, and was Virginia Woolf's rich and light way of dealing with issues between men and women? The longer I lived with Orlando and tried to write a character who was both male and female, the more the notion of the essential human being – that a man and woman both are – predominated.[14]

An auteur in the most contemporary sense, Sally Potter has managed to make contemporary British feature films as international co-productions that challenge the conventions of narrative cinema and gendered points of view, with a unique artistic vision.

Biography

Born in 1949, in the UK, Sally Potter has worked primarily in Britain for many years. Her recent films exploit the possibilities of international co-production. As well as directing, writing and performing in films, Potter has worked as a dancer, choreographer and composer.

Notes

1 Potter expresses this necessity in an April 22, 2009 entry on her blog: http://www.sallypotter.com/money (originally published April 16, 2009 as a reply to a post in a forum titled 'Money Money Money', http://www.sallypotter.com/node/209).

2 Peter Knegt, 'Potter's 'Rage' Finds Unique Home', indiewire May 12, 2009 http://www.indiewire.com/article/potters_rage_finds_unique_home/

3 See Wheeler Winston Dixon (ed.) *Reviewing British Cinema, 1990–92: Essays and Interviews*, New York, SUNY, 1994; Justine Ashby, 'Betty Box, 'the Lady in Charge': Negotiating Space for a Female Producer in Postwar Cinema', in Justine Ashby and Andrew Higson (eds) *British Cinema: Past and Present*, London, Routledge, 2000, pp. 166–78.

4 Such filmmakers include: Carine Adler, Andrea Arnold, Lezli-An Barrett, Zelda Barron, Antonia Bird, Maureen Blackwood, Gurinder Chadha, Christine Edzard, Martha Fiennes, Mandy Fletcher, Coki Giedroyc, Margo Harkin, Beeban Kidron, Hettie McDonald, Mary McMurray, Pat Murphy, Ngozi Onwurah, Angela Pope, Lynne Ramsay, Margaret Tait, Conny Templeton and Jan Worth.

5 Anne Ross Muir, *A Woman's Guide to Jobs in Film and Television*, London, Pandora Press, 1987; Antonia Lant, *Blackout: Reinventing Women for Wartime British Cinema*, Princeton, NJ, Princeton University Press, 1991.

6 Sally Potter, *The Tango Lesson*, London, Faber & Faber, 1997, p. viii.

7 Martin Auty and Nick Roddick, *British Cinema Now*, London, BFI Publishing, 1985; Lester Friedman (ed.) *Fires Were Started: British Cinema and Thatcherism*, University of Minnesota Press, 1993; John Caughie and Kevin Rockett, *The Companion to British and Irish Cinema*, London, Cassell/BFI Publishing, 1996.

8 Sheila Whitaker, 'Declarations of Independence', in Martin Auty and Nick Roddick (eds) *British Cinema Now*, London, BFI Publishing, 1985; Sylvia Harvey, 'The "Other Cinema" in Britain: Unfinished Business in Oppositional and Independent Film, 1929–84', in Charles Barr (ed.) *All Our Yesterdays: 90 Years of British Cinema*, London, BFI Publishing, 1986; Charlotte Brunsdon (ed.) *Films for Women*, London, BFI Publishing, 1986.

9 Laura Mulvey, 'Visual Pleasure and Narrative Cinema', *Screen*, vol. 16, no. 3, 1975 (reprinted in Laura Mulvey, *Visual and Other Pleasures*, Bloomington, Indiana University Press, 1989).

10 Mary Ann Doane, 'Women's Stake: Filming the Female Body', in Constance Penley (ed.) *Feminism and Film Theory*, New York, Routledge,

1988; Lucy Fischer, *Shot/Countershot: Film Tradition and Women's Cinema*, Princeton, NJ, Princeton University Press, 1989; Annette Kuhn, *Women's Pictures: Feminism and Cinema*, London, Routledge, 1982; E. Ann Kaplan, *Women and Film: Both Sides of the Camera*, New York, Routledge, 1983; Pam Cook and Philip Dodd (eds) *Women and Film: A Sight and Sound Reader*, London, Scarlet Press, 1994; Patricia Mellencamp, *A Fine Romance: Five Ages of Film Feminism*, Philadelphia, PA, Temple University Press, 1995.
11 Pam Cook and Philip Dodd, *op. cit.*, p. xiii.
12 Sally Potter, *op. cit.*
13 Andrew Higson (ed.) *Dissolving Views: Key Writings on British Cinema*, London, Cassell, 1996; Andrew Higson, *Waving the Flag: Constructing a National Cinema in Britain*, Oxford, Clarendon Press, 1995; Sarah Street, *British National Cinema*, London, Routledge, 1997.
14 Sally Potter, *Orlando*, London, Faber & Faber, 1994, p. xiv.

Filmography

Jerk (*1969*) short
Black and White (1969)
Play (*1970*) short
Thriller (1979) short
The Gold Diggers (1983)
London Story (1987) short
Orlando (1992)
The Tango Lesson (1997)
The Man Who Cried (2000)
Yes (2006)
Rage (2009)

Documentary (television)

Tears, Laughter, Fear, and Rage (1986)
I Am Ox, I Am Horse, I Am Man, I Am Woman (aka *Soviet Women Filmmakers*, 1990)

Expanded cinema (projected film with live performance)

Combines (1970)
Daily (1970)
The Building (1970)
Hors d'oeuvres (1971)

Further reading

Anne Ciecko, 'Transgender, Transgenre, and the Transnational: Sally Potter's *Orlando*', *Velvet Light Trap*, no. 41, 1998, pp. 19–34.

——'Sex, God, Television, Realism and the British Woman Filmmakers', *Journal of Film and Video*, vol. 51, no. 1, 1999, pp. 22–41.

——'Representing the Spaces of Diaspora in Contemporary Films by British Women', *Cinema Journal*, vol. 38, no. 3, 1999, pp. 67–90.

——'Gender, Genre, and the Politics of Representation in Contemporary British Films by Women', Ph.D. dissertation, University of Pittsburgh, PA, 1997.

Catherine Fowler, *Sally Potter* [Contemporary Film Directors series] University of Illinois Press, 2009.

Penny Florence, 'A Conversation with Sally Potter', *Screen*, vol. 34, no. 3, 1993, pp. 274–85.

Kristi McKim, ' "A State of Loving Detachment": Sally Potter's Impassioned and Intellectual Cinema', http://archive.sensesofcinema.com/contents/directors/06/potter.html

Sophie Meyer, *The Cinema of Sally Potter: A Politics of Love*, London, Wallflower, 2009.

Jean Oppenheimer, 'Production Slate: *Yes*', *American Cinematographer*, June 2005, http://www.theasc.com/magazine/july05/productionslate/page1.html

Sally Potter, http://www.sallypotter.com/blog

K. Widdicombe, 'The Contemporary Auteur: An Interview with Sally Potter', http://www.bfi.org.uk/filmtvinfo/publications/16+/potter.html

JOHN SAYLES

By Mark Jancovich and James Lyons

Characterised by his distance from the Hollywood mainstream, John Sayles appears consistently in profiles and articles as 'the doyen of American independent film-making'.[1] Geoff Andrew refers to him as 'the pioneering indie writer-director [who] is none too bothered about sticking to the safe formulae of the mainstream',[2] whilst Sayles himself has reinforced the sense of the 'extraordinary daring'[3] involved in working repeatedly in a precarious financial situation, stating, in reference to his filmmaking, that 'I'll be lucky to do it again is how I feel. Every movie has been a roll of the dice. So far I've never crapped out'.[4]

Sayles started his career with Roger Corman, scripting low-budget exploitation movies such as *Piranha* (1978), made to cash in on the success of *Jaws*; *The Lady in Red* (1979), a film about the criminal world of the 1930s told from the position of the woman who was with John Dillinger at the Biograph Cinema when he was gunned down by the FBI; *The Howling* (1980), a story of werewolves in contemporary California; and *Battle Beyond the Stars* (1980), a science fiction reworking of *The Magnificent Seven*. These films, rarely seen as significant in themselves, are regarded as activities undertaken to fund Sayles's own projects. As Gavin Smith puts it: 'In the tradition of John Cassavetes, who financed his independent films in the sixties and seventies by acting in mainly minor Hollywood pictures, Sayles works as a journeyman writer for hire, ploughing back his earnings into his own personal projects'.[5]

While this position could be seen as one of dependence, it is rarely presented as such. Rather, Sayles is seen in terms of heroic professional detachment, not only for his time with Corman, but for his work as scriptwriter on such films as *Alligator* (1980), *The Challenge* (1980), *Enormous Changes at the Last Minute* (1982), *The Clan of the Cave Bear* (1986), *Wild Thing* (1987), *Breaking In* (1989), *Men of War* (1994) and *Apollo 13* (1995). Even Sayles has, at times, contributed to such an understanding of these films as somehow separate within his larger body of work, remarking: 'You get too much money for writing crummy exploitation movies anyway, and that's how I make my living'.[6]

The result of this critical discourse has been to generate a hierarchy within Sayles's œuvre, with his scriptwriting for other people more often than not relegated to the margins (for example, see Jack Ryan's book *John Sayles, Filmmaker*, which includes a chapter for each of Sayles's directed films, yet collects all his scriptwriting for others in a single chapter). Such script work is often portrayed as raising the films in question above the normal standard and quality: Smith, for example, claims that Sayles brought 'invention and subversive humour to pop genre chores ... His knack for witty dialogue, realistic characters, and playful, intelligent genre revisionism – and his ability to deliver fast – quickly established Sayles as an in-demand rewriter'.[7] However, this work is still carefully distinguished from that which is seen to construct the 'real' or 'true' Sayles – namely his career as a director.

Rather ironically, Sayles's directed work, carefully separated by critics from his scriptwriting for others, is usually portrayed as breaking down a whole series of borders. For example, the claim is often made that characters in Sayles's movies cannot be easily summed up: that they possess a plethora of seemingly contradictory motivations. The character of Otis Payne in *Lone Star* is often taken to be speaking for Sayles when he says: 'It's not like there's some borderline between the good people and the bad people',[8] reflecting the fact that Sayles's narratives are frequently supposed to concern processes of hybridity, creolisation and the problems of drawing and defining both literal and figurative borders (most notably, *Baby, It's You*, *Matewan*, *City of*

Hope, Passion Fish, The Secret of Roan Inish, Lone Star, Men with Guns and *Limbo*).

Whilst it is possible to stress the use of generic elements in Sayles's films – *Baby, It's You* as teen romance, *Brother from Another Planet* as science fiction, *Matewan* as a Western, *Eight Men Out* as a sports movie, *City of Hope* as family melodrama, and *Lone Star* as either a Western or a detective film – critics often present the generic elements as simply a cover used to smuggle in the 'real' materials. Trevor Johnston claims that *Passion Fish* 'cloaks itself, like many of its predecessors, in approachable generic garb. From his earliest commissioned screenplays, Sayles has been nothing if not resourceful in his mastery of sundry genre formulae'.[9] In this way, genre becomes the sugar that helps the medicine of Sayles's films go down better with audiences. As Kemp argues: 'John Sayles has always taken a fruitfully oblique angle on genre, and *Lone Star* turns the conventions and vocabulary of the Western to its own ends'.[10] Genre becomes something from which critics need to distinguish Sayles: he may use it, but the implication is always that genre films are formulaic and conventional and that, in the tradition of the auteur theory, Sayles proves his quality as a filmmaker by transforming those generic features to which others simply conform.

The intent behind Sayles's supposed manipulation of so-called generic formula is usually understood as a form of political motivation – as the desire to create 'a much more politically and emotionally challenging kind of work'.[11] Kemp refers to him as 'a fiercely political film-maker'[12] while, according to Quart, Sayles himself distinguishes himself from other filmmakers, saying that 'American filmmakers tend to be afraid of politics'.[13] However, the precise nature of Sayles's politics is rarely spelled out beyond the claims that he represents 'something different from what Hollywood was offering, something more serious'.[14] Instead, an aura of political commitment is constructed through continual references to his 'integrity'. Smith quotes approvingly David Thomson's claim that there 'is an emphatic integrity to Sayles',[15] while Geoff Andrew claims that, with 'his talent, integrity and inquisitive attitude to the world, Sayles is rightly regarded as an inspirational influence in US indie movie-making'.[16]

This sense of 'integrity' is not tied to any straightforward commitment, to any specific political position or programme. On the contrary, it is defined largely through Sayles's rejection of partisan politics. Although he is quoted as claiming that there is 'a whole raft of American film criticism that's anti-content, whether it's political or not, because they feel that it's a betrayal of pure film',[17] Sayles's films are carefully distinguished from mere 'message movies' through an emphasis on their concern with complexity. Andrew Ross has claimed that, in Cold War America, many intellectuals came to define the rejection of politics *as* politics.[18] Sayles is the product of a later period – the New Left of the 1960s – but in many ways, the New Left was born out of this legacy.[19] It too rejected the supposed totalitarianism of the old left's idealism, themes also common in commentary upon Sayles. He is reputed to have rejected the ideological purism and sectarianism of left politics[20] and, talking of Kenehan, the labour organiser in *Matewan*, has been quoted as saying:

> The Wobblies were not a very old organization when they were broken apart. He's a guy who had just come to this new religion, who is trying to figure out how to apply it. So he is very likely to get his people killed. Both my novel *Los Gusanos* and the film *City of Hope* are interesting in this regard. They both posit that believers can cause as much trouble as cynics. We might like the believers a little bit more, but whether they're Shi'ites, union men, or pro-lifers, they can cause trouble because they absolutely believe.[21]

It is therefore not surprising to find Kim Newman claim, in his review of *City of Hope*, that 'the most corrupt of Sayles' politicians have some noble motives, while the most apparently honest are potentially crooked'.[22]

Reflecting this duplicity, Sayles can, on occasion, be found to endorse a very different, contradictory relationship to the body of his work. Maltin, for example, quotes him claiming that 'working for Roger [Corman] and with Frances [Doel, Corman's story editor and right-hand woman] was terrific', and that working as a writer for hire does

> not just [support my other films] economically. I think I learned a lot from it. So it helps make me a better filmmaker or better writer when I go back to the fray of my own stuff, but it's something that I would do even if I didn't need to; even if I didn't need the money, because I enjoy it, and you're getting to work for the movies, which is a good deal.[23]

Sayles has stated that he only takes on assignments he thinks he can do well or that he will enjoy. Thus, while he is sometimes shown as contemptuous of genre films, he is also presented as a fan of certain genres – 'I liked Westerns, some science fiction, monster movies like *Them!'*[24] – tastes seen as influential upon his writing: 'About the third grade, eight years old, I started to write stories. They were all rip-offs of *Twilight Zone'*.[25] Nor is it just these genres with which he is associated: 'I have wide taste. I like everything from *Cries and Whispers* to *Enter the Dragon'*.[26]

While he has been opposed to the mainstream, here he is presented as refusing such an opposition, as challenging these hierarchies and oppositions. He is even supposed to have stressed the creative possibilities of refusing to maintain that distinction, and has been quoted as saying, 'On *Battle Beyond the Stars*, Corman said, "If you can make *Seven Samurai* into a western, you can make it into a science fiction film". ' He had another idea to make *Mutiny on the Bounty* in outer space. 'Sometimes there's some hybrid vigour you can get into a genre that way'.[27] Here Sayles emphasises the creative potential of hybridity and boundary crossing, demonstrating that this playfulness with genre was practised and encouraged by popular film, not a subversive strategy of his own: on the contrary, it was something he learned from Corman.

In his discussion of the role of the author, Michel Foucault stresses that this category is a mode of classification that creates 'a relationship of homogeneity, filiation, authentification of some texts by others'.[28] Rather than identifying some pre-existing essence, it produces that which it purports to identify. The figure of the author is constructed in an attempt to identify 'a point where contradictions are resolved, where incompatible elements are at last tied together or organized around a fundamental original contradiction'.[29] It is this notion of the distinctive and unique signature of the individual creator that connects an otherwise diverse and disparate series of texts, and also acts to distinguish these texts from others. The study of authorship, therefore, not only constructs a sense of identity but also otherness, and more importantly it works to patrol the border between the two. The 'fundamental, original contradiction' of the figure of Sayles, as constructed by reviews, interviews and profiles, is thus the paradox of the director defined by an 'integrity' that is, at its core, a refusal of all that integrity embodies – wholeness, clarity, unity and the simple drawing of lines. For all the fluid and heterogeneous identity politics of Sayles's directed films, discussions of those films serve, more often than not, to make distinctions: to patrol the border of an integral Sayles. Ultimately, it may be the John Sayles whose work refutes the borders between blockbusters, exploitation movies and a myriad other genres – the so-called 'writer for hire' – who makes the straightforward telling of the story of authorship more difficult.

Postscript

These observations on Sayles were written in the late 1990s, shortly after the success of *Lone Star*. In critical terms, this point represented 'the high point in Sayles's career',[30] and since then his reputation waned considerably. While still referred to as 'an indie icon',[31] few now position Sayles in the ways described previously, Philip French being a noticeable exception.[32] Indeed, many still praise Sayles's 'forgiving irony',[33] in which most characters 'exhibit a strain of decency'[34] so that even the 'bad guys don't wear black'[35] and 'Sayles doesn't demonise them'.[36] They also praise his supposed avoidance of 'pat solutions or happy endings',[37] so that his films confound expectations and 'you can never be sure what will happen next'.[38] However, Sayles was also increasingly present as a figure lacking integrity during this period, with *Variety* stating that 'John Sayles the storyteller and John Sayles the political progressive haven't always played well together'.[39] He is even accused of a 'tendency to didacticism'[40] that makes his films 'schematic'[41] and can result in characters that are impossible to 'believe in'.[42] In this way, his films are claimed to 'only fitfully suc-ceed in camouflaging the machinery behind their characters'[43] and to feature characters that often conform to mere 'stereotype'[44] and 'cliché'.[45]

This shift in critical position is partly due to a change in Sayles's filmmaking, which is increasingly discussed in relation to Robert Altman, with Sayles being identified as a director of ensemble films,[46] and as a director whose films have become increasingly preoccupied with environmental issues.[47] However, another reason may be due to Sayles's relationship to popular culture. For example, *Sunshine State* is supposed to display 'a profound sense of disappointment at the suf-focating banality and shortsightedness of American popular culture',[48] a position which as we suggested earlier is at odds with the ways in which Sayles has previously fed off popular culture. It is therefore noticeable how many of the films he made after *Lone Star* have avoided the generic features of his earlier efforts (*Men with Guns*, *Limbo*, *Casa de los Babys* and *Sunshine State*). Furthermore, his overt return to more familiar generic territory in his most recent films has seen some of the most positive reviews. For example, while *Silver City* was repeatedly identified as a 'murder-mystery' or a 'noir thriller',[49] *Honeydripper* not only draws on well-established narratives of racial change in the 1950s and 1960s, but also focuses these changes through a story about the transformation of popular music and the emergence of 'rock'n'roll'. It seems that, for all their supposed chal-lenge to traditional genres, Sayles's films fare best when they maintain a close connection with popular genres, but the question still remains whether Sayles's political cachet is in decline. Although he was once a director who represented New Left radicalism for reviewers, it remains to be seen whether political changes have displaced his political orientation. Certainly films such as *Men with Guns* and *Casa de los Babys*, with their locations south of the US border, suggest a growing awareness of global politics, but are perhaps still too focused on the US, while films such as *Limbo*, *Sunshine State* and *Silver City* also display a strong concern with environmental issues, but in ways that also seem to lack resonance with broader political debates. In an era when so many supposedly radical filmmakers are working in the new documentary cinema, it may be the case that the centre of gravity has shifted away from Sayles and towards more overtly polemical and self-promoting figures such as Michael Moore.

Biography

Born in Schenectady, in New York, USA, in 1950. A psychology graduate, Sayles published two novels (*Pride of the Bimbos*, 1975; *Union Dues*, 1977) before writing film scripts for Roger Corman in the late 1970s. He won a prestigious MacArthur Foundation Fellowship in 1983 and directed the television series *Shannon's Deal* (1990). Sayles has continued to combine his own filmmaking with script work for others (e.g. *The Spiderwick Chronicles*, 2007), and in February 2009 *Variety* announced that he was due to script an HBO series based on the childhood of Red Hot Chili Peppers frontman Anthony Kiedis.[50]

Notes

1 Trevor Johnston, 'Sayles Talk', *Sight and Sound*, September 1993, p. 26.
2 Geoff Andrew, 'Going to Extremes', *Time Out*, 19–26 January 2000, p. 18.
3 Jonathan Romney, 'Out on a Limb', *Guardian*, 14 January 2000, p. 6.
4 Pat Aufderheide, 'Filmmaking as Storytelling: An Interview with John Sayles', *Cineaste*, vol. 15, no. 4, 1987, p. 15.
5 Gavin Smith, *Sayles on Sayles*, London, Faber & Faber, 1998, p. ix.
6 Pat Aufderheide, *op. cit.*
7 Gavin Smith, *op. cit.*, p. xi.
8 Philip Kemp, 'Review of *Lone Star*', *Sight and Sound*, October 1996, p. 48.
9 Trevor Johnston, 1993, *op. cit.*
10 Philip Kemp, 1996, *op. cit.*
11 Gary Crowdus and Leonard Quart, 'Where the Hope Is: An Interview with John Sayles', *Cineaste*, vol. 18, no. 4, 1991, p. 7.

12 Philip Kemp, 'Review of *The Secret of Roan Inish*', *Sight and Sound*, August 1997, p. 8.

13 Gary Crowdus and Leonard Quart, *op. cit.*

14 Eliot Asinof (n.d.) 'John Sayles', *Directors Guild of America Web Magazine*. Online. Available HTTP: <http://www.dga.org/magazine/v22–25/john_sayles.htm>.

15 Gavin Smith, 'John Sayles: 'I Don't Want to Blow Anything by People' ', *Film Comment*, vol. 32, no. 3, May/June 1996, p. 57.

16 Geoff Andrew, *op. cit.*, p. 19.

17 Gary Crowdus and Leonard Quart, *op. cit.*

18 Andrew Ross, *No Respect: Intellectuals and Popular Culture*, London, Routledge, 1989.

19 See, for example, Richard Pells, *The Liberal Mind in a Conservative Age*, Middletown, CT, Wesleyan University Press, 1989.

20 See Gavin Smith, 1998, *op. cit.*, p. 21.

21 Ibid., pp. 126–7.

22 Kim Newman, 'Review of *City of Hope*', *Sight and Sound*, August 1991, p. 38.

23 Leonard Maltin (n.d.) 'John Sayles', *Writers Guild of America News*. Online. Available HTTP: <http://www.wga.org/pr/0298/sayles.html>.

24 Gavin Smith, 1998, *op. cit.*, p. 4.

25 Ibid., p. 5.

26 Trevor Johnston, 1993, *op. cit.*, p. 29.

27 Jonathan Romney, *op. cit.*

28 Michel Foucault, 'What is an Author', in John Caughie (ed.) *Theories of Authorship*, London, Routledge, 1986, p. 284.

29 Ibid., pp. 287–8.

30 Emanuel Levy, 'Men with Guns', *Variety*, 4 September 1997.

31 John Anderson, 'Honeydripper', *Variety*, 11 September 2007.

32 Philip French, 'Body of Evidence', *Observer*, 24 July 2005.

33 Roger Ebert, 'Sunshine State', *Chicago Sun Times*, 12 July 2002.

34 Stephen Holden, 'Within a Florida Civics Lesson, Rich Stories', *New York Times*, 21 June, 2002.

35 French, *op. cit.*

36 Ibid.

37 Stephen Holden, 'Film Review; Six Characters in Search of an Infant', *New York Times*, 19 September, 2003.

38 Roger Ebert, 'Limbo', *Chicago Sun Times*, 4 July, 1999.

39 Anderson, *op. cit.*

40 Philip Kemp, 'Limbo', *Sight and Sound*, February 2000.

41 Emmanuel Levy, 'Men With Guns', *Variety*, 4 September, 1997; Stephen Holden, ' 'Limbo': Damaged, and Stranded on an Island', *New York Times*, 4 June 1999; David Ng, 'Frustrated Mothers-to-Be Flounder in Saylesian Purgatory', *Village Voice*, 16 September, 2003.

42 A.O. Scott, 'Venal Handlers and a (Sort of) Innocent Politician', *New York Times*, 17 September, 2004.

43 Stephen Holden, 'Way Down in Harmony, With Mythic Blues Again', *New York Times*, 28 December, 2007. Philip French, 'Body of Evidence', *Observer*, 24 July 2005.

44 Holden, op. cit.
45 Ibid.
46 Philip French, 'Sleazy Does It', *Observer*, 28 July 2002.
47 Peter Bradshaw, 'Sunshine State', *Guardian*, 26 July 2002; Roger Ebert, 'Limbo', *Chicago Sun Times*, 4 July, 1999; 'Silver City: Murder Mystery Meets Political Satire in "Silver City"', *Chicago Sun Times*, 17 September, 2004; 'Sunshine State', *Chicago Sun Times*, 12 July 2002; Philip French, 'Body of Evidence', *Observer*, 24 July 2005; 'Sleazy Does It', *Observer*, 28 July 2002; Stephen Holden, ' 'Limbo': Damaged, and Stranded on an Island', *New York Times*, 4 June 1999; 'Within a Florida Civics Lesson, Rich Stories', *New York Times*, 21 June, 2002; Todd McCarthy, 'Limbo', *Variety*, 31 May, 1999; David Rooney, 'Silver City', 11 September 2004; A. O. Scott, 'Venal Handlers and a (Sort of) Innocent Politician', *New York Times*, 17 September, 2004; Jessica Winter, 'State of Confusion', 18 June, 2002.
48 Holden, 'Within a Florida Civics Lesson, Rich Stories'.
49 Roger Ebert, 'Murder Mystery meets political satire in "Silver City"', *Chicago Sun Times*, 17 September, 2004; French, 'Body of Evidence'; David Rooney, 'Silver City', *Variety*, 11 September, 2004.
50 Michael Schneider, 'Sayles red hot for HBO's "Scar"', *Daily Variety*, February 22, 2009. Online. Available: <http://www.variety.com/article/VR1118000444.html?categoryid=14&cs=1>.

Filmography

Return of the Secaucus 7 (1980)
Lianna (1983)
Baby, It's You (1983)
The Brother from Another Planet (1984)
Matewan (1987)
Eight Men Out (1988)
City of Hope (1991)
Passion Fish (1992)
The Secret of Roan Inish (1994)
Lone Star (1996)
Men with Guns (1997)
Limbo (1999)
Sunshine State (2002)
Casa de los Babys (2003)
Silver City (2004)
Honeydripper (2007)

Further reading

Mark Bould, *The Cinema of John Sayles*, London, Wallflower, 2008.
Dian Carson and Heidi Kenega, eds, *Sayles Talk: New Perspectives on Independent Filmmaker John Sayles*. Detroit, Wayne State University Press, 2005.

Jack Ryan, *John Sayles, Filmmaker*, New York, McFarland, 1998.
Dennis West and Joan M. West, 'Borders and Boundaries: An Interview with John Sayles', *Cineaste*, vol. 22, no. 3, 1996, pp. 14–17.

MARTIN SCORSESE

By George S. Larke-Walsh

Martin Scorsese is both an immensely successful filmmaker and a self-appointed guardian of American cinema history. Since the early 1980s he has campaigned for more durable colour film stock, the preservation and archiving of old American films, and the promotion of cinema history to modern audiences. The latter concern has dominated his own promotional interviews and lectures, resulting in a three part television documentary, *A Personal Journey Through American Movies* (1993). For Scorsese the cinema of the present is always and necessarily influenced by the past. Finally honoured by the Academy of Motion Picture Arts in 2007 for *The Departed*, Scorsese is the 'critical' King of Hollywood. As both a sophisticated East Coast film maker and a Hollywood director, he commands immense critical respect, while juggling big budgets and mainstream connections with large studios. He has delivered star vehicles/box office successes, *Color of Money*, *Cape Fear* and *The Departed*, while bringing to the screen more personal films such as *Mean Streets*, *The Last Temptation of Christ* and *Gangs of New York*.

Religion is a recurrent and highly suggestive theme in Scorsese's film work. While the controversial *The Last Temptation of Christ* stands out in this respect, many of Scorsese's male protagonists have voiced their fascination with religion. *Mean Streets'* Charlie is fixated with the idea of his own spiritual purpose. He is the archetypal selective devotee, his desire to do penance very much at odds with his actions. Scorsese observes: 'he acts like he's doing it for the others, but it's a matter of his own pride'.[1] In *Taxi Driver*, Travis Bickle believes himself to be acting out God's rage against the lowlife of New York. Max Cady's furious acts of revenge in *Cape Fear* derive from a similarly obsessive nature. In *Raging Bull*, Jake La Motta punishes his body in training and in the boxing ring in an attempt to atone for his sins. Scorsese returned to New York City in *Bringing Out the Dead*; God's lonely man of the nineties, a paramedic, is now an angel of mercy. Trained to save lives, Frank Pierce finds redemption in having the courage finally to end one. In terms of these religious themes, all the earlier films seem to be leading towards *The Last Temptation*, while *Bringing Out the Dead* refers back to them all, but is not a culmination of them. Along with *Mean Streets* and *Gangs of New York*, *The Last Temptation* remains one of Scorsese's most personal projects. (He worked on the script with Paul Schrader and frequent collaborator Michael Ballhaus was cinematographer.) The film attracted intense reactions from some religious groups, who picketed cinemas in response to the apparent blasphemy implied by Christ's final temptation. The film, based on Nikos Kazantzakis' novel, has Christ appear to leave the cross and experience married life with Mary Magdalene. Scorsese vigorously defended his film, arguing that it was designed to show Christ as a real man, rather than a faultless spiritual being. As such, the Bronx accents, Christ's (Willem Dafoe) inner emotional struggle and the consistently female image of sin converge – if we are to accept Scorsese's comments – to make this as much a working through of Scorsese's own sense of religious identity as it is a story of Christ. Scorsese insists: 'Jesus has to put up with everything we go through, all the doubts and fears and anger ... he has to deal with all this double, triple guilt on the cross. That's the way I directed it, and that's what I wanted, because my own religious feelings are the same'.[2]

Last Temptation is one of Scorsese's most significant films, displaying an intense self-confidence. The subject matter can be interpreted in at least two ways; as suggesting Christ's humanity on one hand, elevating Scorsese's vision of masculine identity to an omnipotent spiritual level on the other. Not only the influence of religion on personal identity but notions of masculinity and a sense of community are all themes common in Scorsese's work. His earliest features, *Who's that Knocking at My Door?* and *Boxcar Bertha* involve intensely spiritual protagonists. Indeed *Boxcar Bertha* could be seen as the closest precursor to *Last Temptation*: it features a tentative relationship between a prostitute, Bertha (Barbara Hershey – who later plays Mary Magdalene in *Temptation*), and a labour leader, Bill, who is literally crucified on the side of a boxcar at the film's end. *Last Temptation of Christ* suggests an attempt to universalise masculine experience by having Scorsese's favourite themes transported from the usual urban, late twentieth-century setting to biblical times. Picketing the film because Jesus has sex has perhaps served to divert attention away from another, perhaps more uncomfortable theme: that masculine identity is an existential conflict capable of omnipotent self-awareness, while femininity remains confined to earth, sexuality and the notion of original sin. My point is not to assert Scorsese's misogyny, so much as to note the extent to which his films are constructed from belief systems which are unashamedly patriarchal, grounded in Catholicism. In short, women feature mainly on a symbolic level in these films: reduced to Madonna or whore, projections of male inner spiritual conflicts.

The Last Temptation of Christ represents the culmination of Scorsese's obsession with an inner spiritual morality as the ultimate conflict in masculine identity. Positing Christ as an ordinary man also raises man to a level with Christ, as capable of achieving the same sublime identity, or completeness. The actions of Charlie (*Mean Streets*), Travis (*Taxi Driver*), Jake (*Raging Bull*) and Cady (*Cape Fear*) are all legitimated when viewed as part of Scorsese's journey towards salvation through self-knowledge. Perhaps this commonality between protagonists suggests Scorsese's auteur status, his protagonists' inner moral and spiritual life repeatedly reiterated as the film's primary concern. According to the *Cahiers* critics, an auteur film is dominated by the search for self-awareness: 'the individual is trapped in *solitude morale* and can escape from it – transcend it – if he or she comes to see their condition and then extend themselves to others and then to God'.[3] Scorsese's twin obsessions are evident in his work, his campaigning, and in many interviews, his attitude to filmmaking exceeding any simple ambition to produce entertainment. As the filmmaker observes, 'my whole life has been movies and religion. That's it, nothing else'.[4]

Scorsese began his film career in the 1960s, at the tail-end of *Cahiers du Cinema*'s glorification of the auteur. Influenced by the emergence of 'art cinema' within the French New Wave and Italian Neo-realist movements, he was briefly associated with the 'Radical Newsreel Movement', but concentrated on making his name as an independent filmmaker. Scorsese's mainstream successes began in the early 1970s. His early contemporaries were directors such as Francis Ford Coppola, George Lucas, Robert Altman, Brian De Palma and Steven Spielberg. Together they represented a new generation of movie directors that emerged in the early 1970s. This era, aptly labelled 'New Hollywood', occurred mainly as a result of changes in the film industry. While the demise of the studio system meant that directors could no longer expect a studio to back them on a regular basis (each film project involved securing finance), it arguably created room for more experimental films to be produced and thus, for some directors to see themselves as artists in similar ways to the European model. Richard Maltby has noted that these 'movie brat' directors, educated at film schools, 'found obvious material benefits in the enhanced industrial status of the director, in part because they became marketable commodities, even stars, in their own right'.[5]

Scorsese has unashamedly exploited his own status as star director. His critical status, encapsulated in his book, *A Personal Journey with Martin Scorsese Through American Movies* (1997), is founded upon the contention that film is America's primary aesthetic form. Such cinephilic perspectives on American film history are complemented by Scorsese's detailed explanations of his own work. This further supports the notion that he is both a critical and a star presence in the cinema industry, a presence that extends beyond his directorial achievements. His 'star director' presence in interviews, combined with his belief in the aesthetic value of American cinema, produces an effect of critical credibility; that is, Scorsese has the aura of an artist working within the establishment without forfeiting his integrity.

Scorsese's collaborations have been central to his work: editor Thelma Schoonmaker first worked with him on *Who's that Knocking at my Door?*, subsequently editing every film since *Raging Bull* (with the exception of the 2005 documentary, *No Direction Home: Bob Dylan*). Michael Ballhaus, who previously worked with Fassbinder, has been Scorsese's regular cinematographer since *After Hours* (although for certain projects Scorsese has looked elsewhere, using Freddie Francis to shoot *Cape Fear*, for instance). Scorsese's best-known collaboration, that with writer Paul Schrader, ironically extends to only three films: *Taxi Driver*, *Raging Bull*, and *The Last Temptation of Christ*. Nicholas Pileggi has written two screenplays, *Goodfellas* and *Casino*, thus standing out as the 'Mafia influence'. Jay Cocks, who adapted Edith Wharton's *The Age of Innocence*, also adapted Asbury's *Gangs of New York*. Dante Ferretti's immaculate set designs for the period pieces *The Age of Innocence*, *The Aviator* and *Gangs of New York* have been central to the visual impact of these films. Robert De Niro has starred in more Scorsese films than anyone else, though in recent years the director has regularly cast Leonardo Di Caprio. This marks a significant thematic shift in that Di Caprio, though a strong star/actor, lacks the existential angst that De Niro's persona brought to the earlier films.

Di Caprio has central roles in *Gangs of New York*, *The Aviator* and *The Departed*, films that foreground exquisite period detail and sometimes violent spectacle in contrast to the intimacy of earlier works. *The Aviator* explores the life and self destructive behaviour of Hollywood tycoon, Howard Hughes. According to Geoffrey O'Brien, Scorsese treats the action sequences calmly and the domestic sequences as battles, but 'not for one second does *The Aviator* surrender to the delusion of intimacy or real affection in its portrait'.[6]

That is, audiences are not invited into Hughes's psyche, only into his society. The same might be said of Di Caprio's Amsterdam (*Gangs of New York*) or Billy Costigan (*The Departed*). The films detail these characters' suffering, but do so in a largely external fashion, through actions such as murder or socio-political corruption. Rather than the frightening figures played by De Niro – such as La Motta or Bickle – Di Caprio seems more a lost boy in a maelstrom of dirty politics and murderous thieves. If audiences feel anxiety it is more likely emanating from the environment he inhabits than from recognition of any internal angst. In contrast, *Taxi Driver* is the story of 'God's lonely man'. Vietnam veteran Travis Bickle cannot sleep, but day-dreams about ridding New York of all the 'scum and the filth' that populate its streets. Despite his threatening, unpredictable nature, a powerful voice-over invites a degree of audience sympathy for the character.

Scorsese's use of violence is a fundamental, at times controversial, element of his films. *Taxi Driver* builds slowly toward a violent climax, wherein Travis acts out his fantasies. Though far from straightforward thematically, the film seems to suggest that Travis is a confused vigilante who lacks direction. However, the absence of a satisfactory narrative conclusion tends to subvert character motivation, or redemption; this inconsistency of structure and theme has attracted strong reactions from audiences and critics alike. Scorsese was apparently shocked on an opening night: 'everyone was yelling and screaming at the shoot-out. When I made it, I didn't intend to have the audience react with that feeling'.[7] No matter what his intentions, some critics were repelled by Scorsese's vision. Patricia Patterson and Manny Farber, for example, argue that 'what's really disgusting about *Taxi Driver* is not the multi-faced loner but the endless propaganda about the magic of guns'.[8] Their analysis concentrates on the pre-valence of violence in gestures and speech, violence which is intended to display male brotherhood. The association with men and violence as a form of retribution or spiritual awakening has equally disturbed feminist critics. Pam Cook describes *Raging Bull* as an exemplification of masculinity in crisis and *Cape Fear* as a rampage against women. For Cook, Scorsese is a 'master of the masochistic aesthetic'.[9] His films have an ambiguous attitude to violence, with audiences seem-ingly encouraged to gain perverse pleasure from witnessing acts of brutality. Todd McCarthy describes the opening fight scene from *Gangs of New York*, in which 'dozens of urban warriors hack each other to bits', as 'frighteningly violent'.[10] For some critics, then, Scorsese's vision has less to do with the search for salvation through self-knowledge, and more to do with the glorification of man's potential for violence.

Much has been written about Scorsese's films. Writers such as David Thompson, Ian Christie and Lesley Stern frame the filmmaker as auteur, although Stern intercuts Scorsese's ideas with her own experience of cinema, effectively challenging even Scorsese's cinephilia. Stern accepts Scorsese's explanation that *Taxi Driver* pays homage to *The Searchers* (1956), suggesting that the film 'brings out the psychopathic tendencies within the vigilante impulse'.[11] While Robin Wood's response to *Taxi Driver* concentrates on how the 'incoherent narrative' echoes the general malaise afflicting America at that time, Robert Kolker describes a symbolic notion of 'New York-ness' traceable through Scorsese's films in the repetition of certain gestures and speech patterns. Arguably these patterns have a lot to do with the recurrent use of actors such as Robert De Niro, Joe Pesci and Harvey Keitel. None the less this notion of 'New York-ness' points to a distinctive, transgeneric evocation of urban, working class, male communities. Thus the disciples in *The Last Temptation of Christ* echo the bar friends in *Mean Streets*, when they bicker about respect or friendship.

While isolation and crises of identity are key themes, the films necessarily include explorations of community and/or brotherhood against which that isolation can be defined. Scorsese centralises protagonists who are male, urban, working-class and often Italian-American, a formulation of brotherhood that has helped foster a perception of docu-realism in his films. Scorsese's commentary on his personal experiences and community arguably reinforces such perceptions. Yet the use of voiceover narrative draws attention to the subjective and/or construction of fiction – as in *Taxi Driver*, *Goodfellas* and *Casino*. In fact Scorsese excels in juggling audience perceptions with regard to what is 'real' in his films and what is a presentation of a character's imagination. Whether it be the questionable subjectivity of *Taxi Driver*, wherein the ending casts doubts on the whole narration, or *The Age of Innocence*, where Newland Archer's narration veils its subjectivity behind seemingly objective scenes, Scorsese's films are self-conscious explorations of the inner conflicts of his main characters. For instance, a clue to Archer's subjectivity is given in Madame Olenska's reply to one of his letters, filmed as a direct address to camera, but still an image conjured by his desire, rather than an independent occurrence.

Scorsese's appearances in his own films – often as a camera-man, or photographer – remind audiences of who is in control of the images.

He promotes himself as a 'star director', and critics concentrate on his 'personal vision'. In the last few years, he has taken on the role of elder statesman in the movie industry, presenting 'Lifetime Achievement Oscars' at the Academy Awards. Perhaps it was Scorsese's critical authority that averted the threatened demonstrations in March 1999, when he escorted Elia Kazan onto the stage to receive his award. On the one hand, Kazan's artistic achievements with films such as *On The Waterfront* (1956) make him an ideal candidate for Scorsese's patronage. None the less, the effects of Senator McCarthy's interrogation of the filmmaking industry – and it was Kazan's capitulation to HUAC that made the award so controversial – would surely have impacted upon the very form of filmmaking with which Scorsese was associated in the 1960s. That he should publicly 'forgive' Kazan by acknowledging him as an artist, over and above political considerations, perhaps confirms the argument that Scorsese's films are concerned with spiritual, not political conflicts.

Scorsese combines the critical credibility of a semi-independent east coast film maker, and the box office draw of a major Hollywood player with a cinephilic commitment to American film. Amongst the cinematic souls he has saved is his old friend, director Michael Powell, whose *Peeping Tom* (1960) virtually ended his career. Scorsese tirelessly campaigned for its re-release and critical recognition, as part of an ongoing project to restore neglected films and filmmakers to present day audiences. Finally receiving an Academy Award for best director in 2007, Scorsese has successfully cast himself as the defender of movies-as-art.

Biography

Born on November 17th 1942 in Queens, New York City, Martin Scorsese spent most of his childhood in New York's Little Italy on the Lower East Side. He attended Cardinal Hayes High School and then entered Cathedral College junior seminary with a view to joining the priesthood. He left after only one year. Later he attended New York University, first to study English and then Film. He received his Masters Degree in 1966. His first feature, *Who's that Knocking at My Door?*, was shown at the 1967 Chicago Film Festival, but did not gain a theatrical release until 1969. In 1972 Roger Corman provided the backing for him to make *Boxcar Bertha*. Then finally in 1973, *Mean Streets* set him firmly on the road to success. He has been married five times and is still based in New York, with offices on Park Avenue. Highly respected by the industry critics and audiences as a director, screenwriter, producer and actor, he received a lifetime achievement award from the American Film Institute in 1997 and a long awaited best director Oscar for *The Departed* in 2007.

Notes

1 David Thompson and Ian Christie, *Scorsese on Scorsese*, London, Faber & Faber, 1996, p. 48.
2 Richard Corliss, 'Body ... and Blood' in *Film Comment* v24:5, 1988, p. 36.
3 John Hess, 'La Politique Des Auteurs: Pt I: World View as Aesthetic', *Jump Cut* no. 1 May/June, 1974, p. 20.
4 Cited in Blake, 'Redeemed in Blood' in *Journal of Popular Film & TV* Spring 24:1, 1996, p. 2.
5 Richard Maltby, *Hollywood Cinema: An Introduction*, Oxford, Blackwell Publishers, 1995, p. 32.
6 Geoffrey O'Brien, 'Machine Dreams' in *Film Comment*, January/February 2005, p. 25.
7 Thompson and Christie, p. 63.
8 Patricia Patterson and Manny Farber, 'The Power and the Gory' in *Film Comment*, May/June, 1976, p. 28.
9 Pam Cook, '*Cape Fear* and Femininity as Destructive Power' in Cook, P. and Dodds, P. (eds) *Women and Film* BFI, 1993, p. 134. See also her 'Masculinity in Crisis? Tragedy and Identification in *Raging Bull*', *Screen* 23:3/4, 1982.
10 Todd McCarthy, 'Scorsese "Gangs" Up for a Gotham Epic' in *Variety* December 9th–15th, 2002, p. 38.
11 Stern, Lesley, *The Scorsese Connection*, London, BFI, 1995, p. 61.

Filmography

What's a Nice Girl Like You Doing in a Place Like This? (1963) short
It's Not Just You, Murray! (1963) short
The Big Shave (1967) short
Who's that Knocking at My Door? (1969)
Street Scenes (1970)
Boxcar Bertha (1972)
Mean Streets (1973)
Alice Doesn't Live Here Anymore (1974)
Italianamerican (1974)
Taxi Driver (1975)
New York, New York (1977)
The Last Waltz (1978) documentary
American Boy: A Profile of Steven Prince (1978) documentary
Raging Bull (1980)
The King of Comedy (1982)

After Hours (1985)
The Color of Money (1986)
The Last Temptation of Christ (1988)
New York Stories (1989) segment – 'Life Lessons'
GoodFellas (1990)
Cape Fear (1991)
The Age of Innocence (1993)
Casino (1995)
Kundun (1997)
Bringing Out the Dead (1999)
Gangs of New York (2002)
The Aviator (2004)
No Direction Home: Bob Dylan (2005)
The Departed (2006)
Shine a Light (2008)

Further reading

Casillo, R., *Gangster Priest: The Italian American Cinema of Martin Scorsese*, Toronto, University of Toronto Press, (2006).

Friedman, Lawrence, *The Cinema of Martin Scorsese*, Oxford, Roundhouse Publishing, 1997.

Kelly, Mary P., *Martin Scorsese: A Journey*, London, Secker & Warburg, 1991.

LoBrutto, V., *Martin Scorsese: A Biography*, New York, Praeger, (2007).

Kolker, R.P., *A Cinema of Loneliness: Penn, Kubrick, Coppola, Scorsese, Altman*, Oxford University Press, 1980.

STEVEN SODERBERGH

By Jennifer Holt

With twenty features in twenty years, Steven Soderbergh has been one of the most prolific American directors in contemporary American cinema, as well as one of the most difficult to categorise. He is perhaps best known for redefining what an 'independent film' meant to Hollywood in 1989. Previously, the label suggested a renegade, low budget cinema exemplified by the raw experimentalism of John Cassavetes, the fantastic trash of early John Waters, or the bleak irony of Jim Jarmusch – all of which traditionally embraced an aesthetic and profit margin that was incompatible with Hollywood's blockbuster mode. However, with the tremendous success of Soderbergh's debut, *sex, lies and videotape*, an independent film was suddenly something profitable, viable, and appealing to mainstream audiences. As a result, Soderbergh and his film became the cause célèbre of a renewed swell in American independent filmmaking that would eventually spawn Quentin Tarantino, the commercialisation of Sundance, and a distinct shift in Hollywood's industrial practices.

After *sex, lies, and videotape* premiered at the 1989 U.S. Film Festival (which eventually became the Sundance Film Festival), Miramax co-founder Harvey Weinstein won a bidding war for the film's distribution rights. Weinstein then took some significant risks with Soderbergh's first feature that would prove crucial to the film's ultimate success, such as shrewdly manoeuvering the film into the main competition at the Cannes Film Festival. Remarkably, *sex, lies* went on to win Cannes's most prestigious award, the Palme d' Or, beating out stiff competition that included Spike Lee's *Do the Right Thing*. When Cannes jury president Wim Wenders announced the winner, he professed that *sex, lies, and videotape* 'gave us confidence in the future of cinema'. Instantly, Soderbergh – at 26, the youngest director ever to win the festival's top honour – found himself at the centre of a hyperbolic celebration that declared him a wunderkind on the order of Orson Welles. Indeed, critics called his film 'the most impressive and significant cinematic debut since *Citizen Kane*', and went on to compare him to masters of cinema from Woody Allen, Cassavetes, and Roeg to Rohmer, Truffaut, and Godard.

After Soderbergh's success, and surely following Tarantino's stunning debut with *Reservoir Dogs* in 1992, Sundance grew exponentially. It became a virtual supermarket for new talent in the 1990s. The growing recognition and importance of the festival that is often directly linked to the debut of *sex, lies, and videotape* conferred the concept of 'independent' film with extraordinary marketing cachet. However, mainstream Hollywood's ensuing exploitation of the 'independent' label also created an identity crisis of sorts: Is a film's 'independence' determined by its source of funding or its aesthetic, its politics or its narrative concerns? In negotiating these questions and variant uses of the term, one thing became clear: the industrial and artistic issues raised by the phenomenal success of Soderbergh's debut complicated any simple definition of independence for the foreseeable future.

A similar complexity has continued to define Soderbergh's career. As a director, he has navigated through various genres, themes, financing sectors, visual styles and narrative formulas. At first glance, the only consistency to his output might appear to be its inconsistency. He seems to float effortlessly between studio projects and independently financed productions, big-budget star vehicles and artful experiments with unknown actors, and a seemingly inexhaustible list of genres. He has made dark and moody crime dramas, surreal experimental comedy, an impressionistic monologue, an expressionistic thriller, existential science fiction, an epic two-part biopic, a faux docudrama series for television, adaptations of best-sellers, a blockbuster franchise of dazzling hipster heist films, avant-garde larks, and of course *sex, lies*, which was based on a semi-autobiographical script he wrote in about a week.

Sex, lies, and videotape's original and stylish package of understated sensuality and sage commentary on modern relationships impressed both critics and audiences. The film grossed $24.7 million in its initial domestic release, more than 20 times its $1.2 million budget. Internationally, it has earned over $100 million to date. *Sex, lies* thus qualifies as one of the most profitable films of the 1980s, with a better rate of return than most blockbusters. When he accepted his award at Cannes, he joked that it would probably be 'all downhill from here' and for a while that seemed to be true. Soderbergh's follow-up film *Kafka* was a big disappointment for critics and audiences and kicked off a string of underachieving and often confounding films. *King of the Hill* received solid reviews but was also virtually ignored at the theatres. Soderbergh then fell into a personal and professional slump during the lifeless neo-noir production *The Underneath* in 1995. This uninspired 'remake' of *Criss Cross* (1949) based on his own adaptation of Don Tracy's crime novel marked a career low point.

He credited the freedom of his next experience, making the $250,000 stream of consciousness home-movie *Schizopolis*, with reviving his passion for directing. That same year, he also completed *Gray's Anatomy*, the third Spalding Gray monologue to be filmed after *Swimming to Cambodia* (Demme, 1987) and *Monster in a Box* (Broomfield, 1992). Soderbergh dug deep into his visual bag of tricks for this manic, hyper-visual interpretation of Gray's panicky crusade for a medical miracle, but still came up empty-handed at the box office.

After five flops and one commercial hit in eight years, he got a call from previous associates at Universal to direct a hip crime romp based on an Elmore Leonard novel and a Scott Frank script. Soderbergh was 'the beneficiary of being cold', as the director himself put it, since everyone else being considered for the job was either busy or too expensive. With the sexy, energetic *Out of Sight*, Soderbergh's career was resurrected; most audiences and critics praised the film, and he had finally proven he could very capably direct a $50 million film with star power. It also marked the beginning of a long-term collaboration with George Clooney, who would become his producing partner and the star of five more Soderbergh films over the next decade.

True to his unpredictable form, Soderbergh followed *Out of Sight* with *The Limey*, a downbeat, haunting drama about an ex-con who comes to Los Angeles looking for answers after his daughter's death. This custom-made star vehicle for Terrence Stamp matched up two 1960s icons (Stamp and Peter Fonda) in an unforgettable meditation on revenge and regret. Time seems to move in all directions during this film, to the point that it is unclear whether or not Stamp is arriving or leaving, whether the film is set in the present or the past. *The Limey* also sports a significant amount of cinematic reflexivity, but wears it well. Soderbergh himself has described the film as both 'Captain America meets Billy Budd' and '*Get Carter* made by Alain Resnais'. Perhaps its most provocative device comes in the flashbacks showing a much younger Stamp which are actually original clips from *Poor Cow* (Loach, 1967), one of Stamp's early films. Both characters are thieves named Wilson, enlivening both the ghosts of Wilson/ Stamp that occupy the entire film and the intertextuality that characteristically invites the past into most Soderbergh narratives.

Two films followed that represented a critical peak for his career: *Traffic* and *Erin Brockovich*. Based on a true story, *Erin Brockovich* is a high-gloss populist fable about a working-class mother of three turned legal activist for an exploited community. The film was a complete departure from the uncomfortable, dark recesses of *The Limey* and the offbeat visual surprises in *Out of Sight*. Instead, Soderbergh crafted a modern-day *Norma Rae* with perfectly polished edges, and embraced the mass audience with open arms. The very successful star vehicle for Julia Roberts made more money in its opening weekend ($28.2 million) than *sex, lies* did in its entire first run. Soderbergh effectively downplayed his unconventional side and produced a bona-fide mainstream hit, and also brought Hollywood's hottest actress two firsts: a $20 million paycheck (which made Roberts the first female star to earn as much per role as the highest paid men) and an Academy Award for Best Actress.

Remarkably, Soderbergh also delivered the ambitious and aggres-sively stylised *Traffic* that same year. Based on a British TV mini-series and financed by indie USA Films after all of the major studios passed, the film intertwined three related stories across seven cities (with much of the dialogue in Spanish) to piece together the complex and disastrously failed war on drugs. It won him the Academy Award for Best Director, and he also became the first person to be nominated as Best Director for two of the Best Picture nominees in the same year.

Traffic is additionally notable for Soderbergh's work as cinematographer, a job he assumed for the first time since *Schizopolis*. With his return to the camera, he unleashed an innovative and original style; each strand of *Traffic*'s narrative is visually differentiated with light and tone, so the lush and saturated colours of the San Diego cartel boss and his suburban family are distinct from the cool blues of Washington, D.C., and the overexposed, yellow tints of Mexico. Since then, Soderbergh has shot all of his films as of this writing (often credited as Peter Andrews, for his father). He also continues to edit many of his films (sometimes using the alias Mary Ann Bernard, for his mother) and has written six of his own screenplays since *sex, lies, and videotape*. He is uniquely productive as a multi-hyphenate filmmaker, and one of the few A-listers in Hollywood to shoot almost all of the films that he directs.

After his success in 2000, Soderbergh embarked on his most commercial endeavour to date, the *Ocean's* series. Remaking the Rat Pack in a trio of elaborate and glitzy Vegas heist films with an all-star cast, *Ocean's Eleven*, *Ocean's Twelve* and *Ocean's Thirteen* gave him a solid studio hit to count on every few years. The franchise also launched Section Eight, his boutique production company with Clooney on the Warner Brothers lot that was in business through 2006. During this time, Soderbergh was able to leverage the goodwill (and profits) generated by the *Ocean's* success to support independent and emerging directors like Christopher Nolan, Todd Haynes and Richard Linklater with creative freedom and studio-powered distribution. Even as he was on the 'inside' with a blockbuster franchise, a deal with a major studio, and 'the sexiest men alive' as his leading men, Soderbergh helped to sustain the vitality of alternative cinematic visions as a producer.

In between the $80–100 million films, he also continued to direct offbeat and riskier projects – most of which flopped miserably at the box office. *Full Frontal* (2002) was a film within a film, shot largely on digital video in an improvisational manner that attempted to blur the lines between script and reality. It was a harsh commentary about the film industry made in a somewhat Dogme 95-esque manner, with a set of rules that famously included stars driving themselves to set and doing their own hair and makeup. An experimental art film made with some of the biggest stars in Hollywood and a host of his usual players, it was replete with excessive style (direct address, jump cuts, non-linear editing) and conveyed a sense of the disconnection inherent in Los Angeles living. Yet, mostly, the film appeared to critics as a focused and determined effort to bring his winning streak at the box office to a screeching halt. That same year, he also directed *Solaris*, a remake of the 1972 Tarkovsky film based on Stanislaw Lem's short story about a space station where the crew is being visited and tormented by their reincarnated memories. It is a science-fiction mystery that ultimately becomes a philosophical psychodrama about love and regret. While the film put forth a powerful and multi-dimensional exploration of space, time and memory, it proved too enigmatic for audiences and was Soderbergh's first big-budget flop.

Undeterred by commercial failure, Soderbergh continued on a path of relentless experimentation punctuated by two more *Ocean's* films for good measure. A faux-documentary political series for HBO (*K Street*) brought his work to television and a low budget murder mystery set in a Midwestern doll factory put him at the forefront of debates about new distribution practices for independent films. Indeed, the most notable thing about *Bubble* (2005) was the deal it launched: a partnership between Soderbergh and 2929 Entertainment (owned by Mark Cuban and Todd Wagner) to produce six films that would open at the same time, or 'day-and-date', in theatres and on the HDNet cable channel, with a DVD release to follow four days later. This arrangement created a panic among theatre owners; the film was subsequently banned by the major chains and it generated a slew of predictions hailing a new era in film distribution. Soderbergh dismissed the hysteria, saying that *Bubble* was not going to destroy the movie-going experience any more than the ability to get takeout has destroyed the restaurant business. It was, however, at the forefront of the early Video on Demand (VOD) trend for smaller film releases.

Going back to the studio trough after *Bubble*, Soderbergh tried something completely different with *The Good German*, but even George Clooney could not save the black-and-white period piece from itself. It was a romantic noir-influenced drama of espionage and intrigue shot with studio-era equipment to evoke an authentic post-war feel. Full of pastiche, homage and even interesting changes in narration and perspective, *The Good German* was ultimately a failed exercise despite its ambitious and earnest approach. It was savaged by critics, even called a 'toxic *Casablanca*' by one, as it attempted to remake that film's classic ending scene to very little success, only highlighting how much Soderbergh's film paled in comparison to the original.

Soderbergh then moved on to realise a longtime dream of bringing the story of Che Guevara to the screen. Again rejected by the major studios, he persevered and pieced together European financing for the project. *Che Part One: Argentine* and *Che Part Two: Guerrilla* were released together (on a very limited basis) as a 4-hour, 23-minute epic roadshow. The films detailed two distinct periods in the life of the Marxist guerrilla leader: the years leading up to the Cuban revolution, and the years unsuccessfully attempting to spread revolution in Bolivia during 1966/7, both broken up and bound by important scenes of Guevara's testimony before the UN in 1964. Hearkening back to *Traffic* and *The Limey*, *Che* employed a non-linear construction (especially in Part 1), alternating between various stocks, colours, and tones to bring a stylistic commentary on this narrative that went beyond recounting details and events. Rather than a straightforward history lesson – Part 1 ends before going into Havana and Part 2 picks up seven years later – the film is a striking look at the man and the struggles of revolution. The film was available through VOD a few days after it appeared in theatres, becoming the highest profile day-and-date release at the time for IFC. It was also part of Soderbergh's ongoing quest to enact more aggressive distribution strategies as difficult economic times required creative solutions from the film industry, particularly the independent sector.

This type of experimentation was also prominent in his next film, *The Girlfriend Experience*, an intimate look at the world of a high priced call girl (adult film star Sasha Grey) who offers the 'girlfriend experience' of conversation, kissing and a pseudo-relationship which is much more expensive than just sex. Set during the economic meltdown and the homestretch of the 2008 U.S. presidential campaign, the film often conflates sex, business and politics in a rather unflattering view of capitalism and the contemporary cultural moment. It also was available a full month in VOD *before* showing in theatres, continuing to push early digital distribution for independent films as has become Soderbergh's commitment.

With a narrative that folds in on itself multiple times, shuffling time and place without much warning, *The Girlfriend Experience* was a low budget return to his trademark aesthetic of disconnected sound and image and splintered temporality. Using these dynamic manipulations of space and time, Soderbergh is able to comment on his characters from numerous vantage points without shackling himself to any traditional rules of filmmaking. In fact, he seems to enjoy breaking as many conventions as possible, and has crafted a distinct aesthetic by pushing the boundaries of cinematic expression. Although some of his films do adhere to more classical principles (*Kafka*, *King of the Hill*, *Erin Brockovich* and to a lesser extent *sex, lies, and videotape*), Soderbergh's most interesting and challenging work is always that which bears his signature of multi-dimensional narrative. His 'time in a prism' was initially too abstruse for most audiences to embrace (*The Underneath, Schizopolis*) but has since been refined into an artful and inventive, albeit not wholly commercial, design (*Out of Sight, The Limey, Traffic, Che, The Girlfriend Experience*).

In the process of developing this original style, Soderbergh has experimented with many innovative devices to shift and layer time, going far beyond the use of traditional flashbacks. In *The Underneath*, Soderbergh created a labyrinthine, tripartite structure that intercut past, present and future together to suggest their simultaneity in the mind of Michael Chambers (Peter Gallagher). The cues were primarily different tints relative to various time frames, resulting in a type of colour-coded temporal logic. *Out of Sight* refined his non-linear approach and additionally toyed with the nature of time itself in its use of jump cuts, freeze frames, overlaps and flashbacks. The film's lively, sophisticated editing allowed time to stop, start again, and retrace its steps as the narrative unravels. *The Limey* distills this fragmentation further still, taking the overlapping images and sound of *Out of Sight* to a new extreme for mainstream cinema. Dialogue is cut to overlap two or three locations. Wilson's haunting memories of his daughter Jenny, disconnected moments in planes and hotels, and various flashes of fantasy splinter the path of his obsessive quest. Consequently, time does not go forward in *The Limey* as much as it moves in varying concentric circles.

Soderbergh has continued to complicate the notion of linear time with the memories haunting *Solaris*, the asynchronous conversations of *The Girlfriend Experience*, and the meticulous yet totally disjointed chronology of *Che*. Even the *Ocean's* blockbusters play with linearity as the heists unfold. He has also continued to defy all expectations when picking new projects, further diffusing the parameters of 'Indiewood' and setting his own trends with the production, financing and distribution of his films. Instead of being the 'cinematic equivalent of the locust', as he once joked, by making a film that people actually wanted to see only once every nine years, Soderbergh has in fact delivered some of the more fearless and intriguing projects in Hollywood's recent past as he moves boldly – and independently – towards cinema's future.

Biography

Steven Soderbergh was born January 14, 1963 in Georgia and was raised in Baton Rouge, where he started making films at age 13. He moved to Los Angeles in 1987 and two of his scripts went into development with Outlaw Pictures, one of which was *sex, lies, and videotape*. Production began in 1988 and the film premiered in January, 1989, at the U.S. Film Festival.

Filmography

9012 Live (1986) music documentary

sex, lies, and videotape (1989) also screenwriter, editor, uncredited sound editor

Kafka (1991) also editor

King Of The Hill (1993) also screenwriter, editor

Fallen Angels (1993) Showtime television anthology series *The Quiet Room* and *The Professional Man*

The Underneath (1995) also screenwriter – credited as Sam Lowry

Schizopolis (1997) also writer, cinematographer, actor

Gray's Anatomy (1997)

Out Of Sight (1998)

Nightwatch (1998) screenwriter

The Limey (1999)

Erin Brockovich (2000)

Traffic (2000) also cinematographer – credited as Peter Andrews

Ocean's Eleven (2001) also cinematographer – credited as Peter Andrews

Full Frontal (2002) also cinematographer – credited as Peter Andrews

Solaris (2002) also screenwriter, cinematographer – credited as Peter Andrews, and editor – credited as Mary Ann Bernard

K Street 10 episodes (2003) also cinematographer – credited as Peter Andrews, and editor – credited as Mary Ann Bernard

Eros 'Equilibrium' (2004) also screenwriter, cinematographer – credited as Peter Andrews and editor – credited as Mary Ann Bernard

Ocean's Twelve (2004) also cinematographer – credited as Peter Andrews

Bubble (2005) also cinematographer – credited as Peter Andrews, and editor – credited as Mary Ann Bernard

The Good German (2006) also cinematographer – credited as Peter Andrews, and editor – credited as Mary Ann Bernard

Ocean's Thirteen (2007) also cinematographer – credited as Peter Andrews

Che: Part One (2008) also cinematographer – credited as Peter Andrews

Che: Part Two (2008) also cinematographer – credited as Peter Andrews

The Girlfriend Experience (2009) also cinematographer – credited as Peter Andrews

The Informant! (2009) also cinematographer – credited as Peter Andrews, no producer or exec producer credits included

Further reading

Kaufman, Anthony (ed.), *Steven Soderbergh: Interviews*. University Press of Mississippi, 2002.

Soderbergh, Steven and Richard Lester, *Getting Away With It: Or: The Further Adventures of the Luckiest Bastard You Ever Saw*. Faber & Faber Inc., New York, 2000.

Levy, Emanuel, *Cinema of Outsiders: The Rise of American Independent Film*. New York University Press, New York, 1999.

Soderbergh, Steven, *sex, lies, and videotape*. Harper and Row, New York, 1990.

TODD SOLONDZ

By Dean DeFino

In a late scene from writer/director Todd Solondz's *Happiness*, psychiatrist/pederast Bill Maplewood has a frank sexual discussion with his adolescent son, Billy, while awaiting arrest for raping two of the boy's schoolmates. It is an excruciating moment – where father reveals unspeakable desires and son pleads for affirmation of his own sexual self-worth – and the one most often cited in a heated debate that continues to surround the film. Like all controversial art, the cultural meaning of *Happiness* tends to precede it. Rejected by its original distributor (Universal/October Films) for its unflinching look at such sensitive subjects as paedophilia, rape fantasy, incest and adolescent sexuality, *Happiness* was the subject of polemics concerning art and obscenity long before the public had a chance to see it. When it was finally released by Good Machine, a distribution entity created by the film's producers, most critics had already either hailed it for exposing the dysfunction beneath the veneer of American life, or condemned it as prurient and exploitative. The unfortunate effect of such debates is to obscure the individual merits of artists and their work. With controversy, the substance of Solondz's work has been subsumed into others' causes of liberty and morality.

Key to the controversy surrounding *Happiness*, and Solondz's work in general, is his predilection to mix modes, and genre conventions in particular. Film vaults are filled with paedophiles, sex-obsessed adolescents, rapists and suicides, but these figures exist only within accepted narrative boundaries. Child predators are monsters of fantasy (the Kid Catcher in *Chitty-Chitty Bang-Bang*) or fops in comedies of manners (*Lolita*'s Humbert Humbert); emerging sexuality is the stuff of teen comedy (from Andy Hardy to *American Pie*); rapists are the savage 'others' of tragedy (Silas Lynch in *Birth of a Nation*) or the madmen of thrillers (Max Cady in *Cape Fear*); and suicides haunt melodramas (*Ordinary People*). But Solondz mixes and matches these genres. In *Happiness*, a rejected lover on the verge of suicide uses words better suited to *The Way of the World* than *As the World Turns* to berate his jiltor; in a perverse revision of a teen sex comedy, Bill Maplewood masturbates in his car with a teenybopper magazine; and young Billy's angst over his sexual prowess plays as tragedy. In *Palindromes*, the story of Aviva, a thirteen-year-old girl who runs away from home after a botched abortion in search of a man to impregnate her again, is told using the conventions of picaresque and fairytale, with the intermittent intrusion of the *Rosemary's Baby* theme suggesting an element of horror. In *Storytelling*, the mixing of modes is perhaps most overt. In the first section, entitled 'Fiction', characters attempt to exorcise personal sexual humiliations in a creative writing course — only to have their verity questioned by classmates — and in the second section, entitled 'Nonfiction', a documentary filmmaker turns directionless footage from a film he is preparing about high school teenager into a condescending mockery of his subject. Solondz's stories constantly confound stated expectations: not surprising from a filmmaker who refers to his own films as 'sad comedies'.

If Solondz's compulsion to deconstruct expectations marks his work as truly independent (the experience of watching a Solondz film is like no other), it also describes the trajectory of his career. Born and raised in the suburbs of Newark, New Jersey, his love of cinema developed while he was an undergraduate at Yale University. It would lead him briefly to Los Angeles, where he tried his hand at screenwriting in the early 1980s, then to the film school of New York University. Though the technical aspects of filmmaking eluded Solondz — who claims to have had a dispensation excusing him from handling a camera — he distinguished himself as a writer and director: so much so that one of his comic shorts, *Schatt's Last Shot*, was chosen among NYU student work for an industry screening in 1986. The next day, Solondz found himself in the executive offices of 20th Century Fox. *Schatt's Last Shot*, which mines the familiar territory of dysfunctional relationships and the New York art scene, encouraged Fox, and later Columbia, to believe that they had found a Woody Allen for 'Generation X'. He was soon signed to multi-script writing contracts with both companies, writing and directing a feature for the Samuel Goldwyn Company. But when Goldwyn finally released Solondz's first feature, *Fear, Anxiety and Depression* (1989) — which stars the writer/director as Ira Ellis, a neurotic nebbish rehearsing his romantic failures — critics turned on him, audiences barely noticed, and Fox and Columbia terminated his contracts. The film's self-pitying tone and crude humour play more like a parody of Allen's monologic narcissism, and

Solondz's ill-conceived blend of romantic and dark comedy frustrated rather than engaged viewers. In a particularly troubling scene, Ira stands by making desperate jokes while his girlfriend is being raped.

For a time, Solondz chose to accept the judgement of his critics and left filmmaking. Rejected by the Peace Corps, he spent several years teaching English to Russian immigrants (as will a character in *Happiness*), and hiding his professional past. But fear that early failure would be his cinematic legacy eventually led him back. In the early 1990s, he convinced backers to support production of a script written some time before: a dark comedy about a gawkish adolescent, Dawn 'Wiener Dog' Wiener (Heather Matarazzo), who attempts to navigate her way through a world of Jobian torments. If *Fear, Anxiety and Depression* strained against the conventions of the romantic comedy, the setting and characters of *Welcome to the Dollhouse* were custom-made to communicate Solondz's sensibilities. Again, he mixes modes. Dawn Wiener's story is the waking nightmare of the social outcast, told not as surreal horror/fantasy but as a dark comedy of manners. Her daily tortures are neither exaggerated nor justified; they merely occur as a matter of social course. As Dawn's classmate tells her when she asks why no high school boy would ever touch her, 'Sorry, Dawn, that's just the way it is'. The cruel logic of social order stabilises the narrative and allows Solondz to amplify issues raised in the earlier film. For example, sexual aggression: Brandon (Brendan Sexton Jr), the only boy to show interest in Dawn, repeatedly threatens to rape her. She first responds to these threats with fear, then resignation, and a brief romance ensues when, meeting no resistance, Brandon admits his affection for her. By combining the hegemony of social order borrowed from the comedy of manners with dark comedy's cynicism, Solondz is able to resolve the victim/aggressor relationship in one of the film's rare moments of humanity.

Such talents were rewarded when *Dollhouse* won the Grand Jury Prize at the Sundance Film Festival and seven Independent Spirit Awards (including Best Director, Best Feature and Best Debut Performance for Matarazzo and Sexton). Critics hailed Solondz as a visionary of his generation, a harbinger of what was being called the 'New Geek Cinema': an emerging body of work that would give voice to outsiders and the brutalised. Unlike misfit voices to come before it – from James Dean to Johnny Rotten – these would be sustained not by bravado but persistence. Like Dawn Wiener in the very last scene of *Dollhouse*, drowning out the gibes of her fellows by insistently repeating a tune to herself, Solondz's rehearsal of geek life would mediate horror by drowning it out. Many critics read the film as an elegiac revision of Solondz's own past, though the filmmaker admits no more than sympathy with Wiener Dog's plight, describing it as a story of survival and applauding her for resisting the self-destructive impulse.

Solondz's next film would further complicate issues of sympathy and advocacy by giving voice to a set of outsiders many of us would rather not hear: paedophiles and rapists, murderers and thieves, the feared and the despised. If Weiner Dog's tune helps her keep her head above water, these are people deeply submerged in their own desperation and ugliness. *Happiness* is much more raw and direct than Solondz's previous works. If *Fear, Anxiety and Depression* is crudely playful and *Dollhouse* focuses primarily on the complex, somewhat alien social strata of adolescence, *Happiness* is an uncomfortably intimate look at lineaments of the world we all occupy. Where David Lynch uses the manufactured surface of American life as a springboard into a bizarre alternative, Solondz reveals what exists just below its surface, by carefully peeling it away and compelling us to look in. Unlike the news media, which Solondz accuses of exploiting criminal behaviour for titillation or moral grandstanding, *Happiness* stirs the viewer by revealing the subject rather than reading the subtext. The result is disturbing precisely because it is so little mediated. He is careful to avoid letting the camera signify too much, showing us neither the many criminal acts that occur during the course of the film (child rape, murder, theft, etc.), nor the condemnation and punishment of the perpetrators. He employs relatively few cuts, and prefers fixed medium shots, where characters in a scene are framed together. The scene, setting and drama are self-contained.

This level of immediacy is complicated by the comic nature of the film. Comedy is, after all, a matter of perceptual distance; of witnessing from a learned distance the foolish confidence of the victim as he unwittingly approaches the banana peel. Some claim that *Happiness* is little more than a sick joke – where dangers far greater than banana peels await Solondz's unwitting victims – while others more generously describe it as a parody or satire. But if parody refracts genre conventions through a comic hall of mirrors (John Waters's *Serial Mom*, for example), and satire condemns the folly and vice of its subject, Solondz's film refuses to condemn and undercuts generic discourses – where fantasy equals escapism, tragedy catharsis, and comedy pleasure – by subjecting them to opposing forces. What results is not a hybrid like tragicomedy, where alternating discourses heighten each other, but a flattened narrative, where the audience is denied the fear, pity and pleasure we normally associate with tragedy and comedy. His 'sad comedy' rarely compels us to laugh or cry.

Happiness does not lack action, emotion or expressive performances, but because characters are so isolated and closeted, words and actions effect their local space rather than extending it. Solondz's dialogue has drawn comparisons to Hal Hartley and David Mamet, but where these other filmmakers construct elaborate verbal games, Solondz's characters speak plainly out of their isolation. In *Storytelling*, Vi uses the creative writing classroom to reveal her twisted sexual relationship with her teacher, Mr. Scott: not because she hopes to make art from life, but because there is no other venue available to her. In *Palindromes*, the frank dialogue between Aviva and her mother, Joyce, over the abortion of Aviva's baby leads not to the reconciliation one expects from melodrama, but a sober realisation that their genetic and social bonds are insubstantial next to their larger ambitions: for Aviva, motherhood, and for Joyce, some magical restoration of Aviva's innocence. 'Am I a bad mother?' asks Joyce after Aviva returns following her botched abortion and subsequent journey into a world of child predators and religious fanatics. To which Aviva responds blankly, 'Everybody makes mistakes'. The words cut through Joyce with a stone-faced honesty and self-awareness, not irony. Solondz has also been compared to John Cassavetes who similarly favoured an ensemble approach, intimate settings and uncomfortable subject matter, but Solondz's work is far more mannered. Cassavetes relied heavily on improvisation, while Solondz proceeds with a didactic, if ubiquitous, formalism rooted not in art cinema, but in television.

Dollhouse began as a response to the *Wonder Years*, which Solondz saw as a purely fantastical representation of youth. His version tells the story of a family trapped in an ideal that it will never realise – of an *Ozzie and Harriet* family in a *Brady Bunch* home – and of an adolescent who recognises the limitations such an ideal imposes. The film is about naming the pretensions of our existence: the 'dollhouses' in which some of us live (and from which others are excluded), the values we hold (trust, self-love, talent, family, etc.) and what lies behind them. Primary among these values is the pursuit of 'happiness'. Solondz covers similar terrain in the 'Nonfiction' portion of *Storytelling*, where the sitcom simulacrum of the American Dream inhabited by the Livingston family crumbles on the scrutiny of the documentary filmmaker's camera, revealing a core of greed, anger, narcissism, racism and homophobia. In a culture where the very notion of happiness is inextricably tangled up with necessity and ambition, we escape into the relative safety and stability of Andy Taylor's Mayberry and Jerry Seinfeld's Manhattan, where nothing very bad ever happens. But Solondz populates his films with slightly exaggerated versions of television types – the *Brady Bunch* family that really *does* scapegoat the middle child, the Ward Cleaver dad who rapes children – to expose their inherent frailties and contradictions. He even goes so far as to cast actors best known for their television roles, from Louise Lasser, Jon Lovitz and Molly Shannon to Lara Flynn Boyle, John Goodman and Richard Masur.

Solondz is not the first director to mine this vein of popular culture. Perhaps the best example is Quentin Tarantino's resurrection of John Travolta and David Carradine. But if Tarantino fetishises popular icons and forms (gangster myth, pulp novel, blaxploitation film), Solondz transcribes them to exploit and manipulate their functionality. Compare Tarantino's use of Travolta in *Pulp Fiction* to Solondz's of Jon Lovitz in *Happiness*. The first plays very much to type: a cool, sweet, confident tough-guy in danger of losing out to his own self-indulgence. Vincent Vega is a latter-day version of Vinny Barberino from *Welcome Back, Kotter* or Tony Manero from *Saturday Night Fever*. But Lovitz's character, the vengeful suicide spewing words of heartfelt hate and pain, is the ugly, repressed side of Lovitz's glib, self-enclosed liars from countless *Saturday Night Live* sketches. If much of our pleasure in Travolta's *Pulp Fiction* performance depends upon our knowledge of earlier roles (particularly the dancing sequence at Jackrabbit Slim's), what we know about Lovitz complicates our response to this performance. Rather than cutting the bitterness of the scene by playing the false bravado that has made Lovitz famous, he allows associations to sour against his deadpan, making the scene still more bitter. The Lovitz the audience knows from television haunts this version, rather than enlivening it.

More than an interest in and appeal to a television sensibility, Solondz's films exploit specific narrative elements of the form as a way of plugging viewers into an otherwise nebulous narrative order. In the situation comedy, for example, narrative action is merely a structure to support a series of jokes, product placements and public service announcements about teen sex, racism, drugs, and other topics of the day. Sitcoms are designed to deliver messages, not catharsis or clarification, and are driven by inevitability, not revelation or intrigue. Like sitcoms, Solondz's scenes are episodic and self-contained. Though the intricate web of relations in *Happiness* (each character is in some way connected to all the others) has been compared to the multi-narrative work of Robert Altman and Paul Thomas Anderson, Solondz uses it to emphasise how very *disconnected* his characters are from each other. Their deeds and words occur in isolation, in the intimate settings familiar to television viewers: family room, restaurant booth, office. When connected, these scenes reveal not narrative continuity or resolution, but a profound level of misunderstanding or miscommunication (the primary narrative functions of sitcoms). Which is not to say that he deliberately seeks to confound the audience. His decision to cast eight different actors in the role of Aviva in *Palindromes* – including a six-year old black girl, a thirteen-year old boy, and forty-two-year-old Jennifer Jason Leigh – was made not from some Buñuelian impulse to destabilise our notion of 'character', but because he recalled the relative ease with which audiences adapted to the casting shift in *Bewitched*, when Dick Sargent took over the role of Darren for Dick York in the show's sixth season. Audiences are capable of bridging such perceptual gaps, of creating unity from the inherently illogical, and so not confounding our sense of character, but enriching it. If Altman and Anderson revel in tracking shots and elegant editing sequences to establish a unity of action and character, Solondz, by contrast, uses the static staging and fluid casting that are the legacy of television to atomise and flatten characters, so to reveal their vulnerabilities.

Television's ubiquity and flatness allow Solondz to figure grave subjects as forces of gravity. The force that brings a character like Bill Maplewood down is an entropic one: a movement towards self-betrayal, instability and death. Solondz describes Maplewood as one who struggles with, and finally gives into, a desire that he can no longer bury or modulate. He is what the director calls 'a bleeding soul', in a losing battle with a monster living inside of him. And, as with all entropic forces, the inevitable result of this battle is flat, undifferentiated chaos. Solondz is often criticised for being sadistic to his characters, for forcing them to occupy that chaos with no room to navigate, but it is here, ironically, that he discovers the greatest hope. Chaos lacks alterity or 'otherness'. As Solondz explained in a 1998 interview with the *Boston Phoenix*, 'to not dismiss something as other makes us more fully human'. Chaos breeds the desperation that forces a sex offender to reach out to his frustrated son, and the understanding that is only possible through the greatest degree of honesty.

In a world where the bounds of isolation are everyday fortified, where television and information technology mediate our primary contact with the global village and personal revelations are made using electronic aliases, the best and worst truths about ourselves emerge (witness the prevalence of paedophilia on the Internet). Todd Solondz's films attempt to address these truths: not to shock, but to communicate and comprehend all that makes us human. If Bill Maplewood finally does succumb to the monster inside of himself, his confession of weakness is a father's gift to the boy, who imagines his delayed sexual development a measure of personal weakness. In a scene echoing the intimate father–son talks that complete most episodes of *Leave it to Beaver*, Bill Maplewood bears the paternal mantle with a seriousness beyond Ward Cleaver, restoring at highest personal cost his son's self-esteem. In the ultimate mixing of modes, the monster of fantasy attempts to restore the familial order ravaged by tragedy. It is a feat as unlikely as dead Laius restoring blind Oedipus's sight, but what makes *Happiness*, and all of Solondz's work, so controversial is that the film holds out a vague hope that the monster may actually succeed.

Biography

Todd Solondz was born in 1959, in Newark, New Jersey, USA. He graduated from Yale University with a Bachelor of Arts in English (1981), and lived briefly in Los Angeles before enrolling in New York University's film school in 1983 (but dropping out in 1986). After the critical failure of his first feature, *Fear, Anxiety and Depression*, he temporarily abandoned filmmaking and taught English to Russian immigrants in New York City, but returned after a five-year hiatus to make the critically acclaimed *Welcome to the Dollhouse*. He currently lives in New York City.

Filmography

As writer/director

Feelings (1984) student film
Babysitter (1984) student film
Schatt's Last Shot (1985) student film
How I Became a Leading Artistic Figure in New York City's East Village Cultural Landscape (1986) short film for *Saturday Night Live*
Fear, Anxiety and Depression (1989), also actor
Welcome to the Dollhouse (1995; aka *Middle Child*) also producer
Happiness (1998)
Storytelling (2001)
Palindromes (2004)
Life During Wartime (2009)

Further reading

Bert Cardullo, 'The Happiness of Your Friends and Neighbors', *Hudson Review*, vol. 52, no. 3, 1999, pp. 455–62.

Chris Chang, 'Cruel to be Kind: A Brief History of Todd Solondz', *Film Comment*, vol. 34, no. 5, 1998, pp. 72–5.

Andrew Lewis Conn, 'The Bad Review *Happiness* Deserves Or: The Tyranny of Critic-Proof Movies', *Film Comment*, vol. 35, no. 1, 1999, pp. 70–2.

Alice Cross, 'Surviving Adolescence with Dignity: An Interview with Todd Solondz', *Cineaste*, vol. 22, no. 3, 1996, pp. 24–8.

Peter Keough (1998) 'Welcome to the Filmmaker', *Boston Phoenix*. Online. Available HTTP: <http://bostonphoenix.com/archive/movies/98/10/22/SOLONDZ.html> (posted 22 October 1998).

Drew Limsky, 'Sexual Warfare in Naturalist Cinema: The Films of Todd Solondz and Neil LaBute', *Excavatio*, no. 13, 2000, pp. 276–80.

Casey McKittrick, ' 'I Laughed and Cringed at the Same Time': Shaping Pedophilic Discourse Around *American Beauty* and *Happiness*', *Velvet Light Trap*, no. 47, 2001, pp. 3–14.

Walter Metz, 'Woody's Melindas and Todd's Stories: Complex Film Narratives in the Light of Literary Modernism', *Film Comment*, vol. 31, no. 1–2, 2006, pp. 107–31.

Michael Newman, 'Characterization as Social Cognition in *Welcome to the Dollhouse*', *Film Studies: An International Review*, no. 8, 2006, pp. 53–67.

Sigrid Nunez, 'Todd Solondz (Writer and Director)', interview, *The Believer*, vol. 3, no. 1, 2005, pp. 58–67.

Adam Pincus (1996) 'In Profile: Todd Solondz', *Sundance Channel Online*. Online. Available HTTP: <http://www.sundancechannel.com/profile/solondz/> (posted January 1996).

Randy Pitman, 'Fear, Anxiety and Depression' (video review), *Library Journal*, vol. 115, no. 12, 1990, p. 148.

Todd Solondz, *Happiness*, London, Faber & Faber, 1998.

Todd Solondz, *Storytelling*, London, Faber & Faber, 2002.

Todd Solondz, *Welcome to the Dollhouse*, London, Faber & Faber, 1996.

STEVEN SPIELBERG

By Peter Krämer

The Economist rarely deals with movies, and, despite its emphasis on economic news, the film industry makes few appearances on its pages. Yet, in February 2009, the magazine reported that '[t]wo of Hollywood's biggest brands form an unexpected partnership'.[1] While the partners in this financing and distribution deal for about half a dozen films per year were the Walt Disney Company and DreamWorks SKG, the article made it clear that the latter 'is largely Steven Spielberg's outfit', and the two brands mentioned in the title therefore were in fact 'Disney' and 'Spielberg'. Hence, in addition to Spielberg, the director, there is 'Spielberg', the brand, which to a greater or lesser degree is attached to the many dozens of films and television programmes he has been involved with in some capacity, including the output of his two companies Amblin Entertainment (formed in 1984) and DreamWorks SKG (formed in 1994). More broadly, the adjective 'Spielbergian' can be used to refer to films which show Spielberg's influence, even though he was not involved in their production. These include, for example, many of the films made by Robert Zemeckis and Chris Columbus, two of Hollywood's biggest hitmakers since the mid-1980s, who launched their careers by writing scripts for Spielberg productions, Zemeckis for *1941* (1979) and Columbus for *Gremlins* (1984) and *The Goonies* (1985); in addition, Zemeckis' early directorial efforts were produced by Spielberg.

If the adjective 'Spielbergian' and the 'Spielberg' brand have a core meaning, it is perhaps, in the words of *The Economist*, the 'fusing [of] blockbuster spectacle with an unflinching take on family life', especially in films addressed to an all-encompassing family audience.[2] Interestingly, this description also applies to much of Disney's feature film output across the decades (starting with *Snow White and the Seven Dwarfs* in 1937), and to many of Hollywood's biggest hits since 1977, the year of both George Lucas's *Star Wars* and Spielberg's *Close Encounters of the Third Kind*. Indeed, it is possible to write the commercial history of American cinema in terms of the major Hollywood studios' adherence to, or departure from, the ideal of family entertainment, best exemplified by the multi-media offerings of the Disney company.[3] Across the 1960s and early 1970s, the major studios, with the exception of Disney, increasingly turned away from their previous emphasis on family entertainment towards a narrower focus on youth audiences, yet following the success of *Star Wars* and *Close Encounters*, both of which were partly inspired by and admiringly compared to classic Disney movies,[4] Hollywood re-focused much of its attention on hugely successful blockbuster productions suitable for children and their parents as well as teenagers and young adults. Most of these were tied in with a wide range of often child-oriented products, just like Disney films had always been.

Together with George Lucas and the Disney company, Spielberg took the lead as Hollywood's most successful purveyor of family entertainment. It is not just that many of the films he directed or produced from 1977 onwards made it onto the annual lists of the ten top grossing movies and of the ten best performing films on video or DVD; some of Spielberg's movies have outperformed almost *all* of the competition during this period. Thus, in addition to four *Star Wars* films and two Disney releases, the inflation-adjusted list (as of

August 2007) of the twenty-five biggest box office hits in the American domestic market since 1977 ranks *E.T. The Extra-Terrestrial* (1982) at number 2, *Raiders of the Lost Ark* (1981, produced by Lucas) at number 6 and *Jurassic Park* (1993) at number 7, followed by the DreamWorks production *Shrek 2* (2004) at number 12 and three 'Spielbergian' films made by his proteges Robert Zemeckis and Chris Columbus: *Forrest Gump* (1994) at number 9, *Home Alone* (1990) at number 16, and *Back to the Future* (1985, an Amblin production), at number 25.[5] Charts for the foreign market show Spielberg's dominance to be even more pronounced. Due to ticket price inflation and fluctuating exchange rates, foreign box office figures are not comparable across decades, yet this problem can be addressed by dividing the all-time foreign box office chart into five-year periods, starting in 1977.[6] The top five hits for each of the five-year periods up to 2006 include Spielberg's *Close Encounters*, *E.T.*, *Indiana Jones and the Last Crusade* (1989, another Lucas production), *Jurassic Park* and *The Lost World: Jurassic Park* (1997), and also *Home Alone*, *Forrest Gump* as well as Columbus's *Harry Potter and the Sorcerer's Stone* (2001) and *Harry Potter and the Chamber of Secrets* (2002), two films which Spielberg had initially been in negotiations for. Finally, while the top 25 (as of May 2004) of the domestic video and DVD sales chart since the 1970s is dominated by eleven Disney releases, *Jurassic Park* ranks 13th and *E.T.* 25th, whereas *Shrek* is at number 5, the Amblin production *Men in Black* (1997) at number 14, *Harry Potter and the Sorcerer's Stone* at number 15 and *Forrest Gump* at number 22.[7]

It is important to note that, after *Close Encounters*, Spielberg's – and DreamWorks' – biggest hits continued to have strong links to Disney. *Variety* called *E.T.* 'the best Disney film Disney never made',[8] and the *Shrek* films were designed by ex-Disney executive Jeffrey Katzenberg as an irreverent homage to his previous employer's classic animated features. Spielberg freely acknowledged his debt to Disney in his films. He transformed the scene from *Peter Pan* (1953), in which the eternal boy and the Darling children fly across the moon-filled night sky, into the very similar iconic image of Elliot and E.T. riding a bike in the air across the backdrop of a full moon, an image he used as the logo for Amblin. Furthermore, going against the novel's depiction of billionaire amusement park creator John Hammond as a ruthless, greedy, dehumanised tycoon, in his film adaptation of Michael Crichton's *Jurassic Park* Spielberg presented a touching portrait of Hammond as over-enthusiastic, yet kind and gentle, a grandfatherly as well as child-like entertainer, who wants nothing more than to share his enjoyment of technologically created entertainment magic and adventure with all the people in the world, especially children. This is not only Spielberg's self-portrait of the artist-entertainer as an old man, but also a tribute to Uncle Walt.

Given Spielberg's close assocation with Disney and the extraordinary commercial success of his films and of his brand, critical writing about him has long had a tendency to see him only or primarily as a family entertainer, and to judge his films as simplistic, retrograde and conservative. Indeed, academic work on Spielberg's films was initially mostly hostile,[9] whereas biographical and film-analytical books addressed to a general readership were much more sympathetic, even celebratory.[10] Partly because of the enormous and lasting impact of *Schindler's List* (1993) on Spielberg's public image and critical status, and partly because of scholars' desire to survey his life's work once he approached his 60th birthday (in December 2006), in recent years a number of monographs and the first international Spielberg conference, which resulted in a special issue of a scholarly journal, have provided a more rounded account of his directorial oeuvre than had previously been available in academic writing.[11] What emerges from this critical analysis is a new appreciation of Spielberg's highly diverse oeuvre. Across this oeuvre certain stylistic and thematic continuities can be observed; perhaps most pronounced among the latter is the centrality of problematic father figures, and a concern for the historical circumstances giving rise to the large-scale and systematic objectification of human beings.

With this in mind, let's survey Spielberg's career. Although he never finished college, Spielberg was a member of the so-called film school generation, a group of young university-trained filmmakers who entered Hollywood from the late 1960s onwards. Indeed, both his first professional film production, the independently produced short *Amblin'* (1968), and *The Sugarland Express* (1974), his first feature film made for theatrical release, contain elements closely associated with the work of his peers. Both are road movies of sorts, mixing comedy and sentimentality; the former features sex, drugs and folk rock among two hippie-ish characters, while the latter pits a young working class couple against the prison system and the police. While Spielberg's second theatrical feature, *Jaws* (1975), is often seen as the beginning of the modern blockbuster, with its huge budget and wide release during the summer supported by massive television advertising, it can also be understood as the culmination of several of the most successful box office trends of the late 1960s and early 1970s. The film, which became the biggest ever hit at the American box office up to this point, is a best-seller adaptation that combines a focus on male–male relationships and on procedural elements (the science and craft of shark hunting) with a sexually quite explicit opening scene, gory violence, implied demonic horror, a critique of the political establishment, great adventure and the death of one of the central characters.[12] At the same time, both feature films are distinguished by their strong emphasis on family relationships. *The Sugarland Express* revolves around a mother's wish to be reunited with her husband (who gets killed in the process) and her baby, while *Jaws* tells the story of a family man who is held responsible for a boy's death by his mourning mother and who almost gets his own son killed before he finally takes appropriate action to protect his loved ones and his community.

Until *Jaws* Spielberg worked almost exclusively for Universal, the main exception being Fox's *Ace Eli and Rodger of the Skies* (1973), a historical drama about the difficult relationship between an irresponsible barnstorming pilot and his traumatised son, which was based on a story by Spielberg. The reason for Spielberg's long assocation with Universal was that, unlike his peers who tried to make a living as freelance, 'independent' filmmakers, in 1968 Spielberg signed a seven-year contract as a television director with the studio. For the next five years, he directed numerous episodes of television series and made-for-television movies, ranging from medical, legal and crime drama to historical action-drama, science fiction and horror. One of his telefilms, *Duel* (1971), once again a kind of road movie, full of suspense and even a touch of demonic horror, gained a lot of attention and, with added scenes which highlighted dysfunctional family relationships and the male protagonist's weaknesses, received a European theatrical release in 1972/73, in many ways preparing the ground for both *The Sugarland Express* and *Jaws*. *Duel* received considerable critical praise, as did *The Sugarland Express* (famously labeled 'one of the most phenomenal debut films in the history of movies' by Pauline Kael) and *Jaws* (nominated for a Best Picture Oscar).[13]

Despite early critical recognition, Spielberg's control over the production process was initially limited due to the fact that he first worked for television on a studio contract and then, on his first two theatrical features, as a freelancer for the powerful producer team of Richard Zanuck and David Brown. Still, he was mostly able to select the projects he wanted to work on (rather than getting assignments), and was involved both in script development (indeed, he received a story credit for *The Sugarland Express*) and in post-production, although he certainly did not have 'final cut'. After the enormous success of *Jaws*, however, there were few limits to his creative control, and he initially used his newly gained power to write and direct *Close Encounters*, a big-budget Columbia release about a man whose obsessions first drive his family away and then get him to the point where he is willing and able to leave Earth in an alien spaceship. The film was a huge commercial and critical success, gaining Spielberg his first nomination for a Best Director Oscar, while also, for example, being listed as one of the ten best films of the year by the *New York Times* and *Time*, and as the best film of the decade 1968–77 by Stanley Kauffmann of the *New Republic*.[14]

From this point onwards, Spielberg applied his enormous productivity, which had already been in evidence during his Universal years, to an ever wider range of films and television programmes. As noted earlier, he had his greatest commercial success with family entertainment. It is worth pointing out that, at a time when theatrical animation was in deep crisis, Spielberg produced several (partially) animated features, including former Disney animator Don Bluth's *An American Tail* (1986) and *The Land Before Time* (1988, co-produced by George Lucas) as well as Zemeckis' *Who Framed Roger Rabbit?* (1988). These were followed by television series such as *Tiny Toon Adventures* (1990–92) and *Animaniacs* (1993–98). Spielberg's involvement in animation helped to revive the production of animated features first at Disney and then at other companies from the late 1980s onwards.

Somewhat surprisingly, Spielberg was also heavily (but not very successfully) involved in youth and/or adult-oriented comedy and comedy-drama, for example with his own slapstick epic *1941* and his first three films as a producer: Zemeckis' *I Wanna Hold Your Hand* (1978) and *Used Cars* (1980) as well as Michael Apted's *Continental Divide* (1981). Later examples among the films he directed include *Always* (1989), *Catch Me If You Can* (2002) and *The Terminal* (2004). Much more famously, Spielberg directed and produced a number of serious historical dramas, the first three based on high profile novels: *The Color Purple* (1985), *Empire of the Sun* (1987), *Schindler's List* (1993), *Amistad* (1997), *Saving Private Ryan* (1998) and *Munich* (2005). Despite some critical controversy, *The Color Purple* was an unprecedented commercial success for what it was: an almost all-black sentimental drama about domestic abuse and female empowerment. While no-one has ever managed to replicate the success of *The Color Purple*, Spielberg's critically acclaimed hits *Schindler's List* and *Saving Private Ryan* (for both of which he won Best Director Oscars) helped to facilitate a successful revival in Hollywood's production of historical epics.[15] Spielberg complemented these two films with the Shoah Visual History Foundation (launched in 1994) and a series of documentaries about the Holocaust, and with the television mini-series *Band of Brothers* (2001).

Last but not least, with *Artificial Intelligence: A.I.* (2001) and *Minority Report* (2002) and the television mini-series *Taken* (2002) Spielberg has recently expanded his long-standing interest in science fiction into very dark and not particularly child-friendly territory, although with *War of the Worlds* (2005) and *Indiana Jones and the Kingdom of the Crystal Skull* (2008, another Lucas production) he has arguably returned his science fiction to material suitable for the whole family. These last two films are a useful reminder of the centrality of highly problematic father–son relationships (and, to a lesser extent, father–daughter relationships) in Spielberg's work. Indeed, absent, neglectful, irresponsible or abusive fathers or father figures, who are often but not always seen from the perspective of their literal or figurative sons and are sometimes able to redeem themselves, are central in all *Indiana Jones* films, *E.T.*, *The Color Purple*, *Empire of the Sun*, *Hook*, the *Jurassic Park* films, *Schindler's List*, *Minority Report*, *Catch Me If You Can* and *Munich*. It is also noteworthy that both *A.I.* and *Minority Report* revolve centrally around another of Spielberg's central concerns: the willingness of human beings to treat other humans (the pre-cogs in *Minority Report*) or human-like beings (the Mechas in *A.I.*) as objects – as means to an end, as slaves, as despised subhuman entities. These two films depict future societies which are based on such objectification: a police state holding pre-cogs captive so as to prevent future crime, and a consumerist world in which most physical and emotional labour is carried out by sentient, feeling robots, who are destroyed once they are no longer needed. Several of his historical films, including family adventures such as *Indiana Jones and the Temple of Doom*, explore the existence of such large-scale, systematic objectification in the past, most notably through the institution of slavery in *Amistad* and through the stigmatisation, ghettoisation, enslavement and murder of millions of Jews in *Schindler's List*. These films emphasise the desperate need and the diverse opportunities for individuals, even most unlikely heroes like the hedonistic Nazi war profiteer Oskar Schindler, to stand up against such objectification, at least to save a few lives, perhaps even – as in *Minority Report* and *Amistad* – to contribute to overall changes in society.

Biography

Spielberg was born on 18 December 1946, in Cincinatti, USA, to Arnold and Leah Spielberg. He began to make 8mm amateur films (including documentaries, Westerns, war films, thrillers, comedies and science fiction movies) in 1957, moving on to 16mm in 1965 and 35mm in 1967, and worked as an intern at Universal Studios in the summers of 1964 and 1965. From 1965 he studied film at California State College at Long Beach, at the same time continuing his unpaid, informal 'apprenticeship' at Universal. In 1968, he signed a seven-year contract as a television director with Universal and dropped out of college.

Notes

1 'Cinderella Story', *The Economist*, 14 February 2009, pp. 74–5.
2 Ibid.
3 Peter Krämer, 'Disney and Family Entertainment', in Linda Ruth Williams and Michael Hammond (eds), *Contemporary American Cinema*, London: Open University Press, 2006, pp. 265–72, 275–9.
4 Joseph McBride, *Steven Spielberg: A Biography*, London; Faber & Faber, 1997, pp. 262, 289; Peter Krämer, ' 'It's aimed at kids – the kid in everybody': George Lucas, *Star Wars* and Children's Entertainment', in Yvonne Tasker (ed.), *Action and Adventure Cinema*, London: Routledge, 2004, p. 365.
5 Cp. 'Domestic Grosses Adjusted for Ticket Price Inflation', http://wwwboxofficemojo.com/alltime/adjusted.htm (accessed 13 August 2007). The domestic market includes both the US and Canada.
6 Internet Movie Database, 'All-Time Non-USA Box Office', http://www.imdb.com/boxoffice/alltimegross?region-non-us (accessed 12 August 2007). Since Canada is regarded as a part of the American domestic market, it is not counted among foreign markets.
7 'Overall Sellers of All Time (Through May 30, 2004)', *Video Store Magazine*, 20 June 2004, p. 32.
8 *Variety* review reprinted in George Perry, *Steven Spielberg*, London: Orion, 1998, pp. 114–16.
9 Cp. Andrew Gordon, 'Science-Fiction and Fantasy Film Criticism: The Case of Lucas and Spielberg', *Journal of the Fantastic in the Arts*, vol. 2, no. 2 (1989), pp. 81–94.
10 See, for example, McBride, op. cit.; Philip M. Taylor, *Steven Spielberg*, London: Batsford, 1992; Douglas Brode, *The Films of Steven Spielberg*, New York: Citadel, 1995.
11 Warren Buckland, *Directed by Steven Spielberg: Poetics of the Contemporary Hollywood Blockbuster*, New York: Continuum, 2006; Lester D. Friedman, *Citizen Spielberg*, Champaign: University of Illinois Press, 2006; Nigel Morris, *The Cinema of Steven Spielberg: Empire of Light*, London: Wallflower Press, 2007; Andrew M. Gordon, *Empire of Dreams: The Science Fiction and Fantasy Films of Steven Spielberg*, Lanham, MD: Rowman and Littlefield, 2008; Nigel Morris (ed.), 'Steven Spielberg', special issue of the *New Review of Film and Television Studies*, vol. 7, no. 1 (March 2009).

12 Cp. Peter Krämer, *The New Hollywood: From Bonnie and Clyde to Star Wars*, London: Wallflower Press, 2005, Ch. 1.
13 McBride, *op. cit.*, pp. 206–7, 223–4, 255–6.
14 Cobbett Steinberg, *Film Facts*, New York: Facts on File, 1980, pp. 164, 175, 179.
15 Cp. James Russell, *The Historical Epic and Contemporary Hollywood: From Dances with Wolves to Gladiator*, New York: Continuum, 2007.

Filmography

Duel (1971), made-for-television movie (European theatrical release: 1972/3; US theatrical release: 1983)

The Sugarland Express (1974), also co-writer

Jaws (1975)

Close Encounters of the Third Kind (1977; special edition released in 1980), also writer

1941 (1979)

Raiders of the Lost Ark (1981)

E.T. The Extraterrestrial (1982), original idea by Spielberg (uncredited), also co-producer

Twilight Zone – The Movie (1983), 'Segment 2', also producer

Indiana Jones and the Temple of Doom (1984)

The Color Purple (1985), also co-producer

Empire of the Sun (1987), also co-producer

Indiana Jones and the Last Crusade (1989)

Always (1989), also co-producer

Hook (1991)

Jurassic Park (1993)

Schindler's List (1993), also co-producer

The Lost World: Jurassic Park (1997)

Amistad (1997), also co-producer

Saving Private Ryan (1998), also co-producer

Artificial Intelligence: A.I. (2001), also co-writer and co-producer

Minority Report (2002)

Catch Me If You Can (2002)

The Terminal (2004), also co-producer

War of the Worlds (2005)

Munich (2005), also co-producer

Indiana Jones and the Kingdom of the Crystal Skull (2008)

OLIVER STONE

By Martin Fradley

> I don't set out to make movies about big, controversial themes. I just make movies about what has happened to my life … I have to keep

digging into our history to understand what happened to me and my generation.

Oliver Stone[1]

Echoing the endlessly scrutinised amateur footage of commercial aircraft tearing into the World Trade Center, the archetypal Oliver Stone image is located in a traumatic moment in American history captured on celluloid by a different filmmaker entirely. In the lengthy courtroom scenes towards the climax of *JFK*, embattled patriot Jim Garrison (Kevin Costner) insistently plays and *re*-plays the infamous Zapruder film for the benefit of both diegetic jury and extra-textual audience. 'This', he intones, 'is the key *shot*'. What we see – *again and again* – in visceral, fetishistic detail is in many ways a synecdoche for the director's advocacy of political enlightenment through visual and emotional assault. Drawing attention to the minutiae of each grainy frame, Garrison/Stone mobilises Zapruder's unsettling *cinéma vérité* in a rhetorically brutal attempt to awaken his complacent and unwary audience to the disturbing 'truth' of the Kennedy assassination and, in turn, to the dark sociopolitical realities of the postwar United States.

Fifteen years after the release of *JFK*, critics disappointed by *World Trade Center* seemed curiously oblivious to the semiotic parallels between the violent events being depicted. The representations of the notorious seven seconds in Dallas and the 102 minutes on the morning of 11th September 2001 in New York both pivot around disturbingly similar visual and narrative tropes: virginal, sun-drenched blue skies; an unsullied state of *a priori* innocence; the illusory sense of normalcy violently interrupted by a horrific return of the Real; the deep, painful shock of misrecognition. The ejaculatory crimson explosion of Kennedy's skull and the hallucinatory orange fireball that lacerated the glimmering surfaces of downtown Manhattan's twin towers are highly condensed symbolic *images* of profound national trauma. More ideologically overdetermined than they are uncanny, both events function in the popular imagination as *holocaustal events*, episodes which cannot simply be forgotten and put out of mind, but neither can they be adequately remembered. It was perhaps unsurprising that Stone was chosen to direct *World Trade Center*: indeed, alongside *Alexander* and *W.*, the film functions as one part of a loose Stone-helmed post-9/11 trilogy. More significantly, the murder of John F. Kennedy and the global media event of 9/11 both testify to the enduring potency of the moving image, the footage of these primal events now inextricably interwoven with the political mythologies of recent American social and cultural history.

And so the story goes: as product of the baby-boom and the national optimism of Eisenhower's USA, the 1960s were a series of emotionally jarring events for the young William Oliver Stone. Beginning with the shock divorce of his adulterous parents in 1962, Stone's biographical narrative moves irresistibly through the most traumatic episodes of 'the sixties', a period which repeatedly violates the innocence of this prototypical mid-century American son. 'I was a child of distortions', Stone later claimed of his disquieting formative years, 'I thought I was a living a happy life, but discovered it was all a lie'.[2] Films such as *Platoon, Born on the Fourth of July, Nixon* and *JFK* are in turn powerfully melodramatic re-enactments of the key events in this turbulent decade, retrospectively filtered through the stylised subjective prism of the Stone imaginary. Indeed, it is principally the compulsive return *to*, and mythopoetic re-imaginings *of*, this volatile epoch and its aftermath which ensured Stone's status as Hollywood's pre-eminent auteur-*provocateur* for much of his career. Through these portentous quasi-revisionist interrogations of history, power, politics and paranoia in postwar American culture, Stone became arguably the most controversial and written-about Hollywood director of the 1980s and 1990s. Yet this notoriety also underscores his position as director-*star*, for any discussion of Stone's *oeuvre* is also unavoidably a sojourn into the director's biography and, dialectically, evidence of the evolving commodification and celebrification of the Stone persona. Any overview of Stone's career is also, in other words, an illustrative demonstration of the synergistic processes involved in the construction of a marketable auteur discourse.

The symbiotic relationship between Stone's creative output and his iconoclastic persona has been perpetuated and reinforced in both popular and critical representations, extending into discussion of his early screenplays and emergence as a major Hollywood player. It is in his scriptwriting that we uncover the skeletal foundations of the formative Stone aesthetic: lone, invariably flawed male protagonists; a mythic *rite-de-passage* narrative; a classical three-act structure typically involving a quasi-spiritual journey from innocence, through suffering and experience, to a state of knowledge and either redemption or death. The filmmaker's early screenwriting also foregrounds the harsh texture of Stone's sensibilities: a preoccupation with extreme violence and mortality supplemented by coarse, testosterone-driven and often crudely didactic dialogue. (The deserts, snakes and Symbolic Indians come later.) Typified by *Scarface* (DePalma, 1983) and *Midnight Express* (Parker, 1978) – for which Stone won his first Oscar – these films are also notable for their racism, casual misogyny, and an unashamed commitment to visual, thematic and, above all, emotional *excess*. This provocatively dissolute sensibility forms a homologous relationship with the imposing, bear-like charisma of Stone himself, a state of mimesis exacerbated by anecdotal tales of the writer–director's punishing work-rate and substantial recreational appetites. Boundaries between auteur, filmic text and fictional protagonist(s) are further elided in retrospective analyses and the director's ever present self-commentary. Events in *Midnight Express*, for example, mirror Stone's youthful incarceration for drug possession; *Scarface*, meanwhile, becomes his post-rehab 'swan song to cocaine'.[3]

This intertextual relay between on-screen protagonist, personal biography and commercial star image becomes ever more reflexive. Early directorial efforts *Seizure* and *The Hand*, for example, are exploitation horror flicks about self-destructive artists. This thematic terrain is subsequently revisited in both the angsty, introverted *Talk Radio* and, conversely, the sensual extravagance of *The Doors*. *Salvador*'s impassioned exposé of Reagan-era foreign policy atrocities in Latin America, meanwhile, becomes a self-legitimising meditation on the social and ethical role of the creative documentarian, personified here by Jimmy Woods's definitively sleazy photo-journalist. This endlessly narcissistic self-referentiality is unquestionably one of the most consistent features of the Stone canon. 'I don't think Oliver could make a movie without being completely in love with the main character', Stone's wife noted of the director's fawning relationship with Fidel Castro in low-budget documentary *Commandante*.[4] Elsewhere, however, this solipsism becomes more fractious and tormented. In *Nixon*, the generic conservatism of the biopic is compellingly reworked as a fragmented and abyssian portrait of paranoid self-loathing, featuring Tony Hopkins-as-Tricky Dicky-as-Charlie Kane-as-Oliver Stone.

Platoon's promotional campaign was successfully founded on similar auteurist rhetoric. This largely autobiographical film's self-proclaimed importance lay in its unique status as *survivor testimony*; the *storyteller* here granted significance equal to the story itself. The presence of Stone the veteran-*auteur* acted as an extratextual guarantee of *Platoon*'s verisimilitude, particularly as an authentic corrective to the crude Reaganite bombast evident in contemporaneous militaristic fantasies *Rambo* (Cosmatos, 1985) and *Top Gun* (Scott, 1986). Protagonist Chris Taylor (Charlie Sheen) is a direct stand-in for Stone himself: a naïve, middle-class college drop-out who volunteers for duty in Vietnam only to have his patriotic illusions crushed by the purposeless barbarity of the conflict and the profound social divisions among his fellow marines. Serving as mythopoetic reportage from the frontline, *Platoon*'s depiction of an innocent American boy's experiential descent into the abyss of Vietnam is recounted ostensibly to cleanse the doors of perception for Stone's audience: 'Those of us who did make it have an obligation to build again, to teach others what we know, and try with what's left of our lives to find a goodness and a meaning to this life'. *Platoon*'s enduring influence on the combat genre is indisputable. Stone's instinctive feel for the marines' colourful, argot-laden banter and the film's cynical grunt's-eye perspective was directly transferred to coalition-occupied Iraq in HBO's acclaimed *Generation Kill* (2008). Nevertheless, *Platoon*'s purported realism is undermined by its symptomatic political evasions and declamatory excesses: it is telling that the film's most iconic moment is the melancholic slow-motion slaughter of a Christ-like Elias (Willem Dafoe) scored by 'Adagio for Strings'. 'We did not fight the enemy', ponders Taylor in the film's most transparent moment of disavowal, 'we fought ourselves, and the enemy was in us.'

Close identification with his protagonists coupled with a fierce critique of the United States' national trajectory since the 1960s form the cornerstones of the director's mid-career aesthetic. Betrayed by Uncle Sam and denied the regenerative promises of the 1950s, Stone – like *Born on the Fourth of July*'s Ron Kovic – repeatedly presented himself in interviews as an impassioned patriot determined to expose his country's failed idealism. In doing so, the fervent nonconformity of the director/protagonist takes on more than a whiff of Oedipal revolt. Stone's (post)modern messiahs – Taylor, Kovic and Garrison most obviously, but also *Salvador*'s Richard Boyle, *Talk Radio*'s misanthropic Barry Champlain, *The Doors*' Jim Morrison, *Any Given Sunday*'s Tony D'Amato, perhaps even *Natural Born Killers*' amoral lovers Mickey and Mallory – come forth bearing the 'truth' in various guises, only to be met with ridicule and/or aggression by a corrupt, hypocritical establishment. Given the United States' deep-rooted populist traditions, of course, Stone's brash coupling of patriotic fervour with anti-authoritarian dissent is the political equivalent of valorising home-baked apple pie. 'It is not that Stone is un-American', muses John Orr, '[i]t is more that he is *too* American'.[5]

Nevertheless, Stone's reputation as mainstream American cinema's foremost political iconoclast reached its zenith during the prolonged Stateside furore over *JFK*. Denounced as 'the cinematic equivalent of rape',[6] criticisms of *JFK* were virtually indistinguishable from personal attacks on the director himself: critical bullets flew from all directions, with Stone caught in the crossfire as the sacrificial lamb akin to *JFK*'s 'slain father-leader'. With life imitating art to an ever greater degree, Stone's crusade to expose the truth directly echoed the plight of *JFK*'s embattled detective-patriot Garrison, the former styling himself as a righteous postmodern Ahab determined to fulfill his quest regardless of the cost. Claiming to be taking on both the establishment *and* 'official history', the controversy surrounding *JFK* substantially bolstered the credibility of Stone's increasingly irreverent, would-be 'subversive' star image. The box office success of *JFK* effectively heralded the fashionable conspiracism of the 1990s.

Epitomised by *JFK*, Stone's historical docudramas have repeatedly courted controversy in both popular and academic forums. Always already highly contentious generic forms, the hybridised modes of 'infotainment' or 'faction' that Stone has favoured from *Salvador* through to *World Trade Center* and *W.* have all underscored the fluid transactions between the real and the *reel*; that is, the protean synergies that exist between historical object, popular memory and media representation. Instinctively alert to the commercial potency of controversy, Stone claimed that the critical hostility surrounding *JFK* was a symptom of his conspiratorial revelations. However, the true source of the hysteria the film provoked is more usefully traced to related anxieties surrounding the politics of historical representation and the supposed death of authentic memory under the mass-mediated conditions of postmodernity. In the popular cultural imagination the Kennedy assassination ruptures American history: November 1963 forms a national–ideological schism wherein the 1950s and early 1960s are understood as an idyll of innocence and national consensus before an irreversible descent into violence, postnational fragmentation and default cynicism. If the benevolent, paternal President is *JFK*'s mourned lost object, he is also unmistakably the key fetish within the Stone imaginary: the film is at once illustrative of the fraught, unstable relationship between past and present *and* a conspiratorial slice of primal mythology. Yet in its casual elision of the emergent liberationist movements and pivotal social gains that come *after* the Fall of the fabled Camelot, *JFK*'s neurotic fixation upon the spiritual torpor and ideological entropy of the contemporary United States ultimately renders the film more amnesiac than it is revisionist.

Nevertheless, it was *JFK*'s meta-textual audacity that particularly provoked the ire of Stone's many critics. The film's frenzied Eisensteinean montage of history sutured documentary footage, painstakingly accurate reconstructions, monochrome and colour stock, melodrama, archival television reports and Hollywood naturalism in a near-seamless collage of fact, fantasy, hypothesis, conjecture and finger-pointing conspiracy theory. In this way, *JFK* is emblematic of the attentive historiographical (self-)consciousness that has always characterised the director's sojourns in the recent past. While *JFK*'s narrative trajectory moves urgently towards a coherent counter explanation of Kennedy's violent demise, the aggressive polyphony of Stone's formal technique has the effect of relativist distanciation. The veracity of historical narrative here is provisional and illusory, a kinetic *bricolage* of partial truths arbitrarily pieced together for reflexive ends. Form and content collude to devastating effect; in *JFK*, as one wily critic put it, '*montage* is the message'.[7]

Stone's engagements with history have continued to attract criticism on a number of levels: their didactic thrust and sensationalist polemic; the director's melodramatic sensibility, rejection of objectivity and aggressive over-identification with his protagonists; the dramatist's creative refusal to adhere to documented 'facts' and the subsequent creation of composite characters and events; and Stone's persistent use of mythic archetypes to personify historical events and social forces. Stone himself has often adopted a slippery, strategic indeterminacy in response to such accusations: claiming to be a cinematic historian at one juncture, purveyor of 'counter-myth' at another; sometimes adopting a position of postmodern relativism, at others self-deprecatingly shrugging his shoulders.[8]

Indeed, Stone has persistently rejected the dispassionate objectivity of the legitimate historian. Perhaps best understood as a purveyor of cinematic *psycho*histories, Stone's fiery sensibility and emphasis upon the emotional *experience* of recent U.S. history typifies the democratic appeal and affective potency of Hollywood's melodramatic mode. For the director, however, the cathartic emotionalism of his movies reflects a sustained commitment to what he ostentatiously dubs 'Dionysian politics'. This characteristically dualistic philosophy privileges subjective and emotional truths over the intellectual/rational, forcing 'the pure wash of emotion over the mind to let you see the inner myth, the spirit of the thing. Then, when the cold light of reason hits you as you walk out of the theatre, the sense of truth will remain lodged beyond reason in the depths of your being'.[9] Beyond the philosophical mumbo-jumbo, Stone is more honest, if no less ponderous:

> I admit I like excess. I like grandiosity of style. I like characters like Gordon Gekko and Jim Morrison. I believe in the power of excess because through excess I live a larger life. I inflate my life and by inflating my life I live more of the world. I die a more experienced man.[10]

Like both its subject and its creator, *The Doors* is indulgent, pretentious and hugely self-important. At the same time, it is a frantic and entertainingly impressionistic medley of the sights, sounds and, naturally, the excesses of the West Coast's counter-cultural scene in the late 1960s. The political chaos and social upheaval of the period is registered only in the abstract, mapped as it is onto the soundtrack-led narrative and debauched, 'shamanic' charisma of its rock star protagonist (Val Kilmer). In one early scene, Morrison is derided by fellow UCLA students for his incoherent *avant-garde* filmmaking; the film professor – played by Stone – attempts to locate an authoritative source of meaning and turns to the star-to-be: 'Let's ask the filmmaker what *he* thinks'. And what does the filmmaker think? 'I believe in Morrison's incantations. Break on through. Kill the pigs. Destroy. Loot. Fuck your mother. All that shit. Anything goes. Anything'.[11] Well, *obviously*.

'Anything goes', however, neatly encapsulates the ethos behind Stone's increasingly spectacular formal pyrotechnics. Progressively more ambitious and experimental throughout the mid-period of his career, the director's visual grandiloquence reached its apogee with the hyper-expressionism of *Natural Born Killers* and the self-satirising *U-Turn*'s stylistic cartwheels and gleeful hybridity. Knowingly exhibitionist, both films revel in their disparate blend of styles and stocks, free-associative imagery, eclectic and inventive use of sound and music, and general sense of all-encompassing hyperreality. Not insignificantly, these violent but playfully nihilistic fantasies emerged in the wake of their immediate predecessors' failure at the box office. More to the point, the wilful incoherence of *Natural Born Killers'* satire on the debilitating omnipresence of the mass media serves to aggressively reiterate Stone's sledgehammer critique of post-1960s American decline. In his largely pessimistic 1990s films in particular, Stone's cinema locates his homeland's moral and ethical Ground Zero as simultaneously yesterday, today and *always*.

From the outset, Stone's movies have remained almost unremittingly homosocial in focus, obsessively exploring the emotional and institutional kinship between men. There is certainly little room for feminism (or even women) in these often regressively masculinist films. Stone's trademark madonna–whore complex is self-evident throughout his back catalogue. *Alexander* exemplifies one side of the director's polarised view of womanhood: Angelina Jolie plays the emperor's vampish mother as an overbearing, Medusean *femme castrice*. Elsewhere, Maggie Gyllenhaal and Maria Bello's anguished wives in *World Trade Center* – maternal, dutiful, ethereally beautiful – typify the flipside of this rigidly adolescent worldview. The limitations of Stone's depiction of women are underlined in the allegorical imaginary of *Any Given Sunday*, wherein the film's litany of predatory hookers, money-grabbing wives and careerist harpies serves as misogynistic shorthand for an American culture perverted by empty materialism and unethical corporate power. Indeed, it is indicative of Stone's priorities – not to mention the expectations of his audience – that his sole attempt to counter perennial accusations of androcentrism, misogyny and Orientalism, and his one film to feature a central female protagonist – *Heaven and Earth* – was a critical and commercial failure.

This persistent marginalisation of women and often banal heteromasculinist agenda epitomise Stone's fascination with the supposed 'crisis' of American masculinity. To be sure, there is no other filmmaker whose *oeuvre* so directly illustrates Susan Faludi's thesis concerning the befuddled state of manhood in postwar U.S. culture.[12] Embattled 'victims' of a postmodern, post-liberationist culture, Stone's menfolk endlessly strive for a redemptive remasculinisation within a debased (read: 'feminised') social order. That *castration* is one of the most recurrent visual and thematic tropes in Stone's movies tells its own deeply symptomatic story. The melodramatic tragedy of Kovic's 'dead penis' or the preoccupation with Morrison's impotence are exemplary in this respect, both illustrative of the way Stone neurotically maps social trauma across brutalised white male bodies.

Moreover, Stone's fantasies of martyrdom repeatedly eroticise male torment and subjugation. The lurid S&M aesthetic of *Midnight Express* begins this suggestive sense of homosocial desire; the director's adoration of *JFK*'s virile and handsome President, or his fascination with the writhing eroticism of Jim Morrison, only reinforce the erotic economy of these ostensibly heterosexist Stone films. You don't have to look hard to detect the relentless undercurrent of fear and desire projected towards the homosexual. 'You don't know shit', rasps Willie O'Keefe (Kevin Bacon) to an intrigued Jim Garrison in *JFK*, *'because you've never been fucked in the ass'*. The heady locker-room funk that enshrouds the director's preferred stomping ground certainly does not begin and end with *Any Given Sunday*: the homoerotic camaraderie of key scenes in, say, *Platoon* only reiterates the desirously fraught nature of intra-male relationships in Stone's films. To this end, perhaps the most intriguing aspect of *Alexander* was the transparency of its representation of bisexuality. Again, the vigorous masculine charisma of Gordon Gekko exceeds containment in *Wall Street*'s ostensibly simplistic morality play. Michael Douglas's iconic Oscar-winning performance here embodies the pleasures of fraternal seduction via overdetermined metaphors of voracious individualism and material desire. 'Greed' may not be *good*, but it is not without temptation.

Despite continuing to engage with contentious material, Stone's offerings in the 2000s have struggled to gain popular or critical approval. Now entering his sixties, the one-time *enfant terrible* may well be mellowing, even maturing. 'I think I'm getting simpler now as I get older', he admitted while promoting *World Trade Center*. Released against the backdrop of an increasingly nebulous 'War on Terror', the absence of political point-scoring in *World Trade Center* was deemed by many to be a wasted opportunity. In mournfully reimagining 9/11 as an elegiac tale of symbolic death and (national) rebirth, Stone's formal restraint necessarily acknowledges the futility of recreating telegenic imagery always already prosthetically seared into the collective memory. Literal, figurative and semiotic warfare nevertheless remains the key referent and dominant metaphor in the Stone imaginary. Hyper-Oedipal ancient world epic *Alexander* serves primarily as a bombastic Orientalist allegory of Bush-era geopolitical hubris, military adventurism and dubiously 'benevolent' imperialism.

The pop-Freudian dynamic of *Alexander* and *W.* also maintained the director's career-long fascination with the failings of real or symbolic parental figures. Like the doomed singer in *The Doors*, Stone's tragicomedy *W.* depicts the hapless George Bush Jnr. as a perpetual adolescent, the arrested development of the Commander in Chief a metonym for that of American political life more broadly. That Stone's representation succeeds in presenting its subject empathetically is due in no small part to Josh Brolin's comic yet sensitively observed performance. Rapidly shot and strategically released during the latter stages of the 2008 presidential election, *W.* is, tonally and stylistically, a long way removed from the paranoiac *noir* of *Nixon*. Whereas Richard Milhous was knowingly consumed by sinister military–industrial forces beyond his control, Dubya's tragedy is cheerful obliviousness to the political realities of Iraq, Guantanamo Bay and Abu Ghraib. '*I'm the decider*', asserts an enthusiastically delusional Bush as Dick Cheney's (Richard Dreyfuss) hawk glowers appreciatively. *W.* presents Dubya as much a malleable patsy as Lee Harvey Oswald, a guileless puppet whose preeminence underscores Stone's contempt for the ethical vacuity and illusory surface of contemporary American politics. Despite its humour, *W.* insistently grants Bush humanity and pathos: given that the film was released at the *nadir* of Bush's political career, this move stands as arguably one of Stone's bravest commercial decisions. This ambivalence is, however, far from atypical. If Stone's avowed aim in *World Trade Center* was to *de*-politicise the mythic primal event of 9/11, the film nevertheless allows for a variety of interpretations. Dave Karnes (Michael Shannon), the God-fearing marine vowing retribution amidst the smoking rubble of Ground Zero, can be understood as a courageous avenging angel, a propagandist poster boy for the war on terror. Just as easily, this terrifyingly cold-eyed apparition can be read as an unsmiling prophet of the political Right, a murderous augur of the militaristic nightmare to follow.

To this end, both Oliver Stone the celebrity *auteur* and the films that bear his brand name adhere to the multiple logics of Hollywood's commercial aesthetic. A filmmaker once dubbed 'The Most Dangerous Man in America' is also a multiple Oscar-winner. The po-mo relativist/revisionist who directs films based on the eternal truths of classical mythology. A dissenting *avant-garde* filmmaker who helms star-laden, multi-million dollar genre flicks. The populist masculinist-individualist who mourns the lost social idealism of the New Left. The anti-corporate, anti-establishment ideologue who enthusiastically advocates neoliberalism and believes 'McDonalds is good for the world'.[13] An outspoken political iconoclast who adapts Andrew Lloyd Webber for the screen. The Leftist director who makes largely sympathetic biopics about the two most reviled Republican presidents in American history. 'I wonder how I can be all these people at the end of the day. Who am I? The [media] don't know who Oliver Stone is: they have no fucking idea. Oliver Stone is still a mystery – to me too'.[14] The strategic indeterminacy of Hollywood entertainment serves, like the opaque riddle of the Zapruder film, to mystify and conceal as much as it reveals. And the *auteur* – even one with a star image as recognisable and relentlessly foregrounded as Oliver Stone's – is a meaningful presence behind or within the text *only if we choose to see him there*. But which 'Oliver Stone' do we choose to see? Now *that's* (provocative) enfotainment.

Biography

Born in New York, USA, in 1946, Stone volunteered for duty in Vietnam in 1967–68. He has won Academy Awards for Best Director (*Platoon* and *Born on the Fourth of July*) and Best Picture (*Platoon*).

Notes

1 Quoted in Chris Salewicz, *Oliver Stone: The Making of His Movies*, London, Orion, 1997, p. 77.
2 Quoted in James Riordan, *Stone: The Controversies, Excesses and Exploits of a Radical Filmmaker*, London, Aurum Press, 1996, p. 31.
3 Riordan, p. 343.

4 Quoted in Tim Adams, 'Oliver's one-man army', *The Observer Review* 31.08.03, p. 3.
5 John Orr *The Art and Politics of Film*, Edinburgh, Edinburgh University Press, 2000, p. 10; emphasis added.
6 Riordan, *op. cit.*, pp. 423–4.
7 Pat Dowell, 'Last Year at Nuremberg: The Cinematic Strategies of *JFK*', *Cineaste*, 19, 1992, p. 9; emphasis added.
8 Quoted in 'Stone on Stone's image', in Robert Brent Toplin, ed., *Oliver Stone's USA: Film, History and Controversy*, Lawrence, University Press of Kansas, 2000, p. 43.
9 Quoted in James L. Farr, 'The Lizard King or Fake Hero: Oliver Stone, Jim Morrison, and History', in Brent Toplin, *op. cit.*, p. 156.
10 Quoted in Riordan, *op. cit.*, p. 343.
11 Quoted in Norman Kagan, *The Cinema of Oliver Stone*, New York, Continuum Publishing, 2000, p. 181.
12 Susan Faludi *Stiffed: The Betrayal of Modern Man*, London, Chatto & Windus, 1990.
13 Quoted in Marc Cooper, '*Playboy* Interview: Oliver Stone', in Charles L.P. Silet (ed.), *Oliver Stone: Interviews*, Jackson: University Press of Mississippi, 2001, p. 65.
14 Stone, quoted in Salewicz, *op. cit.*, p. 118.

Filmography

Seizure (1974)
The Hand (1981)
Salvador (1986)
Platoon (1986)
Wall Street (1987)
Talk Radio (1988)
Born on the Fourth of July (1989)
The Doors (1991)
JFK (1991)
Heaven and Earth (1993)
Natural Born Killers (1994)
Nixon (1995)
U-Turn (1997)
Any Given Sunday (1999)
Commandante (2003)
Alexander (2004)
World Trade Center (2006)
W. (2008)

Further reading

Frank Beaver, *Oliver Stone: Wakeup Cinema*, New York, Twayne, 1994.
Peter Knight, *Conspiracy Culture: From Kennedy to the X-Files*, London, Routledge, 2000.

Robert Kolker, *A Cinema of Loneliness: Penn, Stone, Kubrick, Scorsese, Spielberg, Altman*, Oxford, Oxford University Press, 2000.

Susan Mackey-Kallis, *Oliver Stone's America: Dreaming the Myth Outward*, Boulder, Colorado, Westview Press, 1996.

Marita Sturken, 'Re-enactment, Fantasy and the Paranoia of History: Oliver Stone's Docudramas', *History and Theory* 36, 1997, pp. 64–79.

QUENTIN TARANTINO

By Glyn White

When *Kill Bill (Volume 1)* announced itself in 2003 as 'The 4th film by Quentin Tarantino' it made clear that 'the auteur of the 1990s'[1] had achieved popular and critical prominence on the basis of relatively few feature-length films. The line capitalised on Tarantino as a brand and a media phenomenon whose impact and influence stemmed not only from directing but also from screenwriting and high visibility as a celebrity. Publicity for *Inglourious Basterds* (2009) was similarly director-led. Most Tarantino screenplays have been published and the man and his work are the subject of at least seven books, supplemented by collections of interviews and opinions and academic texts that use his work to engage with ethics and philosophy. A critical consideration of Tarantino necessitates attention to three key areas: mythology, personality and what might be called 'adjectivity'.

Mythology

The story goes that Quentin Tarantino was a video-store clerk who got his script to the actor Harvey Keitel whose support got *Reservoir Dogs* made and so catapulted Tarantino to directorial stardom. Although there is a kernel of truth in this, there is also a mythological aspect, recalling studio-generated tales of stars discovered as waitresses and gas station attendants. Tarantino may indeed be 'the most famous former video-store clerk in America' and he happily acknowledges his past as 'a film geek', stating that: 'I think my biggest appeal amongst young fans is that they look at me as a fan boy who made it'.[2]

Although Tarantino had almost no directorial experience before *Reservoir Dogs*, the transition from video-store clerk to fêted director is not as sudden as sometimes supposed. Tarantino had trained as an actor and had appeared (as an Elvis impersonator) in an episode of *The Golden Girls*. Indeed, it was his lack of success as an actor that first led him to write. Eventually he quit the video store and supported himself by selling scripts (*True Romance*), revamping outlines (*From Dusk 'til Dawn*) and polishing the work of others. A partial rewrite of *Past Midnight* (1992), a cable TV premiere with Rutger Hauer and Natasha Richardson, gained him an associate producer credit. Thus Tarantino had already achieved a measure of credibility in the industry by the time his script for *Reservoir Dogs* reached Keitel: not so much a video-store clerk turned director, as an industrious Hollywood hopeful getting his break.

The initial idea for Tarantino to direct *Reservoir Dogs* on 16mm for a budget of $30,000 (the fee for the *True Romance* script)[3] was sparked by his desire to act. His connection to directing came through writing and acting and, perhaps unsurprisingly, sensitivity to the needs and talents of actors remains a significant strength as a director. The care taken in assembling the cast of *Reservoir Dogs* is instructive. Whether seasoned or relatively fresh, each actor brings a celluloid past like a rap sheet.[4] Of course, the heist parallel (the filmmaker setting up 'a job', making a good score) also feeds the myth. If the robbery goes badly wrong, the film itself – very much about 'getting away with it' – does not.

Personality

After the success of Steven Soderbergh's *sex, lies, and videotape* in 1989, distributors were keen to spot another crossover hit at the 1992 Sundance Festival. Although it did not win a prize, *Reservoir Dogs* caused controversy and gained attention, later gathering critical plaudits across Europe. The film's box-office and critical kudos allowed Tarantino to set up favourable deals, including the opportunity to hand-pick actors for his next project. Its success also meant other extant Tarantino screenplays quickly went into production. *True Romance*, directed by Tony Scott, brought together another excellent cast and increased Tarantino's stock. Meanwhile, *Natural Born Killers* 'got away' from Tarantino – ultimately against his will – to be adapted in visceral style by Oliver Stone, creating further controversy (and profit). The result was a wave of 'Tarantino' movies appearing, building up expectation for his second directorial project, *Pulp Fiction*, which delivered audiences and acclaim, including the Palme d'Or and an Oscar for Best Script.

In the frenzied media attention that followed, it was clear that Tarantino was good copy, someone who had dreamed of fame, who conceived of himself as a performer and had no difficulty putting himself across (in a sense, Tarantino is his own best acting role, nicely performed in his cameo as director Q.T. in Spike Lee's *Girl 6*). Tarantino emerged as a garrulous autodidact often reckless in his desire to defend an opinion against all comers, whether it is his enjoyment of on-screen violence, or championing Paul Verhoeven's *Showgirls* (1995) and Gus Van Sant's *Psycho* remake (1998). He is fiercely defensive of his films, particularly in discussions of violence (*Reservoir Dogs*' torture scene), racism (use of the 'n' word in *Pulp Fiction*), plagiarism (borrowings from Ringo Lam's *City on Fire* [1987] in *Reservoir Dogs*, or the suggestion that he has taken credit for the work of others in his scripts), and, more recently, collared *Sight and Sound*'s editor over criticism of *Deathproof*.[5]

To Tarantino's credit, he remains a fan as well as a filmmaker, visiting small scale venues and events as well as high profile ones. Furthermore, Roger Avary, the man most often cited as the talent exploited by Tarantino, shared Tarantino's Oscar for *Pulp Fiction*'s writing and Tarantino produced his Paris-set *Killing Zoe* (1994). The mythology, hype and personal contradictions around Tarantino led interviewer Simon Hattenstone to characterise him as:

> the most arrogant, precious, pretentious, unquestioning, solipsistic, self-deluded man I've ever met. So I can't work out why I almost like him. Maybe it's because I don't believe he did shaft his friends. Maybe it's because, however shallow he is, he is also a bit of a genius.[6]

Whether self-aware or narcissistic, Tarantino's self-forged personality has provoked considerable irritation, with critics attacking him for a lack of moral compass or pointing to a lack of life experience. Ian Penman, for instance, dubs Tarantino 'The Man Who Mistook a Video Collection for his Life'.[7] Raised by his mother in an ethnically mixed neighborhood in Los Angeles, Tarantino's fondest memories do appear to be movie-based and his life has been spent dreaming, discussing and obsessing about popular culture. Yet the logic of Penman's criticism would not even allow Ken Loach to operate. Rather than something new, Tarantino represents the extreme of an existing phenomenon: the so-called 'movie brats' of New Hollywood. To some extent, this type of criticism is a backlash against the video-store clerk 'mythology', suggesting that he is somehow not fit to be a director without years of struggle or film-school training at the very least.

Luckily, or perhaps shrewdly, when the backlash first reached critical mass it was *Four Rooms*, the disastrous compendium piece for which Tarantino wrote, directed and acted in only one section, that was the target. Other young festival-hit directors – Allison Anders, Robert Rodriguez and Alexandre Rockwell – shared culpability and, with the possible exception of Rodriguez, came out worse. After this, the Tarantino films of the mid-2000s were slightly guarded by not initially appearing in finalised form (*Kill Bill* split into two volumes, *Deathproof* being premiered within the *Grindhouse* collaboration with Rodriguez) with distributor caution and commercial considerations undoubtedly affecting both releases. However, the war film *Inglourious Basterds* was confidently premiered at Cannes and Tarantino's output has maintained sufficient distinctiveness to justify the adjective 'Tarantinoesque'.

Tarantinoesque

Tom Charity points out that this handy adjective has become pejorative 'critical shorthand for hackneyed, would-be-hip, low-budget crime thrillers', so much so that Tarantino complains: 'It's so broken down to black suits, hipper-than-thou dialogue and people talking about TV shows'.[8] But Tarantinoesque also functions as a 'byword for both pop-culture reference and popular post-modern cinema'.[9] Tarantino's postmodern style is manifested in a variety of ways, such as the use of self-conscious artifice (use of chapters and intertitles, the back projections during *Pulp Fiction*'s cab rides or Mia Wallace's finger-drawing indicated by dotted lines on the screen), his blurring of cultural boundaries, particularly those between exploitation and mainstream cinema,[10] and between genres, for example *From Dusk 'til Dawn*'s mid-movie switch from crime thriller to horror movie, or 'The Bonnie Situation' in *Pulp Fiction*, characterised by Polan as a noir/sitcom hybrid.[11]

A further conspicuous postmodern device is the use of intertextual reference. These references can be internal, as when *True Romance*'s Alabama is mentioned in *Reservoir Dogs* or the Texan lawman Earl MacGraw (Michael Parks) appears in *From Dusk 'til Dawn*, *Kill Bill* and *Deathproof*, or they can be external, as in mentions of Madonna or Lee Marvin in *Reservoir Dogs*. A third aspect involves references to other films through personnel, situations and props: casting Pam Grier in *Jackie Brown*'s title role clearly recalls her memorable blaxploitation roles (*Foxy Brown* [1974], *Coffy* [1973]), and simply placing John Travolta in a dance contest in *Pulp Fiction* conjures up *Saturday Night Fever* (1978). Similarly, the glowing contents of the suitcase in *Pulp Fiction* recall 'the great whatsit' of *Kiss Me Deadly* (1955). When Butch (Bruce Willis) is searching for a weapon in the pawnbroker's after he has decided to return and rescue Marcellus Wallace (Ving Rhames), he finds a trove of items with film-hero resonances; the baseball bat suggests the American vigilante hero of *Walking Tall* (1973), the chainsaw conjures a more psychotic response as in the *Texas Chainsaw Massacre* (1974) or *The Evil Dead II* (1987), while the *katana* he finally, and significantly, selects identifies him with the honourable Japanese heroes of *The Yakuza* (1975) and Kurosawa's *Seven Samurai* (1954). *Kill Bill* references Hong Kong cinema and Bruce Lee's last, unfinished, film through Uma Thurman's costume, blaxploitation by borrowing the soundtrack to Isaac Hayes's *Truck Turner* (1974), and 1970s TV by casting David Carradine, star of action series *Kung Fu* (1972–75), as the assassination guru Bill.

Some celebrate these elements whilst others condemn them as style over substance or, perhaps, spectacle over message. Tarantino's post-modern style draws fire from those who don't like their culture popular, amoral and self-referential and his high profile semblance of art-house independence combined with continued commercial viability remains a goad to his detractors. Such postmodern texts tend to unite critics from left and right against them for their lack of engagement in a grand narrative, whether their preferred narrative is humanist or Marxist. Sharon Willis is certainly right to observe Tarantino films' 'lack of historical specificity or social referentiality' and that their extremes of language and violence offer audiences 'the thrill of transgression with the promise that the ironic frame will manage and contain it'.[12] The question is whether this contract justifies reactions such as Richard Corliss's 'nauseatingly nihilistic' or David Denby's 'crap'.[13] *Inglourious Basterds* lacks 'historical specificity', preferring to reference *The Dirty Dozen* and Italian follow-ups as it depicts an American-army Jewish Guerilla outfit operating behind enemy lines in Europe during World War Two, scalping or otherwise mutilating its victims before revealing, with the assassination of Hitler and his closest advisers, that this is an alternate universe in which revenge for Nazi atrocities is a possibility. Tarantinoesque intertextuality is often seen as 'pastiche', blank parody to use Jameson's judgemental terms,[14] but we might equally regard Tarantino's recy-cling of genre elements as a positive exploration of possibilities within the commercial form. This is a director 'in love with popular culture', determined to provide his audience with new experiences to the extent that he is 'a genre unto himself'.[15]

The rewrite

Tarantino's significance lies in his revamping of genre scenarios, which he accomplishes in three key ways. First, he unapologetically upsets narrative conventions by either placing 'the bad guys' centre stage, or examining the lives of those who would usually be peripheral characters. In *Jackie Brown* it is neither the cops nor the gangsters but the 'mule' who is central, while *Pulp Fiction*'s series of skewed genre set-pieces focuss on the boss's moll (Uma Thurman), and the hitmen's problems disposing of a body. *Deathproof* sets up Butterfly (Vanessa Ferlito) as its 'final girl' using Carol Clover's academic work as a template ('the best piece of film criticism I've ever read'), then allows the villain a victory by killing her off mid-film in a nod to *Psycho*.[16]

Second, Tarantino injects elements of realism into the dialogue and narrative. In dialogue this means essentially banal and digressive phatic conversations (about Madonna or burgers in foreign countries) and the inclusion of jokes and casual bad language that refuse to move the plot forward. Much of this texture may be seen to come from crime writing, particularly that of Elmore Leonard, whose 1992 *Rum Punch* Tarantino adapted for *Jackie Brown*. Leonard's work focuses on characters across a broad social spectrum, but the voices of criminal characters such as Ordell Robbie and Louis Gara (played in *Jackie Brown* by Samuel L. Jackson and Robert De Niro) frequently provide the most interest. The dialogue of Tarantino's protagonists is similarly ripe, anecdotal and comic, combining trivia, bullshit and uncomprehending, or at least uneasy, interracial interaction. Another move towards realism in cinematic narrative is that Tarantino's characters must make toilet trips – at fatal moments in the cases of Clarence Worley (Christian Slater) in *True Romance* and thrice over for Vincent Vega (John Travolta) in *Pulp Fiction*. Furthermore, these characters are made out of vulnerable materials – blood and brains: we (almost) see their bodies sliced, injected, buggered and dismembered.

Third, and perhaps most noticeable, Tarantino uses fragmented, novelistic structures; *Reservoir Dogs* shows us the scenes around a heist rather than the heist itself, placing the emphasis not on the generic narrative question 'will the heist succeed?' but shifting it towards a drawn-out dissection of failure. *Inglourious Basterds* has five chapters, four of which introduce new sets of characters before bringing them together in the climactic fifth. There is a harking back to literary modernism with the interest in perspectival views that is apparent even in the most straightforward of his films as director, *Jackie Brown*, in which the key exchange in the shopping mall is shown three times. In film terms, these fragmented structures refer back to *Citizen Kane* (1941), *The Killers* (1946) or *The Killing* (1956), though there are no inquisitive investigators or documentary-style voice-overs to hold the narrative together.

Such narrative complexity produces either an awkward bind or an intensification of the cinematic experience, depending on one's point of view. Polan suggests that these elements are used to take us places we have not yet been and, as such, are comparable to developments in hypertext, choose-your-own adventure novels and alternative endings to narrative-based computer games.[17] In the cinema, however, we have less control over the temporal progress of the narrative and may be taken to unexpected, uncomfortable places. Douglas Brode has identified the director's urge to take his audience on a 'wild narrative ride',[18] and this is perhaps most easily demonstrated if one thinks of the gamut of one's reactions during the ear-slicing scene in *Reservoir Dogs*. That the ride continues to be Tarantino's main concern is shown by *Kill Bill (Volume 1)* where narrative sequence and logic are overridden by its scheme of action climaxes, or in *Grindhouse* where the attempt to render the jagged excess of exploitation cinema extends beyond (and compromises the integrity of) his own contribution (*Deathproof*).

It is clearly around the issue of audience experience that Tarantino acquires his significance as a filmmaker; few other directors personally monitor audience responses so frequently. Using Tarantino to attack his films and/or his films to attack the perceived values of postmodernity misses the point. This is a filmmaker who works successfully within compromised, commodified, popular culture and has been fortunate enough to be able to write, cast and direct on his own terms. The result, and his chief asset, is that he consistently delivers a distinctive and memorable product.

Biography

Quentin Tarantino was born in 1963, in Tennessee, USA.

Notes

1 Sharon Willis ' 'Style', posture and idiom: Tarantino's figures of masculinity' in Christine Gledhill and Linda Williams, *Reinventing Film Studies*, London, Arnold, 2000, pp. 279–95, p. 284.

2 Paul A. Woods, *Quentin Tarantino: The Film Geek Files*, London, Plexus, 2000, pp. 75, 30, 54.

3 Eventually the budget reached $1.5 million.

4 Previous criminal roles for the *Reservoir Dogs* cast: Keitel (*Mean Streets*, 1973; *Taxi Driver*, 1976), Michael Madsen (*Kill Me Again*, 1989), Tim Roth (*The Hit*, 1984), Steve Buscemi (*King of New York*, 1989; *Miller's Crossing*, 1990; *Billy Bathgate*, 1991), Lawrence Tierney (*Dillinger*, 1945;

The Hoodlum, 1951), Chris Penn (*At Close Range*, 1986; *Mobsters*, 1991), Eddie Bunker (*Straight Time*, 1978; *Runaway Train*, 1985).

5 Nick James (a), 'Tarantino bites back', http://www.bfi.org.uk/sightandsound/feature/49432 (2008).

6 Paul A. Woods, *op. cit.*, p. 165.

7 Ibid., p. 126.

8 Ibid., pp. 152 and 154. This characterisation of Tarantinoesque probably best applies to *Killing Zoe* in which Eric Stoltz (admittedly in a beige suit) rides in a car full of drugged-up amateur terrorists, including a stoned Gary Kemp babbling about *The Prisoner*.

9 Ibid., p. 5.

10 Not between high and low culture though; Tarantino has yet to base a script on Homer's *The Odyssey*.

11 Dana Polan, *Pulp Fiction*, London, BFI, 2000, p. 25.

12 Sharon Willis, *op. cit.*, p. 279

13 Richard Corliss, 'And Now ... Pulp Friction', *Time* 162.16, 2003; David Denby, 'Dead Reckoning', *The New Yorker*, 79.30, 2003, p. 112.

14 See Hal Foster (ed.) *Postmodern Culture*, London, Pluto, 1985, p. 114.

15 Nick James (b) 'Welcome to the grindhouse', *Sight & Sound*, June 2007, pp. 16–18, p. 18; Jack Shadoian, *Dreams and Dead Ends* (2nd edition), Oxford, Oxford University Press, 2003, p. 279.

16 Nick James (a), *op. cit.*

17 Dana Polan, *op. cit.*, p. 35.

18 Douglas Brode, *Money, Women and Guns: Crime Movies from Bonnie and Clyde to Present*, New York, Citadel, 1995, p. 239.

Filmography

Reservoir Dogs (1992) also writer, performer
Pulp Fiction (1994) also co-writer
Four Rooms (1995) 'The Man from Hollywood' segment; also co-writer, performer
Jackie Brown (1997) also screenplay
Kill Bill (Volume 1) (2003) also writer
Kill Bill (Volume 2) (2004) also writer
Deathproof (2007) also writer, performer
Inglourious Basterds (2009) also writer

Further reading

Fred Botting and Scott Wilson, *The Tarantinian Ethics*, London, Sage, 2001.
Ed Gallafent, *Quentin Tarantino*, Longman, 2006.
Richard Greene and K. Silen Mohammad (eds) *Quentin Tarantino and Philosophy*, Open Court, 2007.
Geoff King, *Indiewood, USA*, London, I.B. Tauris, 2009.
Gerald Peary, *Quentin Tarantino: Interviews*, University Press of Mississippi, 1998.

LARS VON TRIER

By Mette Hjort

Lars von Trier is widely regarded as the most important Danish filmmaker since Carl Theodor Dreyer, not only on account of the highly original quality of his cinematic *œuvre*, which insists on creative renewal and innovation, but also because he has chosen to channel his success into various collaborative and milieu-building projects that have helped to renew Danish film. Von Trier's contribution is thus best discussed in terms of his cinematic works, his milieu-building contributions, his particular conception of cinematic creativity, and the personal history by which he takes himself to have been shaped.

The films

Von Trier's relation to the tradition of Danish film is polemical and largely negative, the exception being the filmmaker's considerable admiration for Carl Th. Dreyer. Indeed, von Trier's *Medea* (1988) is based on Dreyer's Medea script from 1965–66, which was never financed or produced, and is clearly a tribute to Dreyer. Von Trier's first feature films did, however, establish a clear preference for English-language filmmaking in an art-cinema vein involving a visual style influenced by a host of international filmmakers, including Andrei Tarkovsky. In spite of his reputation for being brutally demanding of actors, especially female actors, von Trier has worked with a number of international stars (Björk, Harriet Andersson, Lauren Bacall, James Caan, Willem Dafoe, Catherine Deneuve, Ben Gazzara, Nicole Kidman, and Barbara Sukowa). Many of these figures express considerable respect for von Trier's commitment to film-making as a rigorously innovative project, and do so even after their experience of the stringencies of a von Trier production process. Von Trier's films have also provided important breakthroughs for such figures as Jean-Marc Barr, Emily Watson and Charlotte Gainsbourg.

Well aware of the need to build audiences for his work, von Trier has framed most of his feature-length films as constitutive parts of trilogies. To date he has completed two trilogies, the Europa trilogy (encompassing *The Element of Crime*, *Epidemic* and *Europa* [US title: *Zentropa*]), and the Golden Heart trilogy (comprising *Breaking the Waves*, *The Idiots*, and *Dancer in the Dark*). A third trilogy, USA – Land of Opportunities, remains incomplete, with only *Dogville* and *Manderlay* completed, and *Washington* still to be shot.

The Europa trilogy explores a Europe that, although strangely deterritorialised, somehow ends up being largely synonymous with Germany. The trilogy, claims von Trier, pits nature against culture. Each of the three films develops a story centred around an 'inquiring humanist who leaves his home terrain, … journeys out into nature' and ends up being destroyed by the very process in question.[1] In the Golden Heart trilogy, von Trier draws inspiration from popular culture, and especially kitsch, in an attempt to test the extent to which art can accommodate extreme sentimentality. In the USA – Land of Opportunities trilogy, von Trier revives his longstanding interest in Franz Kafka's novel *America*, in order to scrutinise insider/outsider dynamics and institutionalised oppression. The official *Dogville* website draws attention to the films' intended commentary on the United States as a super power: 'I learned when I was very small that if you are strong, you also have to be just and good, and that's not something you see in America at all'.[2]

Ever attuned to the task of marketing, and willing to take up this task in artistically interesting ways, von Trier has made a point of accompanying his work with meta-cultural statements in the form, among other things, of provocative manifestos. Thus, for example, potential interest in the films belonging to the Europa trilogy is activated and heightened by three manifestos. The first calls for 'heterosexual films for, about and by men', the second sings the praises of cinematic trifles, and the third, framed as a confession, characterises von Trier as a mere 'masturbator of the screen'.[3] Most significant of all the manifestos, in terms of global impact, is the so-called Dogme 95 manifesto, about which more below.

In addition to the films included in the trilogies, von Trier's feature films include *Direktøren for det hele* (*The Boss of It All*, 2006) and, most recently, *Antichrist* (2009). Although von Trier's films have garnered awards at many an international film festival, Cannes, and especially its organiser Gilles Jacob, have played a particularly important role in making the Danish filmmaker's work visible to international audiences. *Element of Crime* won the Grand Prix Technique at Cannes, as did *Europa*. *Breaking the Waves* won the Grand Prix at Cannes, and *Dancer in the Dark* the Palme d'Or (as well as the Best Actress award for Icelandic singer Björk). And in 2009 Charlotte Gainsbourg won Cannes's Best Actress award for her role in *Antichrist*.

Milieu building

In 1992 von Trier founded Zentropa Entertainments, together with Peter Aalbæk Jensen whom he had met during his years at the National Film School of Denmark. Zentropa Entertainments is housed in former army barracks in Avedøre, on the outskirts of Copenhagen, and is at this point one of Europe's most significant production companies. The Film Town, where the company is located, is itself a remarkable institutional site. Reflecting von Trier and Aalbæk Jensen's commitment to collectivism, the Film Town fosters a synergy-oriented mode of interaction that encourages collaboration. The Film Town also provides a working environment that is unusually hospitable to women – most of Zentropa's leading producers are women – and immigrants. Von Trier and Aalbæk Jensen's political commitments are further evident in various outreach programmes that have been launched with the Film Town as an institutional base. Station Next, for example, brings schoolchildren in their early teens to the Film Town, where they work with film professionals. Station Next aims to enhance the self-esteem of young people from underprivileged (and often immigrant) backgrounds by fostering the kind of cinephilia that will also help to secure film's cultural survival. Von Trier's interest in milieu building has not been limited to the Danish context. He and several of Zentropa's producers have, for example, been involved in helping to create a Scottish Film Town in Glasgow, together with Scottish producer Gillian Berrie.[4] In terms of his own filmmaking, von Trier's more collectivist projects – the Dogme initiative and the co-authored, competitive film game known as *The Five Obstructions* – have played a crucial milieu-building role. In a small-nation context, von Trier's commitment to collectivism has had the effect of significantly enhancing the profiles of several of his filmmaking colleagues, and thus their opportunities to engage in filmmaking.

Cinematic creativity

In the course of his career, it has become increasingly apparent that von Trier works with a well developed theory of cinematic creativity. Key elements in this theory are: the idea that constraints provide the condition of possibility for creativity; and the idea that provocation stimulates creativity, especially when it is directed at the self in the form of challenges to preferred beliefs and taken-for-granted practices. Von Trier's understanding of creativity is shaped by pedagogical principles adopted by the National Film School of Denmark, where the thinking of the filmmaker (and film school teacher) Jørgen Leth has had a significant impact. Much like Leth, von Trier advocates a rule-governed approach to filmmaking; each of his filmmaking projects has been governed by a strict set of rules, many of them self-imposed and formulated with the intent to challenge himself and thereby to stimulate his own creativity.

Von Trier has often thought of his films as clearly defined experiments designed to test his own capacities, and those of the cinematic medium. In *Dogville*, for example, it was a matter of exploring the idea that deeply engaging cinematic fictions might be produced without the elaborate props and sets of mainstream filmmaking, with only chalk marks on the floor to suggest the film's setting. In *The Boss of It All* von Trier once again imposed restrictions on himself in the form of deprivations:

> *The Boss of It All* has one very perverse twist: it was made without a cameraman. The director was using a new process, 'developed with the intention of limiting human influence', which he has called Automavision. This entails choosing the best possible fixed camera position and then allowing a computer to choose when to tilt, pan or zoom. 'For a long time, my films have been handheld', he explains. 'That has to do with the fact that I am a control freak. With Automavision, the technique was that I would frame the picture first and then push a button on the computer. I was not in control – the computer was in control'.

The aim in this instance was not simply to stimulate the director's own creativity, but to ensure that the relevant actors were suitably challenged by means of 'randomised framing and audio settings'.[5]

Von Trier's approach to cinematic creativity was spelled out most clearly in the Dogme 95 initiative, a project that combined rules with provocation and self-provocation, and canny marketing in the form of a meta-cultural manifesto with a highly effective attempt to level the playing field on which members of small and large nations engage in the game of filmmaking. Von Trier announced the Dogme 95 project in Paris in 1995, at a centennial celebration in honour of film as a medium. Speaking on behalf of the Dogme collective (consisting of von Trier and fellow filmmakers Thomas Vinterberg, Søren Kragh-Jacobsen and Kristian Levring), von Trier condemned the decadence of Hollywood-style filmmaking and proposed a solution in the form of a 'Vow of Chastity'. This Vow required filmmakers to submit to ten rules, many of them at odds with the standard practices of mainstream filmmaking. Among other things, the 'Vow of Chastity' called for location shooting, for the simultaneous recording of sound and image, for hand-held cinematography, and, more generally, for a back-to-basics approach that would eschew the standard ways of manipulating sound and image at various stages of the production process. Initially dismissed as a joke, Dogme 95 went on to become a global movement. The success of the Danish Dogme films, starting with Vinterberg's *Festen* (*The Celebration*, 1998) effectively transformed the landscape of contemporary Danish filmmaking. It helped to make the Danish film milieu a magnet for talent, provided a rationale for a dramatic increase in funding for film, significantly enhanced Danish filmmakers' international opportunities, and helped to establish a collectivist ethos at odds with ungenerous zero-sum mentalities.

Von Trier's *Idioterne* (*The Idiots*) is the second of the Danish Dogme films; it explores what the director refers to as the 'distasteful idea of people who are not in fact retarded pretending to be'.[6] Karen (Bodil Jørgensen), an outsider who initially questions the propriety of pretending to be retarded, has a special place in the group. The film concludes with her playing the idiot where the risks to her personally are greatest, in front of her husband and other family members who have not seen her since the death of her 1-year-old son. She is accompanied by Susanne (Louise Hassing), who learns of her deep grief for the first time and movingly bears witness to Karen's newfound ability to achieve the authenticity that somehow accompanies the project of idiotic pretence. At the level of both form and content, the film reflects von Trier's romantic investment in some of the ideals of the 1960s.[7] In addition, claims von Trier, the aim was to produce a cocktail consisting of 'sickly self-centred idiocy on the part of the group's members, combined with intense sentimentality and emotionally charged scenes'.[8] This insistence on sentimentality is linked to von Trier's intentions in *Breaking the Waves*, whilst recalling his interest in reviving the much maligned and frequently adapted works by the maudlin popular writer, Morten Korch, as well as his remarkably successful attempt in *Dancer in the Dark* to combine certain sentimental qualities with the highly stylised musical genre.[9]

In the context of an exchange about the Dogme rules, von Trier clearly identifies the central role played by the concept of provocation in his cinematic work:

> Specifying all those things the directors aren't allowed to do is in itself a provocation. But the business of not allowing the directors

to be credited was like a punch in the face of all directors. I quite like that. But while there's an externally directed provocation here, there's also an even stronger inwardly directed provocation. What provokes others also provokes me. I've used my name a lot in promoting my films, just as David Bowie – whom I'm a great fan of – has allowed his person to fuse with his work. That's why I decided to provoke myself in this way, just to see what would happen. The provocation is always initially inwardly directed, and then it becomes other-directed as a side effect.[10]

In the case of von Trier, provocation, be it self- or other-directed, may focus on questions of form or theme. It may, that is, be a matter of articulating challenges having to do with the technologies and techniques of filmmaking, but provocation may also involve going against the grain of accepted ways of thinking, about religion, sexuality, art, popular culture and sentimentality.

One of von Trier's earliest works, his graduation film *Befrielses-billeder* (*Images of a Relief*), already manifests the elements of formal and thematic provocation that have since become a defining feature of his work. Set in Denmark in 1945, the film uses a visual style heavily indebted to Tarkovsky to explore the defeat of the German occupiers. The film construes the German Wehrmacht soldier, Leo (Edward Flemming), as a victim, showing his eyes being stabbed out by his Danish lover, Esther (Kirsten Olesen), in a sacrificial scene which has him literally ascending to heaven. If the thematic provocation here is a matter of taking issue with broadly humanist conceptions of the atrocities of the Second World War, the formal provocation takes the form of rule-following. *Images of a Relief*, claims von Trier, is 'incredibly, almost hysterically structured. It's in three parts, and every take refers to a take in the next part'.[11]

Formal and thematic provocation are also recurring features of *Riget* and *Riget 2* (*The Kingdom* and *The Kingdom 2*). Referring to this popular TV series, von Trier explains his repeated characterisation of the David Lynch-inspired hospital programme as 'left-handed work': 'It's not the work of a fine hand, which is also a way of provoking yourself, if you're used to writing with your right hand'.[12] The erotic melodrama *Breaking the Waves* should also, according to the filmmaker, be seen as an instance of self-directed provocation:

once again, [there's] an attempt to provoke myself. I establish a problematic and take things to their logical conclusion, which involves asking whether a sacrifice could be sexual. We know about the sacrifices of saints, so why couldn't a sexual sacrifice be a saintly sacrifice?[13]

Provocation, in short, serves many roles in von Trier's *œuvre*. Among other things the insistence on provocation helps to lend credence to the idea that creativity is linked not so much to untrammelled freedom as it is to precisely defined challenges and clearly articulated constraints.

The person

The significance of a public persona can frequently be traced not only to genuine achievements, but to the complicated dynamics of recognition, gate-keeping and self-staging. In the case of von Trier, the combination of properly relevant cinematic elements and more external sociological or institutional factors is particularly noteworthy. In connection with the success of *Dancer in the Dark* at Cannes in 2000, Kragh-Jacobsen underscored von Trier's creative genius, but also his enviable ability successfully to draw attention to himself and his works. During his years at the National Film School of Denmark, Lars Trier added an aristocratic 'von' to his name, something he had toyed with doing as early as 1975.[14] In the context of modern Danish mentalities committed to notions of radical egalitarianism, this politically incorrect gesture was bound to attract attention. The programmatic and polemical nature of von Trier's many manifestos has served to intensify the public attention surrounding his works. And von Trier has himself often remarked on the highly choreographed nature of the projected image of the dynamic Zentropa duo, which presents the filmmaker as sensitive and a highly phobic artist/intellectual, and his partner, Peter Aalbæk Jensen, as a crass, cigar-smoking producer. Von Trier is widely regarded as a consummate orchestrator, with media events and controversies related to his person often being perceived as staged in some way. For example, the highly publicised controversy surrounding von Trier's discovery that producers Aalbæk Jensen and Vibeke Windeløv had condoned an optical manipulation (in violation of the Dogme rules) of his film *The Idiots* has been thought by some to have been a hoax.

Von Trier has chosen to foreground, rather than obscure, some of the more personal details of his life as a filmmaker, through documentaries and film diaries. Key works here are Stig Björkman's 1997 *Tranceformer: A Portrait of Lars von Trier*, *De ydmygede* (*The Humiliated*, 1998), a film by Jesper Jargil documenting the production of *The*

Idiots, and Katja Forbert Petersen's documentary, *Von Triers 100 øjne* (*Von Trier's 100 Eyes*, 2000), which focuses on the making of *Dancer in the Dark* with 100 stationary cameras (during the song and dance sequences). Of equal importance is von Trier's deeply moving film diary (relating to *The Idiots*), which thematises, among other things, the pathos involved in the filmmaker's changed relation to actors. Whereas von Trier's early career is marked by a somewhat hostile, even fearful, attitude towards actors, his more recent films reflect a new-found openness to working much more intensely with actors.

A recurrent theme in von Trier's personal narrative concerns his relationship to his parents and his childhood home. Particularly revealing is his mother's decision, while dying, to inform von Trier that the Jewish social democrat, Ulf Trier, who had raised him as his son, was not his biological father. Inger Høst's startling claim was that she had single-mindedly sought a mate who would provide the artistic genes she wanted for her offspring. She further claimed that this revelation was meant to spur her son on to further artistic achievements. Von Trier has traced many of his phobias (which impinge on his filmmaking inasmuch as they prohibit travel by air and filming in certain kinds of enclosed spaces), as well as his deep-seated commitment to challenging aesthetic and other conventions, to the free-spirited, radical nature of his childhood home, one which emphasised an unusually high degree of autonomy from the earliest age. Høst's stubborn commitment to fostering an artistic genius also meant that von Trier enjoyed every possible form of support for his artistic undertakings from the earliest age.[15] Von Trier's attempts at crime fiction at the age of 7 were duly recorded by Høst and Trier; camera equipment was readily available when the 10-year-old future filmmaker expressed an interest in the medium. The resultant juvenilia includes a two-minute animated film, *Turen til Squashland* (*The Journey to Squash Land*, 1967), *Nat, skat* (*Goodnight Dear*, 1968) and *En røvsyg oplevelse* (*A Miserable Experience*, 1969).[16]

At the time of writing von Trier is in his early fifties. While the filmmaker is often paralysed by his phobias and recurring depression, there is every reason (especially following a viewing of *Antichrist*) to assume that his capacity to find new ways to provoke himself, and his viewers, is far from exhausted.

Biography

Lars von Trier was born in Copenhagen, Denmark, on 30 April 1956. A student in the Department of Film and Media Studies at the

University of Copenhagen from 1976 to 1979, he attended the National Film School of Denmark between 1979 and 1982.

Notes

1 M. Hjort and I. Bondebjerg (eds) *The Danish Directors: Dialogues on a Contemporary National Cinema*, trans. M. Hjort, Bristol, Intellect Press, 2001.

2 Reproduced on *celebritywonder.com* http://www.celebritywonder.com/movie/2003_Dogville_interview:_lars_von_trier_on_dogville.html (last accessed May 25, 2009).

3 T. Degn Johansen and L.B. Kimergaard (eds) *Sekvens Filmvidenskabelig årbog: Lars von Trier*, University of Copenhagen, Department of Film and Media Studies, 1991, pp. 157–9.

4 M. Hjort, 'Affinitive and Milieu-Building Transnationalism: The Advance Party Project', in Dina Iordanova, David Martin-Jones and Belén Vidal (eds), *Cinema at the Periphery*, Detroit, Wayne State University Press, 2010.

5 G. Macnab, 'I'm a control freak – but I was not in control', *Guardian*, Friday September 22, 2006. http://www.guardian.co.uk/film/2006/sep/22/londonfilmfestival2006.londonfilmfestival

6 Lars von Trier, *Dogme 2: Idioterne, manuskript og dagbog*, Copenhagen, Gyldendal, 1998, p. 173.

7 Ibid., p. 166.

8 Ibid., p. 167.

9 M. Hjort and I. Bondebjerg, *op. cit.*, pp. 214, 218, 233.

10 Ibid., p. 221.

11 P. Schepelern, *Lars von Triers elementer. En filminstruktørs arbejde*, Copenhagen, Rosinante, 1997, p. 63.

12 M. Hjort and I. Bondebjerg, *op. cit.*, p. 219.

13 Ibid., p. 220.

14 S. Björkman, 'Trier on von Trier', *Film*, 9, 2000, p. 11.

15 M. Hjort and I. Bondebjerg, *op. cit.*, p. 211.

16 P. Schepelern, *op. cit.*, pp. 16–17.

Filmography

Orchidégartneren / The Orchid Gardener (1977) short
Menthe – la bienheureuse / Joyful Menthe (1979) short
Nocturne (1980) short
Den sidste detalje / The Last Detail (1981) short
Befrielsesbilleder / Images of a Relief (1982) graduation film, short
The Element of Crime (1984)
Epidemic (1987)
Europa / Zentropa (1991)
Riget / The Kingdom (1994)

Breaking the Waves (1996)
Riget 2 / The Kingdom 2 (1997)
Idioterne / The Idiots (1998)
Dancer in the Dark (2000)
Dogville (2003)
De fem benspænd / The Five Obstructions (with Jørgen Leth, 2003)
Manderlay (2005)
Direktøren for det hele / The Boss of It All (2006)
Antichrist (2009)

Television productions

Medea (1988)
Lærerværelset / The Teachers' Room, 1–6 (1994)
Riget / The Kingdom, 1–4 (1994)
Maraton / Marathon (1996)
Riget 2 / The Kingdom 2, 5–8 (1997)
D-dag / D-Day (2000)

Further reading

C. Bainbridge, *The Cinema of Lars von Trier: Authenticity and Artifice*, London, Wallflower, 2007.

S. Björkman, *Trier om Trier. Samtal med Stig Björkman*, Stockholm, Alfabeta, 1999.

M. Hjort, 'Denmark', in M. Hjort and D. Petrie (eds) *The Cinema of Small Nations*, Edinburgh, Edinburgh University Press, 2007.

——. *Small Nation, Global Cinema*, Minneapolis, University of Minnesota Press, 2005.

M. Hjort (ed.), *Dekalog 01: The Five Obstructions*, London, Wallflower, 2008.

Lars von Trier, *Breaking the Waves*, trans. J. Sydenham, Copenhagen, Peter Kofod, 1996.

——. 'Project Open Film City', *Avedøre*, 27 January 1999. Online. Available: www.zentropafilm.com

——. and N. Vørsel, *Riget* ('The Kingdom'), Copenhagen, Aschehoug, 1995.

J. Stevenson, *Lars von Trier*, London, BFI, 2008.
www.dogme95.dk
www.zentropa-film.com

GUS VAN SANT

By Harry M. Benshoff

Once described by Robin Williams as 'a cross between Mister Rogers and William S. Burroughs', twice-Oscar-nominated filmmaker Gus

Van Sant has successfully traversed both commercial Hollywood and independent arenas.[1] A true renaissance artist, Van Sant has also acted, made music videos (for David Bowie, Elton John, The Red Hot Chili Peppers, etc.), published a novel, released albums of music, and has had numerous gallery showings of his photographs and paintings. His first films were independent shorts and features like *The Discipline of DE*, *Mala Noche* and *Drugstore Cowboy*. His next feature film, *My Own Private Idaho*, helped to define the New Queer Cinema movement of the early 1990s, along with other challenging films by directors like Todd Haynes and Gregg Araki. In the mid-to-late 1990s, Van Sant crossed over into mainstream Hollywood, making films like *To Die For*, *Good Will Hunting*, *Psycho* and *Finding Forrester*. In the twenty-first century, however, he has returned to more independent and experimental projects such as *Gerry*, *Elephant*, *Last Days* and *Paranoid Park*. As of this writing, Van Sant's most recent achievement has been directing the biopic *Milk*. *Milk* won a host of international awards and nominations, and brought Van Sant his second Academy Award nomination for Best Director (the first was for *Good Will Hunting*). Today, despite his dalliance with Hollywood-style filmmaking in the late 1990s, Van Sant is known primarily for his quiet iconoclasm and experimental sensibilities, traits that will undoubtedly continue to inform future film projects.

Like most auteur filmmakers, Van Sant's oeuvre can be readily distinguished by its recurrent thematic and stylistic traits. One of Van Sant's chief thematic interests is the complex interrelated notions of family, home and community, and what those concepts might mean to people who live on the fringes of mainstream society – those whom the so-called Religious Right might describe as having no 'family values' whatsoever. Thus Van Sant's films have centred on poor Hispanic hustlers (*Male Noche*), a pseudo-family of heroin addicts (*Drugstore Cowboy*), an unrequited love affair between teenage male prostitutes (*My Own Private Idaho*), and the politically-emergent gay male community of 1970s San Francisco (*Milk*). Van Sant – a white gay male who grew up in an upper middle class family – has been repeatedly compared to Andy Warhol because of his voyeuristic interest in queer street people and how these characters search for a sense of family by forming such bonds between themselves. One might also compare Van Sant to Jean Genet, in that his sexually queer characters are often one step away from criminally queer ones: murderers are central protagonists in *To Die For*, *Psycho*, *Gerry*, *Elephant* and *Paranoid Park*. One of the most important things about all of these films is Van Sant's refusal either to romanticise or moralise about the denizens of his depicted demimondes. Instead, as with Warhol's blank cinematic gaze, Van Sant allows his viewers to make up their own minds about his characters, their motivations and their actions.

Stylistically, Van Sant incorporates but moves well beyond Warhol's infamously minimalist long take aesthetic. Such shots do appear in Van Sant's work – *Elephant* is constructed as a series of long-take travelling shots – and one might also see the Warhol touch in Van Sant's films *Gerry* and *Last Days*, in which nothing much of importance happens before the camera. However, Van Sant's films are also peppered with flamboyantly surreal stylistic touches, highlighting both the grandeur and the squalor of the Pacific Northwest, the geographic area that he usually calls home. Varying film stocks, expressionist colour design, static insert shots of quotidian objects, slow motion or 'ramping' effects that distort time, and quirky open narrative designs all mark Van Sant's stylistic signature. Motifs such as the use of faux home movie footage (often shot by the actors themselves) appear in films from *Mala Noche* to *Milk*, a visual analog of the director's thematic interest in homely nostalgia. Swirling clouds shot in time lapse photography are another Van Sant motif, suggesting the passage of time as well as the insignificance of individual characters within a quickly-moving cosmos. Other visual techniques are more idiosyncratic, albeit just as memorable: in *Drugstore Cowboy* floating hats and cows (which also appear in Van Sant's paintings) help delineate the heroin-dazed characters. In *My Own Private Idaho*, the image of an old barn falling out of the sky and crashing into the open road crystallises the yearning for (and ultimate failure to find) 'home' for its protagonist.

Van Sant is also known as something of an actor's director, and he has seen his cast members win numerous awards for their quiet, intense performances. Although he started his career working with non-actors (and still occasionally uses them, as in *Elephant*), Van Sant quickly developed a method of both scripted rehearsal and open improvisation that allows his performers to develop their characters without too much interference from the director. Although the subject matter of his films usually requires the acting talents of handsomely scruffy young men, Van Sant has also directed women and older male actors to acclaim: *To Die For* helped turn Nicole Kidman into a major Hollywood star, while Robin Williams and Sean Penn won Oscars for their respective roles in *Good Will Hunting* and *Milk*. Yet it seems to be Van Sant's successful direction of young male actors that often makes them want to work with him. Matt Dillon's career was redefined and revitalized by *Drugstore Cowboy*, Matt Damon was nominated for a best lead actor Oscar for *Good Will Hunting*, while *My Own Private Idaho* gave River Phoenix and Keanu Reeves a chance to stretch their pretty-boy images into something more seriously dramatic. (Van Sant developed an intense relationship with River Phoenix while making *Private Idaho* and was devastated by the young actor's death by drug overdose in 1993; that relationship is fictionalised and allegorised in Van Sant's novel *Pink*.)

Van Sant's best work is both thematically and stylistically queer, using film form to question and explore complex and unique human sexualities that cannot be defined by simplistic labels like gay and straight. As such, the lines between male homosociality and homo-sexuality are frequently blurred in Van Sant's films, as in *My Own Private Idaho*, a film whose narrative is also a blur between the Hollywood-styled buddy/road movie and Shakespearean drama (especially the relationship between Prince Hal and his roguish mentor Falstaff in *Henry IV*). *My Own Private Idaho* explores the various types of relations that exist between men – as fathers and sons, brothers, lovers, friends, mentors, and even as commodities. The complex sexuality of the film's hustlers is one of its queerer aspects. Although narcoleptic Mike (River Phoenix) and Scott (Keanu Reeves) have sex with both men and women for money, Mike comes closest to being traditionally gay, and halfway through the film he confesses his love and desire for Scott (in a scene mostly scripted by actor Phoenix). Scott, on the other hand, is more firmly enmeshed within the power dynamics of male homosociality. He has conflicted power struggles with his two Shakespearean father figures: street mentor Bob (the Falstaff character) and his actual father (the Mayor of Portland). Scott is only 'playing at' being a hustler, and when he assumes his privileged position of wealth and class at the end of the film, he cruelly abandons both Bob and Mike. Ultimately, Mike's search for love and home (represented as his search for his lost mother) leads him back to where he started, neither richer nor much wiser.

After the critical success of *Drugstore Cowboy* and *My Own Private Idaho*, Van Sant directed an adaptation of Tom Robbins's cult novel *Even Cowgirls Get the Blues*. Wildly varying in tone and effect, the film pleased neither critics nor audiences, but Van Sant was already at work on his first film for a major Hollywood studio, Columbia Pictures' *To Die For*. Fans of his independent work wondered if Van Sant was 'selling out' to Hollywood, especially after the mainstream popularity of *Good Will Hunting*, a formulaic male melodrama written by and starring aspiring Hollywood players Matt Damon and Ben Affleck. Although it focuses on the relationships between handsome young working class men in Boston, *Good Will Hunting* is resolutely heterosexist, and even resorts to several old time fag jokes (a walk-on by a prison drag queen, gay-baiting a prissy psychologist played by George Plimpton) in order to bolster its characters' normative heterosexualities. The film's happy ending has Will Hunting learning how to open himself to others, a personal growth symbolised by his learning to love a woman (Minnie Driver). The film is also almost totally devoid of any of Van Sant's quirkier stylistic touches. Instead it plays like a standard Hollywood-style melodrama: talking head conversations are edited in shot/reverse shot configurations, Danny Elfman's soupy score underlines each bathetic emotional climax, and everything is wrapped in a warm sepia glow. The allegedly 'normal' homosocial and heterosexual relations that Van Sant's earlier films would have complicated are here played literally straight, perhaps another reason the film found so much success among mainstream audiences who might have recoiled from Van Sant's earlier (and later) work.

The success of *Good Will Hunting* made Van Sant a hot commodity, and he stayed in Hollywood for two more pictures, *Psycho* and *Finding Forrester*. (He was also involved with the developing *Brokeback Mountain* project, a film that would eventually be directed by Ang Lee in 2005.) Universal's *Psycho*, a perverse (almost) shot-by-shot remake of the Alfred Hitchcock classic (1960), infuriated purists and bored teenagers accustomed to more gory horror film fare. To his credit, Van Sant did try to curb the original project's inherent homophobia, making Norman Bates as straight as he could. Columbia's *Finding Forrester* was another male mentor/troubled student melodrama that seemed to be a cynical attempt to cash in on the success of *Good Will Hunting*. However, after *Finding Forrester* Van Sant returned to the arena of small-budget independent filmmaking, creating films that more closely aligned themselves to his earlier auteur efforts.

Elephant, which won both the Golden Palm and the Best Director award at the Cannes Film Festival, is one of Van Sant's most experimental and provocative independent films. Depicting a high school shooting spree modeled on real life incidents such as the one that occurred at the Columbine High School in 1999, *Elephant* showcases many Van Sant signature touches. The film focuses – in a very detached manner – on a handful of kids from somewhat broken homes during a single day at school, and ends with a stark depiction of mass murder. Using mostly non-professional actors and a coolly detached Beethoven sonata on the sound track, Van Sant's film is both harshly realistic and highly stylised. The film is comprised mostly of lengthy tracking shots that follow the characters through the endless corridors of their high school, a trait that recalls the existential angst of *Last Year at Marienbad* (1961). As in that film, the narrative of *Elephant* constantly loops back in time, showing the same events from different viewpoints. However, despite such moments of potential openness, the characters remain mostly ciphers, a trope emphasised by tracking shots that show only the backs of their heads. In another darkly witty bit of symbolism, one young man even wears a Red Cross lifeguard sweatshirt, its prominent cross referencing and foreshadowing his status as a potential target.

Some viewers dislike *Elephant* because it refuses to explain the reasons for the massacre or place blame on any one character or causal factor. In fact, this is part of the film's point – any number of unknown factors might be the ones that drive teenagers like Alex and Eric to mass murder. Like the parable about the blind men who each make a different interpretation about an elephant – depending on what part of it they feel – *Elephant* allows for multiple interpretations. It depicts a world of drunken and absent parents, jealous teens confused about gender and sexuality who find solace in 'first person shooter' video games, and a U.S. 'gun culture' where assault rifles can be ordered on line and delivered straight to one's front door. Any or all of those factors might play into the tragedy that occurs, the 'elephant in the room' that no one will acknowledge being the everyday violence of American popular culture (football, hunting, video games) or perhaps its inability to deal rationally with teenage sexuality. Indeed, conflicts about gender and sexuality play a major role in the film, as when Brittany, Jordan and Nicole relate stories of jealous violence or binge and purge their lunches in order to stay thin and sexually attractive. Another major sequence takes place at a Gay–Straight Alliance meeting, wherein characters wonder aloud how one can tell who may or may not be gay. That question lingers over the film, and is linked to the killers Alex and Eric when they share a naked kiss in a shower stall before they begin their spree. Further linking the Gay–Straight Alliance to Alex and Eric is the fact that both scenes are photographed in a similar manner: the meeting is shot as a long-take 360-degree circular pan, as is the scene of Alex and Eric in their basement 'lair'.

America's culture of violence and discomfort over queer sexualities are also at the heart of *Milk*, one of the more accessible and audience-pleasing films from Van Sant's twenty-first-century 'independent' output. Whereas *Gerry*, *Elephant*, *Last Days*, and *Paranoid Park* all received sparse distribution in American art houses, *Milk* – a Hollywood/independent hybrid released through Universal Pictures' Focus Features subsidiary – eventually found its way into suburban multiplexes. *Milk* is also Van Sant's most overtly political film to date, dramatising the true story of America's first openly gay elected official, San Francisco City Supervisor Harvey Milk (Sean Penn). Shortly after he attained office, Harvey Milk was assassinated by an unhinged right wing politician named Dan White (Josh Brolin). Although scripted by Dustin Lance Black (*The Journey of Jared Price* [2000], *Big Love* [2006–]) and enacted by upcoming Hollywood hunks like James Franco and Emile Hirsch, Van Sant's *Milk* remains remarkably faithful to the facts of Harvey Milk's life. Milk's story had been told on film once before, in the Oscar-winning documentary *The Times of Harvey Milk* (1984). In fact, footage from *The Times of Harvey Milk* as well as other documentaries and television news shows of the era commingle with recreated scenes throughout *Milk*, a facet of its queer hybrid style that Van Sant wanted to bring to the film since he first became involved with it. A Harvey Milk biopic had notoriously languished in Hollywood 'development hell' for many years, at least since the early 1990s when Oliver Stone was attached to the project. (Van Sant was offered the chance to direct the film at that time, but rejected the opportunity because he did not like the script.)

Rather than wallow in a fuzzy glowing nostalgia – which the lighting crew and cinematographer Harris Savides took pains to eschew – *Milk* uses documentary and television footage as a way to anchor Harvey Milk's life in an actual historical era.[2] Van Sant also uses still photos, various film stocks, and simulated home movie footage to underline his concern with the specific discourses of various visual forms. *Milk's* varying visual style literally underlines the ways and means that cinematic and televisual apparatuses can and do use to construct multiple histories of singular events. Milk too, like many countercultural leaders and queer filmmakers, was acutely aware of the aesthetic nature of political discourse. As the film shows, he was not opposed to staging press conferences or street demonstrations as grand theatrical events. And while the film demonstrates that politics is theatrical, it itself simultaneously attests to the political nature of film art.

Van Sant's concern with temporality is evident throughout *Milk*, as its narrative structure uses multiple framing and book-end devices, relating the past to the future and the 'real' to the 'performed'. Time itself becomes obviously unstuck in the quiet sequence preceding Milk's assassination. In it, Harvey's dimly-lit late night talk on the telephone with Scott – reminiscing about their past and some possible future – is intercut with the harsh light of the next morning, as Dan White sits on his suburban couch, plotting his revenge against Milk and Mayor Moscone (his other victim). The film also features other Van Sant auteur touches: slow-motion shots of falling chads that recall the fizzing bubbles washing over the images of *Drugstore Cowboy*, along with multiple split-screen images of a 'telephone tree' that suggest both the magazine cover pin-ups of *My Own Private Idaho* and Van Sant's Warhol-inspired urge for serial reproduction. Most obviously, the floating Steadicam shots that follow Dan White through the corridors of City Hall the morning of his murderous rampage bring to mind their similar use in *Elephant*.

As of this writing, Van Sant is executive producing *Howl*, a film about Allen Ginsberg's famous Beat poem and the censorship battles it faced. Written and directed by the highly acclaimed gay documentarians Jeffrey Freidman and Robert Epstein, the project suggests Van Sant's continued interest in the history of queer America and its queerer denizens. Hopefully, even if Van Sant returns to Hollywood filmmaking now and then for the financial security it can afford, he will continue to make more personal independent films that reflect his ongoing interest in the marginalised and disenfranchised – those Americans whom mainstream Hollywood films usually choose to ignore.

Biography

Gus Van Sant was born in Louisville, Kentucky, on July 24, 1952, but moved around a lot as a child; his father was a travelling salesman and then a marketing executive for various clothing firms. He studied at the Catlin Gabel School in Portland, Oregon, before attending the Rhode Island School of Design, where he earned a BFA in film. After failing to break into the Hollywood industry in the late 1970s (and working on the aborted feature *Alice in Wonderland*), Van Sant settled in Portland where he made short films and his first feature, the microscopically-budgeted 16mm *Mala Noche*. Van Sant then parlayed that film's festival acclaim into a successful career, eventually becoming a director equally at home in a Hollywood studio or on an independent film set in the Pacific Northwest.

Notes

1 Quoted in Edward Guthman, 'Private Dancer: Independent Filmmaker Gus Van Sant's new movie *Finding Forrester* Explores Similar Themes to

Good Will Hunting but Opens New Ground', *San Francisco Chronicle*, Sunday December 12, 2000, p. 6.
2 See Jean Oppenheimer, 'A High Price for Progress', *American Cinematographer* (December 2008), pp. 29–43.

Filmography

Mala Noche (1985) also writer, editor, producer
Drugstore Cowboy (1989) also writer
My Own Private Idaho (1991) also writer
Even Cowgirls Get the Blues (1993) also writer, editor, executive producer
To Die For (1995)
Good Will Hunting (1997)
Psycho (1998) also producer
Finding Forrester (2000)
Gerry (2002) also writer, editor
Elephant (2003) also writer, editor
Last Days (2005) also writer, editor
Paranoid Park (2007) also writer, editor
Milk (2008)

Further reading

Parish, James Robert. *Gus Van Sant: An Unauthorized Biography*. New York: Thunder's Mouth Press, 2001.
Van Sant, Gus. 'A Conversation with Gus Van Sant [Interview with Todd Haynes]' in *The World Within*. Portland, Oregon: Tin House Books, 2007.
Van Sant, Gus. *Pink*. New York: Anchor Books/Doubleday, 1997.

WONG KAR-WAI

By Julian Stringer

Central to the contemporary Chinese cinema renaissance are the nine feature films made to date by Hong Kong director Wong Kar-wai. Attracting both cult and mainstream attention, these titles have established Wong as one of the key names in the international pantheon of Asian filmmakers. Moreover, with Hong Kong now positioned between its existence as a postcolonial global city and its destiny as part of the Chinese nation state, Wong's films have come to bear the burden of historical representation. Whenever audiences and commentators seek to account for the meaning of new times in Hong Kong they invariably scour his work looking for clues.

Wong's initial ascendancy was dramatic and his ongoing ability to maintain a high public profile is impressive. After writing numerous scripts for TVB and production company Cinema City in the early and mid-1980s, he made his directorial debut a few years later as a member of Hong Kong's 'second wave' (cf. Jacob Cheung, Clara Law, Alex Law). *As Tears Go By*, one of the very best Chinese gangster or Triad movies, showcases Wong's profligate talents by transposing Martin Scorsese's *Mean Streets* (1973) to Mongkok and Lantau Island. While this powerful example of genre revisionism made a few waves in domestic and international waters, Wong really started to attract attention in 1991 for his highly idiosyncratic second feature, the 1960s youth melodrama *Days of Being Wild. Ashes of Time*, a gorgeously shot and edited martial arts epic that combines specifically Asian philosophical wisdoms with a modernist decon-struction of narrative, came next. Before long the trope of comparing Asian filmmakers to Western 'models' (specifically, in Wong's case, Jean-Luc Godard) began to surface when the director's fourth and fifth titles became art-house hits in Europe and the US – both the charming *Chungking Express* and the darker *Fallen Angels* have been identified as 'Hong Kong noir'. Wong won Best Director Award at the 1997 Cannes Film Festival for *Happy Together*, a gay road movie shot largely in Argentina, while *In the Mood for Love*, a romantic melodrama starring Wong stalwarts Maggie Cheung and Tony Leung Chiu-Wai, is roundly considered the director's masterpiece. Its follow-up, the science fiction-themed *2046*, received mixed critical notices but nevertheless consolidated the Wong brand after an extra-ordinary premiere at the Cannes Film Festival. As Davies and Yeh note, these Chinese-language titles have confirmed Wong's global art house credentials at the same time as his films have become steadily less popular with audiences in Hong Kong.[1]

Wong's highly innovative and hugely enjoyable movies have attracted critical attention primarily on the basis of their extraordinary visual qualities. Each contains intriguing graphic designs, flamboyant colour schemes, and a playful manipulation of spatial and temporal relationships. Wong has collaborated productively with Christopher Doyle, the famed Australian cinematographer who has worked in China, Hong Kong, Taiwan, Thailand and the United States along-side such stellar directors as Chen Kaige, Stanley Kwan, Pen-Ek Ratanaruang, Edward Yang, Gus Van Sant and Zhang Yimou. Doyle's preferred shooting style, which mixes startling stop-motion effects with predominantly hand-held camerawork, brilliantly com-plements Wong's plot ambiguities and fragmentary storylines. Indeed, for some Western critics, Wong and Doyle have helped revive what Pier Paolo Pasolini once termed 'the cinema of poetry'.[2]

Ackbar Abbas has pushed such claims one step further by suggesting that Wong also assigns visuality a clear political function. Proposing 'disappearance' as a keyword central to any understanding of Hong Kong's unique cultural identity, Ackbar argues that ever since the signing of the 1984 Sino–British Joint Declaration on the Future of Hong Kong, coming to terms with the politics of disappearance has been the great challenge for the city's cultural workers. In the run-up to Hong Kong's reversion to Chinese sovereignty on July 1 1997, how could a world forever slipping out of sight be re-sited? One answer to that question is provided by the almost dialectical nature of Wong's artistic concerns. *Days of Being Wild*, for instance, with its aimless central characters and shifts in location between Hong Kong and Manila, implies geographic and emotional dislocation so as to 'challenge the definition of Hong Kong culture itself by questioning and dismantling the way we look at things'.[3]

Such ambivalence ties Wong's preoccupations to those of a global audience as much as to a local one. Building on the Hong Kong experience, his success may be partly attributable to a world-wide fascination with the unforeseen effects of large-scale migration and youthful alienation. Certainly, these are subjects that have been of concern to many other Hong Kong filmmakers of the 1980s and 1990s. For example, Peter Chan (*Comrades, Almost a Love Story*, 1996), Mabel Cheung (*An Autumn's Tale*, 1987), Ann Hui (*Song of the Exile*, 1990), Stanley Kwan (*Full Moon in New York*, 1989), and Clara Law (*Autumn Moon*, 1992) have all won acclaim for their explorations of issues of border-crossing, the making of connections in lonely and unfamiliar modern cities, and the symbolism associated with places of transit.

At the same time, Wong's reception also illustrates how Asian filmmakers need to offer something new and distinct if they are to penetrate global image markets. The dynamic compositions and editing patterns of *Ashes of Time*, *Fallen Angels* and *Happy Together* are far removed from the bland 'international style' characteristic of so much 'transnational cinema' of the 1990s. Expressing displacement and contradiction through striking visual form has provided Wong Kar-wai with one of the most easily identifiable trademarks in the business. Moreover, *In the Mood for Love* took such innovation to a whole new level through its nostalgic conjuring of the memory of earlier classic tales of thwarted Chinese passion such as *Spring in a Small Town* (Fei Mu, 1948) – thus paving the way for Tian

Zhuangzhuang's 2002 remake of *Spring* as well as Stanley Kwan's *Everlasting Regret* (2005) and Ang Lee's *Lust, Caution* (2007).

Wong's use of music only adds to the structural ambiguity of his films. Musical collaborators Frankie Chan and Roel A. Garcia are architects of some of contemporary cinema's most astonishingly creative sound designs, and they have incorporated elements from a diverse range of Asian and non-Asian musical cultures into their work. Across the nine titles, the contents of what may be called this global jukebox have included artists like Ernesto Lecuona, Los Indios Tabajaras, Xavia Cugat, the Mamas and the Papas, Massive Attack, the Flying Pickets, Marianne Faithfull, Astor Piazzolla, Caetano Veloso, and the Three Amigos, not to mention Chan and Garcia's own pastiche-like compositions in the styles of raga, techno, new age, ambient and Ennio Morricone. Musical serendipity has proved crucial to the emotional and cognitive appeals of a Wong Kar-wai movie, just as it has helped the soundtrack CDs become cult objects of desire among collectors around the world.

On the other hand, it is interesting to note that despite Wong's recurrent use of Chinese pop stars as actors (Andy Lau, Jacky Cheung, Leslie Cheung, Tony Leung, Faye Wong, Leon Lai, Karen Mok) not that much actual Hong Kong music, or Cantopop, makes it into his films. This strategy of devaluing local music in relation to other kinds of international music can be seen as a tease – denying fans the expected songs by favourite stars (Wong similarly plays around with the iconography of film and pop star images) – and as a clever marketing strategy. After all, a wide range of music on a soundtrack and accompanying CD provides consumers with diverse points of entry and helps a film travel far and wide. Specifically, Wong's work appears more and more to have one eye on the massively expanding mainland market, and one on the markets created out of the various Chinese diasporic communities active throughout the world.

Consider the scene where Faye Wong's character cleans up Cop #663's apartment in *Chungking Express*. For this MTV-like segment, the actress loafs from room to room while her own rendition of the Cranberries' song 'Dreams' (now renamed 'Dream Person') plays on the soundtrack. Faye Wong, a native of Beijing, is adored in Hong Kong and Greater China for pop chartbusters like 1992's 'An Easily Hurt Woman'. At the same time, however, she has also been in the vanguard of Cantonese and Mandarin music's transition to rock during the 1990s (she has covered the work of Sinead O'Connor, collaborated with the Cocteau Twins, and married mainland rock star Dou Wei). Staging this particular scene around Faye Wong's version of 'Dreams', then, does not just exhibit good taste, but also constitutes shrewd marketing. First, it reinforces the importance of processes of indigenisation to popular Hong Kong culture by imaginatively transforming Western source music (cf. the use of a cover version of 'Take My Breath Away', Berlin's smash hit from the Hollywood blockbuster *Top Gun* [1986], during the telephone-booth kissing scene between Andy Lau and Maggie Cheung in *As Tears Go By*, or Danny Chung's version of the Turtles' eponymous 1967 hit that memorably closes *Happy Together*). Second, as the original version of this song will no doubt be familiar to international fans of English-language pop music, a Chinese interpretation may well be expected to prick up the ears of many curious listeners. In other words, Faye Wong's 'Dreams' is neither one thing nor the other; local but not local to Hong Kong, Western but not really Western, from the mainland but not of the mainland.

Questions of marketability have been crucial to the establishment of Wong's international profile in other ways as well. As with the work of fellow Asian cult directors Kitano Takeshi and Tsui Hark, an aura of exclusivity, determined by the vagaries of access, has surrounded the ongoing reception of his films. While Wong Kar-wai has certainly been active on the international film festival circuit, his titles were also initially distributed in many overseas territories at a more subterranean level, on bootleg tapes, laser discs and videocassettes imported from Hong Kong and Japan. Indeed, as a mark of this simultaneous visibility and invisibility, no less than three of his works were included in a list of the Top 30 Unreleased Foreign-Language films of the 1990s compiled by the US magazine *Film Comment* in 1997, even though all were widely available in the US at the time through 'unofficial' sources. Similarly, recent years have seen the early appearance of several Wong titles on Blu-Ray as well as the theatrical release of *Ashes of Time Redux* (a reshaped version of the earlier film) to critical acclaim in 2009. Wong's short film contributions to international omnibus projects – e.g. *The Hire: The Follow* (2001), *Eros* (2004) and *To Each His Own Cinema* (2007) – as well as his work in music videos and commercials have also helped secure cultural capital through appeals to a sense of 'high art' and global fashion consciousness.

Yet when it comes to the coverage Wong's films received in the abundance of Hong Kong film fanzines that flooded the US and European print markets during the 1990s, such 'art cinema' associations are not so easily retained. The mix of populist and experimental tendencies in Wong Kar-wai's films has sometimes made it hard for audiences and critics to separate his output from that of other popular

Hong Kong filmmakers. Unlike the work of Jackie Chan, Ringo Lam, Tsui Hark and John Woo, for example, Wong's Chinese films do not play in Western multiplexes, and yet they are often talked about in the same breath as such commercial fare. Wong may cross-over between the cult and the mainstream, but he has also gained a reputation as a troublesome case, someone who makes life awkward for straight-thinking commentators by injecting established genres with a modernist or avant gardist sensibility. Such tactics can easily confuse audiences and critics more comfortable with clear-cut distinctions and categories.

In many respects, this problem of determining how Wong Kar-wai's films should be identified reproduces the relationship he appears to have with the Hong Kong film industry in general. While Wong's early days included script work for one of the most daring of the city's original post-1979 'New Wave' directors, Patrick Tam (*Final Victory*, 1987), he has also written standard pot-boilers like the patchy sci-fi title *Saviour of the Soul* (Corey Yuen, 1991). Conversely, while Wong as director is renowned for playing around with genre conventions, local filmmakers have themselves played around with Wong's critical reputation by creating their own new genre – the Wong Kar-wai parody movie. These parodies have been produced back-to-back with Wong's own titles, as in Jeff Lau's *The Eagle Shooting Heroes* (1991), which was shot by some of the cast and crew of *Ashes of Time* on breaks during the latter's lengthy schedule, or else are signalled by wordplay (Blackie Ko's 1992 *Days of Being Dumb*), and the spoofing of iconic moments from individual movies – comedian Stephen Chow's interpretation of the final scene from *Days of Being Wild* in his self-directed *From Beijing With Love* (1994) is hilarious. Not to be outdone, Wong has himself shown a healthy propensity for self-mockery by inserting numerous intertextual references into his own films, as in Kaneshiro Takeshiro's studied mimicry, in *Fallen Angels*, of Faye Wong's ditsy body language from *Chungking Express*.

While the highly episodic *Fallen Angels* was seen by some critics in 1995 as a virtual non-stop parody of the established Wong Kar-wai style, no such criticism pertains to the movie that thoroughly consolidated Wong's international reputation, *Happy Together*. Ostensibly influenced by Latin-American Magic Realist authors such as Manuel Puig, the film is perhaps of most significance for focusing attention not just on Wong's astonishing formalism, but also on debates about homosexuality in Asian cinema. At the very least, *Happy Together* should be placed in the company of other titles that bravely explored such subject matter in the months leading up to and after the 1997 handover, namely Stanley Kwan's *Hold You Tight* (1998) and Shu Kei's *A Queer Story* (1996). Wong's contribution to this progressive artistic tendency won praise for its frank portrayal of a gay relationship between two Chinese men (played by Leslie Cheung and Tony Leung) stranded in Argentina. According to some reports, the original plan was to have one of the young gay protagonists discover that his recently deceased father was also homosexual, but that ambitious-sounding storyline was scrapped upon touchdown in South America.

On the other hand, for all the film's success at Cannes and other exhibition sites, *Happy Together* has had an occasionally chequered reception career. In South Korea, for example, it was banned from exhibition at the first Seoul Queer Film and Video Festival on the grounds that it was 'not relevant to the emotional life of the Korean people'.[4] Moreover, in a generally sympathetic piece on the film, Denise Tang points out that the choice of Argentina as the film's location may actually serve to 'reinforce the stereotypical Asian response to homosexuality as a foreign concept'. Because we largely see images of the two central characters in a foreign culture, audiences may be encouraged to view them as ' "cultural exiles", gay Asian men who are traitors of their own ethnicity by the nature of their sexual identity as gay men'.[5] (For his part, Chris Doyle indirectly entered the political fray by 'outing' megastar Leslie Cheung in the written commentary accompanying his photographic record of the shoot, *Don't Cry For Me Argentina*.)[6]

In the Mood for Love moves away from the politics of displacement and travel to return to questions concerning the meaning of 'home' in a climate of change. As with *Days of Being Wild*, it is set in 1960s Hong Kong and depicts an intense, and at times tortuous relationship between a couple who never quite connect with one another during the course of their extra-marital 'affair'. The film's astonishingly vivid images – comprising period sets, sumptuous colours, and clothing designs you cannot help but be fascinated by – almost overwhelm the twists and turns of an already complex and enigmatic narrative structure. Well-chosen musical interludes reconfirm the director's ability to construct highly evocative soundtracks. The critical and commercial success of *In the Mood for Love* showed that Wong and his collaborators could once again offer something new and distinct in the global marketplace.

Wong has experienced mixed fortunes since 2000, though. After the disappointingly lacklustre *2046*, he joined the small band of

Chinese directors (cf. Peter Chan, Tsui Hark, John Woo) who have been invited to make commercial movies in the United States. However, his first English-language title, *My Blueberry Nights*, was given only a limited US release in 2007 and was greeted with mixed acclaim. Of equal significance to his current position in international movie culture is the support he has received from Studio Canal in the financing of both *Blueberry* and the widely-publicised forthcoming feature *Lady from Shanghai* (starring Nicole Kidman). In short, it is largely French money, French film festivals and French critical garlands that bankroll and sustain the Wong Kar-wai bandwagon into the twenty-first century.

Perhaps partly for these very reasons, some commentators claim that Wong Kar-wai has now entered a period of creative decline. If this is true, it hardly matters: he has already enjoyed a brilliant career. Spare a thought instead, then, for Japanese director Shunji Iwai (*Love Letter*, 1995; *April Story*, 1998; *All About Lily Chou Chou*, 2001) – the 'other' hip East Asian pop cinema sensation of the 1990s. Iwai arguably possesses a comparable amount of talent to that of Wong, but the former's international career inexplicably stalled at the very moment when the latter's embarked upon its mighty ascent. Both Wong and Iwai helped to define a hip, youth sensibility among filmmakers and audiences across the pan-Asia region. What would international film culture now look like if the two directors had gone on to have equally successful global careers?

Biography

Wong Kar-wai was born in Shanghai, China, in 1958. He trained in graphic design at Hong Kong Polytechnic and in television drama at TVB. In the 1980s he worked as a scriptwriter at Cinema City.

Notes

1 Darrell William Davis and Emilie Yueh-yu Yeh, *East Asian Screen Industries*, London: British Film Institute, 2008, pp. 151–5.
2 John Orr, *Contemporary Cinema*, Edinburgh, Edinburgh University Press, 1998.
3 Ackbar Abbas, *Hong Kong: Culture and the Politics of Disappearance*, Minneapolis, University of Minnesota Press, 1997, p. 62.
4 'Plug Pulled on 1st Seoul Queer Film and Video Festival'. Online. http://gaylesissues.about.com (20 September, 1997).
5 Denise Tang, 'Popular Dialogues of a "Discreet" Nature', *Asian Cinema*, 10, 1, 1998, p. 201.

6 Christopher Doyle, *Don't Cry For Me Argentina: Happy Together Photographic Journal*, ed. Law Wai Ming, Hong Kong, City Entertainment Books, 1997.

Filmography

(All Hong Kong productions unless indicated)

As Tears Go By (1988)
Days of Being Wild (1991)
Ashes of Time (Hong Kong/Taiwan, 1994)
Chungking Express (1994)
Fallen Angels (1995)
Happy Together (1997)
In the Mood for Love (Hong Kong/France, 2000)
2046 (China/Hong Kong/France, 2004)
My Blueberry Nights (China/France/Hong Kong, 2007)
Ashes of Time Redux (Hong Kong/Taiwan, 2009)

Further reading

Wimal Dissanayake with Dorothy Wong, *Wong Kar-Wai's Ashes of Time*, Hong Kong, Hong Kong University Press, 2003.
Doyle, Christopher, *Backlit By the Moon*, Tokyo, Masakazu Takei, 1996.
Jean-Marc Lalanne *et al.*, *Wong Kar-Wai*, Paris: Editions Dis Voir, 1997.
Lisa Odham Stokes and Michael Hoover, *City On Fire: Hong Kong Cinema*, London, Verso, 1999.
Jeremy Tambling, *Wong Kar-Wai's Happy Together*, Hong Kong, Hong Kong University Press, 2003.
Stephen Teo, *Wong Kar-Wai*, London, British Film Institute, 2005.

JOHN WOO

By Tony Williams

John Woo is the one example of a Hong Kong film director who has successfully managed to transfer his talents from his original national industry to the big budget domains of Hollywood cinema and back again. Unlike Hong Kong contemporaries such as Ringo Lam, Kirk Wong and Ronny Yu, Woo secured his position as a mainstream 'A' film director until his return to China to make *Red Cliff*. His significance represents a fascinating case study in the realm of recent explorations of transnational cinemas, especially in the Chinese context. According to Sheldon Hsiao-peng Lu, 'Film has always been a transnational entity',[1] especially in terms of the very hybridity characteristic of the medium itself. However, in an era where the very idea of a nation state is both debateable and multifaceted, all national cinemas are affected by new patterns of global distribution and international coproductions which render previous definitions of authorship and genre highly unstable. Thus, as well as deserving study as a director in his own right, Woo's situation represents a fertile area for investigation of the various transnational dynamics involving issues of gender, genre, and authorship. Both past and present, his films illustrate these issues as well as problematic questions of creative transformation.

Woo is generally characterised as an 'action director', a successor to Sam Peckinpah's equally misleading label of 'master of violence'. However, a closer examination of Woo's major films from *A Better Tomorrow* onwards (as well as certain previous ones) reveals a director whose vision is definitely at odds with the supposed celebration of violence beloved by certain sectors of fan audiences and lesser talents such as Quentin Tarantino. After *The Killer* and *Hard Boiled* came to the attention of Hollywood executives, the director joined the ranks of foreign talents (both past and present) invited to the tempting world of a big budget industry promising freedom, technological expertise and finance lacking in their home industries. Woo's appearance in Hollywood appeared to offer the possibility of rejuvenating an already-jaded action genre industry in the same manner as the Italian Westerns influenced their national counterparts a generation before. However, as *Hard Target* and *Broken Arrow* revealed, the studios eagerly exploited him as an 'action director', constraining his role on the film set without understanding the complexity of his creative vision. It was not until *Face Off* that Woo was finally allowed the freedom of a director's cut. This gave him the opportunity to display the creative synthesis of talents he perfected in Hong Kong Cinema.

Despite the mixed nature of Woo's pre-1986 work, the nature of his innovative creative breakthrough in 1986 needs examination. Woo began his film apprenticeship in several Hong Kong film studios in the late 1960s and 1970s. One formative influence remains constant throughout his Hong Kong and Hollywood periods, the work of Zhang Che. *One Armed Swordsman* (1967), *Golden Swallow* (1968), *The New One Armed Swordsman* (1971) and *Four Riders* (1974) involved Chinese cultural issues of friendship, betrayal and a melancholy depiction of violence. Before beginning his directing career in 1973, Woo worked with Zhang Che as assistant director on *Boxer from Shantung* and *Blood Brothers*. Woo developed themes within his mentor's cinema reworking borrowed styles and placing themes within a new cultural context in his post-1986 films. *A Better Tomorrow*, *A Better Tomorrow 2*, *The Killer*, *A Bullet in the Head*, and *Hard Boiled* situate the heroic values of Zhang Che's films within a corrupt, post-capitalist, hybrid world of a colony already undergoing a crisis scenario as it moved towards a feared apocalyptic climax in 1997. Although Zhang Che's films usually recognised the vulnerability of traditional Chinese heroic codes in a changing world, Woo developed this theme explicitly and stylistically. In *Last Hurrah for Chivalry*, the heroes are already becoming redundant in their own time to the same extent that Mark, Ken Ho, Mr. Lung, John will be in the more brutal twentieth century worlds of *A Better Tomorrow 1* and *2* and *The Killer*. Woo's apocalyptic nightmarish world of Viet Nam in *A Bullet in the Head* witnesses a similar betrayal of friendship affecting characters in Zhang Che's Ching Dynasty drama *Blood Brothers*. Woo later directed 60 per cent of the Zhang Che reunion film (featuring his former stars such as Ti Lung, David Chiang, Chen Kwan-tai and Danny Lee), *Just Heroes*. Despite the Jean-Pierre Melville, Kubrick and Scorsese influences on *The Killer*, Woo's acclaimed film sees a spiritual and symbiotic kinship developing between investigative cop Inspector Li (Danny Lee) and assassin John (Chow Yun-fat) that approximates the values of the martial-arts films directed by both Zhang Che and Woo such as *The Young Dragons*, *The Dragon Tamers* and *Last Hurrah for Chivalry*. The literal title, 'A Pair of Blood-Splattering Heroes', expresses not just the film's duality but implicit themes of heroic reincarnation in a modern world – another theme fascinating Hong Kong cinema.

Woo's pre-1986 comedies appear to bear little relation to his more achieved films. But, despite their mixed nature, several contain significant features which would characterise his later work. At this stage, the problem involves a lack of creative synthesis. In *Money Crazy* and *From Riches to Rags*, Woo directed Ricky Hui. Although little-known to Western audiences, Ricky Hui is part of a talented team of brothers (the others being Michael and Cantonese pop star Samuel) who have a permanent place in Hong Kong film history for their comedy films satirising various aspects of colony materialism, class and politics during the 1970s and 1980s. John Woo helped Michael Hui to direct his first acclaimed feature *Games Gamblers Play* (1974), which parodied Chinese fascination with gambling, and later acted as associate director on Hui's *The Private Eyes* and *The Contract* (1978). Woo has mentioned his fascination with cartoon-style comedy and the work of Jerry Lewis, influences which also appear in his two Ricky Hui films. Despite the scattershot nature of these films, they both satirise Hong Kong fascination with materialism and the ignoring of serious issues of class exploitation and poverty. In *From Riches to Rags*, the climactic scenes show mental asylum patients representing the worst materialistic attributes of their saner counterparts outside. Woo inserts a parodic homage to *2001* showing patients touching a monolith resembling a block of gold. Later, the patients make Ricky Hui undergo a Russian roulette game borrowed from *The Deer Hunter*, a motif Woo would use once again in *Bullet in the Head*. Woo has described *From Riches to Rags* as a 'satire on avarice', showing his intuitive understanding of both the Hui comedy tradition and the Western movies he borrows from. However, Woo's early experiments in cartoon style appear more creatively in the non-comic *Better Tomorrow* films and *The Killer*, while his keen eye for social injustice also occurs in *A Bullet in the Head* and *Hard Target*. *A Bullet in the Head* treats the issue of greed more seriously in the case of Paul (Waise Lee), who betrays his friends for gold. Woo's first Cinema City production *Laughing Times* sees Charlie Chaplin's little tramp reincarnated in Dean Shek's performance. Together with a reconstituted flower girl and Cantonese Jackie Coogan version of *The Kid*, he successfully battles both poverty and a child prostitution racket headed by Karl Maka. Woo's sympathy for street people revealed in a few significant montages in *Hard Target* is not without precedent in his earlier films. The role of cinematic excess characteristic of Woo's later stylistic gangster films also appears in these early comedy films in an experimental manner still awaiting perfect realisation. This feature did not appear until Woo's association with Tsui Hark's Film Workshop Company.

Before then, Woo had attempted to make a Viet Nam film, *Heroes Shed No Tears*, modelled on a disparate number of sources such as the Japanese *Lone Wolf and Child* series, stylistic traits borrowed from the French director Jean Pierre-Melville, and the action genre cinema he was steadily moving towards. Produced by Tsui Hark and starring former Shaw Brothers hero and Zhang Che discovery Ti Lung in the leading role, *A Better Tomorrow* depicted the tensions affecting the Confucian traditions of family and personal relations within an increasingly ruthless corporate world of post-capitalism. Although concentrating on the tortured odyssey of Ho (Ti Lung), the film rocketed Chow Yun-fat into Hong Kong stardom in the role of Mark Gor, a character modelled on both Alain Delon's Melville roles and the heroic traditions depicted in the Shaw Brothers films of

Zhang Che. Stylistically, *A Better Tomorrow* also represented a creative breakthrough for Woo in terms of an appropriation of dynamic and tonal montage features reminiscent of Sergei Eisenstein. However, despite some elaborate action sequences, *A Better Tomorrow 2* suffered from a growing rift between Hark and Woo concerning the direction the film was to take. Under Tsui Hark's influence, the theme of Lung's (Dean Shek) betrayal by his partners became a dominant motif in a film Woo intended as a 'comic book' serialisation of themes already treated in the previous film. *A Better Tomorrow 2* revealed Woo finally achieving success with the stylistic experiments seen in his comedies *Follow The Star*, *From Riches to Rags*, *To Hell With the Devil*, *Laughing Times* and *Run Tiger Run*.

After leaving the Film Workshop, Woo then engaged on his most poetic film, *The Killer*. Starring Chow Yun-Fat and Danny Lee, the film was a co-production of both Golden Princess and Magnum Films, a company owned by Danny Lee. *The Killer* brought Woo to international attention. Synthesising Eastern and Western cinematic traditions, *The Killer* was a reworking of a Takakura Ken *yakuza-eiga* gangster film *Narazumono* (1964) directed by Ishii Teruo. As Ken Hall demonstrates, *The Killer* represents the best example of Woo's creative interweaving of the disparate traditions of Martin Scorsese, Francis Ford Coppola, Stanley Kubrick, Don Siegel, Robert Aldrich, Jean-Pierre Melville, Alfred Hitchcock, David Lean, Akira Kurosawa, Sergio Leone, Zhang Che and Masaki Kobayashi. Hall also points out the influence of not only *Narazumono* but also *Le Samourai* (1966) and Michael Mann's underrated *Manhunter* (1986) on *The Killer*, especially the kinship between two different protagonists.

Woo's cinematic masterpiece is definitely *A Bullet in the Head*, a dark romantic treatment of friendship, betrayal and social chaos characterised by apocalyptic feelings following the Tiananmen Square massacre and its consequences for Hong Kong in 1997. Creatively re-working themes in Sergio Leone's *Once Upon A Time in America* (1985), Michael Cimino's *The Deer Hunter* (1978) and Sam Peckinpah's *Bring Me The Head of Alfredo Garcia* (1974), Woo directed an epic masterpiece dealing with the corruption of human values under two political master narratives of twentieth century society. Critical of the brutal aspects of communism, Woo sees it tarnished by the same features of greed and violence evident in its political *alter ego* – capitalism, particularly its ruthless Hong Kong counterpart. Frank's (Jackie Cheung) cry to the corrupted Paul, 'Do you measure your friendship in gold?' serves not only as the *leitmotif* for this particular film but also for most of Woo's cinema. Articulating the social justice tenets of Western Christianity and Eastern Confucianism, Woo's cinema often presents a spiritual vision. Like Peckinpah, Woo's work often contains a critique of violence and a sense of mournful melancholia existing beneath the supposedly attractive veneer of screen violence.

After seeking some light relief by directing *Once A Thief* (or 'Jules et Jim in Hong Kong'), Woo directed the work which would lead to Hollywood offers. *Hard Boiled* was as technically accomplished as its Hollywood competitors. It attacked human greed and mourned the loss of old heroic traditions. Like John and Inspector Li in *The Killer*, Tequila (Chow Yun-fat) and undercover agent Tony (Tony Leung Chi-wai) are both symbiotic 'secret sharers' in a quest against the new ruthless Triad culture represented by Johnny Wong (Anthony Wong). Brutally taking over from a kindly older Triad boss, Wong's violent methods appall even his most efficient hit man, 'Mad Dog' (played by Shaw Brothers stalwart Philip Kwok), who refuses to participate in a massacre of innocent civilians in a hospital.

Eventually relocating to America and assisted by business partner Terence Chang, Woo found his first Hollywood film riddled by studio compromises and the interference of its egoistic star, Jean Claude Van Damme. Despite these problems and the dilution of the director's creative style, Woo's *Hard Target* does succeed in its aim of being a modern version of Richard Connell's oft-filmed short story, *The Most Dangerous Game*. Casting a sympathetic eye on the plight of homeless people in the land of the free, a perspective obviously influenced by Woo's own early personal life and the scenes depicted in *Laughing Times*, the director attempted to cast Van Damme in the mould of his Chinese knightly heroes battling the forces of corporate capitalist evil, represented by Lance Henriksen and Arnold Vosloo.

Following an abortive project set in the Amazon with Brad Pitt, Woo and Terence Chang returned to America realising the need to play the studio game and continue working in the industry. They both decided to show Hollywood that they could make as dumb an action film as any American; the result was *Broken Arrow*. Apart from the opening boxing scene between two protagonists, the film was as empty and formulaic as any Bruce Willis or Mel Gibson film. However, *Broken Arrow* did represent Woo's first collaboration with John Travolta, whose influence resulted in the director finally obtaining the first cut on their next film together.

The Paramount production *Face/Off* represents Woo's creative synthesis of Hollywood and Eastern traditions. Although the script had been in development since 1990, the final version came to resemble an action film influenced by Hitchcock's *Strangers on a Train* as well as the double motif seen in both Zhang Che films such as *Blood Brothers* and Woo's own *The Killer* and *Hard Boiled*. (The pre-credit sequence resembled the carousel sequence of *Strangers on A Train*.) *Face/Off* is a key example of recent transnational cinema as well as exemplifying Woo's own status as a bridge between Hollywood and Hong Kong. It again presents two characters who are (and become) blood brothers inhabiting different faces, as well as being a film critical of bureaucratic dehumanisation and contempt for individual lives, as the prison sequence and Archer's threats against Sasha reveal. An earlier version of the script once included a scene where Archer as Castor Troy visits Castor's mother and sees the squalid environment which influenced his antagonist's upbringing. Had the scene survived, it would have added an extra social dimension to the film similar to Woo's view of the street people in *Laughing Times* and *Hard Target*.

Woo's further progress became mixed. *Mission Impossible 2* became a narcissistic Tom Cruise project offering little opportunity for the director's creative cinema, while *Paycheck* appeared as empty as *Broken Arrow*. *Windtalkers* is probably his most accomplished Hollywood film, though it suffered from the post 9/11 jingoistic attitude in American society that allowed no depiction of the grim side of war and its effects on human beings of both sides (even within films set in the past). *Windtalkers* is a deliberate contrast to *Bullet in the Head*, revealing that positive qualities of friendship and personal transformation for the better may emerge from a hellish combat situation. Marine Joe Enders ironically operates as Woo's version of Robert Aldrich's saviour-destroyer hero. Traumatised by battle and the loss of his buddies, he is assigned to protect Yahzee, a Navajo code talker, *and* kill him should he fall into enemy hands. *Windtalkers* not only chronicles the growing friendship between the alienated Marine and Yahzee but also the deep transformation of a man who has lost his faith and become a killer. While Enders begins a spiritual change, Yahzee is in danger of becoming too like his protector until he tells him that killing won't bring his friend back to life. *Windtalkers* reveals the emotional devastation of war for both Americans and Japanese. As a soldier remarks, 'I'm in Saipan with a Zippo on my back roasting human beings', while Enders comments about his lost faith, 'They told me I was a soldier of Christ. Somewhere along the way I must have switched gears'. *Windtalkers* poignantly concludes in the Monument Valley location where it began, but now on John Ford's Point. Reunited with his family, Yahzee performs a ritual ceremony bringing peace and liberation to the tormented spirit of Enders. This is a film where

Woo approximates the epic cinema of his idol David Lean, something he will fully achieve in *Red Cliff*.

Loosely based on China's great national epic *The Romance of the Three Kingdoms*, *Red Cliff* deals with only one incident in that narrative. Woo attempts to return to the actual historical material rather than just 'print the legend'. Hopelessly outnumbered by military and naval forces led by Prime Minister Cao (Fengyi Zhang), a disparate group of allies learn to overcome differences and work together. Rather than focus on legendary heroes such as Guan Yu, Zhao Yun and Lu Bei, Woo emphasises the alliance between Commander Zhou You (Tony Leung) and advisor Zhuge Liang (Takeshi Kaneshiro). Unlike their literary counterparts, both men cooperate for the common good. Woo also highlights the crucial role of women in helping achieve final victory, women such as Zhou's wife Xiao Qiao (Lin Chiling) and her sister Sun Shangxiang (Vickie Zhao). Xiao Qiao delays Cao's attack by strategically using a tea ceremony. Sun Shangxiang infiltrates his camp as a spy supplying valuable information. There she encounters impoverished soldier Pit, who has signed up to put food on the table and exempt his family from three years taxation after victory. Woo again stresses that casualties and victims affect both sides. Following Cao's humiliating defeat, Zhou allows him to live, stating 'There is no victor here'. Earlier Cao had commented, 'This is a matter of honour. Even war must be fair'. Despite its epic dimensions, *Red Cliff* is a film revealing its director's compassion and humanity.

Biography

Born in Guangzhou, the capital of Guangdong Province of South China, in 1946, Wu Yusen and his family moved to Hong Kong when he was young. During his education at Matteo Ricci College in 1967, he joined a student drama group and began making 8mm short films. In 1969, he joined Cathay Film Studios as a production assistant. After moving to Shaw Brothers in 1971, he acted as assistant director to Zhang Che on *Ma Yongzhen/Boxer from Shantung* (1972) and *Ci Ma/Blood Brothers* (1973). He then moved to Golden Harvest to begin directing in 1973. Woo moved to Hollywood in 1992 where he remained until returning to China in 2007.

Note

1 Sheldon Hsiao-peng Lu, *Transnational Chinese Cinemas, Identity, Nationhood, Gender*. Honolulu: University of Hawaii Press, 1997, p. 25.

Filmography (Cantonese and Mandarin titles precede English translations)

As Director

Tit hon yau chang/Tie han rou quing/The Young Dragons. Golden Harvest. 1973/1975.

Nui ji toi kuen kwan yong wooi/Nu zi tai quan ying hui/The Dragon Tamers, aka *Belles of Taekwondo*. Golden Harvest, 1974.

Siu lam moon/The Hand of Death, aka *Countdown in Kung Fu*. Golden Harvest, 1976.

Dai Nui Fa/Dinu Hua/Princess Chang Ping. Golden Harvest, 1976.

Daai saat sing yue siu mooi tau/Dasha xingyu xiaomei tou/Follow the Star. Golden Harvest, 1977.

Faat chin hon/Fa qiuan han/Money Crazy. Golden Harvest, 1978.

Ho hap/Hao xia/Last Hurrah for Chivalry. Golden Harvest, 1978.

Haluo yeguiren/Hello, Late Homecomers. Golden Harvest, 1978.

Chin jok gwaai/Qian zuo guai/From Riches to Rags. Golden Harvest, 1979.

Waat kai si doi/Hua ji shi dai/Laughing Times. Cinema City, 1981.

Moh dang tin si/Mo deng tian shi/To Hell with the Devil. Golden Harvest, 1982.

Baat choi Lam A Jan/Ba cai Lin Ya Zhen/Plain Jane to the Rescue. Golden Harvest, 1982.

Ying hung mo lui/Yingxiong wu lei/Heroes Shed No Tears aka The Sunset Warrior. Golden Harvest. 1983 (released in 1986).

Siu jeung/Xiao jiang/The Time You Need A Friend. Cinema City, 1984.

Leung ji lo foo/Liangzhi lao hu/Run Tiger Run. Cinema City, 1985.

Ying hung boon sik/Yingxiong bense/ A Better Tomorrow. Film Workshop/ Cinema City/Golden Princess, 1986.

Ying hung boon sik 2 /Yingxiong bense 2/A Better Tomorrow 2/ Film Workshop/Cinema City/Golden Princess, 1987.

Dip huet seung hung/Dieuxue shuang xiong/The Killer. Film Workshop/ Magnum/Cinema City/Golden Princess, 1989.

Yi daam kwan ying/Yi dan qun ying/Just Heroes, aka *Tragic Heroes*. Magnum/ Golden Princess, 1990.

Dip huet gaai tau/Diexue jietou/Bullet in the Head. Milestone Films/Golden Princess, 1990.

Jung waang sei hoi/Zongsheng sihai/Once A Thief. Milestone Films/Golden Princess, 1991.

Laat sau san taam/Lashou shentan/Hard Boiled. Milestone Films/Golden Princess, 1992.

Hard Target. Alphaville-Renaissance/Universal, 1993.

Broken Arrow. 20th Century Fox, 1996.

Once A Thief. Alliance Productions/WCG. Television pilot. 1996.

Face/Off. Paramount, 1997.

Black Jack. Alliance Productions/WCG. Television pilot, 1998.

Mission Impossible 2. Paramount, 1999.

Windtalkers. MGM, 2002.

Hostage. TV, 2002.

Paycheck. Paramount, 2003.
The Robinsons Lost in Space. TV, 2004.
Stranglehold. VG, 2007.
Chi bi/Red Cliff. 2008.
Chi bi xia:June zhan tia xia. 2009.

Further reading

Ciecko, Anne T. 'Transnational Action: John Woo, Hong Kong, Hollywood'. In Sheldon Hsiao-peng Lu (ed.) *Transnational Chinese Cinemas: Identity, Nationhood, Gender.* Honolulu: University of Hawaii Press, 1997, pp. 221–39.

Hall, Ken. *John Woo's* The Killer, Hong Kong, Hong Kong University Press, 2009.

Hall Ken. *John Woo: The Films.* Second edition, Jefferson, N.C.: McFarland & Co, 1999.

Stokes, Lisa Odham. 'Interview with John Woo'. *Asian Cult Cinema* 61, 2009.

Stringer, Julian. ' "Your Tender Smiles Give Me Strength": Paradigms of Masculinity in John Woo's *A Better Tomorrow* and *The Killer'. Screen* 38.1 (1997): pp. 25–41.

Williams, Tony. 'Space, Place, and Spectacle: The Crisis Cinema of John Woo'. *Cinema Journal* 36.2 (1997): pp. 67–84.

——John Woo's *Bullet in the Head.* Hong Kong: Hong Kong University Press, 2009.

ZHANG YIMOU

By Haomin Gong

The Opening Ceremony of the 2008 Olympic Games in Beijing astounded the world with its extraordinary glamour, pushing the fame of its director, Zhang Yimou, to a peak. The best-known Chinese film director in the world, Zhang Yimou is a key figure of the so-called 'Fifth Generation', or the New Wave and the New Cinema, in the mid-1980s and the 1990s in Mainland China. Apart from being an established art-house film director, Zhang also shows ingenuity in negotiating with both the global commercial market and domestic political censorship. Thus, he has not only won numerous prizes at various international film festivals, but succeeded in the domestic and international box-office. Zhang's filmmaking is representative of the Chinese national cinema from the 1980s to the present day.

Zhang launched his career as a cinematographer after graduating from the Beijing Film Academy in 1982. He was the cinematographer for several Chinese New Cinema classics: Zhang Junzhao's

One and Eight, Chen Kaige's *Yellow Earth* and *The Big Parade*, and Wu Tianming's *Old Well*. Among these films, *Yellow Earth*, the landmark film of the internationally renowned Fifth Generation, represents a milestone in Chinese film history. Zhang's camerawork in this film is especially remarkable: his distinctive use of long shots and long takes of the landscape not only reflects New Wave experimentation in international cinema, but is also reminiscent of traditional Chinese aesthetics. His new film language effectively challenged the socialist realism that was prevalent in China, and opened a new space for cultural critique. The cinematic artistry that Zhang exhibited in his early career as a cinematographer, especially in his exceptional command of space, colour and visual image, would be further demonstrated in his prominent career as a film director.

Zhang's first film as director, *Red Sorghum,* narrates a legendary story of 'my grandpa' and 'my grandma' working in a distillery for sorghum liquor in the 1930s. The Dionysian spirit of raw energy and liberation expressed in their unconventional lifestyle is captured by Zhang's bold cinematic work, especially his stylistic use of the colour red. The film won the Golden Bear Award at the Berlin Film Festival in 1988, the first major international prize for a Chinese film. It was also a huge box-office hit in China.

After making *Code Name Puma*, a popular entertainment film, Zhang directed his second major work, *Ju Dou*. The film tells a story of a failed resistance against patriarchy, subjugated by feudalist ethics in early twentieth-century China. That the story is set in a traditional dye mill gives Zhang an opportunity to display his genius in the mastery of colours in an extravagant fashion. *Ju Dou* was followed by *Raise the Red Lantern*, another dramatic tragedy about the oppression of humanity set in China's past. The fights among the four wives for their husband's favours, all within the confinement of a traditionally walled complex, are symbolic of China's repressive patriarchal social order. The skilfully framed images in this film create a space of imprisonment and an intense sense of inescapability. Because of the subversive features of these two films, they were banned in China for some time.

The three films discussed above mark the 'classical' stage of Zhang's filmmaking. Films in this stage partake in the 'Cultural Reflection' (*wenhua fansi*) taking place in the 1980s and the 1990s. Probing into China's past, Zhang seeks rejuvenating primitive energy and levels critique at the physical and spiritual oppression in contemporary China. His special focus on female characters is remarkable: the narration of their destinies allows allegories of individual oppression and emancipation to emerge. While Zhang's critique of the present remains implicit in these films about the past, a noticeable shift in narrative tone from *Red Sorghum* to *Ju Dou* and *Raise the Red Lantern* may still be traced to the political turmoil at the turn of the decade. The celebratory sense of exhilaration is inevitably replaced by a much grimmer mood of suppression.

After these films of the mythical past, Zhang explored a new area in his directorial career: contemporary life in China. *The Story of Qiu Ju* tells the story of a peasant woman's stubborn search for justice. Similarly, *Not One Less* concerns a substitute teenage teacher who is determined not to lose any students from a school in a poverty-stricken rural area. The almost unreasonable tenacity shown in these characters reflects Zhang's personal experience. Zhang grew up during the Cultural Revolution (1966–76), when he endured hardship because of his 'bad' family background. While working as a peasant and a factory worker, he developed a special interest in photography, even selling his blood to purchase a camera. When the Mao era came to an end in the late 1970s, Zhang decided to join the Beijing Film Academy; already past the age for admission, he was initially refused. Zhang persevered, petitioning the institute and even the Ministry of Culture. Because of his outstanding portfolio, he was finally admitted to the institute by special exception in 1978.

In *The Story of Qiu Ju* and *Not One Less*, Zhang continued to experiment with cinematic techniques. In order to capture the mood of contemporary society, for example, he hid cameras in the crowd to shoot a number of scenes. In *Not One Less*, non-actors are used to play themselves. These naturalistic approaches give the films a documentary effect quite new in Chinese feature films at the time. Although both films were well received by audiences and state media in China, they aroused controversy abroad. While they both won the Golden Lion Prize at the Venice Film Festival in 1992 and 1999 respectively, *Not One Less* was criticised for being pro-government at Cannes (Zhang pulled the film from the festival). Indeed, these two films are obviously much less provocative in ideological terms: depictions of state officials are highly favourable, for instance. In a way, the films achieved the effect of promoting the state project of 'rule by law' (*fazhi*) and the nationwide Hope Project (*xiwang gongcheng*) to help bring dropout children back to school. Yet, it would be rash to accuse Zhang of becoming a mere spokesperson of the state: critical edges are always embedded in his seemingly innocuous stories. In these two films, apart from his critique of the inadequacy of state mechanisms for solving social problems, Zhang also raises such thought-provoking questions as the conflicts between the rule of law and traditional communal ethics, the widening gap between city and the country, and the disorientation brought about by technical and social modernisation in China. Obviously, Zhang has learned how to negotiate with state censorship while exploring the burgeoning film market.

In 1994, Zhang directed *To Live*, another significant Fifth Generation production. Based on the novel of the same title by Yu Hua, the film examines Chinese history from the 1940s to the 1970s from the perspective of an ordinary person's family history. This large historical scope gives the film an epic sweep and sets it apart from Zhang's other films. Yet, ordinary people make the best of circumstances which seem to be beyond their control and the inevitable tension between the narration of the 'large history' and that of the 'small' family history at different historical stages constitutes the central critique of the film. The fate of the family is constantly determined by the whimsical will of modern political history. Confronted by a series of historical absurdities, the film suggests that an ordinary person can eke out a living by upholding the hope of humanity. Due to its sensitive topic, the film was banned in China. In contrast, its acceptance in the West was phenomenal: it won the Jury's Prize at the Cannes Film Festival in 1994.

With the tremendous success of these films in the international film arena, Zhang has also been severely criticised for 'self-Orientalism': intentionally fabricating the 'Orient' to cater to Western tastes. Critics have accused him of feeding first-world curiosity about the third-world 'Other' by constructing exotic spectacles and rituals and displaying alien backwardness, thus strengthening uneven power relationships in the world. What is missing from this charge, however, is recognition of the fact that Zhang's foray into global film circuits has brought Chinese cinema world recognition after its long-term isolation. Moreover, his cinematic practice has allowed him to exert cultural agency in ways that would otherwise be impossible within China. His effort to 'internationalise' Chinese cinema has introduced new mechanisms of production, distribution and exhibition to Chinese filmmakers, audiences and critics. His transnational filmmaking has also brought a new dimension into what is traditionally understood as national cinema in the condition of globalisation.

Criticism aside, Zhang continued to test his directorial skills in new areas. *Shanghai Triad* and *Keep Cool*, two films about Chinese urban life, have enriched the scope of his filmmaking. *Shanghai Triad* is a gangster film about underworld strife in 1930s' Shanghai, narrated from the viewpoint of the gang's young apprentice, a recent arrival from the countryside. The contrast between innocence and corruption is artfully conveyed through Zhang's nuanced direction of space, light and colour. This film of metropolitan life immediately attracted considerable attention. *Keep Cool* turns its lens to contemporary Beijing. Through Zhang's stylised camerawork, this black comedy nicely captures the noisiness and unrest of the city. The film's *vérité* style would reappear in *Not One Less* and *Happy Times*. Although *Shanghai Triad* and *Keep Cool* were both warmly accepted by the Chinese audience, Zhang was not satisfied with them. While he had intended to prove his directorial ability in the subject of urban life, these films, though respectable, could not compare to his classical works. Arguably, Zhang's personal experience may have prevented him from mastering the urban subject, which the younger 'Sixth Generation' directors would so skilfully capture in their filmmaking. In this sense, *The Road Home* represents Zhang's symbolic return to familiar ground. The film describes the love story of a couple living in the countryside during the 1960s. It paints their love in idyllic and ideal shades as it grows against all political odds at the time. The dichotomous structure of the film accurately conveys the director's glorification of the values of the innocent countryside. Again, stubborn determination becomes a weapon of the weak in an alienating modern world.

In 2000, Zhang made *Happy Times*, a low-budget feature that takes on the contemporary urban subject. This tragicomedy tells a warmhearted story of a group of laid-off workers helping a blind girl survive in the city. While it critically touched on many social problems existing in contemporary China, the film aimed more at the rapidly growing market of the 'New Year Film' (*hesuipian*) in Mainland China.

Another factor contributing to the huge popularity and box-office success of these films is Zhang's interesting relationships with lead actresses. *Shanghai Triad* marked an end to the long-term collaboration between Zhang and Gong Li, who had starred in every important film that Zhang had directed to that point. The development of their personal relationship, both on and off the screen, roughly paralleled Zhang's classical stage. (This relationship was intriguingly staged in the 1989 feature *Terra-Cotta Warrior*, in which they both starred.) It would take Zhang several years to find a new female star, Zhang Ziyi, in *Road Home*, who starred in many of his following productions, including *Hero* and *House of Flying Daggers*. It was not until 2006 that audiences saw Gong again: in Zhang's latest production, *Curse of the Golden Flower*.

In the new millennium, Zhang surprised a great many people by making a drastic shift in filmmaking. Perhaps inspired by the tremendous yet unexpected success of Ang Lee's *Crouching Tiger, Hidden Dragon* in the non-Chinese speaking world, Zhang moved into martial arts films. For him, this is the genre that can best represent the unique spirit of the Chinese people. In 2002, *Hero*, Zhang's first martial arts feature, was released. The biggest film in terms of investment in China at the time, *Hero* was also the most lucrative. Its success in international markets was phenomenal and unprecedented for a Chinese director. The film takes the historical story of the failed assassin of the First Emperor of China, but narrates it in a dramatically different way. Zhang's retelling departs from both the orthodox historical record of the event in Sima Qian's *Records of the Grand Historian* (*Shi ji*), and the two films on the same topic directed by his colleagues: Zhou Xiaowen's *The Emperor's Shadow* (*Qin song*, 1996) and Chen Kaige's *The Emperor and the Assassin* (*Jingke ci Qin wang*, 1998). In Zhang's *Hero*, the assassin Nameless voluntarily surrenders to the King as a result of the latter's preaching on the idea of 'All under Heaven' (*tianxia*). The King begs for an understanding of the wars he has launched to unite *tianxia*: individual sacrifice for this grand cause is thus glorified. Despite huge box-office success, the film understandably aroused enormous controversy. Zhang has been severely criticised for flattering the state ideology of totalitarianism. The film coincided with the rise of China as a world power at the beginning of the twenty-first century. (The film was unprecedentedly given the privilege of opening in the Great Hall of the People, political headquarters of the People's Republic of China.) However, it has also been pointed out that Zhang's distinctive portraits of the King and the assassins imply a critique of totalitarianism. Moreover, his attempt to redefine the spirit of 'knight-errant' (*xia*), which is the metaphysical core of the martial arts (*wuxia*), also deserves critical attention.

This ideological ambivalence aside, *Hero* marks an aesthetic highpoint in Zhang's directorial career. The film's *Rashomon*-like narrative challenges the audience who must decipher it. Distinctive colour schemes are artfully employed to augment the power of narration. Zhang recruited world-renown talents, including actors Jet Li, Zhang Ziyi, and Maggie Cheung, composer Tan Dun, and cinematographer Christopher Doyle, adding to the film's profile and popularity. In this light, *Hero* is an excellent example of a successful negotiation among aesthetics, censorship and commercialism.

His next martial arts film, *House of Flying Daggers*, also displays Zhang's gifts as a filmmaker. The intricately fabricated narrative, compelling images and choreography, all-star cast, and elaborate production – all revealed an ambition to move into the international entertainment film market, after having secured his status in the international art-house film circuit. Both *Hero* and *House of Flying Daggers* were nominated for Best Foreign Language Film at the Academy Awards.

After directing a contemporary family drama, *Riding Alone for Thousands of Miles*, featuring Japanese star Takakura Ken, Zhang devoted himself to making *Curse of the Golden Flower*, another big-budget martial arts film. Its sizeable budget of $45 million made it at the time of release the most expensive film in China. The plot of the film is heavily based on Cao Yu's 1934 play, *Thunderstorm*. However, Zhang set the story in the late Tang Dynasty in 928 AD, skilfully turning the modern classic of Chinese literature into a period feature on screen and therefore producing a blockbuster. This high-profile production inherits the merits of Zhang's previous two martial arts films. It extends his success in negotiating the imperatives of art, politics and the market today.

Over the past two decades, Zhang has continually provided Chinese and international screens with films of high artistic standards. Together with his Fifth Generation colleagues, he greatly changed the cinematic scene in China, which had been plagued by Mao's ideology, and thus gave Chinese cinema its due status in the world. His ability to adapt to changing domestic and global conditions means that Zhang retains his relevance. A prolific and versatile filmmaker, Zhang's film work represents the trajectory of Chinese cinema since the 1980s.

Biography

Zhang Yimou was born in Xi'an, Shaanxi Province, in China, in 1951. He was admitted to the Department of Cinematography of the Beijing Film Academy in 1978, and graduated in 1982.

Filmography

Red Sorghum / *Hong gaoliang* (1987)
Code Name Puma / *Daihao Meizhoubao* (1988)
Ju Dou / *Ju Dou* (1990)
Raise the Red Lantern / *Da hong denglong gaogao gua* (1991)
The Story of Qiu Ju / *Qiu Ju da guansi* (1993)
To Live / *Huozhe* (1994)

Shanghai Triad / *Yao a yao, yao dao waipoqiao* (1995)
Keep Cool / *Youhua haohao shuo* (1997)
Not One Less / *Yige dou buneng shao* (1999)
The Road Home / *Wo de fuqin muqin* (1999)
Happy Times (2000)
Hero / *Yingxiong* (2002)
House of Flying Daggers / *Shimian maifu* (2004)
Riding Alone for Thousands of Miles / *Qianli zou danji* (2005)
Curse of the Golden Flower / *Man cheng jin dai huangjin jia* (2006)

As cinematographer:
One and Eight / *Yige he bage* (1984)
Yellow Earth / *Huang tudi* (1984)
The Big Parade / *Da yuebing* (1985)
Old Well / *Lao jing* (1987) also performer

Further reading

Michael Berry, 'Zhang Yimou: Flying Colors', *Speaking in Images: Interviews with Contemporary Chinese Filmmakers*, New York, Columbia University Press, 2005, pp. 109–40.

M. Christine Boyer, 'Approaching the Memory of Shanghai: The Case of Zhang Yimou and *Shanghai Triad* (1995)', in Mario Gandelsonas (ed.) *Shanghai Reflections: Architecture, Urbanism, and the Search for an Alternative Modernity*, Princeton, Princeton Architectural Press, 2002, pp. 56–87.

Evans Chan, 'Zhang Yimou's *Hero*: The Temptation of Fascism', *Film International*, vol. 2, issue 2, 2004, pp. 14–23.

Rey Chow, 'The Force of Surfaces: Defiance in Zhang Yimou's Films', *Primitive Passions: Visuality, Sexuality, Ethnography, and Contemporary Chinese Cinema*, New York, Columbia University Press, 1995, pp. 142–72.

——, 'The Political Economy of Vision in *Happy Times* and *Not One Less*; or, A Different Type of Migration', *Sentimental Fabulations, Contemporary Chinese Films*, New York, Columbia University Press, 2007, pp. 147–65.

Shuqin Cui, 'Gendered Perspective: The Construction and Representation of Subjectivity and Sexuality in *Ju Dou*', in Sheldon H. Lu (ed.) *Transnational Chinese Cinema: Identity, Nationhood, Gender*, Honolulu, University of Hawaii Press, 1997, pp. 303–29.

Qing Dai, 'Raised Eyebrows for *Raise the Red Lantern*', *Public Culture*, vol. 5, no. 2, 1993, pp. 333–7.

A-chin Hsiau, 'The Moral Dilemma of China's Modernization: Rethinking Zhang Yimou's *Qiu Ju da guansi*', *Modern Chinese Literature* vol. 10, no. 1, 1998, pp. 191–206.

Feng Lan, 'Zhang Yimou's *Hero*: Reclaiming the Martial Arts Film for "All under Heaven"', *Modern Chinese Literature and Culture*, vol. 20, no. 1, 2008, pp. 1–43.

Wendy Larson, 'Zhang Yimou's *Hero*: Dismantling the Myth of Cultural Power', *Journal of Chinese Cinema*, vol. 2, no. 3, 2008, pp. 181–96.

Sheldon H. Lu, 'National Cinema, Cultural Critique, Transnational Capital: The Films of Zhang Yimou', in Lu, *op. cit.*, pp. 105–36.

——, 'Chinese Film Culture at the End of the Twentieth Century: The Case of *Not One Less* by Zhang Yimou', in Sheldon H. Lu and Emilie Yueh-yu Yeh (eds.) *Chinese-Language Film: Historiography, Poetics, Politics*, Honolulu, University of Hawaii Press, 2005, pp. 120–37.

Yuejin Wang, '*Red Sorghum*: Mixing Memory and Desire', in Chris Berry (ed.) *Perspectives on Chinese Cinema*, London, British Film Institute Publishing, 1991, pp. 80–103.

Ming-Bao Yue, 'Visual Agency and Ideological Fantasy in Three Films by Zhang Yimou', in Dissanayake (ed.) *Narratives of Agency: Self-Making in China, India, and Japan*, Minneapolis, University of Minnesota Press, 1996, pp. 56–73.

Xudong Zhang, 'Ideology and Utopia in Zhang Yimou's *Red Sorghum*', *Chinese Modernism in the Era of Reforms: Cultural Fever, Avant-Garde Fiction, and the New Chinese Cinema*, Durham, N.C., Duke University Press, 1997, pp. 306–28.

Yingjin Zhang, 'Ideology of the Body in *Red Sorghum*: National Allegory, National Roots, and Third Cinema', *East-West Film Journal*, vol. 4, no. 2, 1990, pp. 38–53.

ZHANG YUAN

By Zhang Zhen

Two decades after the Tian'anmen Square students democracy movement and its violent suppression, Zhang Yuan and his generation of filmmakers, who emerged in the wake of that traumatic event and the fall of the Berlin Wall, are now in their middle age. Along with many of his peers, Zhang has alternately survived or thrived in a new Chinese economical and cultural order deeply marked by a postsocialist ethos and global capitalism. A leading figure of the so-called 'Sixth Generation' directors and underground cinema of the early 1990s, Zhang Yuan today is certainly no longer the same young maverick associated with the aimlessly rebellious 'Beijing Bastards' featured in his eponymous film of 1992. Since 1999, all of his feature films have been approved by the Chinese censorship board and released to the domestic market. Even many of his earlier 'underground' films are now commercially available on DVD format or online.

Yet a survey of Zhang Yuan's films to date reveals some consistent thematic and stylistic preoccupations. Prefiguring Jia Zhangke and other latecomers, Zhang has a persistent interest in the mixing of the documentary and the fictional, melodramatic realism and theatrical surrealism. This formal experimentation is intertwined with an obsession with the complex psycho-social dynamics and politico-ethical implications of institutional forms of power, desire and individual (re)formation, such as the prison, the police, the school, and their intersections with the reconfigured Chinese family under socialism and postsocialism. His most recent feature, *Little Red Flowers* (2006), set in a post-liberation kindergarten in Beijing, is in many ways a summation of his work, filtered through a historically reflective and cinematically seductive lens.

Zhang Yuan is often regarded as a figurehead of the Sixth Generation directors. Born in Nanjing in 1963, Zhang Yuan graduated from the department of cinematography at the Beijing Film Academy (BFA) in 1989. That year is often seen as the dividing line between the Fifth Generation – the first class to graduate from BFA after the Cultural Revolution in the early 1980s – and the Sixth or even younger generation of graduates from BFA and other institutions, who began to make their first films in the 1990s under the compounded pressures of political censorship and new commercial constraints.

The difference between the two generations is more than genea-logical. The Fifth Generation, by the early 1990s, had consolidated its place both on the international scene and in the Chinese film industry with works such as *Yellow Earth* (Chen Kaige), *Horse Thief* (Tian Zhuangzhuang) and *Red Sorghum* (Zhang Yimou). The younger filmmakers, however, identified themselves as independent from the outset. In this sense, the key differences between the Fifth and Sixth Generations are their distinct social and professional identities as well as their aesthetic outlooks.

After graduating from BFA, Zhang Yuan declined an assigned post at the August First Film Studio, a studio charged with producing military and propaganda films under the aegis of the People's Liberation Army. Instead, he embarked on a precarious independent career. With a shoe-string budget of $1300, he made (as producer, director and co-writer) his first feature, *Mama* (aka *The Tree of the Sun*). The film treats a Beijing librarian who single-handedly cares for her autistic son while confronting social prejudices toward the dis-abled, in addition to dealing with her deteriorating relationship with an unsupportive, long-distance commuting husband. The minimal plot and small unit of characters are characteristic of Zhang Yuan's early films. Shot mostly in black and white, *Mama* also prefigures the documentary sensibility and urban themes that became more pronounced in his subsequent works in particular, and the 'urban generation' cinema in general.[1] The story is based on the life experiences of Qin Yan, the actress who plays the mother. Zhang Yuan interweaves the narrative with a series of video interviews with parents of autistic children. The result is an unusual work that treads a thin line between fiction and documentary, lyricism and realism. The film was hailed as 'audacious', and its creator the 'new face of Chinese cinema' by one French critic.[2]

Mama demonstrated that it was possible to make a 35mm feature film entirely outside the studio system. Although registered with the Xi'an studio (which provided no financial support), the film was not widely distributed in China.[3] *Mama* received the Special Jury Prize at the 1991 Nantes Film Festival. It was screened at the Human Rights Film Festival in New York and at the Asian American Film Festival in Washington DC, among other venues. The exhibition of this debut film at such politically significant rather than glamorous venues initiated a practice associated with Zhang Yuan in particular, and with post-Fifth Generation directors in general. Without sponsorship and evading the restrictions set by the Chinese government, Zhang Yuan and other independent filmmakers have actively sought to connect with an alternative international film culture centred in festivals and art house theatres.

Zhang Yuan's second feature was the controversial *Beijing Bastards*, which created quite a stir when it was spirited out of China and shown at festivals overseas. It was seen as a radical departure from the Fifth Generation cinema, also making Zhang Yuan a 'troublemaker' and thus an emblematic figure of an underground movement, in the eyes of the Chinese censors. Significantly, the film was co-produced by Zhang Yuan and China's foremost rock musician, Cui Jian. Their partnership in fact goes back to Zhang Yuan's filming of Cui Jian's music videos. The rock'n'roll spirit is, to an extent, also the spirit of the Sixth Generation, its iconoclastic and restless rhythm the rhythm of the young urban cinema. The film's slender narrative concerns in part a rock band that is driven out of its rehearsal space. The struggle over urban space would become a leitmotif of many Sixth Generation films, especially those that explicitly tackle the widespread phenomenon of urban reconstruction and dislocation. The pervasive documentary atmosphere of the film is accentuated with footage of Cui Jian's live performances.

The sense of place becomes the central focus of *The Square* (1994), a documentary about Tian'anmen Square, co-directed by Zhang Yuan and Duan Jingchuan. The monumental space in the heart of the capital becomes the protagonist rather than the backdrop of a ceaselessly unfolding history and an everyday drama. Zhang Yuan began this project as a defiant gesture after the government blacklisted him (and several other filmmakers) as punishment for unsanctioned participation in festivals abroad. The film is essentially a 'documentary on the political and social economy' of the square.[4] The camera quietly observes the square and its various occupants and visitors during a 24-hour period. The finished film interweaves political rituals (the raising and lowering of the national flag) with everyday life (children flying kites, tourists posing for photos). The square emerges as a multifaceted space filled with state sanctioned symbolic meanings as well as public memory and leisure activities.

If the Fifth Generation and their representative works were preoccupied with creating cultural myths rooted in rural China and the past, Zhang Yuan, as he underscored, is motivated by a strong concern with contemporary 'social problems and social reality' as experienced or witnessed by the filmmaker.[5] This concern with the 'social', particularly issues concerning relations between public and private, between family ethics and cultural norms, and between the state and marginal social subjects, can be discerned across his oeuvre. It is often articulated through a self-conscious documentary or docudramatic mode, which also generally distinguishes the Sixth generation from its predecessors.

As an unconventional documentarian, Zhang Yuan is obsessed with, in his own words, the 'dialectical relation between subjective consciousness and objective reality'.[6] His next film, *Sons* (1995), initiated by downstairs neighbours who asked him to make a film about their dysfunctional family, pushes that dialectic to its breaking point. The family, torn apart by alcoholism and insanity, stages its past and present drama for the camera.[7] A retired couple, formerly dancers of revolutionary ballets, and their two sons live in a typical Beijing apartment complex, surrounded by neighbours with watchful eyes. The father's love of the bottle and the resultant violence nearly destroys the family. The film's impact comes from its unflinching examination of the modern Chinese family, mental illness, and social reproduction. It also probes questions of representation and performance. The characters play themselves with both restraint and abandon. The mother, who suffers most abuse and shoulders the heaviest burden in the family, both emotionally and financially, is particularly moving when we learn that she has hidden the divorce papers in a drawer, staying on to hold the family together. The sense of 'authenticity' of the film is achieved, according to the director, 'through the process of forgetting it rather than its [deliberate] attainment' – as when family members forget their lines and 'perform' as the situation dictates.[8]

445

The blending of performative spontaneity and directorial involvement, reality and fiction continue to appear in Zhang Yuan's subsequent documentaries. Both *Crazy English* (1999) and *Miss Jing Xing* (2000) are in each case about an extraordinary individual whose convictions and actions generated sensational controversies in contemporary Chinese society. *Crazy English* is a *tour de force* portrayal of Li Yang, the self-made English teacher and motivational speaker who invented an idiosyncratic pedagogy called 'Crazy English', still in vogue today. In the fashion of collective gymnastic, Li Yang delivers speeches and gives demonstrations with animated body language in front of mass assemblies (his company also publishes textbooks, cassettes and CD-ROMs) at all sorts of public venues, including the Forbidden Palace and the Great Wall. His students range from PLA soldiers to primary school pupils. The film opens with Zhang's 'crew' filming while jogging and shouting out loud English phrases together with Li Yang and his followers. Amidst the 'crazy' sound, the cameraman trips and falls, causing chaos. The film captures the 'crazy' spirit of Li Yang's enterprise and the chaotic messages he transmits through his linguistic aerobics. He at once promotes a fierce patriotism (that the Chinese will conquer the world market once they master English) and expresses a strange fascination with the West and the modernity it represents (Li confesses in the film that he has never been abroad). The film is equivocal on Li Yang's crusade to modernise China through mastery of the English language. Yet through the direct investigation of Li Yang's method, the film exposes the ideological confusion shared by him and many Chinese people in an era of rapid transformation.

Miss Jing Xing is a candid yet artful treatment of the sex change undergone by Jing Xing, a gay dancer who returned to China after studying in New York. The one-hour long film, made for the Hong Kong-based entertainment website Tom.com, portrays the outspoken Jing Xing as a cosmopolitan Chinese artist with unconventional cultural and sexual identities. Instead of sensationalising the sex change, Zhang Yuan interweaves the vaguely reenacted surgery shot through a blue filter with Jing Xing's own narration and re-constructions of other significant episodes in her life. Culled from both 35mm and digital video footage shot over the span of several years, the film's multi-layered montage creates a polysemic text suggesting that the significance of Jing Xing's choice is both biological and social. By the end of the film, the crew films Jing Xing in Shanghai where she leads local dancers rehearsing for a major performance in China's largest metropolis. The final images capture Jing Xing leaping in the air, beautiful and strong.

Zhang Yuan treats the theme of marginal sexual identity and the relation between art and erotic desire earlier in a different mode, in perhaps his most stylized film, *East Palace, West Palace* (1996). The minimal yet sophisticated narrative takes place within the walls of a public park where local gay men cruise. A police officer 'picks up' and interrogates A Lan at the police station inside the park throughout the night. Although the result is a theatrical 'chamber piece',[9] the inspiration for the film came from a news report about the way in which a research institute conducts research on AIDS. Unable to access the underground gay circle to study their sexual behaviour, the institute solicits the help of police to haul gay men in for forced interviews, or questioning. Flabbergasted by what he believes to be 'one of the most absurd things' in Chinese society, Zhang Yuan decided to interview gay people himself and 'find out what is different about them'.[10] However, extensive interviews and research led to the decision to make a very different film than a documentary about gay life in Beijing. Perhaps in an attempt to get at the core of the absurdity that first inspired the film, Zhang Yuan and the late writer Wang Xiaobo crafted a script that delivers a politico-ethical meditation on the 'relationship between power and privacy',[11] with a philosophical and aesthetic intensity rarely seen in Chinese cinema. The film goes beyond the showing of the gay underworld in Beijing; in Zhang Yuan's words, it 'introduces how the system works'.[12]

The politics of homosexuality is intimately intertwined with the politics of representation in *East Palace, West Palace*. It is significant that A Lan is a writer who 'confesses' to the officer the formation of his sexual identity. His tales are not so much forced testimony as active (self) representation that explores the erotic and intersubjective nature of language. The allegorical meaning of the narrative proper is given more layers by an embedded subtext from traditional opera, about the ambivalent relationship between a palace guard and a female thief. Through the juxtaposition of these theatrical *gestalts* of power relations, Zhang Yuan's modern tale of gender and sexual politics takes on a symbolic significance.

East Palace, West Palace was again banned in China. The prohibition had more to do with the way the film was made than its content. The film was in fact financed partly by an award from the French Ministry of Culture. As soon as the shooting was completed, the film was smuggled out of China for post-production in France, getting ready for the Cannes Film Festival. When Chinese authorities learned about these 'unofficial' manoeuvers, they confiscated Zhang Yuan's passport to prevent him from travelling to the festival to present this film. After strenuous negotiations, Zhang Yuan was given back his passport and, eventually, granted permission to resume filmmaking as a reinstated director in 1998. The result was to be *Crazy English* and *Seventeen Years*, both produced and released through mostly official channels.

Zhang Yuan, who has been struggling to make art under censors' watchful eyes, seems obsessed with forms of institutional imprisonment and possible liberation from it. *Seventeen Years* both solidified his international statue (Best Director award at the Venice International Film Festival) and won him official and popular acceptance at home. The film centres on a female prisoner getting her Spring Festival's parole for the first time in seventeen years. Touched by a television programme about prisoners meeting their relatives, Zhang Yuan began to visit a number of prisons and interviewed many inmates. The extensive preparation obviously contributed to the film's docu-dramatic quality, accentuated by techniques such as hand-held and hidden cameras during location shooting, on one hand, and the melodramatic handling of the family dynamic, on the other.[13]

The narrative structure of the film is characteristically simple yet inventive. As with *Sons*, the plot involves mainly members of a broken family; yet recalling the operatic subtext in *East Palace, West Palace, Seventeen Years* follows a female warden and the prisoner Tao Lan home on the Chinese New Year's eve. As the story turns into a road movie, the warden gets involved in the life of her subject despite her initial reluctance and indifference. The seemingly linear narrative with a final resolution unfolds in a decidedly historical time and social space. The length of 'seventeen years' does not refer only to youth lost behind bars, but approximately overlaps with the 'new era' of reform since China re-opened its doors in 1979. And 'going home' (as the Chinese title indicates) proves to be an ordeal across an alien and ruthlessly changing urban landscape. The childhood neighbourhood where Tao Lan killed her stepsister in the heat of a trivial argument is lying in ruins. Her mother and stepfather have moved to the suburbs, as have thousands of urban Chinese dwellers following the dismantling of inner cities and old neighbourhoods to make way for department stores, office buildings and expressways. We find Tao Lan utterly confused and lost, for instance, in front of huge advertising bulletin boards showing half-naked women in underwear. The middle part of the film takes place entirely on the street, in the urban maze from which Tao Lan wants to flee back to the prison, now more like a home to her after seventeen years of insulation from the outside world. Here the film is perhaps at its most poignant (more so than the melodramatic happy ending of sorts, as it touches on the merits of reform and a market economy, and on a more complex level, the very nature and possibility of individual freedom and family and communal bonds in a society undergoing tremendous, and at times violent transformation.

Seen mainly as a sensitive portrayal of the Chinese prison system, *Seventeen Years* was received favourably in China. Chinese critics seem to have overlooked (maybe purposely so) the film's more complex dimensions. One critic writes in the state sponsored *Popular Cinema*, 'With the success of *Seventeen Years*, the Sixth Generation has reached the summit of the international film world, and has now its representative work'. During the Beijing premiere Zhang Yuan reportedly went up on the stage with his cast to greet the audience and answer questions. The distance between the *enfant terrible* of Chinese cinema, who had previously only made films to provoke the conventional viewing habits of the Chinese audience, and an audience who had very little knowledge of this baby-faced director with a head of intractable curly hair, seems to have shortened significantly within just a couple of years.

One decade after Zhang Yuan made his debut with the low-budget feature *Mama*, the most famous independent filmmaker found himself quickly adapting to a changed Chinese film culture. The Sixth Generation has also expanded and transformed itself into a broadly defined phenomenon of young urban cinema; its experimental spirit is infused with a deep concern for contemporary social life as well as the desire to reach mainstream audiences and attain commercial success. Zhang Yuan admits, 'I want my films to be accessible to the domestic audience. At the very least, I need to maintain a sensible connection to where I live. Hence, when making *Seventeen Years*, I made up my mind that I must get my films through the censors. To me, emerging from the "underground" and learning how to deal with the censors is a road I must take'.[14]

The state film apparatus, perhaps also realising the inevitability of major change in both domestic and global film structures, is playing the card of patronising, or even seducing, young filmmakers by hiring them for productions at major studios, with the possibility of distributing their works in China. The years 2002 and 2003 saw Zhang Yuan reaping the benefits of his strategic repositioning, making three art-pop films for the domestic market. *Sister Jiang* is an intriguing restaging of a model opera from the Cultural Revolution period, which continues Zhang's fascination with Chinese opera's imprint on contemporary politics and culture. Responding in part to the popular nostalgia for 'red classics' of the socialist era in a time of crass commercialism and moral bankruptcy, Zhang Yuan's postmodern 'remake' is at once ironic and romantic, a sentiment representative of his generation's ambivalent memories of the revolutionary legacy.

Focusing on female desire in China's postrevolutionary imaginary, *I Love You* and *Green Tea*, centre on the 'woman in the city' in the wake of market economy.[15] Unlike the use of mostly professional actors in his earlier 'underground' films, these films capitalise on a cluster of celebrity effects and Christopher Doyle's cinematography for generating popular appeal and box-office receipts. Consistent with his preoccupation with 'extreme' people and emotions, the women portrayed here are also nearly mad or schizophrenic, struggling with their own confused gender and social identities in a frantically commercialising urban environment. These gender performances by a new generation of female stars in the context of postsocialist urban modernity recall similar motifs in the Shanghai melodrama films of the 1930s, which Zhang Yuan often cites as important sources of inspiration. *Green Tea*, in having one actress playing two polarised characters as conjured by the woman's pathological fantasy, also echoes and extends the motif of the female double, or what I call 'phantom sisters', in a number of urban generation films such as Wang Quanan's *Lunar Eclipse* (1999) and Lou Ye's *Suzhou River* (2000).

If outraged innocence and the production of hybrid or 'bastardised' identities in post-1989 China are *leitmotifs* in Zhang Yuan's oeuvre and Sixth and Urban Generation cinema in general, *Little Red Flowers* (2006), adapted from Wang Shuo's autobiographical fiction, recombines his thematic and stylistic pursuits in an intriguing period piece set in a Beijing kindergarten of the early 1950s. Calling it a 'nightmare gone awry', one viewer describes his experience of the film as 'something like watching a Bambi movie that had cockroaches oozing out of crevices in the rockfaces'.[16] The stately and spacious traditional architecture with forbidding red walls and flying eaves, which houses the kindergarten, along with the dreamy scenes of snowy nights, are eerily reminiscent of *East Palace, West Palace*. The film is similarly replete with intertwined signs of eroticism (or emerging sexuality) and power, here staged in a strictly regulated institution – a nursery school as a foundational building block of the socialist state. The four- or five-year-olds here, played by Zhang Yuan's daughter and her classmates, are alternately infantilised or made precocious. The boys still wear open-slit pants (which are normally reserved for infants and younger toddlers) as if to show their arrested development. The boy protagonist, a naughty outsider more or less abandoned by his family to the care of the state, is punished for unsuccessful toilet training and other straying behaviours in the form of physical and social isolation.

Nowhere is the subtle critique of the socialist education system more pronounced than in the conceit of 'little red flowers', referring literally to the paper flowers awarded to pupils with good (or submissive) behaviour and symbolically to the fledgling royal subjects of the party–state. The physical and mental discipline stresses obedience and uniformity – (ranging from gender-specific uniforms and bedding to table manners and toilet visits) – geared toward the training of the socialist citizen. With round-the-clock enrolment and hardly any visible family visits and excursions, the kindergarten is more like an orphanage if not a prison. Yet with the stylised set pieces focusing on the undercurrents of the children's rebellious energy and intimate bonds, accentuated by a frequently counterpuntal sound track, the film reiterates the director's reflections on the hegemonic nature of power and seductive mechanism of discipline. The focus on children and their sexuality and the immediate post-liberation setting allow Zhang Yuan to delve deeper into the historical and psychic sources of the PRC's cultural politics – its paternalistic and authoritarian foundation and its mixed blessings for generations of 'little red flowers' (mal)nourished by its ideological plenitude and material scarcity.

Made in and for a very different time, when China has long emerged from behind the iron curtains of the Cold War and ascended as an economic giant on the world stage, *Little Red Flowers* serves as a cautionary tale about the vulnerable human infrastructure of the nation. As China's social and moral fabric is further torn apart in the wake of a ferocious yet ill-regulated market economy and endemic corruption, would the one-child policy and the commoditised education system be able to produce obedient productive citizens as the party–state was once capable of through both coercion and seduction? What does the future hold for the generation of the young children whose members performed in the film? Would the kind of films that Zhang Yuan makes make a difference in their lives?

Zhang Yuan is sceptical about the power of cinema to effect social change, especially in the context of China's current film system, even though he has been successful in navigating the unpredictable censorship and domestic market in the past decade. The official film policy and mainstream culture continue to suppress probing works by Chinese filmmakers while opening the floodgate for Hollywood and domestic or regional commercial blockbusters. There are speculations as to whether or not Zhang Yuan, the Sixth Generation as a whole and even latecomers such as Jia Zhangke have gone mainstream. At the same time, what is mainstream is also being redefined in a significantly transformed China. The acute concern for a socially fragmented society, an increased awareness of the importance of domestic audience, and the desire to reinvent the cinematic language and revive Chinese cinema, in the face of television's enormous popularity and emerging media such as the Internet, have forced young filmmakers to adjust both their outlook and their tactics. Back in 1994, *Time Magazine* selected Zhang Yuan as one of the hundred young leading figures of the world for the new century. Zhang Yuan did not care much about that title; what he cares about most is that more Chinese people see his films in real or virtual theatres. Zhang Yuan will no doubt continue to make films, but his work is faced with new challenges when the practices of filmmaking and media consumption in China and elsewhere as a whole are heading in new or uncertain directions.

Acknowledgement

I would like to thank the Humanities Council at New York University for a grant-in-aid that enabled the research and writing of an earlier version of this essay. I am also grateful to Zhang Yuan, Wu Lala, Jia Zhijie and the *Time Magazine* Beijing Bureau for providing valuable research material.

Notes

1 For a definition of the term and Zhang Yuan's role in this phenomenon, see my introduction in Zhang Zhen (ed.), *The Urban Generation: Chinese Cinema and Society at the Turn of the Twenty-first Century* (Durham, NC, Duke University Press, 2007).

2 Ange-Dominique Bouzet, 'Un chinois pour trois continents', *Liberation*, 20 December, 1991.

3 Only three prints were sold. The film was reportedly released in China in 1994 and broadcast on cable television. Steven Schwanker, 'Director's Cut', *Far Eastern Economic Review*, November 30, 1995, p. 82.

4 Tony Rayns, 'Provoking Desire', *Sight and Sound*, July 1996, p. 26.

5 Ma Li Ya, ' "Hou diwudai" zhenzhi luxian "cuowu" de dianying daoyan – Zhang Yuan' (The 'post-Fifth Generation', politically 'incorrect' director – Zhang Yuan), *Zhong* (The Chinese), July 1996, pp. 96–100.

6 Ibid., p. 98.

7 In order to make the film, Zhang Yuan had to get special permission for the father to be temporarily released from the mental hospital where he was undergoing treatment.

8 Zhang Yuan, comments made at the Chinese Cultural Studies Workshop, Harvard University, November 4, 1999.

9 Rayns, *op. cit.*, p. 28.

10 Ibid.

11 Cheng Qingsong and Huang Ou, 'Zhang Yuan: Write Freely', in *Wode sheyingji busahuang* (My camera does not lie) (Beijing: Zhonghuo youyi, 2002), p. 123.

12 Schwankert, *op. cit.*

13 Zhang Yuan and his crew obtained special permission to film inside the Tianjin First Prison.

14 Shanyi Sun and Li Xun, *Lights! Camera! Kai Shi! In Depth Interviews with China's New Generation of Movie Directors* (Norwalk, CT: EastBridge, 2008), p. 92.

15 Bérénice Reynaud, 'Zhang Yuan's Imaginary Cities and the Theatricalization of the Chinese "Bastards"', in Zhang Zhen', *op. cit.*, p. 284.

16 Mahlon D. Meyer, ' "Little Red Flowers", or a Nightmare Gone Awry, a Coming of Age Movie for a New Generation in China', *Asian Cinema* (Fall/Winter 2006), p. 182.

Filmography

(All produced in China unless otherwise indicated)

Mama / *Beijing zazhong* (China/Hong Kong, 1993)
The Square / *Guangchang* (co-director: Duan Jingchuang; 1994)
Sons / *Erzi* (1995)
East Palace, West Place / *Donggong Xigong* (China/France, 1996)
Demolition and Relocation / *Dingfzi hu* (1998)
Crazy English / *Fengkuang Yingyu* (1999)
Seventeen Years / *Guonian huijia* (1999)
Miss Jing Xing / *Jing Xing Xiaojie* (2000) documentary made with DV, the first Chinese work of the 'Eighth Art' exhibited on the Internet
I Love You / *Wo ai ni* (2003)
Green Tea / *Lü Cha* (2003)
Little Red Flowers / *Kan shang qu hen mei* (2006)

INDEX

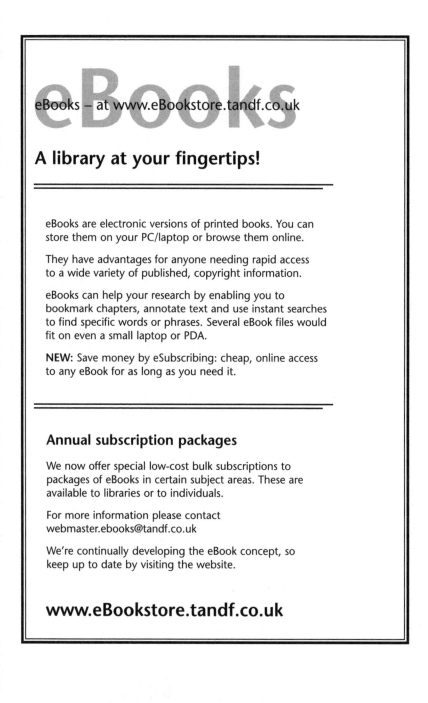